CENTURY 21
Accounting

CENTURY 21 Accounting

INTRODUCTORY COURSE

SIXTH EDITION

Kenton E. Ross, CPA
Professor of Accounting
East Texas State University
Commerce, Texas

Robert D. Hanson
Associate Dean
College of Business Administration
Central Michigan University
Mount Pleasant, Michigan

Claudia Bienias Gilbertson, CPA
Teaching Professor
Anoka-Ramsey Community College
Coon Rapids, Minnesota

Mark W. Lehman, CPA
Instructor
School of Accountancy
Mississippi State University
Starkville, Mississippi

Robert M. Swanson
Professor Emeritus of Business Education
and Office Administration
Ball State University
Muncie, Indiana

South-Western Publishing Co.
BA20FA1

Vice-President/Editor-in-Chief: Dennis M. Kokoruda
Senior Developmental Editor: Carol Volz
Art Director: John Robb
Design Coordinator: Darren Wright
Marketing Manager: Larry Qualls
Coordinating Editor: Mark Beck
Production Manager: Carol Sturzenberger
Senior Production Editor: Mark Cheatham
Production Editor: Kimberlee Kusnerak
Production Editor I: Denise Wheeler
Associate Director/Photo Editing: Devore Nixon
Photo Editor: Kimberly A. Larson

Cover Design: The Optimum Group
Internal Design: Lesiak/Crampton Design

ISBN: 0-538-62955-X

5 6 7 8 9 0 D 99 98

Printed in the United States of America

I(T)P
International Thomson Publishing

South-Western Publishing Co. is an ITP Company. The ITP trademark is used under license.

Preface

This preface is addressed primarily to the student. A complete examination guide for the CENTURY 21 ACCOUNTING learning package is included in the wraparound teacher's edition of this text.

This introductory accounting text will give you a thorough background in the basic accounting procedures used to operate a business. The accounting procedures presented will also serve as a sound background for employment in office jobs and preparation for studying business courses in college. Because the complete accounting cycle is covered for both proprietorships and partnerships, it is easy to see how each employee's job fits into the cycle for a business, an important qualification to employers.

How to Use This Text

This textbook is carefully designed to function as a learning tool. The overall organization is in three parts, with one or more chapters in each part. Part 1 is a special part that has only one chapter. Parts 2 and 3 each consist of several chapters that present a complete accounting cycle. For each part, a business is identified and described and that business is used to illustrate all the concepts for the rest of that part. In addition, each of these parts begins with a chart of accounts that is used throughout the part; it is an excellent preview for the part and serves as a convenient reference as you study each chapter.

Each chapter begins with a set of enabling performance tasks, or learning objectives, that describe what you will be able to do after studying the chapter. The task statements preview the chapter. A list of new terms that are defined and used within the chapter is also printed at the start of the chapter. Begin your study of each chapter with reading the enabling performance tasks and new accounting terms.

Each chapter has a number of headings that should be previewed to help understand the chapter. These headings can also function as a topical outline for a chapter if your studying method includes taking notes in outline format. Abundant illustrations highlight concepts in the chapter narrative. Note that each illustration has both an illustration number that is referenced within the narrative of the chapter and a descriptive caption that describes what is being illustrated. A summary illustration at the end of each chapter ties the main points of the chapter together in graphic terms. All new accounting vocabulary terms are printed in bold type within the sentence that defines the term so these definitions can be easily found.

Special Features

The following special features appear throughout the textbook:

Multicultural Awareness: This feature describes the contributions of a variety of cultures to accounting and business. Some of these features focus on historical contributions while others describe a situation in the United States today. This feature will help strengthen your awareness of the value of diversity in the work force and society.

Professional Business Ethics: The news media are full of stories about unethical behavior in business and the effect of this unethical behavior on businesses and individuals. Boxed features throughout the text present ethical dilemmas that employees and business owners encounter in real life. Chapter 1 discusses ethical behavior in general and presents a 3-step checklist as a model for analyzing ethical decisions.

Global Perspective: Global business topics provide information and activities to enhance preparation for working in the global economy. These topics provide practical real-life information about trading across national boundaries and furnish activities to demonstrate how this information is applied.

Personal Visions in Business: These personality profiles describe individuals in the business world today from a variety of occupations and cultural backgrounds. The individuals portrayed describe how an accounting background can be useful when starting and maintaining your own business and what they have learned about business from their own experiences.

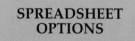

Careers in Accounting: This feature presents a list of job duties for different job titles. This feature can help you select the kinds of jobs you might want to pursue based on the responsibilities of each job.

Spreadsheet Options: Features of spreadsheet software can help streamline business practices. The Spreadsheet Options feature describes some of the techniques used by businesses to make their financial reporting and analysis more efficient.

Applied Mathematics: If accounting is the language of business, then numbers are probably the words of the language. Many different mathematical calculations are involved in accounting for a business. Within a chapter, each time a new mathematical calculation is presented, the formula is highlighted by a color box and the Applied Math Icon appears beside it. The Applied Math Icon is repeated next to end-of-chapter activities that first apply each calculation.

Audit Your Understanding Questions: At the end of each short section of a chapter, a list of questions are given for assessing your grasp of the concepts covered. Self-check answers are provided in Appendix D.

FYI ("For Your Information"): Boxes in the margins emphasize important points from the chapter and sometimes present additional interesting information about accounting and business.

End-of-Chapter Activities

The end of each chapter provides questions, cases, drills, and problems for practicing the new skills learned in the chapter and demonstrating your grasp of the concepts. Each section identifies the enabling performance tasks to be performed. The identifying letters of the tasks are placed in parentheses next to the heading of each activity.

The first section at the end of each chapter presents a list of all the new accounting terms defined in the chapter. You should be sure you know the meaning of each of these terms. This activity is followed by questions that help you review the concepts in the chapter. The next section, called Cases for Critical Thinking, describes case scenarios based on chapter concepts for which you are required to stretch your knowledge to provide the best answer or select the best alternative from those presented. Frequent Applied Communications sections furnish opportunities for honing your communication skills in the context of topics that are related to accounting.

The remaining end-of-chapter activities are drills and problems. The drills require you to analyze procedures from the chapter in a short-answer format. Application Problems apply your new accounting skills as you complete a problem for each section of the chapter. The Mastery Problem is a further application of all the new skills from the chapter in one single problem. The Challenge Problem concludes the chapter by stretching your knowledge to cover new applications. A Recycling Problem is available at the end of the textbook, in Appendix C, to use for additional practice or review. Reinforcement Activities and simulations for each of the accounting cycles are milestone activities that synthesize all the activities from the chapters in the part.

Software

There are four pieces of software that may be used to complete end-of-chapter activities. Each piece of software is represented by an icon. These icons are placed on the appropriate drills and problems that may be completed using the computer.

Automated Accounting: This icon identifies a problem that is appropriate for solving using the *Automated Accounting 6.0* or higher software. A template for this problem is available that contains the chart of accounts and opening balances for selected problems.

Application Program: This icon identifies a problem that is available on the Application Program Disk software.

Accounting Tutorial: This icon identifies a section for which learning can be enhanced using the Accounting Tutorial software.

Spreadsheet Template: This icon identifies a problem for which a template file is available that can be used with commercial spreadsheet software for solving the problem.

All problems that are identified as being appropriate for solving with the use of software can also be completed manually with pencil and paper.

Reference Material

Reference material at the end of the book includes four appendices, a glossary of terms, and an index. Appendix A briefly describes each of the major accounting concepts described in more detail within the text narrative. Appendix B includes information about using a 10-key calculator and computer keypad. Appendix C presents a recycling problem for each chapter in the textbook for additional practice, or review. Appendix D provides the answers to the Audit Your Understanding questions in each chapter so that the questions can be used for self-review. The glossary of terms lists all the terms defined in the text and their definitions for easy reference. The index shows the page location for each topic in the text. This can be useful if you need to look up a topic but do not know where to find it.

ACKNOWLEDGMENTS

We thank the following individuals who contributed to the review process for this edition:

Mrs. Pam Caldwell
Godwin High School
Richmond, Virginia

Ms. Carolyn Francis
Robert E. Lee High School
Baytown, Texas

Mr. Neil Yeager
Cordova High School
Rancho Cordova, California

Dr. Arvella Jones
Commerce High School
Commerce, Texas

Mr. Robert Greer
John Jay High School
San Antonio, Texas

Dr. De Lois Gibson
Cass Technical High School
Detroit, Michigan

Mr. Peter Eisen
Murry Bergtraum High School
New York, New York

Mrs. Linda Songer
Orange Park High School
Orange Park, Florida

Mr. Joe McFarland
Shasta High School
Redding, California

We also appreciate the ongoing feedback provided by the classroom professionals who use CENTURY 21 ACCOUNTING every day.

Contents

PART 3

Accounting for a Merchandising Business Organized as a Partnership

PHOTO CREDITS

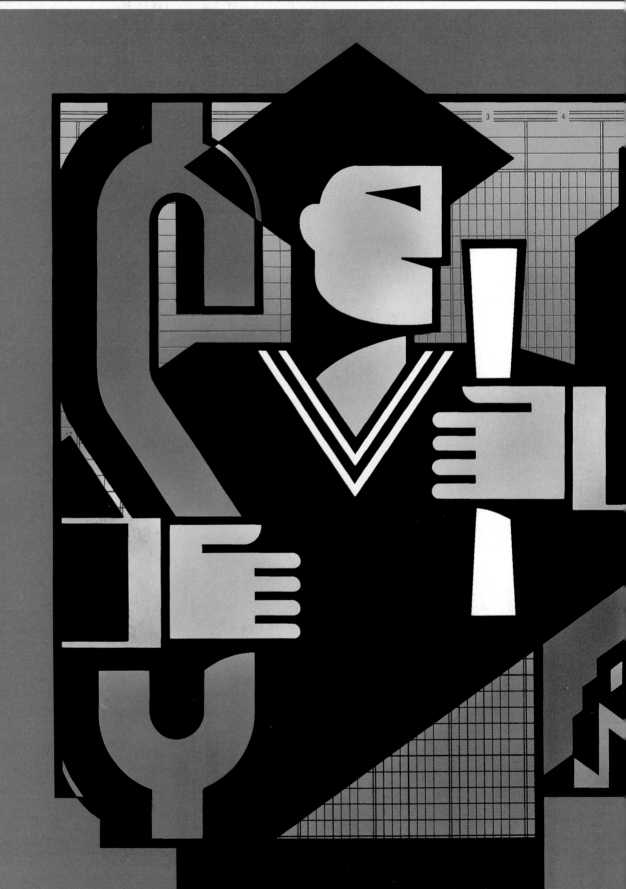

PART 1

Accounting as a Career

GENERAL GOALS

1. Know accounting terminology related to accounting careers.

2. Understand entry-level positions, educational requirements, and career opportunities in accounting.

3. Understand that success in the accounting profession depends on the ability to communicate and make ethical decisions.

1

Accounting Careers: Communication and Ethics in the Workplace

ENABLING PERFORMANCE TASKS

After studying Chapter 1, you will be able to:

a Define accounting terms related to accounting careers.

b Identify how accounting serves as a basis for careers.

c Identify the tasks of various accounting occupations.

d Describe how communication skills are important in reporting accounting information.

e Describe how individuals make ethical business decisions.

TERMS PREVIEW

accounting • accounting system • accounting records • accountant • public accounting firm • private accountant • bookkeeper • accounting clerk • general office clerk • ethics • business ethics

A successful business is involved in numerous financial activities. Summary reports of these financial activities are needed by several people. Owners and managers must understand financial reports to make good business decisions. *How much should be charged for the product or service? Are profits sufficient? Should new products be sold? Should new services be provided? Can costs be decreased?*

Individuals outside the business also use summary reports to make decisions that affect the business. The business' banker uses these summary reports to make loan decisions. *How much should the bank allow the business to borrow? Is the business likely to be able to repay the loan?*

A business must also submit summary reports to certain government agencies. The government requires that the business report financial information when it pays taxes. Other government agencies examine the financial activities of the business to assure that it follows various federal and state laws.

Persons responsible for nonprofit organizations also need accounting information as the basis for making financial decisions. The mayor of a community uses summary reports to determine how taxpayers' money should be spent. *How efficient is the community's water department? Can the community afford to purchase a new fire truck? Must taxes be raised to pay for a new high school building?* Nonprofit organizations, such as churches, public service organizations, and city governments, must keep spending within available financial resources.

Career opportunities exist for individuals to provide businesses, government, and nonprofit organizations with necessary financial information. Many young people choose to prepare for a career in the field of accounting.

FYI

The six largest accounting firms in the United States are referred to as the Big Six. They are:
- Arthur Andersen & Co.
- Coopers & Lybrand
- Deloitte & Touche
- Ernst & Young
- KMPG Peat Marwick
- Price Waterhouse

WHAT IS ACCOUNTING?

To create useful reports, financial information must be maintained in an organized way. Planning, recording, analyzing, and interpreting financial information is called **accounting**. A planned process for providing financial information that will be useful to management is called an **accounting system**. Organized summaries of a business' financial activities are called **accounting records**.

Inaccurate accounting records often contribute to business failure and bankruptcy. Failure to understand accounting information can result in poor business decisions for both businesses and nonprofit organizations. Accounting education helps managers and owners make better business decisions.

Accounting is the language of business. Many individuals in a business complete accounting forms and prepare accounting reports. Owners, managers, and accounting personnel use their knowledge of accounting to understand the information provided in the accounting reports. Regardless of their responsibilities within an organization, individuals can perform their jobs more efficiently if they know the language of business—accounting.

Accounting is used by most individuals in everyday life. Nearly everyone in the United States earns money and must submit income tax reports to the federal and state governments. Everyone, personally or for a business, must plan ways to keep spending within available income. Individuals having accounting skills are better prepared to keep personal financial records.

JOB OPPORTUNITIES IN ACCOUNTING

Accounting positions fit into several classifications that include accountants, bookkeepers, accounting clerks, and other general office workers. An increasing amount of accounting work is done using computers. However, the increase in the use of computers does not appear to be decreasing the need for all kinds of accounting personnel.

Accountants

A person who plans, summarizes, analyzes, and interprets accounting information is called an **accountant**. Accountants prepare various accounting reports and assist owners and managers in making financial decisions. Accountants also supervise the work of other accounting personnel and check the accuracy of financial statements.

CONTROLLER

Accountant needed to maintain accounting system and supervise accounting personnel. Five or more years experience, professional certification, and computer skills required.

ACCOUNTANT

Local business needs an accountant to supervise all accounting functions. Good interpersonal and communications skills are required.

Some accountants work as members of accounting firms that sell accounting services to other businesses. A business selling accounting services to the general public is called a **public accounting firm**. Public accounting firms provide a variety of accounting services to businesses and individuals. These accounting services may include planning an accounting system, preparing accounting reports, and submitting income tax reports to the government. For example, a medical clinic may not need a full-time accountant. The doctor, a nurse, or another office employee may do the day-to-day accounting tasks. The doctor may hire a public accounting firm to help plan the accounting system and analyze, report, and interpret the accounting information.

An accountant who is employed by a single business is called a **private accountant**. The work of private accountants is similar to that done by public accounting firms. However, a private accountant works for only one business.

Bookkeepers

A person who does general accounting work plus some summarizing and analyzing of accounting information is called a **bookkeeper**. In some businesses bookkeepers may supervise the work of other accounting personnel. In small to medium-size businesses, bookkeepers may also help owners and managers interpret accounting information.

BOOKKEEPER

Work without supervision. Experience in general ledger and payroll required. Experience in supervising accounting clerks desirable. Electronic spreadsheet and word processing skills required.

BOOKKEEPER-CLERICAL

Bookkeeper required to supervise accounts receivable and general ledger. Computer and keyboarding skills a must.

Bookkeepers in small businesses may do additional general office work. Many businesses require that bookkeepers have filing and keyboarding skills. Filing skills are needed for storing accounting records. Keyboarding skills are necessary to efficiently use computers to prepare accounting records and reports.

Accounting Clerks

A person who records, sorts, and files accounting information is often called an **accounting clerk**. Some businesses have large amounts of routine accounting tasks that are assigned to accounting clerks.

PAYROLL CLERK

Opening for responsible payroll clerk. Coordination of all payroll activities. Salary depends on training and experience.

ACCOUNTS PAYABLE CLERK

Retail store. Automated system. Will train person with general accounting background.

FYI

Analyzing ethical behavior is discussed in more detail on pages 12–14.

PROFESSIONAL BUSINESS ETHICS

Can I Say This In My Resume?

Kenneth Reed just graduated from high school with one year of high school accounting. Not sure of his long-term career goal, Kenneth decided to apply for a position as bookkeeper with Jackson Industries. In an effort to improve his chances to get the job, Kenneth overstated the leadership experience he had acquired in several part-time jobs. For example, Kenneth's experience as a janitor was exaggerated on his resume as "Asset Maintenance Engineer—accountable for the acquisition and maintenance of productive assets." In the same way, Kenneth's job as a lifeguard was exaggerated as "Recreational Director—responsible for coordinating customers' recreational activities."

Based on the impressive nature of his resume, Kenneth was hired for the bookkeeping position. After one year of employment, Kenneth received above average ratings on his annual employment evaluation. Shortly thereafter, the accountant met Kenneth's former employers and learned the truth of Kenneth's work experience.

The three-step checklist presented in this chapter is useful in determining whether Kenneth demonstrated ethical behavior in preparing his resume.

INSTRUCTIONS Use the following three-step checklist for making ethical decisions. The first activity has been completed for you as follows.

1. Is the action illegal? No. Overstating qualifications is not illegal, but it does provide the employer the opportunity to terminate employment.

2. Does the action violate company or professional standards? No. Since Kenneth was neither an employee of the company nor a member of any profession, this question does not apply.

Accounting clerks are often given a title, such as payroll clerk or accounts payable clerk, to describe the specific accounting activities they perform. These clerks usually work with only a small part of the total accounting system. However, accounting clerks who understand the total accounting system will understand the importance of the work being done. With accounting knowledge and some experience, accounting clerks may earn promotions to more responsible accounting positions.

General Office Clerks

A person who does general kinds of office tasks, including some accounting tasks, is called a **general office clerk**. Many office personnel and computer operators perform some accounting tasks. For example, a secretary may be in charge of a small cash fund. A telephone operator may key-enter sales order information directly into a computer. A computer operator may key-enter data from special accounting documents. Regardless of who completes the accounting activities, the work must be done according to established

3. Who is affected, and how, by the action?

People Affected	Negative	Positive
Kenneth Reed	Could be terminated since management can no longer rely on his honesty. If retained, he could lose any chance of promotion.	Obtains employment.
Other Job Applicants	More highly qualified applicants lost an opportunity for employment.	
Company	Managers may lose trust and may delegate important tasks to other employees.	

As a bookkeeper, Kenneth has been placed in a position of trust. Management must be able to have faith in the accounting records and reports prepared by a bookkeeper. Knowing that Kenneth has the capacity to misrepresent the facts, management may lose faith in Kenneth's honesty.

Kenneth's success in performing the functions of bookkeeper may affect management's decisions. Management may forgive Kenneth for his previous actions since he has proved to be a loyal employee. Although Kenneth may not be terminated, his relationship with management has been damaged.

accounting concepts and procedures. General office clerks with some knowledge of accounting will be able to understand the importance of the accounting tasks they complete.

SECRETARY

Requires 3 years secretarial experience, word processing, communication skills, and bookkeeping experience or accounting education.

SALES REPRESENTATIVE

Direct merchandising company. Key phone orders into automated sales/inventory system. Keyboarding and communications skills required. Knowledge of accounting a plus.

A CAREER IN ACCOUNTING

The career ladder shown in Illustration 1-1 represents the educational requirements and promotional possibilities in accounting careers.

Career Ladder

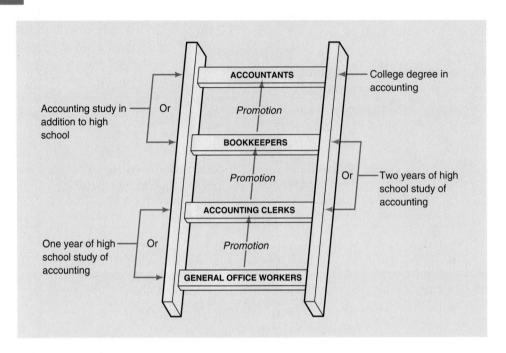

Immediately after high school graduation, individuals may start an accounting career as accounting clerks or general office clerks. A few of the better students may start as bookkeepers. High school study in accounting is useful as preparation for these accounting positions. The study of high school accounting is also good preparation for the study of accounting in college. With experience and additional accounting study, accounting personnel can earn a promotion to a higher position on the career ladder.

Professional Certification

All states require that a candidate pass an examination prepared by the AICPA to be certified as a CPA. The examination is administered twice a year, in May and November.

Almost all persons seeking positions as accountants must complete some study of accounting beyond high school and must gain accounting experience. Most public accountants also earn the Certified Public Accountant (CPA) designation. Each state sets the standards for earning a CPA certificate. Usually, the requirements include the study of college accounting, some accounting experience, and a passing score on a professional test covering all aspects of the accounting field.

Many private accountants often earn certification from a variety of professional accounting organizations. Private accountants can demonstrate their expertise in specific fields of accounting by earning certification such as the Certified Management Accountant (CMA) or the Certified Internal Auditor (CIA).

Professional Organizations

During the past one hundred years accountants have joined to form many professional organizations. The oldest and largest of these organizations is the American Institute of Certified Public Accountants (AICPA). The AICPA has a diverse membership of both public and private accountants. Other organizations, such as the American Woman's Society of Certified Public Accountants, the National Association of Black Accountants, and the International Federation of Accountants provide unique services to meet the needs of their members. Together, these organizations strive to promote job opportunities in accounting, to support and develop the professional skills of their members, and to improve the usefulness of accounting information.

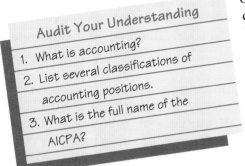

Audit Your Understanding

1. What is accounting?
2. List several classifications of accounting positions.
3. What is the full name of the AICPA?

THE IMPORTANCE OF COMMUNICATION AND ETHICS IN ACCOUNTING

Your knowledge of accounting will provide you with an important skill necessary for success in any profession or business. Yet, accounting knowledge alone will not assure success. Your ability to communicate and make ethical decisions will increase your chances of achieving professional success.

Communication

Effective accounting records can provide individuals with accurate and timely information regarding the financial activities of a business. Yet this information is of little value unless it can be communicated effectively to individuals responsible for making business decisions. Effective communication is essential because managers and accountants must often communicate accounting information to individuals with little or no accounting knowledge. Business leaders emphasize that communication skills are as important as technical skills in achieving career success.

Communication is the transfer of information between two or more individuals. Communication can be either oral or written. Oral communication includes phone conversations, one-on-one meetings, and group meetings. Written communication includes memorandums, letters, and reports.

Effective communication requires both a knowledge of good communication skills and regular practice using those skills. You have learned communication skills in a variety of language and communication classes. This textbook provides you the opportunity

FYI

Examples of other professional associations are: Institute of Management Accountants, American Accounting Association, Work in America Institute, and Families and Work Institute.

to practice your communication and language arts skills. Throughout the textbook you will be presented with a variety of business situations that require you to prepare an oral or written message.

Business Ethics

In your personal life you are faced daily with making decisions between right and wrong. The principles of right and wrong that guide an individual in making decisions are called **ethics**. Your personal ethics enable you to make decisions that consider the impact of your actions on others as well as yourself. Personal ethics are developed throughout your life from your relationships with family, friends, teachers, and other individuals that influence your life.

The use of personal ethics in making business decisions is called **business ethics**. Regardless of your position in an organization, you will be challenged to apply business ethics in making business decisions. The increasing complexity of today's business environment is also increasing the number of difficult business decisions that must be made.

Causes of Unethical Behavior. Unethical behavior occurs when an individual disregards his or her principles of right and wrong by choosing the wrong action. An understanding of the causes of unethical behavior is critical to preventing unethical behavior. Effective managers can identify and correct situations that would allow their employees to make decisions that may be unethical.

Six different factors may cause an individual to make an unethical decision.

1. Excessive emphasis on profits. Business managers are often judged on their ability to increase business profits. The salaries of business managers are often based on the amount of profits earned.
2. Misplaced business loyalty. Business managers often develop a misplaced dedication to their company. Disregarding their business ethics, managers may make decisions that appear to benefit the business without considering the negative impact on others.
3. Personal advancement. Some individuals have a "whatever it takes" attitude toward their personal careers. Their decisions are based solely on the degree that an action will advance their personal careers.
4. Expectation of not getting caught. An individual can recognize that an action is ethically wrong yet select that action because the chance of getting caught is small.
5. Unethical business environment. Individuals working in a business are less likely to apply business ethics if their managers are also making unethical decisions. The ethical environment set by business managers influences the ethical behavior of everyone in the business.

6. Unwillingness to take a stand. How often have you seen something wrong but not taken any action to correct it? Individuals can be unwilling to take a stand against unethical behavior because they fear losing their jobs, missing a deserved promotion, or alienating other employees.

Competition and the pursuit of success are the foundation of the free enterprise system. However, these factors are also common elements of unethical behavior. The desire to gain a competitive edge can motivate some individuals and businesses to make unethical decisions. The pursuit of success can motivate some individuals to overlook their principles of right and wrong. Fortunately, most business leaders now recognize that ethical behavior is the only way to attain long-term success.

Making Ethical Decisions. The increasing complexity of today's business environment requires that you be able to apply ethics in making business decisions. Determining whether an action is ethical can be difficult. In many business situations the line between right and wrong is not clear.

Analyzing a situation is the first step in deciding whether an action is ethical. The following three-step checklist will serve as a guide in collecting all relevant information regarding an action.

Three-step checklist for making ethical decisions:
1. Is the action illegal?
2. Does the action violate company or professional standards?
3. Who is affected, and how, by the action?

1 *Is the action illegal?* Does the action violate international, federal, state, or local laws? You should not consider an action if it is illegal. Obeying the law is in your best interest and the best interest of your business. Individuals will often encourage you to violate laws when the chance of being caught is small or the fine is minimal. Such an approach is shortsighted and does not consider all people who may be effected by the action.

2 *Does the action violate company or professional standards?* Public laws often set only minimum standards of behavior. Many businesses and professions set even higher standards of behavior. Thus, an action may be legal, yet still violate standards of the business or profession. Violating these standards may affect your job security and professional certification. The action may also have a negative effect on your business.

Several professional accounting organizations have adopted codes of professional conduct to assist their members in making ethical decisions. These codes have been written by the organizations' members to encourage their members to act and uphold the professional image of the accounting profession.

Audit Your Understanding

1. What is communication?

2. When does unethical behavior occur?

3. What are the three questions for analyzing ethical situations?

3 *Who is affected, and how, by the action?* If an action is legal and complies with business and professional standards, you must rely on your principles of right and wrong to determine if the action is ethical. Determine how the action affects a variety of people or groups, including the business employees and owners, customers, the local community, and society. In evaluating ethical situations, individuals often fail to consider how their actions affect a wide range of people.

Throughout this textbook you will have the opportunity to analyze common business situations. Use this three-step checklist to help determine whether each action demonstrates ethical behavior.

ACCOUNTING TERMS

EPT(a)

What is the meaning of each of the following?

1. **accounting**
2. **accounting system**
3. **accounting records**
4. **accountant**
5. **public accounting firm**
6. **private accountant**
7. **bookkeeper**
8. **accounting clerk**
9. **general office clerk**
10. **ethics**
11. **business ethics**

QUESTIONS FOR INDIVIDUAL STUDY

EPT(b,e)

1. Who uses summary reports of the financial activities of a business?
2. Why do persons responsible for nonprofit organizations need accounting information?
3. What personal reasons do individuals have for learning accounting facts and procedures?
4. What are the responsibilities of accountants?
5. What accounting services do public accounting firms offer?
6. What is the difference between a private accountant and a public accountant?
7. What does a bookkeeper do?
8. Why do general office clerks need to study accounting?
9. What entry-level accounting jobs might be obtained by persons who have studied high school accounting?
10. How can a person earn a designation as a CPA?
11. Why must managers and accountants have effective communication skills?
12. How are personal ethics developed?
13. What are the causes of unethical behavior?
14. What do most business leaders now recognize about ethical behavior?
15. What is the three-step checklist for collecting information for making an ethical decision?

CASES FOR CRITICAL THINKING

EPT(c,d)

CASE 1 Cynthia's career goal is to be the accountant responsible for her community's accounting system. After completing one year of high school accounting, she hopes to obtain an accounting clerk job in city government. She believes that several years of hard work in city government will provide her with the experience necessary to assume the accountant's job. Do you think Cynthia can reach her goal? Explain.

CASE 2 When planning his high school course selections, Duane selects accounting as a career field. He plans to complete two years of high school accounting study. Duane is not planning to complete any other high school business courses. Duane's school counselor suggests that he also complete at least one year of keyboarding. Should Duane take the counselor's advice? Explain.

APPLIED COMMUNICATIONS

A resume provides a statement of your education, experience, and qualifications for a prospective employer. Your resume should be accurate, honest, and perfect in every respect.

Your resume should include all work experience along with the companies and dates of employment. Education, activities, and interests are all important items that should be included. It is preferable to keep the resume to one typed page.

INSTRUCTIONS:

1. Go to the library and research how to prepare an appropriate resume.
2. Prepare a personal resume that you could send to a prospective employer.

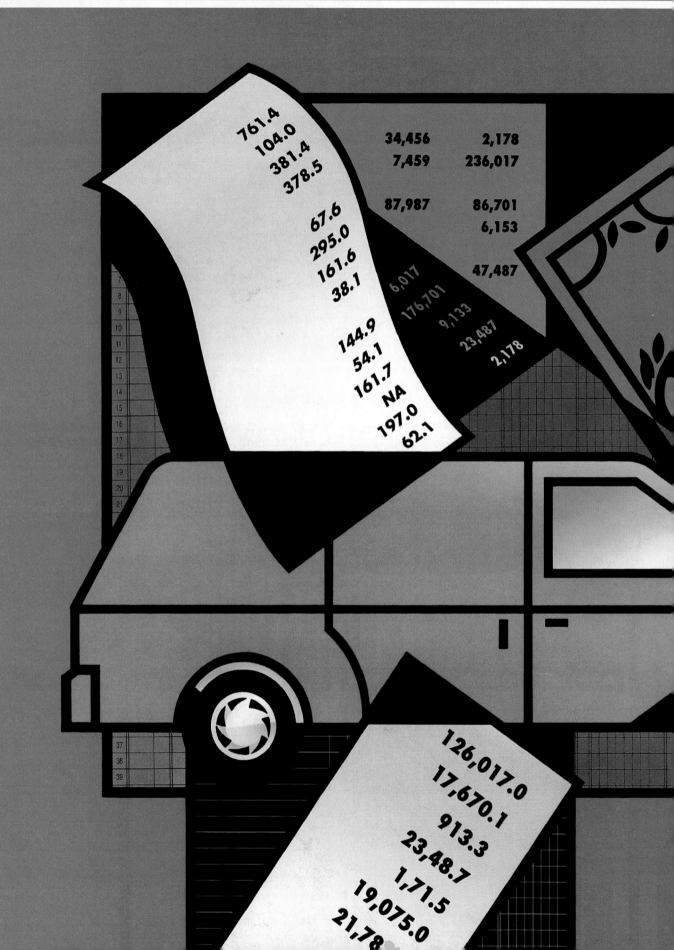

PART 2

Accounting for a Service Business Organized as a Proprietorship

GENERAL GOALS

1. Know accounting terminology related to an accounting system for a service business organized as a proprietorship.

2. Understand accounting concepts and practices related to an accounting system for a service business organized as a proprietorship.

3. Demonstrate accounting procedures used in an accounting system for a service business organized as a proprietorship.

RugCare

CHART OF ACCOUNTS

Balance Sheet Accounts

(100) ASSETS
110 Cash
120 Petty Cash
130 Supplies
140 Prepaid Insurance

(200) LIABILITIES
210 Butler Cleaning Supplies
220 Dale Office Supplies

(300) OWNER'S EQUITY
310 Ben Furman, Capital
320 Ben Furman, Drawing
330 Income Summary

Income Statement Accounts

(400) REVENUE
410 Sales

(500) EXPENSES
510 Advertising Expense
520 Insurance Expense
530 Miscellaneous Expense
540 Rent Expense
550 Repair Expense
560 Supplies Expense
570 Utilities Expense

The chart of accounts for Rugcare is illustrated above for ready reference as you study Part 2 of this textbook.

2

Starting a Proprietorship

ENABLING PERFORMANCE TASKS

After studying Chapter 2, you will be able to:

a Define accounting terms related to starting a service business organized as a proprietorship.

b Identify accounting concepts and practices related to starting a service business organized as a proprietorship.

c Classify accounts as assets, liabilities, or owner's equity.

d Analyze how transactions related to starting a service business organized as a proprietorship affect accounts in an accounting equation.

e Prepare a balance sheet for a service business organized as a proprietorship from information in an accounting equation.

TERMS PREVIEW

service business • proprietorship • asset • equities • liability • owner's equity • accounting equation • transaction • account • account title • account balance • capital • balance sheet

A person who chooses to start a business must make many decisions. To make these decisions, a businessperson needs financial information about the business. To provide the information, many records and reports relating to the business must be kept. In order to create useful records and reports, financial information must be kept in an organized way. Planning, recording, analyzing, and interpreting financial information is known as accounting. A planned process for providing financial information that will be useful to management is known as an accounting system.

THE BUSINESS

A business that performs an activity for a fee is called a **service business.** Ben Furman worked for a service business that cleans carpets for a fee. Mr. Furman wants to be in control of his hours and his earnings. Therefore, he decided to start his own carpet-cleaning business. A business owned by one person is called a **proprietorship.** A proprietorship is also referred to as a sole proprietorship. Mr. Furman has named his new proprietorship *Rugcare*. Rugcare will rent office space and the equipment used to operate the business.

Since a new business is being started, Mr. Furman must design the accounting system that will be used to keep Rugcare's accounting records. In the accounting system, Mr. Furman must be careful to keep Rugcare's accounting records separate from his own personal financial records. For example, Mr. Furman owns a house and a personal car. Rugcare's financial records must *not* include information about Mr. Furman's house, car, or other personal belongings. For example, Mr. Furman must use one checking account for his personal expenses and another checking account for Rugcare. The financial records for Rugcare and Mr. Furman's personal belongings must be kept separate. The accounting concept, *Business Entity*, is applied when a business' financial information is recorded and reported separately from the owner's personal financial information. *(CONCEPT: Business Entity)*

Accounting concepts are described throughout this textbook when an application of a concept first occurs. When additional applications occur, a concept reference, such as *(CONCEPT: Business Entity)*, indicates an application of a specific accounting concept. A brief description of each accounting concept used in this text is also provided in Appendix A.

A complete list of accounting concepts is in Appendix A.

THE ACCOUNTING EQUATION

A business has many items that have value. Rugcare will own items such as cash and supplies that will be used to conduct daily operations. Anything of value that is owned is called an **asset**. Assets have value because they can be used to acquire other assets or be used to operate a business. For example, Rugcare will use cash to buy supplies for the business. Rugcare will then use the asset, supplies, in the operation of the rug-cleaning business.

Financial rights to the assets of a business are called **equities.** A business has two types of equities. (1) Equity of those to whom money is owed. For example, Rugcare may buy some supplies and agree to pay for the supplies at a later date. The business from whom supplies are bought will have a right to some of Rugcare's assets until Rugcare pays for the supplies. An amount owed by a business is called a **liability.** (2) Equity of the owner. Mr. Furman will own Rugcare and invest in the assets of the business. Therefore, he will have a right to decide how the assets will be used. The amount remaining after the value of all liabilities is subtracted from the value of all assets is called **owner's equity.**

The relationship among assets, liabilities, and owner's equity can be written as an equation. An equation showing the relationship among assets, liabilities, and owner's equity is called the **accounting equation.** The accounting equation is most often stated as:

$$\text{Assets} = \text{Liabilities} + \text{Owner's Equity}$$

The accounting equation must be in balance to be correct. Thus, the total of the amounts on the left side of the equation must always equal the total of the amounts on the right side. Before Mr. Furman actually starts the business, Rugcare's accounting equation would show the following amounts.

Assets	=	Liabilities + Owner's Equity
Left side amount		Right side amounts
$0	=	$0 + $0

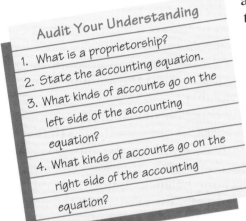

Audit Your Understanding

1. What is a proprietorship?
2. State the accounting equation.
3. What kinds of accounts go on the left side of the accounting equation?
4. What kinds of accounts go on the right side of the accounting equation?

HOW BUSINESS ACTIVITIES CHANGE THE ACCOUNTING EQUATION

FYI

The left side of the accounting equation must always equal the right side.

Business activities change the amounts in the accounting equation. A business activity that changes assets, liabilities, or owner's equity is called a **transaction.** For example, a business that pays cash for supplies is engaging in a transaction. After each transaction, the accounting equation must remain in balance.

The accounting concept, *Unit of Measurement*, is applied when business transactions are stated in numbers that have common values—that is, using a common unit of measurement. *(CONCEPT: Unit of Measurement)* For example, in the United States, business transactions are recorded in dollars. In Switzerland, business transactions are recorded in Swiss francs. The unit of measurement concept is followed so that the financial reports of businesses can be clearly stated and understood in numbers that have comparable values. For example, reports would not be clear if some information was reported in United States dollars and some in Swiss francs.

Received Cash from Owner as an Investment

Mr. Furman uses $10,000.00 of his own money to invest in Rugcare. Rugcare should only be concerned with the effect of this transaction on Rugcare's records. The business should *not* be concerned about Mr. Furman's personal records. *(CONCEPT: Business Entity)*

> *Transaction 1   August 1, 19--. Received cash from owner as an investment, $10,000.00.*

A record summarizing all the information pertaining to a single item in the accounting equation is called an **account**. The name given to an account is called an **account title**. Each part of the accounting equation consists of one or more accounts. For example, one of the asset accounts is titled Cash. The cash account is used to summarize information about the amount of money the business has available.

In the accounting equation shown in Illustration 2-1, the asset account, Cash, is increased by $10,000.00, the amount of cash received by the business. This increase is on the left side of the accounting equation. The amount in an account is called the **account balance**. Before the owner's investment, the account balance of Cash was zero. After the owner's investment, the account balance of Cash is $10,000.00.

ILLUSTRATION 2-1	Receiving cash from owner as an investment changes one asset and owner's equity

	Assets	=	Liabilities	+	Owner's Equity
	Cash	=			Ben Furman, Capital
Beg. Balances	$0		$0		$0
Transaction 1	+10,000				+10,000 (investment)
New Balances	$10,000		$0		$10,000

The account used to summarize the owner's equity in business is called **capital**. The capital account is an owner's equity account. Rugcare's capital account is titled Ben Furman, Capital. In the accounting equation shown in Illustration 2-1, the owner's equity account, Ben Furman, Capital, is increased by $10,000.00. This increase is on the right side of the accounting equation. Before the owner's investment, the account balance of Ben Furman, Capital was zero. After the owner's investment, the account balance of Ben Furman, Capital is $10,000.00.

The accounting equation has changed as a result of the receipt of cash as the owner's investment. However, both sides of the equation are changed by the same amount, $10,000.00. The $10,000.00 increase on the left side of the equation equals the $10,000.00

increase on the right side of the equation. Therefore, the accounting equation is still in balance.

Paid Cash for Supplies

Rugcare needs supplies to operate the business. Ben Furman uses some of Rugcare's cash to buy supplies.

Transaction 2   August 3, 19--. Paid cash for supplies, $1,577.00.

The effect of this transaction on the accounting equation is shown in Illustration 2-2. In this transaction, two asset accounts are changed. One asset, cash, has been exchanged for another asset, supplies. The asset account, Cash, is decreased by $1,577.00, the amount of cash paid out. This decrease is on the left side of the accounting equation. The asset account, Supplies, is increased by $1,577.00, the amount of supplies bought. This increase is also on the left side of the accounting equation.

| **ILLUSTRATION 2-2** | Paying cash for supplies changes two assets |

	Assets			=	**Liabilities**	+	**Owner's Equity**
	Cash	+	Supplies	=			Ben Furman, Capital
Balances	$10,000		$0		$0		$10,000
Transaction 2	−1,577		+1,577				
New Balances	$8,423		$1,577		$0		$10,000

Total of left side:
$8,423 + $1,577 = $10,000

Total of right side:
$10,000

For this transaction, two assets are changed. Therefore, the two changes are both on the left side of the accounting equation. When changes are made on only one side of the accounting equation, the equation must still be in balance. Therefore, if one account is increased, another account on the same side of the equation must be decreased. After this transaction, the new account balance of Cash is $8,423.00. The new account balance of Supplies is $1,577.00. The sum of the amounts on the left side is $10,000.00 (Cash, $8,423.00 + Supplies, $1,577.00). The amount on the right side is also $10,000.00. Therefore, the accounting equation is still in balance.

Paid Cash for Insurance

Insurance premiums must be paid in advance. For example, Rugcare pays a $1,200.00 insurance premium for future insurance coverage.

Transaction 3   August 4, 19--. Paid cash for insurance, $1,200.00.

In return for this payment, Rugcare is entitled to insurance coverage for the length of the policy. The insurance coverage is something of value owned by Rugcare. Therefore, the insurance coverage is an asset. Because insurance premiums are paid in advance, or *prepaid*, the premiums are recorded in an asset account titled Prepaid Insurance.

The effect of this transaction on the accounting equation is shown in Illustration 2-3. In this transaction, two assets are changed. One asset, cash, has been exchanged for another asset, prepaid insurance. The asset account, Cash, is decreased by $1,200.00, the amount of cash paid out. This decrease is on the left side of the accounting equation. The asset account, Prepaid Insurance, is increased by $1,200.00, the amount of insurance bought. This increase is also on the left side of the accounting equation.

ILLUSTRATION 2-3   Paying cash for insurance changes two assets

	Assets			=	Liabilities + Owner's Equity	
	Cash	+ Supplies	+ Prepaid Insurance =			Ben Furman, Capital
Balances	$8,423	$1,577	$0		$0	$10,000
Transaction 3	−1,200		+1,200			
New Balances	$7,223	$1,577	$1,200		$0	$10,000
	Total of left side: $7,223 + $1,577 + $1,200 = $10,000				Total of right side: $10,000	

Since two assets are changed by this transaction, both changes are on the left side of the accounting equation. Since one account is increased, the other account on the same side of the equation must be decreased. After this transaction, the new account balance of Cash is $7,223.00. The new account balance of Prepaid Insurance is $1,200.00. The sum of the amounts on the left side is $10,000.00 (Cash, $7,223.00 + Supplies, $1,577.00 + Prepaid Insurance, $1,200.00). The amount on the right side is also $10,000.00. Therefore, the accounting equation is still in balance.

Bought Supplies on Account

Rugcare needs to buy additional supplies. The supplies are obtained from Butler Cleaning Supplies, which is located in a different city. It is a common business practice to buy items and pay for them at a future date. Another way to state this activity is to say that these items are bought *on account*.

Transaction 4   August 7, 19--. Bought supplies on account from Butler Cleaning Supplies, $2,720.00.

The effect of this transaction on the accounting equation is shown in Illustration 2-4. In this transaction, one asset and one liability are changed. The asset account, Supplies, is increased by $2,720.00, the amount of supplies bought. This increase is on the left side of the accounting equation. Butler Cleaning Supplies will have a claim against some of Rugcare's assets until Rugcare pays for the supplies bought. Therefore, Butler Cleaning Supplies is a liability account. The liability account, Butler Cleaning Supplies, is increased by $2,720.00, the amount owed for the supplies. This increase is on the right side of the accounting equation.

ILLUSTRATION 2-4   Buying supplies on account changes one asset and one liability

	Assets			= Liabilities	+ Owner's Equity
	Cash	+ Supplies	+ Prepaid Insurance =	Butler Cleaning Supplies	+ Ben Furman, Capital
Balances	$7,223	$1,577	$1,200	$0	$10,000
Transaction 4		+2,720		+2,720	
New Balances	$7,223	$4,297	$1,200	$2,720	$10,000

Total of left side:
$7,223 + $4,297 + $1,200 = $12,720

Total of right side:
$2,720 + $10,000 = $12,720

This transaction changes both sides of the accounting equation. When changes are made on both sides of the equation, the change on the left side must equal the change on the right side. After this transaction, the new account balance of Supplies is $4,297.00. The new account balance of Butler Cleaning Supplies is $2,720.00. The sum of the amounts on the left side is $12,720.00 (Cash, $7,223.00 + Supplies, $4,297.00 + Prepaid Insurance, $1,200.00). The sum of the amounts on the right side is also $12,720.00 (Butler Cleaning Supplies, $2,720.00 + Ben Furman, Capital, $10,000.00). Therefore, the accounting equation is still in balance.

FYI

Accountants often refer to GAAP. GAAP is the acronym for Generally Accepted Accounting Principles. These principles are developed by the Financial Accounting Standards Board and are the foundation for all accounting procedures and practices.

Paid Cash on Account

Since Rugcare is a new business, Butler Cleaning Supplies has not done business with Rugcare before. Butler Cleaning Supplies allows Rugcare to buy supplies on account but requires Rugcare to send a check for one-half of the amount immediately. Rugcare will pay the remaining liability at a later date.

Transaction 5   August 11, 19--. Paid cash on account to Butler Cleaning Supplies, $1,360.00.

The effect of this transaction on the accounting equation is shown in Illustration 2-5. In this transaction, one asset and one lia-

ILLUSTRATION 2-5   Paying cash on account changes one asset and one liability

	Assets			=	Liabilities	+	Owner's Equity
	Cash	+ Supplies	+ Prepaid Insurance	=	Butler Cleaning Supplies	+	Ben Furman, Capital
Balances	$7,223	$4,297	$1,200		$2,720		$10,000
Transaction 5	−1,360				−1,360		
New Balances	$5,863	$4,297	$1,200		$1,360		$10,000
	Total of left side: $5,863 + $4,297 + $1,200 = $11,360				Total of right side: $1,360 + $10,000 = $11,360		

bility are changed. The asset account, Cash, is decreased by $1,360.00, the amount of cash paid out. This decrease is on the left side of the accounting equation. After this payment, Rugcare owes less money to Butler Cleaning Supplies. Therefore, the liability account, Butler Cleaning Supplies, is decreased by $1,360.00, the amount paid on account. This decrease is on the right side of the accounting equation.

This transaction changes both sides of the accounting equation. When changes are made on both sides of the equation, the change on the left side must equal the change on the right side. After this transaction, the new account balance of Cash is $5,863.00. The new account balance of Butler Cleaning Supplies is $1,360.00. The sum of the amounts on the left side is $11,360.00 (Cash, $5,863.00 + Supplies, $4,297.00 + Prepaid Insurance, $1,200.00). The sum of the amounts on the right side is also $11,360.00 (Butler Cleaning Supplies, $1,360.00 + Ben Furman, Capital, $10,000.00). Therefore, the accounting equation is still in balance.

Audit Your Understanding

1. What does it mean if the accounting equation is "in balance?"

2. What must be done if a transaction increases the left side of the accounting equation?

3. How can a transaction affect only one side of the accounting equation?

REPORTING FINANCIAL INFORMATION ON A BALANCE SHEET

Periodically a business reports details about its assets, liabilities, and owner's equity. The financial details about assets, liabilities, and owner's equity could be found on the last line of the accounting equation. However, most businesses prepare more formal financial statements that may be copied and sent to interested persons. A financial statement that reports assets, liabilities, and owner's equity on a specific date is called a **balance sheet**.

When a business is started, it is expected that the business will continue to operate indefinitely. For example, Ben Furman assumes that he will own and operate Rugcare for many years. When he retires, he expects to sell Rugcare to someone else who will con-

FYI

Every financial statement has a three-line heading that consists of the name of the company, the name of the statement, and the date.

tinue its operation. The accounting concept, *Going Concern*, is applied when financial statements are prepared with the expectation that a business will remain in operation indefinitely. *(CONCEPT: Going Concern)*

Body of a Balance Sheet

A balance sheet has three major sections. (1) *Assets* are on the left side of the accounting equation. Therefore, Rugcare lists its assets on the left side of the balance sheet. (2) *Liabilities* are on the right side of the accounting equation. Therefore, Rugcare lists its liabilities on the right side of the balance sheet. (3) *Owner's equity* is also on the right side of the accounting equation. Therefore, Rugcare lists its owner's equity on the right side of the balance sheet.

Rugcare's balance sheet, prepared after the transaction on August 11, is shown in Illustration 2-6.

ILLUSTRATION 2-6

Balance sheet for a service business organized as a proprietorship

	Assets			= Liabilities	+ Owner's Equity
	Cash	+ Supplies	+ Prepaid Insurance =	Butler Cleaning Supplies +	Ben Furman, Capital
Balances	$5,863	$4,297	$1,200	$1,360	$10,000

Rugcare			
Balance Sheet			
August 11, 19--			
Assets		**Liabilities**	
Cash	5863 00	Butler Cleaning Supplies	1360 00
Supplies	4297 00	**Owner's Equity**	
Prepaid Insurance	1200 00	Ben Furman, Capital	10000 00
Total Assets	11360 00	Total Liab. and Owner's Eq.	11360 00

Preparing a Balance Sheet

Rugcare's balance sheet is prepared in six steps.

1 Write the *heading* on three lines at the top of the balance sheet. Center each line. The heading for Rugcare's balance sheet is:

Name of the business:	Rugcare
Name of the report:	Balance Sheet
Date of the report:	August 11, 19--

2 Prepare the *assets section* on the LEFT side. Center the word *Assets* on the first line of the wide column on the left side. Under this heading, write each asset account title and

FOREIGN CURRENCY

As our world becomes smaller and global trade increases, more and more United States businesses will get involved in business transactions with companies in foreign countries. Transactions with foreign businesses may be stated in terms of U.S. dollars or the currency of the other country. If the transaction involves foreign currency, the U.S. business must convert the foreign currency into U.S. dollars before the transaction can be re-

corded. *(CONCEPT: Unit of Measurement)*

The value of foreign currency can change daily. The **exchange rate** is the value of foreign currency in relation to the U.S. dollar. Current exchange rates can be found in many daily newspapers or by contacting a bank. The above list of exchange rates is taken from a newspaper. Because the

rates change daily, the current exchange rates could be quite different than these rates which were current when this book was published.

The exchange rate is stated in terms of one unit of foreign currency. Using Germany as an example, the rate means that one German mark is worth .6757 U.S. dollars (or 68

U.S. cents). This rate would be used when exchanging German marks for U.S. dollars.

A **conversion formula** can be used to find out how many foreign currency units can be purchased with one U.S. dollar. The formula is:

---

1 ÷ exchange rate = foreign currency per U.S. dollar

1 dollar ÷ .6757 = 1.4799 marks per dollar

Applying the conversion formula to Germany, one U.S. dollar would buy 1.48 German marks. The formula could be applied to each rate stated above to determine how many foreign currency units can be purchased with one U.S. dollar.

COUNTRY	CURRENCY	U.S. $ EQUIVALENT
Australia	Dollar	.7303
Canada	Dollar	.7908
Germany	Mark	.6757
Hong Kong	Dollar	.12935
Mexico	New Peso	.323154
Peru	New Sol	.7931
South Africa	Rand	.2519

amount. The asset accounts are: Cash, $5,863.00; Supplies, $4,297.00; and Prepaid Insurance, $1,200.00.

3 Prepare the *liabilities section* on the RIGHT side. Center the word *Liabilities* on the first line of the wide column on the right side. Under this heading, write each liability account title and amount. Rugcare has only one liability account to be listed, Butler Cleaning Supplies, $1,360.00.

4 Prepare the *owner's equity section* on the RIGHT side. Center the words *Owner's Equity* on the next blank line of the wide column on the right side. Under this heading, write the owner's equity account title and amount. Rugcare's owner's equity account is Ben Furman, Capital, $10,000.00.

5 Determine if the balance sheet is *in balance*. Use a calculator, if available, or a sheet of scratch paper. Add all the asset amounts on the LEFT side. The total on the left side of Rugcare's balance sheet is $11,360.00 ($5,863.00 + $4,297.00 + $1,200.00). Add the liabilities and owner's equity amounts on the RIGHT side. The total on the right side of Rugcare's balance sheet is $11,360.00 ($1,360.00 + $10,000.00). The total of the LEFT side is the same as the total of the RIGHT side, $11,360.00. Therefore, Rugcare's balance sheet is in balance.

If the balance sheet is NOT in balance, find the errors before completing any more work.

6 Complete the balance sheet. Rule a single line across both amount columns. A single line means that amounts are to be added or subtracted. On the next line, write *Total Assets* in the wide column on the left side. On the same line, write the total asset amount, $11,360.00, in the left amount column. On the same line, write *Total Liabilities and Owner's Equity* in the wide column on the right side. On the same line, write the total liabilities and owner's equity amount, $11,360.00, in the right amount column. Rule double lines below the amount column totals. Double lines mean that the totals have been verified as correct.

When possible, words are spelled in full so there can be no doubt about what word was intended. However, in a few situations, where there is insufficient room to spell the words in full, words may be abbreviated. On Rugcare's balance sheet, it is necessary to abbreviate the words *Total Liab. and Owner's Eq.*

Audit Your Understanding

1. List the three sections of a balance sheet.

2. What kinds of accounts are listed on the left side of a balance sheet?

3. What kinds of accounts are listed on the right side of a balance sheet?

4. What should be done if a balance sheet is not in balance?

SUMMARY OF HOW TRANSACTIONS CHANGE THE ACCOUNTING EQUATION

Changes in the accounting equation caused by Transactions 1 to 5 are summarized in Illustration 2-7 on the following page.

Four basic rules relate to how transactions affect the accounting equation

1 Each transaction changes at least two accounts in the accounting equation.

2 When all the changes occur on one side of the accounting equation, increases on that side must be matched by decreases on the same side. Transactions 2 and 3 are examples of this rule.

3 When a transaction increases one side of the accounting equation, the other side of the equation must also be increased by the same amount. Transactions 1 and 4 are examples of this rule.

4 When a transaction decreases one side of the accounting equation, the other side of the equation must also be decreased by the same amount. Transaction 5 is an example of this rule.

Summary of how transactions change the accounting equation

Four basic rules relate to how transactions affect the accounting equation.

1 Each transaction changes at least two accounts in the accounting equation.

2 When all the changes occur on one side of the accounting equation, increases on that side must be matched by decreases on the same side. Transactions 2 and 3 are examples of this rule.

3 When a transaction increases one side of the accounting equation, the other side of the equation must also be increased by the same amount. Transactions 1 and 4 are examples of this rule.

4 When a transaction decreases one side of the accounting equation, the other side of the equation must also be decreased by the same amount. Transaction 5 is an example of this rule.

Transaction	Assets			= Liabilities +	Owner's Equity
	Cash +	Supplies +	Prepaid Insurance =	Butler Cleaning Supplies +	Ben Furman, Capital
Beginning Balance	$0	$0	$0	$0	$0
1. Received cash from owner as an investment	+10,000				+10,000 (investment)
New Balances	$10,000	$0	$0	$0	$10,000
2. Paid cash for supplies	−1,577	+1,577			
New Balances	$8,423	$1,577	$0	$0	$10,000
3. Paid cash for insurance	−1,200		+1,200		
New Balances	$7,223	$1,577	$1,200	$0	$10,000
4. Bought supplies on account		+2,720		+2,720	
5. New Balances	$7,223	$4,297	$1,200	$2,720	$10,000
Paid cash on account	−1,360			−1,360	
New Balances	$5,863	$4,297	$1,200	$1,360	$10,000

Total of left side:
$5,863 + $4,297 + $1,200 = $11,360

Total of right side:
$1,360 + $10,000 = $11,360

ACCOUNTING TERMS   EPT(a)

What is the meaning of each of the following?

1. **service business**
2. **proprietorship**
3. **asset**
4. **equities**
5. **liability**
6. **owner's equity**
7. **accounting equation**
8. **transaction**
9. **account**
10. **account title**
11. **account balance**
12. **capital**
13. **balance sheet**

1. Which accounting concept is being applied when a business records and reports financial information separate from the owner's personal financial information?
2. What are the two types of equities of a business?
3. What must be true about the accounting equation after each transaction?
4. Which accounting concept is being applied when a business in the United States reports financial information in dollars?
5. What accounts are affected, and how, when the owner invests cash in a business?
6. What accounts are affected, and how, when a business pays cash for supplies?
7. Why is Prepaid Insurance an asset?
8. How are liabilities affected when a business buys supplies on account?
9. How are liabilities affected when a business pays cash for a liability?
10. Which accounting concept is being applied when financial statements are prepared with the expectation that a business will remain in operation indefinitely?
11. What three items are included in the heading of a balance sheet?
12. What six steps are followed in preparing a balance sheet?
13. What do double lines below a column total mean?
14. What are the four basic rules relating to how transactions affect the accounting equation?

CASES FOR CRITICAL THINKING

EPT(a,b)

CASE 1   James Patton starts a new business. Mr. Patton uses his personal car in the business with the expectation that later the business can buy a car. All expenses for operating the car, including license plates, gasoline, oil, tune-ups, and new tires, are paid for out of business funds. Is this an acceptable procedure? Explain.

CASE 2   At the end of the first day of business, Quick Clean Laundry has the following assets and liabilities:

Assets	
Cash	$3,500.00
Supplies	950.00
Prepaid Insurance	1,200.00
Liabilities	
Smith Office Supplies	$ 750.00
Super Supplies Company	1,500.00

The owner, Susan Whiteford, wants to know the amount of her equity in Quick Clean Laundry. Determine this amount and explain what this amount represents.

DRILLS FOR UNDERSTANDING

EPT(c,d,e)

DRILL 2-D1   Classifying assets, liabilities, and owner's equity

TUTORIAL

Use a form similar to the following.

Item	Asset	Liability	Owner's Equity
1. Cash	√		

INSTRUCTIONS:

Classify each item listed below as an asset, liability, or owner's equity. Place a check mark in the appropriate column. Item 1 is given as an example.

1. Cash
2. Alice Jones, Capital
3. Prepaid Insurance
4. Steward Supply Company
5. Supplies
6. Any amount owed
7. Owner's capital account
8. Anything owned

DRILL 2-D2 Determining how transactions change an accounting equation

Use a form similar to the following.

Trans. No.	Assets	=	Liabilities	+ Owner's Equity
1.	+		+	

Transactions
1. Bought supplies on account.
2. Paid cash for insurance.
3. Received cash from owner as an investment.
4. Paid cash for supplies.
5. Paid cash on account to Konroy Company.

INSTRUCTIONS:

Decide which classification(s) are changed by each transaction. Place a plus (+) in the appropriate column if the classification is increased. Place a minus (−) in the appropriate column if the classification is decreased. Transaction 1 is given as an example.

DRILL 2-D3 Determining where items are listed on a balance sheet

Use a form similar to the following.

1	2	3
	Balance Sheet	
Items	Left Side	Right Side
1. Cash	*Asset*	

INSTRUCTIONS:

Classify each item as an asset, liability, or owner's equity. Write the classification in Column 2 or 3 to show where each item is listed on a balance sheet. Item 1 is given as an example.

1. Cash
2. Gretchen Murphy, Capital
3. Supplies
4. Prepaid Insurance
5. Action Laundry
6. Anything owned
7. Any amount owed
8. Owner's capital account

APPLICATION PROBLEMS   EPT(d,e)

PROBLEM 2-1 Determining how transactions change an accounting equation

Frank Mori is starting Mori Repair Shop, a small service business. Mori Repair Shop uses the accounts shown in the following accounting equation. Use a form similar to the following to complete this problem.

Trans. No.	Assets			=	Liabilities		+	Owner's Equity
	Cash +	Supplies +	Prepaid Insurance	=	Swan's Supply Company	+ York Company	+	Frank Mori, Capital
Beg. Bal.	0	0	0		0	0		0
1.	+2,000							+2,000 (investment)
New Bal.	2,000	0	0		0	0		2,000
2.								

Transactions

1. Received cash from owner as an investment, $2,000.00.
2. Paid cash for insurance, $600.00.
3. Bought supplies on account from Swan's Supply Company, $100.00.
4. Bought supplies on account from York Company, $500.00.
5. Paid cash on account to Swan's Supply Company, $100.00.
6. Paid cash on account to York Company, $300.00.
7. Paid cash for supplies, $500.00.
8. Received cash from owner as an investment, $500.00.

INSTRUCTIONS:

For each transaction, complete the following. Transaction 1 is given as an example.

a. Analyze the transaction to determine which accounts in the accounting equation are affected.

b. Write the amount in the appropriate columns using a plus (+) if the account increases or a minus (−) if the account decreases.

c. For transactions that change owner's equity, write in parentheses a description of the transaction to the right of the amount.

d. Calculate the new balance for each account in the accounting equation.

e. Before going on to the next transaction, determine that the accounting equation is still in balance.

PROBLEM 2-2 Preparing a balance sheet from information in an accounting equation

On September 30 the Steffens Company's accounting equation indicated the following account balances.

Trans. No.	Assets				= Liabilities	+ Owner's Equity
	Cash	+ Supplies	+	Prepaid Insurance	= Morton Company	+ Steve Steffens, Capital
New Bal.	1,200	150		300	250	1,400

INSTRUCTIONS:

Using the September 30 balance in the accounting equation, prepare a balance sheet for the Steffens Company.

PROBLEM 2-3 Determining how transactions change an accounting equation and preparing a balance sheet

Nancy Dirks is starting Dirks Company, a small service business. Dirks Company uses the accounts shown in the following accounting equation. Use a form similar to the following to complete this problem.

Trans. No.	Assets				= Liabilities	+ Owner's Equity
	Cash	+ Supplies	+	Prepaid Insurance	= Helfrey Company	+ Nancy Dirks, Capital
Beg. Bal. 1.	0 +350	0		0	0	0 +350 (investment)
New Bal. 2.	350	0		0	0	350

Transactions

1. Received cash from owner as an investment, $350.00.
2. Bought supplies on account from Helfrey Company, $100.00.
3. Paid cash for insurance, $150.00.
4. Paid cash for supplies, $50.00.
5. Received cash from owner as an investment, $300.00.
6. Paid cash on account to Helfrey Company, $75.00.

INSTRUCTIONS:

1. For each transaction, complete the following. Transaction 1 is given as an example.
   a. Analyze the transaction to determine which accounts in the accounting equation are affected.
   b. Write the amount in the appropriate columns, using a plus (+) if the account increases or a minus (−) if the account decreases.
   c. For transactions that change owner's equity, write in parentheses a description of the transaction to the right of the amount.
   d. Calculate the new balance for each account in the accounting equation.
   e. Before going on to the next transaction, determine that the accounting equation is still in balance.
2. Using the final balances in the accounting equation, prepare a balance sheet for Dirks Company. Use July 31 of the current year as the date of the balance sheet.

ENRICHMENT PROBLEMS   EPT(d,e)

MASTERY PROBLEM 2-M Determining how transactions change an accounting equation and preparing a balance sheet

Gregory Morgan is starting a limousine service called Luxury Limo. Luxury Limo uses the accounts shown in the following accounting equation. Use a form similar to the following to complete this problem.

Trans. No.	Assets			=	Liabilities	+	Owner's Equity
	Cash	+ Supplies	+ Prepaid Insurance	=	Limo Supply Company	+	Gregory Morgan, Capital
Beg. Bal.	0	0	0		0		0
1.	+2,000						+2,000 (investment)
New Bal.	2,000	0	0		0		2,000
2.							

Transactions

1. Received cash from owner as an investment, $2,000.00.
2. Paid cash for supplies, $250.00.
3. Bought supplies on account from Limo Supply Company, $300.00.
4. Paid cash for insurance, $600.00.
5. Paid cash on account to Limo Supply Company, $150.00.

INSTRUCTIONS:

1. For each transaction, complete the following. Transaction 1 is given as an example.
   a. Analyze the transaction to determine which accounts in the accounting equation are affected.
   b. Write the amount in the appropriate columns, using a plus (+) if the account increases or a minus (−) if the account decreases.

c. For transactions that change owner's equity, write in parentheses a description of the transaction to the right of the amount.

d. Calculate the new balance for each account in the accounting equation.

e. Before going on to the next transaction, determine that the accounting equation is still in balance.

2. Using the final balances in the accounting equation, prepare a balance sheet for Luxury Limo. Use February 5 of the current year as the date of the balance sheet.

CHALLENGE PROBLEM 2-C Applying accounting concepts to determine how transactions change the accounting equation

Olson Delivery Service, a new business owned by Jerome Olson, uses the accounts shown in the following accounting equation. Use a form similar to the following to complete this problem.

Trans. No.	Assets			=	Liabilities		+	Owner's Equity
	Cash +	Supplies +	Prepaid Insurance	=	Mutual Savings Bank	+	Nelson Supply Co. +	Jerome Olson, Capital
Beg. Bal.	0	0	0		0		0	0
1.	+1,500							+1,500 (investment)
New Bal.	1,500	0	0		0		0	1,500
2.								

Transactions

1. Owner invested cash, $1,500.00.
2. Bought supplies for cash, $400.00.
3. Paid cash for insurance, $240.00.
4. Supplies were bought on account from Nelson Supply Company, $80.00.
5. The owner, Jerome Olson, paid $1,000.00 of his personal cash to Mutual Savings Bank for the car payment on his personal car.
6. Wrote a check for supplies. The supplies were bought from a Canadian company. The supplies cost $120.00 in Canadian dollars, which is equivalent to $100.00 in United States dollars.

INSTRUCTIONS:

For each transaction, complete the following. Transaction 1 is given as an example.

a. Analyze the transaction to determine which business accounts in the accounting equation, if any, are affected. You will need to apply the Business Entity and Unit of Measurement concepts in this problem.

b. If business accounts are affected, determine the appropriate amount of the change. Write the amount in the appropriate columns, using a plus (+) if the account increases or a minus (−) if the account decreases.

c. For transactions that change owner's equity, write in parentheses a description of the transaction to the right of the amount.

d. Calculate the new balance for each account in the accounting equation.

e. Before going on to the next transaction, determine that the accounting equation is still in balance.

Starting a Proprietorship: Changes That Affect Owner's Equity

ENABLING PERFORMANCE TASKS

After studying Chapter 3, you will be able to:

a Define accounting terms related to changes that affect owner's equity for a service business organized as a proprietorship.

b Identify accounting practices related to changes that affect owner's equity for a service business organized as a proprietorship.

c Analyze changes that affect owner's equity for a service business organized as a proprietorship in an accounting equation.

d Prepare a balance sheet for a service business organized as a proprietorship from information in the accounting equation.

TERMS PREVIEW

revenue • expense • withdrawals

A business activity that changes assets, liabilities, or owner's equity is known as a transaction. Chapter 2 describes five transactions involved in starting Rugcare, a proprietorship. Rugcare is now ready to open for business. This chapter presents the transactions that commonly occur during the daily operations of a business. Each of these transactions changes Ben Furman's equity in Rugcare.

HOW TRANSACTIONS CHANGE OWNER'S EQUITY IN AN ACCOUNTING EQUATION

The accounting equation for Rugcare as of August 11, showing the effect of transactions for starting a business, is shown in Illustration 3-1.

The sum of the balances on the left side of the accounting equation, $11,360.00, equals the sum of the balances on the right side of the equation, $11,360.00. The equation is in balance.

Many transactions involved in the daily operations of a business increase or decrease owner's equity. Detailed information about these changes in owner's equity is needed by owners and managers to make sound business decisions.

FYI

Each transaction changes at least two accounts in the accounting equation.

ILLUSTRATION 3-1   Accounting equation after transactions for starting a proprietorship

	Assets			**= Liabilities + Owner's Equity**		
	Cash	+ Supplies +	Prepaid Insurance =	Butler Cleaning Supplies	+	Ben Furman, Capital
Balances	$5,863	$4,297	$1,200	$1,360		$10,000
	Total of left side: $5,863 + $4,297 + $1,200 = $11,360			Total of right side: $1,360 + $10,000 = $11,360		

Received Cash from Sales

A transaction for the sale of goods or services results in an increase in owner's equity. An increase in owner's equity resulting from the operation of a business is called **revenue.** When cash is received from a sale, the total amount of assets and owner's equity is increased.

When Rugcare receives cash for services performed, two accounts in the accounting equation are affected. The asset account, Cash, is increased by the amount of cash received. The owner's equity account, Ben Furman, Capital, is increased by the same amount.

Transaction 6   August 12, 19--. Received cash from sales, $525.00.

The effect of this transaction on the accounting equation is shown in Illustration 3-2. The asset account, Cash, is increased by $525.00, the amount of cash received. This increase is on the left side of the equation. The owner's equity account, Ben Furman, Capital, is also increased by $525.00. This increase is on the right side of the equation.

ILLUSTRATION 3-2   Receiving cash from sales increases assets and owner's equity

	Assets			= Liabilities + Owner's Equity	
	Cash	+ Supplies	+ Prepaid Insurance =	Butler Cleaning Supplies	+ Ben Furman, Capital
Balances	$5,863	$4,297	$1,200	$1,360	$10,000
Transaction 6	+525				+525 (revenue)
New Balances	$6,388	$4,297	$1,200	$1,360	$10,525

Total of left side:
$6,388 + $4,297 + $1,200 = $11,885

Total of right side:
$1,360 + $10,525 = $11,885

When all the changes occur on one side of the accounting equation, increases on that side must be matched by decreases on the same side.

After this transaction is recorded, the sum of the balances on the left side of the equation equals the sum of the balances on the right side, $11,885.00. The equation is still in balance.

In this chapter, three different kinds of transactions that affect owner's equity are described. Therefore, a description of the transaction is shown in parentheses to the right of the amount in the accounting equation. Transaction 6 is a revenue transaction. Therefore, *(revenue)* is shown beside the $525.00 change in owner's equity in Illustration 3-2.

Paid Cash for Expenses

A transaction to pay for goods or services needed to operate a business results in a decrease in owner's equity. A decrease in owner's equity resulting from the operation of a business is called an **expense.** When cash is paid for expenses, the business has less cash. Therefore, the asset account, Cash, is decreased. The owner's equity account, Ben Furman, Capital, is also decreased by the same amount.

Transaction 7   August 12, 19--. Paid cash for rent, $250.00.

The effect of this transaction on the accounting equation is shown in Illustration 3-3. The asset account, Cash, is decreased by $250.00, the amount of cash paid out. This decrease is on the left side of the equation. The owner's equity account, Ben Furman, Capital, is also

ILLUSTRATION 3-3   Paying cash for an expense decreases assets and owner's equity

	Assets			= Liabilities + Owner's Equity	
	Cash	+ Supplies	+ Prepaid Insurance =	Butler Cleaning Supplies	+ Ben Furman, Capital
Balances	$6,388	$4,297	$1,200	$1,360	$10,525
Transaction 7	−250				−250 (expense)
New Balances	$6,138	$4,297	$1,200	$1,360	$10,275
	Total of left side: $6,138 + $4,297 + $1,200 = $11,635			Total of right side: $1,360 + $10,275 = $11,635	

decreased by $250.00. This decrease is on the right side of the equation.

After this transaction is recorded, the sum of the balances on the left side of the equation equals the sum of the balances on the right side, $11,635.00. The equation is still in balance.

Transaction 8   August 12, 19--. Paid cash for telephone bill, $45.00.

Most businesses must make payments for goods and services provided by public utilities, such as telephone companies. These goods and services are often referred to as utilities. In addition to telephone services, electricity, gas, water, and sanitation are also considered to be utilities.

The effect of this transaction on the accounting equation is shown in Illustration 3-4. The asset account, Cash, is decreased by $45.00, the amount of cash paid out. This decrease is on the left side of the equation. The owner's equity account, Ben Furman, Capital, is also decreased by $45.00. This decrease is on the right side of the equation.

> **FYI**
>
> Accounting is not just for accountants. For example, a doctor starting a new practice needs to consider the investment needed to acquire office space, furnishings, and equipment. A doctor must also consider what additional employees must be hired to run the practice.

ILLUSTRATION 3-4   Paying cash for an expense decreases assets and owner's equity

	Assets			= Liabilities + Owner's Equity	
	Cash	+ Supplies	+ Prepaid Insurance =	Butler Cleaning Supplies	+ Ben Furman, Capital
Balances	$6,138	$4,297	$1,200	$1,360	$10,275
Transaction 8	−45				−45 (expense)
New Balances	$6,093	$4,297	$1,200	$1,360	$10,230
	Total of left side: $6,093 + $4,297 + $1,200 = $11,590			Total of right side: $1,360 + $10,230 = $11,590	

After this transaction is recorded, the sum of the balances on the left side of the equation equals the sum of the balances on the right side, $11,590.00. The equation is still in balance.

Other expense transactions might be for advertising, equipment rental or repairs, charitable contributions, and other miscellaneous items. All expense transactions affect the accounting equation in the same way as Transactions 7 and 8.

Paid Cash to Owner for Personal Use

Assets taken out of a business for the owner's personal use are called **withdrawals.** A withdrawal decreases owner's equity. Although an owner may withdraw any kind of asset, usually an owner withdraws cash. The withdrawal decreases the account balance of the withdrawn asset, such as Cash.

Transaction 9   August 12, 19--. Paid cash to owner for personal use, $100.00.

The effect of this transaction on the accounting equation is shown in Illustration 3-5 on the next page. The asset account, Cash, is decreased by $100.00, the amount of cash paid out. This decrease is on the left side of the accounting equation. The owner's equity account, Ben Furman, Capital, is also decreased by $100.00. This decrease is on the right side of the equation.

After this transaction is recorded, the sum of the balances on the left side of the equation equals the sum of the balances on the right side, $11,490.00. The equation is still in balance.

A decrease in owner's equity because of a withdrawal is not a result of the normal operations of a business. Therefore, a withdrawal is not an expense.

Summary of Changes in Owner's Equity

After recording the transactions for starting Rugcare as a proprietorship, the total owner's equity was $10,000.00. Five transactions

FYI

Some organizations were formed to support the interest of professional women. Examples of these organizations are American Society of Women Accountants, National Association for Female Executives, and National Association of Women Business Owners.

ILLUSTRATION 3-5   Paying cash to owner for personal use decreases assets and owner's equity

	Assets				=	Liabilities	+	Owner's Equity
	Cash	+	Supplies	+	Prepaid Insurance =	Butler Cleaning Supplies	+	Ben Furman, Capital
Balances	$6,093		$4,297		$1,200	$1,360		$10,230
Transaction 9	−100							−100 (withdrawal)
New Balances	$5,993		$4,297		$1,200	$1,360		$10,130

Total of left side:
$5,993 + $4,297 + $1,200 = $11,490

Total of right side:
$1,360 + $10,130 = $11,490

have affected owner's equity. In Chapter 2, Ben Furman made a $10,000.00 investment. In this chapter, four transactions that changed owner's equity were recorded in the accounting equation.

Transaction Number	Kind of Transaction	Change in Owner's Equity
6	Revenue	+525.00
7	Expense (rent)	−250.00
8	Expense (telephone)	−45.00
9	Withdrawal	−100.00
	Net change in owner's equity	+130.00

A revenue transaction increased owner's equity. Expense and withdrawal transactions decreased owner's equity. These transactions together increased total owner's equity by $130.00, from $10,000.00 to $10,130.00.

For a business to succeed, revenues must be greater than expenses during most periods of time. An established business should rarely experience a decrease in its owner's equity.

REPORTING A CHANGED ACCOUNTING EQUATION ON A BALANCE SHEET

A balance sheet may be prepared on any date to report information about the assets, liabilities, and owner's equity of a business. The balance sheet prepared in Chapter 2, Illustration 2-6, reports Rugcare's financial condition at the end of business on August 11. The transactions recorded in Chapter 3 have changed the account balances of Cash and Ben Furman, Capital in the accounting equation. A revised balance sheet is prepared to report Rugcare's financial condition after recording these transactions.

The last transaction on August 12 is recorded in the accounting equation as shown in Illustration 3-5. The new account balances in the accounting equation after Transaction 9 are used to prepare the balance sheet. Rugcare's balance sheet as of August 12 is shown in Illustration 3-6.

The August 12 balance sheet is prepared using the same steps as described in Chapter 2.

ILLUSTRATION 3-6 Balance sheet

	Assets			= Liabilities	+ Owner's Equity
	Cash	+ Supplies	+ Prepaid Insurance =	Butler Cleaning Supplies	+	Ben Furman, Capital
New Balances	$5,993	$4,297	$1,200	$1,360	$10,130

Rugcare				
Balance Sheet				
August 12, 19--				
Assets		**Liabilities**	
Cash	5 9 9 3 00	Butler Cleaning Supplies	1 3 6 0 00
Supplies	4 2 9 7 00	**Owner's Equity**	
Prepaid Insurance	1 2 0 0 00	Ben Furman, Capital	10 1 3 0 00
Total Assets	11 4 9 0 00	Total Liab. and Owner's Eq.	11 4 9 0 00

The accounts on the left side of the accounting equation are reported on the left side of Rugcare's balance sheet. The accounts on the right side of the accounting equation are shown on the right side of the balance sheet. The total of the left side of the balance sheet, $11,490.00, is equal to the total of the right side of the balance sheet. The balance sheet is in balance.

A comparison of the August 11 and August 12 balance sheet totals is shown in Illustration 3-7.

The balance sheet has an increase of $130.00 on the left side (Assets) and an increase of $130.00 on the right side (Liabilities + Owner's Equity).

ILLUSTRATION 3-7   Comparison of balance sheet totals

	Assets			= Liabilities +	Owner's Equity
	Cash	+ Supplies	+ Prepaid Insurance =	Butler Cleaning Supplies +	Ben Furman, Capital
August 11	$5,863	$4,297	$1,200	$1,360	$10,000
August 12	$5,993	$4,297	$1,200	$1,360	$10,130
	+$130	$0	$0	$0	+$130

Few businesses need to prepare a balance sheet every day. Many businesses prepare a balance sheet only on the last day of each month. Monthly balance sheets provide business owners and managers with frequent and regular information for making business decisions.

SUMMARY OF TRANSACTIONS THAT AFFECT OWNER'S EQUITY

Revenue, expense, and withdrawal transactions affect owner's equity. A revenue transaction increases owner's equity. Expense and withdrawal transactions decrease owner's equity.

The accounting equation has two sides. The left side of the equation shows assets. The right side of the equation shows liabilities and owner's equity. A transaction changes the account balances of two or more accounts. After each transaction, the total of accounts on the left side must equal the total of accounts on the right side. The effects of the transactions analyzed in Chapters 2 and 3 on the accounting equation are shown in Illustration 3-8 on the following page. After these transactions are recorded, the total of the balances on the left side equals the total of the balances on the right side, $11,490.00. Therefore, the accounting equation is in balance.

The new balances of the accounting equation are used to prepare a balance sheet. The left side of the balance sheet contains asset accounts. The right side contains liability and owner's equity accounts.

Audit Your Understanding

1. What is the heading on the left side of the balance sheet?

2. What are the headings on the right side of the balance sheet?

3. What is the total on the left side of the balance sheet?

4. What is the total on the right side of the balance sheet?

Summary of how transactions affect the accounting equation

Transaction	Assets			= Liabilities +	Owner's Equity
	Cash +	Supplies +	Prepaid Insurance =	Butler Cleaning Supplies +	Ben Furman, Capital
Beginning Balance	$0	$0	$0	$0	$0
1. Received cash from owner as an investment	+10,000				+10,000 (investment)
New Balances	$10,000	$0	$0	$0	$10,000
2. Paid cash for supplies	−1,577	+1,577			
New Balances	$ 8,423	$1,577	$0	$0	$10,000
3. Paid cash for insurance	−1,200		+1,200		
New Balances	$ 7,223	$1,577	$1,200	$0	$10,000
4. Bought supplies on account		+2,720		+2,720	
New Balances	$ 7,223	$4,297	$1,200	$2,720	$10,000
5. Paid cash on account	−1,360			−1,360	
New Balances	$ 5,863	$4,297	$1,200	$1,360	$10,000
6. Received cash from sales	+525				+525 (revenue)
New Balances	$ 6,388	$4,297	$1,200	$1,360	$10,525
7. Paid cash for rent	−250				−250 (expense)
New Balances	$ 6,138	$4,297	$1,200	$1,360	$10,275
8. Paid cash for telephone bill	−45				−45 (expense)
New Balances	$ 6,093	$4,297	$1,200	$1,360	$10,230
9. Paid cash to owner for personal use	−100				−100 (withdrawal)
New Balances	$ 5,993	$4,297	$1,200	$1,360	$10,130

Total of left side:
$5,993 + $4,297 + $1,200 = $11,490

Total of right side:
$1,360 + $10,130 = $11,490

What is the meaning of each of the following?

1. **revenue**
2. **expense**
3. **withdrawals**

1. Why do owners and managers need information about changes in owner's equity?

2. What accounts are affected, and how, when cash is received from sales?

3. How does a cash payment for goods or services needed to operate a business affect owner's equity?

4. What accounts are affected, and how, by a cash payment for an expense?

5. What must be true of the accounting equation after each transaction is recorded?

6. What are four expense transactions other than rent and utilities?

7. Which asset is normally withdrawn by an owner for personal use?

8. What accounts are affected, and how, when an owner withdraws $200.00 for personal use?

9. What transactions decrease owner's equity?

10. What must be true of changes in owner's equity if a business is to be successful?

11. What are three accounts that might be found on the left side of a balance sheet?

12. How often might a business be expected to prepare a balance sheet?

CASE 1 Garcia Books received an investment from its owner, Mrs. Juanita Garcia. This transaction is recorded in the following accounting equation. Is the analysis correct? Explain.

Assets			=	Liabilities	+	Owner's Equity
Cash	+ Supplies	+ Prepaid Insurance =		Panther Supply Company	+	Juanita Garcia, Capital
$1,000	$3,000	$2,000		$2,500		$3,500
+750						
$1,750	$3,000	$2,000		$2,500		$3,500

CASE 2 The manager of Phillip's Department Store prepares a balance sheet at the end of each business day. Is this a satisfactory procedure? Explain.

DRILL 3-D1 Determining how revenue, expense, and withdrawal transactions change an accounting equation

TUTORIAL

Use a form similar to the following.

Trans. No.	Assets					= Liabilities + Owner's Equity		
	Cash	+	Supplies	+	Prepaid Insurance	= Maxwell Company	+	Susan Sanders, Capital
1.	+							+

Transactions

1. Received cash from owner as an investment.
2. Received cash from sales.
3. Paid cash for telephone bill.
4. Paid cash for advertising.
5. Paid cash to owner for personal use.
6. Paid cash for rent.
7. Received cash from sales.
8. Paid cash for equipment repairs.

INSTRUCTIONS:

Decide which accounts in the accounting equation are changed by each transaction. Place a plus (+) in the appropriate column if the account is increased. Place a minus (−) in the appropriate column if the account is decreased. Transaction 1 is given as an example.

DRILL 3-D2 Determining how transactions change an accounting equation

Use a form similar to the following.

Trans. No.	Assets					= Liabilities + Owner's Equity		
	Cash	+	Supplies	+	Prepaid Insurance	= Barrett Company	+	Sue Marist, Capital
1.			+			+		

Transactions

1. Bought supplies on account from Barrett Company.
2. Paid cash for electric bill.
3. Received cash from owner as an investment.
4. Paid cash for insurance.

5. Received cash from sales.

6. Paid cash for rent.

7. Paid cash for supplies.

8. Paid cash for advertising.

9. Paid cash on account to Barrett Company.

10. Paid cash to owner for personal use.

INSTRUCTIONS:

Decide which accounts in the accounting equation are changed by each transaction. Place a plus (+) in the appropriate column if the account is increased. Place a minus (−) in the appropriate column if the account is decreased. Transaction 1 is given as an example.

APPLICATION PROBLEMS   EPT(c,d)

PROBLEM 3-1 Determining how revenue, expense, and withdrawal transactions change an accounting equation

Peter Smith operates a service business called Peter's Service Company. Peter's Service Company uses the accounts shown in the following accounting equation. Use a form similar to the following to complete this problem.

Trans. No.	Assets						= Liabilities + Owner's Equity		
	Cash	+	Supplies	+	Prepaid Insurance	=	Kline Company	+	Peter Smith, Capital
Beg. Bal. 1.	625 −300		375		300		200		1,100 −300 (expense)
New Bal. 2.	325		375		300		200		800

Transactions

1. Paid cash for rent, $300.00.

2. Paid cash to owner for personal use, $150.00.

3. Received cash from sales, $800.00.

4. Paid cash for equipment repairs, $100.00

5. Paid cash for telephone bill, $60.00.

6. Received cash from sales, $650.00.

7. Paid cash for charitable contributions, $35.00.

8. Paid cash for miscellaneous expenses, $25.00.

INSTRUCTIONS:

For each transaction, complete the following. Transaction 1 is given as an example.

a. Analyze the transaction to determine which accounts in the accounting equation are affected.

b. Write the amount in the appropriate columns, using a plus (+) if the account increases or a minus (−) if the account decreases.

c. For transactions that change owner's equity, write in parentheses a description of the transaction to the right of the amount.

d. Calculate the new balance for each account in the accounting equation.

e. Before going on to the next transaction, determine that the accounting equation is still in balance.

PROBLEM 3-2 Determining how transactions change an accounting equation and preparing a balance sheet

Doris Becker operates a typing business called QuickType. QuickType uses the accounts shown in the following accounting equation. Use a form similar to the following to complete this problem.

Trans. No.	Assets			= Liabilities	+ Owner's Equity
	Cash +	Supplies +	Prepaid Insurance	= Teale Company	+ Doris Becker, Capital
Beg. Bal.	500	260	300	100	960
1.	−50				−50 (expense)
New Bal.	450	260	300	100	910
2.					

Transactions
1. Paid cash for equipment repair, $50.00.
2. Received cash from sales, $325.00.
3. Paid cash for supplies, $200.00.
4. Bought supplies on account from Teale Company, $1,200.00.
5. Paid cash for advertising, $200.00.
6. Received cash from sales, $280.00.
7. Paid cash for water bill, $60.00.
8. Paid cash for insurance, $400.00.
9. Paid cash to owner for personal use, $125.00.
10. Received cash from sales, $260.00.
11. Paid cash for equipment rental, $45.00.
12. Paid cash for charitable contributions, $25.00.
13. Received cash from sales, $300.00.
14. Paid cash on account to Teale Company, $100.00.
15. Received cash from owner as an investment, $1,000.00.
16. Paid cash for rent, $600.00.
17. Received cash from sales, $430.00.
18. Paid cash on account to Teale Company, $750.00.

INSTRUCTIONS:

1. For each transaction, complete the following. Transaction 1 is given as an example.
  a. Analyze the transaction to determine which accounts in the accounting equation are affected.
  b. Write the amount in the appropriate columns, using a plus (+) if the account increases or a minus (−) if the account decreases.
  c. For transactions that change owner's equity, write in parentheses a description of the transaction to the right of the amount.

d. Calculate the new balance for each account in the accounting equation.

e. Before going on to the next transaction, determine that the accounting equation is still in balance.

2. Using the final balances in the accounting equation, prepare a balance sheet for Quick-Type. Use the date July 17 of the current year.

MASTERY PROBLEM 3-M **Determining how transactions change an accounting equation and preparing a balance sheet**

Fred Nance operates a service business called Nance Company. Nance Company uses the accounts shown in the following accounting equation. Use a form similar to the following to complete this problem.

Trans. No.	Assets						= Liabilities	+ Owner's Equity
	Cash	+	Supplies	+	Prepaid Insurance	=	Sickle Company	+	Fred Nance, Capital
Beg. Bal.	1,400		300		400		1,500	600
1.	−100							−100 (expense)
New Bal.	1,300		300		400		1,500	500
2.								

Transactions
1. Paid cash for telephone bill, $100.00.
2. Received cash from owner as an investment, $200.00.
3. Paid cash for rent, $500.00.
4. Paid cash for equipment rental, $100.00.
5. Received cash from sales, $895.00.
6. Bought supplies on account from Sickle Company, $600.00.
7. Paid cash for equipment repair, $15.00.
8. Paid cash for miscellaneous expense, $30.00.
9. Received cash from sales, $920.00.
10. Paid cash for advertising, $50.00.
11. Paid cash for charitable contribution, $10.00.
12. Paid cash for supplies, $400.00.
13. Paid cash for advertising, $250.00.
14. Received cash from sales, $795.00.
15. Paid cash on account to Sickle Company, $1,500.00.
16. Paid cash for insurance, $250.00.
17. Received cash from sales, $960.00.
18. Paid cash to owner for personal use, $1,000.00.

INSTRUCTIONS:
1. For each transaction, complete the following. Transaction 1 is given as an example.
    a. Analyze the transaction to determine which accounts in the accounting equation are affected.

b. Write the amount in the appropriate columns, using a plus (+) if the account increases or a minus (−) if the account decreases.

c. For transactions that change owner's equity, write in parentheses a description of the transaction to the right of the amount.

d. Calculate the new balance for each account in the accounting equation.

e. Before going on to the next transaction, determine that the accounting equation is still in balance.

2. Using the final balances in the accounting equation, prepare a balance sheet for Nance Company. Use the date April 30 of the current year.

CHALLENGE PROBLEM 3-C Calculating the missing amounts in an accounting equation

Each of the following statements includes four of the five amounts needed to complete an accounting equation.

Statements

1. Cash, $400.00; Supplies, $300.00; Prepaid Insurance, $800.00; Dexter Company, $500.00.
2. Cash, $200.00; Prepaid Insurance, $400.00; Dexter Company, $250.00; Pat Bouwman, Capital, $900.00.
3. Cash, $300.00; Supplies, $1,000.00; Prepaid Insurance, $750.00; Pat Bouwman, Capital, $1,200.00.
4. Supplies, $2,000.00; Prepaid Insurance, $1,200.00; Dexter Company, $2,400.00; Pat Bouwman, Capital, $3,500.00.
5. Cash, $100.00; Supplies, $2,700.00; Dexter Company, $1,100.00; Pat Bouwman, Capital, $2,500.00.
6. Cash, $250.00; Supplies, $400.00; Prepaid Insurance, $300.00; Pat Bouwman, Capital, $500.00.
7. Cash, $600.00; Supplies, $2,200.00; Prepaid Insurance, $900.00; Dexter Company, $500.00.
8. Supplies, $100.00; Prepaid Insurance, $400.00; Dexter Company, $150.00; Pat Bouwman, Capital, $500.00.

INSTRUCTIONS:

1. Use a form similar to the following. Record the information from each of the statements. Statement 1 is given as an example.

State-ment	Assets			= Liabilities + Owner's Equity	
	Cash +	**Supplies** +	**Prepaid Insurance** =	**Dexter Company** +	**Pat Bouwman, Capital**
1.	400	300	800	500	_____
	Total: _____			Total: _____	

2. Use a form similar to the one shown on page 51. Calculate the sum of the balances on the side of the accounting equation that is complete. The totals of the balances on the left and right sides must be equal for the accounting equation to be in balance.

3. For each line of the form, calculate the amount of the missing item in the accounting equation. Statement 1 is given as an example.

| State-ment | Assets | | | | = Liabilities | + Owner's Equity |
	Cash	+ Supplies	+ Prepaid Insurance	= Dexter Company	+ Pat Bouwman, Capital
1.	400	300	800	500	1,000
	Total: 1,500			Total: 1,500	

4

Analyzing Transactions into Debit and Credit Parts

ENABLING PERFORMANCE TASKS

After studying Chapter 4, you will be able to:

a Define accounting terms related to analyzing transactions into debit and credit parts.

b Identify accounting practices related to analyzing transactions into debit and credit parts.

c Use T accounts to analyze transactions showing which accounts are debited or credited for each transaction.

d Verify the equality of debits and credits for each transaction.

TERMS PREVIEW

T account • debit • credit • chart of accounts • contra account

How business transactions affect accounts in an accounting equation is described in Chapters 2 and 3. Even though the effects of transactions *can* be recorded in an accounting equation, the procedure is not practical in an actual accounting system. Accountants need more detail about the changes affecting each account than will appear in an accounting equation. Also, the number of accounts used by most businesses would make the accounting equation cumbersome to use as a major financial record. Therefore, a separate record is commonly used for each account.

ACCOUNTS

The accounting equation can be represented as a *T*, as shown in Illustration 4-1.

ILLUSTRATION 4-1

Sides of an accounting equation

Assets =	Liabilities + Owner's Equity
Left side	Right side

FYI

Always draw T accounts when analyzing transactions so that you can see the debit and credit sides.

The values of all things owned (assets) are on the left side of the accounting equation. The values of all equities or claims against the assets (liabilities and owner's equity) are on the right side of the accounting equation.

The total of amounts on the left side of the accounting equation must always equal the total of amounts on the right side. Therefore, the total of all assets on the left side of the accounting equation must always equal the total of all liabilities and owner's equity on the right side.

A record summarizing all the information pertaining to a single item in the accounting equation is known as an account. Transactions change the balances of accounts in the accounting equation. Accounting transactions must be analyzed to determine how account balances are changed. An accounting device used to analyze transactions is called a **T account**. The relationship of a T account to the accounts in the accounting equation is shown in Illustration 4-2.

ILLUSTRATION 4-2

Relationship of a T account to the accounting equation

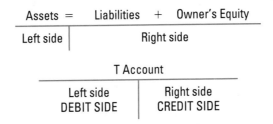

Accountants have special names for amounts recorded on the left and right sides of a T account. An amount recorded on the left side of a T account is called a **debit**. An amount recorded on the right side of a T account is called a **credit**. The T account is the basic device used to analyze the effect of transactions on accounts.

The normal balance side of an asset, liability, or capital account is based on the location of the account in the accounting equation, as shown in Illustration 4-3.

ILLUSTRATION 4-3

Relationship of asset, liability, and capital accounts to the accounting equation

Assets	=	Liabilities	+	Owner's Equity

Left side		Right side	
ASSETS		LIABILITIES	
Left side	Right side	Left side	Right side
Debit side	Credit side	Debit side	Credit side
NORMAL BALANCE			NORMAL BALANCE

OWNER'S CAPITAL ACCOUNT

Left side	Right side
Debit side	Credit side
	NORMAL BALANCE

Asset accounts have normal debit balances (left side) because assets are on the left side of the accounting equation. Liability accounts have normal credit balances (right side) because liabilities appear on the right side of the accounting equation. The owner's capital account has a normal credit balance (right side) because the capital account appears on the right side of the accounting equation.

The sides of a T account are also used to show increases and decreases in account balances, as shown in Illustration 4-4.

ILLUSTRATION 4-4

Increase and decrease sides of asset, liability, and capital accounts

Assets	=	Liabilities	+	Owner's Equity

Left side		Right side	
ASSETS		LIABILITIES	
Left side	Right side	Left side	Right side
Debit side	Credit side	Debit side	Credit side
Normal balance			Normal balance
INCREASE	DECREASE	DECREASE	INCREASE

OWNER'S CAPITAL

Left side	Right side
Debit side	Credit side
	Normal balance
DECREASE	INCREASE

Audit Your Understanding

1. Draw the accounting equation on a T account.

2. What are the two accounting rules that regulate increases and decreases of account balances?

Two basic accounting rules regulate increases and decreases of account balances. (1) Account balances increase on the normal balance side of an account. (2) Account balances decrease on the side opposite the normal balance side of an account.

Asset accounts have normal debit balances; therefore, asset accounts increase on the debit side and decrease on the credit side. Liability accounts have normal credit balances; therefore, liability accounts increase on the credit side and decrease on the debit side. The owner's capital account has a normal credit balance; therefore, the capital account increases on the credit side and decreases on the debit side.

ANALYZING HOW TRANSACTIONS AFFECT ACCOUNTS

Before a transaction is recorded in the records of a business, the information is analyzed to determine which accounts are changed and how. Each transaction changes the balances of at least two accounts. In addition, debits equal credits for each transaction, as shown in Illustration 4-5.

ILLUSTRATION 4-5

Debits equal credits for each transaction

Supplies		Cash	
Left side Debit side Normal balance	Right side Credit side	Left side Debit side Normal balance	Right side Credit side
Increase 1,577.00	Decrease	Increase	1,577.00 Decrease

DEBITS -------------------------------- equal ------------------------------ CREDITS

The total debits, $1,577.00, equal the total credits, $1,577.00, for this transaction.

Four questions are used in analyzing a transaction into its debit and credit parts.

1 What accounts are affected? A list of accounts used by a business is called a **chart of accounts**. The account titles used by Rugcare are found on the chart of accounts on page 18.

2 How is each account classified? Rugcare's accounts are classified as assets, liabilities, owner's equity, revenue, and expenses.

3 How is each account balance changed? Is each account increased or decreased?

4 How is each amount entered in the accounts? The amount is either debited or credited to the account.

For a transaction in which cash is received, the cash account is always increased.

Received Cash from Owner as an Investment

August 1, 19--. Received cash from owner as an investment, $10,000.00.

The effect of this transaction in the accounting equation is shown in Illustration 4-6.

ILLUSTRATION 4-6

How debits and credits affect accounts when receiving cash from owner as an investment

Assets	=	Liabilities	+	Owner's Equity
Left side Cash +10,000.00				Right side Ben Furman, Capital +10,000.00 (investment)

Any Asset		Owner's Capital	
Left side Debit side Normal balance Increase	Right side Credit side Decrease	Left side Debit side Decrease	Right side Credit side Normal balance Increase

Cash		Ben Furman, Capital	
Left side Debit side Normal balance Increase 10,000.00	Right side Credit side Decrease	Left side Debit side Decrease	Right side Credit side Normal balance Increase 10,000.00

DEBITS ---------------------------- equal ---------------------------- CREDITS

Four questions are used to analyze this transaction.

1 *What accounts are affected?* Cash and Ben Furman, Capital.

2 *How is each account classified?* Cash is an asset account with a normal debit balance. Ben Furman, Capital is an owner's equity account with a normal credit balance.

3 *How is each account balance changed?* Cash is increased. Ben Furman, Capital is increased.

4 *How is each amount entered in the accounts?* The asset account, Cash, has a normal debit balance and is increased by a debit, $10,000.00. The owner's equity account, Ben Furman, Capital, has a normal credit balance and is increased by a credit, $10,000.00.

For this transaction, the total debits, $10,000.00, equal the total credits, $10,000.00.

Paid Cash for Supplies

August 3, 19--. Paid cash for supplies, $1,577.00.

The effect of this transaction is shown in Illustration 4-7.

ILLUSTRATION 4-7

How debits and credits affect accounts when paying cash for supplies

Assets		=	Liabilities	+	Owner's Equity

Cash	Supplies
−1,577.00	+1,577.00

Any Asset

Left side	Right side
Debit side	Credit side
Normal balance	
Increase	Decrease

Supplies

Left side	Right side
Debit side	Credit side
Normal balance	
Increase 1,577.00	Decrease

Cash

Left side	Right side
Debit side	Credit side
Normal balance	
Increase	Decrease 1,577.00

DEBITS ------------ equal ------------ CREDITS

FYI

For a transaction in which cash is paid, the cash account is always decreased.

Four questions are used to analyze this transaction.

1 *What accounts are affected?* Cash and Supplies.

2 *How is each account classified?* Cash is an asset account with a normal debit balance. Supplies is an asset account with a normal debit balance.

3 *How is each account balance changed?* Cash is decreased. Supplies is increased.

4 *How is each amount entered in the accounts?* The asset account, Supplies, has a normal debit balance and is increased by a debit, $1,577.00. The asset account, Cash, has a normal debit balance and is decreased by a credit, $1,577.00.

For this transaction, the total debits, $1,577.00, equal the total credits, $1,577.00.

Paid Cash for Insurance

August 4, 19--. Paid cash for insurance, $1,200.00.

The effect of this transaction is shown in Illustration 4-8.

Four questions are used to analyze this transaction.

1 *What accounts are affected?* Cash and Prepaid Insurance.

2 *How is each account classified?* Cash is an asset account with a normal debit balance. Prepaid Insurance is an asset account with a normal debit balance.

MULTICULTURAL AWARENESS

Fra Luca Pacioli

Fra Luca Pacioli, an Italian mathematician, is the "Father of Accounting." He is called this because he was the first person to explain an accounting system in writing. His book, The Method Of Venice, *which first described the double-entry accounting system, was published in 1494.*

ILLUSTRATION 4-8

How debits and credits affect accounts when paying cash for insurance

Assets		=	Liabilities	+	Owner's Equity
Cash −1,200.00	Prepaid Insurance +1,200.00				

Any Asset

Left side Debit side Normal balance Increase	Right side Credit side Decrease

Prepaid Insurance

Left side Debit side Normal balance Increase 1,200.00	Right side Credit side Decrease

Cash

Left side Debit side Normal balance Increase	Right side Credit side Decrease 1,200.00

DEBITS ------------ equal ------------ CREDITS

3 *How is each account balance changed?* Cash is decreased. Prepaid Insurance is increased.

4 *How is each amount entered in the accounts?* The asset account, Prepaid Insurance, has a normal debit balance and is increased by a debit, $1,200.00. The asset account, Cash, has a normal debit balance and is decreased by a credit, $1,200.00.

For this transaction, the total debits, $1,200.00, equal the total credits, $1,200.00.

Bought Supplies on Account

August 7, 19--. Bought supplies on account from Butler Cleaning Supplies, $2,720.00.

The effect of this transaction is shown in Illustration 4-9.
Four questions are used to analyze this transaction.

1 *What accounts are affected?* Supplies and Butler Cleaning Supplies.

2 *How is each account classified?* Supplies is an asset account with a normal debit balance. Butler Cleaning Supplies is a liability account with a normal credit balance.

3 *How is each account balance changed?* Supplies is increased. Butler Cleaning Supplies is increased.

4 *How is each amount entered in the accounts?* The asset account, Supplies, has a normal debit balance and is increased

Always use the four steps of analyzing transactions. This will make the analyzing process easier.

Assets	=	Liabilities + Owner's Equity
Supplies +2,720.00		Butler Cleaning Supplies +2,720.00

Any Asset		Any Liability	
Left side Debit side Normal balance Increase	Right side Credit side Decrease	Left side Debit side Decrease	Right side Credit side Normal balance Increase

Supplies		Butler Cleaning Supplies	
Left side Debit side Normal balance Increase 2,720.00	Right side Credit side Decrease	Left side Debit side Decrease	Right side Credit side Normal balance Increase 2,720.00

DEBITS ---------------------------- equal ---------------------------- CREDITS

by a debit, $2,720.00. The liability account, Butler Cleaning Supplies, has a normal credit balance and is increased by a credit, $2,720.00.

For this transaction, the total debits, $2,720.00, equal the total credits, $2,720.00.

Paid Cash on Account

August 11, 19--. Paid cash on account to Butler Cleaning Supplies, $1,360.00.

The effect of this transaction is shown in Illustration 4-10.

Assets	=	Liabilities + Owner's Equity
Cash −1,360.00		Butler Cleaning Supplies −1,360.00

Any Asset		Any Liability	
Left side Debit side Normal balance Increase	Right side Credit side Decrease	Left side Debit side Decrease	Right side Credit side Normal balance Increase

Cash		Butler Cleaning Supplies	
Left side Debit side Normal balance Increase	Right side Credit side Decrease 1,360.00	Left side Debit side Decrease 1,360.00	Right side Credit side Normal balance Increase

CREDITS ----- equal ------ DEBITS

Four questions are used to analyze this transaction.

1 *What accounts are affected?* Cash and Butler Cleaning Supplies.

2 *How is each account classified?* Cash is an asset account with a normal debit balance. Butler Cleaning Supplies is a liability account with a normal credit balance.

3 *How is each account balance changed?* Cash is decreased. Butler Cleaning Supplies is decreased.

4 *How is each amount entered in the accounts?* The liability account, Butler Cleaning Supplies, has a normal credit balance and is decreased by a debit, $1,360.00. The asset account, Cash, has a normal debit balance and is decreased by a credit, $1,360.00.

For this transaction, the total debits, $1,360.00, equal the total credits, $1,360.00.

Received Cash from Sales

Revenue increases the owner's capital. The increases from revenue could be recorded directly in the owner's capital account. However, to avoid a capital account with a large number of entries and to

■ Joe Arriola ■

AVANTI PRESS, MIAMI, FLORIDA

Cuban-born Joe Arriola is the chairperson and chief executive officer of Avanti Press in Miami, Florida. Avanti Press prints high-quality catalogs and brochures. Clients include Walt Disney Company, Avon, Royal Caribbean Cruise Line, J.C. Penney, and many others. Avanti has sales of over $65 million a year. Winning the Minority Supplier of the Year Award has also attracted national attention and resulted in new business for the firm.

When he was 25 years old Arriola joined his father's printing business, which he began to expand when his father retired. A high school friend, Gene Martinez, helped in the expansion and is now president of the firm. Together, the two friends expanded the firm from 12 employees to over 425. In the process, the small offset printing company expanded into a full-service business offering different kinds of printing, design, photography, copy writing, and graphics. New areas for the

business are telemarketing and fulfillment services for their customers.

Arriola admits that when he and Martinez began the expansion they thought they knew a lot more than they really did about how to run a business. However, with hard work and some luck they prospered. Arriola says, "Back then we worked a lot of twenty-hour days. Now that we've been very successful, we've cut back to 16-hour workdays."

Arriola also maintains that the two best courses he has ever taken were the two years of accounting courses he took in high school in Miami. The accounting courses gave him the background to be able to read and understand financial statements and to communicate with bankers and financial institutions in the language of business, accounting.

Looking back on the early days of his business, Arriola said that the biggest surprise was that he thought "you open your doors, work hard, sell a lot, and make a lot of money. But it's not as easy as that. You have to plan for cash flows so that you can pay your accounts payable, and so many other things that you never thought of."

Personal Visions in Business

summarize revenue information separately from the other records, Rugcare uses a separate revenue account.

August 12, 19--. Received cash from sales, $525.00.

The effect of this transaction is shown in Illustration 4-11.

ILLUSTRATION 4-11   How debits and credits affect accounts when receiving cash from sales

	Assets	=	Liabilities	+	Owner's Equity

Cash
+525.00

Owner's Capital
+525.00 (revenue)

Owner's Capital

Left side	Right side
Debit side	Credit side
	Normal balance
Decrease	Increase

Any Revenue Account

Left side	Right side
Debit side	Credit side
	Normal balance
Decrease	Increase

Cash

Left side	Right side
Debit side	Credit side
Normal balance	
Increase 525.00	Decrease

Sales

Left side	Right side
Debit side	Credit side
	Normal balance
Decrease	Increase 525.00

DEBITS ----------------------------- equal ----------------------------- CREDITS

The owner's capital account has a normal credit balance. A revenue account shows increases in capital. Therefore, a revenue account also has a normal credit balance. Revenue accounts increase on the credit side and decrease on the debit side. Rugcare's revenue account is titled Sales.

Four questions are used to analyze this revenue transaction.

1 What accounts are affected?   Cash and Sales.

2 How is each account classified?   Cash is an asset account with a normal debit balance. Sales is a revenue account with a normal credit balance.

3 How is each account balance changed?   Cash is increased. Sales is increased.

4 How is each amount entered in the accounts?   The asset account, Cash, has a normal debit balance and is increased by a debit, $525.00. The revenue account, Sales, has a normal credit balance and is increased by a credit, $525.00.

For this transaction, the total debits, $525.00, equal the total credits, $525.00.

Paid Cash for an Expense

Expenses decrease the owner's capital. Expenses could be recorded directly in the owner's capital account. However, to avoid a capital account with a large number of entries and to summarize expense information separately from the other records, Rugcare uses separate expense accounts.

The titles of Rugcare's expense accounts are shown on the chart of accounts, page 18. The expense account, Utilities Expense, is used to record all payments of utility bills. These include payments made for electricity, telephone, gas, water, and sanitation.

August 12, 19--. Paid cash for rent, $250.00.

The effect of this transaction is shown in Illustration 4-12.

ILLUSTRATION 4-12   How debits and credits affect accounts when paying cash for an expense

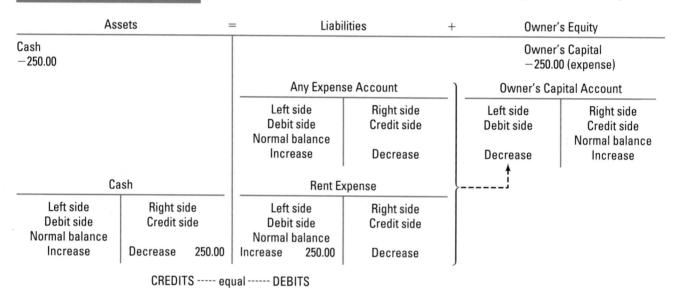

The owner's capital account has a normal credit balance. Decreases in the owner's capital account are shown as debits. An expense account shows decreases in owner's equity. Therefore, an expense account has a normal debit balance. An expense account increases on the debit side and decreases on the credit side.

Four questions are used to analyze this expense transaction.

1 *What accounts are affected?*   Cash and Rent Expense.

2 *How is each account classified?*   Cash is an asset account with a normal debit balance. Rent Expense is an expense account with a normal debit balance.

3 *How is each account balance changed?*   Cash is decreased. Rent Expense is increased.

4 *How is each amount entered in the accounts?* The expense account, Rent Expense, has a normal debit balance and is increased by a debit, $250.00. The asset account, Cash, has a normal debit balance and is decreased by a credit, $250.00.

For this transaction, the total debits, $250.00, equal the total credits, $250.00.

Paid Cash to Owner for Personal Use

Assets taken out of a business for the personal use of the owner are known as withdrawals. Withdrawals are considered to be part of the owner's equity taken out of a business. Therefore, withdrawals decrease the owner's equity. Withdrawals could be recorded as decreases directly in the owner's capital account. However, common accounting practice is to record withdrawals in a separate account to provide a separate record of the withdrawals for each fiscal period. In this way, the owner knows how much has been withdrawn from the business each fiscal period.

An account that reduces a related account on a financial statement is called a **contra account.** The drawing account is a contra capital account because the account shows decreases in capital.

August 12, 19--. Paid cash to owner for personal use, $100.00.

The effect of this transaction is shown in Illustration 4-13.

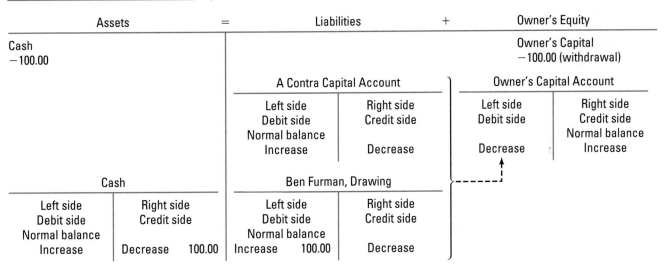

| ILLUSTRATION 4-13 | How debits and credits affect accounts when paying cash to owner for personal use |

The owner's capital account has a normal credit balance. Decreases in the owner's capital account are shown as debits. Because a drawing account shows decreases in capital, a drawing account has a normal debit balance. A drawing account increases on the debit side and decreases on the credit side.

Audit Your Understanding

1. State the four questions to analyze a transaction.

2. Are asset accounts increased on the debit side or credit side?

3. Are liability accounts increased on the debit side or credit side?

4. Is the owner's drawing account increased on the debit side or credit side?

5. Are revenue accounts increased on the debit side or credit side?

6. Are expense accounts increased on the debit side or credit side?

Four questions are used to analyze this transaction.

1 What accounts are affected?   Cash and Ben Furman, Drawing.

2 How is each account classified?   Cash is an asset account with a normal debit balance. Ben Furman, Drawing is a contra capital account with a normal debit balance.

3 How is each account balance changed?   Cash is decreased. Ben Furman, Drawing is increased.

4 How is each amount entered in the accounts?   The contra capital account, Ben Furman, Drawing, has a normal debit balance and is increased by a debit, $100.00. The asset account, Cash, has a normal debit balance and is decreased by a credit, $100.00.

For this transaction, the total debits, $100.00, equal the total credits, $100.00.

SUMMARY OF ANALYZING TRANSACTIONS INTO DEBIT AND CREDIT PARTS

The total debits and total credits for a transaction must be equal, as shown in the following T accounts.

Supplies		Cash	
Debits	Credits	Debits	Credits
1,577.00			1,577.00

DEBITS -------------------- equal ------------------ CREDITS

Debits and credits affect account balances as shown in the following.

Assets	=	Liabilities	+	Owner's Equity
Equation's left side				Equation's right side

Asset Accounts		Liability Accounts		Owner's Capital Account	
Left side Debit side Normal balance Increases	Right side Credit side Decreases	Left side Debit side Decreases	Right side Credit side Normal balance Increases	Left side Debit side Decreases	Right side Credit side Normal balance Increases

Owner's Drawing Account	
Left side Debit side Normal balance Increases	Right side Credit side Decreases

Expense Accounts		Sales	
Left side Debit side Normal balance Increases	Right side Credit side Decreases	Left side Debit side Decreases	Right side Credit side Normal balance Increases

A summary analysis of transactions is shown in Illustration 4-14.

SUMMARY ILLUSTRATION 4-14
Summary analysis of transactions into debit and credit parts

Transaction	Accounts Affected	Account Classification	How is Account Affected?		Entered in Account as a	
			Increase	Decrease	Debit	Credit
Received cash from owner as an investment	Cash Ben Furman, Capital	Asset Owner's Equity	X X		X	X
Paid cash for supplies	Supplies Cash	Asset Asset	X	X	X	X
Paid cash for insurance	Prepaid Insurance Cash	Asset Asset	X	X	X	X
Bought supplies on account	Supplies Butler Cleaning Supplies	Asset Liability	X X		X	X
Paid cash on account	Butler Cleaning Supplies Cash	Liability Asset		X X	X	X
Received cash from sales	Cash Sales	Asset Revenue	X X		X	X
Paid cash for rent	Rent Expense Cash	Expense Asset	X	X	X	X
Paid cash to owner for personal use	Ben Furman, Drawing Cash	Contra Capital Asset	X	X	X	X

What is the meaning of each of the following?

1. **T account**
2. **debit**
3. **credit**
4. **chart of accounts**
5. **contra account**

1. What basic accounting device is used to help analyze transactions?

2. What determines which side of a T account will be the normal balance side?

3. What is the normal balance side of an asset account? Of a liability account? Of a capital account?

4. What two basic accounting rules regulate the increases and decreases of an account?

5. On which sides of a T account are increases and decreases recorded for asset accounts? For liability accounts? For the capital account?

6. What is the relationship between total debits and total credits in accounting records?

7. What accounts are affected, and how, when cash is received from an owner as an investment?

8. What accounts are affected, and how, when cash is paid for supplies?

9. What accounts are affected, and how, when cash is paid for insurance?

10. What accounts are affected, and how, when supplies are bought on account?

11. What accounts are affected, and how, when cash is paid on account?

12. What is the normal balance side of a revenue account?

13. What accounts are affected, and how, when cash is received from sales?

14. What is the normal balance side of an expense account?

15. What accounts are affected, and how, when cash is paid for rent?

16. What is the normal balance side of a drawing account?

17. What accounts are affected, and how, when cash is paid to an owner for personal use?

CASE 1 Sharon Morris records *all* cash receipts as revenue and *all* cash payments as expenses. Is Miss Morris recording her cash receipts and cash payments correctly? Explain your answer.

CASE 2 Thomas Bueler records all investments, revenue, expenses, and withdrawals in his capital account. At the end of each month, Mr. Bueler sorts the information to prepare a summary of what has caused the changes in his capital account balance. To help Mr. Bueler prepare this summary in the future, what changes would you suggest he make in his records?

DRILL 4-D1   Determining the normal balance, increase, and decrease sides for accounts

TUTORIAL

Jeff Dixon owns a service business called HouseClean. HouseClean uses the following accounts.

Cash	Sales
Supplies	Advertising Expense
Prepaid Insurance	Miscellaneous Expense
Miller Supplies	Rent Expense
Wayne Office Supplies	Repair Expense
Jeff Dixon, Capital	Utilities Expense
Jeff Dixon, Drawing	

INSTRUCTIONS:

1. Prepare a T account for each account. Label the debit and credit sides of each account. The T account for Cash is given as an example.
2. For each account, label the side of the T account that is used for each of the following. The T account for Cash is given as an example.
   a. Normal balance
   b. Increase side
   c. Decrease side

Cash

Debit Side	Credit Side

Cash

Debit Side Normal balance Increase	Credit Side Decrease

DRILL 4-D2   Analyzing how transactions affect accounts

Use a form similar to the following. Transaction 1 is given as an example.

1	2	3	4	5	6	7	8	9
Trans. No.	**Accounts Affected**	**Account Classification**	**Account's Normal Balance**		**How is Account Affected?**		**Entered in Account as a**	
			Debit	**Credit**	**(+)**	**(−)**	**Debit**	**Credit**
1.	*Cash*	*Asset*	√		√		√	
	Jeff Dixon, Capital	*Owner's Equity*		√	√			√

Transactions
1. Received cash from owner as an investment.
2. Paid cash for supplies.
3. Paid cash for insurance.
4. Bought supplies on account from Miller Supplies.
5. Received cash from sales.
6. Paid cash on account to Miller Supplies.
7. Paid cash for rent.
8. Paid cash for repairs.
9. Paid cash for miscellaneous expense.
10. Paid cash for telephone bill (utilities expense).
11. Paid cash to owner for personal use.

INSTRUCTIONS:

1. Use the account titles given in Drill 4-D1. In Column 2, write the accounts affected by each transaction.
2. For each account title, write the account classification in Column 3.
3. For each account title, place a check mark in either Column 4 or 5 to indicate the normal balance.
4. For each account title, place a check mark in either Column 6 or 7 to indicate if the account is increased (+) or decreased (−) by this transaction.
5. For each account title, place a check mark in either Column 8 or 9 to indicate if the account is changed by a debit or a credit.

APPLICATION PROBLEMS
EPT(c,d)

PROBLEM 4-1 Analyzing transactions into debit and credit parts

Dixie Conastar owns a business called Conastar Company. Conastar Company uses the following accounts.

Cash	Sales
Supplies	Advertising Expense
Prepaid Insurance	Miscellaneous Expense
Bales Office Supplies	Rent Expense
Dixie Conastar, Capital	Utilities Expense
Dixie Conastar, Drawing	

Transactions

Apr. 1. Received cash from owner as an investment, $5,000.00.
2. Paid cash for supplies, $50.00.
3. Paid cash for insurance, $75.00.
6. Bought supplies on account from Bales Office Supplies, $100.00.
7. Received cash from sales, $400.00.
8. Paid cash for water bill (utilities expense), $25.00.
9. Paid cash for advertising, $40.00.
13. Paid cash on account to Bales Office Supplies, $50.00.
14. Received cash from sales, $400.00.
15. Paid cash for miscellaneous expense, $5.00.
16. Paid cash to owner for personal use, $50.00.
18. Paid cash for rent, $250.00.

INSTRUCTIONS:

April 1.

```
         Cash
  5,000.00 |
```

```
   Dixie Conastar, Capital
            | 5,000.00
```

1. Prepare two T accounts for each transaction. On each T account, write the account title of one of the accounts affected by the transaction.
2. Write the debit or credit amount in each T account to show how the transaction affected that account. T accounts for the first transaction are given as an example.

PROBLEM 4-2 Analyzing transactions into debit and credit parts

Buelah VanBorne owns a business called VanBorne Services. VanBorne Services uses the following accounts.

Cash	Sales
Supplies	Advertising Expense
Prepaid Insurance	Miscellaneous Expense
Fortune Supplies	Rent Expense
Herdle Office Supplies	Repair Expense
Buelah VanBorne, Capital	Utilities Expense
Buelah VanBorne, Drawing	

Transactions

May 1. Received cash from owner as an investment, $2,000.00.
     4. Bought supplies on account from Herdle Office Supplies, $500.00.
     6. Paid cash for rent, $500.00.
     7. Received cash from sales, $400.00.
    11. Paid cash on account to Herdle Office Supplies, $250.00.
    13. Paid cash for repairs, $80.00.
    14. Received cash from sales, $500.00.
    15. Paid cash for supplies, $600.00.
    19. Paid cash for insurance, $240.00.
    20. Bought supplies on account from Fortune Supplies, $50.00.
    21. Paid cash for supplies, $500.00.
    21. Received cash from sales, $750.00.
    25. Paid cash for telephone bill (utilities expense), $90.00.
    26. Paid cash for advertising, $130.00.
    28. Paid cash for miscellaneous expense, $15.00.
    28. Received cash from sales, $520.00.
    29. Paid cash to owner for personal use, $600.00.
    31. Received cash from sales, $400.00.

INSTRUCTIONS:

1. Prepare a T account for each account.
2. Analyze each transaction into its debit and credit parts. Write the debit and credit amounts in the proper T accounts to show how each transaction changes account balances. Write the date of the transaction in parentheses before each amount. The amounts for Transaction 1 are given in T accounts as an example.

Cash	
(1) 2,000.00	

Buelah VanBorne, Capital	
	(1) 2,000.00

ENRICHMENT PROBLEMS   EPT(c,d)

MASTERY PROBLEM 4-M Analyzing transactions into debit and credit parts

James Lands owns a business called LandScape. LandScape uses the following accounts.

Cash	Sales
Supplies	Advertising Expense
Prepaid Insurance	Miscellaneous Expense
Derner Office Supplies	Rent Expense
Janitor Supplies	Repair Expense
James Lands, Capital	Utilities Expense
James Lands, Drawing	

Transactions

June 1. Received cash from owner as an investment, $3,000.00.
     2. Paid cash for supplies, $60.00.
     4. Paid cash for rent, $200.00.
     4. Received cash from sales, $350.00.
     5. Paid cash for repairs, $10.00.
     9. Bought supplies on account from Janitor Supplies, $500.00.
    10. Paid cash for insurance, $100.00.
    11. Received cash from owner as an investment, $900.00.
    11. Received cash from sales, $300.00.
    12. Bought supplies on account from Derner Office Supplies, $50.00.
    15. Paid cash for miscellaneous expense, $5.00.
    16. Paid cash on account to Janitor Supplies, $50.00.

18. Received cash from sales, $400.00.
22. Paid cash for electric bill (utilities expense), $35.00.
23. Paid cash for advertising, $30.00.
25. Received cash from sales, $220.00.
26. Paid cash to owner for personal use, $600.00.
30. Received cash from sales, $100.00.

INSTRUCTIONS:

1. Prepare a T account for each account.
2. Analyze each transaction into its debit and credit parts. Write the debit and credit amounts in the proper T accounts to show how each transaction changes account balances. Write the date of the transaction in parentheses before each amount.

CHALLENGE PROBLEM 4-C Analyzing transactions recorded in T accounts

Edward Burns owns a business for which the following T accounts show the current financial situation.

	Cash				Sales	
(1)	5,000.00	(2)	80.00		(6)	475.00
(6)	475.00	(4)	15.00		(8)	350.00
(8)	350.00	(5)	16.00		(9)	400.00
(9)	400.00	(7)	900.00			
		(10)	150.00			
		(11)	95.00			
		(12)	50.00			

	Supplies			Advertising Expense	
(3)	300.00		(5)	16.00	
(11)	95.00				

	Midwest Supplies				Miscellaneous Expense	
(10)	150.00	(3)	300.00	(4)	15.00	

	Edward Burns, Capital				Rent Expense	
		(1)	5,000.00	(7)	900.00	

	Edward Burns, Drawing			Utilities Expense	
(2)	80.00		(12)	50.00	

INSTRUCTIONS:

1. Use a form similar to the following.

1	2	3	4	5	6
Trans. No.	Accounts Affected	Account Classification	Entered in Account as a		Description of Transaction
			Debit	Credit	
1.	Cash Edward Burns, Capital	Asset Owner's Equity	√	√	Received cash from owner as an investment

2. Analyze each numbered transaction in the T accounts. Write the titles of accounts affected in Column 2. For each account, write the classification of the account in Column 3.
3. For each account, place a check mark in either Column 4 or 5 to indicate if the account is affected by a debit or a credit.
4. For each transaction, write a brief statement in Column 6 describing the transaction. Information for Transaction 1 is given as an example.

5

Journalizing Transactions

ENABLING PERFORMANCE TASKS

After studying Chapter 5, you will be able to:

a Define accounting terms related to journalizing transactions.

b Identify accounting concepts and practices related to journalizing transactions.

c Record selected transactions in a five-column journal.

d Prove equality of debits and credits in a five-column journal.

e Prove cash.

f Forward totals from one journal page to another.

g Rule a five-column journal.

TERMS PREVIEW

journal • journalizing • special amount column • general amount column • entry • double-entry accounting • source document • check • receipt • memorandum • proving cash

As described in Chapter 4, transactions are analyzed into debit and credit parts before information is recorded. A form for recording transactions in chronological order is called a **journal**. Recording transactions in a journal is called **journalizing.**

Transactions could be recorded in the accounting equation. However, generally accepted accounting practice is to make a more permanent record by recording transactions in a journal.

A JOURNAL

Each business uses the kind of journal that best fits the needs of that business. The nature of a business and the number of transactions to be recorded determine the kind of journal to be used.

Journal Form

Rugcare uses a journal that has five amount columns, as shown in Illustration 5-1.

ILLUSTRATION 5-1	Five-column journal

JOURNAL   PAGE

	DATE	ACCOUNT TITLE	DOC. NO.	POST. REF.	GENERAL DEBIT	GENERAL CREDIT	SALES CREDIT	CASH DEBIT	CASH CREDIT	
1										1
2										2
3										3

The five amount columns in Rugcare's journal are General Debit, General Credit, Sales Credit, Cash Debit, and Cash Credit. A journal amount column headed with an account title is called a **special amount column.** Special amount columns are used for frequently occurring transactions. For example, most of Rugcare's transactions involve receipt or payment of cash. A large number of the transactions involve receipt of cash from sales. Therefore, Rugcare uses three special amount columns in its journal: Sales Credit, Cash Debit, and Cash Credit.

Using special amount columns eliminates writing an account title in the Account Title column. Therefore, recording transactions in a journal with special amount columns saves time.

A journal amount column that is not headed with an account title is called a **general amount column.** In Rugcare's journal, the General Debit and General Credit columns are general amount columns.

Accuracy

Information recorded in a journal includes the debit and credit parts of each transaction recorded in one place. The information can be verified by comparing the data in the journal with the source document data to assure that all information is correct.

Chronological Record

Transactions are recorded in a journal by date in the order in which the transactions occur. All the information about each transaction is recorded in one place making the information for a specific transaction easy to locate.

Double-Entry Accounting

Information for each transaction recorded in a journal is called an **entry.** The recording of debit and credit parts of a transaction is called **double-entry accounting.** In double-entry accounting, each transaction affects at least two accounts. Both the debit part and the credit part are recorded for each transaction. This procedure reflects the dual effect of each transaction on the business' records. For example, cash paid for advertising causes (1) a decrease in cash and (2) an increase in expenses. Double-entry accounting assures that debits equal credits.

SOURCE DOCUMENTS

A business paper from which information is obtained for a journal entry is called a **source document.** Each transaction is described by a source document that proves that the transaction did occur. For example, Rugcare prepares a check stub for each cash payment made. The check stub describes information about the cash payment transaction for which the check is prepared. The accounting concept, *Objective Evidence,* is applied when a source document is prepared for each transaction. *(CONCEPT: Objective Evidence)*

A transaction should be journalized only if it actually occurs. The amounts recorded must be accurate and true. Nearly all transactions result in the preparation of a source document. One way to verify the accuracy of a specific journal entry is to compare the entry with the source document. Rugcare uses four source documents: checks, calculator tapes, receipts, and memorandums.

Checks

A business form ordering a bank to pay cash from a bank account is called a **check.** The source document for cash payments is a check. Rugcare makes all cash payments by check. The checks are prenumbered to help Rugcare account for all checks. Rugcare's record of information on a check is the check stub prepared at the same time as the check. A check and check stub prepared by Rugcare are shown in Illustration 5-2.

ILLUSTRATION 5-2   Check and check stub

NO. 1	$ 1,577.00		
Date August 3		19 --	
To Janitorial Supplies Co.			
For Supplies			
BAL. BRO'T. FOR'D.		0	00
AMT. DEPOSITED . . . 8 1 -- Date		10,000	00
SUBTOTAL.		10,000	00
OTHER:			
SUBTOTAL.		10,000	00
AMT. THIS CHECK		1,577	00
BAL. CAR'D. FOR'D.		8,423	00

RUGCARE 623 Walnut Street
Billings, MT 59101-1946

NO. 1   93-109
               929

August 3,   19 --

PAY TO THE ORDER OF Janitorial Supplies Co. $ 1,577.00

One thousand five hundred seventy-seven and no/100   DOLLARS
For Classroom Use Only

Peoples national bank
Billings, MT 59101-2320

FOR Supplies   Ben Furman

⑈09290⑈0941⑈ 43⑈452119⑈

Procedures for preparing checks and check stubs are described in Chapter 7.

Calculator Tapes

Rugcare collects cash at the time services are rendered to customers. At the end of each day, Rugcare uses a printing electronic calculator to total the amount of cash received from sales for that day. By totaling all the individual sales, a single source document is produced for the total sales of the day. Thus, time and space are saved by recording only one entry for all of a day's sales. The calculator tape is the source document for daily sales. *(CONCEPT: Objective Evidence)* A calculator tape used as a source document is shown in Illustration 5-3.

ILLUSTRATION 5-3   Calculator tape used as a source document

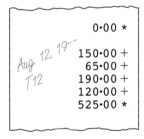

Rugcare dates and numbers each calculator tape. For example, in Illustration 5-3, the number, *T12*, indicates that the tape is for the twelfth day of the month.

Receipts

A business form giving written acknowledgement for cash received is called a **receipt**. When cash is received from sources other than sales, Rugcare prepares a receipt. The receipts are prenumbered to help account for all the receipts. A receipt is the source document

---

FYI

If you misspell words in your written communications, people may mistrust the quality of your accounting skills. Note that in the word receipt the "e" comes before the "i" and there is a silent "p" before the "t" at the end of the word.

for cash received from transactions other than sales. *(CONCEPT: Objective Evidence)* Rugcare's receipt is shown in Illustration 5-4.

ILLUSTRATION 5-4

Receipt used as a source document

No. **1**	Receipt No. **1**
Date _August 1,_ 19 _--_	_August 1,_ 19 _--_
From _Ben Furman_	Rec'd from _Ben Furman_
For _Investment_	For _Investment_
	Ten thousand and no/100 ———————— Dollars
$ 10,000 00	Amount $ 10,000 00
	RUGCARE _Ben Furman_
	Received By
	623 Walnut Street Billings, MT 59101-1946

1. What are the five amount columns in Rugcare's journal?
2. In what order are transactions recorded in a journal?
3. List four types of source documents.
4. Why are source documents important?

Memorandums

A form on which a brief message is written describing a transaction is called a **memorandum**. When no other source document is prepared for a transaction, or when additional explanation is needed about a transaction, Rugcare prepares a memorandum. *(CONCEPT: Objective Evidence)* Rugcare's memorandums are prenumbered to help account for all the memorandums. A brief note is written on the memorandum to describe the transaction. The memorandum used by Rugcare is shown in Illustration 5-5.

ILLUSTRATION 5-5

Memorandum used as a source document

MEMORANDUM	**RUGCARE** 623 Walnut Street Billings, MT 59101-1946 No. **1**
	Bought supplies on account from Butler Cleaning Supplies, $2,720.00
Signed: _Ben Furman_	Date: _August 7, 19--_

RECORDING TRANSACTIONS IN A FIVE-COLUMN JOURNAL

Information for each transaction recorded in a journal is known as an entry. An entry consists of four parts: (1) date, (2) debit, (3) credit, and (4) source document. Before a transaction is recorded in a journal, the transaction is analyzed into its debit and credit parts.

Received Cash from Owner as an Investment

August 1, 19--. Received cash from owner as an investment, $10,000.00. Receipt No. 1.

Cash	
10,000.00	

Ben Furman, Capital	
	10,000.00

The source document for this transaction is Receipt No. 1. *(CONCEPT: Objective Evidence)* The analysis of this transaction is shown in the T accounts.

All T account analysis in Chapter 5 is described in detail in Chapter 4.

The asset account, Cash, is increased by a debit, $10,000.00. The owner's capital account, Ben Furman, Capital, is increased by a credit, $10,000.00. The journal entry for this transaction is shown in Illustration 5-6.

ILLUSTRATION 5-6 Journal entry to record receiving cash from owner as an investment

JOURNAL PAGE *1*

	DATE		ACCOUNT TITLE	DOC. NO.	POST. REF.	GENERAL (1) DEBIT	GENERAL (2) CREDIT	(3) SALES CREDIT	CASH (4) DEBIT	CASH (5) CREDIT	
1	*19--* *Aug.*	*1*	*Ben Furman, Capital*	*R1*			*10 000 00*		*10 000 00*		1

1 ***Date.*** Write the date, *19--, Aug. 1,* in the Date column. This entry is the first one on this journal page. Therefore, the year and month are both written for this entry. Neither the year nor the month are written again on the same page.

2 ***Debit.*** The journal has a special amount column for debits to Cash. The title of the account is in the column heading. Therefore, the account title does not need to be written in the Account Title column. Write the debit amount, *$10,000.00,* in the Cash Debit column.

3 ***Credit.*** Write the title of the account credited, *Ben Furman, Capital,* in the Account Title column. There is no special amount column with the title of the account credited, Ben Furman, Capital, in its heading. Therefore, the credit amount is recorded in the General Credit column. Write the credit amount, *$10,000.00,* in the General Credit column.

FYI

If you draw T accounts for transactions, it will make journalizing easier.

All amounts recorded in the General Debit or General Credit amount columns must have an account title written in the Account Title column.

4 Source document. Write the source document number, *R1*, in the Doc. No. column. The source document number, *R1*, indicates that this is Receipt No. 1.

The source document number is a cross reference from the journal to the source document. If more details are needed about this transaction, a person can refer to Receipt No. 1.

Paid Cash for Supplies

August 3, 19--. Paid cash for supplies, $1,577.00. Check No. 1.

Supplies

| 1,577.00 | |

Cash

| | 1,577.00 |

The source document for this transaction is Check No. 1. *(CONCEPT: Objective Evidence)* The analysis of this transaction is shown in the T accounts.

The asset account, Supplies, is increased by a debit, $1,577.00. The asset account, Cash, is decreased by a credit, $1,577.00. The journal entry for this transaction is shown in Illustration 5-7.

ILLUSTRATION 5-7   Journal entry to record paying cash for supplies

JOURNAL   PAGE *1*

| | | | | | 1 | 2 | 3 | 4 | 5 |
	DATE	ACCOUNT TITLE	DOC. NO.	POST. REF.	GENERAL DEBIT	GENERAL CREDIT	SALES CREDIT	CASH DEBIT	CASH CREDIT	
2	3	*Supplies*	C1		1 5 7 7 00				1 5 7 7 00	2

---

1 Date. Write the date, *3*, in the Date column. This is not the first entry on the journal page. Therefore, the year and month are not written for this entry.

2 Debit. Write the title of the account debited, *Supplies*, in the Account Title column. There is no special amount column with the title of the account debited, Supplies, in its heading. Therefore, the debit amount is recorded in the General Debit column. Write the debit amount, *$1,577.00*, in the General Debit column.

3 Credit. The journal has a special amount column for credits to Cash. The title of the account is in the column heading. Therefore, the account title does not need to be written in the Account Title column. Write the credit amount, *$1,577.00*, in the Cash Credit column.

4 Source document. Write the source document number, *C1*, in the Doc. No. column. The source document number, *C1*, indicates that this is Check No. 1.

FYI

Dollars and cents signs and decimal points are not used when writing amounts on ruled accounting paper. Sometimes a color tint or a heavy vertical rule is used on printed accounting paper to separate the dollars and cents columns.

Paid Cash for Insurance

August 4, 19--. Paid cash for insurance, $1,200.00. Check No. 2.

Prepaid Insurance

1,200.00	

Cash

	1,200.00

The source document for this transaction is Check No. 2. *(CON-CEPT: Objective Evidence)* The analysis of this transaction is shown in the T accounts.

The asset account, Prepaid Insurance, is increased by a debit, $1,200.00. The asset account, Cash, is decreased by a credit, $1,200.00. The journal entry for this transaction is shown in Illustration 5-8.

ILLUSTRATION 5-8 Journal entry to record paying cash for insurance

					GENERAL		SALES	CASH	
					1	2	3	4	5
	DATE	ACCOUNT TITLE	DOC. NO.	POST. REF.	DEBIT	CREDIT	SALES CREDIT	DEBIT	CREDIT
3	4	Prepaid Insurance	C2		1 2 0 0 00				1 2 0 0 00	3

JOURNAL PAGE *1*

1 Date. Write the date, *4*, in the Date column.

2 Debit. Write the title of the account debited, *Prepaid Insurance*, in the Account Title column. There is no special amount column with the title of the account debited, Prepaid Insurance, in its heading. Therefore, the debit amount is recorded in the General Debit column. Write the debit amount, *$1,200.00*, in the General Debit column.

3 Credit. The journal has a special amount column for credits to Cash. The title of the account is in the column heading. Therefore, the account title does not need to be written in the Account Title column. Write the credit amount, *$1,200.00*, in the Cash Credit column.

4 Source document. Write the source document number, *C2*, in the Doc. No. column.

Bought Supplies on Account

August 7, 19--. Bought supplies on account from Butler Cleaning Supplies, $2,720.00. Memorandum No. 1.

Supplies

2,720.00	

Butler Cleaning Supplies

	2,720.00

Rugcare ordered these supplies by telephone. Rugcare wishes to record this transaction immediately. Therefore, a memorandum is prepared that shows supplies were received on account.

The source document for this transaction is Memorandum No. 1. *(CONCEPT: Objective Evidence)* The analysis of this transaction is shown in the T accounts.

The asset account, Supplies, is increased by a debit, $2,720.00. The liability account, Butler Cleaning Supplies, is increased by a credit, $2,720.00. The journal entry for this transaction is shown in Illustration 5-9.

ILLUSTRATION 5-9   Journal entry to record buying supplies on account

	DATE	ACCOUNT TITLE	DOC. NO.	POST. REF.	GENERAL DEBIT	GENERAL CREDIT	SALES CREDIT	CASH DEBIT	CASH CREDIT	
4	7	Supplies	M1		2 7 2 0 00					4
5		Butler Cleaning Supplies				2 7 2 0 00				5

1 Date.   Write the date, 7, in the Date column.

2 Debit.   The journal does not have a special amount column for either the debit to Supplies or credits to Butler Cleaning Supplies. Therefore, both account titles need to be written in the Account Title column. The debit and credit amounts are recorded in the General Debit and General Credit columns. Write the title of the account debited, *Supplies*, in the Account Title column. Write the debit amount, *$2,720.00*, in the General Debit column.

3 Credit.   On the next line, write the title of the account credited, *Butler Cleaning Supplies*, in the Account Title column. Write the credit amount, *$2,720.00*, in the General Credit column on the same line as the account title.

This entry requires two lines in the journal because account titles for both the debit and credit amounts must be written in the Account Title column.

4 Source document.   Write the source document number, *M1*, in the Doc. No. column on the first line of the entry.

Paid Cash on Account

August 11, 19--. Paid cash on account to Butler Cleaning Supplies, $1,360.00. Check No. 3.

The source document for this transaction is Check No. 3. *(CONCEPT: Objective Evidence)* The analysis of this transaction is shown in the T accounts.

The liability account, Butler Cleaning Supplies, is decreased by a debit, $1,360.00. The asset account, Cash, is decreased by a credit, $1,360.00. The journal entry for this transaction is shown in Illustration 5-10.

Butler Cleaning Supplies	
1,360.00	

Cash	
	1,360.00

ILLUSTRATION 5-10   Journal entry to record paying cash on account

	DATE	ACCOUNT TITLE	DOC. NO.	POST. REF.	GENERAL DEBIT	GENERAL CREDIT	SALES CREDIT	CASH DEBIT	CASH CREDIT	
6	11	Butler Cleaning Supplies	C3		1 3 6 0 00				1 3 6 0 00	6

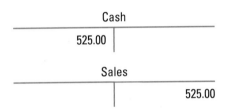

1 **Date.** Write the date, *11*, in the Date column.

2 **Debit.** Write the title of the account debited, *Butler Cleaning Supplies*, in the Account Title column. There is no special amount column with the title of the account debited, Butler Cleaning Supplies, in its heading. Therefore, the debit amount is recorded in the General Debit column. Write the debit amount, *$1,360.00*, in the General Debit column.

3 **Credit.** The journal has a special amount column for credits to Cash. The title of the account is in the column heading. Therefore, the account title does not need to be written in the Account Title column. Write the credit amount, *$1,360.00*, in the Cash Credit column.

4 **Source document.** Write the source document number, *C3*, in the Doc. No. column.

Received Cash from Sales

August 12, 19--. Received cash from sales, $525.00. Tape No. 12.

The source document for this transaction is Calculator Tape No. 12. *(CONCEPT: Objective Evidence)* The analysis of this transaction is shown in the T accounts.

The asset account, Cash, is increased by a debit, $525.00. The revenue account, Sales, is increased by a credit, $525.00. The journal entry for this transaction is shown in Illustration 5-11.

ILLUSTRATION 5-11 Journal entry to record receiving cash from sales

| | DATE | ACCOUNT TITLE | DOC. NO. | POST. REF. | GENERAL | | SALES CREDIT | CASH | |
					DEBIT	CREDIT		DEBIT	CREDIT
7	12 ✓		T12	✓			5 2 5 00	5 2 5 00		7

JOURNAL   PAGE *1*

1 **Date.** Write the date, *12*, in the Date column.

2 **Debit.** The journal has a special amount column for debits to Cash. The title of the account is in the column heading. Therefore, the account title does not need to be written in the Account Title column. Write the debit amount, *$525.00*, in the Cash Debit column.

3 **Credit.** The journal also has a special amount column for credits to Sales. The title of the account is in the column heading. Therefore, the account title does not need to be written in the Account Title column. Write the credit amount, *$525.00*, in the Sales Credit column.

Because both amounts for this entry are recorded in special amount columns, no account titles are written in the

Account Title column. Therefore, a check mark is placed in the Account Title column to show that no account titles need to be written for this transaction. A check mark is also placed in the Post. Ref. column to show that no separate amounts on this line are to be posted individually.

Posting procedures are described in Chapter 6.

4 *Source document.* Write the source document number, *T12*, in the Doc. No. column.

Paid Cash for an Expense

August 12, 19--. Paid cash for rent, $250.00. Check No. 4.

The source document for this transaction is Check No. 4. (*CONCEPT: Objective Evidence*) The analysis of this transaction is shown in the T accounts.

The expense account, Rent Expense, is increased by a debit, $250.00. The asset account, Cash, is decreased by a credit, $250.00. The journal entry for this transaction is shown on line 8 in Illustration 5-12.

Rent Expense	
250.00	

Cash	
	250.00

| **ILLUSTRATION 5-12** | Journal entries to record paying cash for expenses |

JOURNAL

PAGE **1**

	DATE	ACCOUNT TITLE	DOC. NO.	POST. REF.	GENERAL DEBIT	GENERAL CREDIT	SALES CREDIT	CASH DEBIT	CASH CREDIT	
8	12	Rent Expense	C4		2 5 0 00				2 5 0 00	8
9	12	Utilities Expense	C5		4 5 00				4 5 00	9

1 *Date.* Write the date, *12*, in the Date column.

2 *Debit.* Write the title of the account debited, *Rent Expense*, in the Account Title column. There is no special amount column with the title of the account debited, Rent Expense, in its heading. Therefore, the debit amount is recorded in the General Debit column. Write the debit amount, *$250.00*, in the General Debit column.

3 *Credit.* The journal has a special amount column for credits to Cash. The title of the account is in the column heading. Therefore, the account title does not need to be written in the Account Title column. Write the credit amount, *$250.00*, in the Cash Credit column.

4 *Source document.* Write the source document number, *C4*, in the Doc. No. column.

The journal entry shown in Illustration 5-12 includes a cash payment for another expense, Utilities Expense. This transaction is journalized in the same way as the cash payment for rent.

FYI

Accounting is not just for accountants. For example, a performing artist earns revenue from providing a service. Financial decisions must be made such as the cost of doing a performance, the percentage of revenue paid to a manager, travel expenses, and the cost of rehearsal space.

Paid Cash to Owner for Personal Use

August 12, 19--. Paid cash to owner for personal use, $100.00. Check No. 6.

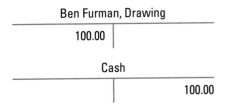

Ben Furman, Drawing

100.00 |

Cash

| 100.00

The source document for this transaction is Check No. 6. *(CONCEPT: Objective Evidence)* The analysis of this transaction is shown in the T accounts.

The contra capital account, Ben Furman, Drawing, is increased by a debit, $100.00. The asset account, Cash, is decreased by a credit, $100.00. The journal entry for this transaction is shown in Illustration 5-13.

ILLUSTRATION 5-13   Journal entry to record paying cash to owner for personal use

| | | | | | | GENERAL | | SALES | CASH | |
	DATE	ACCOUNT TITLE	DOC. NO.	POST. REF.		DEBIT	CREDIT	CREDIT	DEBIT	CREDIT
JOURNAL						1	2	3	4	5
10	12	*Ben Furman, Drawing*	C6			100 00				100 00

PAGE *1*

1 Date. Write the date, *12*, in the Date column.

2 Debit. Write the title of the account debited, *Ben Furman, Drawing*, in the Account Title column. There is no special amount column with the title of the account debited, Ben Furman, Drawing, in its heading. Therefore, the debit amount is recorded in the General Debit column. Write the debit amount, *$100.00*, in the General Debit column.

3 Credit. The journal has a special amount column for credits to Cash. The title of the account is in the column heading. Therefore, the account title does not need to be written in the Account Title column. Write the credit amount, *$100.00*, in the Cash Credit column.

4 Source document. Write the source document number, *C6*, in the Doc. No. column.

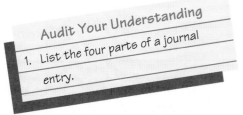

Audit Your Understanding

1. List the four parts of a journal entry.

PROVING AND RULING A JOURNAL

After Rugcare uses all but the last line on a journal page, columns are proved and ruled before totals are carried forward to the next page. At the end of each month, Rugcare also proves and rules the journal.

After all entries on August 20 are recorded, page 1 of Rugcare's journal is filled, as shown in Illustration 5-14 on the next page.

Page 1 is proved and ruled before totals are carried forward to page 2.

Proving a Journal Page

To prove a journal page, Rugcare verifies that the total debits on the page equal the total credits. Three steps are followed in proving a journal page.

☞☞ FYI ☜☜

Instructions are given in Appendix B for using a calculator.

1 *Add each of the amount columns.* Use a calculator if one is available. If a calculator is not available, total the columns on a sheet of paper.

2 *Add the debit column totals, and then add the credit column totals.* The figures from page 1 of Rugcare's journal are below.

Column	Debit Column Totals	Credit Column Totals
General	$ 7,920.00	$12,920.00
Sales		2,319.00
Cash	12,319.00	5,000.00
Totals	$20,239.00	$20,239.00

3 *Verify that the total debits and total credits are equal.* The total debits and the total credits on page 1 of Rugcare's journal are $20,239.00. Because the total debits equal the total credits, page 1 of Rugcare's journal is proved.

ILLUSTRATION 5-14   Completed page 1 of a journal

JOURNAL   PAGE 1

	DATE		ACCOUNT TITLE	DOC. NO.	POST. REF.	GENERAL DEBIT (1)	GENERAL CREDIT (2)	SALES CREDIT (3)	CASH DEBIT (4)	CASH CREDIT (5)	
1	Aug.	1	Ben Furman, Capital	R1			1000000		1000000		1
2		3	Supplies	C1		157700				157700	2
3		4	Prepaid Insurance	C2		120000				120000	3
4		7	Supplies	M1		272000					4
5			Butler Cleaning Supplies				272000				5
6		11	Butler Cleaning Supplies	C3		136000				136000	6
7		12	√	T12	√			52500	52500		7
8		12	Rent Expense	C4		25000				25000	8
9		12	Utilities Expense	C5		4500				4500	9
10		12	Ben Furman, Drawing	C6		10000				10000	10
11		13	Repair Expense	C7		2000				2000	11
12		13	Miscellaneous Expense	C8		2500				2500	12
13		13	√	T13	√			22900	22900		13
14		14	Advertising Expense	C9		6800				6800	14
15		14	√	T14	√			36000	36000		15
16		17	Petty Cash	C10		20000				20000	16
17		17	√	T17	√			35000	35000		17
18		18	Miscellaneous Expense	C11		7000				7000	18
19		18	√	T18	√			32000	32000		19
20		19	√	T19	√			29000	29000		20
21		20	Repair Expense	C12		8500				8500	21
22		20	√	T20	√			24500	24500		22
23		20	Supplies	M2		20000					23
24			Dale Office Supplies				20000				24
25		20	Carried Forward		√	792000	1292000	231900	1231900	500000	25

If the total debits do not equal the total credits, the errors must be found and corrected before any more work is completed.

Ruling a Journal Page

After a journal page is proved, the page is ruled as shown in Illustration 5-14.

1 Rule a single line across all amount columns directly below the last entry to indicate that the columns are to be added.

2 On the next line, write the date, *20*, in the Date column.

3 Write the words, *Carried Forward*, in the Account Title column. A check mark is also placed in the Post. Ref. column to show that nothing on this line needs to be posted.

4 Write each column total below the single line.

5 Rule double lines below the column totals across all amount columns. The double lines mean that the totals have been verified as correct.

Starting a New Journal Page

The column totals from the previous page are carried forward to a new page. The totals are recorded on the first line of the new page as shown in Illustration 5-15.

ILLUSTRATION 5-15	Starting a new journal page

JOURNAL   PAGE *2*

	DATE	ACCOUNT TITLE	DOC. NO.	POST. REF.	GENERAL DEBIT (1)	GENERAL CREDIT (2)	SALES CREDIT (3)	CASH DEBIT (4)	CASH CREDIT (5)	
1	19-- Aug. 20	Brought Forward		✓	7 9 20 00	12 9 20 00	2 3 1 9 00	12 3 1 9 00	5 0 0 0 00	1
2										2

1 Write the page number, *2*, at the top of the journal.

2 Write the date, *19--, Aug. 20*, in the Date column. Because this is the first time that a date is written on page 2, the year, month, and day are all written in the Date column.

3 Write the words, *Brought Forward*, in the Account Title column. A check mark is also placed in the Post. Ref. column to show that nothing on this line needs to be posted.

4 Record the column totals brought forward from the previous page.

Completing a Journal at the End of a Month

Rugcare always proves and rules a journal at the end of each month even if the last page for the month is not full. Page 2 of Rugcare's journal on August 31 is shown in Illustration 5-16.

ILLUSTRATION 5-16 Ruling a journal at the end of a month

JOURNAL PAGE 2

	DATE	ACCOUNT TITLE	DOC. NO.	POST. REF.	GENERAL DEBIT (1)	GENERAL CREDIT (2)	SALES CREDIT (3)	CASH DEBIT (4)	CASH CREDIT (5)	
1	Aug. 20	Brought Forward		✓	7920 00	12920 00	2319 00	12319 00	5000 00	1
2	21	✓	T21	✓			270 00	270 00		2
3	24	✓	T24	✓			300 00	300 00		3
4	25	✓	T25	✓			310 00	310 00		4
5	26	✓	T26	✓			245 00	245 00		5
6	27	Utilities Expense	C13		70 00				70 00	6
7	27	✓	T27	✓			290 00	290 00		7
8	28	Supplies	C14		434 00				434 00	8
9	28	✓	T28	✓			267 00	267 00		9
10	28	Miscellaneous Expense	M3			3 00			3 00	10
11	31	Miscellaneous Expense	C15			7 00			12 00	11
12		Repair Expense				5 00				12
13	31	Ben Furman, Drawing	C16		500 00				500 00	13
14	31	✓	T31	✓			290 00	290 00		14
15	31	Totals			8939 00	12920 00	4291 00	14291 00	6019 00	15

The entries on lines 10, 11, and 12, Illustration 5-16, are described in Chapter 7.

FYI

Double lines ruled below totals mean the totals have been verified as correct.

Proving Page 2 of a Journal. The last page of a journal for a month is proved using the same steps previously described. Then, cash is proved and the journal is ruled. The proof of page 2 of Rugcare's journal is shown below.

Column	Debit Column Totals	Credit Column Totals
General	$ 8,939.00	$12,920.00
Sales		4,291.00
Cash	14,291.00	6,019.00
Totals	$23,230.00	$23,230.00

Page 2 of Rugcare's journal is proved because the total debits are equal to the total credits, $23,230.00.

Proving Cash. Determining that the amount of cash agrees with the accounting records is called **proving cash.** Cash can be proved at any time Rugcare wishes to verify the accuracy of the cash records. However, Rugcare *always* proves cash at the end of a month when the journal is proved. Rugcare uses two steps to prove cash.

1 *Calculate the cash balance.*

Cash on hand at the beginning of the month. . . $0.00

Rugcare began the month with no cash balance. Mr. Furman invested the initial cash on August 1.

Plus total cash received during the month . . . . .   +14,291.00

This amount is the total of the journal's Cash Debit column.

Equals total $14,291.00
Less total cash paid during the month . . . .   − 6,019.00

This amount is the total of the journal's Cash Credit column.

Equals cash balance at the end of the month. . . $ 8,272.00

Checkbook balance on the next unused
check stub . . . . $ 8,272.00

2 *Verify that the cash balance equals the checkbook balance on the next unused check stub in the checkbook.* Because the cash balance calculated using the journal and the checkbook balance are the same, *$8,272.00,* cash is proved.

☞ ☞ FYI ☜ ☜

Always use a straight edge to draw lines.

Ruling a Journal at the End of a Month. A journal is ruled at the end of each month even if the last journal page is not full. Rugcare's journal is ruled as shown in Illustration 5-16.

The procedures for ruling a journal at the end of a month are similar to those for ruling a journal page to carry the totals forward.

Rugcare uses five steps in ruling a journal at the end of each month.

1 Rule a single line across all amount columns directly below the last entry to indicate that the columns are to be added.

2 On the next line, write the date, *31,* in the Date column.

3 Write the word, *Totals,* in the Account Title column.

Some of the column totals will be posted as described in Chapter 6. Therefore, a check mark is not placed in the Post. Ref. column for this line.

4 Write each column total below the single line.

5 Rule double lines below the column totals across all amount columns. The double lines mean that the totals have been verified as correct.

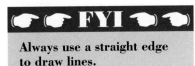

Audit Your Understanding

1. List the formula for proving cash.

2. List the 5 steps to rule a journal at the end of a month.

PROFESSIONAL ACCOUNTING ASSOCIATIONS

Accounting for financial activities of businesses around the world has many similarities as well as differences. In many countries, accounting associations grant a title to designate accountants as professionals in their field.

Qualification requirements for a title designation are generally established by a professional accounting organization. The requirements normally consist of a stated amount of education and experience in accounting. Upon meeting these requirements, individuals are designated with a special ti-

tle. Some countries also have special requirements and title designations for individuals who perform tax

accounting work.

The following is a selected list of countries and their professional account-

ing title designation and the organization that grants that title.

COUNTRY	TITLE	ORGANIZATION
Australia	Chartered Accountant	Institute of Chartered Accountants in Australia
Bangladesh	Chartered Accountant	Institute of Chartered Accountants of Bangladesh
Canada	Chartered Accountant	Canadian Institute of Chartered Accountants
India	Chartered Accountant	Institute of Chartered Accountants of India
Japan	Certified Public Accountant	Japanese Institute of Certified Public Accountants
Mexico	Contador Público (Public Accountant)	Mexican Institute of Public Accountants / Federation of Societies of Public Accountants
Nigeria	Chartered Accountant	Institute of Chartered Accountants of Nigeria
Pakistan	Chartered Accountant	Institute of Chartered Accountants of Pakistan
Republic of China (Taiwan)	Certified Public Accountant	National Federation of Certified Public Accountants / Associations of the Republic of China Chartered Accountants
South Africa	Chartered Accountant	South African Institute of Chartered Accountants

The Summary Illustration on page 90 analyzes the procedure for journalizing transactions.

GENERALLY ACCEPTED ACCOUNTING PRACTICES

In completing accounting work, Rugcare is guided by generally accepted accounting practices, including those shown in Illustration 5-17.

1. Errors are corrected in a way that does not cause doubts about what the correct information is. If an error is recorded, cancel the error by neatly drawing a line through the incorrect item. Write the correct item immediately above the canceled item, as

shown in the Cash Debit column on line 17 of Illustration 5-17.

2. Sometimes an entire entry is incorrect and is discovered before the next entry is journalized. Draw neat lines through all parts of the incorrect entry. Journalize the entry correctly on the next blank line, as shown on lines 18 and 19, Illustration 5-17.

ILLUSTRATION 5-17 Some generally accepted accounting practices

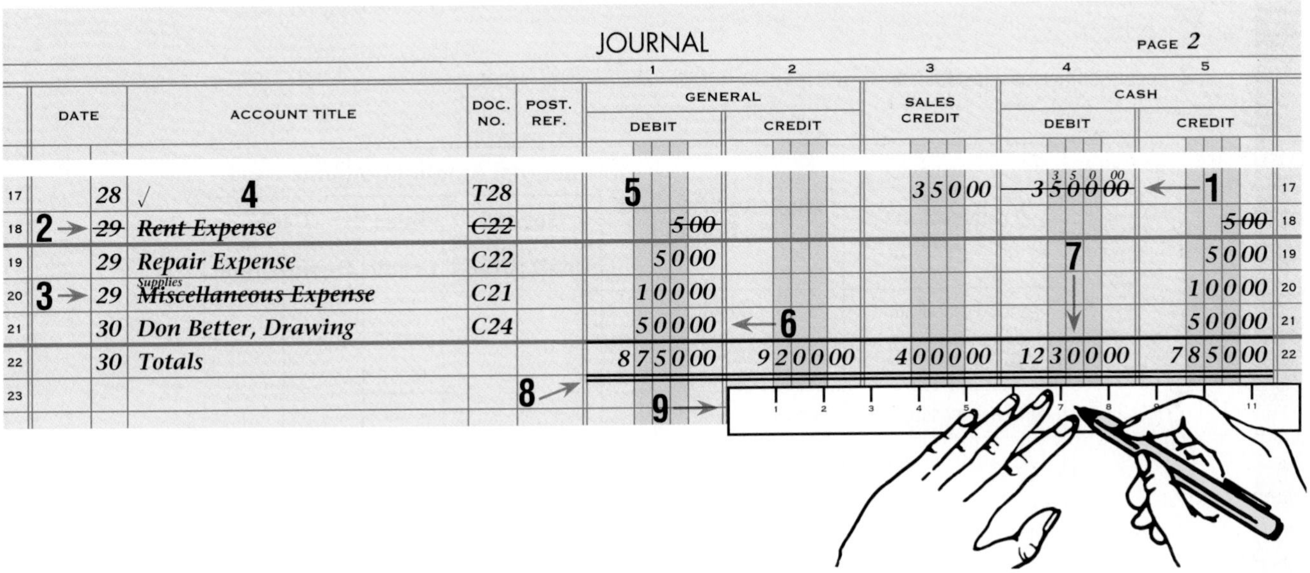

JOURNAL PAGE 2

	DATE		ACCOUNT TITLE	DOC. NO.	POST. REF.	GENERAL DEBIT (1)	GENERAL CREDIT (2)	SALES CREDIT (3)	CASH DEBIT (4)	CASH CREDIT (5)	
17		28	√	T28				350 00	350 00 ~~3 500 00~~		17
18		~~29~~	~~Rent Expense~~	~~C22~~		~~5 00~~				~~5 00~~	18
19		29	Repair Expense	C22		50 00				50 00	19
20		29	Supplies ~~Miscellaneous Expense~~	C21		100 00				100 00	20
21		30	Don Better, Drawing	C24		500 00				500 00	21
22		30	Totals			8 750 00	9 200 00	4 000 00	12 300 00	7 850 00	22
23											

3. Sometimes several correct entries are recorded after an incorrect entry is made. The next blank lines are several entries later. Draw neat lines through all incorrect parts of the entry. Record the correct items on the same lines as the incorrect items, directly above the canceled parts. This procedure is shown on line 20 of Illustration 5-17.
4. Words in accounting records are written in full when space permits. Words may be abbreviated only when space is limited. All items are written legibly.
5. Dollars and cents signs and decimal points are not used when writing amounts on ruled accounting paper. Sometimes a color tint or a heavy vertical rule is used on printed accounting paper to separate the dollars and cents columns.
6. Two zeros are written in the cents column when an amount is in even dollars, such as $500.00. If the cents column is left blank, doubts may arise later about the correct amount.
7. A single line is ruled across amount columns to indicate addition or subtraction as shown on line 21, Illustration 5-17.
8. A double line is ruled across amount columns to indicate that the totals have been verified as correct.
9. Neatness is very important in accounting records so that there is never any doubt about what information has been recorded. A ruler is used to make single and double lines.

Summary of journalizing transactions

1 Analyze transactions

   a. From source document information

Receipts	Calculator Tapes	Checks	Memorandums

   b. Using T accounts

Rent Expense	Cash
50.00	50.00

Debits ⟶ equal ⟶ Credits

   c. Verify for each entry that:

2 Record entries in a journal

Transactions	Written in Account Title Column	Journal Amount Columns Used				
		General		Sales	Cash	
		Debit	Credit	Credit	Debit	Credit
Received cash from owner as an investment	Capital Account Title		✓		✓	
Paid cash for supplies	Supplies	✓				✓
Paid cash for insurance	Prepaid Insurance	✓				✓
Bought supplies on account	Supplies Liability Account Title	✓	✓			
Paid cash on account	Liability Account Title	✓				✓
Received cash from sales	✓			✓	✓	
Paid cash for an expense	Expense Account Title	✓				✓
Paid cash to owner for personal use	Drawing Account Title	✓				✓

3 Prove the journal

   a. Rule a single line across amount columns.

   b. Add amount columns.

   c. Add all debit totals and add all credit totals.

   d. Verify that total debits equal total credits.

4 Prove cash

   a. Cash at beginning + Total cash received = Total
      Total − Total cash paid = Ending cash balance

   b. Verify that the cash balance is the same as the amount shown on the next unused check stub.

5 Complete the journal by ruling double lines across all amount columns.

What is the meaning of each of the following?

1. journal
2. journalizing
3. special amount column
4. general amount column
5. entry
6. double-entry accounting
7. source document
8. check
9. receipt
10. memorandum
11. proving cash

QUESTIONS FOR INDIVIDUAL STUDY   EPT(b)

1. What are the five amount columns in the journal used by Rugcare?

2. Which of the columns in Rugcare's journal are special amount columns?

3. What is the source document for a cash payment transaction?

4. What is the source document for a sales transaction?

5. What is the source document for cash received from transactions other than sales?

6. What is the source document for a transaction when no other source document is prepared or when additional explanation is needed?

7. What are the four parts of a journal entry?

8. What two journal amount columns are used to record cash received from the owner as an investment?

9. What two journal amount columns are used to record cash paid for supplies?

10. What two journal amount columns are used to record cash paid for insurance?

11. What two journal amount columns are used to record supplies bought on account?

12. What two journal amount columns are used to record cash paid on account?

13. What two journal amount columns are used to record cash received from sales?

14. What two journal amount columns are used to record cash paid for an expense?

15. What two journal amount columns are used to record cash paid to the owner for personal use?

16. What is the procedure for proving a journal page?

17. What are the two steps that Rugcare uses in proving cash?

CASES FOR CRITICAL THINKING   EPT(b)

CASE 1 During the summer, Willard Kelly does odd jobs to earn money. Mr. Kelly keeps all his money in a single checking account. He writes checks to pay for personal items and for business expenses. These payments include personal clothing, school supplies, gasoline for his car, and recreation. Mr. Kelly uses his check stubs as his accounting records. Are Mr. Kelly's accounting procedures and records correct? Explain your answer.

CASE 2 In his business, Michael Rock uses a journal with the following columns: Date, Account Title, Check No., Cash Debit, and Cash Credit. Mr. Rock's wife, Jennifer, suggests that he needs three additional amount columns: General Debit, General Credit, and Sales Credit. Mr. Rock states that all his business transactions are for cash, and he never buys on account. Therefore, he does not see the need for more than the Cash Debit and Cash Credit special amount columns. Who is correct, Mr. or Mrs. Rock? Explain your answer.

DRILL 5-D1 Analyzing transactions

This drill provides continuing practice in analyzing transactions into debit and credit parts. Use Rugcare's chart of accounts, page 18.

Transactions
1. Paid cash for supplies, $100.00.
2. Bought supplies on account from Butler Cleaning Supplies, $500.00.
3. Paid cash to owner for personal use, $50.00.
4. Received cash from sales, $300.00.
5. Paid cash for rent, $200.00.
6. Paid cash for insurance, $250.00.
7. Received cash from owner as an investment, $1,000.00.
8. Paid cash for repairs, $25.00.
9. Paid cash for telephone bill, $30.00.
10. Paid cash for advertising, $40.00.
11. Paid cash on account to Butler Cleaning Supplies, $300.00.
12. Paid cash for miscellaneous expense, $3.00.

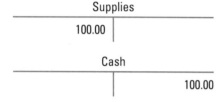

INSTRUCTIONS:

1. For each transaction, prepare two T accounts. On the T accounts, write the account titles affected by the transaction.
2. Write the debit or credit amount in each T account to show how the transaction affected that account. T accounts for Transaction 1 are given as an example.

DRILL 5-D2 Analyzing transactions

This drill continues the practice in analyzing transactions. Mark Jacobs owns a service business called Jacobs Secretarial Services. Jacobs Secretarial Services uses the following accounts.

Cash	Sales
Supplies	Advertising Expense
Prepaid Insurance	Miscellaneous Expense
Gable Supplies	Rent Expense
Mark Jacobs, Capital	Repair Expense
Mark Jacobs, Drawing	Utilities Expense

Use a form similar to the following. Transaction 1 is given as an example.

1	2	3	4	5	6	7
Trans. No.	Accounts Affected	Account Classification	How is Account Affected?		Entered in Account as a	
			(+)	(−)	Debit	Credit
1.	Advertising Expense Cash	Expense Asset	✓	✓	✓	✓

Transactions
1. Paid cash for advertising.
2. Paid cash for repairs.
3. Received cash from owner as an investment.
4. Paid cash for miscellaneous expense.
5. Bought supplies on account from Gable Supplies.

6. Paid cash on account to Gable Supplies.
7. Paid cash for water bill.
8. Paid cash for supplies.
9. Paid cash for rent.
10. Paid cash to owner for personal use.
11. Received cash from sales.
12. Paid cash for insurance.

INSTRUCTIONS:

1. In Column 2, write the titles of the accounts affected by each transaction.
2. For each account title, write the account classification in Column 3.
3. For each account title, place a check mark in either Column 4 or 5 to indicate if each account is increased (+) or decreased (−) by this transaction.
4. For each account title, place a check mark in either Column 6 or 7 to indicate if the amount is entered in the account as a debit or a credit.

APPLICATION PROBLEMS   EPT(c,d,e,f,g)

PROBLEM 5-1 Journalizing transactions

Dorothy Gilbert owns a service business called Lane Company. Lane Company uses the following accounts.

Cash	Sales
Supplies	Advertising Expense
Prepaid Insurance	Miscellaneous Expense
Mertz Supplies	Rent Expense
Dorothy Gilbert, Capital	Repair Expense
Dorothy Gilbert, Drawing	Utilities Expense

INSTRUCTIONS:

1. Journalize the following transactions completed during February of the current year. Use page 1 of a journal similar to the one described in this chapter for Rugcare. Source documents are abbreviated as follows: check, C; memorandum, M; receipt, R; calculator tape, T.

Transactions

Feb. 1. Received cash from owner as an investment, $12,000.00. R1.
    3. Paid cash for rent, $600.00. C1.
    4. Paid cash for insurance, $1,200.00. C2.
    5. Bought supplies on account from Mertz Supplies, $1,500.00. M1.
    6. Paid cash for supplies, $1,000.00. C3.
    7. Paid cash on account to Mertz Supplies, $750.00. C4.
    10. Paid cash for miscellaneous expense, $5.00. C5.
    12. Received cash from sales, $500.00. T12.
    14. Received cash from sales, $450.00. T14.
    17. Paid cash for repairs, $75.00. C6.
    17. Received cash from sales, $300.00. T17.
    20. Received cash from sales, $370.00. T20.
    21. Received cash from sales, $470.00. T21.
    24. Received cash from sales, $400.00. T24.
    25. Paid cash for electric bill, $50.00. C7.
    25. Received cash from sales, $450.00. T25.
    26. Paid cash for advertising, $90.00. C8.
    26. Received cash from sales, $300.00. T26.
    27. Received cash from sales, $350.00. T27.
    28. Paid cash to owner for personal use, $250.00. C9.
    28. Received cash from sales, $500.00. T28.

2. Prove the journal. Rule a single line across all amount columns. Write the amount column totals below the single line.
3. Prove cash. The beginning cash balance on February 1 is zero. The ending cash balance on the next unused check stub is $12,070.00.
4. Rule the journal.

PROBLEM 5-2 Journalizing transactions

Rona Dowling owns a service business called LawnCare. LawnCare uses the following accounts.

Cash	Sales
Supplies	Advertising Expense
Prepaid Insurance	Miscellaneous Expense
Main Office Supplies	Rent Expense
Westley Supplies	Repair Expense
Rona Dowling, Capital	Utilities Expense
Rona Dowling, Drawing	

INSTRUCTIONS:

1. Journalize the following transactions completed during April of the current year. Use page 1 of a journal similar to the one described in this chapter for Rugcare. Source documents are abbreviated as follows: check, C; memorandum, M; receipt, R; calculator tape, T.

Transactions

Apr. 1. Received cash from owner as an investment, $10,000.00. R1.
2. Paid cash for rent, $800.00. C1.
3. Paid cash for insurance, $3,000.00. C2.
6. Bought supplies on account from Westley Supplies, $2,000.00. M1.
7. Paid cash for supplies, $700.00. C3.
8. Paid cash on account to Westley Supplies, $1,000.00. C4.
8. Received cash from sales, $500.00. T8.
9. Paid cash for telephone bill, $60.00. C5.
9. Received cash from sales, $650.00. T9.
10. Paid cash for repairs, $85.00. C6.
10. Received cash from sales, $600.00. T10.
13. Paid cash for miscellaneous expense, $15.00. C7.
13. Received cash from sales, $700.00. T13.
14. Received cash from sales, $650.00. T14.
15. Paid cash to owner for personal use, $350.00. C8.
15. Received cash from sales, $500.00. T15.
16. Paid cash for supplies, $1,000.00. C9.
16. Received cash from sales, $600.00. T16.
17. Received cash from sales, $650.00. T17.
20. Bought supplies on account from Main Office Supplies, $500.00. M2.
20. Received cash from sales, $570.00. T20.
21. Received cash from sales, $670.00. T21.

2. Prove and rule page 1 of the journal. Carry the column totals forward to page 2 of the journal.
3. Use page 2 of the journal. Journalize the following transactions completed during April of the current year.

Apr. 22. Paid cash for electric bill, $55.00. C10.
22. Received cash from sales, $600.00. T22.
23. Bought supplies on account from Main Office Supplies, $50.00. M3.
23. Received cash from sales, $650.00. T23.
24. Paid cash for advertising, $100.00. C11.

24. Received cash from sales, $500.00. T24.
27. Received cash from sales, $550.00. T27.
28. Received cash from sales, $500.00. T28.
29. Paid cash for supplies, $150.00. C12.
29. Received cash from sales, $650.00. T29.
30. Paid cash to owner for personal use, $350.00. C13.
30. Received cash from sales, $500.00. T30.

4. Prove page 2 of the journal.
5. Prove cash. The beginning cash balance on April 1 is zero. The balance on the next unused check stub is $12,375.00.
6. Rule page 2 of the journal.

ENRICHMENT PROBLEMS

MASTERY PROBLEM 5-M Journalizing transactions

APPLICATION

Rachel Frank owns a service business called Frank's Car Wash. Frank's Car Wash uses the following accounts.

Cash	Sales
Supplies	Advertising Expense
Prepaid Insurance	Miscellaneous Expense
Delancy Supplies	Rent Expense
Long Supplies	Repair Expense
Rachel Frank, Capital	Utilities Expense
Rachel Frank, Drawing	

INSTRUCTIONS:

1. Journalize the following transactions completed during June of the current year. Use page 1 of a journal similar to the one described in this chapter for Rugcare. Source documents are abbreviated as follows: check, C; memorandum, M; receipt, R; calculator tape, T.

Transactions

June 1. Received cash from owner as an investment, $18,000.00. R1.
2. Paid cash for rent, $900.00. C1.
3. Paid cash for supplies, $1,500.00. C2.
4. Bought supplies on account from Delancy Supplies, $3,000.00. M1.
5. Paid cash for insurance, $4,500.00. C3.
8. Paid cash on account to Delancy Supplies, $1,500.00. C4.
8. Received cash from sales, $750.00. T8.
9. Paid cash for electric bill, $75.00. C5.
9. Received cash from sales, $700.00. T9.
10. Paid cash for miscellaneous expense, $7.00. C6.
10. Received cash from sales, $750.00. T10.
11. Paid cash for repairs, $100.00. C7.
11. Received cash from sales, $850.00. T11.
12. Received cash from sales, $700.00. T12.
15. Paid cash to owner for personal use, $350.00. C8.
15. Received cash from sales, $750.00. T15.
16. Paid cash for supplies, $1,500.00. C9.
16. Received cash from sales, $650.00. T16.
17. Bought supplies on account from Long Supplies, $750.00. M2.
17. Received cash from sales, $600.00. T17.
18. Received cash from sales, $800.00. T18.
19. Received cash from sales, $750.00. T19.

2. Prove and rule page 1 of the journal. Carry the column totals forward to page 2 of the journal.

3. Use page 2 of the journal. Journalize the following transactions completed during June of the current year.

Transactions

June 22. Bought supplies on account from Long Supplies, $80.00. M3.
22. Received cash from sales, $700.00. T22.
23. Paid cash for advertising, $130.00. C10.
23. Received cash from sales, $650.00. T23.
24. Paid cash for telephone bill, $60.00. C11.
24. Received cash from sales, $600.00. T24.
25. Received cash from sales, $550.00. T25.
26. Paid cash for supplies, $70.00. C12.
26. Received cash from sales, $600.00. T26.
29. Received cash from sales, $750.00. T29.
30. Paid cash to owner for personal use, $375.00. C13.
30. Received cash from sales, $800.00. T30.

4. Prove page 2 of the journal.
5. Prove cash. The beginning cash balance on June 1 is zero. The balance on the next unused check stub is $18,883.00.
6. Rule page 2 of the journal.

CHALLENGE PROBLEM 5-C Journalizing transactions

APPLICATION

Wilbur Moore owns a service business called Moore's Tailors. Moore's Tailors uses the following accounts.

Cash	Sales
Supplies	Advertising Expense
Prepaid Insurance	Miscellaneous Expense
Marker Supplies	Rent Expense
O'Brien Supplies	Repair Expense
Wilbur Moore, Capital	Utilities Expense
Wilbur Moore, Drawing	

INSTRUCTIONS:

1. Use page 1 of a journal similar to the following.

Journal								Page 1
Cash		**Date**	**Account Title**	**Doc. No.**	**Post Ref.**	**General**		**Sales Credit**
Debit	**Credit**					**Debit**	**Credit**	

Journalize the following transactions completed during June of the current year. Source documents are abbreviated as follows: check, C; memorandum, M; receipt, R; calculator tape, T.

Transactions

June 1. Owner invested money, $17,000.00. R1.
2. Wrote a check for supplies, $1,400.00. C1.
3. Paid June rent, $800.00. C2.
4. Wrote a check for insurance, $3,000.00. C3.
5. Bought supplies on account from Marker Supplies, $2,500.00. M1.
7. Received cash from sales, $550.00. T7.

June 9. Paid monthly telephone bill, $70.00. C4.
       9. Wrote a check to Marker Supplies on account, $1,300.00. C5.
      10. Received cash from sales, $550.00. T10.
      11. Paid for miscellaneous expense, $6.00. C6.
      11. Received cash from sales, $550.00. T11.
      12. Wrote a check for repairs, $90.00. C7.
      12. Cash was received from sales, $600.00. T12.
      15. Paid for supplies, $1,300.00. C8.
      15. Total cash sales, $540.00. T15.
      16. Owner withdrew money for personal use, $300.00. C9.
      16. Cash was received from sales, $400.00. T16.
      17. Total cash sales, $780.00. T17.
      18. Bought supplies on account from O'Brien Supplies, $900.00. M2.
      18. Received cash from sales, $600.00. T18.
      19. Wrote a check for supplies, $85.00. C10.
      19. Cash was received from sales, $850.00. T19.

2. Prove and rule page 1 of the journal. Carry the column totals forward to page 2 of the journal.

3. Use page 2 of the journal. Journalize the following transactions completed during June of the current year.

Transactions
June 22. Received cash from sales, $700.00. T22.
      23. Bought supplies on account from Marker Supplies, $95.00. M3.
      23. Received cash from sales, $720.00. T23.
      24. Paid for July advertising, $100.00. C11.
      24. Received cash from sales, $550.00. T24.
      25. Paid water bill, $75.00. C12.
      25. Received cash from sales, $600.00. T25.
      26. Received cash from sales, $450.00. T26.
      29. Wrote a check to O'Brien Supplies on account, $900.00. C13.
      29. Received cash from sales, $630.00. T29.
      30. Owner withdrew cash for personal use, $450.00. C14.
      30. Received cash from sales, $360.00. T30.

4. Prove page 2 of the journal.
5. Prove cash. The cash balance on June 1 is zero. The balance on the next unused check stub is $16,554.00.
6. Rule page 2 of the journal.

6

Posting to a General Ledger

ENABLING PERFORMANCE TASKS

After studying Chapter 6, you will be able to:

a Define accounting terms related to posting from a journal to a general ledger.

b Identify accounting concepts and practices related to posting from a journal to a general ledger.

c Prepare a chart of accounts for a service business organized as a proprietorship.

d Post amounts from a journal to a general ledger.

TERMS PREVIEW

ledger • general ledger • account number • file maintenance • opening an account • posting

Rugcare records transactions in a journal as described in Chapter 5. A journal is a permanent record of the debit and credit parts of each transaction with transactions recorded in chronological order. A journal does not show in one place all the changes in a single account. If only a journal is used, a business must search through all journal pages to find items affecting a single account balance. For this reason, a form is used to summarize in one place all the changes to a single account. A separate form is used for each account.

An account form is based on and includes the debit and credit sides of a T account as shown in Illustration 6-1.

ILLUSTRATION 6-1

Relationship of a T account to an account form

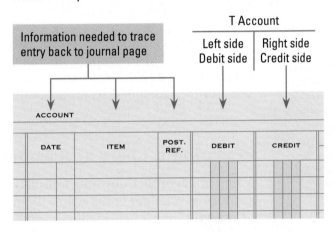

In addition to debit and credit columns, space is provided in the account form for recording the transaction date and journal page number. This information can be used to trace a specific entry back to where a transaction is recorded in a journal.

The major disadvantage of the account form shown in Illustration 6-1 is that no current, up-to-date account balance is shown. If the form in Illustration 6-1 is used, an up-to-date balance must be calculated each time the account is examined. Also, the balance is difficult and time consuming to calculate when an account has a large number of entries. Therefore, a more commonly used account form has Debit and Credit Balance columns as shown in Illustration 6-2. Because the form has columns for the debit and credit balance, it is often referred to as the balance-ruled account form.

ILLUSTRATION 6-2

Account form

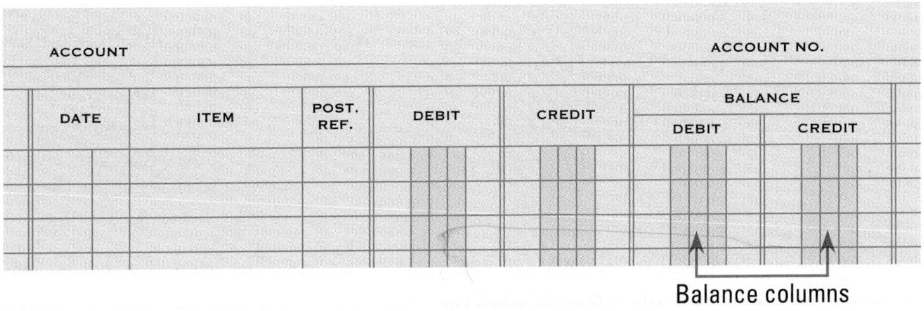

The account balance is calculated and recorded as each entry is recorded in the account. Recording information in an account is described later in this chapter. The T account is a useful device for analyzing transactions into debit and credit parts. However, the balance-ruled account form is more useful as a permanent record of changes to account balances than is the T account. Rugcare uses the balance-ruled account form.

ARRANGING ACCOUNTS IN A GENERAL LEDGER

A group of accounts is called a **ledger**. A ledger that contains all accounts needed to prepare financial statements is called a **general ledger**. The name given to an account is known as an account title. The number assigned to an account is called an **account number**.

Preparing a Chart of Accounts

A list of account titles and numbers showing the location of each account in a ledger is known as a chart of accounts. Rugcare's chart of accounts is shown in Illustration 6-3.

ILLUSTRATION 6-3   Chart of accounts

CHART OF ACCOUNTS

Balance Sheet Accounts	**Income Statement Accounts**
(100) ASSETS	(400) REVENUE
110 Cash	410 Sales
120 Petty Cash	
130 Supplies	(500) EXPENSES
140 Prepaid Insurance	510 Advertising Expense
	520 Insurance Expense
(200) LIABILITIES	530 Miscellaneous Expense
210 Butler Cleaning Supplies	540 Rent Expense
220 Dale Office Supplies	550 Repair Expense
	560 Supplies Expense
(300) OWNER'S EQUITY	570 Utilities Expense
310 Ben Furman, Capital	
320 Ben Furman, Drawing	
330 Income Summary	

ILLUSTRATION 6-4

For ease of use while studying Part 2, Rugcare's chart of accounts is also shown on page 100.

Accounts in a general ledger are arranged in the same order as they appear on financial statements. Rugcare's chart of accounts, Illustration 6-3, shows five general ledger divisions. (1) Assets, (2) Liabilities, (3) Owner's Equity, (4) Revenue, and (5) Expenses.

Numbering General Ledger Accounts

Rugcare assigns a three-digit account number to each account. For example, Supplies is assigned the number *130* as shown in Illustration 6-4.

Account numbers

> 1   3   0   **Supplies**
>
> General ledger division   Location within general ledger division

The first digit of each account number shows the general ledger division in which the account is located. For example, the asset division accounts are numbered in the 100s. Therefore, the number for the asset account, Supplies, begins with a *1*.

The second two digits indicate the location of each account within a general ledger division. The *1* in the account number 130, Supplies, indicates that the account is located in the asset division. The *30* in the account number for Supplies indicates that the account is located between account number 120 and account number 140.

Rugcare initially assigns account numbers by 10s so that new accounts can be added easily. Nine numbers are unused between each account on Rugcare's chart of accounts, Illustration 6-3. For example, numbers 111 to 119 are unused between accounts numbered 110 and 120. New numbers can be assigned between existing account numbers without renumbering all existing accounts. The procedure for arranging accounts in a general ledger, assigning account numbers, and keeping records current is called **file maintenance.**

Unused account numbers are assigned to new accounts. Rugcare records payments for gasoline in Miscellaneous Expense. If Mr. Furman found that the amount paid each month for gasoline had become a major expense, he might decide to use a separate account. The account might be titled Gasoline Expense. Rugcare arranges expense accounts in alphabetic order in its general ledger. Therefore, the new account would be inserted between Advertising Expense and Insurance Expense.

510	Advertising Expense	(Existing account)
	GASOLINE EXPENSE	(NEW ACCOUNT)
520	Insurance Expense	(Existing account)

The number selected for the new account should leave some unused numbers on either side of it for other accounts that might need to be added. The middle, unused account number between existing numbers 510 and 520 is 515. Therefore, 515 is assigned as the account number for the new account.

510	Advertising Expense	(Existing account)
515	GASOLINE EXPENSE	(NEW ACCOUNT)
520	Insurance Expense	(Existing account)

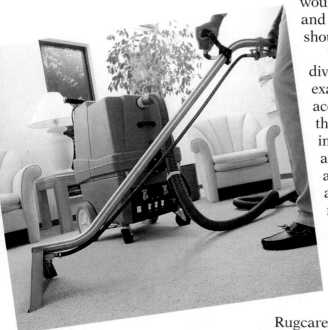

When an account is no longer needed, it is removed from the general ledger and the chart of accounts. For example, if Rugcare were to buy its own equipment and building, there would be no need for the rent expense account. The account numbered 540 would be removed, and that number would become unused and available to assign to another account if the need should arise.

When a new account is added at the end of a ledger division, the next number in a sequence of 10s is used. For example, suppose Rugcare needs to add another expense account, Water Expense, to show more detail about one of the utility expenses. The expense accounts are arranged in alphabetic order. Therefore, the new account would be added at the end of the expense section of the chart of accounts. The last used expense account number is 570, as shown on the chart of accounts, Illustration 6-3. The next number in the sequence of 10s is 580, which is assigned as the number of the new account.

560	Supplies Expense	(Existing account)
570	Utilities Expense	(Existing account)
580	WATER EXPENSE	(NEW ACCOUNT)

Rugcare has relatively few accounts in its general ledger and does not anticipate adding many new accounts in the future. Therefore, a three-digit account number adequately provides for the few account numbers that might be added. However, as the number of general ledger accounts increases, a business may change to four or more digits.

Charts of accounts with more than three digits are described in later chapters.

Opening General Ledger Accounts

Writing an account title and number on the heading of an account is called **opening an account.** A general ledger account is opened for each account listed on a chart of accounts. Accounts are opened and arranged in a general ledger in the same order as on the chart of accounts.

Cash, account number 110, is the first account on Rugcare's chart of accounts. The cash account is opened as shown in Illustration 6-5.

ILLUSTRATION 6-5

Opening an account in a general ledger

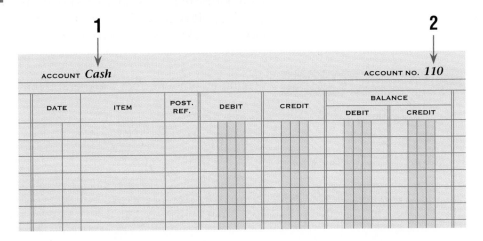

1   **2**

ACCOUNT *Cash*   ACCOUNT NO. *110*

DATE	ITEM	POST. REF.	DEBIT	CREDIT	BALANCE	
					DEBIT	CREDIT

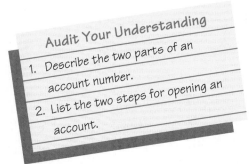

Audit Your Understanding

1. Describe the two parts of an account number.

2. List the two steps for opening an account.

1 Write the account title, *Cash*, after the word *Account* in the heading.

2 Write the account number, *110*, after the words *Account No.* in the heading.

The same procedure is used to open all accounts listed on Rugcare's chart of accounts.

POSTING FROM A JOURNAL TO A GENERAL LEDGER

Transferring information from a journal entry to a ledger account is called **posting**. Posting sorts journal entries so that all debits and credits affecting each account are brought together in one place. For example, all changes to *Cash* are brought together in the cash account.

Amounts in journal entries are recorded in either general amount columns or special amount columns. There are two rules for posting amounts from a journal. (1) Separate amounts in a journal's general amount columns are posted individually to the account written in the Account Title column. (2) Separate amounts in a journal's special amount columns are not posted individually. Instead, the special amount column totals are posted to the account named in the heading of the special amount column.

Posting Separate Amounts

For most, but not all journal entries, at least one separate amount is posted individually to a general ledger account. When an entry in a journal includes an amount in a general amount column and an account title in the Account Title column, the amount is posted individually.

FYI

Each separate amount in the general debit and credit columns is posted individually. The totals of these columns are not posted.

Posting a Separate Amount from a General Debit Column.   Each separate amount in the General Debit and General Credit columns of a journal is posted to the account written in the Account Title column. Posting an amount from the General Debit column is shown in Illustration 6-6.

ILLUSTRATION 6-6   Posting an amount from a General Debit column

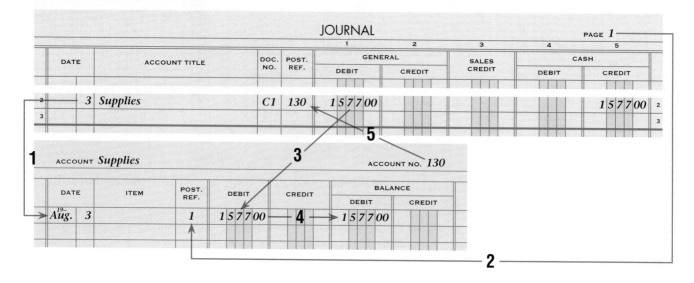

1 Write the date, *19--, Aug. 3*, in the Date column of the account, Supplies.

2 Write the journal page number, *1*, in the Post. Ref. column of the account. Post. Ref. is an abbreviation for Posting Reference.

3 Write the debit amount, *$1,577.00*, in the Debit amount column.

4 Write the new account balance, *$1,577.00*, in the Balance Debit column. Because this entry is the first in the supplies account, the previous balance is zero. The new account balance is calculated as shown below.

	Previous Balance	+	Debit Column Amount	=	New Debit Balance
	$0.00	+	$1,577.00	=	$1,577.00

5 Return to the journal and write the account number, *130*, in the Post. Ref. column of the journal.

The numbers in the Post. Ref. columns of the general ledger account and the journal serve three purposes. (1) An entry in an account can be traced to its source in a journal. (2) An entry in a journal can be traced to where it was posted in an account. (3) If posting is interrupted, the accounting personnel can easily see which entries in the journal still need to be posted. A blank in the Post. Ref. column of the journal indicates that posting for that line still needs to be completed. *Therefore, the posting reference is always recorded in the journal as the last step in the posting procedure.*

A second amount is posted to the supplies account from Rugcare's journal, line 4, as shown in Illustration 6-7.

ILLUSTRATION 6-7   Posting a second amount to an account

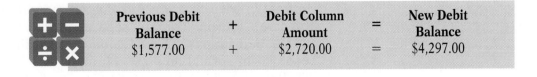

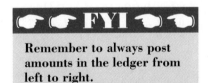

Remember to always post amounts in the ledger from left to right.

1 Write the date, *7*, in the Date column of the account. The month and year are written only once on a page of a ledger account unless the month or year changes.

2 Write the journal page number, *1*, in the Post. Ref. column of the account.

3 Write the debit amount, *$2,720.00*, in the Debit amount column.

4 Write the new account balance, *$4,297.00*, in the Balance Debit column. The new account balance is calculated as shown below.

	Previous Debit Balance	+	Debit Column Amount	=	New Debit Balance
	$1,577.00	+	$2,720.00	=	$4,297.00

5 Return to the journal and write the account number, *130*, in the Post. Ref. column of the journal.

Posting a Separate Amount from a General Credit Column. An amount in the General Credit column of a journal is posted as shown in Illustration 6-8.

ILLUSTRATION 6-8   Posting an amount from a General Credit column

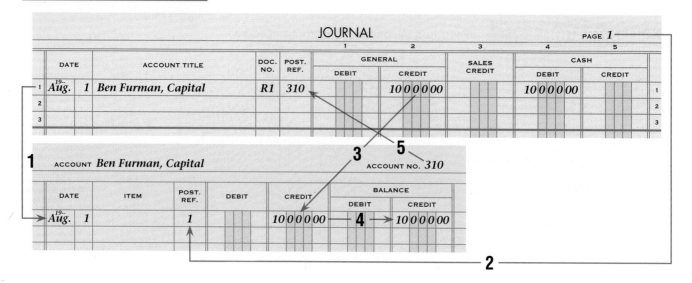

1 Write the date, *19--, Aug. 1*, in the Date column of the account.

2 Write the journal page number, *1*, in the Post. Ref. column of the account.

3 Write the credit amount, *$10,000.00*, in the Credit amount column.

4 Write the new account balance, *$10,000.00*, in the Balance Credit column. The new account balance is calculated as shown below.

Previous Balance	+	Credit Column Amount	=	New Credit Balance
$0.00	+	$10,000.00	=	$10,000.00

5 Return to the journal and write the account number, *310*, in the Post. Ref. column of the journal.

Journal Entries that are not Posted Individually. Several lines in Rugcare's journal contain separate amounts that are not to be posted individually. These include forwarding totals and amounts recorded in special amount columns.

The totals brought forward from page 1 are shown on line 1 of the journal in Illustration 6-9. None of these separate total amounts on line 1 are posted individually to general ledger accounts. To assure that no postings are overlooked, no blank posting reference spaces should be left in the Post. Ref. column of the journal. Therefore, when the totals were forwarded to page 2 of the journal, a check mark was placed in the Post. Ref. column of line 1 to show that no separate amounts are posted individually.

ILLUSTRATION 6-9   Check marks show that amounts are not posted

JOURNAL   PAGE 2

	DATE	ACCOUNT TITLE	DOC. NO.	POST. REF.	GENERAL DEBIT (1)	GENERAL CREDIT (2)	SALES CREDIT (3)	CASH DEBIT (4)	CASH CREDIT (5)	
1	Aug. 20	Brought Forward		√	7 9 2 0 00	12 9 2 0 00	2 3 1 9 00	12 3 1 9 00	5 0 0 00	1
11	31	Miscellaneous Expense	C15	530	7 00				1 2 00	11
12		Repair Expense		550	5 00					12
13	31	Ben Furman, Drawing	C16	320	5 0 0 00				5 0 0 00	13
14	31	√	T31	√			2 9 0 00	2 9 0 00		14
15	31	Totals			8 9 3 9 00	12 9 2 0 00	4 2 9 1 00	14 2 9 1 00	6 0 1 9 00	15
16					(√)	(√)				16
17										17

Check mark indicates that amounts ARE NOT posted individually

Check marks indicate that general amount column totals ARE NOT posted

FYI

Remember that a check mark in the Post. Ref. column means nothing on that line is posted.

Separate amounts in the special amount columns, Sales Credit, Cash Debit, and Cash Credit, are not posted individually. For example, on line 14 of the journal, Illustration 6-9, two separate $290.00 amounts are recorded in two special amount columns, Sales Credit and Cash Debit.

A check mark was placed in the Post. Ref. column on line 14 when the entry was journalized. The check mark indicates that no separate amounts are posted individually from this line. Instead, the totals of the special amount columns are posted.

Posting the Totals of Amount Columns

Separate amounts in special amount columns *are not* posted individually. The separate amounts are part of the special amount column totals. Only the totals of special amount columns *are* posted.

FYI

Remember that only the totals of special amount columns are posted.

Totals of General Debit and General Credit Amount Columns. The General Debit and General Credit columns are not special amount columns because the column headings do not contain the name of an account. All of the separate amounts in the General Debit and General Credit amount columns are posted individually.

Therefore, the column totals *are not* posted. A check mark in parentheses is placed below each general amount column total as shown in Illustration 6-9. The check mark indicates that the totals of the General Debit and General Credit columns are not posted.

A check mark in the Post. Ref. column indicates that amounts are not to be posted individually. On the totals line, the amounts in the special amount columns are posted. Therefore, a check mark is not placed in the Post. Ref. column for the totals line.

Posting the Totals of Special Amount Columns. Rugcare's journal has three special amount columns for which only totals are posted: Sales Credit, Cash Debit, and Cash Credit.

Posting the Total of the Sales Credit Column. The Sales Credit column of a journal is a special amount column with the account title Sales in the heading. Each separate amount in a special amount column could be posted individually. However, all of the separate amounts are debits or credits to the same account. Therefore, an advantage of a special amount column is that only the column total needs to be posted. For example, 14 separate sales transactions are recorded in the Sales Credit column of Rugcare's August journal. Instead of making 14 separate credit postings to Sales, only the column total is posted. As a result, only one posting is needed, which saves 13 postings. The smaller number of postings means 13 fewer opportunities to make a posting error. Posting special amount column totals saves time and results in greater accuracy.

The total of Rugcare's Sales Credit column is posted as shown in Illustration 6-10.

ILLUSTRATION 6-10   Posting the total of the Sales Credit column

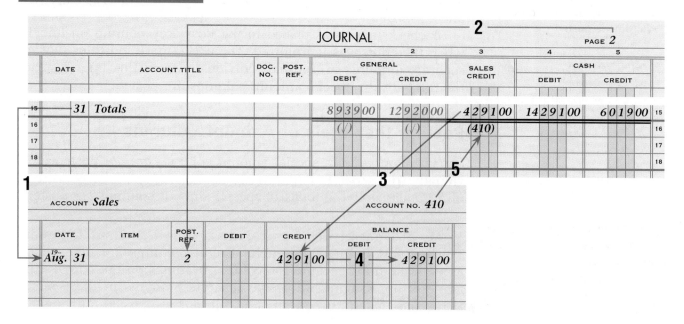

1 Write the date, *19--, Aug. 31,* in the Date column of the account, Sales.

2 Write the journal page number, *2,* in the Post. Ref. column of the account.

3 Write the column total, *$4,291.00,* in the Credit amount column.

4 Write the new account balance, *$4,291.00,* in the Balance Credit column. The new account balance is calculated as shown below.

Previous Balance	+	Credit Column Amount	=	New Credit Balance
$0.00	+	$4,291.00	=	$4,291.00

5 Return to the journal and write the account number in parentheses, *(410),* below the Sales Credit column total.

■ Belinda Hughes ■

BOO-BOO-BABY, INC., NEW YORK, NEW YORK

Belinda Hughes is looking for investors with $250,000 to help turn her company into a large corporation. Her business, Boo-Boo-Baby, Inc., based in New York, makes a designer line of children's coats and accessories. It all started for Hughes, formerly head designer of women's coats in a New York company, when she became an aunt and made her first children's coat in 1986. Then she turned an interest into an opportunity by starting her own company designing children's outerwear.

Hughes started her business with an investment of $15,000 from her personal savings. By 1991 she had sold $240,000 of children's wear and expects solid future growth. Five years after the start of her Boo-Boo-Baby line, her children's coats were carried in over 100 stores across the country, including major department stores such as Macy's, Bloomingdale's, Sak's, and Nordstrom's.

Hughes uses bold colors, unusual fabrics, and her own creative designs to distinguish her products in the large children's apparel market. She describes her coats as "funky" and says, "I design coats so that when people see them, they absolutely must have them."

She has a plan for the future of her business which includes the continued distribution of her coats to major department stores. Her ambitions also include a moderately priced line for chain stores.

Hughes is a graduate of the Parsons School of Design and has strong opinions about the value of education. When asked what she would recommend to students who would like to be successful business owners, she said "a good education is very important." She also believes that a course in accounting is crucial for business success because "you have to know the numbers to succeed." Although her degree is in design, her degree program included business courses. Drawing from personal experience, she emphasized that students should pay attention in school because you can't know today what will be important in real life later.

Personal Visions in Business

Posting the Total of the Cash Debit Column. The Cash Debit column of a journal is posted as shown in Illustration 6-11.

Posting the total of the Cash Debit column

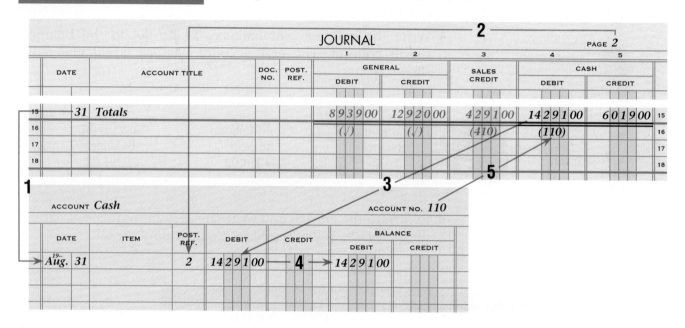

Two zeros are written in the cents column when an amount is in even dollars, such as $500.00. If the cents column is left blank, doubts may arise later about the correct amount.

1 Write the date, *19--, Aug. 31,* in the Date column of the account, Cash.

2 Write the journal page number, *2,* in the Post. Ref. column of the account.

3 Write the column total, *$14,291.00,* in the Debit amount column.

4 Write the new account balance, *$14,291.00,* in the Balance Debit column. The new account balance is calculated as shown below.

	Previous Balance	+	Debit Column Amount	=	New Debit Balance
	$0.00	+	$14,291.00	=	$14,291.00

5 Return to the journal and write the account number in parentheses, *(110),* below the Cash Debit column total.

Posting the Total of the Cash Credit Column. Posting the total of a journal's Cash Credit column is shown in Illustration 6-12.

ILLUSTRATION 6-12   Posting the total of the Cash Credit column

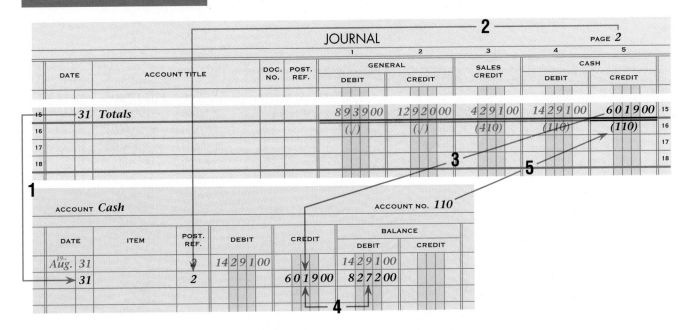

1 Write the date, *31*, in the Date column of the account, Cash.

2 Write the journal page number, *2*, in the Post. Ref. column of the account.

3 Write the column total, *$6,019.00*, in the Credit amount column.

4 Write the new account balance, *$8,272.00*, in the Balance Debit column. The new account balance is calculated as shown below.

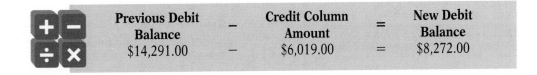

	Previous Debit Balance	−	Credit Column Amount	=	New Debit Balance
	$14,291.00	−	$6,019.00	=	$8,272.00

Whenever the debits in an account exceed the credits, the account balance is a debit. Whenever the credits in an account exceed the debits, the account balance is a credit.

5 Return to the journal and write the account number in parentheses, *(110)*, below the Cash Credit column total.

Journal Page with Posting Completed

Page 2 of Rugcare's August journal, after all posting has been completed, is shown in Illustration 6-13.

ILLUSTRATION 6-13   A journal page after posting has been completed

JOURNAL

PAGE 2

	DATE	ACCOUNT TITLE	DOC. NO.	POST. REF.	GENERAL DEBIT (1)	GENERAL CREDIT (2)	SALES CREDIT (3)	CASH DEBIT (4)	CASH CREDIT (5)	
1	Aug. 20	Brought Forward		√	7 9 2 0 00	12 9 2 0 00	2 3 1 9 00	12 3 1 9 00	5 0 0 00	1
2	21	√	T21	√			2 7 0 00	2 7 0 00		2
3	24	√	T24	√			3 0 0 00	3 0 0 00		3
4	25	√	T25	√			3 1 0 00	3 1 0 00		4
5	26	√	T26	√			2 4 5 00	2 4 5 00		5
6	27	Utilities Expense	C13	570	7 0 00				7 0 00	6
7	27	√	T27	√			2 9 0 00	2 9 0 00		7
8	28	Supplies	C14	130	4 3 4 00				4 3 4 00	8
9	28	√	T28	√			2 6 7 00	2 6 7 00		9
10	28	Miscellaneous Expense	M3	530	3 00				3 00	10
11	31	Miscellaneous Expense	C15	530	7 00				1 2 00	11
12		Repair Expense		550	5 00					12
13	31	Ben Furman, Drawing	C16	320	5 0 0 00				5 0 0 00	13
14	31	√	T31	√			2 9 0 00	2 9 0 00		14
15	31	Totals			8 9 3 9 00	12 9 2 0 00	4 2 9 1 00	14 2 9 1 00	6 0 1 9 00	15
16					(√)	(√)	(410)	(110)	(110)	16
17										17

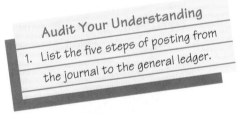

Audit Your Understanding

1. List the five steps of posting from the journal to the general ledger.

General Ledger with Posting Completed

Rugcare's general ledger, after all posting from the August journal is completed, is shown in Illustration 6-14.

The use of the accounts, Income Summary, Insurance Expense, and Supplies Expense, is described in Chapter 8.

ILLUSTRATION 6-14   A general ledger after posting has been completed

ACCOUNT Cash   ACCOUNT NO. 110

DATE	ITEM	POST. REF.	DEBIT	CREDIT	BALANCE DEBIT	BALANCE CREDIT
Aug. 31		2	14 2 9 1 00		14 2 9 1 00	
31		2		6 0 1 9 00	8 2 7 2 00	

ACCOUNT Petty Cash   ACCOUNT NO. 120

DATE	ITEM	POST. REF.	DEBIT	CREDIT	BALANCE DEBIT	BALANCE CREDIT
Aug. 17		1	2 0 0 00		2 0 0 00	

ACCOUNT **Supplies**   ACCOUNT NO. **130**

DATE		ITEM	POST. REF.	DEBIT	CREDIT	BALANCE	
						DEBIT	CREDIT
Aug.¹⁹⁻⁻	3		1	1 5 7 7 00		1 5 7 7 00	
	7		1	2 7 2 0 00		4 2 9 7 00	
	20		1	2 0 0 00		4 4 9 7 00	
	28		2	4 3 4 00		4 9 3 1 00	

ACCOUNT **Prepaid Insurance**   ACCOUNT NO. **140**

DATE		ITEM	POST. REF.	DEBIT	CREDIT	BALANCE	
						DEBIT	CREDIT
Aug.¹⁹⁻⁻	4		1	1 2 0 0 00		1 2 0 0 00	

ACCOUNT **Butler Cleaning Supplies**   ACCOUNT NO. **210**

DATE		ITEM	POST. REF.	DEBIT	CREDIT	BALANCE	
						DEBIT	CREDIT
Aug.¹⁹⁻⁻	7		1		2 7 2 0 00		2 7 2 0 00
	11		1	1 3 6 0 00			1 3 6 0 00

ACCOUNT **Dale Office Supplies**   ACCOUNT NO. **220**

DATE		ITEM	POST. REF.	DEBIT	CREDIT	BALANCE	
						DEBIT	CREDIT
Aug.¹⁹⁻⁻	20		1		2 0 0 00		2 0 0 00

ACCOUNT **Ben Furman, Capital**   ACCOUNT NO. **310**

DATE		ITEM	POST. REF.	DEBIT	CREDIT	BALANCE	
						DEBIT	CREDIT
Aug.¹⁹⁻⁻	1		1		1 0 0 0 0 00		1 0 0 0 0 00

ACCOUNT **Ben Furman, Drawing**   ACCOUNT NO. **320**

DATE	ITEM	POST. REF.	DEBIT	CREDIT	BALANCE DEBIT	BALANCE CREDIT
Aug. 19-- 12		1	1 0 0 00		1 0 0 00	
31		2	5 0 0 00		6 0 0 00	

ACCOUNT **Income Summary**   ACCOUNT NO. **330**

DATE	ITEM	POST. REF.	DEBIT	CREDIT	BALANCE DEBIT	BALANCE CREDIT

ACCOUNT **Sales**   ACCOUNT NO. **410**

DATE	ITEM	POST. REF.	DEBIT	CREDIT	BALANCE DEBIT	BALANCE CREDIT
Aug. 19-- 31		2		4 2 9 1 00		4 2 9 1 00

ACCOUNT **Advertising Expense**   ACCOUNT NO. **510**

DATE	ITEM	POST. REF.	DEBIT	CREDIT	BALANCE DEBIT	BALANCE CREDIT
Aug. 19-- 14		1	6 8 00		6 8 00	

ACCOUNT **Insurance Expense**   ACCOUNT NO. **520**

DATE	ITEM	POST. REF.	DEBIT	CREDIT	BALANCE DEBIT	BALANCE CREDIT

ACCOUNT *Miscellaneous Expense* ACCOUNT NO. *530*

DATE	ITEM	POST. REF.	DEBIT	CREDIT	BALANCE DEBIT	BALANCE CREDIT
Aug. 13		1	25 00		25 00	
18		1	70 00		95 00	
28		2	3 00		98 00	
31		2	7 00		105 00	

ACCOUNT *Rent Expense* ACCOUNT NO. *540*

DATE	ITEM	POST. REF.	DEBIT	CREDIT	BALANCE DEBIT	BALANCE CREDIT
Aug. 12		1	250 00		250 00	

ACCOUNT *Repair Expense* ACCOUNT NO. *550*

DATE	ITEM	POST. REF.	DEBIT	CREDIT	BALANCE DEBIT	BALANCE CREDIT
Aug. 13		1	20 00		20 00	
20		1	85 00		105 00	
31		2	5 00		110 00	

ACCOUNT *Supplies Expense* ACCOUNT NO. *560*

DATE	ITEM	POST. REF.	DEBIT	CREDIT	BALANCE DEBIT	BALANCE CREDIT

ACCOUNT *Utilities Expense* ACCOUNT NO. *570*

DATE	ITEM	POST. REF.	DEBIT	CREDIT	BALANCE DEBIT	BALANCE CREDIT
Aug. 12		1	45 00		45 00	
27		2	70 00		115 00	

The procedures for posting from Rugcare's journal are summarized in Illustration 6-15.

SUMMARY ILLUSTRATION 6-15

Summary of posting to a general ledger

Seven steps are followed in posting amounts from a journal to a general ledger.

1 The date is written in the Date column of the account.

2 The journal page number is written in the Post. Ref. column of the account.

3 The amount is written in the Debit or Credit amount column of the account.

4 A new account balance is calculated and recorded in the Balance Debit or Balance Credit column of the account.

5 An account number is placed in the Post. Ref. column of the journal to show to which account a separate amount on that line has been posted. The account number is written in the journal *as the last step* in the posting procedure.

6 Check marks are placed in parentheses below general amount columns of a journal to show that the totals of these columns *are not* posted.

7 Account numbers are placed in parentheses below special amount column totals of a journal to show that these column totals have been posted.

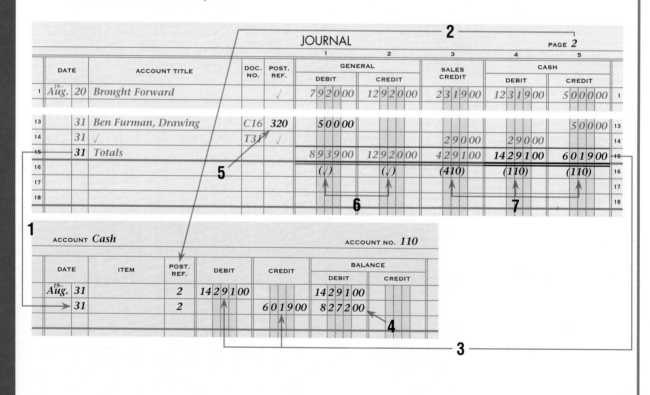

What is the meaning of each of the following?

1. **ledger**
2. **general ledger**
3. **account number**
4. **file maintenance**
5. **opening an account**
6. **posting**

1. Why are general ledger accounts used in an accounting system?
2. In what order are accounts arranged in a general ledger?
3. On Rugcare's chart of accounts, what is indicated by each digit in an account number?
4. Why are unused numbers usually left between account numbers on a chart of accounts?
5. What number is assigned to a new account inserted in a chart of accounts between accounts numbered 530 and 540?
6. What number is assigned to a new account added at the end of a division in which the last account is numbered 550?
7. What are the two steps in opening a new account?
8. Why are amounts posted from a journal to general ledger accounts?

9. What three purposes are served by recording posting reference numbers in journals and accounts?
10. How is a new account balance calculated when the previous balance is a debit and a debit entry is posted?
11. Why are separate amounts in special amount columns of a journal not posted individually?
12. Why are totals of a journal's general amount columns not posted?
13. What is done to indicate that the general amount column totals are not posted?
14. What is done to indicate that a special amount column total in a journal has been posted?
15. How is a new account balance calculated when the previous balance is a debit, a credit entry is posted, and the previous debit balance is larger than the credit entry?

CASE 1   Angela Silva does not use a journal in her business records. She records the debits and credits for each transaction directly in the general ledger accounts. Is Ms. Silva using the correct procedure? Explain your answer.

CASE 2   Philip Westing does the accounting work for his business. When posting, he first transfers all of the information to the general ledger accounts.

Then he returns to the journal and, all at one time, writes the account numbers in the Post. Ref. column of the journal. Diana Young also does the accounting work for her business. When posting, she writes all the account numbers in the Post. Ref. column of the journal before she transfers any information to the accounts. Is Mr. Westing or Miss Young following the correct procedure? Explain your answer.

A fax machine allows a business to send documents anywhere in a matter of minutes using a telephone line. Business managers no longer have to wait days to obtain the information needed to make timely business decisions. Some businesses use fax machines to increase sales, allowing customers to order items without leaving their offices or homes.

Most fax machines in offices are located in one or more central locations and used by a number of different workers for both sending and receiving documents. To facilitate directing the document to the intended receiver, it is usual practice to include a cover sheet in the fax transmission. The cover sheet should include the information below.

1. Name of the person sending the message.
2. Name of the person to receive the message.
3. Phone number of both sending and receiving fax machines.

4. Total number of pages being transmitted, including the cover sheet.

INSTRUCTIONS:

1. Write a memorandum responding to the following scenario: Ben Furman is at the bank applying for a business loan. The bank's loan officer has asked for a list of Rugcare's asset, liability, owner's equity, sales, and expense accounts, and their current balances. Mr. Furman has just called you and asked that you fax him at the bank with this information. In your memorandum include an introductory sentence or paragraph and end with a concluding statement.
2. Prepare a cover sheet for transmitting a fax message. The bank's fax machine telephone number is 800-555-3333. Use your own name and personal telephone number or school telephone number.

DRILLS FOR UNDERSTANDING   EPT(b,c,d)

DRILL 6-D1   Preparing a chart of accounts

The following account descriptions refer to the location of accounts in a chart of accounts similar to the one for Rugcare, page 100.

1. The first asset account
2. The first liability account
3. The first owner's equity account
4. The first revenue account
5. The first expense account
6. The third asset account

7. The fourth expense account
8. The owner's drawing account
9. The cash account
10. The sales account
11. The owner's capital account

Use a form similar to the following. Account description 1 is given as an example.

1	2
Account Description	**Account Number**
1. The first asset account	*110*

INSTRUCTIONS:

1. In Column 1, write the account description.
2. In Column 2, write the account number. Account numbers are assigned by 10s.
3. Check your answers with Rugcare's chart of accounts, page 100. Determine if your answers are the same for each account as shown on the chart of accounts.
4. Cover your answers in Column 2. Practice rapidly recalling the account numbers for each account.

DRILL 6-D2 Analyzing posting from a journal

INSTRUCTIONS:

1. Use completed page 2 of the journal shown in Illustration 6-13. For each of the following lines in that illustration, write the separate amount, if any, that is posted individually. Also, write the account title to which the amount is posted.

    a. Line 6   **c.** Line 10   **e.** Line 12

    b. Line 9   **d.** Line 11   **f.** Line 13

2. Use the general ledger accounts shown in Illustration 6-14. Answer the following questions.

    a. What item or transaction is represented by the amount in the cash account's Credit column?

    b. What item or transaction is represented by the amount in the prepaid insurance account's Debit Balance column?

    c. What item or transaction is represented by the amount in the sales account's Credit column?

    d. Where in the journal is the information found about the item or transaction recorded in the advertising expense account's Debit column?

APPLICATION PROBLEMS   EPT(c,d)

PROBLEM 6-1 Preparing a chart of accounts

Marie Wilson owns a service business called Wilson's Services. Wilson's Services uses the following accounts.

Automobile Expense	Miscellaneous Expense
Bartel Supplies	Novack Office Supplies
Cash	Prepaid Insurance
Insurance Expense	Sales
Marie Wilson, Capital	Supplies
Marie Wilson, Drawing	Supplies Expense

INSTRUCTIONS:

1. Prepare a chart of accounts similar to the one described in this chapter. Arrange expense accounts in alphabetic order. Use 3-digit account numbers and number the accounts within a division by 10s.
2. Two new accounts, Gasoline Expense and Utilities Expense, are to be added to the chart of accounts prepared in Instruction 1. Assign account numbers to the two new accounts.

PROBLEM 6-2 Posting to a general ledger

Don Ley owns a service business called AquaCare. AquaCare's journal, which is needed to complete this problem, is in the working papers that accompany this textbook.

INSTRUCTIONS:

1. Open a general ledger account for each of the following accounts.

Assets	**Revenue**
110 Cash	410 Sales
120 Supplies	**Expenses**
130 Prepaid Insurance	510 Advertising Expense
Liabilities	520 Miscellaneous Expense
210 Donard Supplies	530 Rent Expense
220 Fell Office Supplies	540 Utilities Expense
Owner's Equity	
310 Don Ley, Capital	
320 Don Ley, Drawing	

2. Post the separate amounts on each line of the journal that need to be posted individually.

3. Post the journal's special amount column totals.

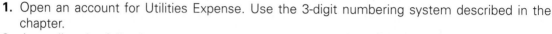

ENRICHMENT PROBLEMS   EPT(d)

MASTERY PROBLEM 6-M Journalizing and posting to a general ledger

AUTOMATED

APPLICATION

Al Hiatt owns a service business called Hiatt Cleaning. Hiatt Cleaning's general ledger accounts are given in the working papers that accompany this textbook.

INSTRUCTIONS:

1. Open an account for Utilities Expense. Use the 3-digit numbering system described in the chapter.

2. Journalize the following transactions completed during November of the current year. Use page 1 of a journal. Source documents are abbreviated as follows: check, C; memorandum, M; receipt, R; calculator tape, T.

Nov. 1. Received cash from owner as an investment, $7,000.00. R1.

    3. Paid cash for rent, $300.00. C1.

    5. Paid cash for insurance, $200.00. C2.

    6. Received cash from sales, $750.00. T6.

    9. Paid cash for miscellaneous expense, $5.00. C3.

    11. Paid cash for supplies, $500.00. C4.

    13. Bought supplies on account from Major Supplies, $600.00. M1.

    13. Received cash from sales, $700.00. T13.

    16. Paid cash for electric bill, $40.00. C5.

    18. Paid cash on account to Major Supplies, $300.00. C6.

    20. Paid cash for advertising, $30.00. C7.

    20. Received cash from sales, $770.00. T20.

    25. Paid cash for supplies, $150.00. C8.

    27. Paid cash for supplies, $100.00. C9.

    27. Received cash from sales, $1,150.00. T27.

    30. Paid cash to owner for personal use, $300.00. C10.

    30. Received cash from sales, $410.00. T30.

3. Prove the journal.

4. Prove cash. The beginning cash balance on November 1 is zero. The balance on the next unused check stub is $8,855.00.

5. Rule the journal.

6. Post from the journal to the general ledger.

CHALLENGE PROBLEM 6-C Journalizing and posting to a general ledger

AUTOMATED

Dee Worthy owns a service business called HouseCare. HouseCare's general ledger accounts are given in the working papers that accompany this textbook.

HouseCare uses the following journal.

JOURNAL								Page
Debit		Date	Account Title	Doc. No.	Post Ref.	**Credit**		
Cash	General					General	Sales	Cash
1								

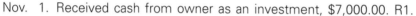

APPLICATION

INSTRUCTIONS:

1. Journalize the following transactions completed during March of the current year. Use page 5 of a journal. Source documents are abbreviated as follows: check, C; memorandum, M; receipt, R; calculator tape, T.

Mar. 1. Owner invested money, $8,000.00. R1.
      3. Paid March rent, $350.00. C1.
      5. Wrote a check for miscellaneous expense, $5.00. C2.
      9. Paid for quarterly insurance, $250.00. C3.
      11. Paid for supplies, $400.00. C4.
      13. Cash sales, $450.00. T13.
      16. Supplies were bought on account from Hartwood Supplies, $700.00. M1.
      18. Hartwood Supplies was paid on account, $350.00. C5.
      19. Paid telephone bill, $60.00. C6.
      20. Cash was received from sales, $1,100.00. T20.
      23. Wrote a check for June advertising, $50.00. C7.
      23. Paid for supplies, $150.00. C8.
      27. Paid for supplies, $150.00. C9.
      27. Received cash from sales, $1,830.00. T27.
      30. Owner withdrew cash for personal use, $400.00. C10.
      31. Received cash from sales, $410.00. T31.

2. Prove the journal.
3. Prove cash. The beginning cash balance on March 1 is zero. The balance on the next unused check stub is $9,625.00.
4. Rule the journal.
5. Post from the journal to the general ledger.

Safety and Health Considerations

ELECTRICAL EQUIPMENT

The following rules protect the operator of the equipment, other persons in the environment, and the equipment itself.

1. Do not unplug equipment by pulling on the electrical cord. Instead, grasp the plug at the outlet and remove it.
2. Do not stretch electrical cords across an aisle where someone might trip over them.
3. Avoid food and beverages near equipment where a spill might result in an electrical short.
4. Do not attempt to remove the cover of equipment for any reason while the power is turned on.
5. Do not attempt to repair equipment while it is plugged in. To avoid damage most repairs should be done by an authorized service technician.
6. Always turn the power off when finished using equipment.
7. Do not overload extension cords.
8. Follow manufacturer recommendations for safe use.
9. Replace frayed electrical cords immediately.

MICROCOMPUTERS

1. To avoid damage to the drives, do not insert pencils or other implements in floppy disk drives.
2. To prevent overheating, avoid blocking air vents.
3. Position keyboards to prevent bumping or dropping them off the work surface.

MONITORS

1. Most manufacturers advise repair by authorized service technicians only.
2. Adjust brightness and focus for comfortable viewing.
3. Avoid glare on the monitor screen.
4. Do not leave fingerprints on the screen. Keep the screen clear of dust. Only use a soft cloth for cleaning the screen.

PRINTERS

1. Do not let jewelry, ties, scarves, loose sleeves, or other clothing get caught in the machinery. This could result in damage to the machinery and could cause personal injury.
2. Exercise caution when using toxic chemicals such as toner in order to avoid spills.

DISKETTES

1. Write/protect all program software to avoid accidental erasure.
2. Do not bend or fold diskettes.
3. Do not write on a diskette with a hard or sharp-pointed pen or pencil; use a felt-tip marker.
4. Do not touch exposed surfaces of diskettes.
5. Be sure the disk drive is not running when you insert or remove a diskette.
6. Keep diskettes away from extreme hot or cold temperatures. Do not leave diskettes in a car during very hot or cold weather.
7. Keep diskettes away from magnetic fields such as transformers and magnets.
8. Store diskettes in the storage envelopes.
9. Keep diskettes away from smoke, ashes, and dust, including chalk dust.
10. Do not leave diskettes in the disk drive for prolonged periods, such as overnight.

Recording Transactions for a Proprietorship

Financial data may be recorded and reported by hand or by machine. An accounting system in which data are recorded and reported mostly by hand is referred to as **manual accounting**. Some businesses use automated machines to speed the recording and reporting process. An accounting system in which data are recorded and reported mostly by using automated machines is **automated accounting**. However, even in automated accounting, some procedures are done by hand.

Rugcare, the service business described in Part 2, uses a manual accounting system. Rugcare's manual journalizing and posting procedures are described in Chapters 5 and 6. Integrating Automated Accounting Topic 1 describes procedures for using automated accounting software to journalize and post Rugcare's transactions. The Automated Accounting Problems contain instructions for using automated accounting software to solve Mastery Problem 6-M and Challenge Problem 6-C, Chapter 6.

COMPUTER PROGRAMMING

A **computer program** is a set of instructions followed by a computer to process data. The programs used to direct the operations of a computer are **software**. An **automated accounting system** is a collection of computer programs designed to automate accounting procedures.

A person needs special training to be a **computer programmer**. Understanding accounting concepts and procedures is helpful to a computer programmer. Just as important, an accountant needs to know basic computer concepts and procedures in order to assist a computer programmer and to use a computer.

AUTOMATED GENERAL LEDGER ACCOUNTING

Automated general ledger accounting is based on the same accounting concepts as a manual accounting system. The only differences are equipment and procedures.

General Ledger Data Base

A pre-arranged file in which data can be entered and retrieved is a **data base**. In automated accounting the general ledger is a data base. A general ledger data base contains general information about the business, the chart of accounts, and financial activity for each account. A model of a computer application stored on a computer disk for repeated use is a **template**. Rugcare stores its general ledger data base as a template.

To perform accounting procedures, the general ledger data base is retrieved from the template. The file is saved as a new file using another file name, which allows the template to remain in its original format. Changes to the original template should be made only when necessary to update the file for future repeated use.

The new file is then used to complete accounting activities. Transaction data may then be recorded in the general ledger accounts. At the end of a fiscal period, financial data are retrieved and financial reports are prepared.

Chart of Accounts Numbering Systems

Chart of accounts numbering systems are similar for both automated and manual accounting. Rugcare's three-digit numbering system is described in Chapter 6. The procedures for arranging accounts in a general ledger, assigning account numbers, and keeping records current are **file maintenance**.

File Maintenance

File maintenance procedures are similar for both automated and manual accounting. In automated accounting the chart of accounts is part of the general ledger data base. The chart of accounts requires maintenance periodically to add and change accounts. File maintenance requires five steps. (1) A chart of accounts input form is prepared. (2) The general ledger data base is retrieved. (3) Data

To save a file under another name, pull down the File menu and choose the Save As menu command. Key the path to the drive and directory that contains the data files. Save your data base with a file name of XXX1A (where XXX are your initials).

from the chart of accounts input form are keyed into the computer to change the chart of accounts. (4) A revised chart of accounts report is prepared to verify the accuracy of the data that was keyed. (5) The revised chart of accounts is stored as part of the general ledger data base.

Adding an Account Within a Ledger Division. Rugcare decided to add a new account titled Gasoline Expense within the expenses division of the chart of accounts. The entry on the chart of accounts input form to add Gasoline Expense is shown on line 1 of Illustration T1-1.

ILLUSTRATION T1-1

Entry for file maintenance

| RUN DATE _08/12/--_ | CHART OF ACCOUNTS | |
| MM DD YY | Input Form | |

	1	2	
	ACCOUNT NUMBER	ACCOUNT TITLE	
1	515	Gasoline Expense	1
2			2
3			3
4			4

A new account number added within a ledger division is determined using procedures described in Chapter 6. Using the unused middle number, the new account number for Gasoline Expense is 515.

510 Advertising Expense   (Existing Account)
515 Gasoline Expense   (NEW ACCOUNT)
520 Insurance Expense   (Existing Account)

Three steps are followed to complete a chart of accounts input form.

1 The run date, _08/12/--_, is written in the space provided at the top of the form. The **run date** is the date to be printed on reports prepared by a computer.

2 Each account number is written in the Account Number column.

3 Each account title is written in the Account Title column just as it will appear on the output. The automated accounting software specifies the maximum number of spaces that can be used for account numbers and account titles. Any account title that contains more than 25 characters must be abbreviated when recorded on the chart of accounts input form. All of Rugcare's account titles fit the 25-character space allowed, so none have to be abbreviated.

Adding an Account at the End of a Ledger Division. A new account number added at the end of a ledger division is determined following procedures described in Chapter 6. The next number in a

Automated Accounting 6.0 software limits account titles to 25 characters. Therefore, abbreviations may be necessary.

sequence of 10 is used for a new account added at the end of a chart of accounts division.

Processing File Maintenance Data

In automated accounting the activities are arranged so that each activity may be selected using a keyboard or some other input device such as a mouse. A list of options from which an activity may be selected is a **menu**. Rugcare's software has a menu bar and a series of pull-down menus. When a menu is selected from the menu bar, a pull-down list of commands will appear. The menu bar shown in Illustration T1-2 contains six different menus. (1) File. (2) Options. (3) Journals. (4) Ledgers. (5) Reports. (6) Help.

ILLUSTRATION T1-2   Menu bar and pull-down file menu

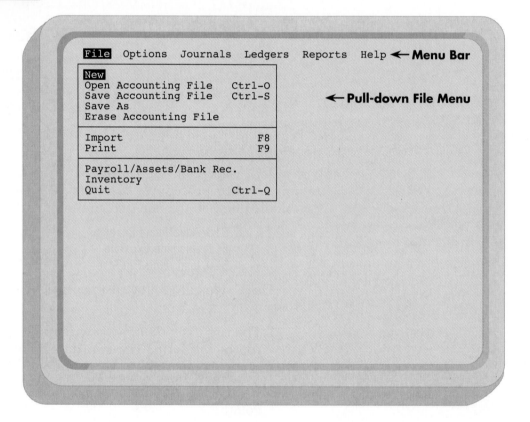

The general ledger data base is retrieved from the template disk by first selecting File from the menu bar. The Open Accounting File command is then chosen from the File menu, as shown in Illustration T1-2, to retrieve a specific general ledger data base from the template disk.

To process file maintenance data, select the Ledgers menu from the menu bar. The Maintain Accounts command is then chosen from the Ledgers menu to display the data entry window for entering file maintenance data. File maintenance data are keyed from the chart of accounts input form. The entry for Gasoline Expense is shown in Illustration T1-3.

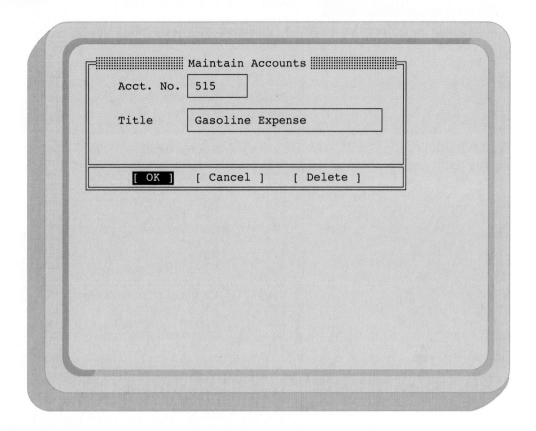

After all file maintenance data have been keyed, the Reports menu is selected from the menu bar. The Accounts command is chosen from the Reports menu to display the Report Selection window. When the Report Selection window appears, select the Chart of Accounts option to display the revised chart of accounts report. The revised chart of accounts report is checked for accuracy by comparing the report with the chart of accounts input form. The revised chart of accounts report, as shown in Illustration T1-4 on the next page, is printed and filed for future reference.

RECORDING TRANSACTIONS

In manual accounting, transactions are analyzed into debit and credit parts as described in Chapter 4 and recorded in a journal as described in Chapter 5. Transaction data are then periodically posted from a journal to a general ledger as described in Chapter 6.

In automated accounting, transactions are also analyzed into debit and credit parts. A general journal input form is used to journalize transactions. After each transaction has been keyed, the software is directed to post to the general ledger accounts.

```
                  Rugcare
             Chart of Accounts
                 08/12/--
-----------------------------------
Account    Account
Number     Title
-----------------------------------
110        Cash
120        Petty Cash
130        Supplies
140        Prepaid Insurance
210        Butler Cleaning Supplies
220        Dale Office Supplies
310        Ben Furman, Capital
320        Ben Furman, Drawing
410        Sales
510        Advertising Expense
515        Gasoline Expense
520        Insurance Expense
530        Miscellaneous Expense
540        Rent Expense
550        Repair Expense
560        Supplies Expense
570        Utilities Expense
```

The following transactions completed by Rugcare are analyzed into debit and credit parts in Chapter 4.

Received Cash from Owner as an Investment

August 1, 19--. Received cash from owner as an investment, $10,000.00. Receipt No. 1.

Dollar and cent signs are not entered on input forms.

The journal entry to record this transaction is on lines 1 and 2 of the general journal input form shown in Illustration T1-5.

The run date, *08/12/--*, is written in the space provided at the top of the input form. The run date indicates the date to be printed on the report.

On line 1, the date, *08/01*, is written in the Date column. The source document number, *R1*, is entered in the Reference column. The cash account number, *110*, is recorded in the Account No. column. The Customer/Vendor No. column is left blank. Entries requiring the use of this column are described in Part 3, Integrating Automated Accounting Topic 4. The amount debited to Cash, *$10,000.00*, is written in the Debit column.

On line 2, the account number for Ben Furman, Capital, *310*, is written in the Account No. column. The Date and Reference numbers are entered only once for each complete transaction. Therefore, the Date and Reference columns are left blank starting with the second line of an entry. The amount credited to Ben Furman, Capital, *$10,000.00*, is recorded in the Credit column.

General journal input form with transactions recorded

	DATE MM/DD	REFERENCE	ACCOUNT NO.	CUSTOMER/ VENDOR NO.	DEBIT	CREDIT	
RUN DATE 08/12/-- MM DD YY		GENERAL JOURNAL Input Form					
1	08/01	R1	110		10000 00		1
2	/		310			10000 00	2
3	/03	C1	130		1577 00		3
4	/		110			1577 00	4
5	/04	C2	140		1200 00		5
6	/		110			1200 00	6
7	/07	M1	130		2720 00		7
8	/		210			2720 00	8
9	/11	C3	210		1360 00		9
10	/		110			1360 00	10
11	/12	T12	110		525 00		11
12	/		410			525 00	12
13	/12	C4	540		250 00		13
14	/		110			250 00	14
15	/12	C5	570		45 00		15
16	/		110			45 00	16
17	/12	C6	320		100 00		17
18	/		110			100 00	18
19	/						19
25	/						25
				PAGE TOTALS	17777 00	17777 00	
				FINAL TOTALS	17777 00	17777 00	

Paid Cash for Supplies

August 3, 19--. Paid cash for supplies, $1,577.00. Check No. 1.

The journal entry to record this transaction is on lines 3 and 4 of Illustration T1-5. Supplies is debited and Cash is credited for $1,577.00.

Paid Cash for Insurance

August 4, 19--. Paid cash for insurance, $1,200.00. Check No. 2.

The journal entry to record this transaction is on lines 5 and 6 of Illustration T1-5. Prepaid Insurance is debited and Cash is credited for $1,200.00.

Bought Supplies on Account

August 7, 19--. Bought supplies on account from Butler Cleaning Supplies, $2,720.00. Memorandum No. 1.

The journal entry to record this transaction is on lines 7 and 8 of Illustration T1-5. Supplies is debited and Butler Cleaning Supplies is credited for $2,720.00.

FYI

Dollar signs and cent signs are not keyed when using Automated Accounting 6.0 software. When the cents are zero (.00), key only the dollar amount. For example, if the amount is 15.00, key 15. The software automatically assigns the .00.

Paid Cash on Account

August 11, 19--. Paid cash on account to Butler Cleaning Supplies, $1,360.00. Check No. 3.

The journal entry to record this transaction is on lines 9 and 10 of Illustration T1-5. Butler Cleaning Supplies is debited and Cash is credited for $1,360.00.

Received Cash from Sales

August 12, 19--. Received cash from sales, $525.00. Tape No. 12.

The journal entry to record this transaction is on lines 11 and 12 of Illustration T1-5. Cash is debited and Sales is credited for $525.00.

Paid Cash for an Expense

August 12, 19--. Paid cash for rent, $250.00. Check No. 4.

The journal entry to record this transaction is on lines 13 and 14 of Illustration T1-5. Rent Expense is debited and Cash is credited for $250.00.

Illustration T1-5 includes a journal entry, lines 15 and 16, for Utilities Expense. This transaction is journalized in the same way as the cash payment for rent.

Paid Cash to Owner for Personal Use

August 12, 19--. Paid cash to owner for personal use, $100.00. Check No. 6.

The journal entry to record this transaction is on lines 17 and 18 of Illustration T1-5. Ben Furman, Drawing is debited and Cash is credited for $100.00.

Completing a General Journal Input Form

After all transactions have been journalized, Rugcare totals the Debit and Credit amount columns. The totals are recorded on the Page Totals line provided at the bottom of the input form.

A journal entry should not be split on two different general journal input forms. Therefore, if a complete journal entry cannot be entered on an input form, a new input form is started. The totals for all pages are then entered *only* on the last page on the Final Totals line. The two totals are compared to assure that debits equal credits. If only one general journal input form is required then the totals are recorded on the Page Totals line and the Final Totals line.

Processing Journal Entries

To process journal entries, the Journals menu is selected from the menu bar. The General Journal command is chosen from the Journals menu to display the data entry window for entering transaction data from the general journal input form. Rugcare keys the

A journal entry should not be split on two different general journal input forms.

transaction data from the general journal input form one line at a time. Lines 1 and 2 are shown entered in Illustration T1-6.

ILLUSTRATION T1-6   Data entry window with a general journal entry recorded

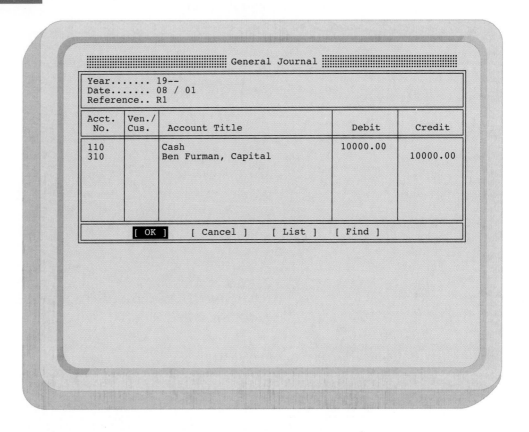

After all lines on the input form have been keyed and posted, the Reports menu is selected from the menu bar. The Journals command is chosen from the Reports menu. The General Journal report is chosen from the Report Selection window. This selection displays the Selection Options screen shown in Illustration T1-7.

The data to be printed on reports can be restricted by specifying the date range or reference numbers as shown on Illustration T1-7. As Rugcare wants to print all transactions recorded on the general journal input form, pushing the *Ok* box directs the software to display a general journal report. The displayed general journal report is checked for accuracy by comparing the report totals, $17,777.00, with the totals on the general journal input form. Because the totals are the same, the general journal report is assumed to be correct. The general journal report is printed, as shown in Illustration T1-8, and is filed for future reference.

To avoid damage to disk drives on the computer, do not insert any implements such as pencils in the disk drive.

Selection Options screen

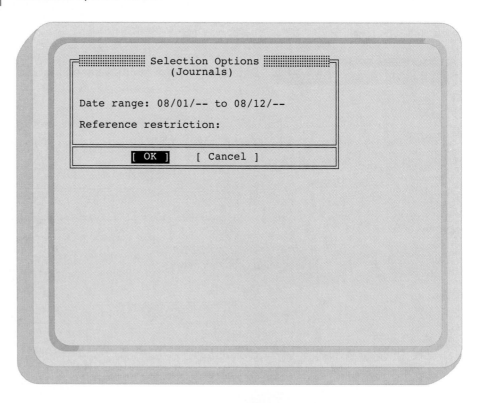

```
┌░░░░░░░░░░ Selection Options ░░░░░░░░░┐
│                (Journals)            │
│                                      │
│ Date range: 08/01/-- to 08/12/--     │
│                                      │
│ Reference restriction:               │
├──────────────────────────────────────┤
│      [ OK ]        [ Cancel ]        │
└──────────────────────────────────────┘
```

General journal report

```
                         Rugcare
                      General Journal
                        08/12/--
-----------------------------------------------------------------
Date   Refer.   V/C Acct.  Title              Debit      Credit
-----------------------------------------------------------------
08/01  R1          110     Cash              10000.00
08/01  R1          310     Ben Furman, Capital            10000.00

08/03  C1          130     Supplies           1577.00
08/03  C1          110     Cash                           1577.00

08/04  C2          140     Prepaid Insurance  1200.00
08/04  C2          110     Cash                           1200.00

08/07  M1          130     Supplies           2720.00
08/07  M1          210     Butler Cleaning Supplies       2720.00

08/11  C3          210     Butler Cleaning Supplies 1360.00
08/11  C3          110     Cash                           1360.00

08/12  T12         110     Cash                525.00
08/12  T12         410     Sales                           525.00

08/12  C4          540     Rent Expense        250.00
08/12  C4          110     Cash                            250.00

08/12  C5          570     Utilities Expense    45.00
08/12  C5          110     Cash                             45.00

08/12  C6          320     Ben Furman, Drawing 100.00
08/12  C6          110     Cash                            100.00
                                              ---------- ----------
                          Totals             17777.00    17777.00
                                              ========== ==========
```

OPTIONAL PROBLEM DB-1A

Rugcare's general ledger data base is on the accounting textbook template. If you wish to complete these file maintenance activities and record transactions using automated accounting software, load the *Automated Accounting 6.0* or higher software. Select Data Base 1A (DB-1A) from the template disk. Read the Problem Instructions screen. Use the completed input forms in Illustrations T1-1 and T1-5, and follow the procedures described to process Rugcare's file maintenance activities and to record transactions.

AUTOMATED ACCOUNTING PROBLEMS

AUTOMATING MASTERY PROBLEM 6-M Journalizing and posting to a general ledger

INSTRUCTIONS:

1. Prepare input forms for Mastery Problem 6-M, Chapter 6.
   a. Prepare a chart of accounts input form to add Utilities Expense to the general ledger chart of accounts using the 3-digit numbering system described in Chapter 6. Use November 30 of the current year as the run date. Hiatt Cleaning uses the following chart of accounts.

Assets	**Revenue**
110 Cash	410 Sales
120 Supplies	**Expenses**
130 Prepaid Insurance	510 Advertising Expense
Liabilities	520 Miscellaneous Expense
210 Major Supplies	530 Rent Expense
Owner's Equity	
310 Al Hiatt, Capital	
320 Al Hiatt, Drawing	

   b. Record Hiatt Cleaning's transactions on a general journal input form. Use November 30 of the current year as the run date.
2. Load the *Automated Accounting 6.0* or higher software. Select data base *F6-M (First-Year Course Problem 6-M)* from the accounting textbook template. Read the Problem Instructions screen.
3. Select File from the menu bar and choose the Save As menu command. Key the path to the drive and directory that contains your data files. Save the data base with a file name of XXX6M (where XXX are your initials).
4. Key the data from the completed chart of accounts input form.
5. Display/print the revised chart of accounts report. Check the report for accuracy.
6. Key the transactions from the completed general journal input form.
7. Display/print the general journal report. Check the report for accuracy by comparing the report totals with the totals on the input form.

AUTOMATING CHALLENGE PROBLEM 6-C Journalizing and posting to a general ledger

INSTRUCTIONS:

1. Prepare input forms for Challenge Problem 6-C, Chapter 6.
2. Load the *Automated Accounting 6.0* or higher software. Select data base *F6-C (First-Year Course Problem 6-C)* from the accounting textbook template. Read the Problem Instructions screen.
3. Select File from the menu bar and choose the Save As menu command. Key the path to the drive and directory that contains your data files. Save the data base with a file name of XXX6C (where XXX are your initials).
4. Key the transactions from the completed general journal input form.
5. Display/print the general journal report. Check the report for accuracy by comparing the report totals with the totals on the input form.

7

Cash Control Systems

ENABLING PERFORMANCE TASKS

After studying Chapter 7, you will be able to:

a Define accounting terms related to using a checking account and a petty cash fund.

b Identify accounting concepts and practices related to using a checking account.

c Prepare business papers related to using a checking account.

d Reconcile a bank statement.

e Establish and replenish a petty cash fund.

f Record selected transactions related to using a checking account and a petty cash fund.

TERMS PREVIEW

checking account • endorsement • blank endorsement • special endorsement • restrictive endorsement • postdated check • bank statement • dishonored check • electronic funds transfer • petty cash • petty cash slip

In accounting, money is usually referred to as cash. Most businesses make major cash payments by check. However, small cash payments for items such as postage and some supplies may be made from a cash fund kept at the place of business.

Because cash transactions occur more frequently than other types of transactions, more chances occur to make recording errors affecting cash. Cash can be transferred from one person to another without any question about ownership. Also, cash may be lost as it is moved from one place to another.

As a safety measure, Rugcare keeps most of its cash in a bank. Because all cash receipts are placed in a bank, Rugcare has written evidence to support its accounting records. Rugcare can compare its record of checks written with the bank's record of checks paid. Greater control of Rugcare's cash and greater accuracy of its cash records result from these procedures.

CHECKING ACCOUNTS

A business form ordering a bank to pay cash from a bank account is known as a check. A bank account from which payments can be ordered by a depositor is called a **checking account**.

Authorizing Signatures

When a checking account is opened, the bank customer must provide a signature on a signature card for the bank records. If several persons are authorized to sign checks, each person's signature must be on the signature card. Checks should always be signed with the same signature as on the signature card. Only Ben Furman is authorized to sign checks for Rugcare.

Depositing Cash

A bank customer prepares a deposit slip each time cash or checks are placed in a bank account. Deposit slips may differ slightly from one bank to another. Each bank designs its own deposit slips to fit the bank's recording machines. However, all deposit slips contain the same basic information as the slip shown in Illustration 7-1.

Checks are listed on a deposit slip according to the bank number on each check. For example, in Illustration 7-1, the number *93-108* identifies the bank on which the $10,000.00 check is written.

When a deposit is made, a bank gives the depositor a receipt. Many banks use a copy of the deposit slip with a printed or stamped verification as the receipt. The printed verification, *AUG 1 19-- D10000.00 RDS*, is shown along the top left edge of the deposit slip in Illustration 7-1. This printed verification means that a total of $10,000.00 was deposited on August 1. The initials *RDS* next to the amount are those of the bank employee who accepted the deposit.

ILLUSTRATION 7-1

Deposit slip

AUG 1 19-- D10000 00 RDS			
	Date *August 1,* 19 --		
Peoples national bank	Currency		
Billings, MT 59101-2320	Coin		
	Checks		
For deposit to the account of 93-109 / 929	*93-108*	*10,000*	*00*
RUGCARE			
623 Walnut Street			
Billings, MT 59101-1946			
	TOTAL	*10,000*	*00*
⑆092901094⑆ 43⑈452119⑈	CUSTOMER RECEIPT		

Rugcare records the August 1 deposit on the next unused check stub, as shown in Illustration 7-2.

ILLUSTRATION 7-2

Deposit recorded on a check stub

NO. **1** $ _____		
Date _____ 19 __		
To _____		
For _____		
BAL. BRO'T. FOR'D.	*0*	*00*
AMT. DEPOSITED	*8 1 --* *10,000*	*00*
SUBTOTAL. .... Date	*10,000*	*00*
OTHER:		
_____		
_____		
SUBTOTAL:		
AMT. THIS CHECK		
BAL. CAR'D. FOR'D.		

After the deposit is recorded on the check stub, a checkbook subtotal is calculated. The balance brought forward on Check Stub No. 1 is zero. The previous balance, $0.00, *plus* the deposit, $10,000.00, *equals* the subtotal, $10,000.00.

Cash receipts are journalized at the time cash is received. Later, the cash receipts are deposited in the checking account. Therefore, no journal entry is needed for deposits because the cash receipts have already been journalized.

Endorsing Checks

Ownership of a check can be transferred. The name of the first owner is stated on a check following the words *Pay to the order of*. Therefore, the person to whom payment is to be made must indi-

FYI

Endorsements should be written in ink so that they cannot be erased and changed by someone else.

cate that ownership of the check is being transferred. One person transfers ownership to another person by signing on the back of a check. A signature or stamp on the back of a check transferring ownership is called an **endorsement.**

An endorsement should be signed exactly as the person's name appears on the front of the check. For example, a check made payable to B.E. Furman is endorsed on the back as *B.E. Furman*. Immediately below that endorsement, Mr. Furman writes his official signature, *Ben Furman*.

Ownership of a check might be transferred several times, resulting in several endorsements. Each endorser guarantees payment of the check. If a bank does not receive payment from the person who signed the check, each endorser is individually liable for payment.

Three types of endorsements are commonly used, each having a specific use in transferring ownership.

Blank Endorsement. An endorsement consisting only of the endorser's signature is called a **blank endorsement.** A blank endorsement indicates that the subsequent owner is whoever has the check. A blank endorsement is shown in Illustration 7-3.

ILLUSTRATION 7-3 Blank endorsement

Endorse here
X   *Ben Furman*

DO NOT WRITE, STAMP, OR SIGN BELOW THIS LINE
Reserved for Financial Institution Use

Federal regulations require that an endorsement be confined to a limited amount of space that is indicated on the back of a check.

If a check with a blank endorsement is lost or stolen, the check can be cashed by anyone who has it. Ownership may be transferred without further endorsement. A blank endorsement should be used *only* when a person is at the bank ready to cash or deposit a check.

Special Endorsement. An endorsement indicating a new owner of a check is called a **special endorsement.** Special endorsements are sometimes known as endorsements in full. A special endorsement is shown in Illustration 7-4.

ILLUSTRATION 7-4 Special endorsement

Endorse here
X
Pay to the order of
Wilman Furman
Ben Furman

DO NOT WRITE, STAMP, OR SIGN BELOW THIS LINE
Reserved for Financial Institution Use

Special endorsements include the words *Pay to the order of* and the name of the new check owner. Only the person or business named in a special endorsement can cash, deposit, or further transfer ownership of the check.

Restrictive Endorsement. An endorsement restricting further transfer of a check's ownership is called a **restrictive endorsement.** A restrictive endorsement limits use of the check to whatever purpose is stated in the endorsement. A restrictive endorsement is shown in Illustration 7-5.

ILLUSTRATION 7-5 Restrictive endorsement

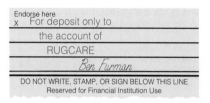

On all checks received, Rugcare stamps a restrictive endorsement which states that the check is for deposit only. This restrictive endorsement prevents unauthorized persons from cashing a check if it is lost or stolen.

Writing Checks

Checks should be written in ink so that no one can alter them.

Rugcare uses printed checks with check stubs attached. Consecutive numbers are preprinted on Rugcare's checks. Consecutive numbers on checks provide an easy way of identifying each check. Also, the numbers help keep track of all checks to assure that none are lost or misplaced.

Preparing Check Stubs. A check stub is a business' record of each check written for a cash payment transaction. *(CONCEPT: Objective Evidence)* To avoid forgetting to prepare a check stub, the check stub is prepared before the check is written. Rugcare's check stub and check are shown in Illustration 7-6.

ILLUSTRATION 7-6 Completed check stub and check

Six steps are used to complete Rugcare's Check Stub No. 1.

1 Write the amount of the check, *$1,577.00*, in the space after the dollar sign at the top of the stub.

2 Write the date of the check, *August 3, 19--*, on the Date line at the top of the stub.

3 Write to whom the check is to be paid, *Janitorial Supplies Co.*, on the To line at the top of the stub.

4 Record the purpose of the check, *Supplies*, on the For line.

5 Write the amount of the check, *$1,577.00*, in the amount column at the bottom of the stub on the line with the words "Amt. this Check."

6 Calculate the new checking account balance, *$8,423.00*, and record the new balance in the amount column on the last line of the stub. The new balance is calculated as shown below.

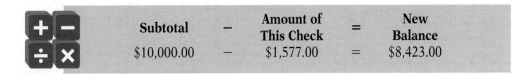

	Subtotal	–	Amount of This Check	=	New Balance
	$10,000.00	–	$1,577.00	=	$8,423.00

Preparing Checks. After the check stub is completed, the check is written. The check shown in Illustration 7-6 is prepared as follows.

1 Write the date, *August 3, 19--*, in the space provided.

> The date should be the month, day, and year on which the check is issued. A check with a future date on it is called a **postdated check.** Most banks will not accept postdated checks because money cannot be withdrawn from a depositor's account until the date on the check.

2 Write to whom the check is to be paid, *Janitorial Supplies Co.*, following the words "Pay to the order of."

> If the person to whom a check is to be paid is a business, use the business' name rather than the owner's name. *(CONCEPT: Business Entity)* If the person to whom the check is to be paid is an individual, use that person's name.

3 Write the amount in figures, *$1,577.00*, following the dollar sign.

> Write the figures close to the printed dollar sign. This practice prevents anyone from writing another digit in front of the amount to change the amount of the check.

4 Write the amount in words, *One thousand five hundred seventy-seven and no/100*, on the line with the word "Dollars."

> This written amount verifies the amount written in figures after the dollar sign. Begin the words at the extreme left. Draw a line through the unused space up to the word "Dollars." This line prevents anyone from writing in additional words to change the amount.

If the amounts in words and in figures are not the same, a bank may pay only the amount in words. Often, when the amounts do not agree, a bank will refuse to pay the check.

5 Write the purpose of the check, *Supplies*, on the line labeled "For."

On some checks this space is labeled "Memo." Some checks do not have a line for writing the purpose of the check.

6 Sign the check.

A check should not be signed until each item on the check and its stub has been verified for accuracy.

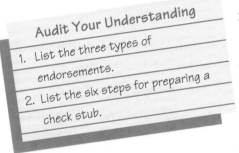
Voiding Checks. Banks usually refuse to accept altered checks. If any kind of error is made in preparing a check, a new check should be prepared. Because checks are prenumbered, all checks not used should be retained for the records. This practice helps account for all checks and assures that no checks have been lost or stolen.

A check that contains errors must be marked so that others will know that it is not to be used. The word *VOID* is written in large letters across both the check and its stub.

When Rugcare records a check in its journal, the check number is placed in the journal's Doc. No. column. If a check number is missing from the Doc. No. column, there is a question whether all checks have been journalized. To assure that all check numbers are listed in the journal, Rugcare records voided checks in the journal. The date is recorded in the journal's Date column. The word *VOID* is written in the Account Title column. The check number is recorded in the Doc. No. column. A check mark is entered in the Post. Ref. column. A dash is placed in the Cash Credit column.

Audit Your Understanding

1. List the three types of endorsements.

2. List the six steps for preparing a check stub.

BANK STATEMENT

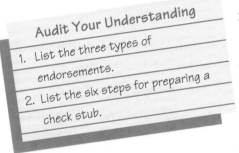
Banks keep separate records for each depositor. Information from deposit slips and checks is recorded daily in depositors' accounts. A report of deposits, withdrawals, and bank balance sent to a depositor by a bank is called a **bank statement**. Rugcare's bank statement for August 27 is shown in Illustration 7-7.

The balance for Rugcare's checking account on August 27, according to the bank's records, is $8,731.00.

When a bank receives checks, the amount of each check is deducted from the depositor's account. Then, the bank stamps the checks to indicate that the check is canceled and is not to be transferred further. Canceled checks are returned to a depositor with a bank statement. Outstanding checks are those checks issued by a depositor but not yet reported on a bank statement. Outstanding deposits are those deposits made at a bank but not yet shown on a bank statement. A bank may assess a charge for maintaining a checking account. Account service charges are also listed on a bank statement.

Banks may have different kinds of checking accounts to fit special needs of depositors. Each bank has its own regulations for its services, and fees are not charged for some checking accounts.

ILLUSTRATION 7-7   Bank statement

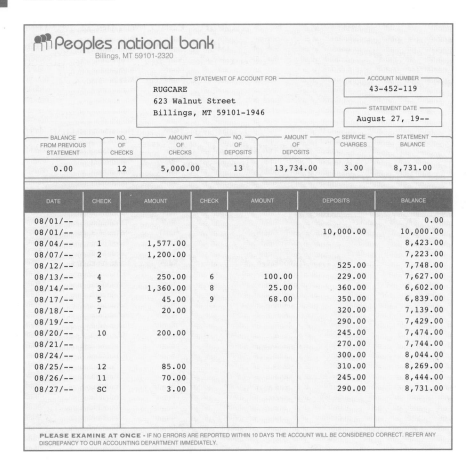

Peoples national bank
Billings, MT 59101-2320

STATEMENT OF ACCOUNT FOR	ACCOUNT NUMBER
RUGCARE 623 Walnut Street Billings, MT 59101-1946	43-452-119
	STATEMENT DATE August 27, 19--

BALANCE FROM PREVIOUS STATEMENT	NO. OF CHECKS	AMOUNT OF CHECKS	NO. OF DEPOSITS	AMOUNT OF DEPOSITS	SERVICE CHARGES	STATEMENT BALANCE
0.00	12	5,000.00	13	13,734.00	3.00	8,731.00

DATE	CHECK	AMOUNT	CHECK	AMOUNT	DEPOSITS	BALANCE
08/01/--						0.00
08/01/--					10,000.00	10,000.00
08/04/--	1	1,577.00				8,423.00
08/07/--	2	1,200.00				7,223.00
08/12/--					525.00	7,748.00
08/13/--	4	250.00	6	100.00	229.00	7,627.00
08/14/--	3	1,360.00	8	25.00	360.00	6,602.00
08/17/--	5	45.00	9	68.00	350.00	6,839.00
08/18/--	7	20.00			320.00	7,139.00
08/19/--					290.00	7,429.00
08/20/--	10	200.00			245.00	7,474.00
08/21/--					270.00	7,744.00
08/24/--					300.00	8,044.00
08/25/--	12	85.00			310.00	8,269.00
08/26/--	11	70.00			245.00	8,444.00
08/27/--	SC	3.00			290.00	8,731.00

PLEASE EXAMINE AT ONCE - IF NO ERRORS ARE REPORTED WITHIN 10 DAYS THE ACCOUNT WILL BE CONSIDERED CORRECT. REFER ANY DISCREPANCY TO OUR ACCOUNTING DEPARTMENT IMMEDIATELY.

Verifying a Bank Statement

Although banks seldom make mistakes, occasionally a check or deposit might be recorded in a wrong account. When a bank statement is received, a depositor should verify its accuracy. If errors are discovered, the bank should be notified at once. However, a bank's records and a depositor's records may differ and still be correct. The difference may exist for several reasons.

1. A service charge may not have been recorded in the depositor's business records.
2. Outstanding deposits may be recorded in the depositor's records but not yet reported on a bank statement.
3. Outstanding checks may be recorded in the depositor's records but not yet reported on a bank statement.
4. A depositor may have made errors in doing arithmetic or in recording information in the business records. The most common mistakes made by depositors are arithmetic errors.
5. The bank may have made an error.

Reconciling a Bank Statement

A bank statement is reconciled by verifying that information on a bank statement and a checkbook are in agreement. Rugcare reconciles a bank statement on the same day that the statement is received. Reconciling immediately is an important aspect of cash control.

Rugcare's canceled checks are received with the bank statement. The returned checks are arranged in numeric order. For each canceled check, a check mark is placed on the corresponding check stub. A check stub with no check mark indicates an outstanding check.

On August 28 Rugcare receives a bank statement dated August 27. Rugcare uses a reconciliation form printed on the back of the bank statement. Rugcare's bank statement reconciliation is shown in Illustration 7-8.

ILLUSTRATION 7-8   Bank statement reconciliation

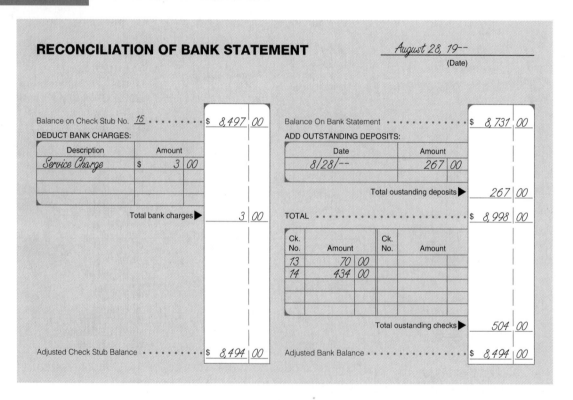

Rugcare uses three steps to reconcile a bank statement.

1 Calculate the adjusted check stub balance.

- Write the date on which the reconciliation is prepared, *August 28, 19--*.

- In the left amount column, list the balance brought forward on Check Stub No. 15, the next unused check stub, *$8,497.00*.

- In the space for bank charges, list any charges. The only such charge for Rugcare is the bank service charge, *$3.00*.

The bank service charge is labeled *SC* on the bank statement.

- Write the adjusted checkbook balance, *$8,494.00*, in the space provided at the bottom of the left amount column. The balance on the check stub, $8,497.00, *minus* the bank's service charge, $3.00, *equals* the adjusted check stub balance, $8,494.00.

2 Calculate the adjusted bank balance.

- Write the ending balance shown on the bank statement, *$8,731.00*, in the right amount column.
- Write the date, *8/28/--* and the amount, *$267.00*, of any outstanding deposits in the space provided. Add the outstanding deposits. Write the total outstanding deposits, *$267.00*, in the right amount column.
- Add the ending bank statement balance to the total outstanding deposits. Write the total, *$8,998.00*, in the space for the Total.
- List the outstanding checks, *Nos. 13 and 14*, and their amounts, *$70.00 and $434.00*, in the space provided. Add the amounts of the outstanding checks, and write the total, *$504.00*, in the right amount column.
- Calculate the adjusted bank balance, and write the amount, *$8,494.00*, in the space provided at the bottom of the right amount column. The total, $8,998.00, *minus* the total outstanding checks, $504.00, *equals* the adjusted bank balance, $8,494.00.

3 Compare adjusted balances.

- The adjusted balances must be the same. The adjusted check stub balance is the same as the adjusted bank balance, *$8,494.00*. Because the two amounts are the same, the bank statement is reconciled. The completed reconciliation form is filed for future reference.
- If the two adjusted balances are not the same, the errors must be found and corrected before any more work is done.

Recording a Bank Service Charge on a Check Stub

The bank deducts the service charge from Rugcare's checking account each month. Although Rugcare did not write a check for the bank service charge, this cash payment must be recorded in Rugcare's accounting records as a cash payment. Rugcare makes a record of a bank service charge on a check stub as shown in Illustration 7-9.

Three steps are used to record a bank service charge on a check stub.

1 Write the words, *Service charge, $3.00*, on the check stub under the heading "Other."

2 Write the amount, *$3.00*, in the check stub's amount column.

FYI

If you study classified advertisements, you will find that many listings for various office workers require the ability to use spreadsheets.

3 Calculate and record the new balance, *$8,494.00*, on the Subtotal line.

ILLUSTRATION 7-9 Bank service charge recorded on a check stub

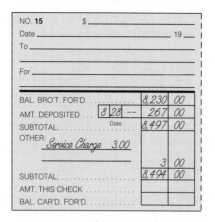

Journalizing a Bank Service Charge

Because the bank service charge is a cash payment for which no check is written, Rugcare prepares a memorandum as the source document. Rugcare's bank service charges are relatively small and occur only once a month. Therefore, a separate ledger account for the expense is not used. Instead, Rugcare records the bank service charge as a miscellaneous expense.

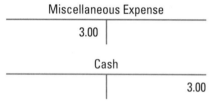

August 28, 19--. Received bank statement showing August bank service charge, $3.00. Memorandum No. 3.

A memorandum is the source document for a bank service charge transaction. *(CONCEPT: Objective Evidence)* The analysis of this transaction is shown in the T accounts.

Miscellaneous Expense is debited for $3.00 to show the increase in this expense account balance. Cash is credited for $3.00 to show the decrease in this asset account balance. The journal entry to record Rugcare's bank service charge is shown in Illustration 7-10.

ILLUSTRATION 7-10 Journal entry to record a bank service charge

| | | | | | GENERAL | | SALES | CASH | |
	DATE	ACCOUNT TITLE	DOC. NO.	POST. REF.	DEBIT	CREDIT	CREDIT	DEBIT	CREDIT
10	28	Miscellaneous Expense	M3		3 00				3 00

JOURNAL   PAGE 2

This entry is journalized using four steps.

1 *Date.* Write the date, *28*, in the Date column.

2 *Debit.* Write the title of the account to be debited, Miscellaneous Expense, in the Account Title column. Record the amount

USING AN ELECTRONIC SPREADSHEET TO PREPARE A BANK RECONCILIATION

Businesses often use forms to prepare accounting reports. The bank reconciliation form in Illustration 7-8 increases the efficiency of verifying a bank statement. Electronic spreadsheet software is another useful tool for preparing accounting reports. Unlike paper forms, however, electronic spreadsheets contain formulas that automatically perform calculations.

An **electronic spreadsheet** displayed on a computer monitor is a group of rows and columns. The space where a column intersects with a row is a **cell**. Cell A17 is located at the intersection of column A and row 17. This is known as the **cell address**.

A spreadsheet prepared for reconciling a bank statement would look like the one in the following illustration. Electronic spreadsheets can be extremely large, having hundreds of columns and thousands of rows.

The power of the electronic spreadsheet comes from the ability to let the software make calculations. This is accomplished by attaching formulas to different cells. This spreadsheet was created with all the formulas necessary to complete a bank reconciliation. For example, the formula at cell I15, +H12+H13, calculates the total outstanding deposits. The spreadsheet adds the values in cells H12 and H13, and displays the value, $1,131.00, in cell I15.

After the bank reconciliation is printed, the same spreadsheet can be used to reconcile other bank statements. Preparing a bank reconciliation using an electronic spreadsheet assures the preparer that the calculations are accurate.

```
         A          B        C     D    E       F      G        H          I
 1  General Ledger: 110                          Date: March 31, 19--
 2  Account Number: 34-2353-26
 3
 4  RECONCILIATION OF BANK STATEMENT
 5
 6  Balance on Check Stub.. 6,234.00       Balance on Bank Statement.. 6,247.00
 7
 8  DEDUCT BANK CHARGES:                   ADD OUTSTANDING DEPOSITS:
 9
10    Description   Amount                 Date                 Amount
11  --------------------------            -------------------------------
12  Service Charge    8.00                 3/30/--                436.00
13                                         3/31/--                695.00
14                                        -------------------------------
15  --------------------------            Total outstanding deposits. 1,131.00
16                                                                 ----------
17  Total bank charges.....    8.00       TOTAL.................... 7,378.00
18                          ----------
19                                        DEDUCT OUTSTANDING CHECKS:
20
21                                        Ck.           Ck.
22                                        No.  Amount   No.  Amount
23                                        -------------------------------
24                                        423   85.00   458    54.00
25                                        455  343.00   459   147.00
26                                        457  523.00
27                                        -------------------------------
28                                        Total outstanding checks... 1,152.00
29                                                                   ----------
30  Adjusted Check Stub
31    Balance.............  6,226.00      Adjusted Bank Balance...... 6,226.00
32                         ==========                               ==========
33
34
35
```

debited to Miscellaneous Expense, *$3.00*, in the General Debit column.

3 *Credit.* Record the amount credited to Cash, *$3.00*, in the Cash Credit column.

4 *Source document.* Write the source document number, *M3*, in the Doc. No. column.

Rugcare reconciled its bank statement on August 28. The entry for the bank service charge is journalized on the same date. Rugcare continues to record entries in the journal until the end of the month as shown in Illustration 6-10, Chapter 6.

- *Receives cash from customers/employees*
- *Issues change and cashes checks*
- *Reconciles cash receipts with cash register balances*
- *Prepares checks for authorized disbursements*
- *Prepares bank deposit slips*

DISHONORED CHECKS

A check that a bank refuses to pay is called a **dishonored check.** Banks may dishonor a check for a number of reasons. (1) The check appears to be altered. (2) The signature of the person who signed the check does not match the one on the signature card at the bank. (3) The amounts written in figures and in words do not agree. (4) The check is postdated. (5) The person who wrote the check has stopped payment on the check. (6) The account of the person who wrote the check has insufficient funds to pay the check.

Issuing a check on an account with insufficient funds is illegal in most states. Altering or forging a check is illegal in all states. A dishonored check may affect the credit rating of the person or business who issued the check. Checking accounts and records should be maintained in such a way that all checks will be honored when presented to the bank.

Sometimes money for a dishonored check can be collected directly from the person or business who wrote the check. Often, however, the value of a dishonored check cannot be recovered and becomes an expense to the business.

Most banks charge a fee for handling dishonored checks that have been previously accepted for deposit. This fee is an expense of the business receiving a dishonored check. Rugcare's bank charges a $5.00 fee for handling dishonored checks. Rugcare attempts to collect the $5.00 fee in addition to the amount of the dishonored check.

Rugcare records a check as a cash debit and deposits the check. When a check is dishonored, the bank deducts the amount of the check plus the fee, $5.00, from Rugcare's checking account. Therefore, Rugcare records a dishonored check in its journal as a cash payment transaction.

Recording a Dishonored Check on a Check Stub

A dishonored check recorded on a check stub is shown in Illustration 7-11.

ILLUSTRATION 7-11

Dishonored check recorded on a check stub

NO. **41**	$ _____
Date	_____ 19 __
To	
For	

BAL. BRO'T. FOR'D.	6,128	00
AMT. DEPOSITED . . .		
SUBTOTAL. . . . . Date	6,128	00
OTHER: *Service Charge* 3.00		
Dis. Check 15.00	18	00
SUBTOTAL:	6,110	00
AMT. THIS CHECK		
BAL. CAR'D. FOR'D.		

The words, *Dishonored check*, are written on the line below the words "Other." The total amount of the dishonored check plus the fee, *$15.00*, is written in the amount column on the same line. A new subtotal is calculated by subtracting the total, $18.00 ($3.00 service charge *plus* $15.00 dishonored check), from the balance brought forward, $6,128.00. The new subtotal, *$6,110.00*, is written on the Subtotal line. A new Balance Carried Forward is not calculated until after Check No. 41 is written.

Journalizing a Dishonored Check

During August, Rugcare received no checks that were subsequently dishonored. However, in November Rugcare did receive a check that was dishonored.

November 29, 19--. Received notice from the bank of a dishonored check, $10.00, plus $5.00 fee; total, $15.00. Memorandum No. 6.

Because Rugcare did not write a check for this cash payment, a memorandum is prepared as the source document. *(CONCEPT: Objective Evidence)*

All checks received are deposited in Rugcare's checking account. The entry for each cash receipts transaction includes a debit to Cash. If a check is subsequently returned as dishonored, the previous cash debit for the amount of the check must be offset by a cash credit. The analysis of this transaction is shown in the T accounts.

Miscellaneous Expense is debited for $15.00 to show the increase in this expense account balance. Cash is credited for $15.00 to show the decrease in this asset account balance. The journal entry to record this transaction is shown in Illustration 7-12.

This entry is journalized using four steps.

Miscellaneous Expense	
15.00	

Cash	
	15.00

1 Date. Write the date, *29*, in the Date column.

2 Debit. Write the title of the account to be debited, Miscellaneous Expense, in the Account Title column. Record the amount debited to Miscellaneous Expense, *$15.00*, in the General Debit column.

3 Credit. Record the amount credited to Cash, *$15.00*, in the Cash Credit column.

4 Source document. Write the source document number, *M6*, in the Doc. No. column.

Audit Your Understanding
1. List the three steps to reconcile a bank statement.
2. Draw T accounts to analyze a dishonored check.

ILLUSTRATION 7-12 Journal entry to record a dishonored check

	DATE	ACCOUNT TITLE	DOC. NO.	POST. REF.	GENERAL DEBIT	GENERAL CREDIT	SALES CREDIT	CASH DEBIT	CASH CREDIT	
					1	2	3	4	5	
19	29	*Miscellaneous Expense*	M6		1 5 00				1 5 00	19

JOURNAL PAGE 10

ELECTRONIC FUNDS TRANSFER

FYI

Individuals can also use a form of electronic funds transfer. Personal accounts can be accessed through Automated Teller Machines (ATMs) to make inquiries, withdraw money, deposit money, and transfer funds from one account to another.

A computerized cash payments system that uses electronic impulses to transfer funds is called **electronic funds transfer.** Many businesses use electronic funds transfer to pay vendors. To use electronic funds transfer (EFT), a business makes arrangements with its bank to process EFT transactions. Arrangements are also made with vendors to accept EFT on account. After arranging for EFT payments on account, a telephone call is all that is needed to transfer funds from the business' account to the vendor's account.

To control cash payments through EFT, the person responsible for requesting transfers should be given a password. The bank should be instructed to not accept EFT requests from any person unable to provide an established password.

Superior Cleaning Service uses electronic funds transfer to make payments on account to vendors. The journal entry for making payments on account through electronic funds transfer is the same as when a check is written. The only change is the source document used to prove that the transaction did occur. Superior Cleaning Service uses a memorandum as the source document for an electronic funds transfer. A note is written on the memorandum to describe the transaction.

Kelson Enterprises	
350.00	

Cash	
	350.00

September 2. Paid cash on account to Kelson Enterprises, $350.00, using EFT. Memorandum No. 10.

The source document for this transaction is Memorandum No. 10. *(CONCEPT: Objective Evidence)* The analysis of this transaction is shown in the T accounts.

The liability account, Kelson Enterprises, is decreased by a debit, $350.00. The asset account, Cash, is decreased by a credit, $350.00.

A cash payment made by EFT is recorded on the check stub as "Other." This procedure keeps the checkbook in balance during the time lag from when the EFT is made until receipt of the bank statement. The EFT payments are verified as part of the regular bank statement reconciliation process. EFT payments are identified in the Check column of the bank statement by the notation *EFT* rather than by a check number.

A summary of procedures for using checking accounts is shown in Illustration 7-13.

FYI

Financial Management Service of the Department of the Treasury issues over 250 million Electronic Funds Transfer (EFT) payments annually.

Summary of checking account procedures

1 A deposit slip is prepared to deposit cash and checks in a checking account.

2 Checks are written to make payments from the checking account.

3 Cash payments transactions are journalized from check stubs.

4 A bank statement showing details of deposits, checks, and service charges.

5 The bank statement is reconciled to assure that the bank statement and checkbook information agree.

6 Bank service changes are journalized and recorded in the checkbook.

7 Dishonored checks are recorded in the checkbook and in the journal.

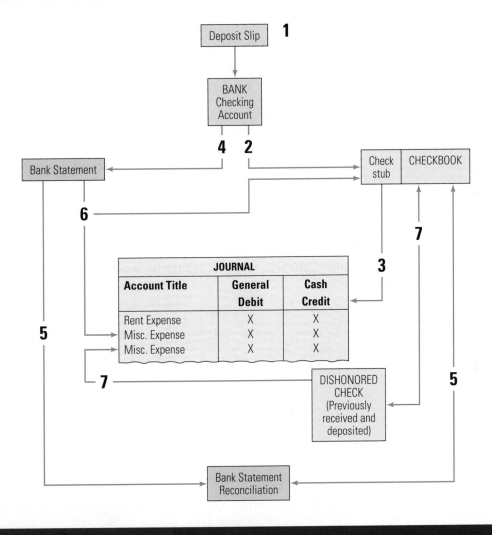

PETTY CASH

An amount of cash kept on hand and used for making small payments is called **petty cash.** Cash control is effective if all cash payments are made by check and cash receipts are deposited in the bank. However, a business usually has some small payments for

Petty Cash

Debit side NORMAL BALANCE Increases	Credit side Decreases

which writing a check is not time or cost effective. Therefore, a business may maintain a separate cash fund for making small cash payments. The actual dollar amount considered to be a small payment differs from one business to another. Mr. Furman has set $5.00 as the maximum amount to be paid at any one time from the petty cash fund.

The petty cash account is an asset with a normal debit balance. The balance of the petty cash account increases on the debit side and decreases on the credit side.

Establishing a Petty Cash Fund

On August 17 Mr. Furman decided that Rugcare needed a petty cash fund of $200.00. This amount should provide for the small cash payments anticipated during a month.

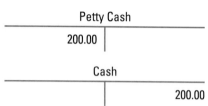

August 17, 19--. Paid cash to establish a petty cash fund, $200.00. Check No. 10.

The source document for this transaction is Check No. 10. (CONCEPT: *Objective Evidence*) The analysis of this transaction is shown in the T accounts.

Petty Cash is debited for $200.00 to show the increase in this asset account balance. Cash is credited for $200.00 to show the decrease in this asset account balance. The journal entry to record this transaction is shown in Illustration 7-14.

ILLUSTRATION 7-14   Journal entry to record establishing a petty cash fund

JOURNAL   PAGE 1

	DATE	ACCOUNT TITLE	DOC. NO.	POST. REF.	GENERAL DEBIT	GENERAL CREDIT	SALES CREDIT	CASH DEBIT	CASH CREDIT	
16	17	*Petty Cash*	C10		2 0 0 00				2 0 0 00	19

This entry is journalized using four steps.

1 Date. Write the date, *17*, in the Date column.

2 Debit. Write the title of the account to be debited, *Petty Cash*, in the Account Title column. Record the amount debited to Petty Cash, *$200.00*, in the General Debit column.

3 Credit. Record the amount credited to Cash, *$200.00*, in the Cash Credit column.

4 Source document. Write the source document number, *C10*, in the Doc. No. column.

Mr. Furman cashed the check and placed the $200.00 in a locked petty cash box kept at Rugcare's place of business. Only Mr. Furman is authorized to make payments from the petty cash fund.

Making Payments from a Petty Cash Fund

Each time a small payment is made from the petty cash fund, Mr. Furman prepares a form showing the purpose and amount of the payment. A form showing proof of a petty cash payment is called a **petty cash slip.**

A petty cash slip used by Rugcare is shown in Illustration 7-15.

ILLUSTRATION 7-15   Petty cash slip

PETTY CASH SLIP	No. 1
Date: *August 18, 19--*	
Paid to: *Bernie's Repair Shop*	
For: *Hose Repair*	$ *5.00*
Account: *Repair Expense*	
Approved: *Ben Furman*	

A petty cash slip shows the following information. (1) Petty cash slip number. (2) Date of petty cash payment. (3) To whom paid. (4) Reason for the payment. (5) Amount paid. (6) Account in which amount is to be recorded. (7) Signature of person approving the petty cash payment.

The petty cash slips are kept in the petty cash box until the fund must be replenished. No entries are made in the journal for the individual petty cash payments.

Replenishing a Petty Cash Fund

As petty cash is paid out, the amount in the petty cash box decreases. Eventually, the petty cash fund must be replenished and the petty cash payments recorded. Rugcare replenishes its petty cash fund whenever the amount on hand is reduced to $75.00. Also, the petty cash fund is always replenished at the end of each month so that all of the expenses are recorded in the month they are incurred.

Rugcare completes four steps in replenishing the petty cash fund.

1 *Prove the petty cash fund.* On August 31 Mr. Furman proves petty cash as shown below.

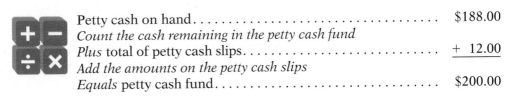

Petty cash on hand.	$188.00
Count the cash remaining in the petty cash fund	
Plus total of petty cash slips.	+ 12.00
Add the amounts on the petty cash slips	
Equals petty cash fund.	$200.00

The last line of the proof must show the same total as the original balance of the petty cash fund, $200.00. If petty cash does not prove, the errors must be found and corrected before any more work is done.

2 *Prepare a petty cash report.* At the end of August, Mr. Furman totals the petty cash slips and prepares a report. Rugcare's August petty cash report is shown in Illustration 7-16.

ILLUSTRATION 7-16   Petty cash report

PETTY CASH REPORT	Date: August 31, 19--		
Explanation	Amounts		
Fund total			200 00
Payments:			
Miscellaneous Expense	7 00		
Repair Expense	5 00		
Less total payments			12 00
Equals recorded amount on hand			188 00
Actual amount on hand			188 00

The report shows that a total of $12.00 has been paid out of petty cash for repairs and miscellaneous expenses. Thus, $12.00 needs to be added to the remaining $188.00 to bring the petty cash fund back to its normal size, $200.00.

3 *Write a check to replenish the petty cash fund.*

4 *Journalize the entry to replenish petty cash.*

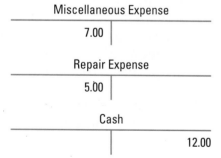

August 31, 19--. Paid cash to replenish the petty cash fund, $12.00: miscellaneous expense, $7.00; repairs, $5.00. Check No. 15.

The source document for this transaction is Check No. 15. *(CONCEPT: Objective Evidence)* The analysis of this transaction is shown in the T accounts.

Miscellaneous Expense is debited for $7.00 and Repair Expense is debited for $5.00 to show the increases in these expense account balances. Cash is credited for $12.00 to show a decrease in this asset account balance.

Unless the petty cash fund is permanently increased or decreased, the balance of the account is always the original amount of the fund. The check issued to replenish petty cash is a credit to Cash and does not affect Petty Cash. When the check is cashed, the money is placed in the petty cash box. The amount in the petty cash box changes as shown below.

		Amount in petty cash box before fund is replenished	$188.00
		Amount from check issued to replenish petty cash	+ 12.00
		Amount in petty cash box after fund is replenished	$200.00

The total amount in the petty cash box, $200.00, is again the same as the balance of the petty cash account. The journal entry to record the transaction to replenish petty cash is shown in Illustration 7-17.

ILLUSTRATION 7-17   Journal entry to record replenishing of petty cash

	DATE	ACCOUNT TITLE	DOC. NO.	POST. REF.	GENERAL DEBIT	GENERAL CREDIT	SALES CREDIT	CASH DEBIT	CASH CREDIT	
11	31	*Miscellaneous Expense*	C15		7 00				12 00	11
12		*Repair Expense*			5 00					12

JOURNAL   PAGE 2

This entry is journalized using four steps.

1 Date.   Write the date, *31*, in the Date column.

2 Debit.   Write the title of the first account to be debited, Miscellaneous Expense, in the Account Title column. Write the amount to be debited to Miscellaneous Expense, *$7.00*, in the General Debit column on the same line as the account title. Write the title of the second account to be debited, Repair Expense, on the next line in the Account Title column. Record the amount to be debited to Repair Expense, *$5.00*, in the General Debit column on the same line as the account title.

3 Credit.   Record the amount to be credited to Cash, *$12.00*, in the Cash Credit column on the first line of this entry.

4 Source document.   Write the source document number, *C15*, in the Doc. No. column.

The check is cashed, and the money is placed in the petty cash box. The amount in the petty cash box is now the original amount of the petty cash fund, $200.00. Petty cash on hand, $188.00, *plus* the cash to replenish, $12.00, *equals* the original amount of the petty cash fund, $200.00. The amount in the petty cash fund is now the same as the balance of the petty cash account, $200.00.

A summary of procedures for using a petty cash fund is shown in Illustration 7-18.

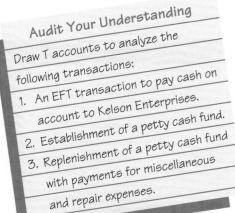

Audit Your Understanding

Draw T accounts to analyze the following transactions:

1. An EFT transaction to pay cash on account to Kelson Enterprises.

2. Establishment of a petty cash fund.

3. Replenishment of a petty cash fund with payments for miscellaneous and repair expenses.

Summary of petty cash fund procedures

1 A check is issued to establish a petty cash fund.

2 The cash payment to establish a petty cash fund is journalized.

3 A petty cash slip is prepared for each payment from the petty cash fund.

4 When the petty cash fund needs to be replenished, a petty cash report is prepared summarizing the petty cash slips.

5 A check is issued to replenish the petty cash fund.

6 The cash payment to replenish petty cash is journalized.

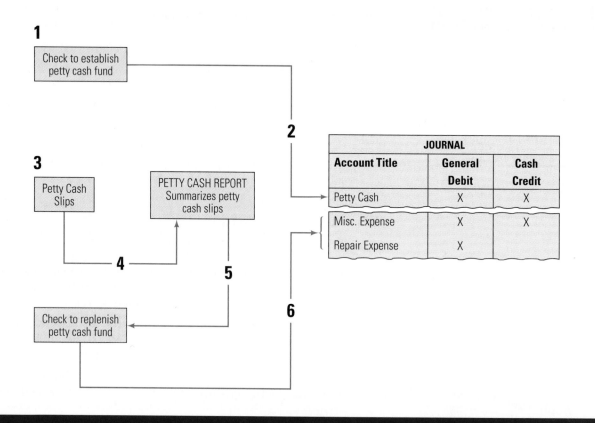

What is the meaning of each of the following?

1. **checking account**
2. **endorsement**
3. **blank endorsement**
4. **special endorsement**
5. **restrictive endorsement**
6. **postdated check**
7. **bank statement**
8. **dishonored check**
9. **electronic funds transfer**
10. **petty cash**
11. **petty cash slip**

QUESTIONS FOR INDIVIDUAL STUDY

1. What evidence does a depositor have that money has been deposited in a checking account?
2. Why is no journal entry made by a business for a deposit in a checking account?
3. Why is the amount written in both numbers and words on a check?
4. What is the most common way of voiding a check?
5. Under what circumstances can a depositor assume that a bank statement reconciliation is correct?
6. Which accounting concept is being applied when a memorandum is prepared for the service charges deducted from a checking account?
7. What accounts are affected, and how, by an entry to record a bank service charge for a checking account?

8. What accounts are affected, and how, when Rugcare is notified that a deposited check has been dishonored?
9. What is the source document for an electronic funds transfer (EFT) transaction?
10. What is the purpose of a petty cash fund?
11. What accounts are affected, and how, when a petty cash fund is established?
12. What is Rugcare's initial record of amounts that have been paid from the petty cash fund?
13. How is the petty cash fund proved?
14. What accounts are affected, and how, by an entry to replenish petty cash when the petty cash slips show payments for miscellaneous expense and repair expense?
15. When is a journal entry made to record payments from the petty cash fund?

CASES FOR CRITICAL THINKING

CASE 1 Iris Velez has a personal checking account in which she maintains a small balance. She receives a bank statement every three months. She files the statement and does not prepare a reconciliation. Sueanne Merker also has a personal checking account in which she maintains a balance of several hundred dollars. She receives bank statements once a month. She prepares a bank statement reconciliation for each bank statement received. Is Mrs. Velez or Ms. Merker following the better procedure? Explain your answer.

CASE 2 Dorset Company decides to establish a petty cash fund. The owner, Edna Dorset, wants to establish a $100.00 petty cash fund and limit payments to $5.00 or less. The manager, Roy Evans, suggests a petty cash fund of $3,000.00 limited to payments of $50.00 or less. Mr. Evans claims this limit will help him avoid writing so many checks. Do you agree with Ms. Dorset or Mr. Evans? Explain your answer.

DRILL 7-D1 Reconciling a bank statement

TUTORIAL

SPREADSHEET

On July 29 of the current year, DeepClean received a bank statement dated July 28. The following information is obtained from the bank statement and from the records of the business.

Bank statement balance	$1,528.00
Bank service charge	2.00
Outstanding deposit, July 28	150.00
Outstanding checks:	
No. 103	70.00
No. 105	35.00
Checkbook balance on Check Stub No. 106	1,575.00

MATHEMATICS

INSTRUCTIONS:

Prepare a bank statement reconciliation. Use July 29 of the current year as the date.

DRILL 7-D2 Reconciling a bank statement

On September 30 of the current year, Ajax Service Co. received a bank statement dated September 29. The following information is obtained from the bank statement and from the records of the business.

Bank statement balance	$3,208.00
Bank service charge	5.00
Outstanding deposits:	
September 29	310.00
September 30	330.00
Outstanding checks:	
No. 214	90.00
No. 215	135.00
No. 217	50.00
Checkbook balance on Check Stub No. 218	3,578.00

INSTRUCTIONS:

Prepare a bank statement reconciliation. Use September 30 of the current year as the date.

DRILL 7-D3 Replenishing a petty cash fund

MATHEMATICS

KeepClean replenished petty cash on the dates shown in Column 2 of the following table. The information in Columns 3 to 5 is obtained from the petty cash reports.

1	2	3	4	5
Trans.	Replenished on	Summary of Petty Cash Slips		
		Supplies	Advertising	Miscellaneous
A	July 31	32.00	25.00	
B	August 31	21.00	20.00	5.00
C	September 30	40.00	20.00	15.00
D	October 31	10.00		20.00

INSTRUCTIONS:

Prepare T accounts for Cash, Supplies, Advertising Expense, and Miscellaneous Expense. Use the T accounts to analyze each transaction given in the table. Label each amount in the T accounts with the corresponding transaction letter.

APPLICATION PROBLEMS   EPT(c,d,e,f)

PROBLEM 7-1   Endorsing checks

For each of the following situations, prepare the appropriate endorsement.

INSTRUCTIONS:

1. Write a blank endorsement. Use your own signature.
2. Write a special endorsement to transfer a check to Delbert Richardson. Use your own signature.
3. Write a restrictive endorsement to deposit a check in the account of OddJobs. Use your own signature.

PROBLEM 7-2   Writing checks

MATHEMATICS

You are authorized to sign checks for OddJobs.

INSTRUCTIONS:

1. Record the balance brought forward on Check Stub No. 50, $1,396.35.
2. Record a deposit of $390.00 made on October 30 of the current year on Check Stub No. 50.
3. Prepare check stubs and write the following checks. Use October 30 of the current year as the date.

Check No. 50. To Corner Garage for repairs, $138.00.
Check No. 51. To OfficeWorld for supplies, $50.00.
Check No. 52. To Dixon Papers for supplies, $15.00.

PROBLEM 7-3   Reconciling a bank statement and recording a bank service charge

Use the bank statement, canceled checks, and check stubs given in the working papers accompanying this textbook.

INSTRUCTIONS:

1. Compare the canceled checks with the check stubs. For each canceled check, place a check mark next to the appropriate check stub number.
2. For each deposit shown on the bank statement, place a check mark next to the deposit amount on the appropriate check stub.
3. Prepare a bank statement reconciliation. Use August 29 of the current year as the date.
4. Record the following transactions on page 8 of a journal. The abbreviation for memorandum is M.

Sept. 1. Received bank statement showing August bank service charge, $5.00. M25.
       1. Received notice from the bank of a dishonored check, $170.00, plus $5.00 fee; total, $175.00. M26.

5. Record the bank service charge and dishonored check on Check Stub No. 165.

PROBLEM 7-4 Paying cash on account using electronic funds transfer

Century Service uses electronic funds transfer to make payments on account.

INSTRUCTIONS:

Journalize the following transactions completed during July of the current year. Use page 8 of a journal. The abbreviation for memo is M.

July 8. Paid cash on account to Central Supply, $268.00, using EFT. M32.
12. Paid cash on account to Lapham Enterprises, $420.00, using EFT. M33.
16. Paid cash on account to Miller Sales, $355.00, using EFT. M34.

PROBLEM 7-5 Establishing and replenishing a petty cash fund

SweepUp established a petty cash fund on August 3 of the current year. At the end of August, the business replenished the petty cash fund.

INSTRUCTIONS:

Journalize the following transactions completed during August of the current year. Use page 10 of a journal. The abbreviation for check is C.

Aug. 3. Paid cash to establish a petty cash fund, $100.00. C57.
31. Paid cash to replenish the petty cash fund, $78.00: supplies, $25.00; miscellaneous expense, $8.00; repairs, $45.00. C97.

ENRICHMENT PROBLEMS   EPT(c,d,e,f)

MASTERY PROBLEM 7-M File maintenance; reconciling a bank statement; journalizing a bank service charge, a dishonored check, and petty cash transactions

Joseph Cruz owns a business called LawnMow. Selected general ledger accounts are given below.

110	Cash	520	Miscellaneous Expense
115	Petty Cash	530	Rent Expense
120	Supplies	535	Repair Expense
130	Prepaid Insurance	540	Supplies Expense
320	Joseph Cruz, Drawing	550	Utilities Expense

INSTRUCTIONS:

1. Journalize the following transactions completed during August of the current year. Use page 20 of a journal. Source documents are abbreviated as follows: check, C; memorandum, M.

Aug. 21. Paid cash to establish a petty cash fund, $100.00. C61.
24. Paid cash for repairs, $135.00. C62.
26. Paid cash for supplies, $40.00. C63.
27. Received notice from the bank of a dishonored check, $35.00, plus $5.00 fee; total, $40.00. M22.
28. Paid cash for miscellaneous expense, $12.00. C64.
31. Paid cash to owner for personal use, $300.00. C65.
31. Paid cash to replenish the petty cash fund, $55.00: supplies, $35.00; miscellaneous expense, $20.00. C66.

2. On August 31 of the current year, LawnMow received a bank statement dated August 30. Prepare a bank statement reconciliation. Use August 31 of the current year as the date. The following information is obtained from the August 30 bank statement and from the records of the business.

Bank statement balance	$1,521.00
Bank service charge................................	5.00
Outstanding deposit, August 31......................	430.00
Outstanding checks, Nos. 65 and 66.	
Checkbook balance on Check Stub No. 67..............	1,601.00

3. Continue using the journal and journalize the following transaction.

Aug. 31. Received bank statement showing August bank service charge, $5.00. M23.

CHALLENGE PROBLEM 7-C Reconciling a bank statement

AUTOMATED

On November 30 of the current year, Johnson Company received a bank statement dated November 29. Miss Johnson placed a check mark beside the amount on each check stub for which a canceled check was received. She also placed a check mark on the check stub beside the amount of each deposit shown on the bank statement. She then prepared a bank statement reconciliation.

The last eight check stubs for the month of November and the bank statement reconciliation are given in the working papers accompanying this textbook. Both the check stubs and reconciliation contain errors.

INSTRUCTIONS:

1. Verify the amounts on the check stubs. Assume that the check amounts in the upper right corner of each stub are correct. Also assume that all deposits have been entered correctly on the check stubs.

2. Draw a line through all incorrect amounts on the check stubs. Write the correct amounts either above or below the incorrect amounts, depending on where space is available.

3. Prepare a correct bank statement reconciliation. Assume that the check marks written beside check and deposit amounts on the check stubs are correct. Therefore, the outstanding deposits and checks are those that are not checked.

Automated Cash Control Systems

Rugcare's manual cash control systems are described in Chapter 7. Integrating Automated Accounting Topic 2 describes procedures for using automated accounting software to reconcile a bank statement. Topic 2 also describes procedures to record selected transactions for using a checking account and petty cash fund. The Automated Accounting Problems contain instructions for using automated accounting software to solve Mastery Problem 7-M and Challenge Problem 7-C, Chapter 7.

RECONCILING A BANK STATEMENT
To reconcile a bank statement using automated accounting software, File is selected from the menu bar. The Payroll/Assets/Bank

Rec. command is selected from the File menu. File is again selected from the menu bar. The Open Data File command is then chosen to retrieve the bank reconciliation data base from the template disk.

System is selected from the menu bar and the Bank Reconciliation option is chosen. Reconciliation is selected from the menu bar. The Reconciliation Data command is then chosen to display the data entry window for keying bank reconciliation data. The following information is obtained from the August 28 bank statement and from the records of Rugcare.

Bank statement balance...............................	$7,586.00
Checkbook balance....................................	8,497.00
Bank service charge	3.00
Outstanding deposit	1,412.00
Outstanding checks:	
No. 13	70.00
No. 14	434.00

The bank statement reconciliation data are keyed as shown in Illustration T2-1.

FYI

To save a file under another name, pull down the File menu and choose the Save As menu command. Key the path to the drive and directory that contains the data files. Save your data base using another file name.

ILLUSTRATION T2-1   Completed bank reconciliation data entry window

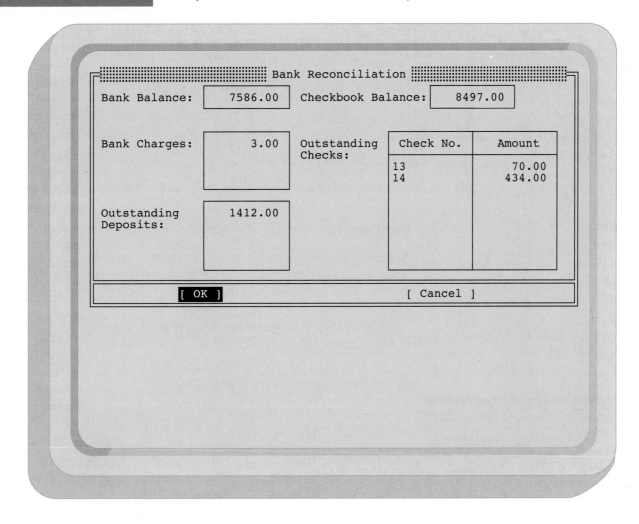

After the bank reconciliation data are keyed, Reports is selected from the menu bar. The Bank Reconciliation command is chosen from the Reports menu to display the bank reconciliation report. The report is checked for accuracy by comparing the Adjusted Checkbook Balance with the Adjusted Bank Balance. As these two totals are the same, the bank statement reconciliation is assumed to be correct. The bank statement reconciliation report is printed, as shown in Illustration T2-2, and filed for future reference.

ILLUSTRATION T2-2   Bank statement reconciliation report

```
                            Rugcare
                       Bank Reconciliation
                           08/28/--

Checkbook Balance                                      8497.00
                                          3.00
                                       ----------
Less Bank Charges                                         3.00
                                                      ----------
Adjusted Checkbook Balance                             8494.00
                                                      ==========


Bank Balance                                           7586.00
                                       1412.00
                                       ----------
Plus Outstanding Deposits                              1412.00
                                13        70.00
                                14       434.00
                                       ----------
Less Outstanding Checks                                 504.00
                                                      ----------
Adjusted Bank Balance                                  8494.00
                                                      ==========
```

RECORDING CASH CONTROL TRANSACTIONS

A general journal input form is used to journalize cash control transactions. Transaction data are journalized on an input form and keyed. The software is directed to post to the general ledger accounts.

Rugcare's cash control transactions are analyzed into debit and credit parts in Chapter 7.

Establishing a Petty Cash Fund

August 17, 19--. Paid cash to establish a petty cash fund, $200.00. Check No. 10.

The journal entry to record this transaction is on lines 1 and 2 of the general journal input form shown in Illustration T2-3. Petty Cash is debited and Cash is credited for $200.00.

General journal input form with transactions recorded

RUN DATE _08,31,--_
MM DD YY

GENERAL JOURNAL
Input Form

	DATE MM/DD	REFERENCE	ACCOUNT NO.	CUSTOMER/ VENDOR NO.	DEBIT	CREDIT	
1	08,17	C10	120		200 00		1
2	/		110			200 00	2
3	,28	M3	530		3 00		3
4	/		110			3 00	4
5	,29	M6	530		15 00		5
6	/		110			15 00	6
7	,31	C15	530		7 00		7
8	/		550		5 00		8
9	/		110			12 00	9
10	/						10
11	/						11
12	/						12
25							25
				PAGE TOTALS	230 00	230 00	
				FINAL TOTALS	230 00	230 00	

Recording a Bank Service Charge

August 28, 19--. Received bank statement showing August bank service charge, $3.00. Memorandum No. 3.

The journal entry to record this transaction is on lines 3 and 4 of Illustration T2-3. Miscellaneous Expense is debited and Cash is credited for $3.00.

Recording a Dishonored Check

August 29, 19--. Received notice from the bank of a dishonored check, $10.00, plus $5.00 fee; total, $15.00. Memorandum No. 6.

The journal entry to record this transaction is on lines 5 and 6 of Illustration T2-3. Miscellaneous Expense is debited and Cash is credited for $15.00.

Replenishing a Petty Cash Fund

☞☞ FYI ☞☞

Dollar and cent signs are not entered on input forms.

August 31, 19--. Paid cash to replenish the petty cash fund, $12.00: miscellaneous expense, $7.00; repairs, $5.00. Check No. 15.

The journal entry to record this transaction is on lines 7 through 9 of Illustration T2-3. Miscellaneous Expense is debited for $7.00. Repair Expense is debited for $5.00. Cash is credited for $12.00.

FYI

After all transactions have been journalized, Rugcare totals the Debit and Credit amount columns. The totals are recorded on the Page Totals and Final Totals lines provided at the bottom of the input form. The totals are compared to assure that debits equal credits.

Processing Cash Control Journal Entries

To process cash control journal entries, File is selected from the menu bar. The Open Accounting File command is chosen from the File menu to retrieve the general ledger data base from the template disk. The Journals menu is selected from the menu bar. The General Journal command is chosen from the Journals menu to key the cash control transaction data.

After all lines on the input form have been keyed and posted, the Reports menu is selected from the menu bar. The Journals command is chosen from the Reports menu. The General Journal report is selected from the Reports Selection menu. This selection displays the Selection Options screen. As Rugcare wants to print all transactions journalized on Illustration T2-3, pushing the *Ok* button directs the software to display a general journal report. The displayed general journal report is checked for accuracy by comparing the report totals, $230.00, with the totals on the general journal input form. Because the totals are the same, the general journal report is assumed to be correct. The general journal report is printed, as shown in Illustration T2-4, and filed for future reference.

ILLUSTRATION T2-4   General journal report

```
                            Rugcare
                        General Journal
                          08/31/--
------------------------------------------------------------------------
Date    Refer.  V/C Acct.  Title                        Debit      Credit
------------------------------------------------------------------------
08/17 C10          120    Petty Cash                   200.00
08/17 C10          110    Cash                                     200.00

08/28 M3           530    Miscellaneous Expense          3.00
08/28 M3           110    Cash                                       3.00

08/29 M6           530    Miscellaneous Expense         15.00
08/29 M6           110    Cash                                      15.00

08/31 C15          530    Miscellaneous Expense          7.00
08/31 C15          550    Repair Expense                 5.00
08/31 C15          110    Cash                                      12.00

                                                      ----------  ----------
                          Totals                        230.00      230.00
                                                      ==========  ==========
```

OPTIONAL PROBLEM DB-2A

Rugcare's general ledger data base is on the accounting textbook template. If you wish to reconcile Rugcare's bank statement using automated accounting software, load the *Automated Accounting 6.0* or higher software. Pull down the File menu from the menu bar and choose the Payroll/Assets/Bank Rec. command. Pull down the File menu and choose the Open Data File command to retrieve Data Base 2A (DB-2A) from the template disk. Read the Problem Instructions screen. Use Illustration T2-1 and follow the procedures described to reconcile Rugcare's bank statement.

OPTIONAL PROBLEM DB-2B

Rugcare's general ledger data base is on the accounting textbook template. If you wish to process Rugcare's cash control transactions using automated accounting software, load the *Automated Accounting 6.0* or higher software. If you just completed Optional Problem DB-2A, you must first load the Accounting System module before you begin. Pull down the File menu and choose the Accounting System command. Pull down the File menu and choose the Open File menu command to retrieve Data Base 2B (DB-2B) from the template disk. Read the Problem Instructions screen. Use Illustration T2-3 and follow the procedures described to process Rugcare's cash control journal entries.

AUTOMATED ACCOUNTING PROBLEMS

AUTOMATING MASTERY PROBLEM 7-M Reconciling a bank statement; journalizing a bank service charge, a dishonored check, and petty cash transactions

INSTRUCTIONS:

1. Journalize transactions from Mastery Problem 7-M, Chapter 7 on a general journal input form. Use August 31 of the current year as the run date.
2. Load the *Automated Accounting 6.0* or higher software. Select data base F7-M (First-Year Course Problem 7-M) from the accounting textbook template. Read the Problem Instructions screen.
3. Select File from the menu bar and choose the Save As menu command. Key the path to the drive and directory that contains your data files. Save the data base with a file name of XXX7M (where XXX are your initials).
4. Key the transactions from the completed general journal input form.
5. Display/print the general journal report. Check the report for accuracy by comparing the report totals with the totals on the input form.
6. Save your file.
7. To complete the bank reconciliation, select File from the menu bar and select the Payroll/Assets/Bank Rec. command. Select File and then the Open Data File command to retrieve data base F7-M from the template disk. The following information is obtained from the bank statement and from the records of the business.

Bank statement balance	$1,521.00
Checkbook balance	1,601.00
Bank service charge	5.00
Outstanding deposit	430.00
Outstanding checks:	
No. 65	300.00
No. 66	55.00

8. Key the bank statement reconciliation data.
9. Display/print the bank statement reconciliation.

AUTOMATING CHALLENGE PROBLEM 7-C Reconciling a bank statement

INSTRUCTIONS:

1. Load the *Automated Accounting 6.0* or higher software. Select File from the menu bar and select the Payroll/Assets/Bank Rec. command. Select File and then the Open Data File command to retrieve data base F7-C from the template disk.
2. Use the manual solution prepared for Challenge Problem 7-C. Key the bank statement reconciliation data.
3. Display/print the bank statement reconciliation.

An Accounting Cycle for a Proprietorship: Journalizing and Posting Transactions

AUTOMATED

Reinforcement activities strengthen the learning of accounting concepts and procedures. Reinforcement Activity 1 is a single problem divided into two parts. Part A includes learnings from Chapters 2 through 7. Part B includes learnings from Chapters 8 through 10. An accounting cycle is completed in Parts A and B for a single business—The Fitness Center.

THE FITNESS CENTER

In May of the current year, Gail Davis starts a service business called The Fitness Center. The business provides exercise facilities for its clients. In addition, Miss Davis, a professional dietician, offers diet and exercise counseling for clients who request her assistance. The business rents the facilities with which it operates, pays the utilities, and is responsible for maintenance. The Fitness Center charges clients for each visit.

CHART OF ACCOUNTS

The Fitness Center uses the following chart of accounts.

CHART OF ACCOUNTS

Balance Sheet Accounts	Income Statement Accounts
(100) ASSETS	**(400) REVENUE**
110 Cash	410 Sales
120 Petty Cash	
130 Supplies	**(500) EXPENSES**
140 Prepaid Insurance	510 Advertising Expense
	520 Insurance Expense
(200) LIABILITIES	530 Miscellaneous Expense
210 Dunnel Supplies	540 Rent Expense
220 Morgan Office Supplies	550 Repair Expense
	560 Supplies Expense
(300) OWNER'S EQUITY	570 Utilities Expense
310 Gail Davis, Capital	
320 Gail Davis, Drawing	
330 Income Summary	

RECORDING TRANSACTIONS

INSTRUCTIONS:

1. Journalize the following transactions completed during May of the current year. Use page 1 of the journal. Source documents are abbreviated as follows: check stub, C; memorandum, M; receipt, R; calculator tape, T.

May 1. Received cash from owner as an investment, $15,000.00. R1.
1. Paid cash for rent, $1,000.00. C1.
2. Paid cash for electric bill, $45.00. C2.
4. Paid cash for supplies, $500.00. C3.
4. Paid cash for insurance, $960.00. C4.
7. Bought supplies on account from Dunnel Supplies, $800.00. M1.
11. Paid cash to establish a petty cash fund, $200.00. C5.
12. Received cash from sales, $550.00. T12.
13. Paid cash for repairs, $25.00. C6.
13. Paid cash for miscellaneous expense, $35.00. C7.
13. Received cash from sales, $185.00. T13.
14. Paid cash for advertising, $100.00. C8.
14. Received cash from sales, $335.00. T14.
15. Paid cash to owner for personal use, $250.00. C9.
15. Paid cash on account to Dunnel Supplies, $300.00. C10.
15. Received cash from sales, $325.00. T15.
18. Paid cash for miscellaneous expense, $100.00. C11.
18. Received cash from sales, $295.00. T18.
19. Received cash from sales, $155.00. T19.
20. Paid cash for repairs, $125.00. C12.
20. Bought supplies on account from Morgan Office Supplies, $150.00. M2.
20. Received cash from sales, $195.00. T20.

2. Prove and rule page 1 of the journal. Carry the column totals forward to page 2 of the journal.

3. Post the separate amounts on each line of page 1 of the journal that need to be posted individually.

4. Use page 2 of the journal. Journalize the following transactions.

May 21. Paid cash for water bill, $110.00. C13.
21. Received cash from sales, $235.00. T21.
25. Paid cash for supplies, $50.00. C14.
25. Received cash from sales, $295.00. T25.
26. Paid cash for miscellaneous expense, $25.00. C15.
26. Received cash from sales, $300.00. T26.
27. Received cash from sales, $195.00. T27.
28. Paid cash for telephone bill, $210.00. C16.
28. Received cash from sales, $275.00. T28.

5. The Fitness Center received a bank statement dated May 27. The following information is obtained from the bank statement and from the records of the business. Prepare a bank statement reconciliation. Use May 29 as the date.

Bank statement balance	$14,312.00
Bank service charge	3.00
Outstanding deposit, May 28	275.00
Outstanding checks:	
No. 14	50.00
No. 15	25.00
No. 16	210.00
Checkbook balance on Check Stub No. 17	14,305.00

6. Continue using page 2 of the journal, and journalize the following transactions.

May 29. Received bank statement showing May bank service charge, $3.00. M3.
    29. Paid cash for supplies, $60.00. C17.
    29. Received cash from sales, $240.00. T29.
    31. Paid cash to replenish the petty cash fund, $17.00: miscellaneous expense, $10.00; repairs, $7.00. C18.
    31. Paid cash to owner for personal use, $250.00. C19.
    31. Received cash from sales, $280.00. T31.

7. Prove page 2 of the journal.
8. Prove cash. The beginning cash balance on May 1 is zero. The balance on the next unused check stub is $14,495.00.
9. Rule page 2 of the journal.
10. Post the separate amounts on each line of page 2 of the journal that need to be posted individually.
11. Post the column totals on page 2 of the journal.

The general ledger prepared in Reinforcement Activity 1, Part A, is needed to complete Reinforcement Activity 1, Part B.

8

Work Sheet for a Service Business

ENABLING PERFORMANCE TASKS

After studying Chapter 8, you will be able to:

a Define accounting terms related to a work sheet for a service business organized as a proprietorship.

b Identify accounting concepts and practices related to a work sheet for a service business organized as a proprietorship.

c Plan adjustments for supplies and prepaid insurance.

d Complete a work sheet for a service business organized as a proprietorship.

e Identify selected procedures for finding and correcting errors in accounting records.

TERMS PREVIEW

fiscal period • work sheet • trial balance • adjustments • income statement • net income • net loss

General ledger accounts contain information needed by managers and owners. Before the information can be used, however, it must be analyzed, summarized, and reported in a meaningful way. The accounting concept, *Consistent Reporting*, is applied when the same accounting procedures are followed in the same way in each accounting period. *(CONCEPT: Consistent Reporting)* For example, in one year a delivery business might report the number of deliveries made. The next year the same business reports the amount of revenue received for the deliveries made. The information for the two years cannot be compared because the business has not been consistent in reporting information about deliveries.

FISCAL PERIODS

The length of time for which a business summarizes and reports financial information is called a **fiscal period**. A fiscal period is also known as an accounting period. Businesses usually select a period of time, such as a month, six months, or a year, for which to summarize and report financial information. The accounting concept, *Accounting Period Cycle*, is applied when changes in financial information are reported for a specific period of time in the form of financial statements. *(CONCEPT: Accounting Period Cycle)* Each business chooses a fiscal period length that meets its needs. Because federal and state tax reports are based on one year, most businesses use a one-year fiscal period. However, because Rugcare is a new business, Mr. Furman wishes to have financial information reported frequently to help him make decisions. For this reason, Rugcare uses a one-month fiscal period.

A fiscal period can begin on any date. However, most businesses begin their fiscal periods on the first day of a month. Rugcare started business on August 1. Therefore, Rugcare's monthly fiscal period is for the period from August 1 through August 31, inclusive. Another business might use a one-year fiscal period from August 1 of one year through July 31 of the next year. Many businesses use a calendar year starting on January 1 and ending on December 31. Businesses often choose a one-year fiscal period that ends during a period of low business activity. In this way, the end-of-year accounting work comes at a time when other business activities are the lightest. For example, a store with a large volume of Christmas holiday sales might prefer to begin its fiscal period on February 1 or March 1.

Most individuals use a one-year fiscal period that begins on January 1 and ends on December 31. This fiscal period corresponds to the period for which they must file income tax returns for the federal and state governments. However, individuals may use a different fiscal period if approved by the Internal Revenue Service.

Financial information may be analyzed, summarized, and reported on any date a business needs the information. However, financial information is always summarized and reported at the end of a fiscal period.

A summary of preparing a work sheet is shown on the Work Sheet Overlay on pages 176A through 176C.

WORK SHEET

A columnar accounting form used to summarize the general ledger information needed to prepare financial statements is called a **work sheet.**

Accountants use a work sheet for four reasons. (1) To summarize general ledger account balances to prove that debits equal credits. (2) To plan needed changes to general ledger accounts to bring account balances up to date. (3) To separate general ledger account balances according to the financial statements to be prepared. (4) To calculate the amount of net income or net loss for a fiscal period.

Journals and ledgers are permanent records of a business and are usually prepared in ink. However, a work sheet is a planning tool and is not considered a permanent accounting record. Therefore, a work sheet is prepared in pencil.

The work sheet has a three-line heading which includes the name of the company, the name of the form, and the time period the work sheet covers.

Preparing the Heading of a Work Sheet

The heading on a work sheet consists of three lines. (1) Name of the business. (2) Name of the report. (3) Date of the report. The heading for Rugcare's work sheet is shown in Illustration 8-1.

ILLUSTRATION 8-1

Heading on a work sheet

Rugcare
Work Sheet
For Month Ended August 31, 19--

The date on Rugcare's work sheet indicates that the work sheet covers the 31 days from August 1 through and including August 31. If the work sheet were for a calendar year fiscal period, it might have a date stated as *For Year Ended December 31, 19--. (CONCEPT: Accounting Period Cycle)*

Preparing a Trial Balance on a Work Sheet

The equality of debits and credits in the general ledger must be proved. The total of all debit account balances must equal the total of all credit account balances. A proof of the equality of debits and credits in a general ledger is called a **trial balance.** Rugcare prepares a trial balance on a work sheet. Rugcare's August 31 trial balance on a work sheet is shown in Illustration 8-2.

FYI

List all general ledger account titles on a work sheet. Even account titles without balances may be affected by adjustments.

Information for the trial balance is taken from the general ledger. General ledger account titles are listed on a trial balance in the same order as listed on the chart of accounts. All the account titles are listed, even if some accounts do not have balances. The accounts that do not have balances in the Trial Balance columns will be needed in other parts of the work sheet.

ILLUSTRATION 8-2

Trial balance on a work sheet

		TRIAL BALANCE	
	ACCOUNT TITLE	DEBIT	CREDIT
1	Cash	8 2 7 2 00	
2	Petty Cash	2 0 0 00	
3	Supplies	4 9 3 1 00	
4	Prepaid Insurance	1 2 0 0 00	
5	Butler Cleaning Supplies		1 3 6 0 00
6	Dale Office Supplies		2 0 0 00
7	Ben Furman, Capital		1 0 0 0 0 00
8	Ben Furman, Drawing	6 0 0 00	
9	Income Summary		
10	Sales		4 2 9 1 00
11	Advertising Expense	6 8 00	
12	Insurance Expense		
13	Miscellaneous Expense	1 0 5 00	
14	Rent Expense	2 5 0 00	
15	Repair Expense	1 1 0 00	
16	Supplies Expense		
17	Utilities Expense	1 1 5 00	
18		15 8 5 1 00	15 8 5 1 00

Rugcare
Work Sheet
For Month Ended August 31, 19--

Seven steps are used in preparing a trial balance on a work sheet.

1 Write the general ledger account titles in the work sheet's Account Title column.

2 Write the general ledger account debit balances in the Trial Balance Debit column. Write the general ledger account credit balances in the Trial Balance Credit column. If an account does not have a balance, the space in the Trial Balance columns is left blank.

3 Rule a single line across the two Trial Balance columns below the last line on which an account title is written. This single line shows that the two columns are to be added.

4 Add both the Trial Balance Debit and Credit columns. Use a calculator if one is available. For Rugcare's work sheet, the totals are Debit, $15,851.00 and Credit, $15,851.00.

5 Check the equality of the two amount column totals. If the two column totals are the same, then debits equal credits in the general ledger accounts. Because the totals, $15,851.00, are the same, the Trial Balance columns on Rugcare's work sheet are in balance.

If the two column totals are not the same and the trial balance is not in balance, recheck the Trial Balance columns to find the error. Other parts of a work sheet are not completed until the Trial Balance columns are proved. Suggestions for locating errors are described later in this chapter.

6 Write each column's total, *$15,851.00*, below the single line.

7 Rule double lines across both Trial Balance columns. The double lines mean that the Trial Balance column totals have been verified as correct.

Complete the Trial Balance columns of the work sheet before going on to the other columns. If the Trial Balance columns are not correct, the remaining columns will also be incorrect.

Planning Adjustments on a Work Sheet

Sometimes a business will pay cash for an expense in one fiscal period, but the expense is not used until a later period. The expense should be reported in the same fiscal period that it is used to produce revenue. The accounting concept, *Matching Expenses with Revenue*, is applied when revenue from business activities and expenses associated with earning that revenue are recorded in the same accounting period. For example, Rugcare buys supplies in quantity in August, but some of the supplies are not used until September. Only the value of the supplies used in August should be reported as expenses in August. In this way, August revenue and the supplies expense associated with earning the August revenue are recorded in the same accounting period. *(CONCEPT: Matching Expenses with Revenue)*

In order to give accurate information on financial statements, some general ledger accounts must be brought up to date at the end of a fiscal period. For example, Rugcare debits an asset account, Supplies, each time supplies are bought. Supplies on hand are items of value owned by a business until the supplies are used. The value of supplies that are used becomes an expense to the business. However, recording an expense each time an individual supply, such as a pencil, is used would be impractical. Therefore, on August 31 the balance of the asset account, Supplies, is the value of all supplies bought rather than the value of only the supplies that

have not been used. The amount of supplies that have been used must be deducted from the asset account, Supplies, and recorded in the expense account, Supplies Expense.

Likewise, the amount of insurance that has been used during the fiscal period is also an expense of the business. When the insurance premium for a year of insurance coverage is paid, the entire amount is debited to an asset account, Prepaid Insurance. Each day during August a portion of the insurance coverage is used. The value of the insurance used is an expense of the business. However, recording each day's amount of insurance used is impractical. Therefore, at the end of a fiscal period, the balance of Prepaid Insurance is the value of all insurance coverage bought, rather than the value of only the insurance coverage that still remains. The amount of the insurance coverage used must be deducted from the asset account, Prepaid Insurance, and recorded in the expense account, Insurance Expense.

Changes recorded on a work sheet to update general ledger accounts at the end of a fiscal period are called **adjustments.** The assets of a business, such as supplies and prepaid insurance, are used to earn revenue. The portion of the assets consumed in order to earn revenue become expenses of the business. The portions consumed are no longer assets but are now expenses. Therefore, adjustments must be made to both the asset and expense accounts for supplies and insurance. After the adjustments are made, the expenses incurred to earn revenue are reported in the same fiscal period as the revenue is earned and reported. *(CONCEPT: Matching Expenses with Revenue)*

A work sheet is used to plan adjustments. Changes are not made in general ledger accounts until adjustments are journalized and posted. The accuracy of the planning for adjustments is checked on a work sheet before adjustments are actually journalized.

Procedures for journalizing Rugcare's adjustments are described in Chapter 10.

Supplies Adjustment. On August 31, before adjustments, the balance of Supplies is $4,931.00, and the balance of Supplies Expense is zero, as shown in the T accounts.

On August 31 Mr. Furman counted the supplies on hand and found that the value of supplies still unused on that date was $2,284.00. The value of the supplies used is calculated as shown below.

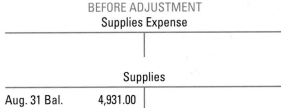

BEFORE ADJUSTMENT

Supplies Expense

Supplies

Aug. 31 Bal.   4,931.00

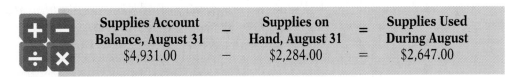

	Supplies Account Balance, August 31	–	Supplies on Hand, August 31	=	Supplies Used During August
	$4,931.00	–	$2,284.00	=	$2,647.00

Four questions are asked in analyzing the adjustment for the asset account, Supplies.

1.	What is the balance of Supplies?...............	$4,931.00
2.	What should the balance be for this account?....	$2,284.00
3.	What must be done to correct the account balance?	
	Decrease	$2,647.00
4.	What adjustment is made?	
	Debit Supplies Expense	$2,647.00
	Credit Supplies.............................	$2,647.00

AFTER ADJUSTMENT

Supplies Expense

Adj. (a)	2,647.00

Supplies

Aug. 31 Bal.	4,931.00	Adj. (a)	2,647.00
(New Bal.	2,284.00)		

The expense account, Supplies Expense, is increased by a debit, $2,647.00, the value of supplies used. The balance of Supplies Expense, $2,647.00, is the value of supplies used during the fiscal period from August 1 to August 31. (CONCEPT: *Matching Expenses with Revenue*)

The asset account, Supplies, is decreased by a credit, $2,647.00, the value of supplies used. The debit balance, $4,931.00, *less* the credit adjustment, $2,647.00, *equals* the new balance, $2,284.00. The new balance of Supplies is the same as the value of supplies on hand on August 31.

Rugcare's supplies adjustment is shown on lines 3 and 16 of the work sheet in Illustration 8-3.

ILLUSTRATION 8-3   Supplies adjustment on a work sheet

		1	2	3	4	
	ACCOUNT TITLE	TRIAL BALANCE		ADJUSTMENTS		
		DEBIT	CREDIT	DEBIT	CREDIT	
3	*Supplies*	4 9 3 1 00			(a) 2 6 4 7 00	3
16	*Supplies Expense*			(a) 2 6 4 7 00		16
17						17
18						18
19						19
20						20

Three steps are used to record the supplies adjustment on the work sheet.

1 Write the debit amount, *$2,647.00*, in the work sheet's Adjustments Debit column on the line with the account title Supplies Expense (line 16).

2 Write the credit amount, *$2,647.00*, in the Adjustments Credit column on the line with the account title Supplies (line 3).

3 Label the two parts of this adjustment with a small letter *a* in parentheses *(a)*. The letter *a* identifies the debit and credit amounts as part of the same adjustment.

SUMMARY OF PREPARATION OF A
WORK SHEET FOR A SERVICE BUSINESS

The following overlay summarizes the preparation of a work sheet. Follow the directions below in using the overlay.

1. Before using the overlay, be sure the pages and transparent overlays are arranged correctly. The correct arrangement is shown below.

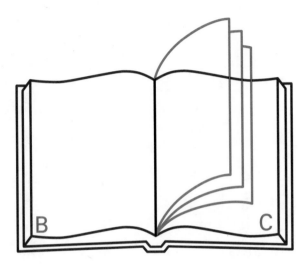

2. Place your book in a horizontal position. Study the steps on page C in preparing the work sheet. You will be able to read the text through the transparent overlays. When directed, carefully lift the transparent overlays and lay them over the work sheet as shown below.

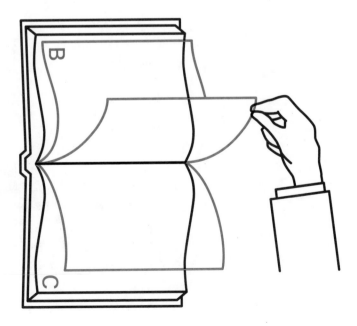

PREPARING A WORK SHEET

To correctly use the insert, read the steps below. Apply the transparent overlays when directed to do so in the steps.

Rugcare

Work Sheet

For Month Ended August 31, 19--

	ACCOUNT TITLE	TRIAL BALANCE DEBIT	TRIAL BALANCE CREDIT	ADJUSTMENTS DEBIT	ADJUSTMENTS CREDIT	INCOME STATEMENT DEBIT	INCOME STATEMENT CREDIT	BALANCE SHEET DEBIT	BALANCE SHEET CREDIT	
1	Cash	827200								1
2	Petty Cash	20000								2
3	Supplies	493100								3
4	Prepaid Insurance	120000								4
5	Butler Cleaning Supplies		136000							5
6	Dale Office Supplies		20000							6
7	Ben Furman, Capital		1000000							7
8	Ben Furman, Drawing	60000								8
9	Income Summary									9
10	Sales		429100							10
11	Advertising Expense	6800								11
12	Insurance Expense									12
13	Miscellaneous Expense	10500								13
14	Rent Expense	25000								14
15	Repair Expense	11000								15
16	Supplies Expense									16
17	Utilities Expense	11500								17
18		1585100	1585100							18
19										19
20										20
21										21
22										22
23										23
24										24
25										25

PREPARING A WORK SHEET

1 Write the heading.

2 Record the trial balance.
- Write the general ledger account titles in the Account Title column.
- Write the account balances in either the Trial Balance Debit or Credit column.
- Rule a single line across the Trial Balance columns.
- Add the Trial Balance columns, and compare the totals.
- Rule double lines across both Trial Balance columns.
  Carefully apply the first overlay.

3 Record the supplies adjustment.
- Write the debit amount in the Adjustments Debit column on the line with the account title Supplies Expense.
- Write the credit amount in the Adjustments Credit column on the line with the account title Supplies.
- Label this adjustment *(a)*.

4 Record the prepaid insurance adjustment.
- Write the debit amount in the Adjustments Debit column on the line with the account title Insurance Expense.
- Write the credit amount in the Adjustments Credit column on the line with the account title Prepaid Insurance.
- Label this adjustment *(b)*.

5 Prove the Adjustments columns.
- Rule a single line across the Adjustments columns.
- Add the Adjustments columns, and compare the totals to assure that they are equal.
- Write the proving totals below the single line.
- Rule double lines across both Adjustments columns.
  Carefully apply the second overlay.

6 Extend all balance sheet account balances.
- Extend the up-to-date asset account balances to the Balance Sheet Debit column.
- Extend the up-to-date liability account balances to the Balance Sheet Credit column.
- Extend the owner's capital and drawing account balances to the Balance Sheet columns.

7 Extend all income statement account balances.
- Extend the up-to-date revenue account balance to the Income Statement Credit column.
- Extend the up-to-date expense account balances to the Income Statement Debit column.
  Carefully apply the third overlay.

8 Calculate and record the net income (or net loss).
- Rule a single line across the Income Statement and Balance Sheet columns.
- Add the columns, and write the totals below the single line.
- Calculate the net income or net loss amount.
- Write the amount of net income (or net loss) below the smaller of the two Income Statement column totals. Write the words *Net Income* or *Net Loss* in the Account Title column.
- Extend the amount of net income (or net loss) to the Balance Sheet columns. Write the amount under the smaller of the two column totals. Write the amount on the same line as the words *Net Income* (or *Net Loss*).

9 Total and rule the Income Statement and Balance Sheet columns.
- Rule a single line across the Income Statement and Balance Sheet columns immediately below the net income (or net loss) amounts.
- Add the net income (or net loss) to the previous column totals. Compare the column totals to assure that totals for each pair of columns are in balance.
- Write the proving totals for each column below the single line.
- Rule double lines across the Income Statement and Balance Sheet columns immediately below the proving totals.

176C

Prepaid Insurance Adjustment. When Rugcare pays for insurance, the amount is debited to the asset account, Prepaid Insurance. However, to debit Insurance Expense daily for the amount of that day's insurance premium used is impractical. Therefore, at the end of a fiscal period, Rugcare's prepaid insurance account does not show the actual value of the remaining prepaid insurance.

BEFORE ADJUSTMENT

Insurance Expense

Prepaid Insurance

Aug. 31 Bal.	1,200.00

On August 31, before adjustments, the balance of Prepaid Insurance is $1,200.00, and the balance of Insurance Expense is zero, as shown in the T accounts.

On August 31 Mr. Furman checked the insurance records and found that the value of insurance coverage remaining was $1,100.00. The value of insurance coverage used during the fiscal period is calculated as shown below.

	Prepaid Insurance Balance, August 31		Insurance Coverage Remaining Unused, August 31		Insurance Coverage Used During August
	$1,200.00	−	$1,100.00	=	$100.00

Four questions are asked in analyzing the adjustment for the asset account, Prepaid Insurance.

1. What is the balance of Prepaid Insurance?......... $1,200.00
2. What should the balance be for this account?.... $1,100.00
3. What must be done to correct the account balance?
   Decrease .... $ 100.00
4. What adjustment is made?
   Debit Insurance Expense...................... $ 100.00
   Credit Prepaid Insurance..................... $ 100.00

AFTER ADJUSTMENT

Insurance Expense

Adj. (b)	100.00

Prepaid Insurance

Aug. 31 Bal.	1,200.00	Adj. (b)	100.00
(New Bal.	1,100.00)		

The expense account, Insurance Expense, is increased by a debit, $100.00, the value of insurance used. The balance of Insurance Expense, $100.00, is the value of insurance coverage used from August 1 to August 31. (CONCEPT: *Matching Expenses with Revenue*)

The asset account, Prepaid Insurance, is decreased by a credit, $100.00, the value of insurance used. The debit balance, $1,200.00, *less* the credit adjustment, $100.00, *equals* the new balance, $1,100.00. The new balance of Prepaid Insurance is the same as the amount of insurance coverage unused on August 31.

Rugcare's prepaid insurance adjustment is shown on lines 4 and 12 of the work sheet in Illustration 8-4.

ILLUSTRATION 8-4 Prepaid insurance adjustment on a work sheet

		1	2	3	4
	ACCOUNT TITLE	TRIAL BALANCE		ADJUSTMENTS	
		DEBIT	CREDIT	DEBIT	CREDIT
1	Cash	8 2 7 2 00				1
2	Petty Cash	2 0 0 00				2
3	Supplies	4 9 3 1 00			(a) 2 6 4 7 00	3
4	Prepaid Insurance	1 2 0 0 00			(b) 1 0 0 00	4
12	Insurance Expense			(b) 1 0 0 00		12
13	Miscellaneous Expense	1 0 5 00				13
14	Rent Expense	2 5 0 00				14
15	Repair Expense	1 1 0 00				15
16	Supplies Expense			(a) 2 6 4 7 00		16
17	Utilities Expense	1 1 5 00				17
18		15 8 5 1 00	15 8 5 1 00	2 7 4 7 00	2 7 4 7 00	18
19						19

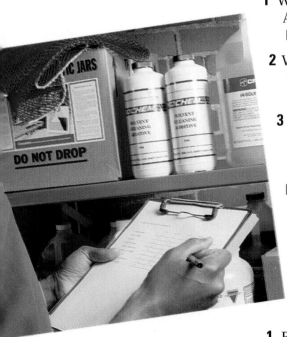

Three steps are used to record the prepaid insurance adjustment on a work sheet.

1 Write the debit amount, *$100.00*, in the work sheet's Adjustments Debit column on the line with the account title Insurance Expense (line 12).

2 Write the credit amount, *$100.00*, in the Adjustments Credit column on the line with the account title Prepaid Insurance (line 4).

3 Label the two parts of this adjustment with a small letter *b* in parentheses *(b)*. The letter *b* identifies the debit and credit amounts as part of the same adjustment.

Proving the Adjustments Columns of a Work Sheet. After all adjustments are recorded in a work sheet's Adjustments columns, the equality of debits and credits for the two columns is proved. Rugcare's completed Adjustments columns are shown in Illustration 8-4.

Three steps are used in proving a work sheet's Adjustments columns.

1 Rule a single line across the two Adjustments columns on the same line as the single line for the Trial Balance columns.

2 Add both the Adjustments Debit and Credit columns. If the two column totals are the same, then debits equal credits for these two columns, and the work sheet's Adjustments columns are in balance. On Rugcare's work sheet, the Adjustments Debit and Credit column totals are $2,747.00. Therefore, the

Adjustments columns on Rugcare's work sheet are in balance. Write each column's total below the single line.

If the two Adjustments column totals are not the same, the Adjustments columns are rechecked and errors corrected before completing the work sheet.

3 Rule double lines across both Adjustments columns. The double lines mean that the totals have been verified as correct.

Extending Financial Statement Information on a Work Sheet

At the end of each fiscal period, Rugcare prepares two financial statements from information on a work sheet. *(CONCEPT: Accounting Period Cycle)* A financial statement that reports assets, liabilities, and owner's equity on a specific date is known as a balance sheet. A financial statement showing the revenue and expenses for a fiscal period is called an **income statement.** The up-to-date account balances on a work sheet are extended to columns for the two financial statements.

Extending Balance Sheet Account Balances on a Work Sheet. The balance sheet accounts are the asset, liability, and owner's equity accounts. Up-to-date balance sheet account balances are extended to the Balance Sheet Debit and Credit columns of the work sheet. The extension of Rugcare's balance sheet account balances is shown on lines 1 through 9 of the work sheet in Illustration 8-5.

Three steps are used in extending balance sheet items on a work sheet.

1 Extend the up-to-date balance of each asset account.

- The balance of Cash in the Trial Balance Debit column is up to date because no adjustment affects this account. Extend the balance of Cash, *$8,272.00,* to the Balance Sheet Debit column. Balances of all asset accounts not affected by adjustments are extended in the same way.

- The balance of Supplies in the Trial Balance Debit column is not up to date because it is affected by an adjustment. Calculate the up-to-date adjusted balance. The debit balance, $4,931.00, *minus* the credit adjustment, $2,647.00, *equals* the up-to-date adjusted balance, $2,284.00. Extend the up-to-date balance, *$2,284.00,* to the Balance Sheet Debit column. The same procedure is used to calculate and extend the up-to-date adjusted balance of the other asset account affected by an adjustment, Prepaid Insurance.

2 Extend the up-to-date balance of each liability account.

- The balance of Butler Cleaning Supplies is the up-to-date balance because no adjustment affects this account. Extend the up-to-date balance, *$1,360.00,* to the Balance Sheet Credit column. The balance of the other liability account is extended in the same way.

FYI

A work sheet is prepared in manual accounting to adjust the accounts and sort amounts needed to prepare financial statements. However, in automated accounting adjustments are prepared from the trial balance and the software automatically generates the financial statements with no need for a work sheet.

ILLUSTRATION 8-5   Balance sheet account balances extended on a work sheet

Rugcare

Work Sheet

For Month Ended August 31, 19--

		1	2	3	4	5	6	7	8	
	ACCOUNT TITLE	TRIAL BALANCE		ADJUSTMENTS		INCOME STATEMENT		BALANCE SHEET		
		DEBIT	CREDIT	DEBIT	CREDIT	DEBIT	CREDIT	DEBIT	CREDIT	
1	Cash	8 2 7 2 00						8 2 7 2 00		1
2	Petty Cash	2 0 0 00						2 0 0 00		2
3	Supplies	4 9 3 1 00			(a) 2 6 4 7 00			2 2 8 4 00		3
4	Prepaid Insurance	1 2 0 0 00			(b) 1 0 0 00			1 1 0 0 00		4
5	Butler Cleaning Supplies		1 3 6 0 00						1 3 6 0 00	5
6	Dale Office Supplies		2 0 0 00						2 0 0 00	6
7	Ben Furman, Capital		10 0 0 0 00						10 0 0 0 00	7
8	Ben Furman, Drawing	6 0 0 00						6 0 0 00		8
9	Income Summary									9
10										10

3 Extend the up-to-date balances of the owner's equity accounts.

- The balance of Ben Furman, Capital in the Trial Balance Credit column is the up-to-date balance because no adjustment affects this account. Extend the balance, *$10,000.00*, to the Balance Sheet Credit column.

- The balance of Ben Furman, Drawing in the Trial Balance Debit column is the up-to-date balance because no adjustment affects this account. Extend the balance, *$600.00*, to the Balance Sheet Debit column.

- Income Summary has no balance in the Trial Balance columns. Therefore, no amount needs to be extended for this account.

Extending Income Statement Account Balances on a Work Sheet. Rugcare's income statement accounts are the revenue and expense accounts. The extension of income statement account balances is shown on lines 10 through 17 of the work sheet in Illustration 8-6.

Two steps are used in extending income statement accounts on a work sheet.

1 Extend the up-to-date balance of the revenue account.

- The balance of Sales in the Trial Balance Credit column is the up-to-date balance because no adjustment affects this account. Extend the balance, *$4,291.00*, to the Income Statement Credit column.

2 Extend the up-to-date balance of each expense account.

- The balance of Advertising Expense in the Trial Balance Debit column is the up-to-date balance because no adjustment affects this account. Extend the balance, *$68.00*, to the Income Statement Debit column. Balances of all expense

Use a ruler when extending amounts on a work sheet to keep track of the line you are on.

ILLUSTRATION 8-6   Income statement account balances extended on a work sheet

Rugcare
Work Sheet
For Month Ended August 31, 19--

	ACCOUNT TITLE	TRIAL BALANCE		ADJUSTMENTS		INCOME STATEMENT		BALANCE SHEET		
		DEBIT	CREDIT	DEBIT	CREDIT	DEBIT	CREDIT	DEBIT	CREDIT	
10	Sales		4 2 9 1 00				4 2 9 1 00			10
11	Advertising Expense	6 8 00				6 8 00				11
12	Insurance Expense			(b) 1 0 0 00		1 0 0 00				12
13	Miscellaneous Expense	1 0 5 00				1 0 5 00				13
14	Rent Expense	2 5 0 00				2 5 0 00				14
15	Repair Expense	1 1 0 00				1 1 0 00				15
16	Supplies Expense			(a) 2 6 4 7 00		2 6 4 7 00				16
17	Utilities Expense	1 1 5 00				1 1 5 00				17
18		15 8 5 1 00	15 8 5 1 00	2 7 4 7 00	2 7 4 7 00					18
19										19

accounts not affected by adjustments are extended in the same way.

- The balance of Insurance Expense in the Trial Balance columns is zero. This zero balance is not the up-to-date balance because this account is affected by an adjustment. Calculate the up-to-date adjusted balance. The debit balance, $0.00, *plus* the debit adjustment, $100.00, *equals* the adjusted balance, $100.00. Extend the up-to-date adjusted debit balance, *$100.00*, to the Income Statement Debit column. The same procedure is used to calculate and extend the up-to-date adjusted balance of each expense account affected by an adjustment.

Calculating and Recording Net Income on a Work Sheet. The difference between total revenue and total expenses when total revenue is greater is called **net income**. Rugcare's August net income is shown on line 19 of the work sheet in Illustration 8-7.

Five steps are used in calculating net income on a work sheet.

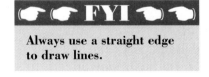

Always use a straight edge to draw lines.

1 Rule a single line across the four Income Statement and Balance Sheet columns.

2 Add both the Income Statement and Balance Sheet columns. Write the totals below the single line.

3 Calculate the net income. Rugcare's net income is calculated as shown below.

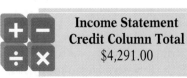

	Income Statement Credit Column Total	−	Income Statement Debit Column Total	=	Net Income
	$4,291.00	−	$3,395.00	=	$896.00

ILLUSTRATION 8-7   Completed work sheet

Rugcare

Work Sheet

For Month Ended August 31, 19--

		1	2	3	4	5	6	7	8	
	ACCOUNT TITLE	TRIAL BALANCE		ADJUSTMENTS		INCOME STATEMENT		BALANCE SHEET		
		DEBIT	CREDIT	DEBIT	CREDIT	DEBIT	CREDIT	DEBIT	CREDIT	
1	Cash	8272 00						8272 00		1
2	Petty Cash	200 00						200 00		2
3	Supplies	4931 00			(a) 2647 00			2284 00		3
4	Prepaid Insurance	1200 00			(b) 100 00			1100 00		4
5	Butler Cleaning Supplies		1360 00						1360 00	5
6	Dale Office Supplies		200 00						200 00	6
7	Ben Furman, Capital		10000 00						10000 00	7
8	Ben Furman, Drawing	600 00						600 00		8
9	Income Summary									9
10	Sales		4291 00				4291 00			10
11	Advertising Expense	68 00				68 00				11
12	Insurance Expense			(b) 100 00		100 00				12
13	Miscellaneous Expense	105 00				105 00				13
14	Rent Expense	250 00				250 00				14
15	Repair Expense	110 00				110 00				15
16	Supplies Expense			(a) 2647 00		2647 00				16
17	Utilities Expense	115 00				115 00				17
18		15851 00	15851 00	2747 00	2747 00	3395 00	4291 00	12456 00	11560 00	18
19	Net Income					896 00			896 00	19
20						4291 00	4291 00	12456 00	12456 00	20
21										21

Rugcare's August work sheet shows a net income because the Income Statement Credit column (revenue) exceeds the Income Statement Debit column (expenses).

4 Write the amount of net income, *$896.00*, below the Income Statement Debit column total. Write the words, *Net Income*, on the same line in the Account Title column.

5 Extend the amount of net income, *$896.00*, to the Balance Sheet Credit column on the same line as the words *Net Income*. The owner's equity account, Ben Furman, Capital, is increased by a credit. Therefore, the net income amount is extended to the Balance Sheet Credit column.

Totaling and Ruling a Work Sheet. Four steps are used in totaling and ruling a work sheet.

1 Rule a single line across the four Income Statement and Balance Sheet columns just below the net income amounts.

2 Add the subtotal and net income amount for each column to get proving totals for the Income Statement and Balance Sheet columns. Write the proving totals below the single line.

Proving totals are used to determine that the debits equal credits for each pair of column totals.

3 Check the equality of the proving totals for each pair of columns. A summary of preparing a work sheet is shown on the Work Sheet Overlay on pages 176A through 176C.

- As shown on line 20 of the work sheet in Illustration 8-7, the proving totals for the Income Statement columns, $4,291.00, are the same.
- As shown on line 20 of the work sheet in Illustration 8-7, the proving totals for the Balance Sheet columns, $12,456.00, are the same.

4 Rule double lines across the Income Statement and Balance Sheet columns. The double lines mean that the totals have been verified as correct.

Calculating and Recording a Net Loss on a Work Sheet. Rugcare's completed work sheet shows a net income. However, a business might have a net loss to report. The difference between total revenue and total expenses when total expenses is greater is called a **net loss**. A net loss on a work sheet is shown in Illustration 8-8.

ILLUSTRATION 8-8 Net loss shown on a work sheet

	ACCOUNT TITLE		5 INCOME STATEMENT DEBIT	6 CREDIT	7 BALANCE SHEET DEBIT	8 CREDIT	
19			2 0 0 0 00	1 9 0 0 00	5 4 0 0 00	5 5 0 0 00	19
20	Net Loss			1 0 0 00	1 0 0 00		20
21			2 0 0 0 00	2 0 0 0 00	5 5 0 0 00	5 5 0 0 00	21
22							22
23							23

Six steps are used in completing a work sheet with a net loss.

1 Rule a single line across the four Income Statement and Balance Sheet columns.

2 Add both the Income Statement and Balance Sheet columns. Write the totals below the single line.

3 The net loss is calculated as shown below.

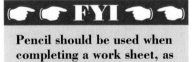

FYI

Pencil should be used when completing a work sheet, as a work sheet is not a permanent record.

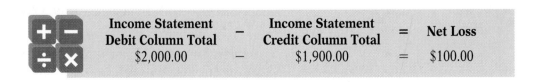

	Income Statement Debit Column Total	−	Income Statement Credit Column Total	=	Net Loss
	$2,000.00	−	$1,900.00	=	$100.00

The Income Statement Debit column total (expenses) is greater than the Income Statement Credit column total (revenue). Therefore, because expenses exceed revenue, there is a net loss.

4 Write the amount of net loss, *$100.00*, below the Income Statement Credit column total. Write the words, *Net Loss*, on the same line in the Account Title column.

5 Extend the amount of net loss, *$100.00*, to the Balance Sheet Debit column on the same line as the words *Net Loss*. The owner's capital account is decreased by a debit. Therefore, a net loss is extended to the Balance Sheet Debit column.

6 Total and rule the work sheet using the same steps as when there is net income.

FINDING AND CORRECTING ERRORS

Some errors in accounting records are not discovered until a work sheet is prepared. For example, a debit to the supplies account may not have been posted from a journal to the general ledger supplies account. The omission may not be discovered until the work sheet's trial balance does not balance. Also, information may be transferred incorrectly from general ledger accounts to the work sheet's trial balance. Additional errors may be made on a work sheet, such as recording adjustment information incorrectly or adding columns incorrectly. In addition, errors may be made in extending amounts to the Income Statement and Balance Sheet columns.

Any errors found on a work sheet must be corrected before any further work is completed. If an incorrect amount is found on a work sheet, erase the error and replace it with the correct amount. If an amount is written in an incorrect column, erase the amount and record it in the correct column. If column totals do not balance, add the columns again.

FYI

Use the Work Sheet Overlay to review the steps for preparing a work sheet.

Checking for Typical Arithmetic Errors

When two column totals are not in balance, subtract the smaller total from the larger total to find the difference. Check the difference between the two amounts against the following guides.

1 *The difference is 1, such as $.01, $.10, $1.00, or $10.00.* For example, if the totals of the two columns are Debit, $12,542.00 and Credit, $12,543.00, the difference between the two columns is $1.00. The error is most likely in addition. Add the columns again.

2 *The difference can be divided evenly by 2.* For example, the difference between two column totals is $48.00. The differ-

Am I a Software Pirate?

Computer software is created by a variety of companies and individuals. Some software is created by large companies that employ many computer programmers. However, a large selection of software is also created by individual computer programmers.

Software created by large companies is typically sold in stores. Included with the software is a user's manual and a license agreement. The license agreement usually states that the company retains legal ownership of the software. The company gives the buyer the right to use the software according to stipulations provided in the license agreement. For example, most companies require that software be used only on a single computer and that no copies be made. Thus, a business with 15 computers is required to purchase 15 copies of the software.

Many individuals also create software. Lacking the financial resources of the large companies, these software authors have developed a concept referred to as "shareware" to distribute their software. Individuals are encouraged to copy shareware and distribute copies to others. In return,

ence, $48.00, *divided* by 2 *equals* $24.00 with no remainder. Look for a $24.00 amount in the Trial Balance columns of the work sheet. If the amount is found, check to make sure it has been recorded in the correct Trial Balance Debit or Credit column. A $24.00 debit amount recorded in a credit column results in a difference between column totals of $48.00. If the error is not found on the work sheet, check the general ledger accounts and journal entries. An entry for $24.00 may have been recorded in an incorrect column in the journal or in an account.

3 ***The difference can be divided evenly by 9.*** For example, the difference between two columns is $45.00. The difference, $45.00, *divided* by 9 *equals* $5.00 with no remainder. When the difference can be divided equally by 9, look for transposed numbers such as 54 written as 45 or 19 written as 91. Also, check for a "slide." A "slide" occurs when numbers are moved to the right or left in an amount column. For example, $12.00 is recorded as $120.00 or $350.00 is recorded as $35.00.

4 ***The difference is an omitted amount.*** Look for an amount equal to the difference. If the difference is $50.00, look for an account balance of $50.00 that has not been extended. Look for any $50.00 amount on the work sheet and determine if it has been handled correctly. Look in the accounts and journals for a $50.00 amount, and check if that amount has been handled correctly. Failure to record a $50.00 account balance will make a work sheet's Trial Balance column totals differ by $50.00.

the individual is instructed to send the author a registration fee if the individual uses the software. Some shareware authors request a specific dollar amount while other authors ask users to pay whatever they consider to be a fair amount.

INSTRUCTIONS Use the three-step checklist to analyze whether each of the following situations demonstrates ethical behavior.

Situation 1. A large company purchased one copy of a copyrighted software program and made numerous copies for use on other computers.

Situation 2. An individual used a shareware program extensively but did not send the shareware author the requested registration fee.

Situation 3. A public university, lacking adequate funds to purchase the required number of copies of a copyrighted electronic spreadsheet program, purchased a single copy and made numerous copies. A label stating "For educational purposes only" was attached to each copy of the software. Students regularly copy the software for personal use.

Between 1960 and 1990 the number of accountants more than doubled.

Checking for Errors in the Trial Balance Columns

1 Have all general ledger account balances been copied in the Trial Balance columns correctly?

2 Have all general ledger account balances been recorded in the correct Trial Balance column?

Correct any errors found and add the columns again.

Checking for Errors in the Adjustments Columns

1 Do the debits equal the credits for each adjustment? Use the small letters that label each part of an adjustment to help check accuracy and equality of debits and credits.

2 Is the amount for each adjustment correct?

Correct any errors found and add the columns again.

Checking for Errors in the Income Statement and Balance Sheet Columns

1 Has each amount been copied correctly when extended to the Income Statement or Balance Sheet column?

2 Has each account balance been extended to the correct Income Statement or Balance Sheet column?

3 Has the net income or net loss been calculated correctly?

4 Has the net income or net loss been recorded in the correct Income Statement or Balance Sheet column?

Correct any errors found and add the columns again.

Checking for Errors in Posting to General Ledger Accounts

Sometimes a pair of work sheet columns do not balance, and an error cannot be found on the work sheet. If this is the situation, check the posting from the journal to the general ledger accounts. As each item in an account or a journal entry is verified, a check mark should be placed next to it. The check mark indicates that the item has been checked for accuracy.

1 Have all amounts that need to be posted actually been posted from the journal?

- For an amount that has not been posted, complete the posting to the correct account.
- In all cases where posting is corrected, recalculate the account balance and correct it on the work sheet.

  When an omitted posting is recorded as described above, the dates in the general ledger accounts may be out of order.

2 Have all amounts been posted to the correct accounts?

- For an amount posted to the wrong account, draw a line through the entire incorrect entry. Recalculate the account balance.
- Record the posting in the correct account. Recalculate the account balance, and correct the work sheet. Make the correction in the general ledger accounts, as shown in Illustration 8-9.

ILLUSTRATION 8-9   Correcting an error in posting to the wrong account

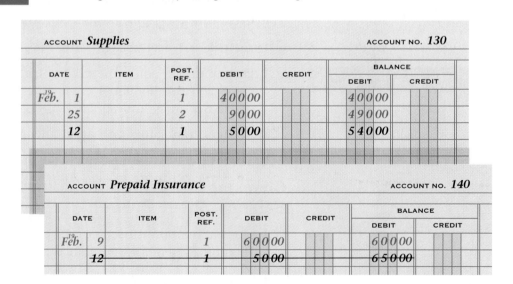

Errors in permanent records should *never* be erased. Erasures in permanent records raise questions about whether important financial information has been altered.

3 Have all amounts been written correctly? Have all amounts been posted to the correct Debit or Credit columns of an account?

- If an amount has been written incorrectly, draw a line through the incorrect amount. Write the correct amount just above the correction in the same space. Recalculate the account balance, and correct the account balance on the work sheet. Correcting an error in writing an amount incorrectly is shown on the first line of the utilities expense account in Illustration 8-10.

ILLUSTRATION 8-10 Correcting an amount written incorrectly and an error in posting to the wrong column of an account

ACCOUNT Utilities Expense						ACCOUNT NO. 570
DATE	ITEM	POST. REF.	DEBIT	CREDIT	BALANCE DEBIT	CREDIT
Sept. 8		1	70 00		~~70 0 00~~ 7 0 00	
17		1	2 7 00	~~2 7 00~~	~~67 3 00~~ 9 7 00	

- For an amount posted to the wrong amount column, draw a line through the incorrect item in the account. Record the posting in the correct amount column. Recalculate the account balance, and correct the work sheet. Correcting an error in posting to a wrong amount column is shown on the second line of the utilities expense account in Illustration 8-10.

Checking for Errors in Journal Entries

1 Do debits equal credits in each journal entry?

2 Is each journal entry amount recorded in the correct journal column?

3 Is information in the Account Title column correct for each journal entry?

4 Are all of the journal amount column totals correct?

5 Does the sum of debit column totals equal the sum of credit column totals in the journal?

6 Have all transactions been recorded?

Some suggestions for correcting errors in journal entries are described in Chapter 5.

Preventing Errors

The best way to prevent errors is to work carefully at all times. Check the work at each step in an accounting procedure. Most errors occur in doing the required arithmetic, especially in adding columns. When possible, use a calculator to add columns. When an error is discovered, do no more work until the cause of the error is found and corrections are made.

FYI

Never erase ink or it will look as if the numbers were altered. Altered numbers arouse suspicion of wrongdoing.

Audit Your Understanding

1. What is the first step in checking for arithmetic errors when two column totals are not in balance?

2. What is one way to check for an error caused by transposed numbers?

3. What term is used to describe an error that occurs when numbers are moved to the right or left in an amount column?

What is the meaning of each of the following?

1. **fiscal period**
2. **work sheet**
3. **trial balance**
4. **adjustments**
5. **income statement**
6. **net income**
7. **net loss**

QUESTIONS FOR INDIVIDUAL STUDY EPT(b)

1. What are typical lengths of fiscal periods?
2. Which accounting concept is being applied when a business summarizes and reports financial information for a fiscal period?
3. What are four reasons for preparing a work sheet?
4. Why is a work sheet prepared in pencil?
5. How is the equality of debits and credits proved in a general ledger?
6. Why is an adjustment for supplies planned at the end of a fiscal period?
7. What accounts are affected, and how, by the adjustment for supplies?
8. After a supplies adjustment, what does the supplies account balance represent?
9. What accounts are affected, and how, by the adjustment for prepaid insurance?
10. Why are the Adjustments columns on a work sheet totaled?
11. What two financial statements are prepared from information on a work sheet?
12. If a work sheet shows a net income, in which two columns will the net income be recorded?
13. How are the amounts in the Income Statement and Balance Sheet columns of a work sheet proved?
14. If two work sheet column totals are not equal and the difference between the totals is one, what is the most likely error?
15. If two work sheet column totals are not equal and the difference between the totals is evenly divisible by nine, what is the most likely error?

CASES FOR CRITICAL THINKING EPT(c,e)

CASE 1 Peter Dowther owns a small business. At the end of a fiscal period, he does not make an adjustment for supplies. Are Mr. Dowther's accounting procedures correct? What effect will Mr. Dowther's procedures have on the business' financial reporting? Explain your answer.

CASE 2 When posting amounts from a journal to general ledger accounts, a $10.00 debit to Supplies is mistakenly posted as a credit to Utilities Expense. Will this error be discovered when the work sheet is prepared? Explain.

DRILLS FOR UNDERSTANDING EPT(d)

DRILL 8-D1 Extending account balances on a work sheet

A partial work sheet form with account titles is given in the working papers that accompany this textbook.

INSTRUCTIONS:

1. Place a check mark in either Column 1 or 2 to indicate the Trial Balance column in which each account's balance will appear. The first account is given as an example.
2. Place a check mark in Columns 5, 6, 7, or 8 to indicate the column to which each up-to-date account balance will be extended.

DRILL 8-D2 Calculating net income or net loss on a work sheet

The column totals from the work sheets of five different businesses are given in the working papers that accompany this textbook.

INSTRUCTIONS:

Complete the following for each company. The amounts for Company A are given as an example.

1. Calculate the amount of net income or net loss. Write the amount on line 2 in the correct columns. Label the amount as *Net Income* or *Net Loss*.
2. Add the amounts in each column. Write the totals on line 3.
3. Verify the accuracy of your proving totals.

APPLICATION PROBLEMS   EPT(c,d,e)

PROBLEM 8-1 Completing a work sheet

On September 30 of the current year, CleanLawn has the following general ledger accounts and balances. The business uses a monthly fiscal period.

Account Titles	Account Balances Debit	Credit
Cash.	$3,000.00	
Petty Cash	100.00	
Supplies.	2,000.00	
Prepaid Insurance	900.00	
Bix Supplies		$ 600.00
OfficeWorld.		100.00
Dorothy Daily, Capital		4,100.00
Dorothy Daily, Drawing	200.00	
Income Summary.	—	—
Sales		2,505.00
Advertising Expense	75.00	
Insurance Expense.	—	
Miscellaneous Expense.	110.00	
Rent Expense.	600.00	
Repair Expense	180.00	
Supplies Expense.	—	
Utilities Expense	140.00	

INSTRUCTIONS:

1. Prepare the heading and trial balance on a work sheet. Total and rule the Trial Balance columns.
2. Analyze the following adjustment information into debit and credit parts. Record the adjustments on the work sheet.

Adjustment Information, September 30

Supplies on hand	$1,100.00
Value of prepaid insurance	600.00

3. Total and rule the Adjustments columns.
4. Extend the up-to-date balances to the Balance Sheet or Income Statement columns.
5. Rule a single line across the Income Statement and Balance Sheet columns. Total each column. Calculate and record the net income or net loss. Label the amount in the Account Title column.
6. Total and rule the Income Statement and Balance Sheet columns.

PROBLEM 8-2 Completing a work sheet

On October 31 of the current year, Village Service Co. has the following general ledger accounts and balances. The business uses a monthly fiscal period.

Account Titles	Account Balances Debit	Credit
Cash.	$4,900.00	
Petty Cash	300.00	
Supplies.	2,500.00	
Prepaid Insurance	2,100.00	
National Supplies		$ 1,400.00
Office Distributors		1,200.00
Wensk Movies		800.00
Susan Haile, Capital.		6,000.00
Susan Haile, Drawing	1,200.00	
Income Summary.	—	—
Sales		20,100.00
Advertising Expense	4,200.00	
Insurance Expense.	—	
Miscellaneous Expense.	600.00	
Rent Expense.	8,000.00	
Repair Expense	2,400.00	
Supplies Expense.	—	
Utilities Expense	3,300.00	

INSTRUCTIONS:

1. Prepare the heading and trial balance on a work sheet. Total and rule the Trial Balance columns.
2. Analyze the following adjustment information into debit and credit parts. Record the adjustments on the work sheet.

Adjustment Information, October 31

Supplies on hand.	$1,500.00
Value of prepaid insurance	900.00

3. Total and rule the Adjustments columns.
4. Extend the up-to-date balances to the Balance Sheet or Income Statement columns.
5. Rule a single line across the Income Statement and Balance Sheet columns. Total each column. Calculate and record the net income or net loss. Label the amount in the Account Title column.
6. Total and rule the Income Statement and Balance Sheet columns.

PROBLEM 8-3 Finding and correcting errors in accounting records

Paul Coty has completed the September monthly work sheet for his business, LeafyLift. The work sheet and general ledger accounts are given in the working papers accompanying this textbook.

Mr. Coty believes that he has made one or more errors in preparing the work sheet. He asks you to help him verify the work sheet.

INSTRUCTIONS:

1. Examine the work sheet and the general ledger accounts. Make a list of the errors you find.
2. Correct any errors you find in the general ledger accounts.
3. Prepare a corrected work sheet.

ENRICHMENT PROBLEMS   EPT(c,d)

MASTERY PROBLEM 8-M Completing a work sheet

On April 30 of the current year, FastGrow has the following general ledger accounts and balances. The business uses a monthly fiscal period.

Account Titles	Account Balances Debit	Credit
Cash.	$5,800.00	
Petty Cash	200.00	

Supplies.	4,000.00	
Prepaid Insurance	1,000.00	
Wheaton Supplies		$ 200.00
Norton Company		115.00
Roger Bently, Capital.		7,200.00
Roger Bently, Drawing	400.00	
Income Summary.	—	—
Sales		5,300.00
Advertising Expense	325.00	
Insurance Expense.	—	
Miscellaneous Expense.	140.00	
Rent Expense.	500.00	
Supplies Expense.	—	
Utilities Expense	450.00	

INSTRUCTIONS:

1. Prepare the heading and trial balance on a work sheet. Total and rule the Trial Balance columns.
2. Analyze the following adjustment information into debit and credit parts. Record the adjustments on the work sheet.

Adjustment Information, April 30

Supplies inventory.	$2,050.00
Value of prepaid insurance.	450.00

3. Extend the up-to-date account balances to the Balance Sheet or Income Statement columns.
4. Complete the work sheet.

CHALLENGE PROBLEM 8-C Completing a work sheet

APPLICATION

Clean and Mow had a small fire in its office. The fire destroyed some of the accounting records. On November 30 of the current year, the end of a monthly fiscal period, the following information was constructed from the remaining records and other sources.

Remains of the general ledger:

Account Titles	Account Balances
Supplies.	$1,800.00
Donna Edwards, Drawing	150.00
Sales	4,000.00
Advertising Expense	420.00
Rent Expense.	700.00
Utilities Expense	490.00

Information from the business' checkbook:
Cash balance on last unused check stub, $3,400.00
Total payments for miscellaneous expense, $60.00
Total payments for insurance, $325.00

Information obtained through inquiries to other businesses:
Owed to Outdoor Supplies, $2,000.00
Value of prepaid insurance, November 30, $250.00

Information obtained by counting supplies on hand after the fire:
Supplies on hand, $1,100.00

INSTRUCTIONS:

1. From the information given, prepare a heading and reconstruct a trial balance on a work sheet. The owner's capital account balance is the difference between the total of all debit account balances minus the total of all credit account balances.
2. Complete the work sheet.

Financial Statements for a Proprietorship

ENABLING PERFORMANCE TASKS

After studying Chapter 9, you will be able to:

a Define the accounting term related to financial statements for a service business organized as a proprietorship.

b Identify accounting concepts and practices related to preparation of financial statements for a service business organized as a proprietorship.

c Prepare an income statement for a service business organized as a proprietorship.

d Analyze an income statement using component percentages.

e Prepare a balance sheet for a service business organized as a proprietorship.

TERMS PREVIEW

component percentage

The financial information needed by managers and owners to make good business decisions can be found in the general ledger accounts. However, the information in the general ledger is very detailed. Therefore, to make this general ledger information more usable, the information is summarized, organized, and reported to the owners and managers.

Also, *all* financial information *must* be reported if good business decisions are to be made. A financial statement with incomplete information is similar to a book with missing pages. The complete story is not told. If a business has both rent and utilities expenses but reports only the rent expense, managers will have incomplete information on which to base decisions. The accounting concept, *Adequate Disclosure*, is applied when financial statements contain all information necessary to understand a business' financial condition. *(CONCEPT: Adequate Disclosure)*

Rugcare prepares two financial statements: an income statement and a balance sheet. Rugcare always prepares financial statements at the end of each monthly fiscal period. *(CONCEPT: Accounting Period Cycle)* The time periods covered by Rugcare's financial statements are shown in Illustration 9-1.

ILLUSTRATION 9-1   Time periods for financial statements

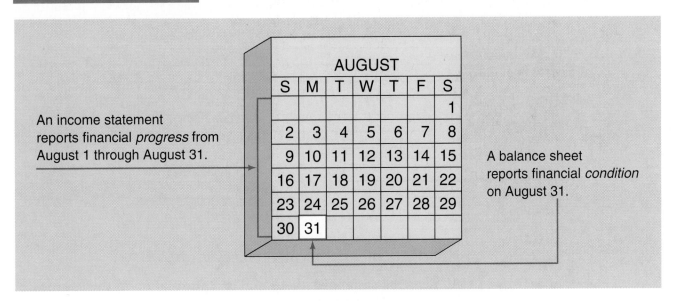

An income statement reports financial *progress* from August 1 through August 31.

A balance sheet reports financial *condition* on August 31.

An income statement reports financial information over a *specific period of time*, indicating the financial *progress* of a business in earning a net income or net loss.

A balance sheet reports financial information on a *specific date*, indicating the financial *condition* of a business. The financial condition of a business refers to its financial strength. If a business has adequate available assets and few liabilities, that business is financially strong. If the business' financial condition is not strong, adverse changes in the economy might cause the business to fail.

INCOME STATEMENT

Revenue is the earnings of a business from business activities. Expenses are the amounts a business pays to operate the business and earn the revenue. The revenue earned and the expenses incurred to earn that revenue are reported in the same fiscal period. (CONCEPT: Matching Expenses with Revenue)

Information needed to prepare financial statements could be obtained from the general ledger accounts. However, a work sheet is prepared to assist in planning the financial statements. Rugcare's income statement information on a work sheet is shown in Illustration 9-2.

Information needed to prepare Rugcare's income statement is obtained from two places on the work sheet. Account titles are obtained from the work sheet's Account Title column. Account balances are obtained from the work sheet's Income Statement columns.

The income statement for a service business has four sections: (1) heading, (2) revenue, (3) expenses, and (4) net income or net loss.

FYI

Information needed to prepare the income statement is obtained from two places on the work sheet. Account titles are obtained from the work sheet's Account Title column. Account balances are obtained from the work sheet's Income Statement columns.

ILLUSTRATION 9-2   Income statement information on a work sheet

	ACCOUNT TITLE		5 INCOME STATEMENT DEBIT	6 INCOME STATEMENT CREDIT	7 BALANCE SHEET DEBIT	8 BALANCE SHEET CREDIT	
10	Sales			4 2 9 1 00			10
11	Advertising Expense		6 8 00				11
12	Insurance Expense		1 0 0 00				12
13	Miscellaneous Expense		1 0 5 00				13
14	Rent Expense		2 5 0 00				14
15	Repair Expense		1 1 0 00				15
16	Supplies Expense		2 6 4 7 00				16
17	Utilities Expense		1 1 5 00				17
18			3 3 9 5 00	4 2 9 1 00			18
19	Net Income		8 9 6 00				19
20			4 2 9 1 00	4 2 9 1 00			20

Heading of an Income Statement

All financial statements have similar information in their three-line headings. (1) The name of the business. (2) The name of the statement. (3) The date of the statement. The three-line heading for Rugcare's income statement is shown in Illustration 9-3.

ILLUSTRATION 9-3   Heading of an income statement

Rugcare
Income Statement
For Month Ended August 31, 19--

The income statement's date shows that this income statement reports information for the one-month fiscal period from August 1 through August 31.

Revenue Section of an Income Statement

Information from the work sheet's Account Title column and Income Statement Credit column is used to prepare the revenue section. The revenue section of an income statement is shown in Illustration 9-4.

Revenue section of an income statement

Revenue:		
Sales		4 2 9 1 00

Write the name of this section, *Revenue:*, at the extreme left of the wide column on the first line. Write the title of the revenue account, *Sales*, on the next line indented about one centimeter. Record the balance of the account, *$4,291.00*, on the same line in the second amount column.

Expenses Section of an Income Statement

Information from the work sheet's Account Title column and Income Statement Debit column is used to prepare the expenses section. The expenses section of Rugcare's income statement is shown in Illustration 9-5.

Expenses section of an income statement

Expenses:		
Advertising Expense	6 8 00	
Insurance Expense	1 0 0 00	
Miscellaneous Expense	1 0 5 00	
Rent Expense	2 5 0 00	
Repair Expense	1 1 0 00	
Supplies Expense	2 6 4 7 00	
Utilities Expense	1 1 5 00	
Total Expenses		3 3 9 5 00

Write the name of this section, *Expenses:*, at the extreme left of the wide column on the next blank line. Write the title of each expense account in the wide column indented about one centimeter. Record the balance of each expense account in the first amount column on the same line as the account title.

To indicate addition, rule a single line across the first amount column under the last expense account balance. Write the words, *Total Expenses*, on the next blank line in the wide column. Record the amount of total expenses, *$3,395.00*, on the same line in the second amount column.

Net Income Section of an Income Statement

The amount of net income is calculated and verified using two steps.

1 The net income is calculated from information on the income statement as shown below.

	Total Revenue	−	Total Expenses	=	Net Income
	$4,291.00	−	$3,395.00	=	$896.00

2 The amount of net income, *$896.00*, is compared with the net income shown on the work sheet, Illustration 9-2. The net income calculated for the income statement and the net income shown on the work sheet must be the same. The net income calculated for Rugcare's income statement, $896.00, is the same as that on the work sheet.

If the net income calculated for the income statement is not the same as that shown on the work sheet, an error has been made. No more work on the income statement should be completed until the error is found and corrected.

A single line is drawn across the second amount column just below the amount of total expenses, as shown in Illustration 9-6.

Write the words, *Net Income*, on the next line at the extreme left of the wide column. On the same line, record the amount of net income, *$896.00*, in the second amount column. Rule double lines across both amount columns below the amount of net income to show that the amount has been verified as correct. Rugcare's completed income statement is shown in Illustration 9-6.

If total expenses exceed total revenue, a net loss is reported on an income statement. When a net loss is reported, write the words, *Net Loss*, in the wide column. Subtract the total expenses from the revenue to calculate the net loss. Record the amount of net loss in the second amount column in parentheses. An amount written in parentheses on a financial statement indicates a negative amount.

Component Percentage Analysis of an Income Statement

For a service business, the revenue reported on an income statement includes two components: (1) total expenses and (2) net income. To make decisions about future operations, Mr. Furman

ILLUSTRATION 9-6   An income statement

Rugcare Income Statement For Month Ended August 31, 19--				% OF SALES
Revenue:				
Sales			4 2 9 1 00	100.0
Expenses:				
Advertising Expense		6 8 00		
Insurance Expense		1 0 0 00		
Miscellaneous Expense		1 0 5 00		
Rent Expense		2 5 0 00		
Repair Expense		1 1 0 00		
Supplies Expense		2 6 4 7 00		
Utilities Expense		1 1 5 00		
Total Expenses			3 3 9 5 00	79.1
Net Income			8 9 6 00	20.9

analyzes relationships between these two income statement components and the total sales. The percentage relationship between one financial statement item and the total that includes that item is called a **component percentage**. On an income statement, component percentages are calculated by dividing the amount of each component by the total amount of sales. Rugcare calculates a component percentage for total expenses and net income. The relationship between each component and total sales is shown in a separate column on the income statement at the right of the amount columns.

Acceptable Component Percentages. For a component percentage to be useful, Mr. Furman needs to know what component percentages are acceptable for businesses similar to Rugcare. Various industry organizations publish average percentages for similar businesses. In the future Mr. Furman could also compare Rugcare's component percentages from one fiscal period with the percentages of previous fiscal periods.

Total Expenses Component Percentage. The total expenses component percentage, based on information from the August income statement shown in Illustration 9-6, is calculated as shown below.

	Total Expenses	÷	Total Sales	=	Total Expenses Component Percentage
	$3,395.00	÷	$4,291.00	=	79.1%

For businesses similar to Rugcare, an acceptable total expenses component percentage is not more than 80.0%. Therefore, Rugcare's percentage, 79.1%, is less than 80.0% and is acceptable.

Net Income Component Percentage.   The net income component percentage, based on information from the August income statement, is calculated as shown below.

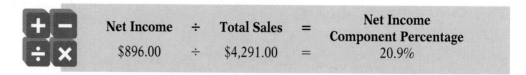

	Net Income	÷	Total Sales	=	Net Income Component Percentage
	$896.00	÷	$4,291.00	=	20.9%

For businesses similar to Rugcare, an acceptable net income component percentage is not less than 20.0%. Therefore, Rugcare's percentage, 20.9%, is greater than 20.0% and is acceptable. The net income component percentage will improve if Rugcare can reduce total expenses in future months. Also, the net income component percentage will improve if Rugcare can increase the amount of revenue in future months.

When there is a net loss, the component percentage for net loss is written in parentheses. A net loss is considered unacceptable.

Income Statement with Two Sources of Revenue

Rugcare receives revenue from only one source, the sale of services for rug and carpet cleaning. Milton Lawn Service receives revenue from two sources, the sale of services to fertilize lawns and the sale of services to trim and care for trees. The business' owner wants to know how much revenue is earned from each source. Therefore, the business uses two revenue accounts: Sales—Lawns and Sales—Tree Care.

When an income statement is prepared for Milton Lawn Service, both revenue accounts are listed, as shown in Illustration 9-7.

ILLUSTRATION 9-7   Revenue section of an income statement showing two sources of revenue

Milton Lawn Service				% OF SALES
Income Statement				
For Month Ended August 31, 19--				
Revenue:				
Sales—Lawns	3 3 6 0 00			
Sales—Tree Care	2 2 5 0 00			
Total Sales			5 6 1 0 00	100.0
Expenses:				

Only the revenue section of Milton Lawn Service's income statement differs from the income statement prepared by Rugcare. Write the section heading, *Revenue:*, at the left of the wide column. Write the titles of both revenue accounts in the wide column indented about one centimeter. Record the balance of each account in the first amount column on the same line as the account title. Total the two revenue account balances. Write the total amount on the next line in the second amount column. Write the words, *Total Sales*, in the wide column indented about one centimeter on the same line as the total revenue amount.

BALANCE SHEET

Information about assets, liabilities, and owner's equity might be obtained from the general ledger accounts or from a work sheet. However, the information is easier to use if reported in an organized manner such as on a balance sheet. Rugcare's balance sheet information on a work sheet is shown in Illustration 9-8.

ILLUSTRATION 9-8   Balance sheet information on a work sheet

	ACCOUNT TITLE	7 BALANCE SHEET DEBIT	8 BALANCE SHEET CREDIT	
1	Cash	8 2 7 2 00		1
2	Petty Cash	2 0 0 00		2
3	Supplies	2 2 8 4 00		3
4	Prepaid Insurance	1 1 0 0 00		4
5	Butler Cleaning Supplies		1 3 6 0 00	5
6	Dale Office Supplies		2 0 0 00	6
7	Ben Furman, Capital		10 0 0 0 00	7
8	Ben Furman, Drawing	6 0 0 00		8
17				17
18		12 4 5 6 00	11 5 6 0 00	18
19	Net Income		8 9 6 00	19
20		12 4 5 6 00	12 4 5 6 00	20

Information needed to prepare Rugcare's balance sheet is obtained from two places on the work sheet. Account titles are obtained from the work sheet's Account Title column. Account balances are obtained from the work sheet's Balance Sheet columns.

A balance sheet has four sections: (1) heading, (2) assets, (3) liabilities, and (4) owner's equity.

Heading of a Balance Sheet

The heading of a balance sheet consists of three lines. (1) The name of the business. (2) The name of the statement. (3) The date of the statement. Rugcare's balance sheet heading is shown in Illustration 9-9.

ILLUSTRATION 9-9   Heading of a balance sheet

Rugcare
Balance Sheet
August 31, 19--

Assets, liabilities, and owner's equity are reported on Rugcare's balance sheet as of a specific date, August 31.

Assets Section of a Balance Sheet

A balance sheet reports information about the elements of the accounting equation.

Assets = Liabilities + Owner's Equity

The assets are on the LEFT side of the accounting equation and on the LEFT side of Rugcare's balance sheet.

The information needed to prepare the assets section is obtained from the work sheet's Account Title column and the Balance Sheet Debit column. The assets section of Rugcare's balance sheet is shown in Illustration 9-10.

ILLUSTRATION 9-10   Assets section of a balance sheet

Assets					
Cash	8 2 7 2 00				
Petty Cash	2 0 0 00				
Supplies	2 2 8 4 00				
Prepaid Insurance	1 1 0 0 00				

Write the title of the section, *Assets*, in the middle of the left wide column. Under the heading write the titles of all asset accounts. Record the balance of each asset account in the left amount column on the same line as the account title.

Equities Section of a Balance Sheet

FYI

The word Liabilities can be abbreviated as "Liab."

Two kinds of equities are reported on a balance sheet: (1) liabilities and (2) owner's equity. Liabilities and owner's equity are on the RIGHT side of the accounting equation and on the RIGHT side of Rugcare's balance sheet.

Liabilities Section of a Balance Sheet. The information needed to prepare the liabilities section is obtained from the work sheet's Account Title column and the Balance Sheet Credit column. The liabilities are reported on a balance sheet as shown in Illustration 9-11.

ILLUSTRATION 9-11

Liabilities section of a balance sheet

					Liabilities			
					Butler Cleaning Supplies	1 3 6 0	00	
					Dale Office Supplies	2 0 0	00	
					Total Liabilities	1 5 6 0	00	

Write the title of the section, *Liabilities*, in the middle of the right wide column. Under this heading write the titles of all liability accounts. Record the balance of each liability account in the right amount column on the same line as the account title. To indicate addition, rule a single line across the right amount column under the last amount. Write the words, *Total Liabilities*, in the right wide column on the next blank line. Record the total of all liabilities, *$1,560.00*, in the right amount column.

FYI

Remember that there are two kinds of equity: Liabilities and Owner's Equity.

Owner's Equity Section of a Balance Sheet. Only the amount of current capital is reported on Rugcare's balance sheet. The amounts needed to calculate the current capital are found in the work sheet's Balance Sheet Debit and Credit columns. The amount of current capital is calculated as shown below.

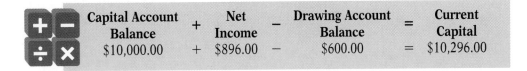

	Capital Account Balance	+	Net Income	−	Drawing Account Balance	=	Current Capital
	$10,000.00	+	$896.00	−	$600.00	=	$10,296.00

The title of the owner's capital account is obtained from the work sheet's Account Title column. Owner's equity is reported on a balance sheet as shown in Illustration 9-12.

FYI

The word Equity can be abbreviated as "Eq."

Write the title of the section, *Owner's Equity*, in the middle of the right wide column on the next line. On the next line, write the title of the owner's capital account, *Ben Furman, Capital*. Record the current amount of owner's equity, *$10,296.00*, in the right amount column.

Rugcare's balance sheet prepared on August 31 is shown in Illustration 9-12. Rule a single line across both amount columns under the last amount in the amount column that is the longest. For Rugcare's balance sheet, the longest column is the right amount

ILLUSTRATION 9-12   A balance sheet

Rugcare					
Balance Sheet					
August 31, 19--					
Assets			**Liabilities**		
Cash	8 2 7 2 00		Butler Cleaning Supplies	1 3 6 0 00	
Petty Cash	2 0 0 00		Dale Office Supplies	2 0 0 00	
Supplies	2 2 8 4 00		Total Liabilities	1 5 6 0 00	
Prepaid Insurance	1 1 0 0 00		*Owner's Equity*		
			Ben Furman, Capital	10 2 9 6 00	
Total Assets	11 8 5 6 00		Total Liab. and Owner's Eq.	11 8 5 6 00	

column. The line is ruled under the amount of Ben Furman's capital, $10,296.00. On the next line, in the right wide column, write the words, *Total Liab. and Owner's Eq.* Record the amount of total liabilities and owner's equity, *$11,856.00*, in the right amount column.

The total assets amount is not recorded at the time the rest of the assets section is prepared. The placement of the total assets line is determined after the equities section is prepared so that the two final totals are on the same line.

Write the words, *Total Assets*, in the left wide column on the same line as the words *Total Liab. and Owner's Eq.* Record the amount of total assets, *$11,856.00*, in the left amount column.

Compare the totals of the two amount columns. Because the totals are the same on both sides of Rugcare's balance sheet, $11,856.00, the balance sheet is in balance. The accounting equation being reported is also in balance.

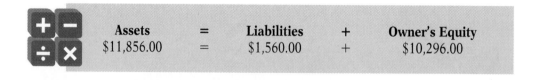

	Assets	=	**Liabilities**	+	**Owner's Equity**
	$11,856.00	=	$1,560.00	+	$10,296.00

If the total assets do not equal the total liabilities and owner's equity, the error or errors must be found and corrected before the balance sheet is completed.

Rule double lines across both the left and right amount columns just below the column totals to show that the totals have been verified as correct.

When a business has a net loss, current capital is calculated as shown below.

	Capital Account Balance	−	**Net Loss**	−	**Drawing Account Balance**	=	**Current Capital**
	$15,000.00	−	$200.00	−	$500.00	=	$14,300.00

ELECTRONIC SPREADSHEETS HELP ANSWER "WHAT IF?" QUESTIONS

Ben Furman analyzes the income statement in Illustration 9-6 to make decisions about Rugcare's future operations. Mr. Furman may analyze several "what if?" questions to determine what action might improve net income and the net income component percentage. What if the amount spent on advertising was increased to $300.00? Mr. Furman estimated that this would increase sales to $5,000.00. However, if sales increase, Rugcare will also need additional supplies to clean more rugs. Therefore, Mr. Furman estimates that supplies expense will increase to $2,900.00.

Electronic spreadsheets eliminate the need to manually erase data and recalculate totals each time a change is made. When data is keyed on the spreadsheet, formulas use the new data to recalculate other values. Formulas may consist of a combination of values, mathematical operations, and cell addresses. The electronic spreadsheet uses the standard mathematical operations of addition (+), subtraction (−), multiplication (*), and division (/). For example,

the formula to calculate the net income component percentage, +E19/E7, divides the value currently displayed at E19 by the value currently displayed at E7.

The analysis indicates that spending $300.00 on advertising would improve net income and the net income component percentage. Mr. Furman will save the spreadsheet on a computer disk for use in answering other "what if?" questions. In the future, Mr. Furman can retrieve the spreadsheet, key new data, and instantly analyze the revised net income and net income component percentage.

```
F7      (P1) +E7/E7
    A        B                C            D         E         F       G
1                                   Rugcare
2                              Income Statement
3                            Projection of Net Income
4                                                               % of
5                                                               Sales
6    Revenue:                                                  -------
7       Sales                                      5,000.00   100.0%
8    Expenses:
9       Advertising Expense              300.00
10      Insurance Expense                100.00
11      Miscellaneous Expense            105.00
12      Rent Expense                     250.00
13      Repair Expense                   110.00
14      Supplies Expense               2,900.00
15      Utilities Expense                115.00
16                                     ----------
17      Total Expenses                             3,880.00    77.6%
18                                                ----------
19   Net Income                                    1,120.00    22.4%
20                                                ======================
```

The current capital, $14,300.00, is reported on the balance sheet in the same way as shown in Illustration 9-12.

Owner's Equity Reported in Detail on a Balance Sheet

Rugcare's balance sheet reports the current capital on August 31 but does not show how this amount was calculated. Rugcare is a small business with relatively few changes in owner's equity to report. Therefore, Ben Furman decided that the business does not need to report all the details in the owner's equity section. However, some businesses prefer to report the details about how owner's equity is calculated.

If Rugcare were to report details about owner's equity, the balance sheet would be prepared as shown in Illustration 9-13.

FYI

The General Accounting Office is the investigative arm of Congress and examines all matters relating to the receipt and disbursement of public funds.

ILLUSTRATION 9-13 Owner's equity reported in detail on a balance sheet

Total Liabilities			1 5 6 0 00
Owner's Equity			
Ben Furman, Capital, August 1		10,000.00	
Net Income	896.00		
Less Ben Furman, Drawing	600.00	296.00	
Ben Furman, Capital, August 31			10 2 9 6 00
Total Liabilities and Owner's Equity			11 8 5 6 00

First, the owner's capital account balance, $10,000.00, is reported. Second, the balance of the drawing account, $600.00, is subtracted from the net income for the fiscal period, $896.00. The difference, $296.00, is added to the previous capital account balance. The current capital, $10,296.00, is recorded as the amount of Ben Furman, Capital on August 31.

A summary of financial statements for a service business organized as a proprietorship is shown in Illustration 9-14.

Audit Your Understanding

1. List the four sections of a balance sheet.

2. What is the formula for calculating current capital?

SUMMARY OF FINANCIAL STATEMENTS FOR A PROPRIETORSHIP

1 An income statement is prepared using information from the Account Title column and Income Statement columns of a work sheet.

2 Component percentages for total expenses and net income are calculated as shown below.

Total Expenses ÷ Total Sales = Total Expenses Component Percentage

Net Income ÷ Total Sales = Net Income Component Percentage

3 A balance sheet is prepared using information obtained from the work sheet's Account Title column and Balance Sheet columns. Current capital to be reported on the balance sheet is calculated as shown below:

$$\text{Capital Account Balance} + \text{Net Income} - \text{Drawing Account Balance} = \text{Current Capital}$$

Summary of financial statements for a proprietorship

1 An income statement is prepared using information from the Account Title column and Income Statement columns of a work sheet.

2 Component percentages for total expenses and net income are calculated as shown below.

Total Expenses ÷ Total Sales = Total Expenses Component Percentage
Net Income   ÷ Total Sales = Net Income Component Percentage

3 A balance sheet is prepared using information obtained from the work sheet's Account Title column and Balance Sheet columns. Current capital to be reported on the balance sheet is calculated as shown below.

$$\text{Capital Account Balance} + \text{Net Income} - \text{Drawing Account Balance} = \text{Current Capital}$$

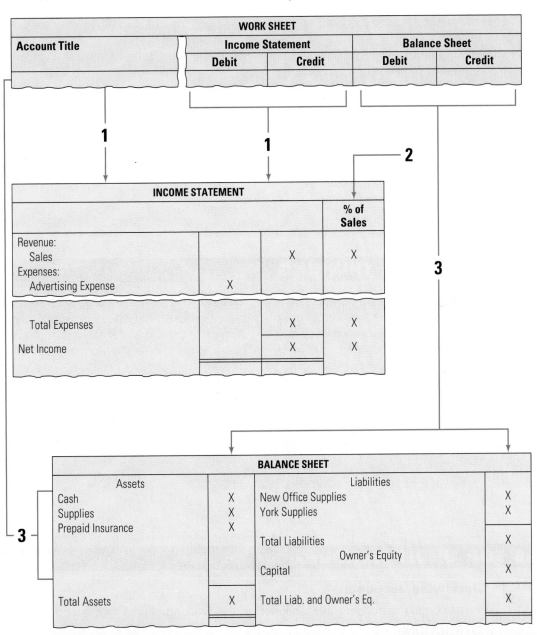

ACCOUNTING TERM

What is the meaning of the following?

1. **component percentage**

QUESTIONS FOR INDIVIDUAL STUDY

EPT(b)

1. Which accounting concept is being applied when all the information about a business' financial condition is reported on financial statements?
2. Which accounting concept is being applied when financial statements are prepared at least once each year?
3. For what period of time does an income statement report financial progress of a business?
4. For what period of time does a balance sheet report financial condition of a business?
5. Which accounting concept is being applied when revenue earned and the expenses incurred to earn that revenue are recorded in the same fiscal period?
6. What does Rugcare do to assist in planning the preparation of financial statements?
7. Where does Rugcare obtain the information for preparing an income statement?
8. What information is found in an income statement heading?
9. What are the two steps in calculating and verifying the net income on Rugcare's income statement?
10. How does Rugcare analyze its income statement?
11. How is revenue shown on an income statement when a business has two sources of revenue?
12. Where does Rugcare obtain the information for preparing a balance sheet?
13. What information is found in a balance sheet heading?

CASES FOR CRITICAL THINKING

EPT(b)

CASE 1 James Worth and Mary Derner each own small businesses. Mr. Worth prepares an income statement and balance sheet at the end of each day for his business. He claims that he needs the information to make business decisions. Mrs. Derner prepares an income statement and balance sheet for her business only at the end of each one-year fiscal period. She claims that she needs the information only at the end of the year when preparing tax reports. Which owner is using the better procedure? Explain your answer.

CASE 2 Ralph Macy owns and manages a business that has produced an average annual net income of $21,600.00 for five years. George Wayne has offered to buy Mr. Macy's business and retain him as manager at a monthly salary of $2,000.00. What should Mr. Macy consider before selling his business and accepting the position as manager?

DRILLS FOR UNDERSTANDING

EPT(b)

DRILL 9-D1 Classifying accounts

A chart containing account titles is given in the working papers that accompany this textbook.

INSTRUCTIONS:

1. For each account title on the chart, place a check mark in either Column 2, 3, 4, 5, or 6 to indicate the classification of each account.

2. Place a check mark in either Column 7 or 8 to indicate on which financial statement each account will be reported.

DRILL 9-D2 Calculating net income or net loss and owner's current capital

A chart containing information for 8 companies is given in the working papers that accompany this textbook.

INSTRUCTIONS:

Complete the following for each company given in the chart.

1. Use the information in Columns 5 and 6. Calculate the amount of net income or net loss for each company. For example, Company A: Revenue, $2,300, − expenses, $900, = net income, $1,400.
2. Calculate the amount of current capital for each company using the net income or net loss from Instruction 1 and the information in Columns 3 and 4. For example, Company A: Capital account balance, $2,320, + net income, $1,400, − drawing, $120, = current capital, $3,600.
3. Use the accounting equation to check the accuracy of your answers in Instructions 1 and 2. For example, Company A: Assets, $5,600, = liabilities, $2,000, + owner's equity, $3,600. If the equation is not in balance, recalculate and correct your answers to Instructions 1 and 2.

APPLICATION PROBLEMS
EPT(c,d,e)

PROBLEM 9-1 Preparing an income statement

The following information is obtained from the work sheet of LawnMow for the month ended June 30 of the current year.

	ACCOUNT TITLE	5 INCOME STATEMENT DEBIT	6 INCOME STATEMENT CREDIT	7 BALANCE SHEET DEBIT	8 BALANCE SHEET CREDIT	
10	*Sales*		3 1 0 0 00			10
11	*Advertising Expense*	3 0 00				11
12	*Insurance Expense*	1 4 0 00				12
13	*Miscellaneous Expense*	6 5 00				13
14	*Rent Expense*	8 0 0 00				14
15	*Supplies Expense*	4 0 0 00				15
16	*Utilities Expense*	7 5 00				16
17		1 5 1 0 00	3 1 0 0 00			17
18	*Net Income*	1 5 9 0 00				18
19		3 1 0 0 00	3 1 0 0 00			19
20						20

INSTRUCTIONS:

Prepare an income statement for the month ended June 30 of the current year. Calculate and record the component percentages for total expenses and net income. Round percentage calculations to the nearest 0.1%.

PROBLEM 9-2 Preparing a balance sheet

The information on page 208 is obtained from the work sheet of LawnMow for the month ended June 30 of the current year.

INSTRUCTIONS:

Prepare a balance sheet for June 30 of the current year.

ACCOUNT TITLE	BALANCE SHEET 7 DEBIT	8 CREDIT	
1 Cash	7 5 3 0 00		1
2 Petty Cash	2 0 0 00		2
3 Supplies	6 8 6 0 00		3
4 Prepaid Insurance	2 5 0 0 00		4
5 Barker Supplies		4 4 0 0 00	5
6 Richmond Office Supplies		1 3 0 0 00	6
7 Clem Sutter, Capital		11 0 0 0 00	7
8 Clem Sutter, Drawing	1 2 0 0 00		8
9 Income Summary			9
16			16
17	18 2 9 0 00	16 7 0 0 00	17
18 Net Income		1 5 9 0 00	18
19	18 2 9 0 00	18 2 9 0 00	19

MASTERY PROBLEM 9-M Preparing financial statements

The following information is obtained from the work sheet of Ace Delivery Service for the month ended July 31 of the current year.

ACCOUNT TITLE	INCOME STATEMENT 5 DEBIT	6 CREDIT	BALANCE SHEET 7 DEBIT	8 CREDIT	
1 Cash			7 5 0 0 00		1
2 Petty Cash			2 0 0 00		2
3 Supplies			7 8 0 0 00		3
4 Prepaid Insurance			2 6 0 0 00		4
5 Down Supplies				4 7 0 0 00	5
6 Melton Office Supplies				1 2 0 0 00	6
7 Clark Smith, Capital				12 0 0 0 00	7
8 Clark Smith, Drawing			1 4 0 0 00		8
9 Income Summary					9
10 Sales		5 6 7 0 00			10
11 Advertising Expense	3 9 0 00				11
12 Insurance Expense	1 9 0 00				12
13 Miscellaneous Expense	1 5 0 00				13
14 Rent Expense	3 0 0 00				14
15 Supplies Expense	2 0 0 00				15
16 Utilities Expense	1 4 0 00				16
17	4 0 7 0 00	5 6 7 0 00	19 5 0 0 00	17 9 0 0 00	17
18 Net Income	1 6 0 0 00			1 6 0 0 00	18
19	5 6 7 0 00	5 6 7 0 00	19 5 0 0 00	19 5 0 0 00	19

INSTRUCTIONS:

1. Prepare an income statement for the month ended July 31 of the current year. Calculate and record the component percentages for total expenses and net income. Round percentage calculations to the nearest 0.1%.

2. Prepare a balance sheet for July 31 of the current year.

CHALLENGE PROBLEM 9-C Preparing financial statements with two sources of revenue and a net loss

The following information is obtained from the work sheet of Mercer Lawn Service for the month ended August 31 of the current year.

	ACCOUNT TITLE	INCOME STATEMENT		BALANCE SHEET		
		DEBIT	CREDIT	DEBIT	CREDIT	
1	Cash			6 0 2 0 00		1
2	Petty Cash			2 0 0 00		2
3	Supplies			6 0 0 0 00		3
4	Prepaid Insurance			2 5 0 0 00		4
5	Choice Supplies				3 0 0 0 00	5
6	Poll Office Supplies				2 0 0 00	6
7	Lydia Roland, Capital				13 0 0 0 00	7
8	Lydia Roland, Drawing			1 3 0 0 00		8
9	Income Summary					9
10	Sales—Lawn Care		4 7 0 0 00			10
11	Sales—Shrub Care		2 6 0 0 00			11
12	Advertising Expense	3 9 0 00				12
13	Insurance Expense	3 0 0 00				13
14	Miscellaneous Expense	4 5 0 00				14
15	Rent Expense	3 0 0 0 00				15
16	Supplies Expense	3 1 0 0 00				16
17	Utilities Expense	2 4 0 00				17
18		7 4 8 0 00	7 3 0 0 00	16 0 2 0 00	16 2 0 0 00	18
19	Net Loss		1 8 0 00	1 8 0 00		19
20		7 4 8 0 00	7 4 8 0 00	16 2 0 0 00	16 2 0 0 00	20

INSTRUCTIONS:

1. Prepare an income statement for the month ended August 31 of the current year. Calculate and record the component percentages for total expenses and net loss. Place the percentage for net loss in parentheses to show that it is for a net loss. Round percentage calculations to the nearest 0.1%.

2. Prepare a balance sheet for August 31 of the current year.

10

Recording Adjusting and Closing Entries for a Service Business

ENABLING PERFORMANCE TASKS

After studying Chapter 10, you will be able to:

a Define accounting terms related to adjusting and closing entries for a service business organized as a proprietorship.

b Identify accounting concepts and practices related to adjusting and closing entries for a service business organized as a proprietorship.

c Record adjusting entries for a service business organized as a proprietorship.

d Record closing entries for a service business organized as a proprietorship.

e Prepare a post-closing trial balance for a service business organized as a proprietorship.

TERMS PREVIEW

adjusting entries • permanent accounts • temporary accounts • closing entries • post-closing trial balance • accounting cycle

Rugcare prepares a work sheet at the end of each fiscal period to summarize the general ledger information needed to prepare financial statements. (CONCEPT: *Accounting Period Cycle*) Financial statements are prepared from information on the work sheet. (CONCEPT: *Adequate Disclosure*)

RECORDING ADJUSTING ENTRIES

Rugcare's adjustments are analyzed and planned on a work sheet. However, these adjustments must be journalized so that they can be posted to the general ledger accounts. Journal entries recorded to update general ledger accounts at the end of a fiscal period are called **adjusting entries.**

Adjusting entries are recorded on the next journal page following the page on which the last daily transactions for the month are recorded. The adjusting entries are entered in the General Debit and General Credit columns of a journal.

Rugcare records two adjusting entries. (1) An adjusting entry to bring the supplies account up to date. (2) An adjusting entry to bring the prepaid insurance account up to date.

Adjusting Entry for Supplies

The information needed to journalize the adjusting entry for supplies is obtained from lines 3 and 16 of Rugcare's work sheet. A partial work sheet and the adjusting entry for supplies are shown in Illustration 10-1.

ILLUSTRATION 10-1   Adjusting entry for supplies recorded in a journal

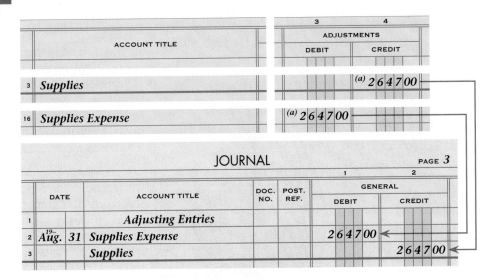

The heading, *Adjusting Entries*, is written in the middle of the Account Title column of the journal. Because no source document is prepared for adjusting entries, the entries are identified with a

heading in the journal. This heading explains all of the adjusting entries that follow. Therefore, the heading is written only once for all adjusting entries.

The date, *19--, Aug. 31*, is written in the Date column. The title of the account debited, *Supplies Expense*, is written in the Account Title column. The debit amount, *$2,647.00*, is recorded in the General Debit column on the same line as the account title. The title of the account credited, *Supplies*, is written on the next line. The credit amount, *$2,647.00*, is recorded in the General Credit column on the same line as the account title.

The effect of posting the adjusting entry for supplies to the general ledger accounts is shown in the T accounts.

Supplies Expense has an up-to-date balance of $2,647.00, which is the value of the supplies used during the fiscal period. Supplies has a new balance of $2,284.00, which is the value of the supplies on hand at the end of the fiscal period.

Supplies Expense			
Adj. (a)	2,647.00		

Supplies			
Bal.	4,931.00	Adj. (a)	2,647.00
(New Bal.	2,284.00)		

■ Tom Richardson ■

HOLDER, MCCALL, AND RICHARDSON, LLP, FORT WORTH, TEXAS

Tom Richardson started his career as a C.P.A., but then he began importing fish. Richardson was in business with a partner in Scotland who bought and shipped fish to the United States by airplane. This seafood importing business led to Richardson's first major exposure to the use of personal computers and software to manage a business and keep its records. During the course of pulling the computer system together, Richardson also connected a Telex to the computer to facilitate transmitting his overseas orders.

After leaving the importing business, Richardson joined a large local accounting firm. He is now a partner in Holder, McCall, and Richardson, LLP, a C.P.A. firm in Fort Worth, Texas. Richardson's firm handles accounting and bookkeeping services for some of its smaller clients using accounting software. As companies become larger, many of them want to bring the accounting

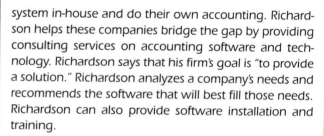

system in-house and do their own accounting. Richardson helps these companies bridge the gap by providing consulting services on accounting software and technology. Richardson says that his firm's goal is "to provide a solution." Richardson analyzes a company's needs and recommends the software that will best fill those needs. Richardson can also provide software installation and training.

Richardson recommends the study of high school accounting for exposure to accounting as a career field. He also recommends a college degree in accounting as an excellent way to learn how a business works. He feels a college degree in accounting can open a lot of doors down the way and is an excellent background for a future as a consultant.

*"***A**ccountants who do not get involved with computers will not be doing much business in ten years," Richardson predicts. "Computer software is constantly offering better and faster solutions to business problems. In fact, the technology field is so dynamic that it is difficult to stay current." Richardson recommends that students include management information system (MIS) courses with their accounting courses so that they are not left behind in the business world.

Personal Visions in Business

Adjusting Entry for Prepaid Insurance

The information needed to journalize the adjusting entry for prepaid insurance is obtained from lines 4 and 12 of Rugcare's work sheet. A partial work sheet and the adjusting entry for prepaid insurance are shown in Illustration 10-2.

Adjusting entry for prepaid insurance recorded in a journal

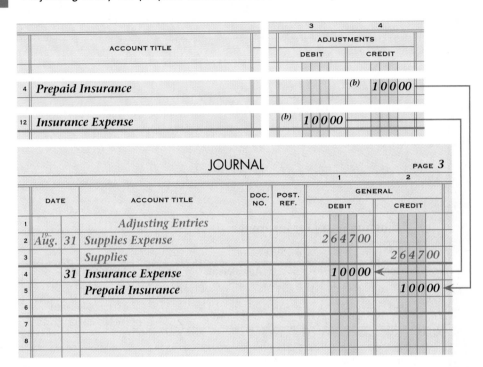

The date, *31,* is written in the Date column. The title of the account debited, *Insurance Expense,* is written in the Account Title column. The debit amount, *$100.00,* is recorded in the General Debit column on the same line as the account title. The title of the account credited, *Prepaid Insurance,* is written on the next line in the Account Title column. The credit amount, *$100.00,* is recorded in the General Credit column on the same line as the account title.

The effect of posting the adjusting entry for insurance to the general ledger accounts is shown in the T accounts.

Insurance Expense has an up-to-date balance of $100.00, which is the value of insurance premiums used during the fiscal period. Prepaid Insurance has a new balance of $1,100.00, which is the value of insurance premiums that remain unused at the end of the fiscal period. *(CONCEPT: Matching Expenses with Revenue)*

The two adjusting entries for a service business organized as a proprietorship are summarized in Illustration 10-3.

Audit Your Understanding

1. Why are adjustments journalized?

2. Where is the information obtained to journalize adjusting entries?

3. What accounts are increased from zero balances after adjusting entries for supplies and prepaid insurance are journalized and posted?

	Insurance Expense
Adj. (b)	100.00

	Prepaid Insurance		
Bal.	1,200.00	Adj. (b)	100.00
(New Bal.	1,100.00)		

Summary of adjusting entries for a service business organized as a proprietorship

1. Adjusting entry for supplies

WORK SHEET				JOURNAL		
Account Title	**Adjustments**			**Account Title**	**General**	
	Debit	**Credit**			**Debit**	**Credit**
Supplies		(a) X		Supplies Expense	X	
				Supplies		X
Supplies Expense	(a) X					

Supplies Expense
Adjusting	

Supplies
Balance	Adjusting

2. Adjusting entry for insurance

WORK SHEET				JOURNAL		
Account Title	**Adjustments**			**Account Title**	**General**	
	Debit	**Credit**			**Debit**	**Credit**
Prepaid Insurance		(b) X		Insurance Expense	X	
				Prepaid Insurance		X
Insurance Expense	(b) X					

Insurance Expense
Adjusting	

Prepaid Insurance
Balance	Adjusting

RECORDING CLOSING ENTRIES

FYI

Permanent accounts are sometimes referred to as real accounts.

Accounts used to accumulate information from one fiscal period to the next are called **permanent accounts**. Permanent accounts are also referred to as real accounts. Permanent accounts include the asset and liability accounts and the owner's capital account. The ending account balances of permanent accounts for one fiscal period are the beginning account balances for the next fiscal period.

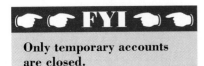

Only temporary accounts are closed.

Accounts used to accumulate information until it is transferred to the owner's capital account are called **temporary accounts.** Temporary accounts are also referred to as nominal accounts. Temporary accounts include the revenue, expense, and owner's drawing accounts plus the income summary account. Temporary accounts show changes in the owner's capital for a single fiscal period. Therefore, at the end of a fiscal period, the balances of temporary accounts are summarized and transferred to the owner's capital account. The temporary accounts begin a new fiscal period with zero balances.

Need for Closing Temporary Accounts

Journal entries used to prepare temporary accounts for a new fiscal period are called **closing entries.** The temporary account balances must be reduced to zero at the end of each fiscal period. This procedure prepares the temporary accounts for recording information about the next fiscal period. Otherwise, the amounts for the next fiscal period would be added to amounts for previous fiscal periods. *(CONCEPT: Matching Expenses with Revenue)* The net income for the next fiscal period would be difficult to calculate because amounts from several fiscal periods remain in the accounts. Therefore, the temporary accounts must start each new fiscal period with zero balances.

To close a temporary account, an amount equal to its balance is recorded in the account on the side opposite to its balance. For example, if an account has a credit balance of $4,291.00, a debit of $4,291.00 is recorded to close the account.

Need for the Income Summary Account

Whenever a temporary account is closed, the closing entry must have equal debits and credits. If an account is debited for $3,000.00 to close the account, some other account must be credited for the same amount. A temporary account titled *Income Summary* is used to summarize the closing entries for the revenue and expense accounts.

The income summary account is unique because it does not have a normal balance side. The balance of this account is determined by the amounts posted to the account at the end of a fiscal period. When revenue is greater than total expenses, resulting in a net income, the income summary account has a credit balance, as shown in the T account.

Income Summary	
Debit side	Credit side
Total expenses	Revenue (greater than expenses)
	(Credit balance is the net income.)

When total expenses are greater than revenue, resulting in a net loss, the income summary account has a debit balance, as shown in the T account on the following page.

Income Summary

Debit side Total expenses (greater than revenue) (Debit balance is the net loss.)	Credit side Revenue

Thus, whether the balance of the income summary account is a debit or a credit depends upon whether the business earns a net income or incurs a net loss. Because Income Summary is a temporary account, the account is also closed at the end of a fiscal period when the net income or net loss is recorded.

Rugcare records four closing entries. (1) An entry to close income statement accounts with credit balances. (2) An entry to close income statement accounts with debit balances. (3) An entry to record net income or net loss and close Income Summary. (4) An entry to close the owner's drawing account.

Information needed to record the four closing entries is found in the Income Statement and Balance Sheet columns of the work sheet.

Closing Entry for an Income Statement Account with a Credit Balance

Rugcare has one income statement account with a credit balance, Sales, as shown on the partial work sheet in Illustration 10-4. This credit balance must be reduced to zero to prepare the account for the next fiscal period. To reduce the balance to zero, Sales is debited for the amount of the balance. Because debits must equal credits for each journal entry, some other account must be credited. The account used for the credit part of this closing entry is Income Summary. The closing entry for Sales is journalized as shown in Illustration 10-4.

ILLUSTRATION 10-4   Closing entry for an income statement account with a credit balance

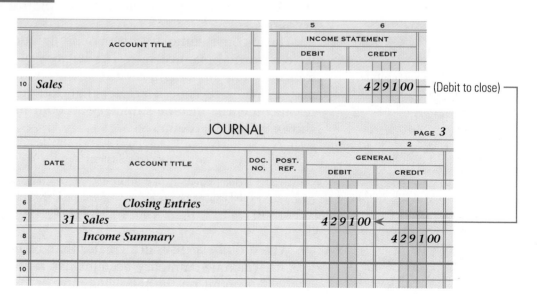

No source document is used for closing entries. Therefore, the heading, *Closing Entries*, is written in the Account Title column of the journal. For Rugcare, this heading is placed in the journal on the first blank line after the last adjusting entry.

The date, *31*, is written on the next line in the Date column. The title of the account debited, *Sales*, is written in the Account Title column. The debit amount, *$4,291.00*, is recorded in the General Debit column on the same line as the account title. The title of the account credited, *Income Summary*, is written in the Account Title column on the next journal line. The credit amount, *$4,291.00*, is recorded in the General Credit amount column on the same line as the account title.

The effect of this closing entry on the general ledger accounts is shown in the T accounts.

The balance of Sales is now zero, and the account is ready for the next fiscal period. The credit balance of Sales is transferred to Income Summary.

	Sales		
Closing	4,291.00	Bal. *(New Bal. zero)*	4,291.00

Income Summary	
	Closing (revenue) 4,291.00

Closing Entry for Income Statement Accounts with Debit Balances

Rugcare has several income statement accounts with debit balances. The seven expense accounts have normal debit balances at the end of a fiscal period, as shown on the partial work sheet in Illustration 10-5, on page 218. The balances of the expense accounts must be reduced to zero to prepare the accounts for the next fiscal period. Each expense account is credited for an amount equal to its balance, and Income Summary is debited for the total of all the expense account balances. The closing entry for the expense accounts is journalized as shown in Illustration 10-5.

The heading for closing entries is written only once. Therefore, the closing entry for expenses starts on the next blank line in the journal.

The date, *31*, is written in the Date column. The title of the account debited, Income Summary, is written in the Account Title column. The amount debited to Income Summary is not entered in the amount column until all expenses have been journalized and the total amount calculated. The account title and balance of each expense account is recorded in the Account Title and General Credit columns. After all expense accounts and their balances have been written in the journal, the credit amounts for this entry are added. The total of all expenses, *$3,395.00*, is recorded in the General Debit column on the same line as the account title, Income Summary.

FYI

The reasons for recording closing entries can be compared to a trip odometer. Closing entries are recorded to prepare the temporary accounts for the next fiscal period by reducing their balances to zero. Likewise a trip odometer must be reset to zero to begin recording the miles for the next trip.

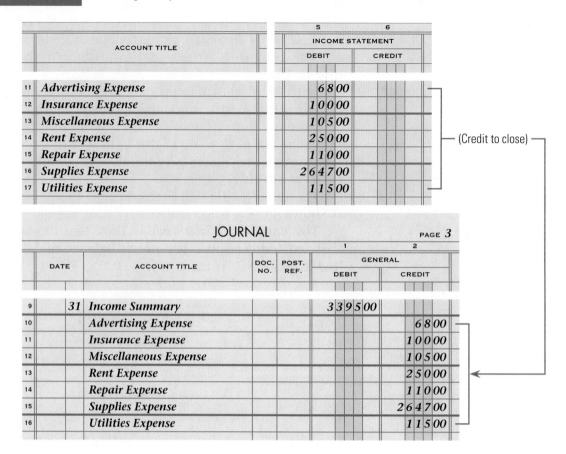

The effect of the closing entry for Rugcare's expense accounts is shown in the T accounts.

Income Summary

Closing (expenses)	3,395.00	Closing (revenue)	4,291.00
		(New Bal.	*896.00)*

Advertising Expense

Bal.	68.00	Closing	68.00
(New Bal. zero)			

Repair Expense

Bal.	110.00	Closing	110.00
(New Bal. zero)			

Insurance Expense

Bal.	100.00	Closing	100.00
(New Bal. zero)			

Supplies Expense

Bal.	2,647.00	Closing	2,647.00
(New Bal. zero)			

Miscellaneous Expense

Bal.	105.00	Closing	105.00
(New Bal. zero)			

Utilities Expense

Bal.	115.00	Closing	115.00
(New Bal. zero)			

Rent Expense

Bal.	250.00	Closing	250.00
(New Bal. zero)			

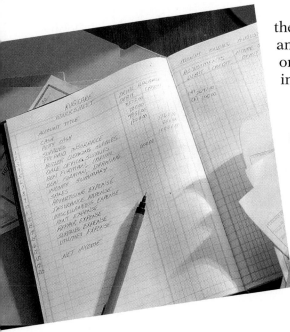

The balance of each expense account is returned to zero, and the accounts are ready for the next fiscal period. The debit balances of the expense accounts are recorded in Income Summary as one debit amount. The balance of Income Summary is the net income for the fiscal period, $896.00.

Closing Entry to Record Net Income or Loss and Close the Income Summary Account

Rugcare's net income is on the partial work sheet shown in Illustration 10-6. The amount of net income increases the owner's capital and, therefore, must be credited to the owner's capital account. The balance of the temporary account, Income Summary, must be reduced to zero to prepare the account for the next fiscal period. The closing entry to record net income and close the income summary account is journalized as shown in Illustration 10-6.

| **ILLUSTRATION 10-6** | Closing entry to record net income and close the income summary account |

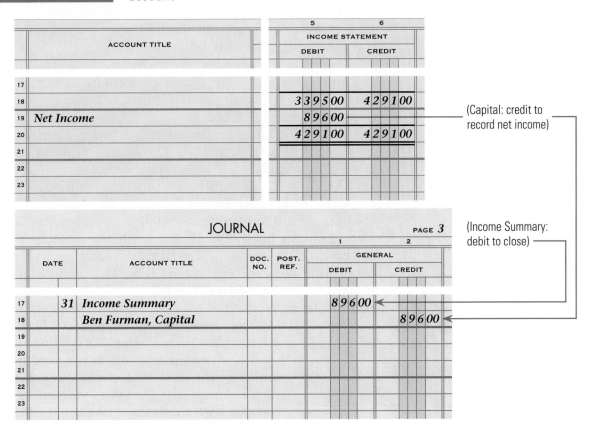

The date, *31*, is written in the Date column. The title of the account debited, *Income Summary*, is written in the Account Title column. The debit amount, *$896.00*, is recorded in the General Debit column on the same line as the account title. The title of the account credited, *Ben Furman, Capital*, is written in the Account Title column on the next line. The credit amount, *$896.00*, is recorded in the General Credit column on the same line as the account title.

The effect of this closing entry on the general ledger accounts is shown in the T accounts.

The debit to the income summary account, $896.00, reduces the account balance to zero and prepares the account for the next fiscal period. The credit, $896.00, increases the balance of the owner's capital account, Ben Furman, Capital.

If the business incurs a net loss, the closing entry is a debit to the owner's capital account and a credit to the income summary account.

Income Summary

Closing (expenses)		Closing (revenue)	
	3,395.00		4,291.00
Closing	896.00	*(New Bal. zero)*	

Ben Furman, Capital

		Bal.	10,000.00
		Closing (net income)	
			896.00
		(New Bal.	*10,896.00)*

Closing Entry for the Owner's Drawing Account

FYI

Most small businesses use the calendar year as their fiscal year because it matches the way the owners have to file their personal income tax returns.

Withdrawals are assets that the owner takes out of a business and which decrease the amount of the owner's equity. The drawing account is a temporary account that accumulates information separately for each fiscal period. Therefore, the drawing account balance is reduced to zero at the end of one fiscal period to prepare the account for the next fiscal period.

The drawing account is neither a revenue nor an expense account. Therefore, the drawing account is not closed through Income Summary. The drawing account balance is closed directly to the owner's capital account.

The closing entry for the owner's drawing account is journalized as shown in Illustration 10-7. The closing entry is on lines 19 and 20 of the journal.

The date, *31*, is written in the Date column. The title of the account debited, *Ben Furman, Capital*, is written in the Account Title column. The debit amount, *$600.00*, is recorded in the General Debit column on the same line with the account title. The title of the account credited, *Ben Furman, Drawing*, is written in the Account Title column on the next line. The credit amount, *$600.00*, is written in the General Credit column on the same line as the account title.

Ben Furman, Capital

Closing	600.00	Bal.	10,000.00
		Net Income	896.00
		(New Bal.	*10,296.00)*

Ben Furman, Drawing

Bal.	600.00	Closing	600.00
(New Bal. zero)			

The effect of the entry to close the drawing account is shown in the T accounts.

The drawing account has a zero balance and is ready for the next fiscal period. The capital account's new balance, $10,296.00, is verified by checking the balance with the amount of capital shown on the balance sheet prepared at the end of the fiscal period. The capital account balance shown on Rugcare's balance sheet in Chapter 9, Illustration 9-12, is $10,296.00. The two amounts are the same, and the capital account balance is verified.

	ACCOUNT TITLE	7	8
		BALANCE SHEET	
		DEBIT	CREDIT
7	Ben Furman, Capital		1000000	7
8	Ben Furman, Drawing	60000		8 — (Credit to close)
9				9
10				10
11				11

JOURNAL   PAGE **3**

	DATE	ACCOUNT TITLE	DOC. NO.	POST. REF.	DEBIT	CREDIT	
6		*Closing Entries*					6
7	31	Sales			429100		7
8		Income Summary				429100	8
9	31	Income Summary			339500		9
10		Advertising Expense				6800	10
11		Insurance Expense				10000	11
12		Miscellaneous Expense				10500	12
13		Rent Expense				25000	13
14		Repair Expense				11000	14
15		Supplies Expense				26470	15
16		Utilities Expense				11500	16
17	31	Income Summary			89600		17
18		Ben Furman, Capital				89600	18
19	31	Ben Furman, Capital			60000		19
20		Ben Furman, Drawing				60000	20
21							21
22							22
23							23

FYI

The Department of Labor estimates that by the year 2005, 25 million jobs will be added to the U.S. economy. Most of these new jobs will be in service businesses.

Closing entries are journalized and posted to prepare temporary accounts for the next fiscal period. The income summary account is used to summarize all revenue and expense accounts before recording net income or net loss in the owner's capital account. A summary of closing entries is shown in Illustration 10-8.

To complete a fiscal period, Rugcare records four journal entries to close temporary accounts.

1 Close income statement accounts with credit balances.

2 Close income statement accounts with debit balances.

3 Record the net income or net loss in the owner's capital account and close Income Summary.

4 Close the owner's drawing account.

Summary of closing entries for a service business organized as a proprietorship

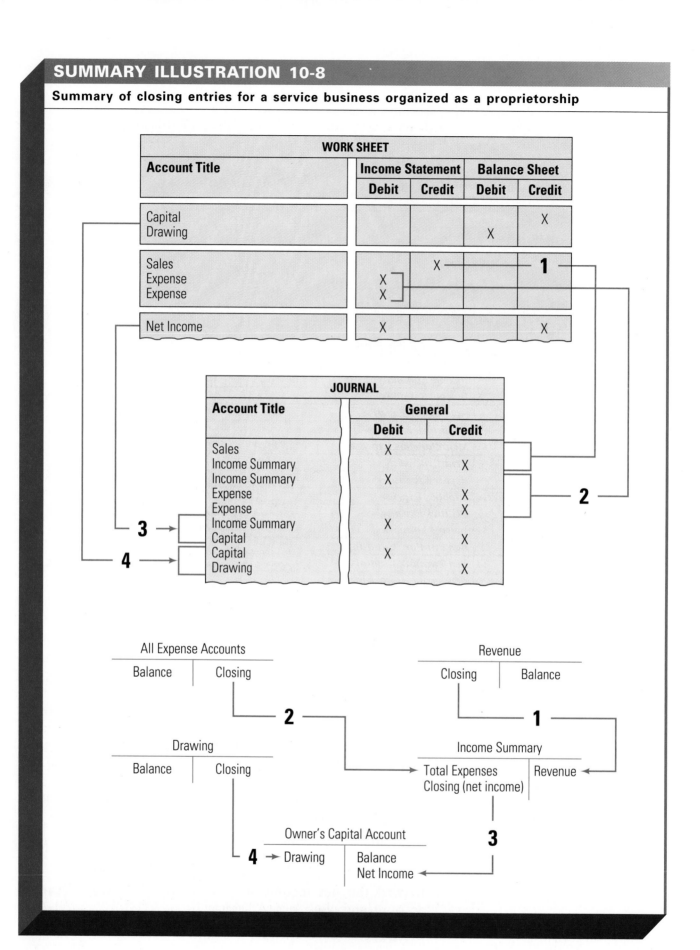

GENERAL LEDGER AFTER ADJUSTING AND CLOSING ENTRIES ARE POSTED

Rugcare's general ledger after the adjusting and closing entries are posted is shown in Illustration 10-9. When an account has a zero balance, lines are drawn in both the Balance Debit and Balance Credit columns. The lines assure a reader that a balance has not been omitted.

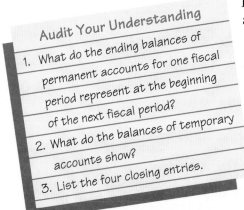

Audit Your Understanding

1. What do the ending balances of permanent accounts for one fiscal period represent at the beginning of the next fiscal period?

2. What do the balances of temporary accounts show?

3. List the four closing entries.

ILLUSTRATION 10-9   General ledger accounts after adjusting and closing entries are posted

ACCOUNT *Cash*   ACCOUNT NO. *110*

DATE	ITEM	POST. REF.	DEBIT	CREDIT	BALANCE DEBIT	BALANCE CREDIT
Aug.¹⁹⁻⁻ 31		2	14 2 9 1 00		14 2 9 1 00	
31		2		6 0 1 9 00	8 2 7 2 00	

ACCOUNT *Petty Cash*   ACCOUNT NO. *120*

DATE	ITEM	POST. REF.	DEBIT	CREDIT	BALANCE DEBIT	BALANCE CREDIT
Aug.¹⁹⁻⁻ 17		1	2 0 0 00		2 0 0 00	

ACCOUNT *Supplies*   ACCOUNT NO. *130*

DATE	ITEM	POST. REF.	DEBIT	CREDIT	BALANCE DEBIT	BALANCE CREDIT
Aug.¹⁹⁻⁻ 3		1	1 5 7 7 00		1 5 7 7 00	
7		1	2 7 2 0 00		4 2 9 7 00	
20		1	2 0 0 00		4 4 9 7 00	
28		2	4 3 4 00		4 9 3 1 00	
31		3		2 6 4 7 00	2 2 8 4 00	

ACCOUNT *Prepaid Insurance*   ACCOUNT NO. *140*

DATE	ITEM	POST. REF.	DEBIT	CREDIT	BALANCE DEBIT	BALANCE CREDIT
Aug.¹⁹⁻⁻ 4		1	1 2 0 0 00		1 2 0 0 00	
31		3		1 0 0 00	1 1 0 0 00	

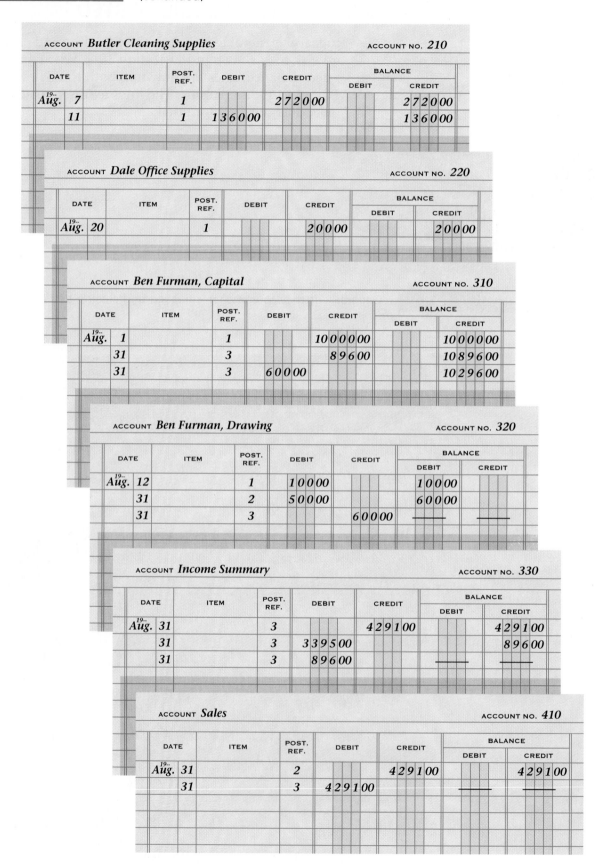

ACCOUNT **Butler Cleaning Supplies** ACCOUNT NO. *210*

DATE	ITEM	POST. REF.	DEBIT	CREDIT	BALANCE DEBIT	BALANCE CREDIT
Aug. 7		1		2 7 2 0 00		2 7 2 0 00
11		1	1 3 6 0 00			1 3 6 0 00

ACCOUNT **Dale Office Supplies** ACCOUNT NO. *220*

DATE	ITEM	POST. REF.	DEBIT	CREDIT	BALANCE DEBIT	BALANCE CREDIT
Aug. 20		1		2 0 0 00		2 0 0 00

ACCOUNT **Ben Furman, Capital** ACCOUNT NO. *310*

DATE	ITEM	POST. REF.	DEBIT	CREDIT	BALANCE DEBIT	BALANCE CREDIT
Aug. 1		1		10 0 0 0 00		10 0 0 0 00
31		3		8 9 6 00		10 8 9 6 00
31		3	6 0 0 00			10 2 9 6 00

ACCOUNT **Ben Furman, Drawing** ACCOUNT NO. *320*

DATE	ITEM	POST. REF.	DEBIT	CREDIT	BALANCE DEBIT	BALANCE CREDIT
Aug. 12		1	1 0 0 00		1 0 0 00	
31		2	5 0 0 00		6 0 0 00	
31		3		6 0 0 00	——	——

ACCOUNT **Income Summary** ACCOUNT NO. *330*

DATE	ITEM	POST. REF.	DEBIT	CREDIT	BALANCE DEBIT	BALANCE CREDIT
Aug. 31		3		4 2 9 1 00		4 2 9 1 00
31		3	3 3 9 5 00			8 9 6 00
31		3	8 9 6 00		——	——

ACCOUNT **Sales** ACCOUNT NO. *410*

DATE	ITEM	POST. REF.	DEBIT	CREDIT	BALANCE DEBIT	BALANCE CREDIT
Aug. 31		2		4 2 9 1 00		4 2 9 1 00
31		3	4 2 9 1 00		——	——

ILLUSTRATION 10-9 General ledger accounts after adjusting and closing entries are posted (continued)

ACCOUNT **Advertising Expense**   ACCOUNT NO. *510*

DATE	ITEM	POST. REF.	DEBIT	CREDIT	BALANCE DEBIT	BALANCE CREDIT
Aug. 14		1	6 8 00		6 8 00	
31		3		6 8 00	———	———

ACCOUNT **Insurance Expense**   ACCOUNT NO. *520*

DATE	ITEM	POST. REF.	DEBIT	CREDIT	BALANCE DEBIT	BALANCE CREDIT
Aug. 31		3	1 0 0 00		1 0 0 00	
31		3		1 0 0 00	———	———

ACCOUNT **Miscellaneous Expense**   ACCOUNT NO. *530*

DATE	ITEM	POST. REF.	DEBIT	CREDIT	BALANCE DEBIT	BALANCE CREDIT
Aug. 13		1	2 5 00		2 5 00	
18		1	7 0 00		9 5 00	
28		2	3 00		9 8 00	
31		2	7 00		1 0 5 00	
31		3		1 0 5 00	———	———

ACCOUNT **Rent Expense**   ACCOUNT NO. *540*

DATE	ITEM	POST. REF.	DEBIT	CREDIT	BALANCE DEBIT	BALANCE CREDIT
Aug. 12		1	2 5 0 00		2 5 0 00	
31		3		2 5 0 00	———	———

ACCOUNT **Repair Expense**   ACCOUNT NO. *550*

DATE	ITEM	POST. REF.	DEBIT	CREDIT	BALANCE DEBIT	BALANCE CREDIT
Aug. 13		1	2 0 00		2 0 00	
20		1	8 5 00		1 0 5 00	
31		2	5 00		1 1 0 00	
31		3		1 1 0 00	———	———

ACCOUNT **Supplies Expense**   ACCOUNT NO. *560*

DATE	ITEM	POST. REF.	DEBIT	CREDIT	BALANCE DEBIT	BALANCE CREDIT
Aug. 31		3	2 6 4 7 00		2 6 4 7 00	
31		3		2 6 4 7 00	———	———

ILLUSTRATION 10-9

General ledger accounts after adjusting and closing entries are posted (concluded)

ACCOUNT *Utilities Expense*					ACCOUNT NO. *570*	
DATE	ITEM	POST. REF.	DEBIT	CREDIT	BALANCE DEBIT	BALANCE CREDIT
Aug.¹⁹⁻⁻ 12		1	45 00		45 00	
27		2	70 00		1 15 00	
31		3		1 15 00	———	———

POST-CLOSING TRIAL BALANCE

The word "Post" means "after." The *Post*-Closing Trial Balance is prepared *after* closing entries.

After the closing entries are posted, Rugcare verifies that debits equal credits in the general ledger accounts by preparing a trial balance. A trial balance prepared after the closing entries are posted is called a **post-closing trial balance.**

Only general ledger accounts with balances are included on a post-closing trial balance. The permanent accounts (assets, liabilities, and owner's capital) have balances and do appear on a post-closing trial balance. Because the temporary accounts (income summary, revenue, expense, and drawing) are closed and have zero balances, they do not appear on a post-closing trial balance. Rugcare's post-closing trial balance is shown in Illustration 10-10.

ILLUSTRATION 10-10

Post-closing trial balance

Rugcare		
Post-Closing Trial Balance		
August 31, 19--		
ACCOUNT TITLE	DEBIT	CREDIT
Cash	8 27 2 00	
Petty Cash	2 00 00	
Supplies	2 28 4 00	
Prepaid Insurance	1 10 0 00	
Butler Cleaning Supplies		1 36 0 00
Dale Office Supplies		2 00 00
Ben Furman, Capital		10 29 6 00
Totals	11 85 6 00	11 85 6 00

Rugcare uses eight steps to prepare a post-closing trial balance.

1 Write the heading on three lines.

2 Write the titles of all general ledger accounts with balances in the Account Title column.

3 On the same line with each account title, write each account's balance in either the Debit or Credit column.

4 Rule a single line across both amount columns below the last amount, and add each amount column.

5 Compare the two column totals. The two column totals must be the same. The total of all debits must equal the total of all credits in a general ledger. The totals of both columns on Rugcare's post-closing trial balance are the same, $11,856.00. Rugcare's post-closing trial balance shows that the general ledger account balances are in balance and ready for the new fiscal period. If the two column totals are not the same, the errors must be found and corrected before any more work is completed.

6 Write the word, *Totals*, on the line below the last account title.

7 Write the column totals, *$11,856.00*, below the single line.

8 Rule double lines across both amount columns to show that the totals have been verified as correct.

Audit Your Understanding

1. Why are lines drawn in both the Balance Debit and Balance Credit columns when an account has a zero balance?

2. Which accounts go on the post-closing trial balance?

3. Why are temporary accounts omitted from a post-closing trial balance?

THE ACCOUNTING CYCLE FOR A SERVICE BUSINESS

Chapters 2 through 10 describe Rugcare's accounting activities for a one-month fiscal period. The series of accounting activities included in recording financial information for a fiscal period is called an **accounting cycle**. *(CONCEPT: Accounting Period Cycle)* Rugcare's accounting cycle is summarized in Illustration 10-11.

For the next fiscal period, the cycle begins again at Step 1.

Summary of an accounting cycle for a service business

1 Source documents are checked for accuracy, and transactions are analyzed into debit and credit parts.

2 Transactions, from information on source documents, are recorded in a journal.

3 Journal entries are posted to the general ledger.

4 A work sheet, including a trial balance, is prepared from the general ledger.

5 Financial statements are prepared from the work sheet.

6 Adjusting and closing entries are journalized from the work sheet.

7 Adjusting and closing entries are posted to the general ledger.

8 Post-closing trial balance of the general ledger is prepared.

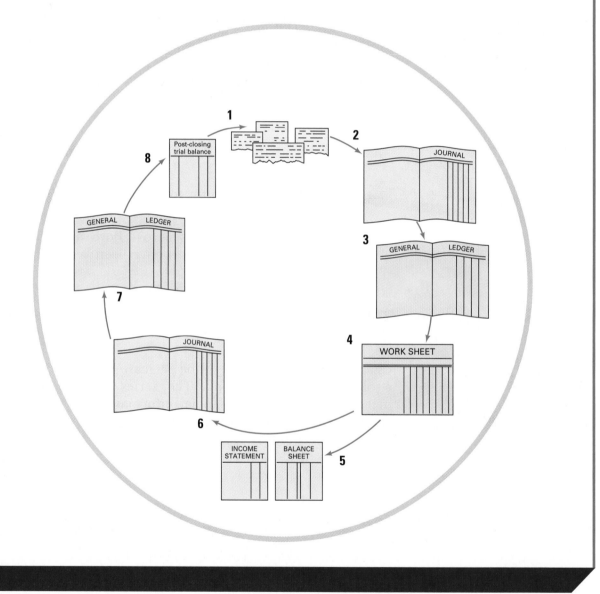

ACCOUNTING TERMS

What is the meaning of each of the following?

1. adjusting entries
2. permanent accounts
3. temporary accounts
4. closing entries
5. post-closing trial balance
6. accounting cycle

QUESTIONS FOR INDIVIDUAL STUDY

1. Which accounting concept is being applied when information in a general ledger is summarized on a work sheet at the end of each fiscal period?
2. How are adjusting entries identified in a journal?
3. What accounts are affected, and how, by the adjusting entry for supplies?
4. What accounts are affected, and how, by the adjusting entry for prepaid insurance?
5. Why are closing entries journalized and posted at the end of a fiscal period?
6. How is the income summary account used?
7. Why is the income summary account considered unique?
8. What kind of balance will the income summary account have if a business has a net income?
9. What four closing entries are recorded by Rugcare?
10. What effect do withdrawals have on the owner's equity?
11. After the closing entries are posted, how is the balance of the capital account verified?
12. Why is a post-closing trial balance prepared after the closing entries have been posted?
13. What are the eight steps of an accounting cycle?

CASES FOR CRITICAL THINKING

CASE 1 Thomas Westcott forgot to journalize and post the adjusting entry for prepaid insurance at the end of the June fiscal period. What effect will this omission have on the records of Mr. Westcott's business as of June 30? Explain your answer.

CASE 2 Jason Fields states that his business is so small that he just records supplies and insurance as expenses when he pays for them. Thus, at the end of a fiscal period, Mr. Fields does not record adjusting and closing entries for his business. Do you agree with his accounting procedures? Explain your answer.

APPLIED COMMUNICATIONS

You have learned that accounting information is used by managers to make business decisions. But exactly what kind of decisions does the owner of a local business make? How does accounting information enable the manager to make better decisions?

INSTRUCTIONS:

Identify a local business of personal interest to you. Write five questions you would ask the manager to learn how accounting information is used to make decisions.

DRILL 10-D1 Determining accounts affected by adjusting and closing entries

Rapid Service Company uses the general ledger accounts that appear on the chart in the working papers that accompany this textbook.

INSTRUCTIONS:

1. For each account title, place a check mark in either Column 2 or 3 to indicate whether the account is affected by an adjusting entry.
2. For each account title, place a check mark in either Column 4 or 5 to indicate whether the account is affected by a closing entry.
3. For each account title, place a check mark in either Column 6 or 7 to indicate whether the account has a balance after the closing entries are posted.

APPLICATION PROBLEM
EPT(c,d,e)

PROBLEM 10-1 Journalizing and posting adjusting and closing entries; preparing a post-closing trial balance

Eiler Company's partial work sheet for the month ended October 31 of the current year is given below. The general ledger accounts are given in the working papers that accompany this textbook. (The general ledger accounts do not show all details for the fiscal period. The "Balance" shown in each account is the account's balance before adjusting and closing entries are posted.)

	ACCOUNT TITLE	ADJUSTMENTS DEBIT	ADJUSTMENTS CREDIT	INCOME STATEMENT DEBIT	INCOME STATEMENT CREDIT	BALANCE SHEET DEBIT	BALANCE SHEET CREDIT	
1	Cash					2 6 0 00		1
2	Supplies		(a) 1 4 5 00			5 6 0 00		2
3	Prepaid Insurance		(b) 1 9 0 00			2 1 0 00		3
4	Kurtz Supplies						3 0 0 00	4
5	Wiley Supplies						9 0 00	5
6	Norma Delk, Capital						2 8 5 0 00	6
7	Norma Delk, Drawing					2 5 0 00		7
8	Income Summary							8
9	Sales				1 1 0 0 00			9
10	Insurance Expense	(b) 1 9 0 00		1 9 0 00				10
11	Miscellaneous Expense			6 5 00				11
12	Rent Expense			3 2 0 00				12
13	Supplies Expense	(a) 1 4 5 00		1 4 5 00				13
14		3 3 5 00	3 3 5 00	7 2 0 00	1 1 0 0 00	3 6 2 0 00	3 2 4 0 00	14
15	Net Income			3 8 0 00			3 8 0 00	15
16				1 1 0 0 00	1 1 0 0 00	3 6 2 0 00	3 6 2 0 00	16
17								17
18								18
19								19

INSTRUCTIONS:

1. Use page 3 of a journal. Journalize and post the adjusting entries.
2. Continue to use page 3 of the journal. Journalize and post the closing entries.
3. Prepare a post-closing trial balance.

MASTERY PROBLEM 10-M Journalizing and posting adjusting and closing entries; preparing a post-closing trial balance

AUTOMATED

Kellerman Services' partial work sheet for the month ended November 30 of the current year is given below. The general ledger accounts are given in the working papers that accompany this textbook. (The general ledger accounts do not show all details for the fiscal period. The "Balance" shown in each account is the account's balance before adjusting and closing entries are posted.)

APPLICATION

INSTRUCTIONS:

1. Use page 3 of a journal. Journalize and post the adjusting entries.
2. Continue to use page 3 of the journal. Journalize and post the closing entries.
3. Prepare a post-closing trial balance.

		ADJUSTMENTS		INCOME STATEMENT		BALANCE SHEET		
ACCOUNT TITLE		DEBIT	CREDIT	DEBIT	CREDIT	DEBIT	CREDIT	
1	Cash					3 5 0 00		1
2	Supplies		(a) 1 9 5 00			7 5 0 00		2
3	Prepaid Insurance		(b) 2 6 0 00			2 8 0 00		3
4	Kern Supplies						5 0 0 00	4
5	Waite Supplies						1 2 0 00	5
6	A. Kellerman, Capital						3 7 2 5 00	6
7	A. Kellerman, Drawing					3 5 0 00		7
8	Income Summary							8
9	Sales				1 5 0 0 00			9
10	Insurance Expense	(b) 2 6 0 00		2 6 0 00				10
11	Miscellaneous Expense			8 5 00				11
12	Rent Expense			4 2 5 00				12
13	Supplies Expense	(a) 1 9 5 00		1 9 5 00				13
14		4 5 5 00	4 5 5 00	9 6 5 00	1 5 0 0 00	4 8 8 0 00	4 3 4 5 00	14
15	Net Income			5 3 5 00			5 3 5 00	15
16				1 5 0 0 00	1 5 0 0 00	4 8 8 0 00	4 8 8 0 00	16

CHALLENGE PROBLEM 10-C Completing end-of-fiscal-period work

AUTOMATED

A trial balance on a work sheet for Reed Company is given in the working papers that accompany this textbook.

INSTRUCTIONS:

1. Complete the work sheet.

Adjustment Information, December 31

Supplies on hand	$980.00
Value of prepaid insurance	700.00

2. Use page 3 of a journal. Journalize the adjusting entries.
3. Continue to use page 3 of the journal. Journalize the closing entries.

End-of-Fiscal-Period Work for a Proprietorship

Chapters 8 through 10 describe Rugcare's manual accounting procedures for completing end-of-fiscal-period work. Integrating Automated Accounting Topic 3 describes procedures for using automated accounting software to complete Rugcare's end-of-fiscal-period work. The Automated Accounting Problems contain instructions for using automated accounting software to solve Mastery Problem 10-M and Challenge Problem 10-C, Chapter 10.

COMPLETING END-OF-FISCAL-PERIOD WORK

In automated accounting end-of-fiscal-period reports are generated by the software. The run date used for all end-of-fiscal-period reports is the ending date of the accounting period. Before printing financial statements, the software is directed to prepare a trial balance. The trial balance is prepared to prove equality of general ledger debits and credits. The trial balance is also used to plan adjustments to general ledger accounts.

Preparing a Trial Balance

To prepare a trial balance, the File menu is selected from the menu bar. The Open Accounting File command is then chosen to retrieve the general ledger data base from the template disk.

The Reports menu is selected from the menu bar. The Ledgers command is then chosen from the Reports menu. The Trial Balance is then selected from the Report Selection menu to display the trial balance as shown in Illustration T3-1.

| ILLUSTRATION T3-1 | Trial balance |

```
                              Rugcare
                           Trial Balance
                            08/31/--
------------------------------------------------------------------
Acct.   Account
Number  Title                               Debit          Credit
------------------------------------------------------------------
110     Cash                              8272.00
120     Petty Cash                         200.00
130     Supplies                          4931.00
140     Prepaid Insurance                 1200.00
210     Butler Cleaning Supplies                         1360.00
220     Dale Office Supplies                              200.00
310     Ben Furman, Capital                             10000.00
320     Ben Furman, Drawing                600.00
410     Sales                                            4291.00
510     Advertising Expense                 68.00
530     Miscellaneous Expense              105.00
540     Rent Expense                       250.00
550     Repair Expense                     110.00
570     Utilities Expense                  115.00
                                         ----------      ----------
        Totals                            15851.00        15851.00
                                         ==========      ==========
```

Recording Adjusting Entries

Adjusting entries are recorded on a general journal input form. Rugcare records two adjusting entries. (1) An adjusting entry to bring the supplies account up to date. (2) An adjusting entry to bring the prepaid insurance account up to date.

Rugcare has the following adjustment data on August 31.

Adjustment Information, August 31

Supplies on hand...............................	$2,284.00
Value of prepaid insurance	1,100.00

The information needed to journalize the adjusting entries is obtained from the trial balance. The expense account, Supplies

Expense, is increased by a debit, $2,647.00, the value of supplies used. The asset account, Supplies, is decreased by a credit, $2,647.00, the value of the supplies used. The journal entry to record this adjustment is on lines 1 and 2 of the general journal input form shown in Illustration T3-2. The abbreviation for adjusting entries, *Adj. Ent.*, is written in the Reference column for each entry.

The expense account, Insurance Expense, is increased by a debit, $100.00, the value of insurance used. The asset account, Prepaid Insurance, is decreased by a credit, $100.00, the value of insurance used. The journal entry to record this adjustment is shown on lines 3 and 4 of Illustration T3-2.

ILLUSTRATION T3-2

General journal report for adjusting entries

RUN DATE *08/31/--*
MM DD YY

GENERAL JOURNAL
Input Form

	DATE MM/DD	REFERENCE	ACCOUNT NO.	CUSTOMER/ VENDOR NO.	DEBIT	CREDIT	
1	*08/31*	*Adj. Ent.*	*560*		*2647 00*		1
2			*130*			*2647 00*	2
3	*31*	*Adj. Ent.*	*520*		*100 00*		3
4			*140*			*100 00*	4
21							21
22							22
23							23
24							24
25							25
			PAGE TOTALS		2747 00	2747 00	
			FINAL TOTALS		2747 00	2747 00	

Processing Adjusting Entries

To process adjusting entries, the Journals menu is selected from the menu bar. The General Journal command is chosen to display the data entry window for keying adjustment data.

After all lines on the input form have been keyed and posted, the Reports menu is selected from the menu bar. The Journals command is selected from the Reports menu. The General Journal report is chosen from the Report Selection menu. This selection displays the Selection Options screen. The *Ok* button is pushed to display the general journal report. The general journal report is checked for accuracy by comparing the report totals, $2,747.00, with the totals on the general journal input form. Because the totals are the same, the general journal report is assumed to be correct. The general journal report is printed, as shown in Illustration T3-3, and filed for future reference.

General journal report for adjusting entries

```
                          Rugcare
                      General Journal
                        08/31/--
---------------------------------------------------------------------
Date   Refer.   V/C Acct.  Title              Debit       Credit
---------------------------------------------------------------------
08/31  Adj.Ent.     560    Supplies Expense    2647.00
08/31  Adj.Ent.     130    Supplies                        2647.00

08/31  Adj.Ent.     520    Insurance Expense    100.00
08/31  Adj.Ent.     140    Prepaid Insurance                100.00

                                              ----------  ----------
                           Totals              2747.00     2747.00
                                              ==========  ==========
```

PROCESSING FINANCIAL STATEMENTS

To process the income statement, the Reports menu is selected from the menu bar. The Financial Statements command is then selected from the menu. The Income Statement option is chosen from the Report Selection window to display the income statement. The income statement is printed, as shown in Illustration T3-4, and filed for future reference.

Income statement

```
                          Rugcare
                      Income Statement
                  For Period Ended 08/31/--
-------------------------------------------------------------------------
                       *****Monthly*****        *****Yearly******
                       Amount     Percent       Amount     Percent
-------------------------------------------------------------------------
Operating  Revenue
-----------------------------------
Sales                  4291.00     100.00       4291.00     100.00
                      ----------  ----------   ----------  ----------
Total Operating Revenue 4291.00    100.00       4291.00     100.00

Operating  Expenses
-----------------------------------
Advertising Expense      68.00       1.58         68.00       1.58
Insurance Expense       100.00       2.33        100.00       2.33
Miscellaneous Expense   105.00       2.45        105.00       2.45
Rent Expense            250.00       5.83        250.00       5.83
Repair Expense          110.00       2.56        110.00       2.56
Supplies Expense       2647.00      61.69       2647.00      61.69
Utilities Expense       115.00       2.68        115.00       2.68
                      ----------  ----------   ----------  ----------
Total Operating Expenses 3395.00    79.12       3395.00      79.12
                      ----------  ----------   ----------  ----------
Net Income              896.00      20.88        896.00      20.88
                      ==========  ==========   ==========  ==========
```

The income statement prepared by Rugcare's automated accounting software provides both current month and yearly amounts and percentages. This additional data allows Mr. Furman to analyze both monthly and yearly performance. As the month of August was Rugcare's first month of operation, monthly and yearly amounts are the same.

To process the balance sheet, the Reports menu is selected from the menu bar. The Financial Statements command is then selected from the Reports menu. The Balance Sheet option is selected from the Report Selection window to display the balance sheet. The balance sheet is printed, as shown in Illustration T3-5, and filed for future reference.

A balance sheet may be prepared in one of two forms: (1) account form or (2) report form. An account form of balance sheet lists assets on the left and equities on the right. Rugcare's manual accounting system uses the account form of balance sheet. A report form of balance sheet lists the assets, liabilities, and owner's equity vertically. Illustration T3-5 is a report form of balance sheet.

To prevent the computer from overheating, avoid blocking air vents.

| **ILLUSTRATION T3-5** | Balance sheet |

```
                                    Rugcare
                                 Balance Sheet
                                   08/31/--

Assets
----------
Cash                                  8272.00
Petty Cash                             200.00
Supplies                              2284.00
Prepaid Insurance                     1100.00
                                    ----------
Total Assets                                        11856.00
                                                    ==========
Liabilities
--------------------
Butler Cleaning Supplies              1360.00
Dale Office Supplies                   200.00
                                    ----------
Total Liabilities                                    1560.00

Owner's  Equity
----------------------------
Ben Furman, Capital                  10000.00
Ben Furman, Drawing                   -600.00
Net Income                             896.00
                                    ----------
Total Owner's Equity                                10296.00
                                                    ----------
Total Liabilities & Equity                          11856.00
                                                    ==========
```

Closing Temporary Accounts

In automated accounting the software contains instructions for closing temporary accounts. The Options menu is selected from the menu bar. The Period-End Closing command is selected from the Options menu to close all temporary accounts.

Processing a Post-Closing Trial Balance

After the financial statements have been prepared and closing entries have been posted, a post-closing trial balance is prepared. A **post-closing trial balance** is a trial balance that is prepared after closing entries have been posted.

To process a post-closing trial balance, the Reports menu is selected from the menu bar. The Ledgers menu command is selected and the Trial Balance is then chosen from the Report Selection menu. The post-closing trial balance is printed, as shown in Illustration T3-6, and is filed for future reference.

| ILLUSTRATION T3-6 | Post-closing trial balance |

```
                         Rugcare
                      Trial Balance
                       08/31/--
-----------------------------------------------------------------
Acct.    Account
Number   Title                          Debit          Credit
-----------------------------------------------------------------
110      Cash                         8272.00
120      Petty Cash                    200.00
130      Supplies                     2284.00
140      Prepaid Insurance            1100.00
210      Butler Cleaning Supplies                      1360.00
220      Dale Office Supplies                           200.00
310      Ben Furman, Capital                          10296.00
                                      ---------       ---------
         Totals                      11856.00         11856.00
                                      =========       =========
```

COMPARISON OF MANUAL AND AUTOMATED ACCOUNTING CYCLE

The accounting cycle is the same for both manual and automated accounting, only the procedures change. A comparison is shown in Illustration T3-7.

Manual Accounting Cycle	Automated Accounting Cycle
Analyze source documents	Analyze source documents
Record transactions in a journal	Record transactions on an input form and key
Post journal entries	Select posting command
Prepare a work sheet	Print a trial balance
(Adjustments are planned on the work sheet)	Analyze adjusting entries using the trial balance; record adjusting entries on input form, key, and post
Prepare financial statements	Print financial statements
Journalize and post adjusting entries	(Adjusting entries already recorded)
Record closing entries	Select closing command
Prepare a post-closing trial balance	Print a post-closing trial balance

OPTIONAL PROBLEM DB-3A

Rugcare's general ledger data base is on the accounting textbook template. If you wish to process Rugcare's end-of-fiscal-period work using automated accounting software, load the *Automated Accounting 6.0* or higher software. Select Data Base 3A (DB-3A) from the template disk. Read the Problem Instructions screen. Use Illustration T3-2 and follow the procedures described to process Rugcare's end-of-fiscal-period work.

AUTOMATED ACCOUNTING PROBLEMS

AUTOMATING MASTERY PROBLEM 10-M **Journalizing and posting adjusting entries; end-of-fiscal-period work for a proprietorship**

INSTRUCTIONS:

1. Use the end-of-fiscal period work for Mastery Problem 10-M, Chapter 10. Use November 30 of the current year as the run date.

2. Load the *Automated Accounting 6.0* or higher software. Select data base F10-M (First-Year Course Problem 10-M) from the accounting textbook template. Read the Problem Instructions screen.

3. Select File from the menu bar and choose the Save As menu command. Key the path to the drive and directory that contains your data files. Save the data base with a file name of XXX10M (where XXX are your initials).

4. Display/print a trial balance.

5. Record the adjusting entries on a general journal input form using the following information. Use the account numbers from the trial balance that was printed in Instruction 4.

Adjustment Information, November 30

Supplies on hand.	$750.00
Value of prepaid insurance.	280.00

6. Key the adjusting entries from the general journal input form.

7. Display/print the general journal report.
8. Display/print the income statement.
9. Display/print the balance sheet.
10. Perform period-end closing.
11. Display/print the post-closing trial balance.

AUTOMATED

AUTOMATING CHALLENGE PROBLEM 10-C Completing end-of-fiscal period work

INSTRUCTIONS:

1. Load the *Automated Accounting 6.0* or higher software. Select data base F10-C from the accounting textbook template. Read the Problem Instructions screen.

2. Select File from the menu bar and choose the Save As menu command. Key the path to the drive and directory that contains your data files. Save the data base with a file name of XXX10C (where XXX are your initials).

3. Display/print a trial balance.

4. Record the adjusting entries on a general journal input form using the following information. Use the account numbers from the trial balance that was printed in Instruction 3.

Adjustment Information, December 31

Supplies on hand.	$980.00
Value of prepaid insurance.	700.00

5. Key the adjusting entries from the general journal input form.

6. Display/print the general journal report.

7. Display/print the income statement.

8. Display/print the balance sheet.

9. Perform period-end closing.

10. Display/print the post-closing trial balance.

An Accounting Cycle for a Proprietorship: End-of-Fiscal-Period Work

AUTOMATED

The general ledger prepared in Reinforcement Activity 1, Part A, is needed to complete Reinforcement Activity 1, Part B.

Reinforcement Activity 1, Part B, includes end-of-fiscal-period activities studied in Chapters 8 through 10.

WORK SHEET

INSTRUCTIONS:

12. Prepare a trial balance on a work sheet. Use a one-month fiscal period ended May 31 of the current year.

13. Analyze the following adjustment information into debit and credit parts. Record the adjustments on the work sheet.

Adjustment Information, May 31

Supplies on hand $515.00
Value of prepaid insurance 800.00

14. Total and rule the Adjustments columns.

15. Extend the up-to-date account balances to the Balance Sheet and Income Statement columns.

16. Complete the work sheet.

FINANCIAL STATEMENTS

17. Prepare an income statement. Figure and record the component percentages for sales, total expenses, and net income. Round percentage calculations to the nearest 0.1%.

18. Prepare a balance sheet.

ADJUSTING ENTRIES

19. Use page 3 of the journal. Journalize and post the adjusting entries.

CLOSING ENTRIES

20. Continue using page 3 of the journal. Journalize and post the closing entries.

POST-CLOSING TRIAL BALANCE

21. Prepare a post-closing trial balance.

This simulation covers the transactions completed by Video Transfer, a service business organized as a proprietorship. Video Transfer begins business on September 1 of the current year. The business produces personal videos for such events as weddings and family reunions. In addition, the business also transfers home movies and slides to video tape.

The activities included in the accounting cycle for Video Transfer are listed below. The company uses a journal and a general ledger similar to those described for Rugcare in Part 2.

This simulation is available from the publisher in either manual or automated versions.

The following activities are included in this simulation.

1. Journalizing transactions in a journal.

2. Forwarding column totals to a new journal page.

3. Preparing a bank statement reconciliation and recording a bank service charge.

4. Proving cash.

5. Proving and ruling a journal.

6. Posting from a journal to a general ledger.

7. Preparing a trial balance on a work sheet.

8. Recording adjustments on a work sheet.

9. Completing a work sheet.

10. Preparing financial statements (income statement and balance sheet).

11. Journalizing and posting adjusting entries.

12. Journalizing and posting closing entries.

13. Preparing a post-closing trial balance.

PART 3

Accounting for a Merchandising Business Organized as a Partnership

Access to Capital
Management Talent
Ease of Formation
× Benefits

GENERAL GOALS

1. Know accounting terminology related to an accounting system for a merchandising business organized as a partnership.

2. Understand accounting concepts and practices related to an accounting system for a merchandising business organized as a partnership.

3. Demonstrate accounting procedures used in an accounting system for a merchandising business organized as a partnership.

CHART OF ACCOUNTS
GENERAL LEDGER

Balance Sheet Accounts

(1000) ASSETS
1110 Cash
1120 Petty Cash
1130 Accounts Receivable
1140 Merchandise Inventory
1145 Supplies—Office
1150 Supplies—Store
1160 Prepaid Insurance

(2000) LIABILITIES
2110 Accounts Payable
2120 Employee Income Tax Payable
2130 FICA Tax Payable
2140 Sales Tax Payable
2150 Unemployment Tax Payable—Federal
2160 Unemployment Tax Payable—State
2170 Health Insurance Premiums Payable
2180 U.S. Savings Bonds Payable
2190 United Way Donations Payable

(3000) OWNERS' EQUITY
3110 Amy Kramer, Capital
3120 Amy Kramer, Drawing
3130 Dario Mesa, Capital
3140 Dario Mesa, Drawing
3150 Income Summary

Income Statement Accounts

(4000) OPERATING REVENUE
4110 Sales

(5000) COST OF MERCHANDISE
5110 Purchases

(6000) OPERATING EXPENSES
6110 Advertising Expense
6120 Credit Card Fee Expense
6130 Insurance Expense
6140 Miscellaneous Expense
6150 Payroll Taxes Expense
6160 Rent Expense
6170 Salary Expense
6175 Supplies Expense—Office
6180 Supplies Expense—Store
6190 Utilities Expense

SUBSIDIARY LEDGERS

Accounts Receivable Ledger

110 Ashley Delivery
120 Autohaus Service
130 Friendly Auto Service
140 Keystone Delivery
150 Powell Rent-A-Car
160 Wood Sales & Service

Accounts Payable Ledger

210 Antelo Supply
220 Bell Office Products
230 Filtrex Tires
240 Nilon Motor Parts
250 Q-Ban Distributors
260 Veloz Automotive

The charts of accounts for CarLand are illustrated above for ready reference as you study Part 3 of this textbook.

11

Journalizing Purchases and Cash Payments

ENABLING PERFORMANCE TASKS

After studying Chapter 11, you will be able to:

a Define accounting terms related to purchases and cash payments for a merchandising business.

b Identify accounting concepts and practices related to purchases and cash payments for a merchandising business.

c Analyze purchases and cash payments transactions for a merchandising business.

d Journalize purchases and cash payments transactions for a merchandising business.

TERMS PREVIEW

partnership • partner • merchandising business • merchandise • cost of merchandise • markup • vendor • purchase on account • invoice • purchase invoice • terms of sale • correcting entry

Rugcare, the business described in Part 2, is owned by one person. A business owned by one person is known as a proprietorship.

Businesses often require the skills of more than one person. Many businesses also need more capital than one owner can provide. Therefore, some businesses are owned by two or more persons. A business in which two or more persons combine their assets and skills is called a **partnership.** Each member of a partnership is called a **partner.** Partners must agree on how each partner will share the business' profit or loss. As in proprietorships, reports and financial records of the business are kept separate from the personal records of the partners. *(CONCEPT: Business Entity)*

Rugcare, the business described in Part 2, sells services for a fee. A business that sells a service for a fee is known as a service business. However, many other businesses purchase goods to sell. A business that purchases and sells goods is called a **merchandising business.** Goods that a merchandising business purchases to sell are called **merchandise.** The selling of merchandise rather than a service is what makes the activities of a merchandising business different from those of a service business.

CarLand, the business described in this part, is a merchandising business organized as a partnership. The business is owned by Amy Kramer and Dario Mesa. The business purchases and sells automotive supplies. CarLand rents the building in which the business is located as well as the equipment used for operation. CarLand expects to make money and continue in business indefinitely. *(CONCEPT: Going Concern)*

USING AN EXPANDED JOURNAL

A service business generally has a large number of cash transactions and a limited number of noncash transactions. Noncash transactions are those that do not involve either the receipt or payment of cash. Rugcare uses a 5-column journal to record all cash and noncash transactions.

Need for Expanded Journal

CarLand, a merchandising business, has many noncash and other frequently occurring transactions that affect single accounts. CarLand could use the same journal as the one used by Rugcare. However, without adding more special amount columns to the journal, the large number of transactions would require many entries in the General Debit and Credit columns.

Form of Expanded Journal

To save time and space in journalizing transactions, CarLand uses an 11-column journal. The journal includes additional special amount columns for recording frequently occurring transactions that affect single accounts. A journal expanded to provide for the recording of frequently occurring transactions that affect single accounts is shown in Illustration 11-1.

ILLUSTRATION 11-1   Amount columns of an expanded journal

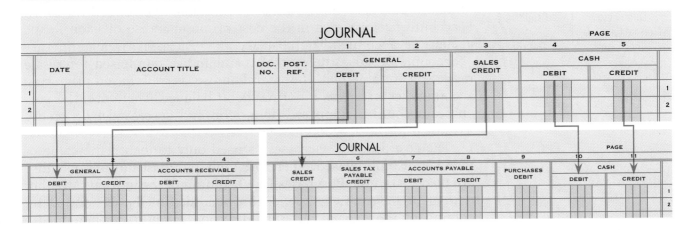

An expanded journal is commonly used by small merchandising businesses in which only one person records transactions. Amy Kramer records all transactions for CarLand.

CarLand's journal, Illustration 11-1, has special amount columns for the recording of frequently occurring transactions related to the purchasing and selling of merchandise. The columns are arranged to make accurate journalizing and posting easier. Debit and credit columns for Cash, Accounts Receivable, and Accounts Payable are arranged in pairs. This arrangement helps avoid errors in recording amounts in the wrong columns. All columns are placed to the right of the Account Title column. The General Debit and Credit amount columns are placed first so that amounts in these columns will be close to the titles in the Account Title column.

The number and arrangement of columns in a journal is determined by the type and frequency of transactions. CarLand determined that the journal described above would best meet the needs of the business.

JOURNALIZING PURCHASES OF MERCHANDISE

The cost account, Purchases, is only used to record the value of merchandise purchased. All other items bought, such as supplies, are recorded in the appropriate asset account.

The price a business pays for goods it purchases to sell is called **cost of merchandise**. The selling price of merchandise must be greater than the cost of merchandise for a business to make a profit. The amount added to the cost of merchandise to establish the selling price is called **markup**. Revenue earned from the sale of merchandise includes both the cost of merchandise and markup. Only the markup increases capital. Accounts for the cost of merchandise are kept in a separate division of the general ledger. The cost of merchandise division is shown in CarLand's chart of accounts, page 244.

In addition to purchasing merchandise to sell, a merchandising business also buys supplies and other assets for use in the business. A business from which merchandise is purchased or supplies or other assets are bought is called a **vendor.**

The account used for recording the cost of merchandise purchased to sell is titled Purchases. Purchases is classified as a cost account because it is in the cost of merchandise division in the chart of accounts. The cost account, Purchases, is a temporary account. Because the cost of merchandise purchased for resale reduces capital when the merchandise is purchased, the cost account, Purchases, has a normal debit balance. Therefore, the purchases account is increased by a debit and decreased by a credit, as shown in the T account.

The cost account, Purchases, is used only to record the value of merchandise purchased. Therefore, only purchases of merchandise are recorded in the Purchases Debit column of the journal. All other items bought, such as supplies, are recorded in the General Debit column of the journal. Merchandise and other items bought are recorded and reported at the price agreed upon at the time the transactions occur. The price agreed upon at the time the transaction occurs may be lower than the given price. The accounting concept, *Historical Cost,* is applied when the actual amount paid for merchandise or other items bought is recorded. *(CONCEPT: Historical Cost)*

Purchases	
Debit side	Credit side
Normal balance	
Increase	Decrease

Purchase of Merchandise for Cash

CarLand pays cash for some purchases. All cash payments are made by check.

November 2, 19--. Purchased merchandise for cash, $483.00. Check No. 259.

Purchases	
483.00	

Cash	
	483.00

A cash purchase transaction increases the purchases account balance and decreases the cash account balance.

Because the purchases account has a normal debit balance, Purchases is debited for $483.00 to show the increase in this cost account. The cash account also has a normal debit balance. Therefore, Cash is credited for $483.00 to show the decrease in this asset account.

The journal entry to record this transaction is shown in Illustration 11-2.

ILLUSTRATION 11-2   Journal entry to record a purchase of merchandise for cash

	DATE	ACCOUNT TITLE	DOC. NO.	POST. REF.	PURCHASES DEBIT	CASH DEBIT	CASH CREDIT	
					9	10	11	
1	Nov. 2	√	C259	√	4 8 3 00		4 8 3 00	1
2								2

PAGE *21*   JOURNAL   PAGE *21*

The date, *19--, Nov. 2,* is recorded in the Date column. Both the debit and credit amounts will be recorded in special amount columns. Therefore, a check mark is placed in the Account Title column to show that no account title needs to be written. The check number, *C259,* is recorded in the Doc. No. column. Both the debit and credit amounts will be posted as part of special amount column totals. Therefore, a check mark is placed in the Post. Ref. column to show that amounts on this line are not to be posted individually. The debit to Purchases, *$483.00,* is entered in the Purchases Debit column. The credit to Cash, *$483.00,* is entered in the Cash Credit column.

Purchase of Merchandise on Account

A transaction in which the merchandise purchased is to be paid for later is called a **purchase on account.** Some businesses that purchase on account from only a few vendors keep a separate general ledger account for each vendor to whom money is owed. Businesses that purchase on account from many vendors will have many accounts for vendors. To avoid a bulky general ledger, the total amount owed to all vendors can be summarized in a single general ledger account. A liability account that summarizes the amounts owed to all vendors is titled Accounts Payable. CarLand uses an accounts payable account.

The liability account, Accounts Payable, has a normal credit balance. Therefore, the accounts payable account is increased by a credit and decreased by a debit, as shown in the T account.

When a vendor sells merchandise to a buyer, the vendor prepares a form showing what has been sold. A form describing the goods sold, the quantity, and the price is called an **invoice.** An invoice used as a source document for recording a purchase on account transaction is called a **purchase invoice.** *(CONCEPT: Objective Evidence)* A purchase invoice received by CarLand is shown in Illustration 11-3.

Accounts Payable	
Debit side	Credit side
	Normal balance
Decrease	Increase

ILLUSTRATION 11-3   Purchase invoice

			REC'D 11/02/-- P74		

veloz automotive
2611 Industrial
Fremont, NH 03044-2672

TO: CarLand
1374 Parklane
Rockville, RI 02873-4121

DATE: 10/26/--
INV. NO.: 2768
TERMS: 30 days
ACCT. NO.: 260

QUANTITY	CAT. NO.	DESCRIPTION	UNIT PRICE	TOTAL
8	4422	All-season tires	73.00	584.00 ✓
6	4424	All-season tires	73.00	438.00 ✓
12	6620	Floor mats	16.00	192.00 ✓
12	7715	Seat covers	45.00	540.00 ✓
		Total		1,754.00
				Pst

A purchase invoice lists the quantity, the description, the price of each item, and the total amount of the invoice. A purchase invoice provides the information needed for recording a purchase on account.

When CarLand receives a purchase invoice, a date and a number are stamped in the upper right-hand corner. The date stamped is the date the invoice is received. CarLand received the invoice in Illustration 11-3 on 11/02/--. This date should not be confused with the vendor's date on the invoice, 10/26/--. CarLand assigns numbers in sequence to easily identify all purchase invoices. The number stamped on the invoice, *P74*, is the number assigned by CarLand to this purchase invoice. This number should not be confused with the invoice number, *2768*, assigned by the vendor. Each vendor uses a different numbering system. Therefore, vendor invoice numbers could not be recorded in sequence, which would make it impossible to detect a missing invoice.

A buyer needs to know that all items ordered have been received and that the prices are correct. The check marks on the invoice show that the items have been received and that amounts have been checked and are correct. The initials near the total are those of the person at CarLand who checked the invoice.

An agreement between a buyer and a seller about payment for merchandise is called the **terms of sale.** The terms of sale on the invoice, Illustration 11-3, are 30 days. These terms mean that payment is due within 30 days from the date of the invoice. The invoice is dated October 26. Therefore, payment must be made by November 25.

November 2, 19--. Purchased merchandise on account from Veloz Automotive, $1,754.00. Purchase Invoice No. 74.

A purchase on account transaction increases the amount owed to a vendor. This transaction increases the purchases account balance and increases the accounts payable account balance.

Because the purchases account has a normal debit balance, Purchases is debited for $1,754.00 to show the increase in this cost account. The accounts payable account has a normal credit balance. Therefore, Accounts Payable is credited for $1,754.00 to show the increase in this liability account.

The journal entry to record this purchase on account transaction is shown in Illustration 11-4.

Purchases

| 1,754.00 | |

Accounts Payable

| | 1,754.00 |

ILLUSTRATION 11-4   Journal entry to record a purchase of merchandise on account

PAGE *21*		JOURNAL						
						7 ACCOUNTS PAYABLE	8	9 PURCHASES DEBIT
DATE		ACCOUNT TITLE	DOC. NO.	POST. REF.		DEBIT	CREDIT	
2	2	*Veloz Automotive*	P74				1 7 5 4 00	1 7 5 4 00

The date, *2*, is written in the Date column. No special amount column is provided for Veloz Automotive Therefore, the vendor name, *Veloz Automotive*, is recorded in the Account Title column. CarLand's purchase invoice number, *P74,* is entered in the Doc. No. column. The credit to Accounts Payable, *$1,754.00,* is recorded in the Accounts Payable Credit column. The debit to Purchases, *$1,754.00,* is recorded in the Purchases Debit column.

The debit to Purchases and the credit to Accounts Payable are recorded in special amount columns. Therefore, writing the titles of either general ledger account in the Account Title column is not necessary. However, the name of the vendor is written in the Account Title column to show to whom the amount is owed. The way CarLand keeps records of the amount owed to each vendor is described in Chapter 13.

JOURNALIZING BUYING SUPPLIES

CarLand buys supplies for use in the business. Supplies are not recorded in the purchases account because supplies are not intended for sale. Cash register tapes and price tags are examples of supplies used in a merchandising business.

Buying Supplies for Cash

CarLand buys most of its supplies for cash.

November 5, 19--. Paid cash for office supplies, $87.00. Check No. 261.

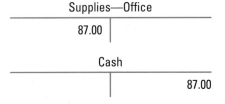

Supplies—Office	
87.00	

Cash	
	87.00

FYI

Supplies are not recorded in the Purchases account because supplies are not intended for sale.

This transaction increases the office supplies account balance and decreases the cash account balance.

Because the office supplies account has a normal debit balance, Supplies—Office is debited for $87.00 to show the increase in this asset account. The cash account also has a normal debit balance. Therefore, Cash is credited for $87.00 to show the decrease in this asset account.

The journal entry to record this buying supplies for cash transaction is shown in Illustration 11-5, page 252.

The date, *5*, is recorded in the Date column. No special amount column is provided for Supplies—Office. Therefore, the account title, *Supplies—Office*, is written in the Account Title column. The check number, *C261,* is entered in the Doc. No. column. The debit to Supplies—Office, *$87.00,* is recorded in the General Debit column. The credit to Cash, *$87.00,* is recorded in the Cash Credit column.

ILLUSTRATION 11-5   Journal entry to record buying supplies for cash

					1	2		10	11	
PAGE *21*		JOURNAL							PAGE *21*	
					GENERAL			CASH		
DATE	ACCOUNT TITLE	DOC. NO.	POST. REF.	DEBIT	CREDIT		DEBIT	CREDIT	
6	5	*Supplies—Office*	C261		8 7 00				8 7 00	6
7										7
8										8

Buying Supplies on Account

CarLand usually buys supplies for cash. Occasionally, however, CarLand buys some supplies on account.

November 6, 19--. Bought store supplies on account from Antelo Supply, $160.00. Memorandum No. 43.

When CarLand buys supplies on account, an invoice is received from the vendor. This invoice is similar to the purchase invoice received when merchandise is purchased. To assure that no mistake is made, a memorandum is attached to the invoice noting that the invoice is for supplies and not for purchases. Memorandum 43 is shown in Illustration 11-6.

ILLUSTRATION 11-6   Memorandum for buying supplies on account

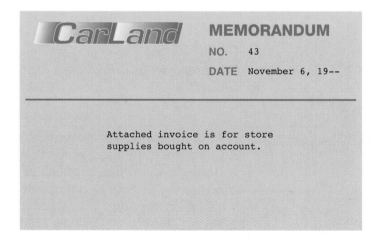

```
CarLand    MEMORANDUM

           NO.   43

           DATE  November 6, 19--


           Attached invoice is for store
           supplies bought on account.
```

Supplies—Store

160.00 |

Accounts Payable

| 160.00

This transaction increases the store supplies account balance and increases the accounts payable account balance.

Because the store supplies account has a normal debit balance, Supplies—Store is debited for $160.00 to show the increase in this asset account. The accounts payable account has a normal credit balance. Therefore, Accounts Payable is credited for $160.00 to show the increase in this liability account.

The journal entry to record this buying supplies on account transaction is shown in Illustration 11-7.

ILLUSTRATION 11-7   Journal entry to record buying supplies on account

								1	2		7	8
PAGE *21*		JOURNAL										
								GENERAL			ACCOUNTS PAYABLE	
	DATE	ACCOUNT TITLE	DOC. NO.	POST. REF.				DEBIT	CREDIT		DEBIT	CREDIT
9	6	*Supplies—Store*	M43					1 6 0 00				
10		*Antelo Supply*										1 6 0 00

The date, 6, is written in the Date column. No special amount column is provided for Supplies—Store Therefore, the account title, *Supplies—Store*, is recorded in the Account Title column. The memorandum number, *M43*, is entered in the Doc. No. column. The debit to Supplies—Store, *$160.00*, is written in the General Debit column on the same line. An account title is also required for the credit part of the entry. Therefore, the vendor name, *Antelo Supply*, is recorded in the Account Title column on the next line. The credit to Accounts Payable, *$160.00*, is entered in the Accounts Payable Credit column on the same line.

JOURNALIZING CASH PAYMENTS

Most of CarLand's cash payments are to vendors or for expenses. Payment to vendors is made according to the terms of sale on the purchase invoices. Payment for an expense is usually made at the time the expense occurs.

Cash Payment on Account

CarLand pays by check for all cash purchases and for payments on account.

November 7, 19--. Paid cash on account to Filtrex Tires, $970.00, covering Purchase Invoice No. 72. Check No. 263.

This cash payment on account transaction decreases the amount owed to vendors. This transaction decreases the accounts payable account balance and decreases the cash account balance.

Because the accounts payable account has a normal credit balance, Accounts Payable is debited for $970.00 to show the decrease in this liability account. The cash account has a normal debit balance. Therefore, Cash is credited for $970.00 to show the decrease in this asset account.

Accounts Payable
970.00 |

Cash
| 970.00

The journal entry to record this cash payment on account transaction is shown in Illustration 11-8.

ILLUSTRATION 11-8   Journal entry to record a cash payment on account

PAGE 21		JOURNAL			7 ACCOUNTS PAYABLE DEBIT	8 CREDIT	10 CASH DEBIT	11 PAGE 21 CREDIT	
	DATE	ACCOUNT TITLE	DOC. NO.	POST. REF.	DEBIT	CREDIT	DEBIT	CREDIT	
13	7	Filtrex Tires	C263		970 00			970 00	13
14									14
15									15
16									16

The date, 7, is written in the Date column. No special amount column is provided for Filtrex Tires. Therefore, the vendor name, *Filtrex Tires*, is recorded in the Account Title column. The check number, *C263*, is entered in the Doc. No. column. The debit to Accounts Payable, *$970.00*, is written in the Accounts Payable Debit column. The credit to Cash, *$970.00*, is written in the Cash Credit column.

Cash Payment of an Expense

CarLand usually pays for an expense at the time the transaction occurs.

November 9, 19--. Paid cash for advertising, $125.00. Check No. 265.

This cash payment increases the advertising expense account balance and decreases the cash account balance.

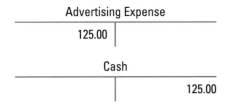

Advertising Expense

| 125.00 | |

Cash

| | 125.00 |

Because the advertising expense account has a normal debit balance, Advertising Expense is debited for $125.00 to show the increase in this expense account. The cash account also has a normal debit balance. Therefore, Cash is credited for $125.00 to show the decrease in this asset account.

The journal entry to record this cash payment of an expense transaction is shown in Illustration 11-9.

ILLUSTRATION 11-9   Journal entry to record a cash payment of an expense

| | | | | | | GENERAL | | CASH | |
| | | | | | | 1 | 2 | 10 | 11 |
	DATE	ACCOUNT TITLE	DOC. NO.	POST. REF.		DEBIT	CREDIT	DEBIT	CREDIT
17	9	Advertising Expense	C265			125 00			125 00	17

PAGE *21* — JOURNAL — PAGE *21*

The date, *9*, is written in the Date column. No special amount column is provided for Advertising Expense. Therefore, the account title, *Advertising Expense*, is recorded in the Account Title column. The check number, *C265*, is entered in the Doc. No. column. The debit to Advertising Expense, *$125.00*, is written in the General Debit column. The credit to Cash, *$125.00*, is written in the Cash Credit column.

Cash Payment to Replenish Petty Cash

The account title Petty Cash is used only when establishing the petty cash account.

CarLand deposits all cash in a bank. Some cash, however, is kept in a petty cash fund for making change at the cash register and for making small cash payments. CarLand has a petty cash fund of $500.00, which is replenished whenever the petty cash on hand drops below $200.00.

> *November 9, 19--. Paid cash to replenish the petty cash fund, $301.00: office supplies, $58.00; store supplies, $65.00; advertising, $92.00; miscellaneous, $86.00. Check No. 266.*

Supplies—Office

| 58.00 | |

Supplies—Store

| 65.00 | |

Advertising Expense

| 92.00 | |

Miscellaneous Expense

| 86.00 | |

Cash

| | 301.00 |

This cash payment increases the balances of the supplies accounts and several expense accounts and decreases the cash account balance.

The supplies accounts have normal debit balances. Therefore, Supplies—Office is debited for $58.00 and Supplies—Store is debited for $65.00 to show the increases in these two asset accounts. The expense accounts also have normal debit balances. Therefore, Advertising Expense is debited for $92.00 and Miscellaneous Expense is debited for $86.00 to show the increases in these expense accounts. The cash account has a normal debit balance. Therefore, Cash is credited for $301.00, the total amount needed to replenish the petty cash fund, to show the decrease in this asset account.

The journal entry to record this cash payment to replenish petty cash transaction is shown in Illustration 11-10.

	PAGE 21		JOURNAL			1	2			10	11		
				DOC. NO.	POST. REF.	**GENERAL**				**CASH**			
	DATE	ACCOUNT TITLE				DEBIT	CREDIT			DEBIT	CREDIT		
18	9	Supplies—Office		C266		5 8 00					3 0 1 00		18
19		Supplies—Store				6 5 00							19
20		Advertising Expense				9 2 00							20
21		Miscellaneous Expense				8 6 00							21

The date, 9, is written once in the Date column, line 18. No special amount columns are provided for any of the accounts for which the petty cash fund was used. Therefore, the account titles are recorded in the Account Title column. The check number, C266, is entered once in the Doc. No. column, line 18. The debit amounts are written in the General Debit column. The credit amount is recorded in the Cash Credit column.

JOURNALIZING OTHER TRANSACTIONS

Most transactions of merchandising businesses are related to purchasing and selling merchandise. A merchandising business, however, has other transactions that must be recorded. CarLand records these other transactions in its journal.

Withdrawals by Partners

Amy Kramer, Drawing	
Debit side Normal balance Increase	Credit side Decrease

Dario Mesa, Drawing	
Debit side Normal balance Increase	Credit side Decrease

The two assets generally taken out of a merchandising business by owners are cash and merchandise.

Assets taken out of a business for the personal use of an owner are known as withdrawals. The two assets generally taken out of a merchandising business are cash and merchandise. Withdrawals reduce the amount of a business' capital. The account titles of the partners' drawing accounts are Amy Kramer, Drawing and Dario Mesa, Drawing. The drawing accounts are classified as contra capital accounts. Since capital accounts have credit balances, partners' drawing accounts have normal debit balances. Therefore, the drawing accounts are increased by a debit and decreased by a credit, as shown in the T accounts.

Withdrawals could be recorded as debits directly to the partners' capital accounts. However, withdrawals are normally recorded in separate accounts so that the total amounts are easily determined for each accounting period.

Cash Withdrawal. When either Amy Kramer or Dario Mesa withdraws cash from CarLand, a check is written for the payment.

November 10, 19--. Dario Mesa, partner, withdrew cash for personal use, $1,500.00. Check No. 267.

Dario Mesa, Drawing

| 1,500.00 | |

Cash

| | 1,500.00 |

This cash withdrawal increases Dario Mesa's drawing account balance and decreases the cash account balance.

Because the drawing account has a normal debit balance, Dario Mesa, Drawing is debited for $1,500.00 to show the increase in this contra capital account. The cash account also has a normal debit balance. Therefore, Cash is credited for $1,500.00 to show the decrease in this asset account.

The journal entry to record this cash withdrawal is shown in Illustration 11-11.

ILLUSTRATION 11-11   Journal entry to record a cash withdrawal by a partner

						GENERAL		CASH	
	DATE	ACCOUNT TITLE	DOC. NO.	POST. REF.	DEBIT	CREDIT	DEBIT	CREDIT	
22	10	*Dario Mesa, Drawing*	C267		1 5 0 0 00			1 5 0 0 00	22

PAGE *21*   JOURNAL   PAGE *21*

The date, *10*, is written in the Date column. No special amount column is provided for Dario Mesa, Drawing. Therefore, the contra capital account title, *Dario Mesa, Drawing*, is recorded in the Account Title column. The check number, *C267*, is entered in the Doc. No. column. The debit to Dario Mesa, Drawing, *$1,500.00*, is written in the General Debit column. The credit to Cash, *$1,500.00*, is written in the Cash Credit column.

Merchandise Withdrawal. A partner may also withdraw merchandise for personal use.

> *November 12, 19--. Dario Mesa, partner, withdrew merchandise for personal use, $200.00. Memorandum No. 44.*

This merchandise withdrawal increases Dario Mesa's drawing account balance and decreases the purchases account balance.

Because the drawing account has a normal debit balance, Dario Mesa, Drawing is debited for $200.00 to show the increase in this contra capital account. The purchases account also has a normal debit balance. Therefore, Purchases is credited for $200.00 to show the decrease in this cost account.

The journal entry to record this merchandise withdrawal is shown in Illustration 11-12.

Dario Mesa, Drawing

| 200.00 | |

Purchases

| | 200.00 |

ILLUSTRATION 11-12   Journal entry to record a merchandise withdrawal by a partner

PAGE *21*   JOURNAL

						GENERAL	
	DATE	ACCOUNT TITLE	DOC. NO.	POST. REF.	DEBIT	CREDIT	
26	12	*Dario Mesa, Drawing*	M44		2 0 0 00		
27		*Purchases*				2 0 0 00	

The date, *12*, is written in the Date column. Neither a Drawing Debit nor a Purchases Credit column is provided in the journal because merchandise withdrawals do not occur frequently. Therefore, the account title, *Dario Mesa, Drawing*, is recorded in the Account Title column. The memorandum number, *M44*, is entered in the Doc. No. column. The debit to Dario Mesa, Drawing, *$200.00*, is written in the General Debit column. The account title, *Purchases*, is recorded in the Account Title column on the next line. The credit to Purchases, *$200.00*, is entered in the General Credit column.

Correcting Entry

Errors may be made even though care is taken in recording transactions. Simple errors may be corrected by ruling through the incorrect item, as described in Chapter 5. However, a transaction may have been improperly journalized and posted to the ledger. When an error in a journal entry has already been posted, the incorrect journal entry should be corrected with an additional journal entry. A journal entry made to correct an error in the ledger is called a **correcting entry**.

> *November 13, 19--. Discovered that a payment of cash for advertising in October was journalized and posted in error as a debit to* Miscellaneous Expense *instead of* Advertising Expense, *$120.00. Memorandum No. 45.*

If an accounting error is discovered, a memorandum is prepared describing the correction to be made. The source document for a correcting entry is the memorandum. *(CONCEPT: Objective Evidence)* A memorandum for this correcting entry is shown in Illustration 11-13.

ILLUSTRATION 11-13   Memorandum for a correcting entry

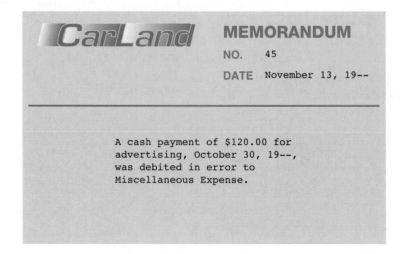

To correct the error, an entry is made to add $120.00 to the advertising expense account. The entry must also deduct $120.00 from the miscellaneous expense account. The correcting entry increases the advertising expense account balance and decreases the miscellaneous expense account balance.

Because the advertising expense account has a normal debit balance, Advertising Expense is debited for $120.00 to show the increase in this expense account. The miscellaneous expense account also has a normal debit balance. Therefore, Miscellaneous Expense is credited for $120.00 to show the decrease in this expense account.

The journal entry to record this correcting entry is shown in Illustration 11-14.

Advertising Expense	
120.00	

Miscellaneous Expense	
	120.00

ILLUSTRATION 11-14   Journal entry to record a correcting entry

	DATE	ACCOUNT TITLE	DOC. NO.	POST. REF.	GENERAL DEBIT	GENERAL CREDIT
28	13	Advertising Expense	M45		1 2 0 00	
29		Miscellaneous Expense				1 2 0 00
30						
31						
32						
33						
34						

PAGE 21 — JOURNAL

Audit Your Understanding

1. When cash is paid on account, what is the effect on the cash account?

2. What are two assets normally withdrawn by the partners of a business?

3. What is a correcting entry?

The date, *13*, is written in the Date column. The account title, *Advertising Expense*, is recorded in the Account Title column. The memorandum number, *M45*, is entered in the Doc. No. column. The debit to Advertising Expense, *$120.00*, is entered in the General Debit column. The account title, *Miscellaneous Expense*, is written in the Account Title column on the next line. The credit to Miscellaneous Expense, *$120.00*, is recorded in the General Credit column.

The chart shown in Illustration 11-15 summarizes the entries for purchases, cash payments, and other transactions in an expanded journal.

Summary of entries for purchases, cash payments, and other transactions in an expanded journal

TRANSACTION	JOURNAL										
	1	2	3	4	5	6	7	8	9	10	11
	GENERAL		ACCOUNTS RECEIVABLE		SALES CREDIT	SALES TAX PAYABLE CREDIT	ACCOUNTS PAYABLE		PURCHASES DEBIT	CASH	
	DEBIT	CREDIT	DEBIT	CREDIT			DEBIT	CREDIT		DEBIT	CREDIT
Purchase merchandise for cash									X		X
Purchase merchandise on account								X	X		
Buying supplies for cash	X										X
Buying supplies on account	X							X			
Cash payment on account							X				X
Cash payment of an expense	X										X
Cash payment to replenish petty cash	X										X
Cash withdrawal	X										X
Merchandise withdrawal	X	X									

What is the meaning of each of the following?

1. **partnership**
2. **partner**
3. **merchandising business**
4. **merchandise**
5. **cost of merchandise**
6. **markup**
7. **vendor**
8. **purchase on account**
9. **invoice**
10. **purchase invoice**
11. **terms of sale**
12. **correcting entry**

QUESTIONS FOR INDIVIDUAL STUDY   EPT(b)

1. Why would two or more persons want to own a single business?

2. What makes the activities of a merchandising business different from those of a service business?

3. What are noncash transactions?

4. Why does CarLand use an 11-column journal rather than a 5-column journal like the one used by Rugcare?

5. What is the title of the account that shows the cost of merchandise purchased for sale?

6. What is the account classification of Purchases?

7. Which accounting concept is being applied when merchandise and other items bought are recorded and reported at the price agreed upon at the time the transactions occur?

8. What accounts are affected, and how, when merchandise is purchased for cash?

9. Why is a check mark placed in the Account Title column of an expanded journal for a cash purchase transaction?

10. Why would a business use a single general ledger account to summarize the amount owed to all vendors?

11. What is the name of the liability account that summarizes the amounts owed to all vendors?

12. Why does CarLand use its own set of sequential purchase invoice numbers rather than using the numbers assigned by vendors?

13. What accounts are affected, and how, when merchandise is purchased on account?

14. Why are the account titles (Purchases and Accounts Payable) for a purchase on account entry not written in the Account Title column in the expanded journal?

15. Why are supplies bought recorded in a separate supplies account rather than in the purchases account?

16. What accounts are affected, and how, when store supplies are bought on account?

17. What accounts are affected, and how, when a cash payment on account is made?

18. How does CarLand use a petty cash fund?

19. What accounts are affected, and how, when a withdrawal of merchandise is made?

20. When should a journal entry be made to correct errors in recording transactions?

CASE 1 Deborah Butler owns and operates a gift shop in a downtown shopping area. Because of a shopping mall that has opened in one of the suburbs, the gift shop's business has been declining. Ms. Butler has an opportunity to move the business to the shopping mall. Additional capital, however, is required to move and operate the business in a new location. The local bank has agreed to lend the money needed. The business hours would be extended at the new location. The business would also be open seven days a week. The extended hours plus the expected increase in business would require the hiring of one additional employee. Ms. Butler has been contacted by Fred Chaney, a person with similar merchandising experience, who would like to become a partner. As an alternative to borrowing cash, Mr. Chaney would provide the capital necessary to move the business to the new location. For the capital provided, Mr. Chaney would share equally in the net income or loss of the business. Mr. Chaney would also share equally in the operation of the business. Should Ms. Butler (1) borrow the money from the bank or (2) bring in a partner? Explain your answer.

CASE 2 Daryl Hodges is a high school student who works part-time in a local clothing store. As part of his duties, he records daily transactions in a journal. One day he asks the owner: "You use the purchase invoice as your source document for recording purchases of merchandise on account. You use a memorandum as your source document for recording the entry when supplies are bought on account. Why don't you use the invoice for both entries?" How would you respond to this question?

DRILL 11-D1 Analyzing transactions into debit and credit parts

INSTRUCTIONS:

Prepare two T accounts for each of the following transactions. Use the T accounts to analyze each transaction. Use account titles similar to CarLand's, as shown in the chart of accounts, page 244. The partners' names are Irma Gilbert and Alex Jensen. The first transaction is given as an example.

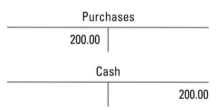

	Purchases	
200.00		

	Cash	
		200.00

1. Purchased merchandise for cash, $200.00.
2. Purchased merchandise on account from Klein Co., $900.00.
3. Paid cash for office supplies, $75.00.
4. Bought store supplies on account from Central Supply, $240.00.
5. Bought office supplies on account from Cratin Supply, $125.00.
6. Purchased merchandise for cash, $175.00.
7. Paid cash for office supplies, $70.00.
8. Paid cash on account to Matson Company, $750.00.
9. Purchased merchandise on account from Garber Company, $1,200.00.
10. Paid cash for advertising, $85.00.
11. Irma Gilbert, partner, withdrew cash for personal use, $1,000.00.
12. Alex Jensen, partner, withdrew cash for personal use, $1,000.00.
13. Irma Gilbert, partner, withdrew merchandise for personal use, $130.00.
14. Paid cash on account to Butler Enterprises, $360.00.

15. Discovered that a transaction for office supplies bought last month was journalized and posted in error as a debit to Prepaid Insurance instead of Supplies—Office, $60.00.

16. Alex Jensen, partner, withdrew merchandise for personal use, $95.00.

The solution to Drill 11-D1 is needed to complete Drill 11-D2.

DRILL 11-D2 Analyzing journal entries

The solution to Drill 11-D1 is needed to complete Drill 11-D2.

INSTRUCTIONS:

A form for analyzing transactions is given in the working papers that accompany this textbook. Based on the answers in Drill 11-D1, write the amounts in the amount columns to be used to journalize each transaction. Transaction 1 is given as an example in the working papers.

APPLICATION PROBLEM
EPT(c,d)

PROBLEM 11-1 Journalizing purchases, cash payments, and other transactions

Mary Demski and Eileen Ivan, partners, own a gift shop.

INSTRUCTIONS:

Journalize the following transactions completed during September of the current year. Use page 21 of a journal similar to the one described in this chapter for CarLand. Source documents are abbreviated as follows: check, C; memorandum, M; purchase invoice, P.

Sept. 1. Purchased merchandise for cash, $150.00. C220.

     1. Purchased merchandise on account from Kemp Fashions, $1,350.00. P60.

     2. Paid cash for office supplies, $75.00. C221.

     2. Purchased merchandise on account from Bonner & Co., $740.00. P61.

     3. Purchased merchandise on account from Burton Fabrics, $585.00. P62.

     4. Paid cash for office supplies, $55.00. C222.

     7. Bought store supplies on account from Pulver Supply, $135.00. M42.

     7. Purchased merchandise for cash, $120.00. C223.

     8. Paid cash for telephone bill, $120.00. C224.

     9. Bought office supplies on account from Lorand Supply, $85.00. M43.

    11. Purchased merchandise for cash, $110.00. C225.

    12. Paid cash for store supplies, $60.00. C226.

    14. Mary Demski, partner, withdrew cash for personal use, $1,200.00. C227.

    14. Eileen Ivan, partner, withdrew cash for personal use, $1,200.00. C228.

    18. Paid cash on account to Kemp Fashions, $1,350.00, covering P60. C229.

    21. Paid cash for advertising, $87.00. C230.

    22. Paid cash on account to Bonner & Co., $740.00, covering P61. C231.

    24. Mary Demski, partner, withdrew merchandise for personal use, $160.00. M44.

    25. Discovered that a transaction for office supplies bought in August was journalized and posted in error as a debit to Purchases instead of Supplies—Office, $88.00. M45.

    26. Paid cash on account to Burton Fabrics, $585.00, covering P62. C232.

    29. Eileen Ivan, partner, withdrew merchandise for personal use, $120.00. M46.

    30. Paid cash to replenish the petty cash fund, $305.00: office supplies, $63.00; store supplies, $51.00; advertising, $88.00; miscellaneous, $103.00. C233.

    30. Paid cash on account to Pulver Supply, $135.00, covering M42. C234.

MASTERY PROBLEM 11-M Journalizing purchases, cash payments, and other transactions

APPLICATION

Sylvia Prior and Julia Steger, partners, own a bookstore.

INSTRUCTIONS:

Journalize the following transactions completed during November of the current year. Use page 23 of a journal similar to the one described in this chapter for CarLand. Source documents are abbreviated as follows: check, C; memorandum, M; purchase invoice, P.

Nov. 2. Paid cash for rent, $1,250.00. C261.
2. Sylvia Prior, partner, withdrew cash for personal use, $1,500.00. C262.
2. Julia Steger, partner, withdrew cash for personal use, $1,500.00. C263.
3. Purchased merchandise for cash, $130.00. C264.
4. Paid cash on account to BFL Publishing, $920.00, covering P71. C265.
4. Purchased merchandise on account from Quality Books, $1,450.00. P74.
5. Paid cash for office supplies, $48.00. C266.
7. Julia Steger, partner, withdrew merchandise for personal use, $42.00. M32.
9. Paid cash for electric bill, $154.00. C267.
9. Paid cash on account to Quality Books, $1,235.00, covering P72. C268.
10. Bought store supplies on account from Carson Supply Co., $106.00. M33.
11. Paid cash on account to Matson Book Service, $975.00, covering P73. C269.
14. Purchased merchandise on account from Falk Book Co., $1,525.00. P75.
16. Paid cash for store supplies, $62.00. C270.
16. Sylvia Prior, partner, withdrew merchandise for personal use, $64.00. M34.
17. Bought store supplies on account from Gray Supplies, $214.00. M35.
18. Purchased merchandise for cash, $145.00. C271.
18. Paid cash to replenish the petty cash fund, $302.00: office supplies, $73.00; store supplies, $47.00; advertising, $92.00; miscellaneous, $90.00. C272.
19. Paid cash on account to Quality Books, $1,450.00, covering P74. C273.
21. Purchased merchandise on account from Voss Publishing, $925.00. P76.
24. Paid cash on account to Falk Book Co., $1,525.00, covering P75. C274.
26. Discovered that a transaction for office supplies bought in October was journalized and posted in error as a debit to Purchases instead of Supplies—Office, $94.00. M36.
28. Bought store supplies on account from Carson Supply, $118.00. M37.
30. Purchased merchandise for cash, $68.00. C275.

CHALLENGE PROBLEM 11-C Journalizing correcting entries

A review of Meir Decorating's accounting records for last month revealed the following errors.

INSTRUCTIONS:

Journalize the needed correcting entries on page 8 of a journal similar to the one described in this chapter for CarLand. Use December 2 of the current year.

Dec. 2. Merchandise withdrawn by Alice Reyes, partner, was journalized and posted in error as a credit to Cash instead of Purchases, $116.00. M35.
2. Office supplies bought for cash were journalized and posted in error as a debit to Purchases instead of Supplies—Office, $95.00. M36.
2. A check written for advertising was journalized and posted in error as a debit to Miscellaneous Expense instead of Advertising Expense, $125.00. M37.
2. Store supplies bought on account were journalized and posted in error as a debit to Utilities Expense instead of Supplies—Store, $52.00. M38.
2. Merchandise purchased on account was journalized and posted in error as a debit to Supplies—Office instead of Purchases, $850.00. M39.

Dec. 2. A check written for rent was journalized and posted in error as a debit to Salary Expense instead of Rent Expense, $1,200.00. M40.

2. A cash withdrawal by Harold Atkins, partner, was journalized and posted in error as a credit to Purchases instead of Cash, $200.00. M41.

2. A check written for miscellaneous expense was journalized and posted in error as a debit to Supplies Expense—Store instead of Miscellaneous Expense, $89.00. M42.

2. Office supplies bought for cash were journalized and posted in error as a debit to Prepaid Insurance instead of Supplies—Office, $160.00. M43.

2. A check written for store supplies was journalized and posted in error as a debit to Supplies—Office instead of Supplies—Store, $151.00. M44.

12

Journalizing Sales and Cash Receipts

ENABLING PERFORMANCE TASKS

After studying Chapter 12, you will be able to:

a Define accounting terms related to sales and cash receipts for a merchandising business.

b Identify accounting concepts and practices related to sales and cash receipts for a merchandising business.

c Analyze sales and cash receipts transactions for a merchandising business.

d Journalize sales and cash receipts transactions for a merchandising business.

e Prove and rule a journal.

TERMS PREVIEW

customer • sales tax • cash sale • credit card sale • sale on account • sales invoice

Purchases and sales of merchandise are the two major activities of a merchandising business. A person or business to whom merchandise or services are sold is called a **customer.** Rugcare, described in Part 2, sells services. CarLand, described in this part, sells merchandise. Other businesses may sell both services and merchandise.

SALES TAX

Laws of most states and some cities require that a tax be collected from customers for each sale made. A tax on a sale of merchandise or services is called a **sales tax.** Sales tax rates are usually stated as a percentage of sales. Regardless of the tax rates used, accounting procedures are the same.

Every business collecting a sales tax needs accurate records of the amount of tax collected. Businesses must file reports with the proper government unit and pay the amount of sales tax collected. Records need to show (1) total sales and (2) total sales tax. The amount of sales tax collected by CarLand is a business liability until paid to the state government. Therefore, the sales tax amount is recorded in a separate liability account titled *Sales Tax Payable.* The liability account, Sales Tax Payable, has a normal credit balance. This account is increased by a credit and decreased by a debit, as shown in the T account.

Sales Tax Payable	
Debit side	Credit side
	Normal balance
Decrease	Increase

CarLand operates in a state with a 6% sales tax rate. A customer must pay for the price of the goods plus the sales tax. The total amount of a sale of merchandise priced at $200.00 is calculated as shown below.

Price of Goods	×	Sales Tax Rate	=	Sales Tax
$200.00	×	6%	=	$12.00
Price of Goods	**+**	**Sales Tax**	**=**	**Total Amount Received**
$200.00	+	$12.00	=	$212.00

A customer must pay $212.00 for the merchandise ($200.00 for the goods plus $12.00 for the sales tax). CarLand records the price of goods sold, the sales tax, and the total amount received.

JOURNALIZING SALES AND CASH RECEIPTS FOR SALES

A sale of merchandise may be (1) for cash or (2) on account. A sale of merchandise increases the revenue of a business. Regardless of when payment is made, the revenue should be recorded at the time of a sale, not on the date cash is received. For example, on June 15 CarLand sells merchandise on account to a customer. The customer pays CarLand for the merchandise on July 12. CarLand records the revenue on June 15, the date of the sale. The accounting concept, *Realization of Revenue,* is applied when revenue is recorded at the time goods or services are sold. *(CONCEPT: Realization of Revenue)*

Cash and Credit Card Sales

CarLand sells most of its merchandise for cash. A sale in which cash is received for the total amount of the sale at the time of the transaction is called a **cash sale.** CarLand also sells merchandise to customers who have a bank approved credit card. A sale in which a credit card is used for the total amount of the sale at the time of the transaction is called a **credit card sale.** Major bank approved credit cards include VISA, MasterCard, Discover Card, and Carte Blanche. CarLand accepts all major bank approved credit cards from customers. A customer who uses a credit card promises to pay the amount due for the credit card transaction to the bank issuing the credit card.

CarLand prepares a credit card slip for each credit card sale. At the end of each week, these credit card slips are included with CarLand's bank deposit. CarLand's bank accepts the credit card slips the same way it accepts checks and cash for deposit. The bank increases CarLand's bank account by the total amount of the credit card sales deposited. If a credit card was issued by another bank, CarLand's bank sends the credit card slips to the issuing bank. The bank that issues the credit card then bills the customer and collects the amount owed. The bank that accepts and processes the credit card slips for a business charges a fee for this service. This fee is included on CarLand's monthly bank statement.

Cash and credit card sales are both revenue items that increase the revenue account, Sales. Because the bank accepts credit card slips the same way it accepts cash, CarLand's bank account increases after each deposit as though cash had been deposited. Therefore, CarLand combines all cash and credit card sales and records the two revenue items as a single cash sales transaction.

> *November 7, 19--. Recorded cash and credit card sales, $6,450.00, plus sales tax, $387.00; total, $6,837.00. Cash Register Tape No. 7.*

CarLand uses a cash register to list all cash and credit card sales. When a transaction is entered on the cash register, a paper tape is printed as a receipt for the customer. The cash register also internally accumulates data about total cash and credit card sales.

At the end of each week, a cash register tape is printed showing total cash and credit card sales. The tape is removed from the cash register and marked with a *T* and the date (T7). The cash register tape is used by CarLand as the source document for weekly cash and credit card sales transactions. *(CONCEPT: Objective Evidence)*

A cash and credit card sales transaction increases the balances of the cash account, the sales account, and the sales tax payable account.

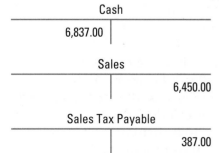

Because the asset account, Cash, has a normal debit balance, Cash is debited for the total sales and sales tax, $6,837.00, to show the increase in this asset account. The sales account has a normal credit balance. Therefore, Sales is credited for the total price of all goods sold, $6,450.00, to show the increase in this revenue account. The sales tax payable account also has a normal credit balance. Therefore, Sales Tax Payable is credited for the total sales tax, $387.00, to show the increase in this liability account.

The journal entry to record this cash and credit card sales transaction is shown in Illustration 12-1.

ILLUSTRATION 12-1   Journal entry to record cash and credit card sales

PAGE 21	JOURNAL			5	6		10	11	PAGE 21
				SALES CREDIT	SALES TAX PAYABLE CREDIT		CASH		
DATE	ACCOUNT TITLE	DOC. NO.	POST. REF.				DEBIT	CREDIT	
14	7 √		T7	√	6 4 5 0 00	3 8 7 00	6 8 3 7 00		14

The date, *7*, is written in the Date column. Special amount columns are provided for all accounts in this transaction. Therefore, a check mark is placed in the Account Title column to show that no account title needs to be written. The cash register tape number, *T7*, is recorded in the Doc. No. column. A check mark is also placed in the Post. Ref. column to show that amounts on this line do not need to be posted individually. The credit to Sales, *$6,450.00*, is written in the Sales Credit column. The credit to Sales Tax Payable, *$387.00*, is recorded in the Sales Tax Payable Credit column. The debit to Cash, *$6,837.00*, is entered in the Cash Debit column.

Sales on Account

A sale for which cash will be received at a later date is called a **sale on account.** A sale on account is also referred to as a charge sale. CarLand sells on account only to businesses. Other customers must either pay cash or use a credit card.

CarLand summarizes the total due from all charge customers in a general ledger account titled *Accounts Receivable.* Accounts Receivable is an asset account with a normal debit balance. Therefore, the accounts receivable account is increased by a debit and decreased by a credit, as shown in the T account.

Accounts Receivable	
Debit side Normal balance Increase	Credit side Decrease

When merchandise is sold on account, the seller prepares a form showing what has been sold. A form describing the goods sold, the quantity, and the price is known as an invoice. An invoice used as a source document for recording a sale on account is called a **sales invoice.** *(CONCEPT: Objective Evidence)* A sales invoice is also referred to as a sales ticket or a sales slip. The sales invoice used by CarLand is shown in Illustration 12-2.

ILLUSTRATION 12-2   Sales invoice

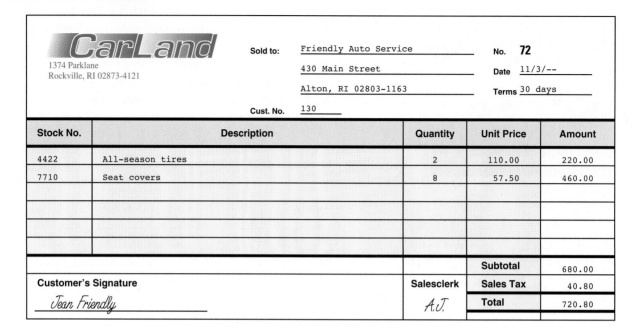

The seller considers an invoice for a sale on account to be a sales invoice. The same invoice is considered by the customer to be a purchase invoice.

A sales invoice is prepared in duplicate. The original copy is given to the customer. The carbon copy is used as the source document for the sale on account transaction. *(CONCEPT: Objective Evidence)* Sales invoices are numbered in sequence. The number 72 is the number of the sales invoice issued to Friendly Auto Service.

FYI

About 115 million people in the United States use credit cards to buy goods and services.

November 3, 19--. Sold merchandise on account to Friendly Auto Service, $680.00, plus sales tax, $40.80; total, $720.80. Sales Invoice No. 72.

A sale on account transaction increases the amount to be collected later from a customer. Payment for this sale will be received at a later date. However, the sale is recorded at the time the sale is made because the sale has taken place and payment is due to CarLand. *(CONCEPT: Realization of Revenue)*

Because the accounts receivable account has a normal debit balance, Accounts Receivable is debited for the total sales and sales tax, $720.80, to show the increase in this asset account. The sales account has a normal credit balance. Therefore, Sales is credited for the price of the goods, $680.00, to show the increase in this revenue account. The sales tax payable account also has a normal credit balance. Therefore, Sales Tax Payable is credited for the amount of sales tax, $40.80, to show the increase in this liability account.

The journal entry to record this sale on account transaction is shown in Illustration 12-3.

Accounts Receivable	
720.80	

Sales	
	680.00

Sales Tax Payable	
	40.80

INTERNATIONAL WORK WEEK

American business offices normally operate Monday through Friday, eight hours a day, with a 30 to 45 minute lunch break. However, that is not necessarily true in other countries. When doing business internationally, the business day must be taken into consideration when telephone communication is made.

For example, in Spain, many businesses close at 2:00 p.m. so that employees may eat lunch with their families. The office reopens at 5:00 p.m. and stays open until about 8:00 p.m.

In the People's Republic of China, employees usually work Monday through Saturday, eight hours a day, with lunch from 1:00 p.m. to 2:00 p.m.

Before attempting to telephone or fax communication to foreign countries, the time differences and working hours must be taken into consideration. The following chart shows the time zones around the world.

World Time Zone Map

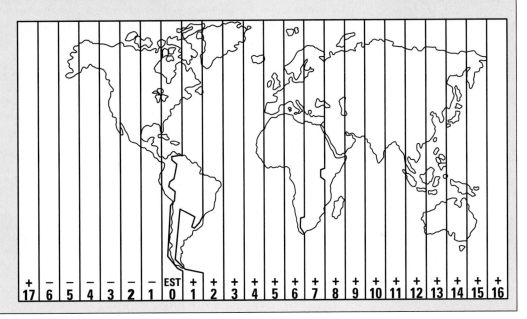

ILLUSTRATION 12-3   Journal entry to record a sale on account

| | | | | | ACCOUNTS RECEIVABLE | | SALES CREDIT | SALES TAX PAYABLE CREDIT |
| PAGE 21 | | JOURNAL | | | 3 | 4 | 5 | 6 |
DATE	ACCOUNT TITLE		DOC. NO.	POST. REF.	DEBIT	CREDIT		
3	Friendly Auto Service		S72		720 80		680 00	40 80

The date, *3*, is written in the Date column. The customer name, *Friendly Auto Service,* is recorded in the Account Title column. The sales invoice number, *S72*, is entered in the Doc. No. column. The debit to Accounts Receivable *$720.80*, is written in the Accounts Receivable Debit column. The credit to Sales, *$680.00*, is recorded in the Sales Credit column. The credit to Sales Tax Payable, *$40.80*, is entered in the Sales Tax Payable Credit column.

The debit and credit amounts are recorded in special amount columns. Therefore, writing the titles of the ledger accounts in the Account Title column is not necessary. However, the name of the customer is written in the Account Title column to show from whom the amount is due. CarLand's procedures for keeping records of the amounts to be collected from each customer are described in Chapter 13.

Cash Receipts on Account

When cash is received on account from a customer, CarLand prepares a receipt. The receipts are prenumbered so that all receipts can be accounted for. Receipts are prepared in duplicate. The original copy of the receipt is given to the customer. The carbon copy of the receipt is used as the source document for the cash receipt on account transaction. *(CONCEPT: Objective Evidence)*

November 6, 19--. Received cash on account from Autohaus Service, $1,802.00, covering S65. Receipt No. 86.

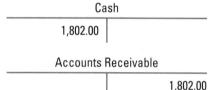

A cash receipt on account transaction decreases the amount to be collected from a customer. This transaction increases the cash account balance and decreases the accounts receivable account balance.

Because the cash account has a normal debit balance, Cash is debited for the amount of cash received, $1,802.00, to show the increase in this asset account. The accounts receivable account also has a normal debit balance. Therefore, Accounts Receivable is credited for $1,802.00 to show the decrease in this asset account.

The journal entry to record this cash receipt on account transaction is shown in Illustration 12-4.

ILLUSTRATION 12-4   Journal entry to record a cash receipt on account

	DATE	ACCOUNT TITLE	DOC. NO.	POST. REF.	ACCOUNTS RECEIVABLE DEBIT	ACCOUNTS RECEIVABLE CREDIT	CASH DEBIT	CASH CREDIT	
11	6	*Autohaus Service*	R86			1 8 0 2 00	1 8 0 2 00		11
12									12

PAGE *21* — JOURNAL — PAGE *21*

The date, *6*, is written in the Date column. The customer name, *Autohaus Service,* is recorded in the Account Title column. The receipt number, *R86*, is entered in the Doc. No. column. The credit to **Accounts Receivable**, *$1,802.00*, is written in the Accounts Receivable Credit column. The debit to **Cash**, *$1,802.00*, is recorded in the Cash Debit column.

The Summary Illustration on page 277 summarizes the entries for sales and cash receipts transactions in an expanded journal.

PROVING AND RULING AN EXPANDED JOURNAL

A journal is proved and ruled whenever a journal page is filled and always at the end of a month.

Totaling and Proving an Expanded Journal Page

After all November 14 entries are recorded, page 21 of CarLand's journal is filled. Page 21 is totaled and proved before column totals are forwarded to page 22. To prove a journal page, CarLand uses a calculator to verify that the total debit amounts equal the total credit amounts. CarLand's debit totals equal the credit totals on page 21 of the journal. Therefore, the equality of debits and credits has been proved.

Ruling an Expanded Journal Page to Carry Totals Forward

After a journal page has been proved, the journal must be prepared for forwarding. CarLand's journal column totals prepared for forwarding are shown on line 34, Illustration 12-5 on pages 274 and 275.

Five steps are followed to rule CarLand's journal.

1 Rule a single line across all amount columns directly below the last entry to indicate that the columns are to be added.

2 On the next line write the date, *14*, in the Date column.

3 Write the words, *Carried Forward*, in the Account Title column. A check mark is also placed in the Post. Ref. column to show that nothing on this line needs to be posted.

4 Write each column total below the single line.

5 Rule double lines below the column totals across all amount columns to show that the totals have been verified as correct.

Starting a New Expanded Journal Page

The totals from the previous journal page are carried forward to the next journal page. The totals are recorded on the first line of the new page. Column totals brought forward to a new page are shown on line 1, Illustration 12-6 on pages 274 and 275.

PAGE *21*   JOURNAL

	DATE		ACCOUNT TITLE	DOC. NO.	POST. REF.	GENERAL DEBIT	GENERAL CREDIT	ACCOUNTS RECEIVABLE DEBIT	ACCOUNTS RECEIVABLE CREDIT	
1	*Nov.* ¹⁹⁻⁻	2	✓	C259	✓					1
2		2	*Veloz Automotive*	P74						2
32		14	*Powell Rent-A-Car*	R89					3 1 8 00	32
33		14	✓	T14	✓					33
34		14	*Carried Forward*		✓	4 2 9 3 00	3 2 0 00	3 3 9 2 00	3 9 7 5 00	34

PAGE *22*   JOURNAL

	DATE	ACCOUNT TITLE	DOC. NO.	POST. REF.	GENERAL DEBIT	GENERAL CREDIT	ACCOUNTS RECEIVABLE DEBIT	ACCOUNTS RECEIVABLE CREDIT	
1	*Nov.* ¹⁹⁻⁻ 14	*Brought Forward*		✓	4 2 9 3 00	3 2 0 00	3 3 9 2 00	3 9 7 5 00	1
2									2
3									3
4									4

Four steps are followed for forwarding totals.

1 Write the page number, *22,* at the top of the journal.

2 Write the date, *19--, Nov. 14,* in the Date column.

3 Write the words, *Brought Forward,* in the Account Title column. A check mark is also placed in the Post. Ref. column to show that nothing on this line needs to be posted.

4 Record the column totals brought forward from page 21 of the journal.

Proving an Expanded Journal at the End of a Month

Equality of debits and credits in a journal is proved at the end of each month. The proof for CarLand's journal, Illustration 12-7 on pages 276 and 277, is calculated as follows.

ILLUSTRATION 12-5   Journal prepared for forwarding (right page)

PAGE *21*

	5	6	7	8	9	10	11	
	SALES CREDIT	SALES TAX PAYABLE CREDIT	ACCOUNTS PAYABLE DEBIT	ACCOUNTS PAYABLE CREDIT	PURCHASES DEBIT	CASH DEBIT	CASH CREDIT	
1					483 00		483 00	1
2				1754 00	1754 00			2
32						318 00		32
33	5100 00	306 00				5406 00		33
34	14750 00	885 00	5360 00	11690 00	12013 00	16218 00	9656 00	34

ILLUSTRATION 12-6   Journal totals brought forward to a new page (right page)

PAGE *22*

	5	6	7	8	9	10	11	
	SALES CREDIT	SALES TAX PAYABLE CREDIT	ACCOUNTS PAYABLE DEBIT	ACCOUNTS PAYABLE CREDIT	PURCHASES DEBIT	CASH DEBIT	CASH CREDIT	
1	14750 00	885 00	5360 00	11690 00	12013 00	16218 00	9656 00	1
2								2
3								3
4								4

Col. No.	Column Title	Debit Totals	Credit Totals
1	General Debit	$15,686.22	
2	General Credit		$ 2,029.02
3	Accounts Receivable Debit	9,222.00	
4	Accounts Receivable Credit		7,950.00
5	Sales Credit		31,600.00
6	Sales Tax Payable Credit		1,896.00
7	Accounts Payable Debit	10,820.00	
8	Accounts Payable Credit		15,870.00
9	Purchases Debit	14,773.00	
10	Cash Debit	32,224.00	
11	Cash Credit		23,380.20
	Totals	$82,725.22	$82,725.22

FYI

Double lines below totals show that the totals have been verified as correct.

The two totals, *$82,725.22*, are equal. Equality of debits and credits in CarLand's journal for November is proved.

	DATE	ACCOUNT TITLE	DOC. NO.	POST. REF.	GENERAL		ACCOUNTS RECEIVABLE		
					1 DEBIT	**2** CREDIT	**3** DEBIT	**4** CREDIT	
15	30	✓	T30	✓					15
16	30	Totals			15 686 22	2 029 02	9 222 00	7 950 00	16
17									17
18									18
19									19
20									20

PAGE 23   JOURNAL

Proving Cash at the End of a Month

CarLand's cash proof at the end of November is calculated as shown below.

Cash on hand at the beginning of the month . . . . (November 1 balance of cash account in general ledger)	$14,706.20
Plus total cash received during the month . . . . (Cash Debit column total, line 16, Illustration 12-7)	32,224.00
Equals total	$46,930.20
Less total cash paid during the month . . . . (Cash Credit column total, line 16, Illustration 12-7)	23,380.20
Equals cash balance on hand at end of the month . . .	$23,550.00
Checkbook balance on the next unused check stub . .	$23,550.00

Since the balance on the next unused check stub is the same as the cash proof, cash is proved.

☞☞ FYI ☜☜

When cash is proved, it must always equal the amount on the next unused check stub.

Ruling an Expanded Journal at the End of a Month

CarLand's journal is ruled at the end of each month. CarLand's expanded journal totaled and ruled at the end of November is shown on line 16, Illustration 12-7. Five steps are followed to rule a journal.

> **1** Rule a single line across all amount columns directly below the last entry to indicate that the columns are to be added.

PAGE 23

	5	6	7	8	9	10	11
	SALES CREDIT	SALES TAX PAYABLE CREDIT	ACCOUNTS PAYABLE DEBIT	ACCOUNTS PAYABLE CREDIT	PURCHASES DEBIT	CASH DEBIT	CASH CREDIT
15	1 1 5 0 00	6 9 00				1 2 1 9 00		15
16	31 6 0 0 00	1 8 9 6 00	10 8 2 0 00	15 8 7 0 00	14 7 7 3 00	32 2 2 4 00	23 3 8 0 20	16
17								17
18								18
19								19
20								20

Audit Your Understanding

1. How is a journal proved before column totals are forwarded to a new page?

2. List the four steps for starting a new expanded journal page.

3. How is cash proved for an expanded journal?

2 On the next line write the date, *30*, in the Date column.

3 Write the word, *Totals*, in the Account Title column.

4 Write each column total below the single line.

5 Rule double lines across all amount columns to show that the totals have been verified as correct.

Some of the column totals will be posted as described in Chapter 13. Therefore, a check mark is not placed in the Post. Ref. column for this line.

The chart shown in Illustration 12-8 summarizes the entries for sales and cash receipts transactions in an expanded journal.

SUMMARY ILLUSTRATION 12-8

Summary of entries for sales and cash receipts transactions in an expanded journal

TRANSACTION	JOURNAL										
	1 GENERAL DEBIT	2 GENERAL CREDIT	3 ACCOUNTS RECEIVABLE DEBIT	4 ACCOUNTS RECEIVABLE CREDIT	5 SALES CREDIT	6 SALES TAX PAYABLE CREDIT	7 ACCOUNTS PAYABLE DEBIT	8 ACCOUNTS PAYABLE CREDIT	9 PURCHASES DEBIT	10 CASH DEBIT	11 CASH CREDIT
Cash and credit card sale					X	X				X	
Sale on account			X		X	X					
Cash receipt on account				X						X	

What is the meaning of each of the following?

1. **customer**
2. **sales tax**
3. **cash sale**
4. **credit card sale**
5. **sale on account**
6. **sales invoice**

QUESTIONS FOR INDIVIDUAL STUDY EPT(b)

1. What are the two major activities of a merchandising business?
2. How are sales tax rates usually stated?
3. Why must every business that collects a sales tax keep accurate records of the amount of tax collected?
4. What two amounts must sales tax records show?
5. Why is sales tax collected considered a liability?
6. What is the normal balance of the sales tax payable account, and how is the account increased and decreased?
7. Which accounting concept is being applied when revenue is recorded at the time a sale is made, regardless of when payment is made?
8. Which accounting concept is being applied when a cash register tape is used as the source document for cash and credit card sales?
9. How often does CarLand journalize cash sales?
10. What accounts are affected, and how, for a cash and credit card sales transaction?
11. Why is a check mark placed in the Account Title column of an expanded journal when journalizing cash and credit card sales?
12. What is another name used for a sale on account?
13. What is the title of the general ledger account used to summarize the total amount due from all charge customers?
14. What is the source document for a sale on account transaction?
15. What are other names used for a sales invoice?
16. What accounts are affected, and how, for a sale on account transaction?
17. Which amount columns in a journal are used to record a sale on account transaction?
18. What accounts are affected, and how, for a cash receipt on account transaction?
19. How often is the equality of debits and credits in a journal proved?
20. How often is a journal page ruled?

CASES FOR CRITICAL THINKING EPT(b)

CASE 1 Carrie and Karl Lott, partners, operate a shoe store. A 5-column journal similar to the one described in Chapter 5 is used to record all transactions. The business sells merchandise for cash and on account. The business also purchases most of its merchandise on account. Mrs. Lott asked an accountant to check the accounting system and recommend changes. The accountant suggests that an expanded journal similar to the one described in Chapters 11 and 12 be used. Which journal would be better? Why?

CASE 2 Amy Pryor, an accountant for a sporting goods store, has noted a major increase in overdue amounts from charge customers. All invoice amounts from sales on account are due within 30 days. The amounts due have reduced the amount of cash available for the day-to-day operation of the business. Miss Pryor recommends that the business (1) stop all sales on account and (2) begin accepting bank credit cards. The owner is reluctant to accept the recommendations because the business might lose some reliable customers who do not have credit cards. Also, the business will have increased expenses because of the credit card fee. How would you respond to Miss Pryor's recommendations? What alternatives might the owner consider?

How often have you heard people complain about the rising costs of products? The tendency for prices to increase over time is referred to as inflation. Increasing prices reduce what an individual or company can purchase with the same amount of money.

INSTRUCTIONS:

The following table represents the prices for selected consumer goods in 1980. Copy the table and add a column for the current year and a column for the percent of change. Use the newspaper and identify current prices for the products listed. Determine the percentage change in the price of each item. If an item decreased in price, can you explain the reason for the decrease?

COMPARISON OF PRICES FOR SELECTED CONSUMER ITEMS 1980 AND 19--

Item	1980 Price
19-inch color television	$439.00
Cassette tape.	6.95
Milk (gallon)	1.99
Ground beef (pound)	1.69
Eggs, medium (dozen).	.69
Raisin bran	1.39
Film, 12 exposures	1.13
Theater ticket.	3.50
Motor oil (quart)	.84
Refrigerator (19.1 cu. ft.).	679.00

DRILLS FOR UNDERSTANDING

EPT(c,d)

DRILL 12-D1 Analyzing transactions into debit and credit parts

TUTORIAL

INSTRUCTIONS:

Prepare T accounts for each of the following transactions. Use the T accounts to analyze each transaction. A 5% sales tax has been added to each sale. The first transaction is given as an example.

1. Recorded cash and credit card sales, $1,500.00, plus sales tax, $75.00; total, $1,575.00.

2. Sold merchandise on account to Steven Kramer, $300.00, plus sales tax, $15.00; total, $315.00.

3. Sold merchandise on account to Mark Fields, $360.00, plus sales tax, $18.00; total, $378.00.

4. Received cash on account from Jackson White, $157.50.

5. Received cash on account from Gloria Burton, $68.25.

6. Recorded cash and credit card sales, $1,750.00, plus sales tax, $87.50; total, $1,837.50.

The solution to Drill 12-D1 is needed to complete Drill 12-D3.

Cash	
1,575.00	

Sales	
	1,500.00

Sales Tax Payable	
	75.00

DRILL 12-D2 Analyzing sales transactions

MATHEMATICS

INSTRUCTIONS:

1. Prepare a T account for each of the following accounts: Cash, Accounts Receivable, Sales, and Sales Tax Payable.

2. Using the T accounts, analyze the following transactions. Add a 6% sales tax to each sale. Write the transaction number in parentheses to the left of each amount. The first transaction is given as an example.

1. Recorded cash and credit card sales, $2,700.00.
2. Sold merchandise on account to Melissa Bedo, $180.00.
3. Sold merchandise on account to Kim Lea, $170.00.
4. Received cash on account from Maria Jones, $148.40.
5. Received cash on account from Jack Mumford, $79.50.
6. Recorded cash and credit card sales, $2,375.00.

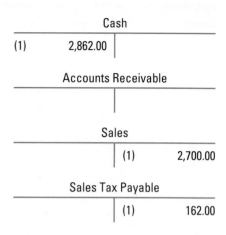

Cash	
(1) 2,862.00	

Accounts Receivable	

Sales	
	(1) 2,700.00

Sales Tax Payable	
	(1) 162.00

DRILL 12-D3 Analyzing journal entries

The solution to Drill 12-D1 is needed to complete Drill 12-D3.

INSTRUCTIONS:

A form for analyzing journal entries is given in the working papers that accompany this textbook. Based on the answers in Drill 12-D1, write the amounts in the amount columns to be used to journalize each transaction. Transaction 1 is given as an example in the working papers.

APPLICATION PROBLEM   EPT(c,d,e)

PROBLEM 12-1 Journalizing sales and cash receipts

Mark Butler and Betty Rivers, partners, own a tennis equipment and clothing store.

INSTRUCTIONS:

1. Journalize the following transactions completed during September of the current year. Use page 16 of a journal similar to the one described in this chapter. A 4% sales tax has been added to each sale. Source documents are abbreviated as follows: receipt, R; sales invoice, S; cash register tape, T.

Sept. 1. Sold merchandise on account to Valerie Seeley, $50.00, plus sales tax, $2.00; total, $52.00. S66.

2. Sold merchandise on account to Jill Folker, $125.00, plus sales tax, $5.00; total, $130.00. S67.

4. Sold merchandise on account to Jerome Hodges, $85.00, plus sales tax, $3.40; total, $88.40. S68.

5. Received cash on account from Rita Picken, $140.40, covering S62. R93.

5. Recorded cash and credit card sales, $2,360.00, plus sales tax, $94.40; total, $2,454.40. T5.

7. Received cash on account from Karla Doyle, $182.00, covering S63. R94.

9. Sold merchandise on account to Anthony Zolte, $115.00, plus sales tax, $4.60; total, $119.60. S69.

12. Recorded cash and credit card sales, $2,890.00, plus sales tax, $115.60; total, $3,005.60. T12.

12. Received cash on account from Jonathan Ames, $50.40, covering S64. R95.

14. Received cash on account from Robert Hall, $67.60, covering S65. R96.

15. Sold merchandise on account to Beth Klein, $115.00, plus sales tax, $4.60; total, $119.60. S70.

Sept. 17. Received cash on account from Valerie Seeley, $52.00, covering S66. R97.

19. Recorded cash and credit card sales, $2,810.00, plus sales tax, $112.40; total, $2,922.40. T19.

25. Received cash on account from Jill Folker, $130.00, covering S67. R98.

26. Sold merchandise on account to Jill Folker, $75.00, plus sales tax, $3.00; total, $78.00. S71.

26. Recorded cash and credit card sales, $2,650.00, plus sales tax, $106.00; total, $2,756.00. T26.

28. Received cash on account from Jerome Hodges, $88.40, covering S68. R99.

29. Sold merchandise on account to Karla Doyle, $95.00, plus sales tax, $3.80; total, $98.80. S72.

30. Recorded cash and credit card sales, $1,540.00, plus sales tax, $61.60; total, $1,601.60. T30.

2. Total the journal. Prove the equality of debits and credits.

3. Rule the journal.

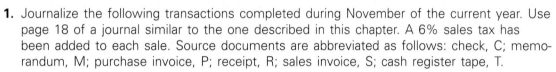

ENRICHMENT PROBLEMS   EPT(c,d,e)

MASTERY PROBLEM 12-M Journalizing transactions

APPLICATION

MATHEMATICS

Kevin Sykes and David Webb, partners, own a bicycle and motorcycle store.

INSTRUCTIONS:

1. Journalize the following transactions completed during November of the current year. Use page 18 of a journal similar to the one described in this chapter. A 6% sales tax has been added to each sale. Source documents are abbreviated as follows: check, C; memorandum, M; purchase invoice, P; receipt, R; sales invoice, S; cash register tape, T.

Nov. 2. Paid cash for rent, $1,250.00. C244.

2. Kevin Sykes, partner, withdrew cash for personal use, $600.00. C245.

2. David Webb, partner, withdrew cash for personal use, $600.00. C246.

3. Paid cash for electric bill, $130.00. C247.

3. Purchased merchandise on account from Vista Cycle Co., $2,275.00. P58.

4. Paid cash on account to Daley Motorcycles, $1,360.00, covering P56. C248.

5. Sold merchandise on account to Loree Adams, $1,130.00, plus sales tax, $67.80; total, $1,197.80. S61.

5. Paid cash for office supplies, $62.00. C249.

6. Purchased merchandise for cash, $165.00. C250.

7. Recorded cash and credit card sales, $5,850.00, plus sales tax, $351.00; total, $6,201.00. T7.

9. Sold merchandise on account to Victor Droste, $358.00, plus sales tax, $21.48; total, $379.48. S62.

9. Received cash on account from Wayne Ivory, $1,775.50, covering S57. R112.

11. Bought office supplies on account from Walden Supply, $68.00. M43.

12. Purchased merchandise for cash, $180.00. C251.

12. Received cash on account from Robert Melvin, $996.40, covering S58. R113.

13. Paid cash on account to Action Cycles, $1,365.00, covering P57. C252.

14. David Webb, partner, withdrew merchandise for personal use, $385.00. M44.

Nov. 14. Recorded cash and credit card sales, $2,680.00, plus sales tax, $160.80; total, $2,840.80. T14.

16. Kevin Sykes, partner, withdrew cash for personal use, $600.00. C253.

16. David Webb, partner, withdrew cash for personal use, $600.00. C254.

17. Purchased merchandise on account from United Bicycle Co., $825.00. P59.

18. Purchased merchandise for cash, $196.00. C255.

18. Bought store supplies on account from Baker Supply, $92.00. M45.

19. Paid cash on account to Walden Supply, $68.00, covering M43. C256.

21. Recorded cash and credit card sales, $2,430.00, plus sales tax, $145.80; total, $2,575.80. T21.

23. Discovered that a payment of cash for advertising in October was journalized and posted in error as a debit to Miscellaneous Expense instead of Advertising Expense, $125.00. M46.

23. Paid cash for office supplies, $44.00. C257.

2. Prepare page 18 of the journal for forwarding. Total the amount columns. Prove the equality of debits and credits, and record the totals to be carried forward on line 32.

3. Record the totals brought forward on line 1 of page 19 of the journal. Prove the equality of debits and credits again.

4. Journalize the following transactions on page 19 of the journal.

Nov. 23. Received cash on account from Esther Lorand, $630.70, covering S59. R114.

24. Sold merchandise on account to Celia Sotelo, $325.00, plus sales tax, $19.50; total, $344.50. S63.

27. Purchased merchandise on account from Cycle World, $1,240.00. P60.

27. Paid cash for advertising, $85.00. C258.

28. Recorded cash and credit card sales, $2,680.00, plus sales tax, $160.80; total, $2,840.80. T28.

28. Received cash on account from Leonard Kane, $1,147.00, covering S60. R115.

30. Sold merchandise on account to Jonathan Hunt, $45.00, plus sales tax, $2.70; total, $47.70. S64.

30. Paid cash to replenish the petty cash fund, $301.00: office supplies, $62.00; store supplies, $71.00; advertising, $88.00; miscellaneous, $80.00. C259.

30. Recorded cash and credit card sales, $640.00, plus sales tax, $38.40; total, $678.40. T30.

5. Total page 19 of the journal. Prove the equality of debits and credits.

6. Prove cash. The November 1 cash account balance in the general ledger was $9,431.00. On November 30 the balance on the next unused check stub was $21,511.40.

7. Rule page 19 of the journal.

CHALLENGE PROBLEM 12-C Journalizing transactions

The columns of a journal may be arranged in different ways. For example, the journal used in this chapter is referred to as an expanded journal. All of the amount columns are to the right of the Account Title column. However, another arrangement is to have the amount columns divided by the Account Title column. Some of the amount columns are to the left and some are to the right of the Account Title column.

INSTRUCTIONS:

1. Use a journal with the columns arranged as follows.

Cash		Date	Account Title	Doc. No.	Post Ref.	General		Accts. Rec.		Sales Cr.	Sales Tax Pay. Cr.	Accts. Payable		Purchases Dr.
Dr.	Cr.					Dr.	Cr.	Dr.	Cr.			Dr.	Cr.	

2. Use the transactions and instructions for Mastery Problem 12-M. Complete all of the instructions using the journal above.

13

Posting to General and Subsidiary Ledgers

ENABLING PERFORMANCE TASKS

After studying Chapter 13, you will be able to:

a Define accounting terms related to posting to ledgers.

b Identify accounting practices related to posting to ledgers.

c Post to a general ledger from a journal.

d Open accounts in ledgers.

e Post to subsidiary ledgers from a journal.

f Prepare subsidiary schedules.

TERMS PREVIEW

subsidiary ledger • accounts payable ledger • accounts receivable ledger • controlling account • schedule of accounts payable • schedule of accounts receivable

A journal provides a permanent record of transactions listed in chronological order. Journal entries are sorted and summarized by transferring information to ledger accounts. Transferring information from journal entries to ledger accounts is known as posting. Posting information from a journal to ledger accounts summarizes in one place transactions affecting each account.

LEDGERS AND CONTROLLING ACCOUNTS

A business' size, number of transactions, and type of transactions determine the number of ledgers used in an accounting system.

General Ledger

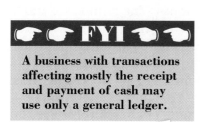

A ledger that contains all accounts needed to prepare financial statements is known as a general ledger. A general ledger sorts and summarizes all information affecting income statement and balance sheet accounts. A business with transactions involving mostly the receipt and payment of cash may use only a general ledger. Rugcare, described in Part 2, uses only a general ledger. CarLand also uses a general ledger. CarLand's general ledger chart of accounts is on page 244. However, because of the business' size and the number and type of transactions, CarLand also uses additional ledgers in its accounting system.

Subsidiary Ledgers

A business needs to know the amount owed each vendor as well as the amount to be collected from each charge customer. Therefore, a separate account is needed for each vendor and each customer. A general ledger could contain an account for each vendor and for each customer. However, a business with many vendors and customers would have a bulky general ledger and a long trial balance. CarLand eliminates these problems by keeping a separate ledger for vendors and a separate ledger for customers. Each separate ledger s summarized in a single general ledger account. A ledger that is summarized in a single general ledger account is called a **subsidiary dger.** A subsidiary ledger containing only accounts for vendors m whom items are purchased or bought on account is called an **counts payable ledger.** A subsidiary ledger containing only counts for charge customers is called an **accounts receivable ger.**

trolling Accounts

otal amount owed to all vendors is summarized in a single al ledger account, Accounts Payable. The total amount to be collected from all charge customers is summarized in a single general ledger account, Accounts Receivable.

An account in a general ledger that summarizes all accounts in a subsidiary ledger is called a **controlling account.** The balance of a controlling account equals the total of all account balances in its related subsidiary ledger. Thus, the balance of the controlling account, Accounts Payable, equals the total of all vendor account balances in the accounts payable subsidiary ledger. The balance of the controlling account, Accounts Receivable, equals the total of all charge customer account balances in the accounts receivable subsidiary ledger.

POSTING TO A GENERAL LEDGER

Daily general ledger account balances are usually not necessary. Balances of general ledger accounts are needed only when financial statements are prepared. Posting from a journal to a general ledger can be done periodically throughout a month. The number of transactions determines how often to post to a general ledger. A business with many transactions would normally post more often than a business with few transactions. Posting often helps keep the work load evenly distributed throughout a month. However, posting must always be done at the end of a month. CarLand uses the same 4-column general ledger account form and posting procedures as described for Rugcare in Chapter 6.

Posting a Journal's General Amount Columns

Amounts recorded in a journal's general amount columns are amounts for which no special amount columns are provided. Therefore, separate amounts in a journal's General Debit and General Credit columns *ARE* posted individually to the accounts written in the journal's Account Title column. The posting of the General Debit entry on line 6 of CarLand's journal is shown in Illustration 13-1.

ILLUSTRATION 13-1   Posting from a journal's General Debit column

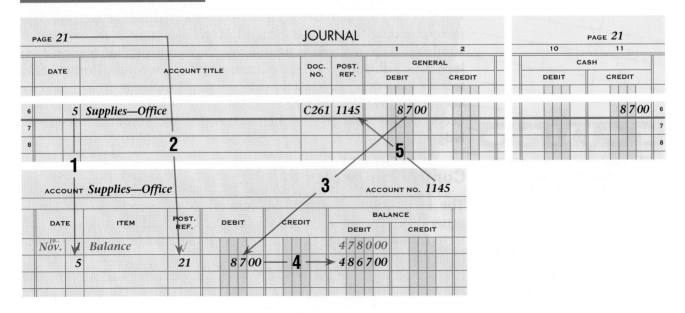

Five steps are followed to post the debit entry to the general ledger.

1 Write the date, *5*, in the Date column of the account.

2 Write the journal page number, *21*, in the Post. Ref. column of the account.

3 Write the debit amount, *$87.00*, in the account's Debit amount column.

4 Add the amount in the Debit amount column to the previous balance in the Balance Debit column ($4,780.00 + $87.00 = $4,867.00). Write the new account balance, *$4,867.00*, in the Balance Debit column.

5 Write the general ledger account number, *1145*, in the Post. Ref. column of the journal.

Posting a Journal's Special Amount Columns

CarLand's journal has nine special amount columns. Separate amounts written in these special amount columns *ARE NOT* posted individually to the general ledger. Separate amounts in a special

■ **Jan Robbins** ■

NAS, INC.

Jan Robbins owns NAS, Inc., a systems engineering company that specializes in government contracting. NAS, Inc. employs approximately 200 workers. Robbins is of Cherokee Indian heritage and wondered when she started her business whether she would encounter any discrimination. She was surprised to find that there was discrimination, not because she is a Native American, but because she is a woman. The industry she had entered, systems engineering for government contracts, was dominated by males who considered it to be an industry just for men. However, Robbins has worked hard and succeeded. She also finds that attitudes toward women in business are changing so that women starting out today should not face as much discrimination as she did.

Robbins worked as a sales representative for an adver-

tising agency before starting NAS, Inc. She also did some copywriting for an advertising agency. When she started her business, she started small because she had only a small amount of savings to invest. She began by being willing to work on even the smallest government contracts, usually as a subcontractor to the contractor who had won the contract.

Robbins attributes her ability to set up her business to the year of accounting she studied in high school. She says that it helped her set up her expenses and to understand the language that businesses use every day. Robbins strongly believes in the value of business courses for success and especially favors courses in accounting and banking as preparation for entrepreneurship.

Asked about her basic philosophy of business, Robbins replied, "No one plans to fail, they just fail to plan. A day doesn't pass that I don't think of that statement."

Personal Visions in Business

amount column all affect the same general ledger account. Therefore, only the totals of special amount columns *ARE* posted to the general ledger. Each special amount column total is posted to the general ledger account listed in the column heading. Posting of the Cash Credit amount column total is shown in Illustration 13-2.

ILLUSTRATION 13-2 Posting the Cash Credit column total

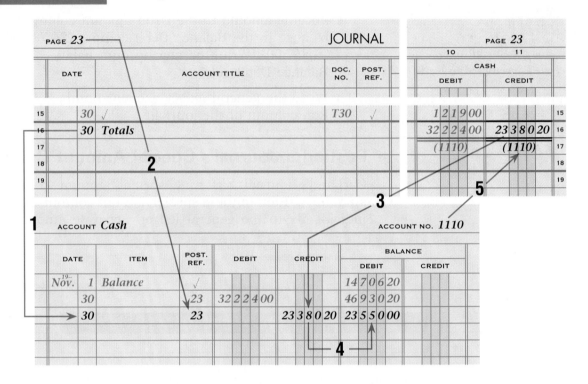

Five steps are followed to post the Cash Credit column total.

1 Write the date, *30,* in the Date column of the account.

2 Write the journal page number, *23,* in the Post. Ref. column of the account.

3 Write the Cash Credit column total, *$23,380.20,* in the account's Credit amount column.

4 Subtract the amount in the Credit amount column from the previous balance in the Balance Debit column ($46,930.20 − $23,380.20 = $23,550.00). Write the new account balance, *$23,550.00,* in the Balance Debit column.

5 Return to the journal and write the general ledger account number, *1110,* in parentheses below the Cash Credit column total.

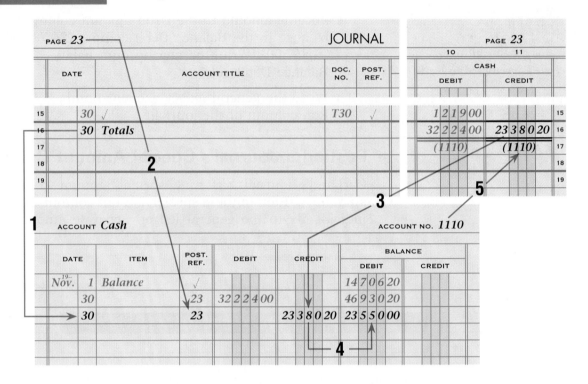

FYI

Posting must always be done at the end of the month.

Rules for Posting a Journal's Column Totals

Rules for posting a journal's column totals are shown in Illustration 13-3.

ILLUSTRATION 13-3 Rules for posting a journal's column totals

PAGE *23* — JOURNAL

	DATE	ACCOUNT TITLE	DOC. NO.	POST. REF.	GENERAL DEBIT	GENERAL CREDIT	ACCOUNTS RECEIVABLE DEBIT	ACCOUNTS RECEIVABLE CREDIT	
16	30	*Totals*			15 68 6 22	2 0 29 02	9 2 22 00	7 9 50 00	16
17					(√)	(√)	(1130)	(1130)	17
18									18
19									19

General amount column totals ARE NOT posted

Special amount column totals ARE posted

A check mark is placed in parentheses below the General Debit and General Credit column totals to indicate that the two amount column totals *ARE NOT* posted. The general ledger account number of the account listed in the column heading is written in parentheses below the special amount column totals to show that the totals *ARE* posted.

OPENING A NEW PAGE FOR AN ACCOUNT IN A GENERAL LEDGER

The number of entries that may be recorded on each general ledger account form depends on the number of lines provided. When all lines have been used, a new page is prepared. The account title, account number, and account balance are recorded on the new page.

On November 1 CarLand prepared a new page for Cash in the general ledger because the existing page was full. On that day, the account balance was $14,706.20. The new page for Cash in the general ledger is shown in Illustration 13-4.

ILLUSTRATION 13-4 Opening a new page for an account in a general ledger

ACCOUNT *Cash*   ACCOUNT NO. *1110*

DATE	ITEM	POST. REF.	DEBIT	CREDIT	BALANCE DEBIT	BALANCE CREDIT
Nov. 1	*Balance*	√			14 70 6 20	

The account title and account number are written on the heading at the top of the new page. The date, *19--, Nov. 1,* is recorded in the Date column. The word *Balance* is written in the Item column. A check mark is placed in the Post. Ref. column to show that the entry has been carried forward from a previous page rather than posted from a journal. The account balance, *$14,706.20,* is written in the Balance Debit column.

ASSIGNING ACCOUNT NUMBERS TO SUBSIDIARY LEDGER ACCOUNTS

CarLand assigns a vendor number to each account in the accounts payable ledger. A customer number is also assigned to each account in the accounts receivable ledger. A three-digit number is used. The first digit identifies the division in which the controlling account appears in the general ledger. The second two digits show each account's location within a subsidiary ledger. Accounts are assigned by 10s beginning with the second digit. Accounts in the subsidiary ledgers can be located by either number or name.

The vendor number for Antelo Supply is 210. The first digit, *2,* shows that the controlling account is a liability, Accounts Payable. The second and third digits, *10,* show the vendor number assigned to Antelo Supply.

The customer number for Ashley Delivery is 110. The first digit, *1,* shows that the controlling account is an asset, Accounts Receivable. The second and third digits, *10,* show the customer number assigned to Ashley Delivery.

The procedure for adding new accounts to subsidiary ledgers is the same as described for Rugcare's general ledger in Chapter 6. Accounts are arranged in alphabetic order within the subsidiary ledgers. New accounts are assigned the unused middle number. If the proper alphabetic order places a new account as the last account, the next number in the sequence of 10s is assigned. CarLand's chart of accounts for the subsidiary ledgers is on page 244.

FYI

Account numbers are assigned by 10s. A new account is assigned the unused middle number which places it in the correct alphabetic order.

POSTING TO AN ACCOUNTS PAYABLE LEDGER

When the balance of a vendor account in an accounts payable ledger is changed, the balance of the controlling account, Accounts Payable, is also changed. The total of all vendor account balances in the accounts payable ledger equals the balance of the controlling account, Accounts Payable. The relationship between the accounts payable ledger and the general ledger controlling account, Accounts Payable, is shown in Illustration 13-5.

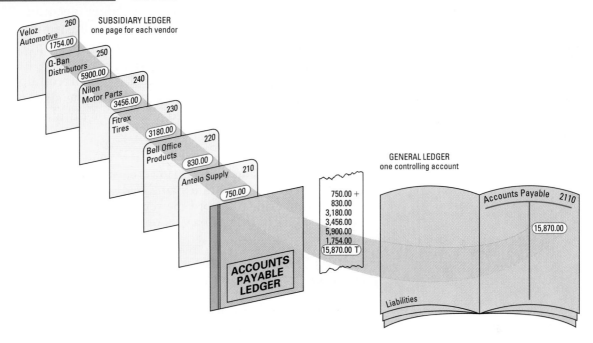

Accounts Payable Ledger Form

CarLand uses the 3-column accounts payable subsidiary account form shown in Illustration 13-6.

ILLUSTRATION 13-6

Three-column account form used in an accounts payable ledger

VENDOR *Veloz Automotive*						VENDOR NO. *260*
DATE	ITEM	POST. REF.	DEBIT	CREDIT	CREDIT BALANCE	

Information to be recorded in the accounts payable ledger is essentially the same as that recorded in the 4-column general ledger account. The information includes the date, posting reference, debit or credit amount, and new account balance. Accounts payable are liabilities, and liabilities have normal credit balances. Therefore, the Debit Balance column is usually not needed for the accounts payable ledger accounts. The accounts payable account form is the same as the general ledger account form except that there is no Debit Balance column.

Accounts in CarLand's accounts payable ledger are arranged in alphabetic order and kept in a loose-leaf binder. Periodically, accounts for new vendors are added and accounts no longer used are removed from the accounts payable ledger. If the number of accounts becomes large enough to make a loose-leaf binder inappropriate, ledger pages may be kept in a file cabinet.

Opening Vendor Accounts

Each new account is opened by writing the vendor name and vendor number on the heading of the ledger account. The account opened for Veloz Automotive is shown in Illustration 13-6.

The vendor name is obtained from the first purchase invoice received. The vendor number is assigned using the three-digit numbering system described on page 290. The correct alphabetic order for Veloz Automotive places the account as the sixth account in the accounts payable subsidiary ledger. Vendor number 260 is assigned to Veloz Automotive.

Some businesses record both the vendor name and vendor address on the ledger form. However, the address information is usually kept in a separate name and address file. This practice eliminates having to record the vendor address on the ledger form each time a new ledger page is opened or the address changes.

FYI

A new vendor account is opened by writing the vendor name and vendor number on the heading of the ledger account and placing it in alphabetic order.

Posting from a Journal to an Accounts Payable Ledger

Each entry in the Accounts Payable columns of a journal affects the vendor named in the Account Title column. CarLand posts each amount in these two columns often. Posting often keeps each vendor account balance up to date. Totals of Accounts Payable special amount columns are posted to the general ledger at the end of each month.

Posting a Credit to an Accounts Payable Ledger. Posting a credit for a purchase on account from the journal to the accounts payable ledger is shown in Illustration 13-7.

ILLUSTRATION 13-7   Posting a credit to an accounts payable ledger

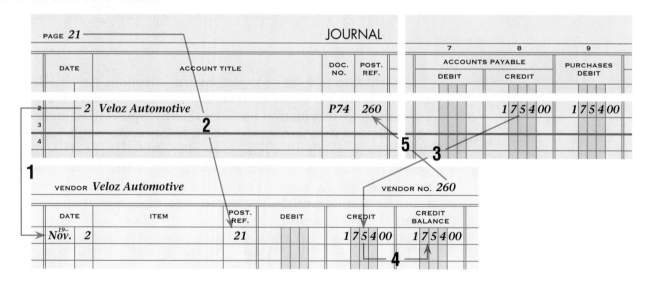

Five steps are followed to post the entry on line 2 of the journal to the accounts payable ledger.

1 Write the date, *19--, Nov. 2,* in the Date column of the account.

2 Write the journal page number, *21,* in the Post. Ref. column of the account.

3 Write the credit amount, *$1,754.00,* in the Credit amount column of the account for Veloz Automotive.

4 Add the amount in the Credit amount column to the previous balance in the Credit Balance column. (Veloz Automotive has no previous balance; therefore, $0 + $1,754.00 = $1,754.00.) Write the new account balance, *$1,754.00,* in the Credit Balance column.

5 Write the vendor number, *260,* in the Post. Ref. column of the journal. The vendor number shows that the posting for this entry is complete.

The controlling account in the general ledger, Accounts Payable, is also increased by this entry. At the end of the month, the journal's Accounts Payable Credit column total is posted to the controlling account, Accounts Payable.

Posting a Debit to an Accounts Payable Ledger. The same steps are followed to post a debit to a vendor account as are used to post a credit. However, the debit amount is entered in the Debit amount column of the vendor account. The debit amount is subtracted from the previous credit balance. Posting a cash payment on account from the journal to the accounts payable ledger is shown in Illustration 13-8.

The controlling account in the general ledger, Accounts Payable, is decreased by this entry. At the end of the month, the journal's

---

ILLUSTRATION 13-8   Posting a debit to an accounts payable ledger

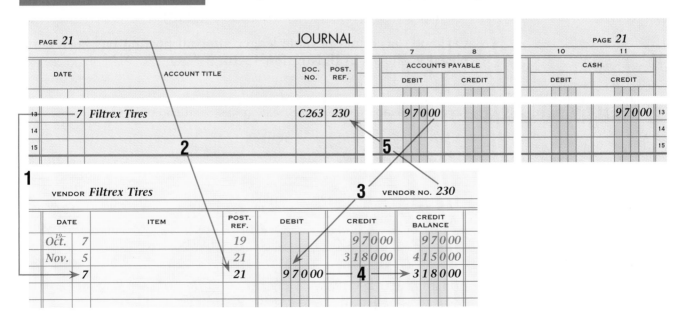

Accounts Payable Debit column total is posted to the controlling account, Accounts Payable.

Opening a New Page for a Vendor in an Accounts Payable Ledger

The number of entries that may be recorded on each account form depends on the number of lines provided. When all lines have been used, a new page is prepared. The vendor name, vendor number, and account balance are recorded on the new page.

On November 1 CarLand prepared a new page for Nilon Motor Parts in the accounts payable ledger because the existing page was full. On that day, the account balance was $4,840.00. The new page for Nilon Motor Parts in the accounts payable ledger is shown in Illustration 13-9.

ILLUSTRATION 13-9

Opening a new page for a vendor in the accounts payable ledger

VENDOR Nilon Motor Parts						VENDOR NO. 240
DATE	ITEM	POST. REF.	DEBIT	CREDIT	CREDIT BALANCE	
Nov. 1	Balance	✓			4 8 4 0 00	

The vendor name and vendor number are written at the top of the account page. The date, *19--, Nov. 1*, is recorded in the Date column. The word *Balance* is written in the Item column. A check mark is placed in the Post. Ref. column to show that the amount has been carried forward from a previous page rather than posted from a journal. The account balance, *$4,840.00*, is written in the Credit Balance column.

Completed Accounts Payable Ledger

CarLand's accounts payable ledger after all posting has been completed is shown in Illustration 13-10.

ILLUSTRATION 13-10

Accounts payable ledger after posting has been completed

VENDOR Antelo Supply					VENDOR NO. 210
DATE	ITEM	POST. REF.	DEBIT	CREDIT	CREDIT BALANCE
Oct. 12		19		4 3 0 00	4 3 0 00
Nov. 6		21		1 6 0 00	5 9 0 00
12		21	4 3 0 00		1 6 0 00
23		22		5 9 0 00	7 5 0 00

VENDOR *Bell Office Products*   VENDOR NO. *220*

DATE		ITEM	POST. REF.	DEBIT	CREDIT	CREDIT BALANCE
Oct.¹⁹⁻⁻	23		20		620 00	620 00
Nov.	23		22	620 00		———
	24		22		830 00	830 00

VENDOR *Filtrex Tires*   VENDOR NO. *230*

DATE		ITEM	POST. REF.	DEBIT	CREDIT	CREDIT BALANCE
Oct.¹⁹⁻⁻	7		19		970 00	970 00
Nov.	5		21		3180 00	4150 00
	7		21	970 00		3180 00

VENDOR *Nilon Motor Parts*   VENDOR NO. *240*

DATE		ITEM	POST. REF.	DEBIT	CREDIT	CREDIT BALANCE
Nov.¹⁹⁻⁻	1	Balance	✓			4840 00
	4		21		3456 00	8296 00
	20		22	4840 00		3456 00

VENDOR *Q-Ban Distributors*   VENDOR NO. *250*

DATE		ITEM	POST. REF.	DEBIT	CREDIT	CREDIT BALANCE
Nov.¹⁹⁻⁻	1	Balance	✓			3960 00
	6		21	3960 00		———
	13		21		3140 00	3140 00
	20		22		2760 00	5900 00

VENDOR *Veloz Automotive*   VENDOR NO. *260*

DATE		ITEM	POST. REF.	DEBIT	CREDIT	CREDIT BALANCE
Nov.¹⁹⁻⁻	2		21		1754 00	1754 00

An error in posting may cause a business to overpay or underpay its vendors.

POSTING TO AN ACCOUNTS RECEIVABLE LEDGER

When the balance of a customer account in an accounts receivable ledger is changed, the balance of the controlling account, Accounts Receivable, is also changed. The total of all customer account balances in the accounts receivable ledger equals the balance of the controlling account, Accounts Receivable. The relationship between the accounts receivable ledger and the general ledger controlling account, Accounts Receivable, is shown in Illustration 13-11.

ILLUSTRATION 13-11 Relationship of accounts receivable ledger and general ledger controlling account

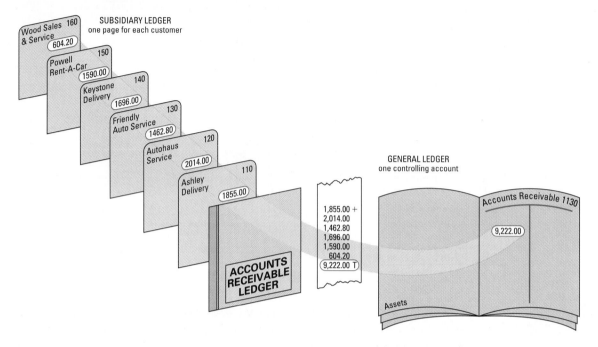

Accounts Receivable Ledger Form

CarLand uses the 3-column accounts receivable subsidiary account form shown in Illustration 13-12.

ILLUSTRATION 13-12 Three-column account form used in an accounts receivable ledger

CUSTOMER *Friendly Auto Service*					CUSTOMER NO. *130*	
DATE	ITEM	POST. REF.	DEBIT	CREDIT	DEBIT BALANCE	

The accounts receivable account form is similar to the one used for the accounts payable ledger. Accounts receivable are assets, and assets have normal debit balances. Therefore, the form used in the accounts receivable ledger has a Debit Balance column instead of a Credit Balance column.

Accounts in CarLand's accounts receivable ledger are arranged in alphabetic order and kept in a loose-leaf binder. Periodically, accounts for new customers are added and accounts no longer used are removed from the accounts receivable ledger. The customer number 130 had been assigned to a former customer. That account, however, had been removed from the ledger. Therefore, customer number 130 is available for assignment to Friendly Auto Service.

Some businesses record both the customer name and customer address on the ledger form. However, the address information is usually kept in a separate name and address file. This practice eliminates having to record the customer address on the ledger form each time a new ledger page is opened or the address changes.

Opening Customer Accounts

Procedures for opening customer accounts are similar to those used for opening vendor accounts. The customer name is obtained from the first sales invoice prepared for a customer. The customer number is assigned using the three-digit numbering system described on page 290. The customer name and customer number are written on the heading of the ledger account. The account opened for Friendly Auto Service is shown in Illustration 13-12.

Posting from a Journal to an Accounts Receivable Ledger

Separate amounts in a journal's general amount columns are posted individually.

Each entry in the Accounts Receivable columns of a journal affects the customer named in the Account Title column. Each amount listed in these two columns is posted to a customer account in the accounts receivable ledger often. Posting often keeps each customer account balance up to date. Totals of Accounts Receivable special amount columns are posted to the general ledger at the end of each month.

Posting a Debit to an Accounts Receivable Ledger. Posting a debit for a sale on account from the journal to the accounts receivable ledger is shown in Illustration 13-13.

Five steps are followed to post the entry on line 4 of the journal to the accounts receivable ledger.

1 Write the date, *3*, in the Date column of the account.

2 Write the journal page number, *21*, in the Post. Ref. column of the account.

3 Write the debit amount, *$720.80*, in the Debit amount column of the account for Friendly Auto Service.

4 Add the amount in the Debit amount column to the previous balance in the Debit Balance column ($265.00 + $720.80 = $985.80). Write the new account balance, *$985.80*, in the Debit Balance column.

5 Write the customer number, *130*, in the Post. Ref. column of the journal. The customer number shows that the posting for this entry is completed.

ILLUSTRATION 13-13 Posting a debit to an accounts receivable ledger

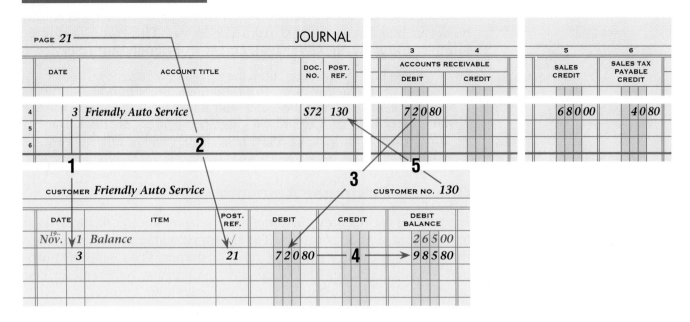

The controlling account in the general ledger, Accounts Receivable, is also increased by this entry. At the end of the month, the journal's Accounts Receivable Debit column total is posted to the controlling account, Accounts Receivable.

Posting a Credit to an Accounts Receivable Ledger. The same steps are followed to post a credit to a customer account as are used to post a debit. However, the credit amount is written in the Credit amount column of the customer account. The credit amount is subtracted from the previous debit balance. Posting a cash receipt on account from the journal to the accounts receivable ledger is shown in Illustration 13-14.

The controlling account in the general ledger, Accounts Receivable, is decreased by this entry. However, the amount is not posted individually to the accounts receivable account. At the end of the month, the amount, *$318.00*, is posted as part of the special amount column total to Accounts Receivable.

Opening a New Page for a Customer in an Accounts Receivable Ledger

Procedures for opening a new page in an accounts receivable ledger are similar to those for an accounts payable ledger. The customer name and customer number are written at the top of the new account page. The date is recorded in the Date column. The word *Balance* is written in the Item column. A check mark is placed in the Post. Ref. column to show that the amount has been carried forward from a previous page rather than posted from a journal. The account balance is recorded in the Debit Balance column.

Audit Your Understanding

1. What is the title of the balance amount column of the accounts payable ledger form? Why?

2. How is a new vendor account opened?

3. List the five steps for posting to the accounts payable ledger.

4. What is the title of the balance amount column of the accounts receivable ledger form? Why?

ILLUSTRATION 13-14 Posting a credit to an accounts receivable ledger

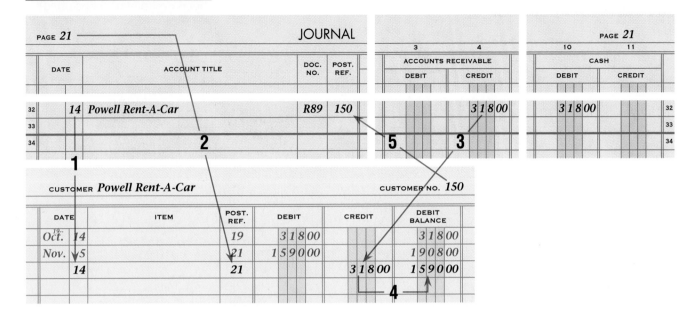

Completed Accounts Receivable Ledger

CarLand's accounts receivable ledger after all posting has been completed is shown in Illustration 13-15.

ILLUSTRATION 13-15 Accounts receivable ledger after posting has been completed

CUSTOMER *Ashley Delivery* **CUSTOMER NO.** *110*

DATE	ITEM	POST. REF.	DEBIT	CREDIT	DEBIT BALANCE
Nov. 1	Balance	✓			2 4 9 1 00
9		21	4 7 7 00		2 9 6 8 00
16		22	1 3 7 8 00		4 3 4 6 00
17		22		2 4 9 1 00	1 8 5 5 00

CUSTOMER *Autohaus Service* **CUSTOMER NO.** *120*

DATE	ITEM	POST. REF.	DEBIT	CREDIT	DEBIT BALANCE
Nov. 1	Balance	✓			1 8 0 2 00
6		21		1 8 0 2 00	————
18		22	2 0 1 4 00		2 0 1 4 00

CUSTOMER *Friendly Auto Service*   CUSTOMER NO. *130*

DATE		ITEM	POST. REF.	DEBIT	CREDIT	DEBIT BALANCE
Nov.	1	Balance	✓			2 6 5 00
	3		21	7 2 0 80		9 8 5 80
	24		22	7 4 2 00		1 7 2 7 80
	25		22		2 6 5 00	1 4 6 2 80

CUSTOMER *Keystone Delivery*   CUSTOMER NO. *140*

DATE		ITEM	POST. REF.	DEBIT	CREDIT	DEBIT BALANCE
Oct.	10		19	9 5 4 00		9 5 4 00
Nov.	10		21		9 5 4 00	—
	24		22	3 1 8 00		3 1 8 00
	29		22	1 3 7 8 00		1 6 9 6 00

CUSTOMER *Powell Rent-A-Car*   CUSTOMER NO. *150*

DATE		ITEM	POST. REF.	DEBIT	CREDIT	DEBIT BALANCE
Oct.	14		19	3 1 8 00		3 1 8 00
Nov.	5		21	1 5 9 0 00		1 9 0 8 00
	14		21		3 1 8 00	1 5 9 0 00

CUSTOMER *Wood Sales & Service*   CUSTOMER NO. *160*

DATE		ITEM	POST. REF.	DEBIT	CREDIT	DEBIT BALANCE
Nov.	1	Balance	✓			2 1 2 0 00
	11		21	6 0 4 20		2 7 2 4 20
	13		21		9 0 1 00	1 8 2 3 20
	20		22		1 2 1 9 00	6 0 4 20

PROVING THE ACCURACY OF POSTING

A single error in posting to a ledger account may cause the trial balance to be out of balance. An error in posting may cause the cash account balance to disagree with the actual cash on hand. An error in posting may also cause the income to be understated or overstated on an income statement. An error in posting may also cause a business to overpay or underpay its vendors. Posting must be accurate to assure correct account balances. Therefore, to prove the accuracy of posting, three things are done. (1) Cash is proved. (2) Subsidiary schedules are prepared to prove that the total of the balances in the subsidiary ledgers equals the balance of the controlling account in the general ledger. (3) A trial balance is prepared to prove that debits equal credits in the general ledger.

Preparation of a trial balance is described in Chapter 16.

Proving Cash

The method used to prove cash is described in Chapter 12. The cash proof total is compared with the balance on the next unused check stub in the checkbook.

Proving the Subsidiary Ledgers

A controlling account balance in a general ledger must equal the sum of all account balances in a subsidiary ledger. CarLand proves the accounts payable and accounts receivable subsidiary ledgers at the end of each month.

Proving Accounts Payable. A listing of vendor accounts, account balances, and total amount due all vendors is called a **schedule of accounts payable.** A schedule of accounts payable is prepared after all entries in a journal are posted. CarLand's schedule of accounts payable, prepared on November 30, is shown in Illustration 13-16.

ILLUSTRATION 13-16   Schedule of accounts payable

CarLand	
Schedule of Accounts Payable	
November 30, 19--	
Antelo Supply	750 00
Bell Office Products	830 00
Filtrex Tires	3180 00
Nilon Motor Parts	3456 00
Q-Ban Distributors	5900 00
Veloz Automotive	1754 00
Total Accounts Payable	15870 00

The balance of Accounts Payable in the general ledger is $15,870.00. The total of the schedule of accounts payable is $15,870.00. Because the two amounts are the same, the accounts payable ledger is proved.

Proving Accounts Receivable. A listing of customer accounts, account balances, and total amount due from all customers is called a **schedule of accounts receivable.** A schedule of accounts receivable is prepared after all entries in a journal are posted. CarLand's schedule of accounts receivable, prepared on November 30, is shown in Illustration 13-17.

ILLUSTRATION 13-17   Schedule of accounts receivable

CarLand	
Schedule of Accounts Receivable	
November 30, 19--	
Ashley Delivery	1 8 5 5 00
Autohaus Service	2 0 1 4 00
Friendly Auto Service	1 4 6 2 80
Keystone Delivery	1 6 9 6 00
Powell Rent-A-Car	1 5 9 0 00
Wood Sales & Service	6 0 4 20
Total Accounts Receivable	9 2 2 2 00

The balance of Accounts Receivable in the general ledger is $9,222.00. The total of the schedule of accounts receivable is $9,222.00. Because the two amounts are the same, the accounts receivable ledger is proved.

A summary of the posting steps from Rugcare's journal is in Chapter 6. The steps described for Rugcare also apply to posting from an expanded journal. However, special amount columns and controlling accounts require an additional set of posting steps.

Audit Your Understanding

1. How are the accounts payable and accounts receivable subsidiary ledgers proved at the end of the month?

2. What accounts are listed on a schedule of accounts payable?

3. How does a schedule of accounts receivable prove the accounts receivable ledger?

SUMMARY ILLUSTRATION 13-18

Summary of posting

Separate amounts in General columns *ARE* posted individually. Totals of General Debit and Credit columns *ARE NOT* posted.

POST. REF.	GENERAL 1 DEBIT	GENERAL 2 CREDIT	
1150	2 5 00		→ + |
6110	1 5 00		→ + | Separate amounts *ARE* posted individually
6140	5 5 00		→ + |
√			
	15 6 8 6 22	2 0 2 9 02	← Totals *ARE NOT* posted
	(√)	(√)	

Summary of posting

Totals of special amount columns *ARE* posted to the account named in the column heading. Separate amounts in special columns *ARE NOT* posted individually unless the columns affect a controlling account.

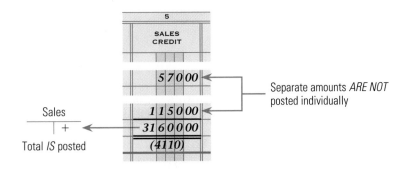

Separate amounts and total amounts are posted from special columns for controlling accounts. Separate amounts in the Accounts Receivable Debit and Credit columns *ARE* posted individually to customer accounts. As the last posting step, a customer number is written in the Post. Ref. column of the journal.

Totals of special columns *ARE* posted to the controlling accounts named in the column headings. The total of an Accounts Receivable Debit column is posted as a debit to **Accounts Receivable** in the general ledger. The total of an Accounts Receivable Credit column is posted as a credit to **Accounts Receivable** in the general ledger. As a last posting step, an account number is placed in parentheses under the total of a special amount column.

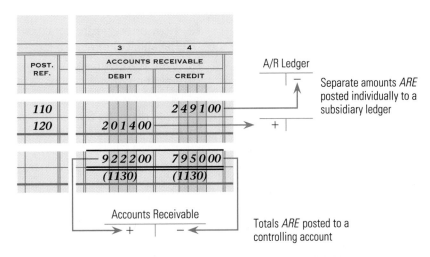

The same principles used for Accounts Receivable amount columns also apply to Accounts Payable amount columns in a journal.

What is the meaning of each of the following?

1. **subsidiary ledger**
2. **accounts payable ledger**
3. **accounts receivable ledger**
4. **controlling account**
5. **schedule of accounts payable**
6. **schedule of accounts receivable**

QUESTIONS FOR INDIVIDUAL STUDY   EPT(b)

1. How is journal entry information sorted and summarized?
2. What determines the number of ledgers used in an accounting system?
3. What ledger contains all accounts needed to prepare an income statement and a balance sheet?
4. What type of business would generally use a single ledger?
5. Why would a business keep a separate account for each vendor and each customer?
6. Why would a business keep a separate ledger for vendors and a separate ledger for customers?
7. What is the title of the general ledger controlling account for vendors?
8. What is the title of the general ledger controlling account for customers?
9. Why is posting to a general ledger done only periodically throughout the month?
10. What determines the frequency of posting to a general ledger?
11. Why are amounts recorded in a journal's general amount columns posted individually?
12. Why are separate amounts in special amount columns not posted individually to the general ledger?
13. Why is a check mark placed in parentheses below the General Debit and General Credit column totals?
14. What does the first digit in a vendor or customer number identify?
15. Why does the 3-column account form used in an accounts payable ledger have a Credit Balance column?
16. Why is posting of separate amounts in the Accounts Payable columns done often?
17. How often are the totals of the Accounts Payable columns of a journal posted?
18. Why is a check mark entered in the Post. Ref. column when a new page is opened for a vendor?
19. Why does the 3-column account form used in an accounts receivable ledger have a Debit Balance column?
20. How are subsidiary ledgers proved at the end of a month?

CASES FOR CRITICAL THINKING   EPT(b)

CASE 1 Automart purchased merchandise on account six weeks ago for $400.00 from Belview Supply. A check for $400.00 was sent three weeks ago in payment of the account. Although no additional purchases have been made, Automart recently received a bill from Belview Supply that listed the balance due as $800.00. What probably caused this error? When would the error probably be discovered?

CASE 2 Leon Reyes observes his accountant at work and says, "You post each individual accounts receivable entry in the journal. Then you post the totals of the Accounts Receivable columns. You are posting these entries twice, which will make the records wrong." The accountant does not agree that the posting procedure is incorrect. Is Mr. Reyes or his accountant correct? Why?

DRILL 13-D1   Analyzing transactions of a merchandising business

INSTRUCTIONS:

Prepare T accounts for each of the following transactions. Use the T accounts to analyze each transaction. A 6% sales tax has been added to each sale. The first transaction is given as an example.

Accounts Receivable	
127.20	

Sales	
	120.00

Sales Tax Payable	
	7.20

1. Sold merchandise on account to Sarah Burke, $120.00, plus sales tax, $7.20; total, $127.20.
2. Paid cash on account to Casa Enterprises, $950.00.
3. Paid cash for rent, $1,250.00.
4. Discovered that a payment for advertising was journalized and posted in error as a debit to Miscellaneous Expense instead of Advertising Expense, $125.00.
5. Paid cash for office supplies, $80.00.
6. Recorded cash and credit card sales, $1,850.00, plus sales tax, $111.00; total, $1,961.00.
7. Joyce Berling, partner, withdrew merchandise for personal use, $90.00.
8. Purchased merchandise on account from Irvine Products, $1,640.00.
9. Received cash on account from Carl Downing, $227.90.
10. Purchased merchandise for cash, $130.00.
11. Michael Zolty, partner, withdrew cash for personal use, $700.00.
12. Bought store supplies on account from Carter Supply, $315.00.

The solution to Drill 13-D1 is needed to complete Drill 13-D2.

DRILL 13-D2   Analyzing, journalizing, and posting transactions of a merchandising business

The solution to Drill 13-D1 is needed to complete Drill 13-D2.

INSTRUCTIONS:

A form for analyzing transactions is provided in the working papers that accompany the textbook.

1. Based on the answers in Drill 13-D1, place a check mark in the amount columns to be used to journalize each transaction.

A form for analyzing posting is provided in the working papers that accompany this textbook.

2. Based on the answers to Instruction 1, place a check mark in the proper column to indicate whether the amount will or will not be posted individually to the ledgers.

PROBLEM 13-1   Opening accounts and posting to ledgers from a journal

The journal for Carpet Magic is given in the working papers accompanying this textbook.

INSTRUCTIONS:

1. Open new pages for the following accounts in the general ledger. Record the balances as of September 1 of the current year.

Account No.	Account Title	Account Balance
1110	Cash	$ 18,300.00
1130	Accounts Receivable	8,470.00
1150	Supplies—Office	3,680.00
1160	Supplies—Store	4,260.00
1170	Prepaid Insurance	1,560.00
2110	Accounts Payable	10,555.00
2120	Sales Tax Payable	1,235.00
3120	Diane Engler, Drawing	8,000.00
3140	Paul Sisco, Drawing	8,340.00
4110	Sales	172,420.00
5110	Purchases	96,500.00
6110	Advertising Expense	1,860.00
6140	Miscellaneous Expense	1,310.00
6160	Rent Expense	8,000.00

2. Open new pages for the following vendor accounts in the accounts payable ledger. Record the balances as of September 1 of the current year.

Vendor No.	Vendor Name	Purchase Invoice No.	Account Balance
210	Crown Carpet Co.	52	$2,575.00
220	Marlow Industries	53	4,220.00
230	Superior Carpeting	—	—
240	V & P Carpet Co.	51	3,760.00

3. Open new pages for the following customer accounts in the accounts receivable ledger. Record the balances as of September 1 of the current year.

Customer No.	Customer Name	Sales Invoice No.	Account Balance
110	Cameo Shoe Store	44	$3,680.00
120	Paula Hughs	42	1,850.00
130	Elsa Leyba	43	2,940.00
140	Scott Ward	—	—

4. Post the separate items recorded in the following columns of the journal. (a) General Debit and Credit. (b) Accounts Receivable Debit and Credit. (c) Accounts Payable Debit and Credit.

5. Post the totals of the special columns of the journal.

6. Prepare a schedule of accounts payable. Compare the total of the schedule with the balance of the controlling account, Accounts Payable, in the general ledger. If the totals are not the same, find and correct the errors.

7. Prepare a schedule of accounts receivable. Compare the total of the schedule with the balance of the controlling account, Accounts Receivable, in the general ledger. If the totals are not the same, find and correct the errors.

ENRICHMENT PROBLEMS
EPT(c,e,f)

MASTERY PROBLEM 13-M Posting to ledgers from a journal

The journal and ledgers for Anton Leather Goods are given in the working papers accompanying this textbook.

INSTRUCTIONS:

1. Post the separate items recorded in the following columns of the journal. (a) General Debit and Credit. (b) Accounts Receivable Debit and Credit. (c) Accounts Payable Debit and Credit.

2. Post the totals of the special columns of the journal.
3. Prepare a schedule of accounts payable and a schedule of accounts receivable. Prove the accuracy of the subsidiary ledgers by comparing the schedule totals with the balances of the controlling accounts in the general ledger. If the totals are not the same, find and correct the errors.

CHALLENGE PROBLEM 13-C Journalizing and posting business transactions

AUTOMATED

The general, accounts payable, and accounts receivable ledgers for Par Golf Products are given in the working papers accompanying this textbook. Use the following account titles.

GENERAL LEDGER

Account No.	Account Title	Account No.	Account Title
1110	Cash	3140	Lawrence Phipps, Drawing
1130	Accounts Receivable	3150	Income Summary
1140	Merchandise Inventory	4110	Sales
1150	Supplies—Office	5110	Purchases
1160	Supplies—Store	6110	Advertising Expenses
2110	Accounts Payable	6140	Miscellaneous Expenses
2120	Sales Tax Payable	6160	Rent Expense
3120	Maria Adolpho, Drawing	6190	Utilities Expense

ACCOUNTS PAYABLE LEDGER

Vendor No.	Vendor Name
210	Artex Golf Products
220	Ecola Golf Equipment
230	Garcia Supply
240	Patton Golf Co.
250	Valiant Golf Co.

ACCOUNTS RECEIVABLE LEDGER

Customer No.	Customer Name
110	William Backus
120	Linda Boge
130	Jonathan Dunbar
140	James Patco
150	Bertha Welsh

INSTRUCTIONS:

1. Journalize the following transactions completed during November of the current year. Use page 18 of a journal similar to the one described in this chapter. Add a 6% sales tax to all sales transactions. Source documents are abbreviated as follows: check, C; memorandum, M; purchase invoice, P; receipt, R; sales invoice, S; cash register tape, T.

Nov. 2. Wrote a check for rent, $950.00. C275.
    3. Received an invoice from Valiant Golf Co. for merchandise purchased on account, $1,625.00. P76.
    4. Paid for merchandise, $119.00. C276.
    5. A check was received in payment on account from Linda Boge, $678.40, covering S50. R45.
    7. Ecola Golf Equipment was paid on account, $1,965.00, covering P72. C277.
    7. Cash and credit card sales, $4,730.00. T7.
       Posting. Post the items that are to be posted individually.
    9. Maria Adolfo, partner, withdrew merchandise for personal use, $165.00. M35.
    11. Merchandise was sold on account to James Patco, $255.00. S54.
    12. Discovered that a transaction for store supplies bought for cash was journalized and posted in error as a debit to Advertising Expense instead of Supplies—Store, $93.00. M36.
    14. Store supplies were bought on account from Garcia Supply, $215.00. M37.
    14. Cash and credit card sales, $4,840.00. T14.
       Posting. Post the items that are to be posted individually.
    16. Cash was withdrawn by Maria Adolfo, partner, for personal use, $1,200.00. C278.

Nov. 16. Cash was withdrawn by Lawrence Phipps, partner, for personal use, $1,200.00. C279.

17. Wrote a check for electric bill, $183.50. C280.

20. Wrote a check to Valiant Golf Co. on account, $2,680.00, covering P73. C281.

21. Recorded cash and credit card sales, $4,480.00. T21.

   Posting. Post the items that are to be posted individually.

23. Artex Golf Products was paid on account, $2,430.00, covering P74. C282.

24. Jonathan Dunbar bought merchandise on account, $1,095.00. S55.

26. Received payment on account from Bertha Welsh, $233.20, covering S51. R46.

26. Merchandise was purchased on account from Patton Golf Co., $1,285.00. P77.

27. A check was received in payment on account from William Backus, $795.00, covering S52. R47.

28. Received an invoice on account from Artex Golf Products for merchandise purchased on account, $2,325.00. P78.

28. Merchandise was sold on account to Bertha Welsh, $1,095.00. S56.

28. Recorded cash and credit card sales, $4,630.00. T28.

   Posting. Post the items that are to be posted individually.

30. Replenish the petty cash fund, $302.00: office supplies, $48.00; store supplies, $62.00; advertising, $74.00; miscellaneous, $118.00. C283.

30. Recorded cash and credit card sales, $840.00. T30.

   Posting. Post the items that are to be posted individually.

2. Total the journal. Prove the equality of debits and credits.

3. Prove cash. The balance on the next unused check stub is $28,218.30.

4. Rule the journal.

5. Post the totals of the special columns of the journal.

6. Prepare a schedule of accounts payable and a schedule of accounts receivable. Prove the accuracy of the subsidiary ledgers by comparing the schedule totals with the balances of the controlling accounts in the general ledger. If the totals are not the same, find and correct the errors.

Recording Transactions for a Partnership

CarLand, the merchandising business described in Part 3, uses a manual accounting system. CarLand's manual journalizing procedures for purchases, cash payments, sales, and cash receipts are described in Chapters 11 and 12. Manual posting procedures are described in Chapter 13. Integrating Automated Accounting Topic 4 describes procedures for using automated accounting software to journalize and post CarLand's transactions. The Automated Accounting Problem contains instructions for using automated accounting software to solve Challenge Problem 13-C, Chapter 13.

AUTOMATED ACCOUNTING PROCEDURES FOR CARLAND

A group of journal entries is a **batch**. CarLand uses five input forms to batch transaction data for automated accounting.

1. Purchases journal input form for purchases on account.
2. Cash payments journal input form for cash payments.
3. Sales journal input form for sales on account.
4. Cash receipts journal input form for cash receipts.
5. General journal input form for all other transactions.

FILE MAINTENANCE

CarLand's chart of accounts for the general and subsidiary ledgers is on page 244. CarLand uses the same procedures as described for Rugcare in Part 2 to maintain its general ledger chart of accounts. The subsidiary ledgers are also a part of the general ledger data base on the template disk. Procedures for adding or changing a subsidiary account are the same as for a general ledger account. (1) An input form is prepared. (2) The data base is retrieved. (3) Data from the input form are keyed. (4) A revised chart of accounts, vendor list, or customer list is displayed to verify the accuracy of the data keyed. (5) The revised chart of accounts or subsidiary ledger lists are stored as part of the general ledger data base on the template disk.

RECORDING PURCHASES

CarLand batches purchases on account transactions and records them on a purchases journal input form.

Purchase of Merchandise on Account

November 2, 19--. Purchased merchandise on account from Veloz Automotive, $1,754.00. Purchase Invoice No. 74.

The journal entry to record this transaction is on line 1 of the purchases journal input form shown in Illustration T4-1.

ILLUSTRATION T4-1   Purchases journal input form with transactions recorded

RUN DATE _11/30/--_
MM DD YY

PURCHASES JOURNAL
Input Form

	DATE MM/DD	VENDOR NO.	INVOICE NO.	INVOICE AMOUNT	ACCOUNT NO.	DEBIT	CREDIT	
1	11 02	260	P74	1754 00	5110	1754 00		1
2	05	240	P75	3456 00	5110	3456 00		2
3	05	230	P76	3180 00	5110	3180 00		3
4	13	250	P77	3140 00	5110	3140 00		4
5	20	250	P78	2760 00	5110	2760 00		5
25								25

NOTE: A credit to Accounts Payable is made automatically by the software.

The run date, *11/30/--*, is written in the space provided at the top of the input form.

On line 1, the date of the transaction, *11/02*, is recorded in the Date column. The vendor number, *260*, is entered in the Vendor No. column. The source document number, *P74*, is written in the

Invoice No. column. The invoice amount, *$1,754.00*, is recorded in the Invoice Amount column. The general ledger account number for Purchases, *5110*, is entered in the Account No. column. The debit amount, *$1,754.00*, is written in the Debit column. The Credit column is left blank. The software automatically records the credit to Accounts Payable for a purchases on account transaction.

RECORDING CASH PAYMENTS

CarLand batches cash payments and records them on a cash payments journal input form. CarLand has two types of cash payments. (1) Direct payments. (2) Payments on account. A direct payment transaction does not affect Accounts Payable. Whereas, a payment on account transaction does affect Accounts Payable.

Purchase of Merchandise for Cash

A purchase of merchandise for cash transaction is a direct payment not affecting Accounts Payable.

> *November 2, 19--. Purchased merchandise for cash, $483.00. Check No. 259.*

The journal entry to record this transaction is on line 1 of the cash payments journal input form shown in Illustration T4-2.

ILLUSTRATION T4-2   Cash payments journal input form with transactions recorded

RUN DATE 11/30/-- (MM DD YY)

CASH PAYMENTS JOURNAL
Input Form

	DATE MM/DD	VENDOR NO.	CHECK NO.	ACCOUNTS PAY. DEBIT	ACCOUNT NO.	DEBIT	CREDIT	
1	11/02		C259		5110	483 00		1
2	02		C260		6160	1500 00		2
3	05		C261		1145	87 00		3
4	06	250	C262	3960 00				4
5	07	230	C263	970 00				5
6	09		C264		6190	300 00		6
7	09		C265		6110	125 00		7
8	09		C266		1145	58 00		8
9					1150	65 00		9
10					6110	92 00		10
11					6140	86 00		11
12	10		C267		3140	1500 00		12
13	12	210	C268	430 00				13
14	15		C272		3120	1500 00		14
15	20	240	C273	4840 00				15
16	23	220	C274	620 00				16
25								25

NOTE: A credit to Cash is made automatically by the software.

The run date, *11/30/--*, is written in the space provided at the top of the form.

On line 1, the date of the transaction, *11/02*, is entered in the Date column. The Vendor No. column is left blank because a purchase of merchandise for cash transaction does not affect a vendor account. The source document number, *C259*, is recorded in the Check No. column. The Accounts Pay. Debit column is left blank. The general ledger account number for Purchases, *5110*, is written in the Account No. column. The amount, *$483.00*, is entered in the Debit column. The software automatically makes the credit to Cash, *$483.00*. Therefore, the Credit column is left blank.

Buying Supplies for Cash

A buying supplies for cash transaction is a direct payment not affecting accounts payable.

> *November 5, 19--. Paid cash for office supplies, $87.00. Check No. 261.*

The journal entry to record this transaction is on line 3 of Illustration T4-2. The entry is similar to other direct payment transactions.

Cash Payment on Account

A cash payment on account transaction affects both the controlling account Accounts Payable and a vendor account in an accounts payable subsidiary ledger.

> *November 6, 19--. Paid cash on account to Q-Ban Distributors, $3,960.00. Check No. 262.*

The journal entry to record this transaction is on line 4 of Illustration T4-2.

The date of the transaction, *06*, is written in the Date column. The vendor number, *250*, is entered in the Vendor No. column. The check number, *C262*, is written in the Check No. column. The amount, *$3,960.00*, is recorded in the Accounts Pay. Debit column. The Account No., Debit, and Credit columns are left blank.

Cash Payment of an Expense

A cash payment of an expense transaction is a direct cash payment not affecting Accounts Payable.

> *November 9, 19--. Paid cash for advertising, $125.00. Check No. 265.*

The journal entry to record this transaction is on line 7 of Illustration T4-2. This journal entry is similar to other direct payments.

Cash Payment to Replenish Petty Cash

A cash payment to replenish petty cash transaction is a direct payment not affecting Accounts Payable.

The run date is usually the date of the last transaction or the last day of a fiscal period.

A direct payment does not affect accounts payable.

November 9, 19--. Paid cash to replenish the petty cash fund, $301.00: office supplies, $58.00; store supplies, $65.00; advertising, $92.00; miscellaneous, $86.00. Check No. 266.

The journal entry to record this transaction is on lines 8 through 11 of Illustration T4-2. This journal entry is similar to other direct payments.

RECORDING OTHER TRANSACTIONS

CarLand batches transactions that are not recorded on any of the other input forms and records them on a general journal input form.

Buying Supplies on Account

November 6, 19--. Bought store supplies on account from Antelo Supply, $160.00. Memorandum No. 43.

The run date, 11/30/--, is written in the space provided at the top of the form.

The journal entry to record this transaction is on lines 1 and 2 of the general journal input form shown in Illustration T4-3. Supplies—Store is debited and Accounts Payable is credited for $160.00.

ILLUSTRATION T4-3   General journal input form with transactions recorded

RUN DATE _11/30/--_   MM DD YY

GENERAL JOURNAL
Input Form

	DATE MM/DD	REFERENCE	ACCOUNT NO.	CUSTOMER/ VENDOR NO.	DEBIT	CREDIT	
1	11/06	M43	1150		160 00		1
2	/		2110	210		160 00	2
3	/12	M44	3140		200 00		3
4	/		5110			200 00	4
5	/13	M45	6110		120 00		5
6	/		6140			120 00	6
7	/20	M46	3120		250 00		7
8	/		5110			250 00	8
9	/23	M47	1150		590 00		9
10	/		2110	210		590 00	10
11	/24	M48	1145		830 00		11
12	/		2110	220		830 00	12
25	/						25
				PAGE TOTALS	2150 00	2150 00	
				FINAL TOTALS	2150 00	2150 00	

Withdrawal of Merchandise by a Partner

November 12, 19--. Dario Mesa, partner, withdrew merchandise for personal use, $200.00. Memorandum No. 44.

The journal entry to record this transaction is on lines 3 and 4 of the general journal input form shown in Illustration T4-3. Dario Mesa, Drawing is debited and Purchases is credited for $200.00.

Correcting Entry

November 13, 19--. Discovered that a payment of cash for advertising in October was journalized and posted in error as a debit to Miscellaneous Expense instead of Advertising Expense, $120.00. Memorandum No. 45.

The journal entry to record this transaction is on lines 5 and 6 of the general journal input form shown in Illustration T4-3. Advertising Expense is debited and Miscellaneous Expense is credited for $120.00.

PROCESSING PURCHASES, CASH PAYMENTS, AND OTHER TRANSACTIONS

The general ledger data base is retrieved from the template disk. To process purchases, the Journals menu is selected from the menu bar. The Purchases Journal command is chosen from the Journals menu to display the data entry window for keying transaction data.

After all transaction data have been keyed and posted, the Reports menu is selected from the menu bar. The Journals command is chosen to display the Report Selection window. The Purchases Journal report is selected from the Report Selection window. As CarLand wants to print all transactions from 11/01/-- to 11/30/--, the *Ok* button is pushed to display the purchases journal report. The displayed report is checked for accuracy by comparing the report with the purchases journal input form. The purchases journal report is printed, as shown in Illustration T4-4, and filed for future reference.

The petty cash account is only used when establishing petty cash.

| **ILLUSTRATION T4-4** | Purchases journal report |

```
                              CarLand
                         Purchases Journal
                             11/30/--
-----------------------------------------------------------------------
Date    Refer.    V/C Acct.   Title                   Debit      Credit
-----------------------------------------------------------------------
11/02   P74           5110    Purchases              1754.00
11/02   P74       260 2110    AP/Veloz Automotive                1754.00

11/05   P75           5110    Purchases              3456.00
11/05   P75       240 2110    AP/Nilon Motor Parts               3456.00

11/05   P76           5110    Purchases              3180.00
11/05   P76       230 2110    AP/Filtrex Tires                   3180.00

11/13   P77           5110    Purchases              3140.00
11/13   P77       250 2110    AP/Q-Ban Distributors              3140.00

11/20   P78           5110    Purchases              2760.00
11/20   P78       250 2110    AP/Q-Ban Distributors              2760.00
                                                    ----------  ----------
                              Totals               14290.00    14290.00
                                                    ==========  ==========
```

To process cash payments, the Journals menu is selected from the menu bar. The Cash Payments command is chosen from the Journals menu to display the data entry window for keying transaction data.

After all transactions have been keyed and posted, a cash payments journal report is displayed. The same steps are followed as for displaying the purchases journal report. However, Cash Payments Journal is selected from the Report Selection window. The displayed report is checked for accuracy by comparing the report with the cash payments journal input form. The cash payments report is printed, as shown in Illustration T4-5, and filed for future reference.

ILLUSTRATION T4-5 Cash payments journal report

```
                              CarLand
                        Cash Payments Journal
                             11/30/--
-----------------------------------------------------------------------
Date   Refer.   V/C Acct.  Title                        Debit      Credit
-----------------------------------------------------------------------
11/02  C259         5110   Purchases                    483.00
11/02  C259         1110   Cash                                    483.00

11/02  C260         6160   Rent Expense                1500.00
11/02  C260         1110   Cash                                   1500.00

11/05  C261         1145   Supplies--Office              87.00
11/05  C261         1110   Cash                                     87.00

11/06  C262     250 2110   AP/Q-Ban Distributors       3960.00
11/06  C262         1110   Cash                                   3960.00

11/07  C263     230 2110   AP/Filtrex Tires             970.00
11/07  C263         1110   Cash                                    970.00

11/09  C264         6190   Utilities Expense            300.00
11/09  C264         1110   Cash                                    300.00

11/09  C265         6110   Advertising Expense          125.00
11/09  C265         1110   Cash                                    125.00

11/09  C266         1145   Supplies--Office              58.00
11/09  C266         1150   Supplies--Store               65.00
11/09  C266         6110   Advertising Expense           92.00
11/09  C266         6140   Miscellaneous Expense         86.00
11/09  C266         1110   Cash                                    301.00

11/10  C267         3140   Dario Mesa, Drawing         1500.00
11/10  C267         1110   Cash                                   1500.00

11/12  C268     210 2110   AP/Antelo Supply             430.00
11/12  C268         1110   Cash                                    430.00

11/15  C272         3120   Amy Kramer, Drawing         1500.00
11/15  C272         1110   Cash                                   1500.00

11/20  C273     240 2110   AP/Nilon Motor Parts        4840.00
11/20  C273         1110   Cash                                   4840.00

11/23  C274     220 2110   AP/Bell Office Products      620.00
11/23  C274         1110   Cash                                    620.00

                                                     ----------  ----------
                           Totals                     16616.00    16616.00
                                                     ==========  ==========
```

To process other transactions, the Journals menu is selected from the menu bar. The General Journal command is chosen from the Journals menu to display the data entry window for keying transactions.

After all transactions have been keyed and posted, a general journal report is displayed. The same steps are followed as for displaying the purchases journal report. However, General Journal is selected from the Report Selection window. The displayed general journal report is checked for accuracy by comparing the report totals, *$2,150.00*, with the totals on the general journal input form. Because the totals are the same, the general journal report is assumed to be correct. The general journal report is printed, as shown in Illustration T4-6, and filed for future reference.

ILLUSTRATION T4-6 General journal report

```
                            CarLand
                        General Journal
                           11/30/--
-----------------------------------------------------------------
Date   Refer.   V/C  Acct.  Title                 Debit    Credit
-----------------------------------------------------------------
11/06  M43           1150   Supplies--Store       160.00
11/06  M43      210  2110   AP/Antelo Supply                160.00

11/12  M44           3140   Dario Mesa, Drawing   200.00
11/12  M44           5110   Purchases                       200.00

11/13  M45           6110   Advertising Expense   120.00
11/13  M45           6140   Miscellaneous Expense           120.00

11/20  M46           3120   Amy Kramer, Drawing   250.00
11/20  M46           5110   Purchases                       250.00

11/23  M47           1150   Supplies--Store       590.00
11/23  M47      210  2110   AP/Antelo Supply                590.00

11/24  M48           1145   Supplies--Office      830.00
11/24  M48      220  2110   AP/Bell Office Products         830.00

                                              ----------  ----------
                            Totals            2150.00     2150.00
                                              ==========  ==========
```

PROVING THE ACCOUNTS PAYABLE SUBSIDIARY LEDGER

A general ledger controlling account balance must equal the sum of all account balances in a subsidiary ledger. CarLand proves the accounts payable subsidiary ledger at the end of each month.

To prove the accounts payable ledger, the Reports menu is selected from the menu bar. The Ledgers command is chosen to display the Report Selection window. General Ledger and Schedule of Accounts Payable are selected from the Report Selection window. As CarLand wants to print the transaction activity in only the general ledger controlling account, Accounts Payable, Account No. 2110 to 2110 is keyed as the account number range. After keying the account number range, the *Ok* button is pushed to display the general ledger account, Accounts Payable. The accounts payable account is printed as shown in Illustration T4-7. The schedule of accounts payable is then displayed. The total of the schedule of accounts payable is compared to the balance of the accounts payable account. As the two amounts are the same, *$15,870.00*, the accounts payable ledger is proved. The schedule of accounts payable is printed, as shown in Illustration T4-8, and filed for future reference.

ILLUSTRATION T4-7   Accounts payable account

```
                            CarLand
                         General Ledger
                            11/30/--
----------------------------------------------------------------------
Account          Journal   Date  Refer.    Debit     Credit    Balance
----------------------------------------------------------------------
2110-Accounts Payable
                 Bal. Fwd.                                    10820.00
                 Purchases 11/02 P74                 1754.00  12574.00
                 Purchases 11/05 P75                 3456.00  16030.00
                 Purchases 11/05 P76                 3180.00  19210.00
                 Cash Pymt 11/06 C262   3960.00               15250.00
                 General   11/06 M43                  160.00  15410.00
                 Cash Pymt 11/07 C263    970.00               14440.00
                 Cash Pymt 11/12 C268    430.00               14010.00
                 Purchases 11/13 P77                 3140.00  17150.00
                 Purchases 11/20 P78                 2760.00  19910.00
                 Cash Pymt 11/20 C273   4840.00               15070.00
                 Cash Pymt 11/23 C274    620.00               14450.00
                 General   11/23 M47                  590.00  15040.00
                 General   11/24 M48                  830.00  15870.00
```

ILLUSTRATION T4-8   Schedule of accounts payable

```
                          CarLand
                 Schedule of Accounts Payable
                          11/30/--
---------------------------------------------------------
Account
Number   Name                              Balance
---------------------------------------------------------
210      Antelo Supply                      750.00
220      Bell Office Products               830.00
230      Filtrex Tires                     3180.00
240      Nilon Motor Parts                 3456.00
250      Q-Ban Distributors                5900.00
260      Veloz Automotive                  1754.00
                                         ----------
         Total                            15870.00
                                         ==========
```

RECORDING SALES ON ACCOUNT

CarLand batches sales on account transactions and records them on a sales journal input form.

November 3, 19--. Sold merchandise on account to Friendly Auto Service, $680.00, plus sales tax, $40.80; total, $720.80. Sales Invoice No. 72.

The journal entry to record this transaction is on lines 1 and 2 of the sales journal input form shown in Illustration T4-9.

ILLUSTRATION T4-9   Sales journal input form with transactions recorded

RUN DATE __11/30/--__
MM DD YY

SALES JOURNAL
Input Form

	DATE MM/DD	CUSTOMER NO.	INVOICE NO.	INVOICE AMOUNT	ACCOUNT NO.	DEBIT	CREDIT	
1	11 03	130	S72	720 80	4110		680 00	1
2	/				2140		40 80	2
3	05	150	S73	1590 00	4110		1500 00	3
4	/				2140		90 00	4
5	09	110	S74	477 00	4110		450 00	5
6	/				2140		27 00	6
7	11	160	S75	604 20	4110		570 00	7
8	/				2140		34 20	8
9	16	110	S76	1378 00	4110		1300 00	9
10	/				2140		78 00	10
11	18	120	S77	2014 00	4110		1900 00	11
12	/				2140		114 00	12
13	24	130	S78	742 00	4110		700 00	13
14	/				2140		42 00	14
15	24	140	S79	318 00	4110		300 00	15
16	/				2140		18 00	16
17	29	140	S80	1378 00	4110		1300 00	17
18	/				2140		78 00	18
25	/							25

NOTE: A debit to Accounts Receivable is made automatically by the software.

The run date, *11/30/--*, is written in the space provided at the top of the form.

On line 1, the date of the transaction, *11/03*, is entered in the Date column. The customer number, *130*, is recorded in the Customer No. column. The source document number, *S72*, is written in the Invoice No. column. The invoice amount, *$720.80*, is written in the Invoice Amount column. The general ledger account number for Sales, *4110*, is entered in the Account No. column. The Debit column is left blank. The software automatically makes the debit to the accounts receivable account. The sale on account amount, $680.00, is recorded in the Credit column.

On line 2 for a sales on account transaction, the Date, Customer No., and Invoice Amount columns are left blank. The general ledger account number for Sales Tax Payable, 2140, is written in the Account No. column. The sales tax amount, $40.80, is entered in the Credit column.

RECORDING CASH RECEIPTS

CarLand batches cash receipts and records them on a cash receipts journal input form. Two types of cash receipts are recorded. (1) Receipts on account. (2) Direct receipts. A receipt on account transaction affects Accounts Receivable. Whereas, a direct receipt transaction does not affect Accounts Receivable.

Cash Receipt on Account

November 6, 19--. Received cash on account from Autohaus Service, $1,802.00. Receipt No. 86.

The journal entry to record this transaction is on line 1 of the cash receipts journal input form shown in Illustration T4-10.

Always remember to record the run date before beginning a problem.

| ILLUSTRATION T4-10 | Cash receipts journal input form with transactions recorded |

RUN DATE 11/30/-- MM DD YY

CASH RECEIPTS JOURNAL
Input Form

	DATE MM/DD	CUSTOMER NO.	REFERENCE	ACCOUNTS REC. CREDIT	ACCOUNT NO.	DEBIT	CREDIT	
1	11 06	120	R86	1802 00				1
2	07		T7		4110		6450 00	2
3	/				2140		387 00	3
4	10	140	R87	954 00				4
5	13	160	R88	901 00				5
6	14	150	R89	318 00				6
7	14		T14		4110		5100 00	7
8	/				2140		306 00	8
9	17	110	R90	2491 00				9
10	20	160	R91	1219 00				10
11	21		T21		4110		5100 00	11
12	/				2140		306 00	12
13	25	130	R92	265 00				13
14	28		T28		4110		5100 00	14
15	/				2140		306 00	15
16	30		T30		4110		1150 00	16
17	/				2140		69 00	17
25	/							25

NOTE: A debit to Cash is made automatically by the software.

The run date, *11/30/--*, is written in the space provided at the top of the form.

On line 1, the date of the transaction, *11/06*, is entered in the Date column. The customer number, *120*, is recorded in the Customer No. column. The source document number, *R86*, is written in the Reference column. The amount of the cash receipt on account, *$1,802.00*, is entered in the Accounts Rec. Credit column. The software automatically makes the debit to *Cash*. Therefore, the Account No. and Debit columns are left blank.

Cash and Credit Card Sales

A cash or credit card sales transaction is a direct receipt not affecting Accounts Receivable.

November 7, 19--. Recorded cash and credit card sales, $6,450.00 plus sales tax, $387.00; total, $6,837.00. Cash Register Tape No. 7.

The journal entry to record this transaction is on lines 2 and 3 of Illustration T4-10.

On line 2, the date of the transaction, *07*, is written in the Date column. The source document number, *T7*, is entered in the Reference column. The software automatically makes the debit to Cash. Therefore, the Debit column is left blank. The general ledger account number for Sales, *4110*, is recorded in the Account No. column. The amount of the sale, *$6,450.00*, is written in the Credit column.

On line 3, the general ledger account number for Sales Tax Payable, *2140*, is entered in the Account No. column. The sales tax payable amount, *$387.00*, is recorded in the Credit column.

PROCESSING SALES AND CASH RECEIPTS

To process sales on account, the Journals menu is selected from the menu bar. The Sales Journal command is chosen from the Journals menu to display the data entry window for keying transaction data.

Display your work before printing to make sure the information is correct. This will save you time and paper.

After all sales on account transactions have been keyed and posted, the Reports menu is selected from the menu bar. The Journals command is chosen to display the Report Selection window. The Sales Journal report is selected from the Report Selection window. As CarLand wants to prints all transactions from 11/01/-- to 11/30/--, the *Ok* button is pushed to display the Sales Journal report. The displayed report is checked for accuracy by comparing the report with the sales journal input form. The sales journal report is printed, as shown in Illustration T4-11, and filed for future reference.

```
                              CarLand
                           Sales Journal
                             11/30/--
------------------------------------------------------------------------
Date   Refer.   V/C Acct.  Title                        Debit      Credit
------------------------------------------------------------------------
11/03  S72      130 1130   AR/Friendly Auto Service      720.80
11/03  S72          4110   Sales                                    680.00
11/03  S72          2140   Sales Tax Payable                         40.80

11/05  S73      150 1130   AR/Powell Rent-A-Car         1590.00
11/05  S73          4110   Sales                                   1500.00
11/05  S73          2140   Sales Tax Payable                         90.00

11/09  S74      110 1130   AR/Ashley Delivery            477.00
11/09  S74          4110   Sales                                    450.00
11/09  S74          2140   Sales Tax Payable                         27.00

11/11  S75      160 1130   AR/Wood Sales & Service       604.20
11/11  S75          4110   Sales                                    570.00
11/11  S75          2140   Sales Tax Payable                         34.20

11/16  S76      110 1130   AR/Ashley Delivery           1378.00
11/16  S76          4110   Sales                                   1300.00
11/16  S76          2140   Sales Tax Payable                         78.00

11/18  S77      120 1130   AR/Autohaus Service          2014.00
11/18  S77          4110   Sales                                   1900.00
11/18  S77          2140   Sales Tax Payable                        114.00

11/24  S78      130 1130   AR/Friendly Auto Service      742.00
11/24  S78          4110   Sales                                    700.00
11/24  S78          2140   Sales Tax Payable                         42.00

11/24  S79      140 1130   AR/Keystone Delivery          318.00
11/24  S79          4110   Sales                                    300.00
11/24  S79          2140   Sales Tax Payable                         18.00

11/29  S80      140 1130   AR/Keystone Delivery         1378.00
11/29  S80          4110   Sales                                   1300.00
11/29  S80          2140   Sales Tax Payable                         78.00
                                                        ---------- ----------
                           Totals                        9222.00    9222.00
                                                        ========== ==========
```

To process cash receipts, the Journals menu is selected from the menu bar. The Cash Receipts command is chosen from the Journals menu to display the data entry window for keying transaction data.

After all transactions have been keyed and posted, the Reports menu is selected from the menu bar. The Journals command is chosen to display the Report Selection window. The Cash Receipts Journal report is selected from the Report Selection window. As CarLand wants to print all transactions from 11/01/-- to 11/30/--, the *Ok* button is pushed to display the Cash Receipts report. The displayed report is checked for accuracy by comparing the report to the cash receipts journal input form. The cash receipts journal report is printed, as shown in Illustration T4-12, and is filed for future reference.

Cash receipts journal report

```
                              CarLand
                       Cash Receipts Journal
                            11/30/--
---------------------------------------------------------------------------
Date   Refer.   V/C Acct.   Title                    Debit         Credit
---------------------------------------------------------------------------
11/06  R86          1110    Cash                    1802.00
11/06  R86      120 1130    AR/Autohaus Service                   1802.00

11/07  T7           1110    Cash                    6837.00
11/07  T7           4110    Sales                                 6450.00
11/07  T7           2140    Sales Tax Payable                      387.00

11/10  R87          1110    Cash                     954.00
11/10  R87      140 1130    AR/Keystone Delivery                   954.00

11/13  R88          1110    Cash                     901.00
11/13  R88      160 1130    AR/Wood Sales & Service                901.00

11/14  R89          1110    Cash                     318.00
11/14  R89      150 1130    AR/Powell Rent-A-Car                   318.00

11/14  T14          1110    Cash                    5406.00
11/14  T14          4110    Sales                                 5100.00
11/14  T14          2140    Sales Tax Payable                      306.00

11/17  R90          1110    Cash                    2491.00
11/17  R90      110 1130    AR/Ashley Delivery                    2491.00

11/20  R91          1110    Cash                    1219.00
11/20  R91      160 1130    AR/Wood Sales & Service               1219.00

11/21  T21          1110    Cash                    5406.00
11/21  T21          4110    Sales                                 5100.00
11/21  T21          2140    Sales Tax Payable                      306.00

11/25  R92          1110    Cash                     265.00
11/25  R92      130 1130    AR/Friendly Auto Service               265.00

11/28  T28          1110    Cash                    5406.00
11/28  T28          4110    Sales                                 5100.00
11/28  T28          2140    Sales Tax Payable                      306.00

11/30  T30          1110    Cash                    1219.00
11/30  T30          4110    Sales                                 1150.00
11/30  T30          2140    Sales Tax Payable                       69.00

                                                   ----------    ----------
                            Totals                 32224.00      32224.00
                                                   ==========    ==========
```

PROVING THE ACCOUNTS RECEIVABLE SUBSIDIARY LEDGER

CarLand proves the accounts receivable subsidiary ledger at the end of each month.

To prove the accounts receivable ledger, the Reports menu is selected from the menu bar. The Ledgers command is chosen to display the Report Selection window. General Ledger and Schedule of Accounts Receivable are selected from the Report Selection window. As CarLand wants to print the transaction activity only in the general ledger controlling account, Accounts Receivable, Account No. 1130 to 1130 is keyed as the account number range. After keying the account number range, the *Ok* button is pushed to display the general ledger account, Accounts Receivable. The accounts receivable account is printed as shown in Illustration T4-13. The schedule of accounts receivable is then displayed. The total of the schedule of accounts receivable is compared to the accounts receivable account balance. As the two amounts are the same, *$9,222.00*, the accounts receivable ledger is proved. The schedule of accounts receivable is printed, as shown in Illustration T4-14 on page 324, and is filed for future reference.

ILLUSTRATION T4-13   Accounts receivable account

```
                              CarLand
                          General Ledger
                            11/30/--
--------------------------------------------------------------------
Account          Journal   Date   Refer.    Debit     Credit   Balance
--------------------------------------------------------------------
1130-Accounts Receivable
                 Bal. Fwd.                                     7950.00
                 Sales    11/03  S72       720.80              8670.80
                 Sales    11/05  S73      1590.00             10260.80
                 Cash Rcpt 11/06 R86                 1802.00   8458.80
                 Sales    11/09  S74       477.00              8935.80
                 Cash Rcpt 11/10 R87                  954.00   7981.80
                 Sales    11/11  S75       604.20              8586.00
                 Cash Rcpt 11/13 R88                  901.00   7685.00
                 Cash Rcpt 11/14 R89                  318.00   7367.00
                 Sales    11/16  S76      1378.00              8745.00
                 Cash Rcpt 11/17 R90                 2491.00   6254.00
                 Sales    11/18  S77      2014.00              8268.00
                 Cash Rcpt 11/20 R91                 1219.00   7049.00
                 Sales    11/24  S78       742.00              7791.00
                 Sales    11/24  S79       318.00              8109.00
                 Cash Rcpt 11/25 R92                  265.00   7844.00
                 Sales    11/29  S80      1378.00              9222.00
```

```
                        CarLand
              Schedule of Accounts Receivable
                        11/30/--
      ---------------------------------------------
      Account
      Number      Name                     Balance
      ---------------------------------------------
      110         Ashley Delivery          1855.00
      120         Autohaus Service         2014.00
      130         Friendly Auto Service    1462.80
      140         Keystone Delivery        1696.00
      150         Powell Rent-A-Car        1590.00
      160         Wood Sales & Service      604.20
                                          ----------
                  Total                    9222.00
                                          ==========
```

OPTIONAL PROBLEM DB-4A

CarLand's general ledger data base is on the accounting textbook template. If you wish to process CarLand's purchases, cash payments, and other transactions using automated accounting software, load the *Automated Accounting 6.0* or higher software. Select Data Base 4A (DB-4A) from the template disk. Read the Problem Instructions screen. Use the completed purchases, cash payments, general journal input forms, Illustrations T4-1, T4-2, and T4-3, and follow the procedures described to process CarLand's purchases, cash payments, and other transactions.

OPTIONAL PROBLEM DB-4A

CarLand's general ledger data base is on the accounting textbook template. If you wish to process CarLand's sales and cash receipts transactions using automated accounting software, load the *Automated Accounting 6.0* or higher software. Continue using Data Base 4A (DB-4A) from the template disk. Use the completed sales and cash receipts journal input forms, Illustrations T4-9 and T4-10, and follow the procedures described to process CarLand's sales and cash receipts.

AUTOMATED ACCOUNTING PROBLEM

AUTOMATING CHALLENGE PROBLEM 13-C   Recording transactions for a partnership

INSTRUCTIONS:

1. Journalize the transactions from Challenge Problem 13-C, Chapter 13 on the appropriate input forms. Use November 30 of the current year as the run date.
2. Load the *Automated Accounting 6.0* or higher software. Select data base F13-C (First-Year Course Problem 13-C) from the accounting textbook template. Read the Problem Instructions screen.
3. Select File from the menu bar and choose the Save As menu command. Key the path to the drive and directory that contains your data files. Save the data base with a file name of XXX13C (where XXX are your initials).
4. Key the data from the completed purchases journal input form.
5. Display/print the purchases journal report.
6. Key the data from the completed cash payments journal input form.
7. Display/print the cash payments journal report.
8. Key the data from the completed general journal input form.

9. Display/print the general journal report.
10. Display/print the accounts payable account.
11. Display/print the schedule of accounts payable.
12. Key the data from the completed sales journal input form.
13. Display/print the sales journal report.
14. Key the data from the cash receipts journal input form.
15. Display/print the cash receipts journal report.
16. Display/print the accounts receivable account.
17. Display/print the schedule of accounts receivable.

14

Preparing Payroll Records

ENABLING PERFORMANCE TASKS

After studying Chapter 14, you will be able to:

a Define accounting terms related to payroll records.

b Identify accounting practices related to payroll records.

c Calculate employee earnings and deductions.

d Complete payroll records.

e Prepare payroll checks.

TERMS PREVIEW

salary • pay period • payroll • total earnings • payroll taxes • withholding allowance • Medicare • FICA tax • federal unemployment tax • state unemployment tax • payroll register • tax base • net pay • automatic check deposit • employee earnings record • pegboard

CarLand employs several people to work in the business. These employees record the time they work for CarLand each day. Periodically CarLand pays its employees for the number of hours each employee has worked. The money paid for employee services is called a **salary.** The period covered by a salary payment is called a **pay period.** A business may decide to pay employee salaries every week, every two weeks, twice a month, or once a month. CarLand uses a semimonthly pay period. Employees are paid twice a month, on the 15th and last day of each month.

The total amount earned by all employees for a pay period is called a **payroll.** The payroll is reduced by state and federal taxes and other deductions, such as health insurance, to determine the amount paid to all employees. Special payroll records support the recording of payroll transactions in a journal. The business also uses these records to inform employees of their annual earnings and to prepare payroll reports for the government.

PAYROLL TIME CARDS

A payroll system must include an accurate record of the time each employee has worked. Several methods are used for keeping time records. One of the more frequently used methods is a time card. Time cards are used as the basic source of information to prepare a payroll.

Some time cards only require employees to record the total hours worked each day. Employees who record the total hours worked each day usually complete time cards by hand.

A business may use a time card that requires employees to record their arrival and departure times. CarLand uses a time clock to record the daily arrival and departure times of its employees. The time card for Patrick S. Turner for the pay period December 1–15 is shown in Illustration 14-1.

ILLUSTRATION 14-1

Payroll time card

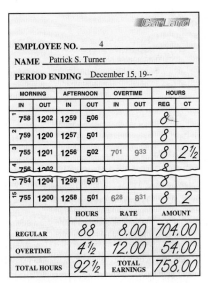

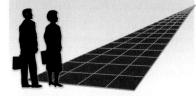
Analyzing a Payroll Time Card

Mr. Turner's employee number is at the top of the card. Below the employee number are the employee name and the ending date of the pay period.

CarLand's time cards have three sections, Morning, Afternoon, and Overtime, with In and Out columns under each section. When Mr. Turner reported for work on December 1, he inserted the card in the time clock. The clock recorded his time of arrival, 7:58, on the first line of the time card. The other entries on this line indicate that he left for lunch at 12:02. He returned at 12:59 and left for the day at 5:06. On December 3 he worked overtime, starting at 7:01 and leaving at 9:33.

CarLand calculates overtime pay for each employee who works more than 8 hours in one day. No employee works more than 5 days in any one week.

Calculating Hours Worked

The first task in preparing a payroll is to calculate the number of hours worked by each employee. Four steps are followed to calculate employee hours worked.

1 Calculate the number of regular hours for each day and enter the amounts in the Hours Reg column.

> Mr. Turner works 8 hours during a normal day. The hours worked on December 3, the third line of the time card, are calculated using the arrival and departure times imprinted on the time card. Times are rounded to the nearest quarter hour to calculate the hours worked.

	Departure Time	−	Arrival Time	=	Hours Worked
Morning:					
Time card	12:01		7:55		
Nearest quarter hour	12:00	−	8:00	=	4:00
Afternoon:					
Time card	5:02		12:56		
Nearest quarter hour	5:00	−	1:00	=	4:00
Total regular hours worked on December 3					8:00

> The hours worked in the morning and afternoon are calculated separately. The morning departure time of 12:01 is rounded to the nearest quarter hour, 12:00. The rounded arrival time, 8:00, *subtracted* from the departure time, 12:00, *equals* the morning hours worked. Hours worked of 4:00 means that Mr. Turner worked 4 hours and no (00) minutes. The total regular hours worked, *8*, is recorded in the Hours Reg column on line 3 of the time card.

2 Calculate the number of overtime hours for each day and enter the amounts in the Hours OT column.

Overtime hours for December 3 are calculated using the same procedure as for regular hours.

	Departure Time	−	Arrival Time	=	Hours Worked
Time card	9:33		7:01		
Nearest quarter hour	9:30	−	7:00	=	2:30

The hours worked of 2:30 means that Mr. Turner worked 2 hours and 30 minutes (½ hour) of overtime. Therefore, 2½ is recorded in the Hours OT column.

3 Add the hours worked in the Hours Reg and OT columns. Enter the totals in the spaces provided at the bottom of the time card.

Mr. Turner worked 88 regular hours (8 hours × 11 days) and 4½ overtime hours during the semimonthly pay period. Therefore, *88* is recorded in the Regular Hours space at the bottom of the card and *4½* is recorded in the Overtime Hours space.

4 Add the Hours column to calculate the total hours. Enter the total in the Hours column at the bottom of the time card.

Mr. Turner worked 88 regular hours and 4½ overtime hours for a total of 92½ hours. Total hours, *92½*, are entered in the Total Hours space.

Calculating Employee Total Earnings

Once the total regular and overtime hours are determined, employee earnings can be calculated. The total pay due for a pay period before deductions is called **total earnings.** Total earnings are sometimes referred to as gross pay or gross earnings. Four steps are followed to calculate employee total earnings.

1 Enter the rate for regular time in the Rate column. Calculate the regular earnings by multiplying regular hours times the regular rate.

Mr. Turner's regular hourly rate, *$8.00,* is entered in the Regular Rate space. The regular earnings are calculated as shown below.

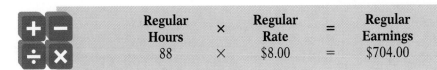

	Regular Hours	×	Regular Rate	=	Regular Earnings
	88	×	$8.00	=	$704.00

The amount of regular earnings, *$704.00,* is entered in the Regular Amount space.

2 Enter the rate for overtime in the Rate column.

Mr. Turner is paid 1½ times his regular rate for overtime work. The overtime rate for Mr. Turner is calculated as shown below.

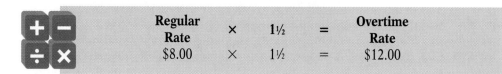

	Regular Rate	×	1½	=	Overtime Rate
	$8.00	×	1½	=	$12.00

The overtime rate, *$12.00*, is entered in the Overtime Rate space.

3 Calculate the overtime earnings by multiplying overtime hours times the overtime rate.

The overtime earnings for Mr. Turner are calculated as shown below.

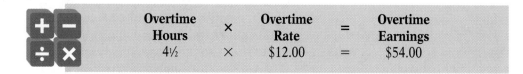

	Overtime Hours	×	Overtime Rate	=	Overtime Earnings
	4½	×	$12.00	=	$54.00

The amount of overtime earnings, $54.00, is entered in the Overtime Amount space.

4 Add the Amount column to calculate the total earnings.

The total earnings for Mr. Turner are calculated as shown below.

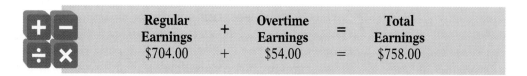

	Regular Earnings	+	Overtime Earnings	=	Total Earnings
	$704.00	+	$54.00	=	$758.00

The amount of total earnings, $758.00, is entered in the Total Earnings space.

CarLand owes Mr. Turner $758.00 for his work during the pay period ending December 15. However, taxes and other deductions must be subtracted from total earnings to determine the actual amount CarLand will pay Mr. Turner. Therefore, CarLand will not pay Mr. Turner the entire $758.00.

FYI

Total earnings are sometimes referred to as gross pay or gross earnings.

Audit Your Understanding

1. What is a payroll?

2. How does CarLand calculate overtime earnings?

3. How many hours were worked by an employee who arrived at 8:29 and departed at 12:02?

4. What are the total earnings of an employee who worked 40 hours and earns $10.00 per hour?

PAYROLL TAXES

Taxes based on the payroll of a business are called **payroll taxes.** A business is required by law to withhold certain payroll taxes from employee salaries. A business is also required to pay additional payroll taxes. All payroll taxes are based on employee total earnings. Therefore, accurate and detailed payroll records must be maintained. Errors in payroll records could cause incorrect payroll tax payments. Federal and state governments may charge a business a penalty for failure to pay correct payroll taxes when they are due.

FYI

Payroll taxes withheld represent a liability for the employer until payment is made.

Payroll taxes withheld represent a liability for the employer until payment is made. Federal payroll taxes may be paid to a Federal Reserve Bank. The taxes may also be paid to a bank authorized to receive such funds for the government. Local and state governments that assess payroll taxes also designate how, when, and where a business will pay the liability for employee taxes withheld.

Employee Income Tax

A business must withhold federal income taxes from employee total earnings. Federal income taxes withheld must be forwarded periodically to the federal government. Federal income tax is withheld from employee earnings in all 50 states. Employers in many states also are required to withhold state, city, or county income taxes from employee earnings.

The information used to determine the amount of income tax withheld is identified on Form W-4, Employee's Withholding Allowance Certificate. The completed Form W-4 for Mr. Turner is shown in Illustration 14-2.

ILLUSTRATION 14-2 Form W-4, Employee's Withholding Allowance Certificate

Form **W-4**
Department of the Treasury
Internal Revenue Service

Employee's Withholding Allowance Certificate

▶ For Privacy Act and Paperwork Reduction Act Notice, see reverse.

OMB No. 1545-0010
19 --

1 Type or print your first name and middle initial — Last name: Patrick S. Turner

2 Your social security number: 450-70-6432

Home address (number and street or rural route): 1625 Northland Drive

3 ☐ Single ☒ Married ☐ Married, but withhold at higher Single rate.
Note: *If married, but legally separated, or spouse is a nonresident alien, check the Single box.*

City or town, state, and ZIP code: Rockville, RI 02873

4 If your last name differs from that on your social security card, check here and call 1-800-772-1213 for more information . ▶ ☐

5 Total number of allowances you are claiming (from line G above or from the Worksheets on back if they apply) — 5: 4

6 Additional amount, if any, you want deducted from each paycheck . . . . — 6: $ -0-

7 I claim exemption from withholding and I certify that I meet **ALL** of the following conditions for exemption:

- Last year I had a right to a refund of **ALL** Federal income tax withheld because I had **NO** tax liability; **AND**
- This year I expect a refund of **ALL** Federal income tax withheld because I expect to have **NO** tax liability; **AND**
- This year if my income exceeds $600 and includes nonwage income, another person cannot claim me as a dependent.

If you meet all of the above conditions, enter the year effective and "Exempt" here . . . ▶ 7 19

8 Are you a full-time student? (**Note:** *Full-time students are not automatically exempt.*) . . . . 8 ☒ Yes ☐ No

Under penalties of perjury, I certify that I am entitled to the number of withholding allowances claimed on this certificate or entitled to claim exempt status.

Employee's signature ▶ Patrick S. Turner **Date ▶** June 27 , 19 --

9 Employer's name and address (Employer: Complete 9 and 11 only if sending to the IRS) | 10 Office code (optional) | 11 Employer identification number

Information from the completed Form W-4 is used when a business calculates the amount of federal income taxes to be withheld. Employers are required to have on file a current Form W-4 for all employees. The amount of income tax withheld is based on employee marital status and withholding allowances.

Marital Status. Employees identify on Form W-4 whether they are married or single. A married employee will have less income tax withheld than a single employee with the same total earnings.

> Mr. Turner checked the married box for item 3 of the Form W-4 shown in Illustration 14-2.

Withholding Allowance. A deduction from total earnings for each person legally supported by a taxpayer is called a **withholding allowance.** The larger the number of the withholding allowances claimed, the smaller the income tax withheld from employee salaries.

> Mr. Turner claimed four withholding allowances, one each for himself, his wife, and his two children. The number of withholding allowances was recorded in item 5 of the Form W-4.

Most employees are required to have federal income taxes withheld from their salaries. An exemption from withholding is available for certain low-income and part-time employees. The employee must meet the requirements listed in the instructions which accompany Form W-4. The requirements are very restrictive. Most students with part-time jobs who live with their parents do *not* qualify for the exemption. Students who earn over $500 in salary or any interest from a savings or checking account are not eligible to claim the exemption.

> The federal government occasionally changes the way income taxes are withheld from employee total earnings. The Form W-4 shown in Illustration 14-2 was the form in use when the materials for this textbook were prepared. Employers must be aware of changes in tax laws and forms. If Form W-4 is changed, an employer must obtain a new W-4 from each employee.

Employee and Employer Social Security Tax

The federal social security law includes three programs.

1. Old-age, survivors, and disability insurance benefits for qualified employees and their spouses, widows or widowers, dependent children, and parents.
2. Payments to senior citizens for the cost of certain hospital and related services. The federal health insurance program for people who have reached retirement age is called **Medicare.**
3. Grants to states that provide benefits for persons temporarily unemployed and for certain relief and welfare purposes.

> Each employee must have a social security number. Current law requires that most infants who are at least one year old by the

Many hospitals encourage new mothers to apply for social security numbers for their infants before leaving the hospital.

USING FUNCTIONS TO PREPARE A PAYROLL REGISTER

Many computations are required to prepare a payroll register. When computations require many values, formulas with individual cell references can become burdensome. For example, the formula to compute the total regular wages at G17 would be +G10+G11+G12+G13+G14+G15. A lengthy formula can sometimes by replaced with a function which is a short-cut formula. Functions make keying easier and more efficient.

A typical function begins with the @ sign, followed by the function name, and ending with cell references. The name of the function describes what calculation will be performed. The cell refer-

ences identify the location of values to be used in the computation. The most common function, @SUM, computes the sum of the values in a range of cells. The function @SUM(G10..G15) would add the amounts in cells G10 through G15 to compute total regular wages.

In subsequent payroll periods, Ms. Bauch may have different earnings or change her number of withholding allowances. The electronic spreadsheet will use these new values to determine the correct income tax withholding from the data base. The electronic spreadsheet can perform this task instantly and accurately.

```
     A       B        C       D    E  F      G        H        I   J   K
1                                                            PAYROLL REGISTER
2    Semimonthly Period Ended:    December 15, 19--
3
4                                           Earnings
5                                  ----------------------------    ----------
6                          No.                                     Federal
7    Empl.              Mar. of                                    Income
8    No.  Employee's Name St.  All.  Regular Overtime   Total        Tax
9    ----------------------------------  ----------------------    ----------
10      2 Bauch, Mary R.    2    2     660.00             660.00      57.00
11      5 Clay, Richard P.  1    1      80.00              80.00        .00
12      1 Javorski, Adam B. 2    2     384.00   18.00     402.00      17.00
13      6 Maggio, Brenda A. 1    1      40.00              40.00        .00
14      4 Turner, Patrick S.2    4     704.00   54.00     758.00      45.00
15      3 Wilkes, Samuel R. 1    1     616.00             616.00      73.00
16                                  ----------------------------    ----------
17                                  2,484.00   72.00   2,556.00     192.00
18                                  ============================    =========
19
20
  G17    (,2) @SUM(G10..G15)
```

end of a tax year have a social security number. Therefore, most employees will have received their social security number as a child. Employees without social security numbers can apply for a number at the nearest Social Security office.

FICA Tax. A federal tax paid by employees and employers for old-age, survivors, disability, and hospitalization insurance is called **FICA tax.** FICA is the abbreviation for the Federal Insurance Contributions Act. FICA tax is based on the total earnings of the employees. Employers are required to withhold FICA tax from a specified amount of employee salary paid in a calendar year. In addition, employers must pay the same amount of FICA tax as withheld from employee salaries.

Federal Unemployment Tax. A federal tax used for state and federal administrative expenses of the unemployment program is

FICA is an acronym for Federal Insurance Contributions Act.

called **federal unemployment tax.** This tax is paid entirely by employers.

State Unemployment Tax. A state tax used to pay benefits to unemployed workers is called **state unemployment tax.** This tax is usually paid by employers. The Social Security Act specifies certain standards for unemployment compensation laws. Therefore, a high degree of uniformity exists in state unemployment laws. However, details of state unemployment laws do differ. Because of these differences, employers must know the requirements of the states in which they operate.

Retention of Records. Employers are required to retain all payroll records showing payments and deductions. Some records must be retained longer than others. Records pertaining to social security tax payments and deductions must be retained for four years. The length of time state unemployment tax payment records must be retained varies from state to state.

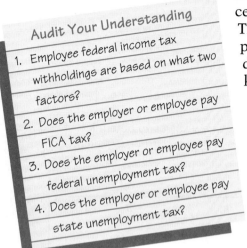

Audit Your Understanding

1. Employee federal income tax withholdings are based on what two factors?

2. Does the employer or employee pay FICA tax?

3. Does the employer or employee pay federal unemployment tax?

4. Does the employer or employee pay state unemployment tax?

PAYROLL REGISTER

A business form used to record payroll information is called a **payroll register.** A payroll register summarizes the total earnings and payroll withholdings of all employees. CarLand's payroll register for the semimonthly period ended December 15 is shown in Illustration 14-3.

Regular, overtime, and total earnings are recorded in a payroll register from information on time cards. Amounts deducted for payroll taxes, health insurance, and charitable contributions are calculated and recorded in a payroll register. Also, the total amount

ILLUSTRATION 14-3   Payroll register

					EARNINGS			DEDUCTIONS							
	EMPL. NO.	EMPLOYEE'S NAME	MARITAL STATUS	NO. OF ALLOWANCES	REGULAR	OVERTIME	TOTAL	FEDERAL INCOME TAX	FICA TAX	HEALTH INSURANCE	OTHER		TOTAL	NET PAY	CHECK NO.
1	2	Bauch, Mary R.	M	2	660 00		660 00	57 00	52 80	38 00	B	5 00	152 80	507 20	419
2	5	Clay, Richard P.	S	1	80 00		80 00	00	6 40				6 40	73 60	420
3	1	Javorski, Adam B.	M	2	384 00	18 00	402 00	17 00	32 16	38 00			87 16	314 84	421
4	6	Maggio, Brenda A.	S	1	40 00		40 00	00	3 20				3 20	36 80	422
5	4	Turner, Patrick S.	M	4	704 00	54 00	758 00	45 00	60 64	50 00	B uw	10 00 / 10 00	175 64	582 36	423
6	3	Wilkes, Samuel R.	S	1	616 00		616 00	73 00	49 28	32 00			154 28	461 72	424
7		Totals			2484 00	72 00	2556 00	192 00	204 48	158 00	B uw	15 00 / 10 00	579 48	1976 52	

SEMIMONTHLY PERIOD ENDED *December 15, 19--*   PAYROLL REGISTER   DATE OF PAYMENT *December 15, 19--*

to be paid to each employee and the check number of each payroll check are recorded in a payroll register.

The two partners of CarLand, Amy Kramer and Dario Mesa, are not listed on the payroll register. Owners of partnerships are not employees of the company. Cash payments to partners are recorded as withdrawals rather than as salaries.

Recording Earnings in a Payroll Register

The employee number, name, marital status, and withholding allowances are listed in a payroll register. Employee earnings for a pay period are written in the appropriate columns of a payroll register.

Recorded on line 5 of the payroll register are Mr. Turner's employee number, *4*, and name, *Turner, Patrick S.* Also recorded are Mr. Turner's marital status, *M* for married; the number of withholding allowances, *4*; regular earnings, *$704.00*; overtime earnings, *$54.00*; and total earnings, *$758.00*. This information is obtained from Mr. Turner's Form W-4 and time card.

Recording Deductions in a Payroll Register

The deductions section of a payroll register is used to record the payroll taxes and other deductions withheld from employee earnings. Also, some companies deduct amounts for retirement plans. These deductions will vary from one company to another depending on policies established between management and employees.

Five steps are followed to calculate and record deductions.

1 The Federal Income Tax column is used to record the amount of federal income tax withheld from employee earnings. This amount is determined from tables furnished by the federal government. Portions of the tables showing the tax to be withheld are shown in Illustration 14-4.

Mr. Turner's federal income tax on total earnings of $758.00 is found in the table for married persons. Since CarLand pays its payroll twice a month, the table for a semimonthly pay period is used. The proper wage bracket is from $740.00 to $760.00. The income tax to be withheld is the amount shown on this line under the column for four allowances, $45.00.

No federal income tax was withheld from the earnings of Richard Clay and Brenda Maggio. Although they are students who work part-time, they are not exempt from federal income tax withholding. They did not, however, have enough total earnings *in this pay period* to require any income tax to be withheld. Federal income tax withholding tables are also available for daily, weekly, biweekly, and monthly pay periods. The tables in Illustration 14-4 are those available when materials for this textbook were prepared.

2 The FICA Tax column is used to record the amount deducted for social security tax. FICA tax is calculated by multiplying

Businesses must withhold federal income tax from employee total earnings in all fifty states.

Businesses must withhold state and local income tax from employee total earnings in many states.

ILLUSTRATION 14-4 Section of income tax withholding tables for semimonthly pay period

SEMIMONTHLY PAYROLL PERIOD — MARRIED PERSONS

SEMIMONTHLY MARRIED PERSONS

And the wages are–		And the number of withholding allowances claimed is–										
At least	But less than	0	1	2	3	4	5	6	7	8	9	10
		The amount of income tax to be withheld shall be–										
$0	$130											
130	135	1										
135	140	2										
140	145	2										
145	150	3										
400	410	42	30	17	5							
410	420	43	31	19	7							
420	430	45	33	20	8							
430	440	46	34	22	10							
440	450	48	36	23	11							
450	460	49	37	25	13							
460	470	51	39	26	14	2						
470	480	52	40	28	16	3						
480	490	54	42	29	17	5						
490	500	55	43	31	19	6						
500	520	57	45	33	21	9						
520	540	60	48	36	24	12						
540	560	63	51	39	27	15	3					
560	580	66	54	42	30	18	6					
580	600	69	57	45	33	21	9					
600	620	72	60	48	36	24	12					
620	640	75	63	51	39	27	15	2				
640	660	78	66	54	42	30	18	5				
660	680	81	69	57	45	33	21	8				
680	700	84	72	60	48	36	24	11				
700	720	87	75	63	51	39	27	14	2			
720	740	90	78	66	54	42	30	17	5			
740	760	93	81	69	57	45	33	20	8			
760	780	96	84	72	60	48	36	23	11			
780	800	99	87	75	63	51	39	26	14	2		
800	820	102	90	78	66	54	42	29	17	5		
820	840	105	93	81	69	57	45	32	20	8		
840	860	108	96	84	72	60	48	35	23	11		
860	880	111	99	87	75	63	51	38	26	14	2	
880	900	114	102	90	78	66	54	41	29	17	5	
900	920	117	105	93	81	69	57	44	32	20	8	
920	940	120	108	96	84	72	60	47	35	23	11	
940	960	123	111	99	87	75	63	50	38	26	14	2
960	980	126	114	102	90	78	66	53	41	29	17	5
980	1,000	129	117	105	93	81	69	56	44	32	20	8
1,000	1,020	132	120	108	96	84	72	59	47	35	23	11
1,020	1,040	135	123	111	99	87	75	62	50	38	26	14
1,040	1,060	138	126	114	102	90	78	65	53	41	29	17
1,060	1,080	141	129	117	105	93	81	68	56	44	32	20
1,080	1,100	144	132	120	108	96	84	71	59	47	35	23
1,100	1,120	147	135	123	111	99	87	74	62	50	38	26
1,120	1,140	150	138	126	114	102	90	77	65	53	41	29
1,140	1,160	153	141	129	117	105	93	80	68	56	44	32
1,160	1,180	156	144	132	120	108	96	83	71	59	47	35
1,180	1,200	159	147	135	123	111	99	86	74	62	50	38
1,200	1,220	162	150	138	126	114	102	89	77	65	53	41
1,220	1,240	165	153	141	129	117	105	92	80	68	56	44
1,240	1,260	168	156	144	132	120	108	95	83	71	59	47
1,260	1,280	171	159	147	135	123	111	98	86	74	62	50
1,280	1,300	174	162	150	138	126	114	101	89	77	65	53
1,300	1,320	177	165	153	141	129	117	104	92	80	68	56
1,320	1,340	180	168	156	144	132	120	107	95	83	71	59
1,340	1,360	183	171	159	147	135	123	110	98	86	74	62
1,360	1,380	187	174	162	150	138	126	113	101	89	77	65
1,380	1,400	192	177	165	153	141	129	116	104	92	80	68

total earnings by the tax rate. From time to time, Congress changes the tax rate used to calculate FICA taxes. A FICA tax rate of 8% is used to illustrate the FICA tax calculations in this textbook. The FICA tax for Mr. Turner is calculated as shown below.

Total Earnings	×	FICA Tax Rate	=	FICA Tax Deduction
$758.00	×	8%	=	$60.64

Congress has limited the amount of FICA tax that each individual must pay. The FICA tax is not calculated on total earnings over a specific maximum amount. The maximum amount of earnings on which a tax is calculated is called a **tax base.**

The FICA tax rate is a combination of two different tax rates: (1) a tax for old-age, survivors, and disability and (2) a

SEMIMONTHLY PAYROLL PERIOD — SINGLE PERSONS

And the wages are—		And the number of withholding allowances claimed is—										
At least	But less than	0	1	2	3	4	5	6	7	8	9	10
		The amount of income tax to be withheld shall be—										
$0	$45											
45	50	1										
50	55	1										
55	60	2										
60	65	3										
65	70	4										
70	75	4										
75	80	5										
80	85	6										
85	90	7										
380	390	51	39	27	15	2						
390	400	53	41	28	16	4						
400	410	54	42	30	18	5						
410	420	56	44	31	19	7						
420	430	57	45	33	21	8						
430	440	59	47	34	22	10						
440	450	60	48	36	24	11						
450	460	62	50	37	25	13	1					
460	470	63	51	39	27	14	2					
470	480	65	53	40	28	16	4					
480	490	66	54	42	30	17	5					
490	500	68	56	43	31	19	7					
500	520	70	58	46	33	21	9					
520	540	73	61	49	36	24	12					
540	560	76	64	52	39	27	15	3				
560	580	79	67	55	42	30	18	6				
580	600	82	70	58	45	33	21	9				
600	620	85	73	61	48	36	24	12				
620	640	88	76	64	51	39	27	15	3			
640	660	91	79	67	54	42	30	18	6			
660	680	94	82	70	57	45	33	21	9			
680	700	97	85	73	60	48	36	24	12			
700	720	100	88	76	63	51	39	27	15	2		
720	740	103	91	79	66	54	42	30	18	5		
740	760	106	94	82	69	57	45	33	21	8		
760	780	109	97	85	72	60	48	36	24	11		
780	800	112	100	88	75	63	51	39	27	14	2	
800	820	118	103	91	78	66	54	42	30	17	5	
820	840	123	106	94	81	69	57	45	33	20	8	
840	860	129	109	97	84	72	60	48	36	23	11	
860	880	135	112	100	87	75	63	51	39	26	14	2
880	900	140	118	103	90	78	66	54	42	29	17	5
900	920	146	123	106	93	81	69	57	45	32	20	8
920	940	151	129	109	96	84	72	60	48	35	23	11
940	960	157	134	112	99	87	75	63	51	38	26	14
960	980	163	140	117	102	90	78	66	54	41	29	17
980	1,000	168	146	123	105	93	81	69	57	44	32	20
1,000	1,020	174	151	128	108	96	84	72	60	47	35	23
1,020	1,040	179	157	134	111	99	87	75	63	50	38	26
1,040	1,060	185	162	140	117	102	90	78	66	53	41	29
1,060	1,080	191	168	145	122	105	93	81	69	56	44	32
1,080	1,100	196	174	151	128	108	96	84	72	59	47	35
1,100	1,120	202	179	156	134	111	99	87	75	62	50	38
1,120	1,140	207	185	162	139	116	102	90	78	65	53	41
1,140	1,160	213	190	168	145	122	105	93	81	68	56	44
1,160	1,180	219	196	173	150	128	108	96	84	71	59	47
1,180	1,200	224	202	179	156	133	111	99	87	74	62	50
1,200	1,220	230	207	184	162	139	116	102	90	77	65	53
1,220	1,240	235	213	190	167	144	122	105	93	80	68	56
1,240	1,260	241	218	196	173	150	127	108	96	83	71	59

SEMIMONTHLY SINGLE PERSONS

tax for Medicare. The two taxes also have different tax bases. The FICA tax rates and bases used in this text are shown below.

	Tax Rate	Tax Base
Old-age, survivors, and disability	6.5%	earnings up to $55,500
Medicare	1.5%	earnings up to $130,200
Total	8.0%	

Therefore, the effective FICA tax rate for earnings up to the tax base of $55,500 is 8.0% (6.5% + 1.5%). The additional FICA tax rate for earnings from $55,500 to $130,200 is 1.5%.

Before calculating Mr. Turner's FICA tax, his accumulated earnings are compared to the tax base. Between January 1 and December 1, Mr. Turner has earned $16,794.00. Since his earnings are less than either tax base, the total FICA tax of 8.0%

of earnings ($758.00 × 8% = $60.64) is recorded in the payroll register. If Mr. Turner had accumulated earnings over $55,500.00 but not yet $130,200.00, only the Medicare portion of FICA tax (1.5% of earnings) would be owed. If Mr. Turner had accumulated earnings over $130,200.00, no FICA tax would be owed and no amount would have been recorded in the payroll register.

3 The Health Insurance column is used to record health insurance premiums. Full-time employees of CarLand participate in a group health insurance plan to take advantage of lower group rates.

Mr. Turner's semimonthly health insurance premium is $50.00. Premiums are set by the insurance company and are usually based on the employee marital status and whether coverage is for an individual or a family. Some health insurance premiums may be based on the number of individuals covered.

Information from Form W-4 determines how much federal income tax is to be withheld.

4 The Other column is used to record voluntary deductions requested by an employee. Entries are identified by code letters. CarLand uses the letter *B* to identify amounts withheld for buying U.S. Savings Bonds. *UW* is used to identify amounts withheld for employee contributions to United Way.

Mr. Turner has authorized CarLand to withhold $10.00 each pay period to buy U.S. Savings Bonds for him. Mr. Turner has also authorized that $10.00 be withheld as a contribution to the United Way.

5 The Total column is used to record total deductions. All deductions on a line for each employee are added. The total deductions for Mr. Turner are calculated as shown below.

	Federal Income Tax	+	FICA Tax	+	Health Insurance	+	Other	=	Total Deductions
	$45.00	+	$60.64	+	$50.00	+	$20.00	=	$175.64

Calculating Net Pay in a Payroll Register

The total earnings paid to an employee after payroll taxes and other deductions is called **net pay**. Net pay is calculated by subtracting total deductions from total earnings. The Net Pay column is used to record the amount. The net pay for Mr. Turner is calculated as shown below.

	Total Earnings	–	Total Deductions	=	Net Pay
	$758.00	–	$175.64	=	$582.36

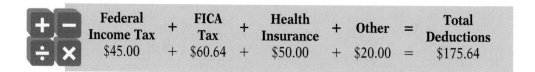

Completing a Payroll Register

After the net pay has been recorded for each employee, the word *Totals* is written in the Employee name column and each amount column is totaled. A separate total is shown for each different type of deduction in the Other column. Accuracy of these totals is verified by subtracting the Total Deductions column total from the Total Earnings column total as shown below.

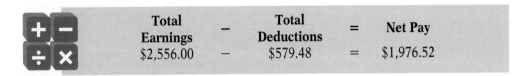

	Total Earnings	−	Total Deductions	=	Net Pay
	$2,556.00	−	$579.48	=	$1,976.52

The net pay calculated above, $1,976.52, is compared to the total of the Net Pay column. The payroll register is proved because these amounts are equal. After the payroll register is proved, a double rule is drawn below the totals, and the register is given to a partner of the company for approval.

Before checks are written for employee net pay, the payroll calculations are checked for accuracy. A partner approves the payroll after the accuracy is verified. After each check is written, the check number is recorded in the Ck. No. column.

PAYROLL CHECKS

CarLand pays its employees with checks written on a special payroll checking account. A check for the total net pay is written on CarLand's general checking account. The check is deposited in the payroll checking account. Illustration 14-5 shows the check written for the December 1-15 pay period. The check amount, $1,976.52, is the total of the Net Pay column of the payroll register in Illustration 14-3.

ILLUSTRATION 14-5 Check for total net pay

No. **287**	
Date *12/15* 19 -- $ *1,976.52*	
To *Payroll Account*	
005972165	
For *Payroll for December 1-15*	
Bal. Bro't For'd	3,261 94
Amt. Deposited	
Total	3,261 94
Amt. This Check	1,976 52
Bal. Car'd For'd	1,285 42

GENERAL ACCOUNT   No. **287**   57-63 / 115

CarLand   *December 15,* 19 --

Pay to the order of *Payroll Account 005972165* $ *1,976.52*

One thousand nine hundred seventy-six and 52/100 Dollars
FOR CLASSROOM USE ONLY

FIRST SECURITY BANK OF ROCKVILLE

Dario Mesa

⑈011500638⑈ 005972164⑈

The information used to prepare payroll checks is taken from a payroll register. The payroll check for Mr. Turner is shown in Illustration 14-6. A special payroll check form is used that has a detachable stub for recording earnings and amounts deducted. Employees keep the stubs for a record of deductions and cash received.

ILLUSTRATION 14-6   Payroll check with detachable stub

Check No. **423**		PAYROLL ACCOUNT		57-63 / 115

PERIOD ENDING | 12 | 15 | -- |

EARNINGS $ 758.00

REG. $ 704.00
O.T. $ 54.00

DEDUCTIONS $ 175.64

INC. TAX $ 45.00
FICA TAX $ 60.64
HEALTH INS. $ 50.00
OTHER $ 10.00 / 10.00

NET PAY $ 582.36

December 15, 19 --   No. **423**

Pay to the order of Patrick S. Turner $ 582.36

Five hundred eighty-two and 36/100 ———— Dollars
FOR CLASSROOM USE ONLY

FIRST SECURITY BANK OF ROCKVILLE   *CarLand*

Dario Mesa

⑆011500638⑆ 005972165⑈

The two deductions for FICA tax would normally be shown separately on a payroll check stub. For simplicity, illustrations in this textbook will show the FICA tax as a single amount on payroll check stubs.

Payroll Bank Account

A separate checking account for payroll checks helps to protect and control payroll payments. The exact amount needed to pay the payroll is deposited in the special payroll account. If amounts on checks are altered or unauthorized payroll checks are prepared, the amount in the special payroll account would be insufficient to cover all the checks. Thus, the bank and CarLand would be alerted quickly to an unauthorized payroll check. Also, since payroll checks are drawn on the separate account, any balance in this account will correspond to the sum of outstanding payroll checks.

FYI

Using a separate checking account for payroll checks provides internal control and helps to prevent fraud.

Automatic Check Deposit

Employees may authorize an employer to deposit payroll checks directly in their checking account at a specific bank. Depositing payroll checks directly to an employee's checking or savings account in a specific bank is called **automatic check deposit**. When automatic check deposit is used, the employer sends the check to the employee's bank for deposit.

Electronic Funds Transfer

A computerized cash payments system that uses electronic impulses to transfer funds is known as electronic funds transfer (EFT). Some businesses deposit employee net pay directly to each employee bank account through EFT. When EFT is used, the bank's computer deducts the amount of net pay from the business' bank account and adds the amount to each employee bank account. The payroll must still be calculated, but individual checks are not written and do not have to be distributed. Under this system, each employee receives a statement of earnings and deductions similar to the detachable stub on a payroll check.

EMPLOYEE EARNINGS RECORDS

A business form used to record details affecting payments made to an employee is called an **employee earnings record.** This information is recorded each pay period. The record includes earnings, deductions, net pay, and accumulated earnings for the calendar year. Employee earnings records enable the company to complete required tax forms at the end of the year.

Recording Information in an Employee Earnings Record

CarLand keeps all employee earnings records on cards. One card for each employee is used for each quarter in the calendar year. After a payroll register has been prepared, the payroll data for each employee are recorded on each employee earnings record. The December 15 payroll register data for Patrick S. Turner are recorded on his fourth quarter employee earnings record shown in Illustration 14-7, page 342.

Quarterly totals are used in the preparation of payroll reports required by the government. The accumulated earnings are also used to determine if the employee has earned more than the FICA tax base.

Analyzing an Employee Earnings Record

Accumulated earnings are also called year-to-date earnings.

Mr. Turner's employee number, name, social security number, and other payroll data are entered at the top of his fourth quarter employee earnings record.

Amount columns of an employee earnings record are the same as amount columns of a payroll register. Amounts opposite an employee name in a payroll register are recorded in the corresponding columns of the employee earnings record. The pay period ending December 15 is the fifth pay period in the fourth quarter. Therefore, Mr. Turner's earnings and deductions for that pay period are entered on line 5 of his employee earnings record.

The earnings record also has an Accumulated Earnings column. The first entry in this column is the accumulated earnings at the end of the previous quarter. Accumulated earnings of $13,918.00 were carried forward from the third quarter earnings record to the fourth quarter earnings record, as shown in Illustration 14-7.

ILLUSTRATION 14-7   Employee earnings record

EARNINGS RECORD FOR QUARTER ENDED *September 30, 19--*

EMPLOYEE NO. **4** | **Turner** (LAST NAME) | **Patrick** (FIRST) | **S.** (MIDDLE INITIAL) | MARITAL STATUS **M** | WITHHOLDING ALLOWANCES **4**

	10 ACCUMULATED EARNINGS
	9 3 7 6 00
	10 1 9 0 00
	10 8 7 4 00
	11 6 9 2 00
	12 4 5 6 00
	13 8 1 4 00
	13 9 1 8 00
	13 9 1 8 00

EARNINGS RECORD FOR QUARTER ENDED *December 31, 19--*

EMPLOYEE NO. **4** | **Turner** (LAST NAME) | **Patrick** (FIRST) | **S.** (MIDDLE INITIAL) | MARITAL STATUS **M** | WITHHOLDING ALLOWANCES **4**

RATE OF PAY **$8.00** PER HR. SOCIAL SECURITY NO. **450-70-6432** POSITION **Sales Clerk**

		EARNINGS			DEDUCTIONS						
PAY PERIOD		1	2	3	4	5	6	7	8	9	10
NO.	ENDED	REGULAR	OVERTIME	TOTAL	FEDERAL INCOME TAX	FICA TAX	HEALTH INSURANCE	OTHER	TOTAL	NET PAY	ACCUMULATED EARNINGS
1	10/15	6 4 0 00	6 0 00	7 0 0 00	3 9 00	5 6 00	5 0 00	B 1 0 00 / UW 1 0 00	1 6 5 00	5 3 5 00	14 6 1 8 00
2	10/31	7 6 8 00		7 6 8 00	4 8 00	6 1 44	5 0 00	B 1 0 00 / UW 1 0 00	1 7 9 44	5 8 8 56	15 3 8 6 00
3	11/15	7 0 4 00		7 0 4 00	3 9 00	5 6 32	5 0 00	B 1 0 00 / UW 1 0 00	1 6 5 32	5 3 8 68	16 0 9 0 00
4	11/30	7 0 4 00		7 0 4 00	3 9 00	5 6 32	5 0 00	B 1 0 00 / UW 1 0 00	1 6 5 32	5 3 8 68	16 7 9 4 00
5	12/15	7 0 4 00	5 4 00	7 5 8 00	4 5 00	6 0 64	5 0 00	B 1 0 00 / UW 1 0 00	1 7 5 64	5 8 2 36	17 5 5 2 00
6	12/31	6 4 0 00		6 4 0 00	3 0 00	5 1 20	5 0 00	B 1 0 00 / UW 1 0 00	1 5 1 20	4 8 8 80	18 1 9 2 00
7											
	QUARTERLY TOTALS	4 1 6 0 00	1 1 4 00	4 2 7 4 00	2 4 0 00	3 4 1 92	3 0 0 00	B 6 0 00 / UW 6 0 00	1 0 0 1 92	3 2 7 2 08	

OTHER DEDUCTIONS: B—U.S. SAVINGS BONDS; UW—UNITED WAY

Total earnings for a pay period are added to the accumulated earnings in the previous line to calculate the new total accumulated earnings. Accumulated earnings are sometimes referred to as year-to-date earnings. Mr. Turner's accumulated earnings as of December 15 are calculated as shown below.

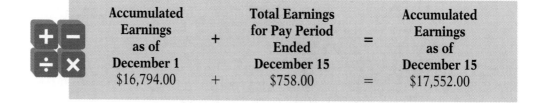

	Accumulated Earnings as of December 1		Total Earnings for Pay Period Ended December 15		Accumulated Earnings as of December 15
	$16,794.00	+	$758.00	=	$17,552.00

The Accumulated Earnings column shows the total earnings for Mr. Turner since the first of the year. The amounts in the Accumulated Earnings column supply an up-to-date reference for an employee's year-to-date earnings. When employee earnings reach the tax base, certain payroll taxes do not apply. For example, employers pay state and federal unemployment taxes only on a specified amount of each employee earnings. FICA taxes are also paid only on a specified amount of earnings.

Quarterly totals will be calculated on Mr. Turner's employee earnings record after the payroll for the pay period ended December 31 is recorded. The Quarterly Totals line provides space for the totals for the quarter. The accuracy of the quarterly totals is verified with the same steps used to verify payroll register totals. The Total Deductions column total is subtracted from the Total Earnings column total as shown below.

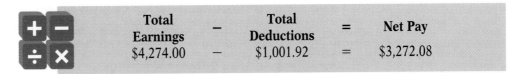

	Total Earnings	–	Total Deductions	=	Net Pay
	$4,274.00	–	$1,001.92	=	$3,272.08

The net pay calculated above, $3,272.08, is compared to the total of the Net Pay column. The earnings record is proved because these amounts are equal. These totals are needed to prepare required government reports.

PROCESSING A PAYROLL USING A PEGBOARD

Preparing a payroll requires calculating, recording, and reporting payroll information. Each business selects a system for processing the payroll that results in adequate control for the least amount of cost.

A special device used to write the same information at one time on several forms is called a **pegboard**. One type of pegboard is shown in Illustration 14-8.

ILLUSTRATION 14-8   A pegboard

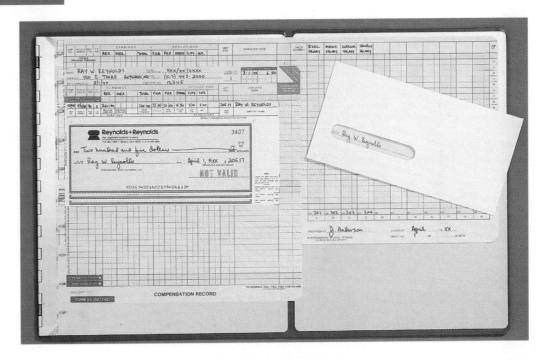

The name pegboard comes from the pegs along one side of the board. The forms used with this device have holes punched along one side. Each of the forms is placed on the pegs. Thus, the line on each form on which information is to be written is aligned one below the other.

When a payroll is recorded, a page of the payroll register is attached to the pegboard. Next, the employee earnings record is properly positioned on top of the payroll register page. Then the check is positioned on top of both of these sheets. As the check stub is written, the carbonless paper imprints the same information on the employee earnings record and the payroll register. The information is written only once. However, the information is recorded on three different records at the same time. Recording information on several forms with one writing is referred to as the write-it-once principle.

The pegboard has two major purposes. First, the pegboard provides a solid writing base for writing on the forms by hand. Second, information is recorded on several forms with one writing, thus saving time and reducing the chance of error.

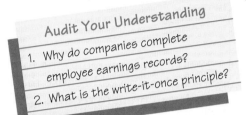

Audit Your Understanding

1. Why do companies complete employee earnings records?

2. What is the write-it-once principle?

SUMMARY ILLUSTRATION 14-9

Summary of preparing payroll records

1 A time card is used to record employee hours worked and to calculate regular, overtime, and total earnings. Payroll taxes are calculated using tax tables and information on the Form W-4. This information is recorded for each employee in a payroll register.

2 A check is written on a general checking account for the total of the Net Pay column on the payroll register. The check is deposited in a special payroll checking account.

3 Payroll checks are written on the special payroll checking account for the net pay of each employee.

4 Information from the payroll register is recorded on each employee earnings record.

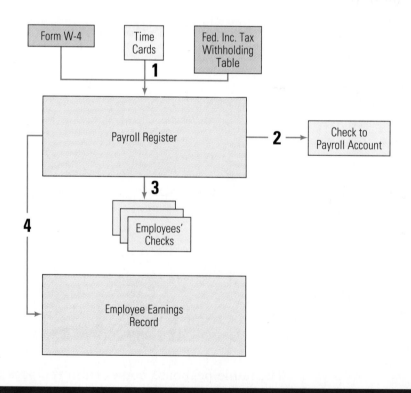

What is the meaning of each of the following?

1. salary
2. pay period
3. payroll
4. total earnings
5. payroll taxes
6. withholding allowance
7. Medicare
8. FICA tax
9. federal unemployment tax
10. state unemployment tax
11. payroll register
12. tax base
13. net pay
14. automatic check deposit
15. employee earnings record
16. pegboard

QUESTIONS FOR INDIVIDUAL STUDY
EPT(b)

1. How often may a business decide to pay its employees?
2. What information is presented at the top of a time card?
3. To calculate hours worked to the nearest quarter hour, how would an arrival time of 7:54 be rounded?
4. On what amount are employee payroll taxes based?
5. What factors determine the amount of federal income tax withheld from an employee?
6. How does the number of withholding allowances affect the amount of federal income tax withheld?
7. Who pays FICA tax?
8. How long must records pertaining to social security tax payments and deductions be retained?
9. What is the source of the earnings amounts reported in a payroll register?
10. Why are partners of a company not listed in the company's payroll register?
11. How is the amount of federal income tax withheld from employee salaries determined?
12. Under what circumstances can an employee who is not exempt from federal income tax withholding have no tax withheld on a payroll register?
13. What must an employer know to be able to calculate the amount of FICA tax to be withheld from the salary of an employee?
14. How is a payroll register proved?
15. What amount is deposited into a payroll checking account?
16. Where is the information obtained to prepare a payroll check?
17. What is the major purpose of the Accumulated Earnings column of an employee earnings record?
18. What are two major purposes for using a pegboard for processing a payroll?

CASES FOR CRITICAL THINKING
EPT(b,e)

CASE 1 Kilton Hardware currently requires each employee to inform the accounting clerk of the total hours worked each day during the pay period. The total number of hours worked by all employees has been steadily increasing during the prior pay periods. The new store manager has suggested that a time clock be installed to record arrival and departure times. The accounting clerk believes the current system is satisfactory. Do you agree with the new manager or the accounting clerk? Explain your response.

CASE 2 A banker has recommended that Tillman Construction Company open a second checking account. The company would write payroll checks on the new checking account. The company's 50 employees are currently paid with checks written on its general checking account. Do you agree with the banker's recommendation? Explain the reason for your decision.

The employees of Ritter Company currently use time cards and a time clock to record their arrival and departure times. Management plans to replace the time clock with a device that reads a magnetic strip on the back of each employee's name badge. The name badge is scanned by the badge reader in the same manner that credit cards are scanned. Since the badge reader is connected to a computer, the information is recorded directly to a computer file. Thus, the new system will enable management to make daily analyses of employee hours and pro-ductivity. Management expects this information will allow its managers to make more timely decisions and increase profits.

INSTRUCTIONS:

Assume you are the payroll clerk for Ritter Company. Write a memo to the employees informing them of the new system. Because some employees may not be happy with this new system, be sure to include reasons why the policy is being implemented.

DRILLS FOR UNDERSTANDING   EPT(c)

DRILL 14-D1   Calculating employee total earnings

Information taken from employee time cards is given in the working papers accompanying this textbook.

INSTRUCTIONS:

For each employee, calculate the amount of regular, overtime, and total earnings. Overtime hours are paid at one and one-half times the regular rate.

DRILL 14-D2   Determining payroll taxes withholding

Information taken from a semimonthly payroll register is given in the working papers accompanying this textbook.

INSTRUCTIONS:

1. Determine the federal income tax that must be withheld for each of the eight employees. Use the tax withholding tables shown in Illustration 14-4.

2. Calculate the amount of FICA tax that must be withheld for each employee using an 8% tax rate. None of the eight employees has accumulated earnings greater than the tax base.

APPLICATION PROBLEMS   EPT(c,d,e)

PROBLEM 14-1   Completing payroll time cards

Employee time cards are given in the working papers accompanying this textbook.

INSTRUCTIONS:

1. Calculate the regular, overtime, and total hours worked by each employee. Any hours over the regular 8-hour day are considered overtime. Record the hours on the time cards.

2. Determine the regular, overtime, and total earnings for each employee. The overtime rate is 1½ times the regular rate. Complete the time cards.

PROBLEM 14-2 Preparing a semimonthly payroll

The information for the semimonthly pay period April 1–15 of the current year is given in the working papers accompanying this textbook.

INSTRUCTIONS:

1. Prepare a payroll register. The date of payment is April 15. Use the federal income tax withholding tables in Illustration 14-4 to find the income tax withholding for each employee. Calculate FICA tax withholding using an 8% tax rate. None of the employee accumulated earnings has exceeded the FICA tax base.
2. Prepare a check for the total amount of the net pay. Make the check payable to Payroll Account, and sign your name as partner of City Hardware Company. The beginning check stub balance is $8,365.79.
3. Prepare payroll checks for Jill V. Gunter, Check No. 765, and Ronald E. Webb, Check No. 769. Sign your name as a partner of City Hardware Company. Record the two payroll check numbers in the payroll register.

PROBLEM 14-3 Preparing an employee earnings record

Derrick M. Hammond's earnings for the six semimonthly pay periods in April, May, and June of the current year are given in the working papers accompanying this textbook.

The following additional data about Derrick Hammond are needed to complete the employee earnings record.

1. Employee number: 32
2. Marital status: married
3. Withholding Allowances: 2
4. Rate of pay: regular, $14.00
5. Social security number: 218-78-2164
6. Position: service manager
7. Accumulated earnings for the first quarter: $7,928.00
8. Deductions from total earnings:
   a. Health insurance: $40.00 each semimonthly pay period
   b. U.S. Savings Bonds: $10.00 each semimonthly pay period
   c. Federal income tax: determined each pay period by using the withholding tables in Illustration 14-4
   d. FICA taxes: 8% of total earnings each pay period

INSTRUCTIONS:

1. Prepare an employee earnings record for Derrick Hammond for the second quarter of the year.
2. Verify the accuracy of the completed employee earnings record. The Quarter Total for Regular and Overtime Earnings should equal the Quarter Total for Net Pay plus Total Deductions. The Quarter Total for Total Earnings should equal the end-of-quarter Accumulated Earnings minus the beginning-of-quarter Accumulated Earnings.

ENRICHMENT PROBLEMS   EPT(c,d,e)

MASTERY PROBLEM 14-M Preparing a semimonthly payroll

The following information is for the semimonthly pay period May 15–31 of the current year.

| Employee | | Marital Status | No. of Allow- ances | Earnings | | Deductions | |
No.	Name			Regular	Overtime	Health Insurance	Savings Bonds
3	Abney, Patricia D.	M	2	$512.00	$12.80	$30.00	$10.00
6	Blanks, Wilma E.	S	1	576.00	21.60		
8	Fitts, Deborah S.	M	3	624.00	11.70	38.00	5.00
1	Greer, Daniel J.	M	2	399.00	34.20	30.00	5.00
5	Habig, Vincent W.	S	1	672.00			
9	Jones, Phyllis M.	M	2	608.00	79.80	30.00	10.00
10	Malloy, Timothy R.	S	2	544.00	10.20	30.00	10.00
2	Paxton, Alice Y.	M	4	496.00		44.00	
4	Tait, Michelle D.	S	1	640.00	36.00		
7	Walzak, Thomas T.	S	1	472.00			15.00

INSTRUCTIONS:

1. Prepare a payroll register. The date of payment is May 31. Use the income tax withholding tables in Illustration 14-4 to find the income tax withholding for each employee. Calculate FICA tax withholding using an 8% tax rate. None of the employee accumulated earnings has exceeded the FICA tax base.

2. Prepare a check for the total amount of the net pay. Make the check payable to Payroll Account, and sign your name as a partner of Mercer Company. The beginning check stub balance is $10,287.20.

3. Prepare payroll checks for Daniel Greer, Check No. 426, and Michelle Tait, Check No. 431. Sign your name as a partner of Mercer Company. Record the two payroll check numbers in the payroll register.

CHALLENGE PROBLEM 14-C Calculating piecework wages

SPREADSHEET

Production workers in factories are frequently paid on the basis of the number of units they produce. This payroll method is referred to as the piecework incentive wage plan. Most piecework incentive wage plans include a guaranteed hourly rate to employees regardless of the number of units they produce. This guaranteed hourly rate is referred to as the base rate.

Time and motion study engineers usually determine the standard time required for producing a single unit. Assume, for example, that time studies determine that one-third of an hour is the standard time required to produce a unit. Then the standard rate for an 8-hour day would be 24 units (8 hours divided by 1/3 hour = 24 units per day). If a worker's daily base pay is $66.00, the incentive rate per unit is $2.75 ($66.00 divided by 24 units = $2.75 per unit). Therefore, the worker who produces 24 or fewer units per day is paid the base pay, $66.00. However, each worker is paid an additional $2.75 for each unit over 24 produced each day.

Southern Woodworks Company has eight employees in production departments that are paid on a piecework incentive wage plan. The following standard and incentive wage rates are listed by department.

Department	Standard Production per Employee	Incentive Rate per Unit
Cutting	30 units per day	$2.30
Assembly	20 units per day	$4.10
Finishing	40 units per day	$1.80

Each employee worked eight hours a day during the semimonthly pay period, August 1–15. Payroll records for August 1–15 are summarized in the following table.

Employee		Marital Status	No. of Allow-ances	Guaranteed Daily Rate	Units Produced per Day									
No.	Name				Pay Period August 1–15									
					2	3	4	5	6	9	10	11	12	13
	Cutting Department													
C2	Simpson, Alan J.	S	1	$69.00	29	32	31	34	28	27	30	32	36	26
C4	Creek, Janice A.	M	1	$69.00	32	31	28	29	27	29	31	32	27	28
C8	Pate, Marie S.	M	2	$69.00	31	28	27	24	31	33	32	29	30	29
	Assembly Department													
A1	Meese, Frank K.	S	1	$82.00	20	21	19	19	18	18	19	21	20	21
A6	Harris, Kevin E.	M	3	$82.00	25	21	17	18	19	21	20	20	21	18
A7	Martin, Angela M.	S	1	$82.00	22	24	25	21	20	19	23	21	18	17
	Finishing Department													
F5	Quinn, Karen A.	M	2	$72.00	41	40	38	39	42	43	41	40	38	37
F3	Raines, Jon S.	M	2	$72.00	37	37	38	38	39	38	40	41	41	42

INSTRUCTIONS:

Prepare a payroll register. The earnings column headed *Incentive* is used instead of Overtime. The date of payment is August 16. Use the income tax withholding tables in Illustration 14-4. Calculate the employee FICA tax withholding using an 8% tax rate. None of the employees has health insurance or other deductions.

15

Payroll Accounting, Taxes, and Reports

ENABLING PERFORMANCE TASKS

After studying Chapter 15, you will be able to:

a Identify accounting concepts and practices related to payroll accounts, taxes, and reports.

b Analyze payroll transactions.

c Journalize and post payroll transactions.

d Prepare selected payroll tax reports.

Payroll information for each pay period is recorded in a payroll register. Each pay period the payroll information for each employee is also recorded on each employee earnings record. Separate payroll accounts for each employee are not kept in the general ledger. Instead, accounts are kept in the general ledger to summarize total earnings and deductions for all employees.

The payroll register and employee earnings records provide all the payroll information needed to prepare a payroll and payroll tax reports. Journal entries are made to record the payment of the payroll and the employer payroll taxes. In addition, various quarterly and annual payroll tax reports are required to report the payment of payroll taxes.

RECORDING A PAYROLL

The payroll register for CarLand's semimonthly pay period ended December 15 is shown in Illustration 15-1, on page 352.

Analyzing Payment of a Payroll

The column totals of a payroll register provide the debit and credit amounts needed to journalize a payroll. CarLand's December 15 payroll is summarized in the following T accounts.

Employee Income Tax Payable	
	Dec. 15 192.00

FICA Tax Payable	
	Dec. 15 204.48

Health Insurance Premiums Payable	
	Dec. 15 158.00

Salary Expense	
Dec. 15 2,556.00	

U.S. Savings Bonds Payable	
	Dec. 15 15.00

United Way Donations Payable	
	Dec. 15 10.00

Cash	
	Dec. 15 1,976.52

The Total Earnings column total, $2,556.00, is the salary expense for the period. Salary Expense is debited for this amount.

The Federal Income Tax column total, $192.00, is the amount withheld from employee salaries for federal income tax. The amount withheld is a liability of the business until the taxes are sent to the federal government. Employee Income Tax Payable is credited for $192.00 to record this liability.

The FICA Tax column total, $204.48, is the amount withheld from salaries of all employees for FICA tax. The amount withheld

CAREERS IN ACCOUNTING

PAYROLL CLERK

- *Compiles payroll data from time cards and personnel records*
- *Calculates wages and deductions*
- *Posts to payroll records*
- *Prepares and issues paychecks*
- *Prepares periodic reports of earnings, taxes, and deductions*
- *Records data concerning transfer of employees*

ILLUSTRATION 15-1   Payroll register

	EMPL. NO.	EMPLOYEE'S NAME	MARITAL STATUS	NO. OF ALLOWANCES	EARNINGS			DEDUCTIONS					NET PAY	CHECK NO.	
					1	2	3	4	5	6	7	8	9		
					REGULAR	OVERTIME	TOTAL	FEDERAL INCOME TAX	FICA TAX	HEALTH INSURANCE	OTHER	TOTAL			
1	2	Bauch, Mary R.	M	2	660 00		660 00	57 00	52 80	38 00	B 5 00	152 80	507 20	419	1
2	5	Clay, Richard P.	S	1	80 00		80 00	00	6 40			6 40	73 60	420	2
3	1	Javorski, Adam B.	M	2	384 00	18 00	402 00	17 00	32 16	38 00		87 16	314 84	421	3
4	6	Maggio, Brenda A.	S	1	40 00		40 00	00	3 20			3 20	36 80	422	4
5	4	Turner, Patrick S.	M	4	704 00	54 00	758 00	45 00	60 64	50 00	B 10 00 / UW 10 00	175 64	582 36	423	5
6	3	Wilkes, Samuel R.	S	1	616 00		616 00	73 00	49 28	32 00		154 28	461 72	424	6
7		Totals			2484 00	72 00	2556 00	192 00	204 48	158 00	B 15 00 / UW 10 00	579 48	1976 52		7

SEMIMONTHLY PERIOD ENDED *December 15, 19--*   PAYROLL REGISTER   DATE OF PAYMENT *December 15, 19--*

FYI

Other payroll deductions may include a deduction for savings bonds and United Way contributions.

is a liability of the business until the tax is paid to the government. FICA Tax Payable is credited for $204.48.

The Health Insurance column total, $158.00, is the amount withheld from salaries for health insurance premiums. The amount withheld is a liability of the business until the premiums are paid to the insurance company. Health Insurance Premiums Payable is credited for $158.00 to record this liability.

The Other column of the deductions section may contain more than one total. Two types of *Other* deductions are recorded in Car-Land's payroll register. The $15.00 Other column total identified with the letter B is withheld to buy savings bonds for employees. The $10.00 total identified with the letters *UW* is withheld for employee United Way pledges. Until these amounts have been paid by the employer, they are liabilities of the business. U.S. Savings Bonds Payable is credited for $15.00. United Way Donations Payable is credited for $10.00.

The Net Pay column total, $1,976.52, is the net amount paid to employees. Cash is credited for $1,976.52. A check for the total net pay amount, $1,976.52, is written on CarLand's general checking account. This amount is deposited in a special payroll checking account used only for employee payroll checks. Individual payroll checks are then written on the special payroll checking account.

Journalizing Payment of a Payroll

December 15, 19--. Paid cash for semimonthly payroll, $1,976.52 (total payroll, $2,556.00, less deductions: employee income tax, $192.00; FICA tax, $204.48; health insurance premiums, $158.00; U.S. Savings Bonds, $15.00; United Way donations, $10.00). Check No. 287.

The journal entry to record payment of CarLand's December 15 payroll is shown in Illustration 15-2.

The date, *15*, is written in the Date column. The title of the account debited, *Salary Expense*, is recorded in the Account Title col-

ILLUSTRATION 15-2 Journal entry to record a payroll

JOURNAL

					1	2		10	11	
	DATE	ACCOUNT TITLE	DOC. NO.	POST. REF.	GENERAL			CASH		
					DEBIT	CREDIT		DEBIT	CREDIT	
21	15	*Salary Expense*	C287		2 5 5 6 00				1 9 7 6 52	21
22		*Employee Income Tax Payable*				1 9 2 00				22
23		*FICA Tax Payable*				2 0 4 48				23
24		*Health Insurance Premiums Payable*				1 5 8 00				24
25		*U.S. Savings Bonds Payable*				1 5 00				25
26		*United Way Donations Payable*				1 0 00				26

Total Earnings is the debit amount for Salary Expense. Net pay is the credit amount for cash.

umn. The check number, *C287,* is entered in the Doc. No. column. The amount debited to Salary Expense, *$2,556.00,* is written in the General Debit column. On the same line, the net amount paid to employees, *$1,976.52,* is written in the Cash Credit column. Five liability accounts are credited for the amounts deducted from employee salaries. The five account titles are written in the Account Title column. The five credit amounts are written in the General Credit column.

Posting the Journal Entry for Payment of a Payroll

Amounts recorded in the General columns of a journal are posted individually to general ledger accounts. After the December 15 payroll entry is posted, the liability and salary expense accounts appear as shown in Illustration 15-3.

ILLUSTRATION 15-3 General ledger accounts after journal entry for payment of a payroll is posted

ACCOUNT *Employee Income Tax Payable* ACCOUNT NO. *2120*

DATE	ITEM	POST. REF.	DEBIT	CREDIT	BALANCE	
					DEBIT	CREDIT
15		24		1 9 2 00		1 9 2 00

ACCOUNT *FICA Tax Payable* ACCOUNT NO. *2130*

DATE	ITEM	POST. REF.	DEBIT	CREDIT	BALANCE	
					DEBIT	CREDIT
15		24		2 0 4 48		2 0 4 48

ILLUSTRATION 15-3

General ledger accounts after journal entry for payment of a payroll is posted (concluded)

ACCOUNT Health Insurance Premiums Payable						ACCOUNT NO. 2170	
DATE	ITEM	POST. REF.	DEBIT	CREDIT	BALANCE		
					DEBIT	CREDIT	
Dec. 1	Balance	✓				5 2 4 00	
15		24		1 5 8 00		6 8 2 00	

ACCOUNT U.S. Savings Bonds Payable						ACCOUNT NO. 2180	
DATE	ITEM	POST. REF.	DEBIT	CREDIT	BALANCE		
					DEBIT	CREDIT	
Dec. 1	Balance	✓				1 0 00	
15		24		1 5 00		2 5 00	

ACCOUNT United Way Donations Payable						ACCOUNT NO. 2190	
DATE	ITEM	POST. REF.	DEBIT	CREDIT	BALANCE		
					DEBIT	CREDIT	
Dec. 1	Balance	✓				4 0 00	
15		24		1 0 00		5 0 00	

ACCOUNT Salary Expense						ACCOUNT NO. 6170	
DATE	ITEM	POST. REF.	DEBIT	CREDIT	BALANCE		
					DEBIT	CREDIT	
Dec. 1	Balance	✓			54 9 5 2 00		
15		24	2 5 5 6 00		57 5 0 8 00		

The credit to Cash, $1,976.52, is not posted separately to the cash account. The amount is included in the journal's Cash Credit column total that is posted at the end of the month.

RECORDING EMPLOYER PAYROLL TAXES

Employers must pay to the government the taxes withheld from employee earnings. CarLand has withheld federal income tax and FICA tax from employee salaries. The amounts withheld are liabilities to the business until they are actually paid to the government. In addition, employers must pay several of their own payroll taxes. Employer payroll taxes are business expenses.

Calculating Employer Payroll Taxes

Most employers must pay three separate payroll taxes. These taxes are (1) employer FICA tax, (2) federal unemployment tax, and (3) state unemployment tax. Employer payroll taxes expense is based on a percentage of employee earnings.

Employer FICA Tax. CarLand withheld $204.48 in FICA tax from employee wages for the pay period ended December 15. CarLand owes the same amount of FICA taxes as the amount withheld from employees. Therefore, CarLand's FICA tax for the pay period ended December 15 is also $204.48.

Congress sets the FICA tax rate for employees and employers. Periodically, Congress may change the tax rate and tax base. The FICA tax rate is a combination of two different tax rates: (1) a tax for old-age, survivors, and disability and (2) a tax for Medicare. The two taxes also have different tax bases. The FICA tax rates and bases used in this text are shown below.

	Tax Rate	Tax Base
Old-age, survivors, and disability	6.5%	earnings up to $55,500
Medicare	1.5%	earnings up to $130,200
Total	8.0%	

Therefore, the effective FICA tax rate for earnings up to the tax base of $55,500 is 8.0% (6.5% + 1.5%). The additional FICA tax rate for earnings from $55,500 to $130,200 is 1.5%.

The FICA tax is the only payroll tax paid by *both* the employees and the employer. Employees pay 8% of their total earnings up to a tax base of $55,500.00 and 1.5% of their total earnings up to $130,200.00 as a FICA tax. Employers also pay FICA tax on each employee's earnings using the same tax rates and tax bases.

Federal Unemployment Tax. Federal unemployment insurance laws require that employers pay taxes for unemployment compensation. These tax funds are used to pay workers benefits for limited periods of unemployment and to administer the unemployment compensation program. All of the federal unemployment tax is paid by the employer.

The federal unemployment tax for most businesses is 0.8% of total earnings of each employee up to a tax base of *$7,000.00* during a calendar year. The total earnings of CarLand's December 1-15 pay period subject to the federal unemployment tax is referred to as unemployment taxable earnings. The amount of unemployment taxable earnings is calculated as shown in Illustration 15-4.

Accumulated earnings are calculated on each employee earnings record. Patrick S. Turner's accumulated earnings as of November 30, *$16,794.00*, are recorded in the first column. Total earnings for Mr. Turner for the December 15 pay period, *$758.00*, are recorded

ILLUSTRATION 15-4   Total earnings subject to federal unemployment tax

	Accumulated Earnings as of Nov. 30, 19--	Total Earnings for Dec. 15, 19-- Pay Period	Unemployment Taxable Earnings
CarLand			
Taxable Earnings			
for December 15, 19-- Pay Period			
Bauch, Mary R.	$14,520.00	$660.00	$ —
Clay, Richard P.	2,160.00	80.00	80.00
Javorski, Adam B.	5,792.50	402.00	402.00
Maggio, Brenda A.	1,680.00	40.00	40.00
Turner, Patrick S.	16,794.00	758.00	—
Wilkes, Samuel R.	4,976.50	616.00	616.00
			$1,138.00

in the second column. Since the accumulated earnings for Mr. Turner are greater than $7,000.00, none of his current earnings are subject to federal unemployment tax. Thus, the amount of unemployment taxable earnings recorded in the third column is zero, which is represented by a dash.

The accumulated earnings for Samuel R. Wilkes, $4,976.50, are less than $7,000.00. Therefore, his total earnings for the December 15 pay period are subject to federal unemployment tax. Total earnings for Mr. Wilkes for the December 15 pay period, *$616.00*, are recorded in the Unemployment Taxable Earnings column.

The total earnings for the pay period are entered in the Unemployment Taxable Earnings column for employees whose accumulated earnings are less than $7,000.00. The sum of the Unemployment Taxable Earnings Column, $1,138.00, is the amount used to calculate federal unemployment tax.

CarLand's federal unemployment tax is calculated as shown below.

Unemployment Taxable Earnings	×	Federal Unemployment Tax Rate	=	Federal Unemployment Tax
$1,138.00	×	0.8%	=	$9.10

State Unemployment Tax. Most states require that employers pay unemployment tax of 5.4% on the first $7,000.00 earned by each employee. The unemployment taxable earnings used to calculate the federal unemployment tax are also used to calculate the state unemployment tax. The unemployment taxable earnings subject to the state unemployment tax are calculated in Illustration 15-4. Thus, the state employment tax to be paid by CarLand is calculated as shown below.

	Unemployment Taxable Earnings	×	State Unemployment Tax Rate	=	State Unemployment Tax
	$1,138.00	×	5.4%	=	$61.45

Journalizing Employer Payroll Taxes

Employer payroll taxes are paid to the government at a later date. However, the liability is incurred when salaries are paid. Therefore, the transaction to record employer payroll taxes expense is journalized on the same date the payroll is journalized. The salary expense and the employer payroll taxes expense are, therefore, both recorded in the same accounting period.

Payroll Taxes Expense

275.03	

FICA Tax Payable

	204.48

Unemployment Tax Payable—Federal

	9.10

Unemployment Tax Payable—State

	61.45

December 15, 19--. Recorded employer payroll taxes expense, $275.03, for the semimonthly pay period ended December 15. Taxes owed are: FICA tax, $204.48; federal unemployment tax, $9.10; state unemployment tax, $61.45. Memorandum No. 54.

Payroll Taxes Expense is debited for $275.03 to show the increase in the balance of this expense account. Three liability accounts are credited to show the increase in payroll tax liabilities. FICA Tax Payable is credited for $204.48. Unemployment Tax Payable—Federal is credited for $9.10. Unemployment Tax Payable—State is credited for $61.45.

CarLand's journal entry to record the employer payroll taxes expense is shown in Illustration 15-5.

ILLUSTRATION 15-5   Journal entry to record employer payroll taxes

						GENERAL		CASH		
PAGE *24*		JOURNAL			1	2		10	11 PAGE *24*	
	DATE	ACCOUNT TITLE	DOC. NO.	POST. REF.	DEBIT	CREDIT		DEBIT	CREDIT	
27	15	*Payroll Taxes Expense*	M54		2 7 5 03					27
28		*FICA Tax Payable*				2 0 4 48				28
29		*Unemployment Tax Payable—Federal*				9 10				29
30		*Unemployment Tax Payable—State*				6 1 45				30
31										31

The date, *15*, is written in the Date column. The title of the account debited, *Payroll Taxes Expense*, is written in the Account Title column. The memorandum number, *M54*, is entered in the Doc. No. column. The debit amount, *$275.03*, is entered in the General Debit column. The titles of the liability accounts are entered in the Account Title column. The amounts credited to the liability accounts are entered in the General Credit column.

Posting an Employer Payroll Taxes Entry

After the entry for the employer payroll taxes is posted, the accounts involved appear as shown in Illustration 15-6.

ILLUSTRATION 15-6   General ledger accounts after journal entry for employer payroll taxes expense is posted

ACCOUNT *FICA Tax Payable*   ACCOUNT NO. *2130*

DATE	ITEM	POST. REF.	DEBIT	CREDIT	BALANCE DEBIT	BALANCE CREDIT
15		24		2 04 48		2 04 48
15		24		2 04 48		4 08 96

ACCOUNT *Unemployment Tax Payable—Federal*   ACCOUNT NO. *2150*

DATE	ITEM	POST. REF.	DEBIT	CREDIT	BALANCE DEBIT	BALANCE CREDIT
Dec. 1	Balance	✓				4 0 48
15		24		9 10		4 9 58

ILLUSTRATION 15-6   General ledger accounts after journal entry for employer payroll taxes expense is posted (concluded)

ACCOUNT **Unemployment Tax Payable—State**   ACCOUNT NO. **2160**

DATE		ITEM	POST. REF.	DEBIT	CREDIT	BALANCE	
						DEBIT	CREDIT
Dec.¹⁹⁻⁻	1	Balance	√				2 7 3 22
	15		24		6 1 45		3 3 4 67

ACCOUNT **Payroll Taxes Expense**   ACCOUNT NO. **6150**

DATE		ITEM	POST. REF.	DEBIT	CREDIT	BALANCE	
						DEBIT	CREDIT
Dec.¹⁹⁻⁻	1	Balance	√			6 7 3 8 96	
	15		24	2 7 5 03		7 0 1 3 99	

FYI

A job description is a list of basic responsibilities and tasks for a particular job.

The FICA Tax Payable account has two credits. The first credit, $204.48, is the FICA tax withheld from *employee* wages for the semimonthly period ended December 15. This amount was posted from the journal entry that recorded payment of the payroll, Illustration 15-2. The second credit, $204.48, is the *employer* liability for FICA tax. This amount was posted from the journal entry that recorded the employer payroll taxes, Illustration 15-5.

Summary of Amounts Posted to the General Ledger

Both the employees and employer owe payroll taxes. Federal income tax and FICA tax are withheld from employee salaries. An equal amount of FICA tax is owed by the employer. The employer must also record federal and state unemployment taxes. The payroll taxes resulting from CarLand's December 1–15 pay period are summarized on page 360.

	Employees	Employer
Federal Income Tax	$192.00	—
FICA Tax	204.48	$204.48
Federal Unemployment Tax	—	9.10
State Unemployment Tax	—	61.45
Total	$396.48	$275.03

Only the employer payroll taxes, $275.03, are recorded as payroll taxes expense in CarLand's general ledger accounts. The payroll taxes of both the employees and the employer create liabilities to the business which must be paid at times specified by the government.

REPORTING WITHHOLDING AND PAYROLL TAXES

Each employer is required by law to periodically report the payroll taxes withheld from employee salaries and the employer payroll taxes due the government. Some reports are submitted quarterly and others are submitted annually.

Employer Quarterly Federal Tax Return

Each employer must file a quarterly federal tax return showing the federal income tax and FICA taxes due the government. This information is submitted every three months on Form 941, Employer's Quarterly Federal Tax Return. Form 941 is filed before the last day of the month following the end of a calendar quarter. CarLand's Form 941 for the calendar quarter ended December 31 is shown in Illustration 15-7, page 361. The information needed to prepare Form 941 is obtained from employee earnings records.

Total earnings, *$15,192.85*, are recorded on line 2 of Form 941. This amount is the sum of the fourth quarter total earnings of all CarLand employees. The amount of total earnings, *$15,192.85*, is also recorded on the line to the left of line 6a and 7. The income tax withheld, *$1,168.00*, is recorded on line 3 of Form 941. The amount is the total of the fourth quarter federal income tax withheld from CarLand's employees.

The social security (FICA) taxes due are calculated as shown below.

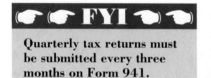

	Total Earnings	×	FICA Tax Rate	=	Social Security (FICA) Tax
Old-age, survivors, and disability	$15,192.85	×	13%	=	$1,975.07
Medicare	$15,192.85	×	3%	=	$ 455.79
TOTAL					$2,430.86

ILLUSTRATION 15-7   Form 941, Employer's Quarterly Federal Tax Return

Form 941
(Rev. January 19--)
Department of the Treasury
Internal Revenue Service

4141

Employer's Quarterly Federal Tax Return

▶ See Circular E for more information concerning employment tax returns.

Please type or print.

OMB No. 1545-0029
Expires 5-31-93

Your name, address, employer identification number, and calendar quarter of return. (If not correct, please change.)

If address is different from prior return, check here ▶

Name (as distinguished from trade name)	Date quarter ended
CarLand	December 31, 19--
Trade name, if any	Employer identification number
	31-0429632
Address (number and street)	City, state, and ZIP code
1374 Parklane	Rockville, RI 02873-4121

T
FF
FD
FP
I
T

IRS Use

1 1 1 1 1 1 1 1 1 1   2   3 3 3 3 3   4 4 4
5 5 5   6   7   8 8 8 8 8   9 9 9   10 10 10 10 10 10 10 10 10 10

If you do not have to file returns in the future, check here . . . ▶ ☐   Date final wages paid . . . ▶ _____

If you are a seasonal employer, see **Seasonal employers** on page 2 and check here . ▶ ☐

1	Number of employees (except household) employed in the pay period that includes March 12th ▶	**1**		6

2	Total wages and tips subject to withholding, plus other compensation . . . . ▶	**2**	$15,192	85
3	Total income tax withheld from wages, tips, pensions, annuities, sick pay, gambling, etc. . . ▶	**3**	1,168	00
4	Adjustment of withheld income tax for preceding quarters of calendar year (see instructions) ▶	**4**	-0-	
5	Adjusted total of income tax withheld (line 3 as adjusted by line 4—see instructions)	**5**	1,168	00
6a	Taxable social security wages (Complete line 7) $ 15,192 85 × 13% (.13) =	**6a**	1,975	07
b	Taxable social security tips $ -0- × 13% (.13) =	**b**	-0-	
7	Taxable Medicare wages and tips . . . . $ 15,192 85 × 3% (.03) =	**7**	455	79
8	Total social security and Medicare taxes (add lines 6a, 6b, and 7)	**8**	2,430	86
9	Adjustment of social security and Medicare taxes (see instructions for required explanation) .	**9**	-0-	
10	Adjusted total of social security and Medicare taxes (line 8 as adjusted by line 9—see instructions) . . ▶	**10**	2,430	86
11	Backup withholding (see instructions)	**11**	-0-	
12	Adjustment of backup withholding tax for preceding quarters of calendar year	**12**	-0-	
13	Adjusted total of backup withholding (line 11 as adjusted by line 12)	**13**	-0-	
14	**Total taxes** (add lines 5, 10, and 13)	**14**	3,598	86
15	Advance earned income credit (EIC) payments made to employees, if any . . . . ▶	**15**	-0-	
16	Net taxes (subtract line 15 from line 14). **This should equal line IV below** (plus line IV of Schedule A (Form 941) if you have treated backup withholding as a separate liability)	**16**	3,598	86
17	**Total deposits for quarter,** including overpayment applied from a prior quarter, from your records . . ▶	**17**	3,598	86
18	**Balance due** (subtract line 17 from line 16). This should be less than $500. Pay to Internal Revenue Service ▶	**18**	-0-	
19	**Overpayment,** if line 17 is more than line 16, enter excess here ▶ $ _____ and check if to be: ☐ Applied to next return **OR** ☐ Refunded.			

Record of Federal Tax Liability (You must complete if line 16 is $500 or more and Schedule B is not attached.) See instructions before checking these boxes.
If you made deposits using the 95% rule, check here ▶ ☐   If you are a first time 3-banking-day depositer, check here . . . ▶ ☐

Show tax liability here, **not deposits.** The IRS gets deposit data from FTD coupons.

DO NOT Show Federal Tax Deposits Here

Date wages paid		First month of quarter		Second month of quarter		Third month of quarter
1st through 3rd	A		I		Q	
4th through 7th	B		J		R	
8th through 11th	C		K		S	
12th through 15th	D	602.60	L	572.65	T	600.96
16th through 19th	E		M		U	
20th through 22nd	F		N		V	
23rd through 25th	G	592.65	O	596.80	W	633.20
26th through the last	H		P		X	
Total liability for month	I	1,195.25	II	1,169.45	III	1,234.16
IV Total for quarter (add lines **I, II,** and **III**). This should equal line 16 above . . . . ▶						3,598.86

Sign Here

Under penalties of perjury, I declare that I have examined this return, including accompanying schedules and statements, and to the best of my knowledge and belief, it is true, correct, and complete.

Signature ▶ *Amy Kramer*   Print Your Name and Title ▶ *Partner*   Date ▶ 1/24/--

For Paperwork Reduction Act Notice, see page 2.   Cat. No. 17001Z

The 13% tax rate is the sum of the *employee* 6.5% FICA tax rate and the employer 6.5% FICA tax rate for old-age, survivors, and disability tax. The 3% tax rate is the sum of the *employee* 1.5% FICA tax rate and the *employer* 1.5% FICA tax rate for Medicare tax. The total FICA tax amount, $2,430.86, is recorded on line 8 of Form 941.

CarLand is required to pay the federal government the sum of the FICA tax and federal income tax withheld. The amount of the payment is calculated as shown below.

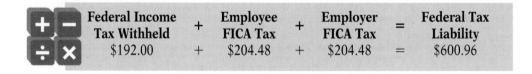

Federal Income Tax Withheld	+	FICA Tax	=	Total Payment
$1,168.00	+	$2,430.86	=	$3,598.86

Federal Income Tax withheld is copied from line 3 to line 5. FICA Tax is copied from line 8 to line 10. The total payment owed to the federal government, *$3,598.86,* is recorded on line 14 of Form 941.

The lower section of Form 941 lists the amounts and dates when payroll taxes were withheld from employees and are owed by the employer. For the pay period ended December 15, the amount of taxes owed is calculated as shown below.

Federal Income Tax Withheld	+	Employee FICA Tax	+	Employer FICA Tax	=	Federal Tax Liability
$192.00	+	$204.48	+	$204.48	=	$600.96

The federal tax liability for the December 15 pay period, *$600.96,* is recorded on line T of Form 941. The December 15 pay period ended in the third month of the quarter between the 12th and 15th of the month. The December 15 pay period is, therefore, recorded on line T.

Employer Annual Report to Employees of Taxes Withheld

Each employer who withholds income tax and FICA tax from employee earnings must furnish each employee with an annual report of these withholdings. The report shows total year's earnings and the amounts withheld for taxes for an employee. These amounts are obtained from the employee earnings records. The report is prepared on the Internal Revenue Service Form W-2, Wage and Tax Statement.

Employers are required to furnish Form W-2 to each employee by January 31 of the next year. If an employee ends employment before December 31, Form W-2 must be furnished within 30 days of the last date of employment.

FYI

Form W-2 shows the total year's earnings and the amounts withheld for taxes for each employee.

The Form W-2 prepared by CarLand for Patrick S. Turner is shown in Illustration 15-8.

ILLUSTRATION 15-8   Form W-2, Wage and Tax Statement

1 Control number	22222	For Official Use Only ▶ OMB No. 1545-0008			
2 Employer's name, address, and ZIP code CarLand 1374 Parklane Rockville, RI 02873-4121			6 Statutory employee ☐ Deceased ☐ Pension plan ☐ Legal rep. ☐ 942 emp. ☐ Subtotal ☐ Deferred compensation ☐ Void ☐		
			7 Allocated tips	8 Advance EIC payment	
			9 Federal income tax withheld 1,032.00	10 Wages, tips, other compensation 18,192.00	
3 Employer's identification number 31-0429632	**4 Employer's state I.D. number**		11 Social security tax withheld 1,182.48	12 Social security wages 18,192.00	
5 Employee's social security number 450-70-6432			13 Social security tips	14 Medicare wages and tips 18,192.00	
19a Employee's name (first, middle initial, last) Patrick S. Turner			15 Medicare tax withheld 272.88	16 Nonqualified plans	
 1625 Northland Drive Rockville, RI 02873-5073 **19b Employee's address and ZIP code**			17 See Instrs. for Form W-2	18 Other	
20 /////	21 /////		22 Dependent care benefits	23 Benefits included in Box 10	
24 State income tax	25 State wages, tips, etc.	26 Name of state	27 Local income tax	28 Local wages, tips, etc.	29 Name of locality

Copy A For Social Security Administration   Department of the Treasury—Internal Revenue Service

Form **W-2 Wage and Tax Statement 19--**

Four copies (A to D) of Form W-2 are prepared for each employee. Copies B and C are given to the employee. The employee attaches Copy B to a personal federal income tax return and keeps Copy C for a personal record. The employer sends Copy A to the Social Security Administration and keeps Copy D for the business' records.

Businesses in states with state income tax must prepare additional copies of Form W-2. The employee attaches the additional copy to the personal state income tax return.

Employer Annual Reporting of Payroll Taxes

Form W-3, Transmittal of Income and Tax Statements, is sent to the Social Security Administration by February 28 each year. Form W-3 reports the previous year's earnings and payroll taxes withheld for all employees. Attached to Form W-3 is Copy A of each employee Form W-2. A Form W-3 prepared by CarLand is shown in Illustration 15-9 on the next page.

ILLUSTRATION 15-9   Form W-3, Transmittal of Income and Tax Statements

DO NOT STAPLE

1 Control number				
	33333	For Official Use Only ▶ OMB No. 1545-0008		

☐ Kind of Payer ▶	2 941/941E ☒ Military ☐ 943 ☐ CT-1 ☐ 942 ☐ Medicare govt. emp. ☐	3 Employer's state I.D. number	5 Total number of statements
		4	6

6 Establishment number	7 Allocated tips	8 Advance EIC payments
9 Federal income tax withheld 4,612.00	10 Wages, tips, and other compensation 60,153.00	11 Social security tax withheld 3,909.95
12 Social security wages 60,153.00	13 Social security tips	14 Medicare wages and tips 60,153.00
15 Medicare tax withheld 902.29	16 Nonqualified plans	17 Deferred compensation

18 Employer's identification number 31-0429632	19 Other EIN used this year
20 Employer's name CarLand	21 Dependent care benefits
1374 Parklane Rockville, RI 02873-4121	23 Adjusted total social security wages and tips 60,153.00
	24 Adjusted total Medicare wages and tips 60,153.00
	25 Income tax withheld by third-party payer

22 Employer's address and ZIP code (If available, place label over Boxes 18 and 20.)

Under penalties of perjury, I declare that I have examined this return and accompanying documents, and, to the best of my knowledge and belief, they are true, correct, and complete.

Signature ▶ *Amy Kramer*   Title ▶ *Partner*   Date ▶ *2/27/--*

Telephone number ____ *(401) 555-9368* ____

Form **W-3 Transmittal of Income and Tax Statements 19--**   Department of the Treasury Internal Revenue Service

---

Audit Your Understanding

1. What is the FICA tax rate employers must pay on employees?

2. What is the federal unemployment tax rate employers must pay on employees?

At the end of a calendar year, employers must also report to the federal and state governments a summary of all earnings paid to employees during the twelve months.

Employers with more than 250 employees have different procedures for reporting withholding tax information. The information is sent to the Internal Revenue Service in computer files rather than the actual Forms W-2 and W-3.

PAYING WITHHOLDING AND PAYROLL TAXES

At least quarterly, employers must pay to the federal government the federal income taxes and FICA taxes withheld from employee salaries. The payment also includes the amount of employer FICA taxes.

Paying the Liability for Employee Income Tax and FICA Tax

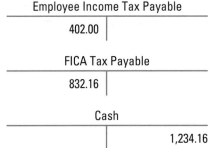

Tax rates change periodically. Always check the most current tax information before calculating an amount for any tax.

Employee withheld income tax, employee FICA tax, and employer FICA tax are paid periodically in a combined payment. Tax payments are made to banks authorized by the Internal Revenue Service to accept these payments or to a Federal Reserve bank. The timing of these tax payments is based on the amount of taxes owed. A payment is accompanied by a Form 8109, Federal Tax Deposit Coupon, which shows the amount and purpose of the payment.

In December, CarLand withheld $402.00 from employee salaries for federal income taxes. The liability for FICA tax for December is $832.16. This amount includes both the employer share and the amounts withheld from employees. CarLand's federal tax payment is sent January 15 to an authorized bank with Form 8109 as shown in Illustration 15-10.

| ILLUSTRATION 15-10 | Form 8109, Federal Tax Deposit Coupon for withheld income tax and FICA taxes |

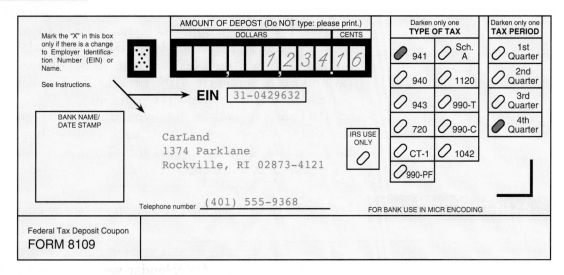

The type of tax, federal income and FICA taxes, is identified by marking the 941 circle. These taxes are reported to the government using Form 941. The calendar quarter is identified on the right side of the form.

Employee Income Tax Payable

402.00	

FICA Tax Payable

832.16	

Cash

	1,234.16

January 15, 19--. Paid cash for liability for employee income tax, $402.00, and for FICA tax, $832.16; total, $1,234.16. Check No. 305.

The balances of the liability accounts are reduced by this transaction. Therefore, Employee Income Tax Payable is debited for $402.00. FICA Tax Payable is debited for $832.16. The balance of the Cash account is decreased by a credit for the total payment, $1,234.16.

The journal entry to record payment of these liabilities is shown in Illustration 15-11 on the next page.

The date, *15*, is written in the Date column. The titles of the two accounts debited, *Employee Income Tax Payable* and *FICA Tax Payable*, are written in the Account Title column. The check number, *C305*, is entered in the Doc. No. column. The two debit amounts are entered in the General Debit column. The amount of the credit to Cash, *$1,234.16*, is recorded in the Cash Credit column.

| ILLUSTRATION 15-11 | Journal entry to record payment of liability for employee income tax and FICA tax |

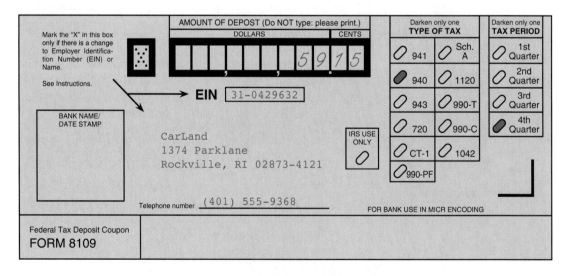

	DATE		ACCOUNT TITLE	DOC. NO.	POST. REF.	GENERAL DEBIT	GENERAL CREDIT	CASH DEBIT	CASH CREDIT	
25		15	*Employee Income Tax Payable*	*C305*		402 00			1234 16	25
26			*FICA Tax Payable*			832 16				26
27										27

PAGE 27 — JOURNAL — *PAGE 27*

Paying the Liability for Federal Unemployment Tax

Federal unemployment tax is usually paid after the end of each quarter. Federal unemployment tax is paid to the federal government by sending the check to a designated bank. The payment for federal unemployment tax is similar to the one required for income tax and FICA tax. Form 8109, Federal Tax Deposit Coupon, accompanies the unemployment tax payment.

CarLand's federal unemployment tax at the end of December 31 is $59.15. A payment is made each quarter but no report is due until the end of the year. CarLand's Form 8109 for the fourth quarter is shown in Illustration 15-12.

| ILLUSTRATION 15-12 | Form 8109, Federal Tax Deposit Coupon for federal unemployment tax |

The type of tax, federal unemployment tax, is identified by marking the 940 circle since this tax is reported to the government using Form 940. The calendar quarter is identified on the right side of the form.

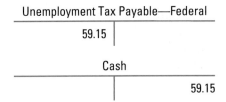

Unemployment Tax Payable—Federal

59.15	

Cash

	59.15

January 31, 19--. Paid cash for federal unemployment tax liability for quarter ended December 31, $59.15. Check No. 318.

The balance of the liability account is reduced by this transaction. Therefore, Unemployment Tax Payable—Federal is debited for $59.15. The balance of the asset account, Cash, is decreased by a credit for the payment, $59.15.

The journal entry to record payment of the liability for federal unemployment taxes is shown in Illustration 15-13.

The date, *31*, is written in the Date column. The title of the account debited, *Unemployment Tax Payable—Federal*, is written in the Account Title column. The check number, *C318*, is entered in the Doc. No. column. The check amount, *$59.15*, is entered in the General Debit and Cash Credit columns.

ILLUSTRATION 15-13   Journal entry to record payment of liability for federal unemployment tax

PAGE 28		JOURNAL						
					GENERAL		**CASH**	
DATE	ACCOUNT TITLE	DOC. NO.	POST. REF.		DEBIT	CREDIT	DEBIT	CREDIT
27	31	*Unemployment Tax Payable—Federal*	C318		59 15			59 15	27
28									28

Paying the Liability for State Unemployment Tax

State requirements for reporting and paying state unemployment taxes vary. In general, employers are required to pay the state unemployment tax during the month following each calendar quarter.

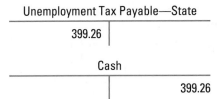

Unemployment Tax Payable—State

399.26	

Cash

	399.26

January 31, 19--. Paid cash for state unemployment tax liability for quarter ended December 31, $399.26. Check No. 319.

The liability account is reduced by this transaction. Therefore, Unemployment Tax Payable—State is debited for $399.26. The balance of the asset account, Cash, is decreased by a credit, $399.26.

The journal entry to record payment of the liability for state unemployment tax is shown in Illustration 15-14.

ILLUSTRATION 15-14   Journal entry to record payment of liability for state unemployment tax

PAGE 28		JOURNAL						
					GENERAL		**CASH**	
DATE	ACCOUNT TITLE	DOC. NO.	POST. REF.		DEBIT	CREDIT	DEBIT	CREDIT
28	31	*Unemployment Tax Payable—State*	C319		399 26			399 26	28

The date, *31*, is written in the Date column. The title of the account debited, *Unemployment Tax Payable—State*, is written in the Account Title column. The check number, *C319*, is entered in the Doc. No. column. The check amount, *$399.26*, is entered in the General Debit and Cash Credit columns.

The entries to journalize a payroll and payroll taxes are summarized in Illustration 15-15.

SUMMARY ILLUSTRATION 15-15

Summary of payroll accounting, taxes, and reports

The payroll register provides the amounts required to journalize the payroll. Employer payroll taxes are calculated and recorded in the journal. Later, the employee and employer payroll taxes are paid to the federal and state governments.

	1	2	10	11
ACCOUNT TITLE	**GENERAL**		**CASH**	
	DEBIT	**CREDIT**	**DEBIT**	**CREDIT**
Pay the Payroll:				
Salary Expense	X			X
Employee Income Tax Payable		X		
FICA Tax Payable		X		
Health Insurance Premiums Payable		X		
U.S. Savings Bonds Payable		X		
United Way Donations Payable		X		
Record Employer Payroll Taxes:				
Payroll Taxes Expense	X			
FICA Tax Payable		X		
Unemployment Tax Payable—Federal		X		
Unemployment Tax Payable—State		X		
Pay Employee and Employer Taxes:				
Employee Income Tax Payable	X			X
FICA Tax Payable	X			X
Unemployment Tax Payable—Federal	X			X
Unemployment Tax Payable—State	X			X

Tax	Who Pays the Tax	
	Employee	**Employer**
Federal Income Tax	X	
FICA Tax	X	X
Federal Unemployment Tax		X
State Unemployment Tax		X

1. Why does a business need to keep payroll information about individual employees?
2. What two business forms provide the payroll information needed about individual employees?
3. What accounts are affected, and how, by an entry to record a payroll?
4. Where is the amount obtained that is used to write a payroll check?
5. What are the three payroll taxes paid by most employers?
6. What is the only payroll tax paid by both the employee and the employer?
7. What amount is used to calculate federal unemployment tax?
8. When is the transaction to record employer payroll taxes expense journalized?
9. What accounts are affected, and how, by an entry to record employer payroll taxes?
10. Where is the information obtained that is needed to prepare a quarterly federal tax return, Form 941?

11. What amounts are used to calculate the tax liability for a pay period as reported on the quarterly federal tax return, Form 941?
12. What information is reported on a Form W-2, Wage and Tax Statement?
13. Who receives a completed Form W-2, Wage and Tax Statement?
14. What should an employee do with Copies B and C of Form W-2, Wage and Tax Statement, received from an employer?
15. What is the purpose of Form W-3, Transmittal of Income and Tax Statements?
16. What payroll taxes are deposited using Form 8109, Federal Tax Deposit Coupon?
17. What accounts are affected, and how, by an entry to record payment of an employer liability for federal unemployment tax?

CASES FOR CRITICAL THINKING

EPT(b)

CASE 1 The partners of Smith and Tyson have decided to hire a sales manager. They agree that the business can only afford to pay the manager a salary of $30,000.00. The accounting clerk informs the partners that hiring the manager will cost the business more than the $30,000.00 salary. Do you agree with the accounting clerk? Explain your response.

CASE 2 Miller Manufacturing had total salary expense for the month of November of $40,000.00. Sandra Peterson, accounting clerk, calculated the November employer FICA tax as $3,200.00 ($40,000.00 × 8%). Samuel Grissom, accountant, stated that the FICA taxes withheld from employee earnings were $2,850.00. What is the most likely reason for the difference between Ms. Peterson's and Mr. Grissom's calculations for FICA taxes? Explain.

DRILLS FOR UNDERSTANDING

EPT(b)

DRILL 15-D1   Analyzing payroll transactions

INSTRUCTIONS:

1. Prepare the following T accounts for four different businesses: Cash, Employee Income Tax Payable, FICA Tax Payable, Unemployment Tax Payable—Federal, Unemployment Tax Payable—State, Payroll Taxes Expense, and Salary Expense.

Business	Total Earnings	Federal Income Tax Withheld	Employee FICA Tax	Employer FICA Tax	Federal Unemployment Tax	State Unemployment Tax
A	$ 9,000.00	$1,350.00	$ 720.00	$ 720.00	$ 72.00	$486.00
B	4,200.00	590.00	336.00	336.00	33.60	226.80
C	12,600.00	2,016.00	1,008.00	1,008.00	100.80	680.40
D	7,800.00	1,140.00	624.00	624.00	62.40	421.20

2. Use T accounts to analyze the following payroll entries for each business. (a) Entry to record payment of a payroll. (b) Entry to record employer payroll taxes.

DRILL 15-D2 Calculating employer payroll taxes

Payroll information taken from a payroll register and employee earnings records is given in the working papers accompanying this textbook.

INSTRUCTIONS:

1. Calculate the amount of earnings subject to unemployment taxes. Unemployment taxes are owed on the first $7,000.00 of earnings for each employee.
2. Calculate the amount of employer payroll taxes owed for the May 1–15 pay period. Employer payroll tax rates are as follows: FICA, 8%; federal unemployment, 0.8%; state unemployment, 5.4%.

APPLICATION PROBLEMS

EPT(b,c,d)

PROBLEM 15-1 Journalizing and posting payment of semimonthly payrolls

Lambert's payroll register has the following totals for two semimonthly pay periods, August 1–15 and August 16–31 of the current year.

Period	Total Earnings	Deductions				Net Pay
		Federal Income Tax	FICA Tax	Other	Total	
Aug. 1–15.	$3,670.00	$514.00	$293.60	B $90.00	$897.60	$2,772.40
Aug. 16–31.	$3,180.00	$437.00	$254.40	B $75.00	$766.40	$2,413.60

Other Deductions: B—U.S. Savings Bonds

INSTRUCTIONS:

1. Journalize payment of the two payrolls on page 17 of a journal. The first payroll was paid by Check No. 756 on August 15 of the current year. The second payroll was paid by Check No. 768 on August 31 of the current year.
2. Post the items that are to be posted individually. The balances in the general ledger as of August 1 of the current year are recorded in the accounts.

The general ledger accounts used in Problem 15-1 are needed to complete Problem 15-2.

PROBLEM 15-2 Calculating, journalizing, and posting employer payroll taxes

The general ledger accounts used in Problem 15-1 are needed to complete Problem 15-2.

Lambert's semimonthly payroll register totals are shown in Problem 15-1. Employer payroll tax rates are as follows: FICA, 8%; federal unemployment, 0.8%; state unemployment, 5.4%. Unemployment taxes are owed on the first $7,000.00 of earnings for each employee.

Information about accumulated earnings and total earnings for the August 1–15 pay period is given in the working papers accompanying this textbook.

INSTRUCTIONS:

1. Calculate the amount of earnings subject to unemployment taxes for the August 1–15 pay period.
2. Calculate the employer payroll tax amounts for the August 1–15 pay period.
3. Journalize the employer payroll taxes on page 18 of a journal. Use the date of August 15 of the current year. The source document is Memorandum No. 75.
4. Post the items that are to be posted individually.
5. Total earnings for the August 16–31 pay period are given in the working papers. Calculate the employer payroll taxes for the August 16–31 pay period. Calculate August 15 accumulated earnings by adding total earnings for the August 1–15 pay period to the July 31 accumulated earnings.
6. Journalize the employer payroll taxes on page 18 of a journal. Use the date of August 31 of the current year. The source document is Memorandum No. 82.
7. Post the items that are to be posted individually.

PROBLEM 15-3 Reporting employer quarterly withholding and payroll taxes

The following payroll data is for Jenson Clothing Company for the second quarter of the current year.

Date Paid	Total Earnings	Federal Income Tax Withheld	Employee FICA Tax Withheld
April 15	$2,825.00	$416.00	$226.00
April 30	2,987.00	438.00	238.96
May 15	3,142.00	468.00	251.36
May 31	2,936.00	428.00	234.88
June 15	3,212.00	489.00	256.96
June 30	2,849.00	422.00	227.92

Additional Data

1. Company address: 669 Eagle Street, Warrenville, IL 62325-4600
2. Employer identification number: 60-8909267
3. Number of employees: 5
4. Federal tax payments have been made on May 15, June 15, and July 15.

INSTRUCTIONS:

Prepare a Form 941, Employer's Quarterly Federal Tax Return, for Jenson Clothing Company. The return is for the second quarter of the current year. Use the date July 21. Sign your name as a partner of the company.

PROBLEM 15-4 Calculating and journalizing withholding and payroll taxes

The following payroll data is for Hawbecker Company for the first quarter of the current year.

Period	Total Earnings	Federal Income Tax Withheld
March	$12,537.00	$2,138.00
First Quarter	37,293.00	—

In addition, total earnings are subject to 8% employee and 8% employer FICA tax. The federal unemployment tax rate is 0.8% and the state unemployment tax rate is 5.4% of total earnings. No total earnings have exceeded the tax base for calculating unemployment taxes.

INSTRUCTIONS:

1. Calculate the appropriate liability amount of FICA tax for March. Journalize the payment of the federal income tax and FICA tax liabilities on page 7 of a journal. The taxes were paid by Check No. 785 on April 3 of the current year.

2. Calculate the appropriate federal unemployment tax liability for the first quarter. Journalize payment of this liability in the journal. The tax was paid by Check No. 802 on April 30 of the current year.

3. Calculate the appropriate state unemployment tax liability for the first quarter. Journalize payment of this liability in the journal. The tax was paid by Check No. 803 on April 30 of the current year.

ENRICHMENT PROBLEMS   EPT(b,c)

MASTERY PROBLEM 15-M   Journalizing and posting payroll transactions

AUTOMATED

APPLICATION

Star Equipment completed payroll transactions during the period April 1 to May 15 of the current year. Payroll tax rates are as follows: FICA, 8%; federal unemployment, 0.8%; state unemployment, 5.4%. The company buys savings bonds for employees as accumulated withholdings reach the necessary amount to purchase a bond. No total earnings have exceeded the tax base for calculating unemployment taxes.

The balances in the general ledger as of April 1 of the current year are recorded in the working papers accompanying this textbook.

CHART OF ACCOUNTS

Account Number	Account Title	Account Number	Account Title
1110	Cash	2150	Unemployment Tax Pay.—Fed.
1130	Accounts Receivable	2160	Unemployment Tax Pay.—St.
1140	Merchandise Inventory	2180	U.S. Savings Bonds Pay.
2110	Accounts Payable	3150	Income Summary
2120	Employee Income Tax Pay.	6150	Payroll Taxes Expense
2130	FICA Tax Payable	6170	Salary Expense

INSTRUCTIONS:

1. Journalize the following transactions on page 14 of a journal. Source documents are abbreviated as follows: check, C, and memorandum, M.

Apr. 15. Paid cash for liability for employee income tax, $945.00, and for FICA tax, $984.99; total, $1,929.99. C356.

15. Paid cash for semimonthly payroll, $2,463.52 (total payroll, $3,256.00, less deductions: employee income tax, $482.00; FICA tax, $260.48; U.S. Savings Bonds, $50.00). C357.

15. Recorded employer payroll taxes expense. M25.

15. Paid cash for U.S. Savings Bonds for employees, $250.00. C358.

30. Paid cash for semimonthly payroll, $2,527.36, (total payroll, $3,358.00, less deductions: employee income tax, $512.00; FICA tax, $268.64; U.S. Savings Bonds, $50.00). C376.

30. Recorded employer payroll taxes expense. M29.

30. Paid cash for federal unemployment tax liability for quarter ended March 31, $147.75. C377.

30. Paid cash for state unemployment tax liability for quarter ended March 31, $997.30. C378.

Posting. Post the items that are to be posted individually.

May 15. Paid cash for liability for employee income tax, $994.00, and for FICA tax, $1,058.24; total, $2,052.24. C405.

15. Paid cash for semimonthly payroll, $2,373.40 (total payroll, $3,145.00, less deductions: employee income tax, $470.00; FICA tax, $251.60; U.S. Savings Bonds, $50.00). C406.

May 15. Recorded employer payroll taxes expense. M36.

> *Posting.* Post the items that are to be posted individually.

2. Prove and rule the journal.

CHALLENGE PROBLEM 15-C Journalizing and posting payroll transactions

AUTOMATED

APPLICATION

Danner Hardware completed payroll transactions during the period January 1 to April 30 of the current year. Payroll tax rates are as follows: FICA, 8%; federal unemployment, 0.8%; and state unemployment, 5.4%. The company buys savings bonds for employees as the accumulated withholdings reach the necessary amount to purchase a bond. No total earnings have exceeded the tax base for calculating unemployment taxes.

The balances in the general ledger as of January 1 of the current year are recorded in the working papers accompanying this textbook.

CHART OF ACCOUNTS

Account Number	Account Title	Account Number	Account Title
1110	Cash	2150	Unemployment Tax Pay.—Fed.
1130	Accounts Receivable	2160	Unemployment Tax Pay.—St.
1140	Merchandise Inventory	2180	U.S. Savings Bonds Pay.
2110	Accounts Payable	3150	Income Summary
2120	Employee Income Tax Pay.	6150	Payroll Taxes Expense
2130	FICA Tax Payable	6170	Salary Expense

INSTRUCTIONS:

1. Journalize the following transactions on page 1 of a journal. Source documents are abbreviated as follows: check, C, and memorandum, M.

Jan. 2. Wrote a check for 12 U.S. Savings Bonds at $25.00 each for employees. C143.
   15. Paid the December liability for employee income tax and for FICA tax. C152.
   31. Wrote a check for federal unemployment tax liability for quarter ended December 31. C158.
   31. Wrote a check for state unemployment tax liability for quarter ended December 31. C159.
   31. Paid January payroll, $6,283.04 (total payroll, $8,487.00, less deductions: employee income tax, $1,425.00; FICA tax, $678.96; U.S. Savings Bonds, $100.00). C164.
   31. Recorded employer payroll taxes expense. M95.

> *Posting.* Post the items that are to be posted individually.

Feb. 15. Wrote a check for January liability for employee income tax and for FICA tax. C170.
   28. Paid February payroll, $6,348.16 (total payroll, $8,598.00, less deductions: employee income tax, $1,462.00; FICA tax, $687.84; U.S. Savings Bonds, $100.00). C180.
   28. Recorded employer payroll taxes expense. M104.

> *Posting.* Post the items that are to be posted individually.

Mar. 15. Wrote a check for February liability for employee income tax and for FICA tax. C195.
   31. Paid March payroll, $6,660.76 (total payroll, $9,028.00, less deductions: employee income tax, $1,545.00; FICA tax, $722.24; U.S. Savings Bonds, $100.00). C206.
   31. Recorded employer payroll taxes expense. M113.

> *Posting.* Post the items that are to be posted individually.

Apr. 1. Paid cash for 12 U.S. Savings Bonds at $25.00 each for employees. C207.
   15. Wrote a check for March liability for employee income tax and for FICA tax. C218.
   30. Wrote a check for federal unemployment tax liability for quarter ended March 31. C224.
   30. Wrote a check for state unemployment tax liability for quarter ended March 31. C225.

> *Posting.* Post the items that are to be posted individually.

2. Prove and rule the journal.

Recording Payroll Transactions

CarLand's manual journalizing and posting procedures for payroll transactions are described in Chapter 15. Integrating Automated Accounting Topic 5 describes procedures for using automated accounting software to journalize and post CarLand's payroll transactions. The Automated Accounting Problems contain instructions for using automated accounting software to solve the April payroll transactions from Mastery Problem 15-M and Challenge Problem 15-C, Chapter 15.

AUTOMATED PAYROLL ACCOUNTING PROCEDURES FOR CARLAND

CarLand uses two input forms to batch payroll transaction data for automated accounting.

1. Cash payments journal input form for all cash payments.
2. General journal input form for all other transactions.

Recording Payment of a Payroll

CarLand uses a cash payments journal input form to journalize payment of a payroll.

> *December 15, 19--. Paid cash for semimonthly payroll, $1,976.52 (total payroll, $2,556.00, less deductions: employee income tax, $192.00; FICA tax, $204.48; health insurance premiums, $158.00; U.S. Savings Bonds, $15.00; United Way donations, $10.00). Check No. 287.*

The journal entry to record this transaction is on lines 1 through 6 of the cash payments journal input form shown in Illustration T5-1.

ILLUSTRATION T5-1   Cash payments journal input form with payroll transactions recorded

RUN DATE 12/15/--   MM DD YY

CASH PAYMENTS JOURNAL
Input Form

	DATE MM/DD	VENDOR NO.	CHECK NO.	ACCOUNTS PAY. DEBIT	ACCOUNT NO.	DEBIT	CREDIT	
1	12/15		C287		6170	2556 00		1
2					2120		192 00	2
3					2130		204 48	3
4					2170		158 00	4
5					2180		15 00	5
6					2190		10 00	6
25								25

NOTE: A credit to Cash is made automatically by the software.

The run date, *12/15/--*, is written in the space provided at the top of the form.

On line 1, the date of the transaction, *12/15*, is entered in the Date column. The source document number, *C287*, is recorded in the Check No. column. The general ledger account number for Salary Expense, *6170*, is written in the Account No. column. The debit amount, *$2,556.00*, is written in the Debit column.

On lines 2 through 6, the account numbers for the payroll liabilities are written in the Account No. column. The credit amounts are entered in the Credit column. The software automatically makes the credit to Cash, *$1,976.52.*

Recording Employer Payroll Taxes

CarLand journalizes employer payroll taxes on a general journal input form.

> *December 15, 19--. Recorded employer payroll taxes expense, $275.03, for the semimonthly pay period ended December 15. Taxes owed are: FICA tax, $204.48; federal unemployment tax, $9.10; state unemployment tax, $61.45. Memorandum No. 54.*

The journal entry to record this transaction is on lines 1 through 4 of the general journal input form shown in Illustration T5-2.

ILLUSTRATION T5-2

General journal input form with employer taxes recorded

RUN DATE _12/15/--_ MM DD YY

GENERAL JOURNAL
Input Form

	DATE MM/DD	REFERENCE	ACCOUNT NO.	CUSTOMER/ VENDOR NO.	DEBIT	CREDIT	
1	12/15	M54	6150		275 03		1
2	/		2130			204 48	2
3	/		2150			9 10	3
4	/		2160			61 45	4
25	/						25
				PAGE TOTALS	275 03	275 03	
				FINAL TOTALS	275 03	275 03	

The run date, *12/15/--,* is written in the space provided at the top of the input form.

On line 1, the date of the transaction, *12/15,* is entered in the Date column. The source document number, *M54,* is recorded in the Reference column. The general ledger account number for Payroll Taxes Expense, *6150,* is written in the Account No. column. The debit amount, *$275.03,* is entered in the Debit column.

On lines 2 through 4, the account numbers for the payroll taxes are recorded in the Account No. column. The credit amounts are written in the Credit column.

After the employer payroll taxes transaction has been journalized, CarLand totals the Debit and Credit columns. The totals are recorded on the Page Totals and Final Totals lines provided at the bottom of the input form.

Processing a Payroll Payment and Employer Payroll Taxes

To process a cash payment, the Journals menu is selected from the menu bar. The Cash Payments Journal command is selected from

the Journals menu to display the data entry window for keying payroll data.

After the payroll payment has been keyed and posted, the Reports menu is selected from the menu bar. The Journals command is chosen to display the Report Selection window. The Cash Payments Journal is selected from the Report Selection window. As CarLand wants to print all transactions from 12/01/-- to 12/15/--, the *Ok* button is pushed to display the cash payments report. The report is checked for accuracy by comparing the report with the cash payments journal input form. The cash payments journal report is printed, as shown in Illustration T5-3, and filed for future reference.

ILLUSTRATION T5-3   Cash payments journal report with a payroll payment recorded

```
                              CarLand
                       Cash Payments Journal
                            12/15/--
--------------------------------------------------------------------------
Date    Refer.   V/C Acct.   Title                      Debit      Credit
--------------------------------------------------------------------------
12/15   C287         6170    Salary Expense            2556.00
12/15   C287         2120    Employee Income Tax Pay.               192.00
12/15   C287         2130    FICA Tax Payable                       204.48
12/15   C287         2170    Health Ins. Premiums Pay.              158.00
12/15   C287         2180    U.S. Savings Bonds Pay.                 15.00
12/15   C287         2190    United Way Donations Pay.               10.00
12/15   C287         1110    Cash                                  1976.52

                                                      ----------  ----------
                             Totals                     2556.00    2556.00
                                                      ==========  ==========
```

To process general journal entries, the Journals menu is selected from the menu bar. The General Journal command is chosen from the Journals menu to display the data entry window for keying transaction data.

After all lines on the input form have been keyed and posted, the general journal report is displayed. The same steps are followed as for displaying the cash payments journal report. However, the General Journal is selected from the Report Selection window. The report is checked for accuracy by comparing the report totals, *$275.03*, with the totals on the general journal input form. Because the totals are the same, the general journal report is assumed to be correct. The general journal report is printed, as shown in Illustration T5-4, and is filed for future reference.

PAYING WITHHOLDING AND PAYROLL TAXES

CarLand journalizes the payment of withholding and payroll taxes on a cash payments journal input form.

General journal report with employer payroll taxes recorded

```
                              CarLand
                           General Journal
                             12/15/--
----------------------------------------------------------------------
Date   Refer.   V/C  Acct.   Title                    Debit     Credit
----------------------------------------------------------------------
12/15  M54           6150    Payroll Taxes Expense    275.03
12/15  M54           2130    FICA Tax Payable                   204.48
12/15  M54           2150    Unemployment Tax Pay--Fed            9.10
12/15  M54           2160    Unemployment Tax Pay--St.           61.45

                                                     ----------  ----------
                             Totals                   275.03     275.03
                                                     ==========  ==========
```

Recording Payment of Employee Income Tax and FICA Tax

January 15, 19--. Paid cash for liability for employee income tax, $402.00, and for FICA tax, $832.16; total, $1,234.16. Check No. 305.

The journal entry to record this transaction is on lines 1 and 2 of the cash payments journal input form shown in Illustration T5-5.

Cash payments journal input form with withholding and payroll taxes recorded

RUN DATE *01/31/--*
MM DD YY

CASH PAYMENTS JOURNAL
Input Form

	DATE MM/DD	VENDOR NO.	CHECK NO.	ACCOUNTS PAY. DEBIT	ACCOUNT NO.	DEBIT	CREDIT	
1	01/15		C305		2120	402 00		1
2	/				2130	832 16		2
3	/31		C318		2150	59 15		3
4	/31		C319		2160	399 26		4
25	/							25

NOTE: A credit to Cash is made automatically by the software.

For the purpose of this illustration, check numbers 306–317 have been omitted.

Paying the Liability for Federal Unemployment Tax

January 31, 19--. Paid cash for federal unemployment tax liability for quarter ended December 31, $59.15. Check No. 318.

The journal entry to record this transaction is on line 3 of Illustration T5-5.

Paying the Liability for State Unemployment Tax

January 31, 19--. Paid cash for state unemployment tax liability for quarter ended December 31, $399.26. Check No. 319.

The journal entry to record this transaction is on line 4 of Illustration T5-5.

Processing the Payment of Withholding and Payroll Taxes

To process the cash payment for withholding and payroll taxes, the transaction data are keyed from the cash payments journal input form. After all lines have been keyed and posted, a cash payments report is displayed. The displayed cash payments report is checked for accuracy by comparing the report with the cash payments journal input form. After accuracy has been verified, the cash payments report is printed, as shown in Illustration T5-6, and is filed for future reference.

| ILLUSTRATION T5-6 | Cash payments journal report with withholding and payroll taxes recorded |

```
                            CarLand
                      Cash Payments Journal
                           01/31/--
-------------------------------------------------------------------------
Date   Refer.   V/C Acct.   Title                    Debit       Credit
-------------------------------------------------------------------------
01/15  C305         2120    Employee Income Tax Pay.  402.00
01/15  C305         2130    FICA Tax Payable          832.16
01/15  C305         1110    Cash                                  1234.16

01/31  C318         2150    Unemployment Tax Pay--Fed  59.15
01/31  C318         1110    Cash                                    59.15

01/31  C319         2160    Unemployment Tax Pay--St. 399.26
01/31  C319         1110    Cash                                   399.26
                                                     ---------- ----------
                            Totals                    1692.57    1692.57
                                                     ========== ==========
```

OPTIONAL PROBLEM DB-5A

CarLand's general ledger data base is on the accounting textbook template. If you wish to process CarLand's December payroll transactions using automated accounting software, load the *Automated Accounting 6.0* or higher software. Select Data Base 5A (DB-5A) from the template disk. Read the Problem Instructions screen. Using the completed cash payments and general journal input forms, Illustrations T5-1, T5-2, and T5-5, follow the procedures described to process CarLand's payroll transactions.

AUTOMATED ACCOUNTING PROBLEMS

AUTOMATING MASTERY PROBLEM 15-M Journalizing and posting payroll transactions

INSTRUCTIONS:

1. Journalize transactions for the month of April *only* from Mastery Problem 15-M, Chapter 15, on the appropriate input forms. Use April 30 of the current year as the run date.
2. Load the *Automated Accounting 6.0* or higher software. Select data base F15-M (First-Year Course Problem 15-M) from the accounting textbook template. Read the Problem Instructions screen.
3. Select File from the menu bar and choose the Save As menu command. Key the path to the drive and directory that contains your data files. Save the data base with a file name of XXX15M (where XXX are your initials).
4. Key the data from the completed cash payments journal input form.
5. Display/print the cash payments journal report.
6. Key the data from the completed general journal input form.
7. Display/print the general journal report.

AUTOMATING CHALLENGE PROBLEM 15-C Journalizing and posting payroll transactions

INSTRUCTIONS:

1. Journalize transactions for the month of January *only* from Challenge Problem 15-C, on the appropriate input forms. Use January 31 of the current year as the run date.
2. Load the *Automated Accounting 6.0* or higher software. Select data base F15-C from the accounting textbook template. Read the Problem Instructions screen.
3. Select File from the menu bar and choose the Save As menu command. Key the path to the drive and directory that contains your data files. Save the data base with a file name of XXX15C (where XXX are your initials).
4. Key the data from the completed cash payments journal input form.
5. Display/print the cash payments journal report.
6. Key the data from the completed general journal input form.
7. Display/print the general journal report.

An Accounting Cycle for a Partnership: Journalizing and Posting Transactions

Reinforcement Activity 2 reinforces learnings from Part 3, Chapters 11 through 18. Activities cover a complete accounting cycle for a merchandising business organized as a partnership. Reinforcement Activity 2 is a single problem divided into two parts. Part A includes learnings from Chapters 11 through 15. Part B includes learnings from Chapters 16 through 18.

The accounting work of a single merchandising business for the last month of a yearly fiscal period is used in this reinforcement activity. The records kept and reports prepared, however, illustrate the application of accounting concepts for all merchandising businesses.

CLEARVIEW OPTICAL

Tara Bruski and James Myler, partners, own and operate ClearView Optical, a merchandising business. The business sells a complete line of fashion, sun, and sport eyewear. ClearView is located in a downtown shopping area and is open for business Monday through Saturday. A monthly rent is paid for the building and fixtures. ClearView accepts credit cards from customers.

CHART OF ACCOUNTS

ClearView Optical uses the chart of accounts shown on the next page.

JOURNAL AND LEDGERS

The journal and ledgers used by ClearView Optical are listed in the following chart. Models of the journal and ledgers are shown in the textbook illustrations given in the chart.

Journal and Ledgers	Chapter	Illustration Number
Expanded journal.	12	12-5
Accounts payable ledger	13	13-10
Accounts receivable ledger	13	13-15
General ledger.	16	16-1

CLEARVIEW OPTICAL
CHART OF ACCOUNTS

Balance Sheet Accounts

(1000) ASSETS
1110 Cash
1120 Petty Cash
1130 Accounts Receivable
1140 Merchandise Inventory
1145 Supplies—Office
1150 Supplies—Store
1160 Prepaid Insurance

(2000) LIABILITIES
2110 Accounts Payable
2120 Employee Income Tax Payable
2130 FICA Tax Payable
2140 Sales Tax Payable
2150 Unemployment Tax Payable—Federal
2160 Unemployment Tax Payable—State
2170 Health Insurance Premiums Payable
2180 U.S. Savings Bonds Payable
2190 United Way Donations Payable

(3000) OWNERS' EQUITY
3110 Tara Bruski, Capital
3120 Tara Bruski, Drawing
3130 James Myler, Capital
3140 James Myler, Drawing
3150 Income Summary

Income Statement Accounts

(4000) OPERATING REVENUE
4110 Sales

(5000) COST OF MERCHANDISE
5110 Purchases

(6000) OPERATING EXPENSES
6110 Advertising Expense
6120 Credit Card Fee Expense
6130 Insurance Expense
6140 Miscellaneous Expense
6150 Payroll Taxes Expense
6160 Rent Expense
6170 Salary Expense
6175 Supplies Expense—Office
6180 Supplies Expense—Store
6190 Utilities Expense

SUBSIDIARY LEDGERS

Accounts Receivable Ledger

110 Theresa Abbey
120 Nancy Bonner
130 Jonathan Doran
140 Irma Iznaga
150 Brian Patco
160 Norman Witte

Accounts Payable Ledger

210 A & B Optical Co.
220 Central Office Supply
230 Kosh Optical Lab
240 Optical Imports
250 Trend Optics Co.
260 Weaver Supply

RECORDING TRANSACTIONS

The December 1 account balances for the general and subsidiary ledgers are given in the working papers accompanying this textbook.

INSTRUCTIONS:

1. Journalize the following transactions on page 23 of a journal. A 6% sales tax has been added to each sale. Source documents are abbreviated as follows: check, C; memorandum, M; purchase invoice, P; receipt, R; sales invoice, S; cash register tape, T.

Dec. 1. Paid cash for rent, $1,000.00. C272.
   1. Tara Bruski, partner, withdrew cash for personal use, $1,200.00. C273.
   1. James Myler, partner, withdrew cash for personal use, $1,200.00. C274.
   2. Paid cash for electric bill, $288.50. C275.
   2. Received cash on account from Nancy Bonner, $344.50, covering S64. R82.
   3. Paid cash for miscellaneous expense, $60.00. C276.
   3. Paid cash on account to Trend Optics Co., $483.80, covering P73. C277.
   4. Sold merchandise on account to Theresa Abbey, $375.00, plus sales tax, $22.50; total, $397.50. S67.
   5. Recorded cash and credit card sales, $4,830.00, plus sales tax, $289.80; total, $5,119.80. T5.
       Posting. Post the items that are to be posted individually.
   7. Sold merchandise on account to Jonathan Doran, $385.00, plus sales tax, $23.10; total, $408.10. S68.
   7. Received cash on account from Norman Witte, $360.40, covering S65. R83.
   8. Bought office supplies on account from Central Office Supply, $293.00. M43.
   9. Purchased merchandise on account from Optical Imports, $1,125.00. P77.
   9. Bought store supplies on account from Weaver Supply, $275.00. M44.
   10. Tara Bruski, partner, withdrew merchandise for personal use, $250.00. M45.
   10. Paid cash for office supplies, $145.00. C278.
   10. Discovered that a payment of cash for advertising in November was journalized and posted in error as a debit to Miscellaneous Expense instead of Advertising Expense, $125.00. M46.
   11. Paid cash on account to Kosh Optical Lab, $975.80, covering P74. C279.
   11. Purchased merchandise on account from Trend Optics Co., $860.00. P78.
   12. Paid cash for store supplies, $220.00. C280.
   12. Recorded cash and credit card sales, $5,940.00, plus sales tax, $356.40; total, $6,296.40. T12.
       Posting. Post the items that are to be posted individually.
   14. James Myler, partner, withdrew merchandise for personal use, $325.00. M47.
   14. Purchased merchandise on account from Kosh Optical Lab, $2,730.00. P79.
   14. Sold merchandise on account to Brian Patco, $140.00, plus sales tax, $8.40; total, $148.40. S69.
   14. Paid cash for advertising, $345.00. C281.
   15. Paid cash on account to A & B Optical Co., $1,060.40, covering P75. C282.
   15. Received cash on account from Irma Iznaga, $683.70, covering S66. R84.
   15. Sold merchandise on account to Nancy Bonner, $410.00, plus sales tax, $24.60; total, $434.60. S70.
       Posting. Post the items that are to be posted individually.

2. Prove and rule page 23 of the journal.

3. Carry the column totals forward to page 24 of the journal.

4. Journalize the following transactions on page 24 of the journal.

Dec. 15. Paid cash for semimonthly payroll, $1,751.80 (total payroll, $2,315.00, less deductions: employee income tax, $181.00; FICA tax, $185.20; health insurance, $142.00; U.S. Savings Bonds, $25.00; United Way donations, $30.00). C283.

Dec. 15. Recorded employer payroll taxes, $250.30, for the semimonthly pay period ended December 15. Taxes owed are: FICA tax, $185.20; federal unemployment tax, $8.40; and state unemployment tax, $56.70. M48.

19. Recorded cash and credit card sales, $5,760.00, plus sales tax, $345.60; total, $6,105.60. T19.

23. Paid cash on account to Optical Imports, $1,840.00, covering P76. C284.

26. Recorded cash and credit card sales, $5,820.00, plus sales tax, $349.20; total, $6,169.20. T26.

Posting. Post the items that are to be posted individually.

ClearView Optical's bank charges a fee for handling the collection of credit card sales deposited during the month. The credit card fee is deducted from ClearView Optical's bank account. The amount is then shown on the bank statement. The credit card fee is recorded in the journal as a reduction in cash.

Dec. 28. Recorded credit card fee expense, $285.20. M49. (Debit Credit Card Fee Expense; credit Cash.)

30. Purchased merchandise on account from A & B Optical Co., $1,620.00. P80.

31. Paid cash to replenish the petty cash fund, $304.00: office supplies, $62.00; store supplies, $59.00; advertising, $87.00; miscellaneous, $96.00. C285.

31. Paid cash for semimonthly payroll, $1,882.00 (total payroll, $2,460.00, less deductions: employee income tax, $184.20; FICA tax, $196.80; health insurance, $142.00; U.S. Savings Bonds, $25.00; United Way donations, $30.00). C286.

31. Recorded employer payroll taxes, $263.92, for the semimonthly pay period ended December 31. Taxes owed are: FICA tax, $196.80; federal unemployment tax, $8.66; and state unemployment tax, $58.46. M50.

31. Received bank statement showing December bank service charge, $4.50. M51.

31. Recorded cash and credit card sales, $3,240.00, plus sales tax, $194.40; total, $3,434.40. T31.

Posting. Post the items that are to be posted individually.

5. Total page 24 of the journal. Prove the equality of debits and credits.
6. Prove cash. The balance on the next unused check stub was $34,918.00.
7. Rule the journal.
8. Post the totals of the special columns of the journal.
9. Prepare a schedule of accounts payable and a schedule of accounts receivable. Prove the accuracy of the subsidiary ledgers by comparing the schedule totals with the balances of the controlling accounts in the general ledger. If the totals are not the same, find and correct the errors.

The ledgers used in Reinforcement Activity 2, Part A, are needed to complete Reinforcement Activity 2, Part B.

Stellar Attractions Pegboard Payroll System provides experience in preparing records using a pegboard and no-carbon-required forms. When data are entered on the statement of earnings and deductions stub on the check, the employee earnings record and the payroll register are simultaneously prepared. Posting is eliminated. The following activities are included in the accounting cycle for Stellar Attractions. This business simulation is available from the publisher.

Activities in Stellar Attractions:

1. Preparing necessary forms for new employees.

2. Completing time cards by entering summary data.

3. Assembling forms on a pegboard: checks with earnings and deductions stubs, employee earnings records, and payroll register. All records are completed with one writing.

4. Recording time card summary data on the statement of earnings and deductions stubs of checks on the pegboard.

5. Determining appropriate deductions using tax tables and figuring net pay.

6. Recording deductions and net pay on the statement of earnings and deductions stubs.

7. Totaling, proving, ruling, and filing the payroll register. Filing employee earnings records.

8. Separating, writing, and signing payroll checks.

9. Totaling and proving employee earnings records for the end of the quarter and year to date.

10. Preparing quarterly and annual reports.

16

Work Sheet for a Merchandising Business

ENABLING PERFORMANCE TASKS

After studying Chapter 16, you will be able to:

a Define accounting terms related to a work sheet for a merchandising business.

b Identify accounting concepts and practices related to a work sheet for a merchandising business.

c Plan adjustments on a work sheet for a merchandising business.

d Complete a work sheet for a merchandising business.

TERMS PREVIEW

inventory • **merchandise inventory**

Management decisions about future business operations are often based on financial information. Financial information shows whether a profit is being made or a loss is being incurred. Profit or loss information helps an owner or manager determine future changes. Financial information is also needed to prepare required tax reports. A business summarizes financial information at least once each fiscal period. CarLand uses a one-year fiscal period that begins on January 1 and ends on December 31. Therefore, CarLand summarizes its financial information on December 31 of each year.

GENERAL LEDGER WITH POSTING COMPLETED

CarLand's completed general ledger on December 31, after all transactions have been posted, is shown in Illustration 16-1, pages 388 through 393. No entries have been posted in the following accounts: Income Summary, Insurance Expense, Supplies Expense—Office, and Supplies Expense—Store. Transactions during the year did not affect these accounts.

AN 8-COLUMN WORK SHEET FOR A MERCHANDISING BUSINESS

A columnar accounting form on which the financial information needed to prepare financial statements is summarized is known as a work sheet. A work sheet is used to plan adjustments and sort financial statement information. A work sheet may be prepared whenever a business wishes to summarize and report financial information. A work sheet is always prepared at the end of each fiscal period because financial statements are prepared at the end of each fiscal period. (CONCEPT: Accounting Period Cycle) CarLand prepares a work sheet and financial statements annually.

Work sheets for service and merchandising businesses are similar. CarLand's work sheet is similar to the one used by Rugcare described in Chapter 8. CarLand's work sheet, however, also includes accounts for accounts receivable, merchandise inventory, accounts payable, sales tax, and purchases.

RECORDING A TRIAL BALANCE ON A WORK SHEET

To prove the equality of debits and credits in the general ledger, a trial balance is prepared. CarLand prepares a trial balance in the Trial Balance columns of a work sheet. CarLand's trial balance on December 31 is shown in Illustration 16-2, page 394.

ILLUSTRATION 16-1   General ledger with posting completed

ACCOUNT *Cash*   ACCOUNT NO. *1110*

DATE		ITEM	POST. REF.	DEBIT	CREDIT	BALANCE	
						DEBIT	CREDIT
Dec.¹⁹⁻	1	Balance	✓			23 55 00 00	
	31		25	30 98 4 00		54 53 4 00	
	31		25		30 30 0 43	24 23 3 57	

ACCOUNT *Petty Cash*   ACCOUNT NO. *1120*

DATE		ITEM	POST. REF.	DEBIT	CREDIT	BALANCE	
						DEBIT	CREDIT
Jan.¹⁹⁻	1	Balance	✓			5 00 00	

ACCOUNT *Accounts Receivable*   ACCOUNT NO. *1130*

DATE		ITEM	POST. REF.	DEBIT	CREDIT	BALANCE	
						DEBIT	CREDIT
Dec.¹⁹⁻	1	Balance	✓			9 22 2 00	
	31		25	8 69 2 00		17 91 4 00	
	31		25		8 58 2 00	9 33 2 00	

ACCOUNT *Merchandise Inventory*   ACCOUNT NO. *1140*

DATE		ITEM	POST. REF.	DEBIT	CREDIT	BALANCE	
						DEBIT	CREDIT
Jan.¹⁹⁻	1	Balance	✓			225 40 0 00	

ACCOUNT *Supplies—Office*   ACCOUNT NO. *1145*

DATE		ITEM	POST. REF.	DEBIT	CREDIT	BALANCE	
						DEBIT	CREDIT
Dec.¹⁹⁻	1	Balance	✓			4 98 0 00	
	3		24	1 60 00		5 14 0 00	
	9		24	86 00		5 22 6 00	
	18		25	1 24 00		5 35 0 00	
	31		25	50 00		5 40 0 00	

ACCOUNT *Supplies—Store*   ACCOUNT NO. *1150*

DATE		ITEM	POST. REF.	DEBIT	CREDIT	BALANCE	
						DEBIT	CREDIT
Dec.¹⁹⁻	1	Balance	✓			5 13 0 00	
	7		24	2 30 00		5 36 0 00	
	31		25	73 00		5 43 3 00	
	31		25	3 47 00		5 78 0 00	

ILLUSTRATION 16-1 General ledger with posting completed (continued)

ACCOUNT *Prepaid Insurance*   ACCOUNT NO. *1160*

DATE	ITEM	POST. REF.	DEBIT	CREDIT	BALANCE DEBIT	BALANCE CREDIT
Dec. 1	Balance	✓			4 8 4 0 00	

ACCOUNT *Accounts Payable*   ACCOUNT NO. *2110*

DATE	ITEM	POST. REF.	DEBIT	CREDIT	BALANCE DEBIT	BALANCE CREDIT
Dec. 1	Balance	✓				15 8 7 0 00
31		25	15 5 4 5 59			3 2 4 41
31		25		10 1 2 7 49		10 4 5 1 90

ACCOUNT *Employee Income Tax Payable*   ACCOUNT NO. *2120*

DATE	ITEM	POST. REF.	DEBIT	CREDIT	BALANCE DEBIT	BALANCE CREDIT
Dec. 1	Balance	✓				3 8 4 00
15		24	3 8 4 00		—	—
15		24		1 9 2 00		1 9 2 00
31		25		2 1 0 00		4 0 2 00

ACCOUNT *FICA Tax Payable*   ACCOUNT NO. *2130*

DATE	ITEM	POST. REF.	DEBIT	CREDIT	BALANCE DEBIT	BALANCE CREDIT
Dec. 1	Balance	✓				8 1 7 92
15		24	8 1 7 92		—	—
15		24		2 0 4 48		2 0 4 48
15		24		2 0 4 48		4 0 8 96
31		25		2 1 1 60		6 2 0 56
31		25		2 1 1 60		8 3 2 16

ACCOUNT *Sales Tax Payable*   ACCOUNT NO. *2140*

DATE	ITEM	POST. REF.	DEBIT	CREDIT	BALANCE DEBIT	BALANCE CREDIT
Dec. 1	Balance	✓				1 8 9 6 00
15		24	1 8 9 6 00		—	—
31		25		1 7 6 0 00		1 7 6 0 00

ILLUSTRATION 16-1   General ledger with posting completed (continued)

ACCOUNT **Unemployment Tax Payable—Federal**   ACCOUNT NO. **2150**

DATE		ITEM	POST. REF.	DEBIT	CREDIT	BALANCE DEBIT	BALANCE CREDIT
Dec.¹⁹⁻⁻	1	Balance	√				40 48
	15		24		9 10		49 58
	31		25		9 57		59 15

ACCOUNT **Unemployment Tax Payable—State**   ACCOUNT NO. **2160**

DATE		ITEM	POST. REF.	DEBIT	CREDIT	BALANCE DEBIT	BALANCE CREDIT
Dec.¹⁹⁻⁻	1	Balance	√				2 73 22
	15		24		61 45		3 34 67
	31		25		64 59		3 99 26

ACCOUNT **Health Insurance Premiums Payable**   ACCOUNT NO. **2170**

DATE		ITEM	POST. REF.	DEBIT	CREDIT	BALANCE DEBIT	BALANCE CREDIT
Dec.¹⁹⁻⁻	1	Balance	√				5 24 00
	15		24		1 58 00		6 82 00
√	31		25		1 58 00		8 40 00

ACCOUNT **U.S. Savings Bonds Payable**   ACCOUNT NO. **2180**

DATE		ITEM	POST. REF.	DEBIT	CREDIT	BALANCE DEBIT	BALANCE CREDIT
Dec.¹⁹⁻⁻	1	Balance	√				10 00
	15		24		15 00		25 00
	31		25		15 00		40 00

ACCOUNT **United Way Donations Payable**   ACCOUNT NO. **2190**

DATE		ITEM	POST. REF.	DEBIT	CREDIT	BALANCE DEBIT	BALANCE CREDIT
Dec.¹⁹⁻⁻	1	Balance	√				40 00
	15		24		10 00		50 00
	31		25		10 00		60 00

ACCOUNT **Amy Kramer, Capital**   ACCOUNT NO. **3110**

DATE		ITEM	POST. REF.	DEBIT	CREDIT	BALANCE DEBIT	BALANCE CREDIT
Jan.¹⁹⁻⁻	1	Balance	√				101 11 8 00

ILLUSTRATION 16-1   General ledger with posting completed (continued)

ACCOUNT *Amy Kramer, Drawing*   ACCOUNT NO. *3120*

DATE		ITEM	POST. REF.	DEBIT	CREDIT	BALANCE	
						DEBIT	CREDIT
Dec.¹⁹⁻⁻	1	Balance	√			16 7 0 0 00	
	15		24	1 5 0 0 00		18 2 0 0 00	

ACCOUNT *Dario Mesa, Capital*   ACCOUNT NO. *3130*

DATE		ITEM	POST. REF.	DEBIT	CREDIT	BALANCE	
						DEBIT	CREDIT
Jan.¹⁹⁻⁻	1	Balance	√				101 2 2 8 00

ACCOUNT *Dario Mesa, Drawing*   ACCOUNT NO. *3140*

DATE		ITEM	POST. REF.	DEBIT	CREDIT	BALANCE	
						DEBIT	CREDIT
Dec.¹⁹⁻⁻	1	Balance	√			17 1 0 0 00	
	15		24	1 5 0 0 00		18 6 0 0 00	

ACCOUNT *Income Summary*   ACCOUNT NO. *3150*

DATE	ITEM	POST. REF.	DEBIT	CREDIT	BALANCE	
					DEBIT	CREDIT

ACCOUNT *Sales*   ACCOUNT NO. *4110*

DATE		ITEM	POST. REF.	DEBIT	CREDIT	BALANCE	
						DEBIT	CREDIT
Dec.¹⁹⁻⁻	1	Balance	√				323 2 6 6 00
	31		25		29 3 3 4 00		352 6 0 0 00

ACCOUNT *Purchases*   ACCOUNT NO. *5110*

DATE		ITEM	POST. REF.	DEBIT	CREDIT	BALANCE	
						DEBIT	CREDIT
Dec.¹⁹⁻⁻	1	Balance	√			148 1 7 2 51	
	31		25	10 1 2 7 49		158 3 0 0 00	

ACCOUNT *Advertising Expense*   ACCOUNT NO. *6110*

DATE		ITEM	POST. REF.	DEBIT	CREDIT	BALANCE	
						DEBIT	CREDIT
Dec.¹⁹⁻⁻	1	Balance	√			4 8 6 0 00	
	4		24	1 6 5 00		5 0 2 5 00	
	16		25	8 3 00		5 1 0 8 00	
	22		25	3 9 2 00		5 5 0 0 00	

ILLUSTRATION 16-1   General ledger with posting completed (continued)

ACCOUNT **Credit Card Fee Expense**   ACCOUNT NO. **6120**

DATE		ITEM	POST. REF.	DEBIT	CREDIT	BALANCE DEBIT	BALANCE CREDIT
Dec.¹⁹⁻	1	Balance	√			2 1 7 5 00	
	28		25	7 1 5 00		2 8 9 0 00	

ACCOUNT **Insurance Expense**   ACCOUNT NO. **6130**

DATE		ITEM	POST. REF.	DEBIT	CREDIT	BALANCE DEBIT	BALANCE CREDIT

ACCOUNT **Miscellaneous Expense**   ACCOUNT NO. **6140**

DATE		ITEM	POST. REF.	DEBIT	CREDIT	BALANCE DEBIT	BALANCE CREDIT
Dec.¹⁹⁻	1	Balance	√			1 7 3 2 15	
	9		24	3 9 00		1 7 7 1 15	
	17		25	1 6 3 00		1 9 3 4 15	
	22		25	1 0 6 00		2 0 4 0 15	
	31		25	1 4 2 00		2 1 8 2 15	

ACCOUNT **Payroll Taxes Expense**   ACCOUNT NO. **6150**

DATE		ITEM	POST. REF.	DEBIT	CREDIT	BALANCE DEBIT	BALANCE CREDIT
Dec.¹⁹⁻	1	Balance	√			6 7 3 8 96	
	15		24	2 7 5 03		7 0 1 3 99	
	31		25	2 8 5 76		7 2 9 9 75	

ACCOUNT **Rent Expense**   ACCOUNT NO. **6160**

DATE		ITEM	POST. REF.	DEBIT	CREDIT	BALANCE DEBIT	BALANCE CREDIT
Dec.¹⁹⁻	1	Balance	√			16 5 0 0 00	
	1		24	1 5 0 0 00		18 0 0 0 00	

ACCOUNT **Salary Expense**   ACCOUNT NO. **6170**

DATE		ITEM	POST. REF.	DEBIT	CREDIT	BALANCE DEBIT	BALANCE CREDIT
Dec.¹⁹⁻	1	Balance	√			54 9 5 2 00	
	15		24	2 5 5 6 00		57 5 0 8 00	
	31		25	2 6 4 5 00		60 1 5 3 00	

ILLUSTRATION 16-1   General ledger with posting completed (concluded)

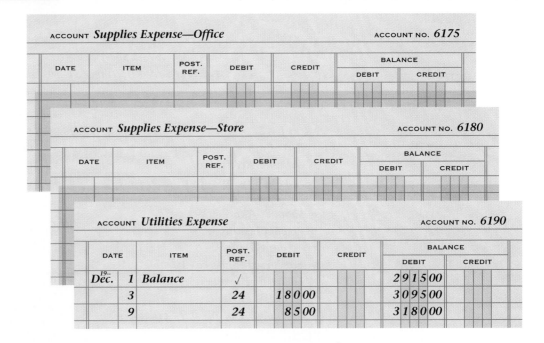

ACCOUNT *Supplies Expense—Office*					ACCOUNT NO. *6175*	
DATE	ITEM	POST. REF.	DEBIT	CREDIT	BALANCE DEBIT	CREDIT

ACCOUNT *Supplies Expense—Store*					ACCOUNT NO. *6180*	
DATE	ITEM	POST. REF.	DEBIT	CREDIT	BALANCE DEBIT	CREDIT

ACCOUNT *Utilities Expense*					ACCOUNT NO. *6190*	
DATE	ITEM	POST. REF.	DEBIT	CREDIT	BALANCE DEBIT	CREDIT
Dec. 1	Balance	✓			2 9 1 5 00	
3		24	1 8 0 00		3 0 9 5 00	
9		24	8 5 00		3 1 8 0 00	

FYI

A trial balance is prepared to prove the equality of debits and credits in the general ledger.

General ledger accounts are listed in the work sheet's Account Title column in the same order in which they appear in the general ledger. All accounts are listed regardless of whether there is a balance or not. Listing all accounts reduces the possibility of overlooking an account that needs to be brought up to date.

PLANNING ADJUSTMENTS ON A WORK SHEET

After posting is completed at the end of a fiscal period, some general ledger accounts, such as the two supplies accounts and the prepaid insurance account, are not up to date. Adjustments for supplies and prepaid insurance are described in Chapter 8. In addition to supplies and prepaid insurance, CarLand needs to adjust the merchandise inventory account. Changes recorded on a work sheet to update general ledger accounts at the end of a fiscal period are known as adjustments.

Adjustments are planned in the Adjustments columns of a work sheet. Adjustments recorded on a work sheet are for planning purposes only. The general ledger account balances are not changed until entries are journalized and posted. Journal entries made to bring general ledger accounts up to date are known as adjusting entries.

Merchandise Inventory Adjustment

The amount of goods on hand is called an **inventory**. The amount of goods on hand for sale to customers is called **merchandise inventory**. The general ledger account in which merchandise inventory is

MULTICULTURAL AWARENESS

Peru

In some ancient civilizations, such as the Incan civilization in Peru, recordkeepers memorized business transactions and transmitted them by reciting them when necessary. The Incan recordkeepers used small ropes of different colors and sizes, and knotted and joined them in different ways to help remember financial data. These ropes, called "quipu," were one of the earliest means of recording transactions.

ILLUSTRATION 16-2   Trial balance on a work sheet

		TRIAL BALANCE	
	ACCOUNT TITLE	DEBIT	CREDIT
1	Cash	24 2 3 3 57	
2	Petty Cash	5 0 0 00	
3	Accounts Receivable	9 3 3 2 00	
4	Merchandise Inventory	225 4 0 0 00	
5	Supplies—Office	5 4 0 0 00	
6	Supplies—Store	5 7 8 0 00	
7	Prepaid Insurance	4 8 4 0 00	
8	Accounts Payable		10 4 5 1 90
9	Employee Income Tax Payable		4 0 2 00
10	FICA Tax Payable		8 3 2 16
11	Sales Tax Payable		1 7 6 0 00
12	Unemploy. Tax Payable—Federal		5 9 15
13	Unemploy. Tax Payable—State		3 9 9 26
14	Health Insurance Premiums Payable		8 4 0 00
15	U.S. Savings Bonds Payable		4 0 00
16	United Way Donations Payable		6 0 00
17	Amy Kramer, Capital		101 1 1 8 00
18	Amy Kramer, Drawing	18 2 0 0 00	
19	Dario Mesa, Capital		101 2 2 8 00
20	Dario Mesa, Drawing	18 6 0 0 00	
21	Income Summary		
22	Sales		352 6 0 0 00
23	Purchases	158 3 0 0 00	
24	Advertising Expense	5 5 0 0 00	
25	Credit Card Fee Expense	2 8 9 0 00	
26	Insurance Expense		
27	Miscellaneous Expense	2 1 8 2 15	
28	Payroll Taxes Expense	7 2 9 9 75	
29	Rent Expense	18 0 0 0 00	
30	Salary Expense	60 1 5 3 00	
31	Supplies Expense—Office		
32	Supplies Expense—Store		
33	Utilities Expense	3 1 8 0 00	
34		569 7 9 0 47	569 7 9 0 47
35			

CarLand
Work Sheet
For Year Ended December 31, 19--

recorded is titled *Merchandise Inventory*. Merchandise Inventory is an asset account with a normal debit balance, as shown in the T account.

Merchandise Inventory	
Debit side	Credit side
Normal balance	
Increase	Decrease

Analyzing a Merchandise Inventory Adjustment. CarLand's merchandise inventory account on January 1, the beginning of the fiscal year, has a debit balance of $225,400.00, as shown in the T account.

Merchandise Inventory

Jan. 1 Bal. 225,400.00	

When preparing a trial balance, all accounts must be listed whether they have a balance or not.

BEFORE ADJUSTMENT
Income Summary

Merchandise Inventory

Jan. 1 Bal. 225,400.00	

When an account that requires adjusting does not have a related expense account, the temporary account Income Summary is used.

AFTER ADJUSTMENT
Income Summary

Adj. (a) 13,200.00	

Merchandise Inventory

Jan. 1 Bal. 225,400.00	Adj. (a) 13,200.00
(New Bal. 212,200.00)	

The balance of the merchandise inventory account on December 31, the end of the fiscal year, is the same amount, $225,400.00. The January 1 and December 31 balances are the same because no entries have been made in the account during the fiscal year. The changes in inventory resulting from purchases and sales transactions have not been recorded in the merchandise inventory account.

During a fiscal period, the amount of merchandise on hand increases each time merchandise is purchased. However, all purchases are recorded in the purchases account. The amount of merchandise on hand decreases each time merchandise is sold. However, all sales are recorded in the sales account. This procedure makes it easier to quickly determine the total purchases and sales during a fiscal period. The merchandise inventory account balance, therefore, must be adjusted to reflect the changes resulting from purchases and sales during a fiscal period.

The two accounts used to adjust the merchandise inventory are Merchandise Inventory and Income Summary. The T accounts show the merchandise inventory and income summary accounts before the merchandise inventory adjustment is made.

Before the adjustment, the merchandise inventory account has a January 1 debit balance of $225,400.00. The merchandise inventory account balance, however, is not up to date. The actual count of merchandise on December 31 shows that the inventory is valued at $212,200.00. Therefore, the merchandise inventory account balance must be adjusted to show the current value of merchandise on hand.

Most accounts needing adjustment at the end of a fiscal period have a related temporary account. For example, when the account Supplies is adjusted, Supplies Expense is the related expense account, a temporary account. Merchandise Inventory, however, does not have a related expense account. Therefore, Income Summary, a temporary account, is used to adjust the merchandise inventory account at the end of a fiscal period.

Four questions are asked in analyzing the adjustment for merchandise inventory.

1. What is the balance of Merchandise Inventory?... $225,400.00
2. What should the balance be for this account? .. $212,200.00
3. What must be done to correct the account balance? Decrease .... $ 13,200.00
4. What adjustment is made?
   Debit Income Summary .... $ 13,200.00
   Credit Merchandise Inventory............... $ 13,200.00

The merchandise inventory adjustment is shown in the T accounts.

Income Summary is debited and Merchandise Inventory is credited for $13,200.00. The beginning debit balance of Merchandise Inventory, $225,400.00, *minus* the adjustment credit amount, $13,200.00, *equals* the ending debit balance of Merchandise Inventory, $212,200.00.

Recording a Merchandise Inventory Adjustment on a Work Sheet.
The merchandise inventory adjustment is shown on lines 4 and 21 in the work sheet's Adjustments columns in Illustration 16-3.

ILLUSTRATION 16-3   Merchandise inventory adjustment on a work sheet

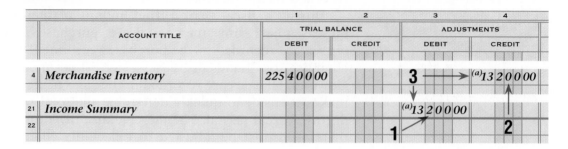

Three steps are used to record CarLand's adjustment for merchandise inventory on a work sheet.

1 Write the debit amount, *$13,200.00,* in the Adjustments Debit column on the line with the account title Income Summary (line 21).

2 Write the credit amount, *$13,200.00,* in the Adjustments Credit column on the line with the account title Merchandise Inventory (line 4).

3 Label the two parts of this adjustment with the small letter a in parentheses, *(a).*

AFTER ADJUSTMENT
Merchandise Inventory

Jan. 1 Bal.	245,600.00	
Adj. (a)	5,200.00	
(New Bal.	*250,800.00)*	

Income Summary

| | | Adj. (a) | 5,200.00 |

If the amount of merchandise inventory on hand is greater than the balance of Merchandise Inventory, opposite entries would be made—debit Merchandise Inventory and credit Income Summary. For example, Kobrin Company's merchandise inventory account on January 1 has a debit balance of $245,600.00. The count of merchandise on December 31 shows that the inventory is valued at $250,800.00. The merchandise on hand is $5,200.00 *greater* than the balance of Merchandise Inventory. This merchandise inventory adjustment is shown in the T accounts.

Merchandise Inventory is debited and Income Summary is credited for $5,200.00.

Supplies Adjustments

CarLand uses office and store supplies in the daily operation of the business. The amount of supplies *not used* during a fiscal period represents an asset. The amount of supplies used during a fiscal period represents an expense. Accurate financial reporting includes recording expenses in the fiscal period in which the expenses contribute to earning revenue. *(CONCEPT: Matching Expenses with Revenue)*

Supplies—Office

Dec. 31 Bal.	5,400.00

Analyzing an Office Supplies Inventory Adjustment.
CarLand's office supplies account on December 31, the end of the fiscal period, has a debit balance of $5,400.00, as shown in the T account.

The account balance for Supplies—Office, $5,400.00, includes two items. (1) The account balance on January 1. (2) The cost of office supplies bought during the year. The account balance does not reflect the value of any office supplies *used* during the year (an expense). Therefore, the office supplies account balance must be adjusted to show the value of office supplies on hand on December 31. The amount of supplies on hand on December 31 is determined by counting the supplies on hand and calculating the value.

The two accounts used to adjust office supplies are Supplies—Office and Supplies Expense—Office. The T accounts show the two accounts before the adjustment is made.

Before the adjustment, the office supplies account has a December 31 debit balance of $5,400.00. However, office supplies have been used throughout the fiscal period. These changes in office supplies were not recorded in the office supplies account. Therefore, the office supplies account balance is not up to date. The actual count of office supplies on December 31 shows that the value of the office supplies inventory is $1,460.00. The office supplies account balance must be adjusted to show the current value of the office supplies inventory.

Four questions are asked in analyzing the adjustment for office supplies inventory.

FYI

The adjustment for supplies is the amount of supplies used.

BEFORE ADJUSTMENT
Supplies Expense—Office

Supplies—Office

Dec. 31 Bal.	5,400.00

1. What is the balance of Supplies—Office? $5,400.00
2. What should the balance be for this account? $1,460.00
3. What must be done to correct the account
   balance? Decrease $3,940.00
4. What adjustment is made?
   Debit Supplies Expense—Office.................. $3,940.00
   Credit Supplies—Office $3,940.00

AFTER ADJUSTMENT
Supplies Expense—Office

Adj. (b)	3,940.00

Supplies—Office

Dec. 31 Bal.	5,400.00	Adj. (b)	3,940.00
(New Bal.	*1,460.00)*		

The office supplies inventory adjustment is shown in the T accounts.

Supplies Expense—Office is debited and Supplies—Office is credited for $3,940.00. The beginning debit balance of Supplies—Office, $5,400.00, *minus* the adjustment credit amount, $3,940.00, *equals* the ending debit balance of Supplies—Office, $1,460.00.

Recording Supplies Inventory Adjustments on a Work Sheet.
CarLand makes a similar adjustment for store supplies. The steps in recording the *two* supplies inventory adjustments are the same as those described for Rugcare in Chapter 8. The *two* supplies inventory adjustments are shown in the Adjustments columns of the work sheet in Illustration 16-4 on page 398. The adjustment for Supplies—Office is labeled *(b)* and is shown on lines 5 and 31. The adjustment for Supplies—Store is labeled *(c)* and is shown on lines 6 and 32.

| | ACCOUNT TITLE | TRIAL BALANCE | | ADJUSTMENTS | |
		DEBIT	CREDIT	DEBIT	CREDIT
		1	2	3	4
5	*Supplies—Office*	5 4 0 00			(b) 3 9 4 0 00
6	*Supplies—Store*	5 7 8 0 00			(c) 3 2 6 0 00
31	*Supplies Expense—Office*			(b) 3 9 4 0 00	
32	*Supplies Expense—Store*			(c) 3 2 6 0 00	
33					
34					

Prepaid Insurance Adjustment

> **FYI**
>
> The adjustment for prepaid insurance is the amount of insurance used or expired.

Payment for insurance protection is paid in advance. The value of prepaid insurance *not expired* during a fiscal period is an asset. The value of prepaid insurance *expired* during a fiscal period is an expense.

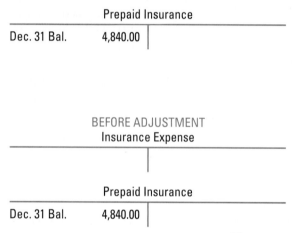

Prepaid Insurance

Dec. 31 Bal.   4,840.00

BEFORE ADJUSTMENT
Insurance Expense

Prepaid Insurance

Dec. 31 Bal.   4,840.00

Analyzing a Prepaid Insurance Adjustment. Car-Land's prepaid insurance account on December 31, the end of the fiscal period, has a debit balance of $4,840.00, as shown in the T account.

The account balance for Prepaid Insurance, $4,840.00, includes two items. (1) The account balance on January 1. (2) The cost of insurance premiums paid during the year. The account balance does not reflect the value of the insurance expired during the year (an expense). Therefore, the prepaid insurance account balance must be adjusted to bring the balance up to date. *(CONCEPT: Matching Expenses with Revenue)*

The two accounts used to adjust the prepaid insurance account are Prepaid Insurance and Insurance Expense. The T accounts show the two accounts before the adjustment is made.

Before the adjustment, the prepaid insurance account has a December 31 debit balance of $4,840.00. The account balance, however, is not up to date. The value of the prepaid insurance *not expired* is determined to be $2,200.00. The prepaid insurance account balance must be adjusted to show its current value.

Four questions are asked in analyzing the adjustment for prepaid insurance.
1. What is the balance of Prepaid Insurance?............$4,840.00
2. What should the balance be for this account?.....$2,200.00
3. What must be done to correct the account balance? Decrease $2,640.00
4. What adjustment is made?
    Debit Insurance Expense.......................................$2,640.00
    Credit Prepaid Insurance....................................$2,640.00

> **Audit Your Understanding**
>
> 1. What is a work sheet?
> 2. Why is a trial balance prepared?
> 3. What account must a merchandising business adjust that a service business does not?
> 4. What accounts are used for the adjustment for merchandise inventory?

AFTER ADJUSTMENT

Insurance Expense

Adj. (d)	2,640.00	

Prepaid Insurance

Dec. 31 Bal.	4,840.00	Adj. (d)	2,640.00
(New Bal.	*2,200.00)*		

The prepaid insurance adjustment is shown in the T accounts.

Insurance Expense is debited and Prepaid Insurance is credited for $2,640.00. The beginning debit balance of Prepaid Insurance, $4,840.00, *minus* the adjustment credit amount, $2,640.00, *equals* the ending debit balance of Prepaid Insurance, $2,200.00.

Recording a Prepaid Insurance Adjustment on a Work Sheet. The steps in recording the prepaid insurance adjustment on a work sheet are the same as those followed by Rugcare in Chapter 8. The adjustment for Prepaid Insurance is labeled *(d)* and is shown in the Adjustments columns on lines 7 and 26 of the work sheet in Illustration 16-5.

ILLUSTRATION 16-5   Prepaid insurance adjustment on a work sheet

		1	2	3	4
	ACCOUNT TITLE	TRIAL BALANCE		ADJUSTMENTS	
		DEBIT	CREDIT	DEBIT	CREDIT
7	*Prepaid Insurance*	4 8 4 0 00			(d) 2 6 4 0 00
26	*Insurance Expense*			(d) 2 6 4 0 00	
27					
28					
29					

COMPLETING A WORK SHEET

CarLand follows the same procedures for completing a work sheet as described for Rugcare in Chapter 8 with the exception of the income summary account. Rugcare sells a service, not merchandise. Therefore, Rugcare has no amount recorded in the income summary account, a related account used to adjust Merchandise Inventory. CarLand sells merchandise. Therefore, the income summary account is used as the related account to adjust Merchandise Inventory. The merchandise inventory adjustment reflects the increases and decreases in the amount of goods on hand resulting from sales and purchases. Therefore, the amount recorded in Income Summary is extended to the work sheet's Income Statement Debit or Credit column. An Income Summary debit amount is extended to the Income Statement Debit column. An Income Summary credit amount is extended to the Income Statement Credit column. CarLand's completed work sheet is shown in Illustration 16-6 on pages 400 and 401.

Illustration 16-7 on page 402 summarizes the steps followed in completing an 8-column work sheet for a merchandising business.

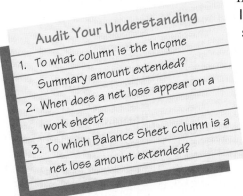

Audit Your Understanding

1. To what column is the Income Summary amount extended?

2. When does a net loss appear on a work sheet?

3. To which Balance Sheet column is a net loss amount extended?

ILLUSTRATION 16-6

Completed work sheet for a merchandising business

CarLand

Work Sheet

For Year Ended December 31, 19--

ACCOUNT TITLE	TRIAL BALANCE DEBIT	TRIAL BALANCE CREDIT	ADJUSTMENTS DEBIT	ADJUSTMENTS CREDIT	INCOME STATEMENT DEBIT	INCOME STATEMENT CREDIT	BALANCE SHEET DEBIT	BALANCE SHEET CREDIT	
Cash	2423357						2423357		1
Petty Cash	50000						50000		2
Accounts Receivable	933200						933200		3
Merchandise Inventory	22540000			(a)1320000			21220000		4
Supplies—Office	540000			(b)394000			146000		5
Supplies—Store	578000			(c)326000			252000		6
Prepaid Insurance	484000			(d)264000			220000		7
Accounts Payable		1045190						1045190	8
Employee Income Tax Payable		40200						40200	9
FICA Tax Payable		83216						83216	10
Sales Tax Payable		176000						176000	11
Unemployment Tax Payable—Federal		5915						5915	12
Unemployment Tax Payable—State		39926						39926	13
Health Insurance Premiums Payable		84000						84000	14
U.S. Savings Bonds Payable		4000						4000	15
United Way Donations Payable		6000						6000	16
Amy Kramer, Capital		10111800						10111800	17
Amy Kramer, Drawing	1820000						1820000		18
Dario Mesa, Capital		10122800						10122800	19
Dario Mesa, Drawing	1860000						1860000		20

	Trial Balance Debit	Trial Balance Credit	Adjustments Debit	Adjustments Credit	Income Statement Debit	Income Statement Credit	Balance Sheet Debit	Balance Sheet Credit	
21 Income Summary			(a) 13 2 0 0 00		13 2 0 0 00				21
22 Sales		352 6 0 0 00				352 6 0 0 00			22
23 Purchases	158 3 0 0 00				158 3 0 0 00				23
24 Advertising Expense	5 5 0 0 00				5 5 0 0 00				24
25 Credit Card Fee Expense	2 8 9 0 00				2 8 9 0 00				25
26 Insurance Expense			(d) 2 6 4 0 00		2 6 4 0 00				26
27 Miscellaneous Expense	2 1 8 2 15				2 1 8 2 15				27
28 Payroll Taxes Expense	7 2 9 9 75				7 2 9 9 75				28
29 Rent Expense	18 0 0 0 00				18 0 0 0 00				29
30 Salary Expense	60 1 5 3 00				60 1 5 3 00				30
31 Supplies Expense—Office			(b) 3 9 4 0 00		3 9 4 0 00				31
32 Supplies Expense—Store			(c) 3 2 6 0 00		3 2 6 0 00				32
33 Utilities Expense	3 1 8 0 00				3 1 8 0 00				33
34	569 7 9 0 47	569 7 9 0 47	23 0 4 0 00	23 0 4 0 00	280 5 4 4 90	352 6 0 0 00	289 2 4 5 57	217 1 9 1 47	34
35 Net Income					72 0 5 5 10			72 0 5 5 10	35
36					352 6 0 0 00	352 6 0 0 00	289 2 4 5 57	289 2 4 5 57	36

Summary of an 8-column work sheet for a merchandising business

1 Prepare a trial balance in the Trial Balance columns.

2 Analyze and record adjustments in the Adjustments columns.

3 Extend balance sheet items to the work sheet's Balance Sheet columns.

4 Extend income statement items, including Income Summary, to the work sheet's Income Statement columns.

5 Total the Income Statement and Balance Sheet columns.

6 Calculate the net income or net loss. If the Income Statement Credit column total (revenue) is larger than the Debit column total (costs and expenses), a net income has occurred. If the Income Statement Debit column total (costs and expenses) is larger than the Credit column total (revenue), a net loss has occurred. CarLand's net income is calculated as shown below.

Income Statement Credit Column Total	−	Income Statement Debit Column Total	=	Net Income
$352,600.00	−	$280,544.90	=	$72,055.10

7 Extend the amount of net income or net loss to the Balance Sheet Debit or Credit column. When a net income occurs, the net income amount is extended to the Balance Sheet Credit amount column, as shown on line 35. When a net loss occurs, the net loss amount is extended to the Balance Sheet Debit amount column.

8 Total the four Income Statement and Balance Sheet amount columns.

9 Check that the totals for each pair of columns are in balance. As shown on line 36, the totals for the Income Statement columns, $352,600.00, are the same. The totals for the Balance Sheet columns, $289,245.57, are also the same. CarLand's work sheet is in balance.

ACCOUNT TITLE	TRIAL BALANCE DEBIT	TRIAL BALANCE CREDIT	ADJUSTMENTS DEBIT	ADJUSTMENTS CREDIT	INCOME STATEMENT DEBIT	INCOME STATEMENT CREDIT	BALANCE SHEET DEBIT	BALANCE SHEET CREDIT	
1 Cash	24 233 57						24 233 57		1
2 Petty Cash	5 000 00						5 000 00		2
4 Merchandise Inventory	225 400 00			(a)13 200 00			212 200 00		4
5 Supplies—Office	5 400 00			(b) 3 940 00			1 460 00		5
8 Accounts Payable		10 451 90						10 451 90	8
19 Dario Mesa, Capital		101 228 00						101 228 00	19
20 Dario Mesa, Drawing	18 600 00						18 600 00		20
21 Income Summary			(a)13 200 00		13 200 00				21
22 Sales		352 600 00				352 600 00			22
23 Purchases	158 300 00				158 300 00				23
32 Supplies Expense—Store			(c) 3 260 00		3 260 00				32
33 Utilities Expense	3 180 00				3 180 00				33
34	569 790 47	569 790 47	23 040 00	23 040 00	280 544 90	352 600 00	289 245 57	217 190 47	34
35 Net Income					72 055 10			72 055 10	35
36					352 600 00	352 600 00	289 245 57	289 245 57	36
37									37

A 10-COLUMN WORK SHEET FOR A MERCHANDISING BUSINESS

Some large merchandising businesses *with many accounts to be adjusted* at the end of a fiscal period may use a 10-column work sheet. A 10-column work sheet includes an additional pair of amount columns titled *Adjusted Trial Balance*, as shown in the 10-column work sheet in Illustration 16-8, pages 404 and 405.

After adjustments have been recorded, the balance for each account listed in the Trial Balance columns is extended to the Adjusted Trial Balance columns. The Adjusted Trial Balance columns are then totaled to prove equality of debits and credits after adjustments. Following proof of debits and credits, amounts in the Adjusted Trial Balance columns are extended to the Balance Sheet and Income Statement columns. The Income Statement and Balance Sheet columns are totaled and ruled the same way as on an 8-column work sheet.

■ Bryan Choi ■
ARCHITECTS ASSOCIATED, DAYTON OHIO

Bryan Choi has been an architect all of his professional life. Bryan Choi is also a planner; he sets goals and works toward them. Before he started his own architectural firm, he planned for fifteen years. He started working in a large company, then went to a medium-sized company, and then to a small company, to learn everything there was to know about going into business for yourself.

Choi also knew for a long time that he would eventually start his own business. Therefore he saved diligently for that day. Choi says, "I started small and took very few risks. That's why I succeeded where others had failed." Because he planned for so long, there were none of the surprises that first-time entrepreneurs often

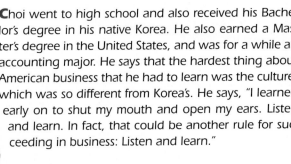

encounter, such as underestimating the need for beginning capital.

Students who ask Choi what they need to do to succeed hear, "Learn to manage your time wisely. Set goals, establish good working habits, and continue to work at whatever it is you want to do until you master it."

Choi went to high school and also received his Bachelor's degree in his native Korea. He also earned a Master's degree in the United States, and was for a while an accounting major. He says that the hardest thing about American business that he had to learn was the culture, which was so different from Korea's. He says, "I learned early on to shut my mouth and open my ears. Listen and learn. In fact, that could be another rule for succeeding in business: Listen and learn."

Personal Visions in Business

ILLUSTRATION 16-8   Ten-column work sheet (left page)

CarLand

Work Sheet

For Year Ended December 31, 19--

	ACCOUNT TITLE	TRIAL BALANCE		ADJUSTMENTS		
		DEBIT	CREDIT	DEBIT	CREDIT	
1	Cash	24 23 3 57				1
2	Petty Cash	5 00 00				2
3	Accounts Receivable	9 33 2 00				3
4	Merchandise Inventory	225 40 0 00			(a) 13 20 0 00	4
5	Supplies—Office	5 40 0 00			(b) 3 94 0 00	5
6	Supplies—Store	5 78 0 00			(c) 3 26 0 00	6
7	Prepaid Insurance	4 84 0 00			(d) 2 64 0 00	7
8	Accounts Payable		10 45 1 90			8
9	Employee Income Tax Payable		4 02 00			9
10	FICA Tax Payable		8 32 16			10
11	Sales Tax Payable		1 76 0 00			11
29	Rent Expense	18 00 0 00				29
30	Salary Expense	60 15 3 00				30
31	Supplies Expense—Office			(b) 3 94 0 00		31
32	Supplies Expense—Store			(c) 3 26 0 00		32
33	Utilities Expense	3 18 0 00				33
34		569 79 0 47	569 79 0 47	23 04 0 00	23 04 0 00	34
35	Net Income					35
36						36

Any business with adjustments to make at the end of a fiscal period could use either an 8-column or a 10-column work sheet. However, completing two extra amount columns when most of the account balances *are not* adjusted requires extra time and work. Account balances not adjusted must be extended from the Trial Balance columns to the Adjusted Trial Balance columns. Whereas, with an 8-column work sheet, account balances *not* adjusted are extended directly to the Balance Sheet or Income Statement columns. CarLand prefers to use an 8-column work sheet because only four adjustments are needed at the end of each fiscal period.

ILLUSTRATION 16-8 Ten-column work sheet (right page)

	5	6	7	8	9	10	
	ADJUSTED TRIAL BALANCE		INCOME STATEMENT		BALANCE SHEET		
	DEBIT	CREDIT	DEBIT	CREDIT	DEBIT	CREDIT	
1	24 2 33 57				24 2 33 57		1
2	5 00 00				5 00 00		2
3	9 33 2 00				9 33 2 00		3
4	212 2 00 00				212 2 00 00		4
5	1 46 0 00				1 46 0 00		5
6	2 52 0 00				2 52 0 00		6
7	2 20 0 00				2 20 0 00		7
8		10 4 51 90				10 4 51 90	8
9		4 02 00				4 02 00	9
10		8 32 16				8 32 16	10
11		1 76 0 00				1 76 0 00	11
29	18 0 00 00		18 0 00 00				29
30	60 1 53 00		60 1 53 00				30
31	3 94 0 00		3 94 0 00				31
32	3 26 0 00		3 26 0 00				32
33	3 18 0 00		3 18 0 00				33
34	592 8 30 47	592 8 30 47	280 5 44 90	352 6 00 00	289 2 45 57	217 1 90 47	34
35			72 0 55 10			72 0 55 10	35
36			352 6 00 00	352 6 00 00	289 2 45 57	289 2 45 57	36

What is the meaning of each of the following?

1. **inventory**
2. **merchandise inventory**

1. Why do some general ledger accounts not have any entries posted and, therefore, zero balances at the end of a fiscal period?

2. Why is a work sheet used at the end of a fiscal period?

3. Which accounting concept is being applied when a work sheet is prepared at the end of each fiscal period?

4. Why are all general ledger accounts listed on the Trial Balance columns of a work sheet?

5. Which of CarLand's general ledger accounts need to be brought up to date at the end of a fiscal period?

6. What type of account is Merchandise Inventory, and what is its normal balance?

7. Why are the beginning and ending balances of the merchandise inventory account before adjustments the same?

8. What accounts are affected, and how, by the adjustment for merchandise inventory?

9. What does the amount of supplies not used during a fiscal period represent to a business?

10. Which accounting concept is being applied when expenses are recorded in the same accounting period in which the expenses contribute to earning revenue?

11. What two items are included in CarLand's office supplies account balance before adjustment?

12. What accounts are affected, and how, by the adjustment for office supplies inventory?

13. What two items are included in CarLand's prepaid insurance account balance before adjustment?

14. What accounts are affected, and how, by a prepaid insurance adjustment?

15. What type of merchandising business might use a 10-column work sheet?

16. What two additional amount columns are found on a 10-column work sheet?

CASE 1 After completing a work sheet, Kramer Merchandising Outlet finds that through an oversight, paper bags still in boxes were overlooked in calculating the supplies inventory. The value of the paper bags overlooked is $50.00. Joseph Kramer suggests that the accountant not worry about such a small amount because the oversight does not have any effect on balancing the Income Statement and Balance Sheet columns of the work sheet. Mr. Kramer further indicates that the oversight will be corrected anyway when the store supplies are counted at the end of the next fiscal period. The accountant recommends that the work sheet be redone to reflect the recalculated supplies inventory. Do you agree with Mr. Kramer or the accountant? Explain your answer.

CASE 2 Quality Shoes paid $1,440.00 for a one-year fire insurance policy. The company prepares an income statement and balance sheet every three months. However, the accountant prepares a prepaid insurance adjustment only at the end of the year. Rachel Delfield, one of the partners in the business, thinks the prepaid insurance should be adjusted every three months. Who is correct? Why?

DRILL 16-D1 Analyzing adjusting entries

TUTORIAL

The following chart contains adjustment information related to the preparation of work sheets for three businesses.

Business	Account Title and Balance		End-of-Fiscal-Period Information	
A	1. Merchandise Inventory	$148,000.00	Merchandise inventory	$134,000.00
	2. Supplies—Office	5,750.00	Office supplies inventory	4,200.00
	3. Supplies—Store	4,920.00	Store supplies inventory	3,840.00
	4. Prepaid Insurance	1,860.00	Value of prepaid insurance	1,240.00
B	1. Merchandise Inventory	$182,000.00	Merchandise inventory	$166,000.00
	2. Supplies—Office	4,680.00	Office supplies inventory	3,460.00
	3. Supplies—Store	5,930.00	Store supplies inventory	4,320.00
	4. Prepaid Insurance	2,520.00	Value of prepaid insurance	1,260.00
C	1. Merchandise Inventory	$166,500.00	Merchandise inventory	$178,000.00
	2. Supplies—Office	5,460.00	Office supplies inventory	4,520.00
	3. Supplies—Store	6,480.00	Store supplies inventory	4,960.00
	4. Prepaid Insurance	2,160.00	Value of prepaid insurance	1,080.00

A form for analyzing transactions is given in the working papers accompanying this textbook.

INSTRUCTIONS:

For each business, analyze the adjustments for merchandise inventory adjustment, office supplies inventory adjustment, store supplies inventory adjustment, and prepaid insurance adjustment. List the accounts affected and the amounts for each of the adjustments. List the account titles in Column 3 and the amounts in either Column 4 or 5. Adjustment 1 for Business A is given as an example in the working papers.

DRILL 16-D2 Extending balance sheet and income statement items

MATHEMATICS

Madison Enterprise's partially completed work sheet is given in the working papers accompanying this textbook.

INSTRUCTIONS:

1. Extend the balance sheet items to the Balance Sheet columns of the work sheet.
2. Extend the income statement items to the Income Statement columns of the work sheet.
3. Complete the work sheet.
   a. Total the Income Statement and Balance Sheet columns.
   b. Calculate and record the net income or net loss.
   c. Total and rule the Income Statement and Balance Sheet columns.

APPLICATION PROBLEMS

EPT(c,d)

PROBLEM 16-1 Completing a work sheet

Eastside Supply's trial balance as of December 31 of the current year is recorded on a work sheet in the working papers accompanying this textbook.

1. Analyze the following adjustment information, and record the adjustments on the work sheet.

Adjustment Information, December 31

Merchandise inventory	$196,610.00
Office supplies inventory	1,410.00
Store supplies inventory	2,450.00
Value of prepaid insurance	1,935.00

2. Calculate and record the net income or net loss.

3. Complete the work sheet.

PROBLEM 16-2 Completing a work sheet

Jomar's trial balance as of December 31 of the current year is recorded on a work sheet in the working papers accompanying this textbook.

INSTRUCTIONS:

1. Analyze the following adjustment information, and record the adjustments on the work sheet.

Adjustment Information, December 31

Merchandise inventory	$246,600.00
Office supplies inventory	1,790.00
Store supplies inventory	1,510.00
Value of prepaid insurance	2,300.00

2. Calculate and record the net income or net loss.

3. Complete the work sheet.

ENRICHMENT PROBLEMS   EPT(c,d)

MASTERY PROBLEM 16-M Completing a work sheet

APPLICATION

Marine Supply's trial balance as of December 31 of the current year is recorded on a work sheet in the working papers accompanying this textbook.

INSTRUCTIONS:

Use the following adjustment information. Complete the work sheet.

Adjustment Information, December 31

Merchandise inventory	$208,600.00
Office supplies inventory	1,855.00
Store supplies inventory	2,355.00
Value of prepaid insurance	1,575.00

CHALLENGE PROBLEM 16-C Completing a 10-column work sheet

Ultimate Fashion's trial balance as of December 31 of the current year is recorded on a work sheet in the working papers accompanying this textbook.

INSTRUCTIONS:

Use the adjustment information given on the next page. Complete the 10-column work sheet.

Adjustment Information, December 31

Merchandise inventory...............	$205,370.00
Office supplies inventory.............	2,160.00
Store supplies inventory.............	2,195.00
Value of prepaid insurance...........	1,320.00

17

Financial Statements for a Partnership

ENABLING PERFORMANCE TASKS

After studying Chapter 17, you will be able to:

a Define accounting terms related to financial statements for a merchandising business organized as a partnership.

b Identify accounting concepts and practices related to financial statements for a merchandising business organized as a partnership.

c Prepare an income statement for a merchandising business organized as a partnership.

d Analyze an income statement using component percentages for a merchandising business organized as a partnership.

e Prepare a distribution of net income statement for a merchandising business organized as a partnership.

f Prepare an owners' equity statement for a merchandising business organized as a partnership.

g Prepare a balance sheet for a merchandising business organized as a partnership.

TERMS PREVIEW

cost of merchandise sold • gross profit on sales • distribution of net income statement • owners' equity statement • supporting schedule

The financial activities of a business are recorded in journals and ledgers during a fiscal period. At the end of a fiscal period, a work sheet is prepared to organize and summarize this financial information. The completed work sheet is used to prepare financial statements. Financial statements provide the primary source of information needed by owners and managers to make decisions on the future activity of a business.

All financial information must be reported in order to make sound business decisions. The financial statements should provide information about a business' financial condition, changes in this financial condition, and the progress of operations. *(CONCEPT: Adequate Disclosure)*

Comparing financial condition and progress for more than one fiscal period also helps owners and managers make sound business decisions. Therefore, financial information must be reported the same way from one fiscal period to the next. *(CONCEPT: Consistent Reporting)*

FINANCIAL STATEMENTS FOR A PARTNERSHIP

A business organized as a partnership prepares four financial statements to report financial progress and condition. A partnership prepares an income statement and a balance sheet similar to those used by a proprietorship. A partnership also prepares two additional financial statements. One statement reports the distribution of net income or net loss for each partner. The other statement reports the changes in owners' equity for the fiscal period.

INCOME STATEMENT

An income statement is prepared using a completed work sheet.

An income statement is used to report a business' financial progress. Merchandising businesses report revenue, cost of merchandise sold, gross profit on sales, expenses, and net income or loss. Current and previous income statements can be compared to determine the reasons for increases or decreases in net income. This comparison is helpful in making management decisions about future operations.

Preparing an Income Statement

Information from a completed work sheet is used to prepare an income statement. CarLand's income statement information on a work sheet for the year ended December 31 is shown in Illustration 17-1 on page 412.

The income statement of a merchandising business has three main sections. (1) Revenue section. (2) Cost of merchandise sold section. (3) Expenses section. The total original price of all merchandise sold during a fiscal period is called the **cost of merchandise sold**. *(CONCEPT: Historical Cost)* Cost of merchandise sold is

ILLUSTRATION 17-1   Income statement information on a work sheet

		1	2	3	4	5	6	7	8
	ACCOUNT TITLE	TRIAL BALANCE		ADJUSTMENTS		INCOME STATEMENT		BALANCE SHEET	
		DEBIT	CREDIT	DEBIT	CREDIT	DEBIT	CREDIT	DEBIT	CREDIT
4	Merchandise Inventory	225400 00			(a)13200 00			212200 00		4
22	Sales		352600 00				352600 00			22
23	Purchases	158300 00				158300 00				23
24	Advertising Expense	5500 00				5500 00				24
25	Credit Card Fee Expense	2890 00				2890 00				25
26	Insurance Expense			(d)2640 00		2640 00				26
27	Miscellaneous Expense	2182 15				2182 15				27
28	Payroll Taxes Expense	7299 75				7299 75				28
29	Rent Expense	18000 00				18000 00				29
30	Salary Expense	60153 00				60153 00				30
31	Supplies Expense—Office			(b)3940 00		3940 00				31
32	Supplies Expense—Store			(c)3260 00		3260 00				32
33	Utilities Expense	3180 00				3180 00				33
34		569790 47	569790 47	23040 00	23040 00	280544 90	352600 00	289245 57	217190 47	34
35	Net Income					72055 10			72055 10	35
36						352600 00	352600 00	289245 57	289245 57	36
37										37

sometimes known as cost of goods sold or cost of sales. CarLand's completed income statement is shown in Illustration 17-2.

CarLand uses seven steps in preparing an income statement.

1 Write the income statement heading on three lines.

2 Prepare the revenue section. Use the information from the Income Statement Credit column of the work sheet.

- Write the name of this section, *Revenue:*, at the extreme left of the wide column on the first line.
- Write the title of the revenue account, Sales, on the next line, indented about one centimeter.
- Write the balance of the sales account, *$352,600.00*, in the second amount column. For CarLand, this amount is also the total of the revenue section.

    For businesses with more than one source of revenue, each revenue account title is listed in the wide column. Each account balance is written in the first amount column. The words *Total Revenue* are written in the wide column on the next line below the last revenue account title. The total amount of revenue is written in the second amount column.

3 Prepare the cost of merchandise sold section.

- Write the name of this section, *Cost of Merchandise Sold:*, at the extreme left of the wide column.

Every financial form has a three-line heading.

ILLUSTRATION 17-2 Income statement for a merchandising business

CarLand				
Income Statement				
For Year Ended December 31, 19--				
				% OF SALES
Revenue:				
Sales			352 600 00	100.0
Cost of Merchandise Sold:				
Merchandise Inventory, January 1, 19--	225 400 00			
Purchases	158 300 00			
Total Cost of Mdse. Available for Sale	383 700 00			
Less Mdse. Inventory, December 31, 19--	212 200 00			
Cost of Merchandise Sold			171 500 00	48.6
Gross Profit on Sales			181 100 00	51.4
Expenses:				
Advertising Expense	5 500 00			
Credit Card Fee Expense	2 890 00			
Insurance Expense	2 640 00			
Miscellaneous Expense	2 182 15			
Payroll Taxes Expense	7 299 75			
Rent Expense	18 000 00			
Salary Expense	60 153 00			
Supplies Expense—Office	3 940 00			
Supplies Expense—Store	3 260 00			
Utilities Expense	3 180 00			
Total Expenses			109 044 90	30.9
Net Income			72 055 10	20.4

- Indent about one centimeter on the next line, and write the items needed to calculate cost of merchandise sold. Write the amount of each item in the first amount column.

Beginning merchandise inventory, January 1 . . . . . . $ 225,400.00
(This amount is the debit balance of Merchandise Inventory in the Trial Balance Debit column of the work sheet.)

Plus purchases made during the fiscal period . . . . . . +158,300.00
(This amount is the debit balance of Purchases in the Income Statement Debit column of the work sheet.)

Equals total cost of merchandise available for sale during the fiscal period. . . . . $ 383,700.00

Less ending merchandise inventory, December 31 . . −212,200.00
(This amount is the debit balance of Merchandise Inventory in the Balance Sheet Debit column of the work sheet.)

Equals cost of merchandise sold during the fiscal period. . . . . $ 171,500.00

- Indent about one centimeter on the next line, and write the words *Cost of Merchandise Sold.* Write the cost of merchandise sold amount, *$171,500.00,* in the second amount column.

4 Calculate the gross profit on sales. The revenue remaining after cost of merchandise sold has been deducted is called **gross profit on sales.**

- Write the words *Gross Profit on Sales* on the next line at the extreme left of the wide column.
- Write the gross profit on sales amount, *$181,100.00,* in the second amount column. (Total revenue, $352,600.00, *less* cost of merchandise sold, $171,500.00, *equals* gross profit on sales, $181,100.00.)

5 Prepare the expenses section. Use the information from the Income Statement Debit column of the work sheet.

- Write the name of this section, *Expenses:*, at the extreme left of the wide column.
- Indent about one centimeter on the next line, and list the expense account titles in the order in which they appear on the work sheet. Write the amount of each expense account balance in the first amount column.
- Indent about one centimeter, and write the words *Total Expenses* on the next line in the wide column below the last expense account title. Total the individual expense amounts and write the total, *$109,044.90,* in the second amount column on the total line.

6 Calculate the net income.

- Write the words *Net Income* on the next line at the extreme left of the wide column.
- Write the net income amount, *$72,055.10,* in the second amount column on the net income line. (Gross profit on sales, $181,100.00, *less* total expenses, $109,044.90, *equals* net income, $72,055.10.)

   Verify accuracy by comparing the amount of net income calculated on the income statement, $72,055.10, with the amount on the work sheet, $72,055.10. The two amounts must be the same.

7 Rule double lines across both amount columns to show that the income statement has been verified as correct.

Amounts are listed in the first amount column of the financial statement and totaled in the second column. These are amount columns, not debit and credit columns.

Analyzing an Income Statement Showing a Net Income

For a merchandising business, every sales dollar reported on the income statement includes four components. (1) Cost of merchandise sold. (2) Gross profit on sales. (3) Total expenses. (4) Net income. To help make decisions about future operations, CarLand analyzes relationships between these four income statement com-

INTERNATIONAL TELEPHONE COMMUNICATION

When placing direct telephone or fax calls to the United States and Canada, a simple system is followed. Each telephone number is preceded by a "1," which allows direct dialing without the assistance of an operator. The number is then followed by a three-digit area code and a 7-digit telephone number as shown below:

```
1        XXX      XXX-XXXX
Direct   Area     Telephone
Dial     Code     Number
```

However, when calling other countries, the procedure is somewhat more involved. It is necessary to first dial the International Access Code, which is "011." This International Access Code allows you to dial a foreign country direct without the assistance of an operator.

The next set of digits that follows is the country code. Every country in the world has a country code. The country code can be one or more digits.

The country code is then followed by a city code. The city code can also be one or more digits. This is then followed by the telephone number of the receiving party as follows:

```
011           XX       XX     XXX-XXXX
International
Access        Country  City   Local
Code          Code     Code   Number
```

Not all countries have direct dialing. So before making international phone calls, you should check with your local telephone company for information.

The chart below illustrates selected country codes and city codes.

CITY	COUNTRY CODE	CITY CODE
London, England (inner city)	44	71
Frankfurt, Germany	49	69
Keelung, Taiwan	886	32
Barcelona, Spain	34	3
Innsbruck, Austria	43	5222
Helsinki, Finland	358	0
Athens, Greece	30	1
Canberra, Australia	61	62
Cape Town, South Africa	27	21
Oslo, Norway	47	2

ponents and sales. The percentage relationship between one financial statement item and the total that includes that item is known as a component percentage. On an income statement, component percentages are calculated by dividing the amount of each component by the amount of sales. CarLand calculates a component percentage for cost of merchandise sold, gross profit on sales, total expenses, and net income. The relationship between each component and sales is shown in a separate column on the income statement.

Acceptable Component Percentages

FYI

Unacceptable component percentages serve as a warning that management action is necessary.

For a component percentage to be useful, a business must know acceptable percentages. This information is determined by making comparisons with prior fiscal periods as well as with industry standards that are published by industry organizations. Based on these sources, CarLand determines the acceptable component percentages shown in the following table.

Income Statement Items	Acceptable Component Percentages	Actual Component Percentages
Sales	100.0%	100.0%
Cost of merchandise sold	not more than 50.0%	48.6%
Gross profit on sales	not less than 50.0%	51.4%
Total expenses	not more than 32.0%	30.9%
Net income	not less than 18.0%	20.4%

Each percentage represents the amount of each sales dollar that is considered acceptable. For example, CarLand determines that no more than 50 cents, or 50.0%, of each sales dollar should be devoted to cost of merchandise sold.

Cost of Merchandise Sold Component Percentage. The cost of merchandise sold is a major cost. Therefore, this cost must be kept as low as possible. Analysis of CarLand's income statement, Illustration 17-2, shows that the cost of merchandise sold is 48.6% of sales. This component percentage is calculated as shown below.

Cost of Merchandise Sold	÷	Sales	=	Cost of Merchandise Sold Component Percentage
$171,500.00	÷	$352,600.00	=	48.6%

The component percentage for cost of merchandise sold, 48.6%, is *less than* the maximum acceptable percentage, 50.0%. Therefore, CarLand's component percentage for cost of merchandise sold is considered acceptable.

Gross Profit on Sales Component Percentage. Gross profit must be large enough to cover total expenses and the desired amount of net income. CarLand determines that at least 50 cents, or 50.0%, of each sales dollar should result in gross profit. Analysis of Car-Land's income statement shows that the component percentage for gross profit on sales is 51.4%. This component percentage is calculated as shown below.

Gross Profit on Sales	÷	Sales	=	Gross Profit on Sales Component Percentage
$181,100.00	÷	$352,600.00	=	51.4%

The component percentage for gross profit on sales, 51.4%, is *not less than* the minimum acceptable percentage, 50.0%. Therefore, CarLand's component percentage for gross profit on sales is considered acceptable.

Negative amounts are written in parentheses.

Total Expenses Component Percentage. Total expenses must be less than gross profit on sales to provide a desirable net income. CarLand determines that no more than 32 cents, or 32.0%, of each sales dollar should be devoted to total expenses. Analysis of Car-

Land's income statement shows that the component percentage for total expenses is 30.9%. This component percentage is calculated as shown below.

	Total Expenses	÷	Sales	=	Total Expenses Component Percentage
	$109,044.90	÷	$352,600.00	=	30.9%

The component percentage for total expenses, 30.9%, is *not more than* the maximum acceptable percentage, 32.0%. Therefore, CarLand's component percentage for total expenses is considered acceptable.

Net Income Component Percentage. The component percentage for net income shows the progress being made by a business. CarLand determines that at least 18 cents, or 18.0%, of each sales dollar should result in net income. Analysis of CarLand's income statement shows that the component percentage for net income is 20.4%. This component percentage is calculated as shown below.

	Net Income	÷	Sales	=	Net Income Component Percentage
	$72,055.10	÷	$352,600.00	=	20.4%

The component percentage for net income, 20.4%, is *not less than* the minimum acceptable percentage, 18.0%. Therefore, CarLand's component percentage for net income is considered acceptable.

Analyzing an Income Statement Showing a Net Loss

When a business' total expenses are greater than the gross profit on sales, the difference is known as a net loss. For example, the income statement shown in Illustration 17-3 on page 418 shows a net loss of $3,770.00 for the fiscal period.

Total expenses, $109,120.00, *less* gross profit on sales, $105,350.00, *equals* net loss, $3,770.00. The net loss amount, *$3,770.00*, is written in parentheses in the second amount column on the line with the words *Net Loss*. An amount written in parentheses on a financial statement indicates a negative amount.

Autoworks uses the same acceptable component percentages as CarLand. Analysis of the income statement, Illustration 17-3, indicates unacceptable component percentages. (1) The component percentage for cost of merchandise sold, 53.3%, is *more than* the maximum acceptable component percentage, 50.0%. (2) The component percentage for gross profit on sales, 46.7%, is *less than* the minimum acceptable component percentage, 50.0%. (3) The component percentage for total expenses, 48.4%, is *more than* the maximum acceptable component percentage, 32.0%. (4) Because a net

The Uniform Partnership Act is a law that governs partnerships in most states.

loss occurred, the component percentage for net income, (1.67%), means that Autoworks lost 1.67 cents on each sales dollar. The net loss amount, $3,770.00, is considered unacceptable.

ILLUSTRATION 17-3   Income statement showing a net loss

Autoworks Income Statement For Year Ended December 31, 19--			% OF SALES
Revenue:			
Sales		225 40 0 00	100.0
Cost of Merchandise Sold:			
Merchandise Inventory, January 1, 19--	243 20 0 00		
Purchases	138 90 0 00		
Total Cost of Mdse. Available for Sale	382 10 0 00		
Less Mdse. Inventory, December 31, 19--	262 05 0 00		
Cost of Merchandise Sold		120 05 0 00	53.3
Gross Profit on Sales		105 35 0 00	46.7
Expenses:			
Advertising Expense	5 20 0 00		
Credit Card Fee Expense	3 12 0 00		
Insurance Expense	1 05 0 00		
Miscellaneous Expense	2 39 0 00		
Payroll Taxes Expense	8 34 0 00		
Rent Expense	14 40 0 00		
Salary Expense	62 31 0 00		
Supplies Expense—Office	4 62 0 00		
Supplies Expense—Store	4 28 0 00		
Utilities Expense	3 41 0 00		
Total Expenses		109 12 0 00	48.4
Net Loss		(3 77 0 00)	(1.67)

Actions to Correct Unacceptable Component Percentages

The goal of any business is to earn an acceptable net income. When component percentages are not acceptable, regardless of whether a net income or net loss occurred, management action is necessary.

Unacceptable Component Percentage for Gross Profit on Sales. The component percentage for gross profit on sales is directly related to sales revenue and cost of merchandise sold. An unacceptable component percentage for gross profit on sales requires one of three actions. (1) Increase sales revenue. (2) Decrease cost of merchandise sold. (3) Increase sales revenue and also decrease cost of merchandise sold.

Increasing sales revenue while keeping the cost of merchandise sold the same will increase gross profit on sales. To increase sales

revenue, management may consider increasing the markup on merchandise purchased for sale. However, a business must be cautious on the amount of the markup increase. If the increase in markup is too large, a decrease in sales revenue could occur for two reasons. (1) The sales price is beyond what customers are willing to pay. (2) The sales price is higher than what competing businesses charge for the same merchandise.

Decreasing the cost of merchandise sold while keeping the sales revenue the same will also increase gross profit on sales. To decrease cost of merchandise sold, management should review purchasing practices. For example, would purchasing merchandise in larger quantities or from other vendors result in a lower cost?

Combining a small increase in sales revenue and a small decrease in the cost of merchandise sold may also result in an acceptable component percentage for gross profit on sales.

Unacceptable Component Percentage for Total Expenses. Each expense account balance must be reviewed to determine if major increases have occurred. This review should include comparisons with prior fiscal periods as well as with industry standards. Actions must then be taken to reduce any expenses for which major increases have occurred or that are beyond industry standards.

Unacceptable Component Percentage for Net Income. If the component percentages for cost of merchandise sold, gross profit on sales, and total expenses are brought within acceptable ranges, net income will also be acceptable.

DISTRIBUTION OF NET INCOME STATEMENT

Partnerships must file tax returns with the IRS to report how income was divided among the partners.

A partnership's net income or net loss may be divided in any way agreed upon by the partners. Amy Kramer and Dario Mesa, partners in CarLand, agreed to share net income or net loss equally.

A partnership distribution of net income or net loss is usually shown on a separate financial statement. A partnership financial statement showing net income or loss distribution to partners is called a **distribution of net income statement.**

Preparing a Distribution of Net Income Statement

The net income, $72,055.10, from the income statement shown in Illustration 17-2 is used to prepare the distribution of net income statement. CarLand's distribution of net income statement is shown in Illustration 17-4 on page 420.

CarLand uses seven steps in preparing a distribution of net income statement.

1 Write the heading of the distribution of net income statement on three lines.

ILLUSTRATION 17-4 Distribution of net income statement for a partnership

CarLand				
Distribution of Net Income Statement				
For Year Ended December 31, 19--				
Amy Kramer				
50.0% of Net Income	36	0 2 7	55	
Dario Mesa				
50.0% of Net Income	36	0 2 7	55	
Net Income	72	0 5 5	10	

2 Write one partner's name, *Amy Kramer,* on the first line at the extreme left of the wide column.

3 Indent about one centimeter on the next line, and write Amy Kramer's share of net income as a percentage, *50.0% of Net Income.* Write Miss Kramer's share of net income, *$36,027.55* (50.0% × $72,055.10), in the amount column on the same line.

4 Write the other partner's name, *Dario Mesa,* on the next line at the extreme left of the wide column.

5 Indent about one centimeter on the next line, and write Dario Mesa's share of net income as a percentage, *50.0% of Net Income.* Write Mr. Mesa's share of net income, *$36,027.55* (50.0% × $72,055.10), in the amount column on the same line.

6 Write the words *Net Income* on the next line at the extreme left of the wide column. Add the distribution of net income for Amy Kramer, $36,027.55, and for Dario Mesa, $36,027.55. Write the total amount, *$72,055.10,* in the amount column. Verify accuracy by comparing the total amount, $72,055.10, with the net income reported on the income statement, $72,055.10. The two amounts must be the same.

7 Rule double lines across the amount column to show that the distribution of net income statement has been verified as correct.

Distribution of Net Income Statement with Unequal Distribution of Earnings

Regardless of how earnings are shared, the steps in preparing a distribution of net income statement are the same. The only difference is the description of how

Audit Your Understanding

1. What is the major difference between the income statement for a merchandising business and a service business?

2. How is the cost of merchandise sold calculated?

3. How can the amount of net income calculated on the income statement be verified?

4. What is the result if total expenses are greater than gross profit on sales?

the earnings are to be shared by the partners. A distribution of net income statement with unequal shares of earnings is shown in Illustration 17-5.

ILLUSTRATION 17-5

Distribution of net income statement with unequal distribution of earnings

Central Sporting Goods		
Distribution of Net Income Statement		
For Year Ended December 31, 19--		
Dolores Demski		
60.0% of Net Income	40 8 0 0 00	
Linda Kemp		
40.0% of Net Income	27 2 0 0 00	
Net Income	68 0 0 0 00	

Dolores Demski and Linda Kemp are partners in a business. Because Mrs. Demski spends more time in the business than Ms. Kemp, the partners agree to share net income or loss unequally. Mrs. Demski gets 60.0% of net income or loss. Ms. Kemp gets 40.0% of net income or loss. With a net income of $68,000.00, Mrs. Demski receives 60.0%, or $40,800.00. Ms. Kemp receives 40.0%, or $27,200.00.

OWNERS' EQUITY STATEMENT

The amount of net income earned is important to business owners. Owners are also interested in changes that occur in owners' equity during a fiscal period. A financial statement that summarizes the changes in owners' equity during a fiscal period is called an **owners' equity statement**. Business owners can review an owners' equity statement to determine if owners' equity is increasing or decreasing and what is causing the change. Three factors can change owners' equity. (1) Additional investments. (2) Withdrawals. (3) Net income or net loss.

Preparing an Owners' Equity Statement

An owners' equity statement shows information about changes during a fiscal period in each partner's capital. Information needed to prepare an owners' equity statement is obtained from the distribution of net income statement and the general ledger capital and drawing accounts. The distribution of net income statement shows each partner's share of net income or net loss. Three kinds of information are obtained from each partner's capital and drawing account. (1) Beginning capital amount. (2) Any additional investments made during the fiscal period. (3) Each partner's withdrawal of assets during the fiscal period.

The general ledger capital and drawing accounts of Amy Kramer and Dario Mesa, partners, are shown in Illustration 17-6 on page 422.

ILLUSTRATION 17-6 Partners' capital and drawing accounts

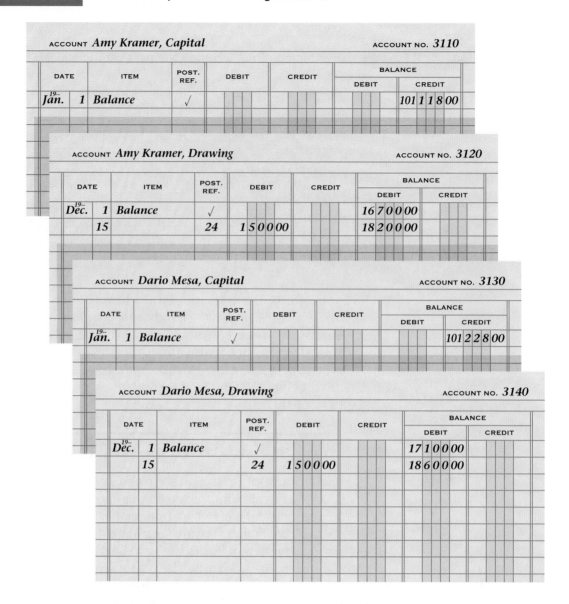

ACCOUNT *Amy Kramer, Capital* ACCOUNT NO. *3110*

DATE		ITEM	POST. REF.	DEBIT	CREDIT	BALANCE	
						DEBIT	CREDIT
Jan.	1	Balance	✓				101 1 1 8 00

ACCOUNT *Amy Kramer, Drawing* ACCOUNT NO. *3120*

DATE		ITEM	POST. REF.	DEBIT	CREDIT	BALANCE	
						DEBIT	CREDIT
Dec.	1	Balance	✓			16 7 0 0 00	
	15		24	1 5 0 0 00		18 2 0 0 00	

ACCOUNT *Dario Mesa, Capital* ACCOUNT NO. *3130*

DATE		ITEM	POST. REF.	DEBIT	CREDIT	BALANCE	
						DEBIT	CREDIT
Jan.	1	Balance	✓				101 2 2 8 00

ACCOUNT *Dario Mesa, Drawing* ACCOUNT NO. *3140*

DATE		ITEM	POST. REF.	DEBIT	CREDIT	BALANCE	
						DEBIT	CREDIT
Dec.	1	Balance	✓			17 1 0 0 00	
	15		24	1 5 0 0 00		18 6 0 0 00	

Neither Amy Kramer nor Dario Mesa invested any additional capital during the year ended December 31. The beginning and ending capital balances, therefore, are the same as recorded in the accounts on January 1. Both partners withdrew cash and merchandise during the year ended December 31.

CarLand's owners' equity statement, prepared for the year ended December 31, is shown in Illustration 17-7.

CarLand uses seven steps in preparing an owners' equity statement.

1 Write the heading of the owners' equity statement on three lines.

2 Write the name, *Amy Kramer,* on the first line at the extreme left of the wide column.

3 Calculate the net increase in capital for Amy Kramer.

ILLUSTRATION 17-7   Owners' equity statement

CarLand							
Owners' Equity Statement							
For Year Ended December 31, 19--							
Amy Kramer							
Capital, January 1, 19--				101 1 1 8 00			
Share of Net Income	36 0 2 7 55						
Less Withdrawals	18 2 0 0 00						
Net Increase in Capital				17 8 2 7 55			
Capital, December 31, 19--						118 9 4 5 55	
Dario Mesa							
Capital, January 1, 19--				101 2 2 8 00			
Share of Net Income	36 0 2 7 55						
Less Withdrawals	18 6 0 0 00						
Net Increase in Capital				17 4 2 7 55			
Capital, December 31, 19--						118 6 5 5 55	
Total Owners' Equity, December 31, 19--						237 6 0 1 10	

- Indent about one centimeter on the next line, and write the words *Capital, January 1, 19--.* Write the beginning capital amount, *$101,118.00,* in the second amount column on the same line. (This amount is obtained from Miss Kramer's capital account in the general ledger.)

- Indent about one centimeter on the next line, and write the words *Share of Net Income.* On the same line, write Miss Kramer's share of net income amount, *$36,027.55,* in the first amount column. (This amount is obtained from the distribution of net income statement.)

- Indent about one centimeter on the next line, and write the words *Less Withdrawals.* On the same line, write the withdrawals amount, *$18,200.00,* in the first amount column. (This amount is obtained from Miss Kramer's drawing account in the general ledger.)

- Indent about one centimeter on the next line, and write the words *Net Increase in Capital.* Write the net increase in capital amount, *$17,827.55,* on the same line in the second amount column. (The share of net income, $36,027.55, *less* withdrawals, $18,200.00, *equals* the net increase in capital, $17,827.55.)

- Indent about one centimeter on the next line, and write the words *Capital, December 31, 19--.* Write the December 31 capital amount, *$118,945.55,* on the same line in the third amount column. (The January 1 capital, $101,118.00, *plus* the net increase in capital, $17,827.55, *equals* the December 31 capital, $118,945.55.)

4 Write the name, *Dario Mesa,* on the next line at the extreme left of the wide column.

5 Calculate the net increase in capital for Dario Mesa.

- Indent about one centimeter on the next line, and write the words *Capital, January 1, 19--.* On the same line, write the beginning capital amount, *$101,228.00,* in the second amount column.

- Indent about one centimeter on the next line, and write the words *Share of Net Income.* On the same line, write Mr. Dario's share of net income amount, *$36,027.55,* in the first amount column.

- Indent about one centimeter on the next line, and write the words *Less Withdrawals.* On the same line, write the withdrawals amount, *$18,600.00,* in the first amount column.

- Indent about one centimeter on the next line, and write the words *Net Increase in Capital.* On the same line, write the difference, *$17,427.55,* in the second amount column.

- Indent about one centimeter on the next line, and write the words *Capital, December 31, 19--.* On the same line, write the December 31 capital amount, *$118,655.55,* in the third amount column.

6 Write the words *Total Owners' Equity, December 31, 19--* on the next line at the extreme left of the wide column. On the same line, write the total amount, *$237,601.10,* in the third amount column.

7 Rule double lines across the three amount columns to show that the totals have been verified as correct.

Some businesses include the owners' equity statement information as part of the balance sheet. An example of this method of reporting changes in owner's equity is shown in Illustration 9-13, Chapter 9.

Owners' Equity Statement with an Additional Investment and a Net Loss

On December 31 the capital accounts of Kevin Blaine and David Lamont showed additional investments of $10,000.00 each. Also, the income statement, Illustration 17-3, showed a net loss of $3,770.00. The partners agreed to share net income or net loss equally. The owners' equity statement for Autoworks is shown in Illustration 17-8.

BALANCE SHEET

Some management decisions can best be made after owners have determined the amount of assets, liabilities, and owners' equity. Owners could obtain some of the information needed by inspect-

Autoworks									
Owners' Equity Statement									
For Year Ended December 31, 19--									
Kevin Blaine									
Capital, January 1, 19--	104 3 0 0 00							
Plus Additional Investment	10 0 0 0 00							
Total		114 3 0 0 00						
Share of Net Loss	1 8 8 5 00							
Plus Withdrawals	14 8 0 0 00							
Net Decrease in Capital		16 6 8 5 00						
Capital, December 31, 19--			97 6 1 5 00					
David Lamont									
Capital, January 1, 19--	102 8 0 0 00							
Plus Additional Investment	10 0 0 0 00							
Total		112 8 0 0 00						
Share of Net Loss	1 8 8 5 00							
Plus Withdrawals	15 1 0 0 00							
Net Decrease in Capital		16 9 8 5 00						
Capital, December 31, 19--			95 8 1 5 00					
Total Owners' Equity, December 31, 19--			193 4 3 0 00					

FYI

A balance sheet reports a business' financial condition on a specific date.

ing general ledger accounts. The information needed might also be found on a work sheet. However, the information is easier to use when organized and reported on a balance sheet. A balance sheet reports a business' financial condition on a specific date. A balance sheet may be prepared in account form or report form. Rugcare, described in Chapter 9, uses the account form. CarLand uses the report form.

Preparing a Balance Sheet

The information used to prepare a balance sheet is obtained from two sources. (1) The Balance Sheet columns of a work sheet, as shown in Illustration 17-9 on page 426. (2) The owners' equity statement, as shown in Illustration 17-7.

CarLand's completed balance sheet on December 31, the last day of the fiscal year, is shown in Illustration 17-10 on page 427.

CarLand uses six steps in preparing a balance sheet.

1 Write the balance sheet heading on three lines.

2 Prepare the assets section of the balance sheet. Use information from the work sheet given in Illustration 17-9.

- Write the section title, *Assets,* on the first line in the middle of the wide column.

- Beginning on the next line, at the extreme left of the wide column, write the asset account titles in the order in which

ILLUSTRATION 17-9 Balance sheet information on a work sheet

ACCOUNT TITLE	TRIAL BALANCE		ADJUSTMENTS		INCOME STATEMENT		BALANCE SHEET		
	DEBIT	CREDIT	DEBIT	CREDIT	DEBIT	CREDIT	DEBIT	CREDIT	
1 Cash	24 233 57						24 233 57		1
2 Petty Cash	500 00						500 00		2
3 Accounts Receivable	9 332 00						9 332 00		3
4 Merchandise Inventory	225 400 00			(a)13 200 00			212 200 00		4
5 Supplies—Office	5 400 00			(b) 3 940 00			1 460 00		5
6 Supplies—Store	5 780 00			(c) 3 260 00			2 520 00		6
7 Prepaid Insurance	4 840 00			(d) 2 640 00			2 200 00		7
8 Accounts Payable		10 451 90						10 451 90	8
9 Employee Income Tax Pay.		402 00						402 00	9
10 FICA Tax Payable		832 16						832 16	10
11 Sales Tax Payable		1 760 00						1 760 00	11
12 Unemploy. Tax Pay.—Fed.		59 15						59 15	12
13 Unemploy. Tax Pay.—State		399 26						399 26	13
14 Health Ins. Premiums Pay.		840 00						840 00	14
15 U.S. Savings Bonds Pay.		40 00						40 00	15
16 United Way Donations Pay.		60 00						60 00	16
17									17
18									18

they appear on the work sheet. Write the balance of each asset account in the first amount column.

- Write the words *Total Assets* on the next line below the last asset account title. Total the individual asset amounts, and write the total assets, *$252,445.57,* on the same line in the second amount column.

3 Prepare the liabilities section of the balance sheet. Use information from the work sheet given in Illustration 17-9.

- Write the section title, *Liabilities,* on the next line in the middle of the wide column.

- Beginning on the next line, at the extreme left of the wide column, write the liability account titles in the order in which they appear on the work sheet. Write the balance of each liability account in the first amount column.

- Write the words *Total Liabilities* on the next line below the last liability account title. Total the individual liability amounts, and write the total liabilities, *$14,844.47,* on the same line in the second amount column.

4 Prepare the owners' equity section of the balance sheet. Use information from the owners' equity statement given in Illustration 17-7.

- Write the section title, *Owners' Equity,* on the next line in the middle of the wide column.

- Write the account title, Amy Kramer, Capital, on the next line at the extreme left of the wide column. On the same line,

ILLUSTRATION 17-10   Balance sheet for a partnership

CarLand				
Balance Sheet				
December 31, 19--				
Assets				
Cash	24 2 3 3 57			
Petty Cash	5 0 0 00			
Accounts Receivable	9 3 3 2 00			
Merchandise Inventory	212 2 0 0 00			
Supplies—Office	1 4 6 0 00			
Supplies—Store	2 5 2 0 00			
Prepaid Insurance	2 2 0 0 00			
Total Assets		252 4 4 5 57		
Liabilities				
Accounts Payable	10 4 5 1 90			
Employee Income Tax Payable	4 0 2 00			
FICA Tax Payable	8 3 2 16			
Sales Tax Payable	1 7 6 0 00			
Unemployment Tax Payable—Federal	5 9 15			
Unemployment Tax Payable—State	3 9 9 26			
Health Insurance Premiums Payable	8 4 0 00			
U.S. Savings Bonds Payable	4 0 00			
United Way Donations Payable	6 0 00			
Total Liabilities		14 8 4 4 47		
Owners' Equity				
Amy Kramer, Capital	118 9 4 5 55			
Dario Mesa, Capital	118 6 5 5 55			
Total Owners' Equity		237 6 0 1 10		
Total Liabilities and Owners' Equity		252 4 4 5 57		

Verify accuracy of the balance sheet by comparing the total amount of assets and the total amount of liabilities and owner's equity. The two amounts must be the same.

write the amount of Amy Kramer's current capital, *$118,945.55,* in the first amount column.

- Write the account title, Dario Mesa, Capital, on the next line at the extreme left of the wide column. On the same line, write the amount of Dario Mesa's current capital, *$118,655.55,* in the first amount column.

- Write the words *Total Owners' Equity* on the next line at the extreme left of the wide column. Add the two capital amounts, and write the total, *$237,601.10,* on the same line in the second amount column.

5 Total the liabilities and owners' equity sections of the balance sheet.

- Write the words *Total Liabilities and Owners' Equity* on the next line at the extreme left of the wide column. Total the liabilities and owners' equity, and write the total, $252,445.57, on the same line in the second amount column.

Verify accuracy by comparing the total amount of assets and the total amount of liabilities and owners' equity. These two amounts must be the same. The two amounts, $252,445.57, are the same. The balance sheet is assumed to be correct.

6 Rule double lines across both amount columns below Total Assets and below Total Liabilities and Owners' Equity. These two sets of double lines show that the amounts have been verified as correct.

Supporting Schedules for a Balance Sheet

A report prepared to give details about an item on a principal financial statement is called a **supporting schedule**. A supporting schedule is sometimes referred to as a supplementary report or an exhibit.

CarLand prepares two supporting schedules to accompany the balance sheet. The supporting schedules are a schedule of accounts payable and a schedule of accounts receivable. A balance sheet shows only the accounts payable total amount. The account balance for each vendor is not shown. When detailed information is needed, a supporting schedule of accounts payable is prepared showing the balance for each vendor. A balance sheet also shows only the accounts receivable total amount. When information about the account balance for each customer is needed, a supporting schedule of accounts receivable is prepared. CarLand's supporting schedules on December 31 are similar to the supporting schedules for November 30 shown in Chapter 13.

The chart shown in Illustration 17-11 summarizes the financial statements for a partnership.

Summary of financial statements for a partnership

1 Information from the completed work sheet is used to prepare the income statement.

2 Information from the income statement is used to prepare the distribution of net income statement.

3 Information from the distribution of net income statement and the general ledger capital and drawing accounts is used to prepare the owners' equity statement.

4 Information from the completed work sheet and the owners' equity statement is used to prepare the balance sheet.

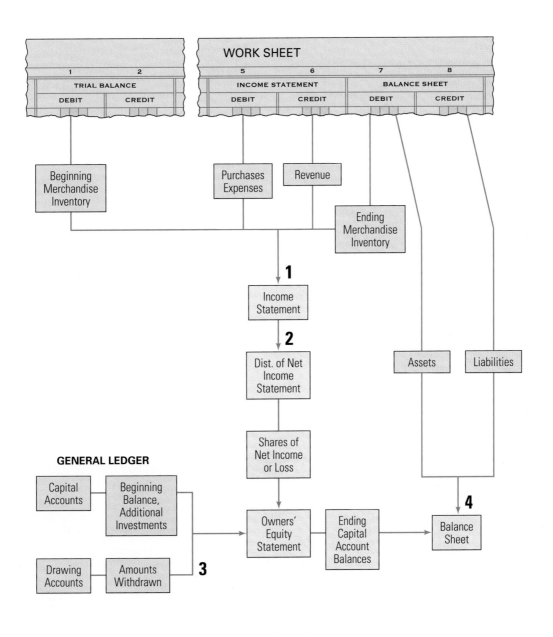

What is the meaning of each of the following?

1. **cost of merchandise sold**
2. **gross profit on sales**
3. **distribution of net income statement**
4. **owners' equity statement**
5. **supporting schedule**

1. Why is a work sheet prepared at the end of a fiscal period?
2. What is the primary source of information needed by owners and managers to make decisions on future activities of a business?
3. Which accounting concept is being applied when financial statements contain all information necessary for a reader to understand a business' financial condition and progress?
4. Which accounting concept is being applied when accounting principles are applied the same way in preparing financial statements from one fiscal period to the next?
5. Which financial statement reports the financial progress of a business?
6. How may income statements be used to determine reasons for increases or decreases in net income?
7. Where does a business find the information needed to prepare an income statement?
8. What are the three main sections of an income statement for a merchandising business?
9. How is the cost of merchandise sold calculated?
10. How is the gross profit on sales calculated?
11. How is net income calculated?
12. What four component percentages does CarLand calculate to analyze its income statement?
13. How does a business determine acceptable component percentages?
14. How is net loss calculated?
15. What are two reasons why an increase in markup could result in a decrease in sales revenue?
16. Why does a partnership prepare a distribution of net income statement?
17. Why do businesses prepare an owners' equity statement?
18. What three factors can cause changes in owners' equity to occur?
19. Where does a business find the information needed to prepare an owners' equity statement?
20. Which financial statement reports the financial condition of a business?

CASE 1   Jun Mori and Victoria Leben, partners, compared their current income statement with their income statement of a year ago. They noted that sales were 15.0% higher than a year ago. They also noted that the total expenses were 20.0% higher than a year ago. What type of analysis should be done to determine whether the increase in expenses is justified?

CASE 2   Rhoda Chalupa and Jonathan Fulton are partners in a paint and decorating store. The store operates on a yearly fiscal period. At the end of each year, an accountant is hired to prepare financial statements. At the end of each month during the year, Mrs. Chalupa prepares a work sheet. The work sheet is prepared to determine if the business made or lost money that month. The accountant suggests that monthly financial statements also be prepared. Mrs. Chalupa believes, however, that the monthly work sheet is sufficient to determine how the business is doing. Do you agree with Mrs. Chalupa or the accountant? Why?

A long written report should contain numerous headings. A heading enables the reader to focus on the primary idea of the next section. An outline is a special document that lists only the headings of a report. By reviewing an outline before and after reading a report, the reader can gain a better understanding of the relationship among the topics being presented.

Each chapter of this textbook is similar to a long report. Headings are used to separate and emphasize major concepts.

INSTRUCTIONS:

Prepare an outline of this chapter.

DRILLS FOR UNDERSTANDING

EPT(c,d,e)

DRILL 17-D1 Calculating the cost of merchandise sold

Information from the work sheets of three businesses is given in the working papers accompanying this textbook.

INSTRUCTIONS:

Calculate the cost of merchandise sold for each business.

DRILL 17-D2 Calculating net income or loss

Information from the work sheets of three businesses is given in the working papers accompanying this textbook.

INSTRUCTIONS:

Calculate the net income or loss for each business.

DRILL 17-D3 Calculating component percentages

Information from the income statements of three businesses is given in the working papers accompanying this textbook.

INSTRUCTIONS:

Calculate component percentages for cost of merchandise sold, gross profit on sales, total expenses, and net income for each business. Round percentage calculations to the nearest 0.1%.

DRILL 17-D4 Calculating the distribution of net income or loss

Information concerning net income or loss distribution for three businesses is given in the working papers accompanying this textbook.

INSTRUCTIONS:

1. Assume that each business earned a net income of $64,000.00. What is the amount of income to be distributed to each partner in each business?
2. Assume that each business had a net loss of $8,000.00. What is the amount of loss to be distributed to each partner in each business?

APPLICATION PROBLEMS

EPT(c,d,e,f,g)

PROBLEM 17-1 Preparing financial statements

The work sheet for Midwest Supply for the year ended December 31 of the current year is provided in the working papers accompanying this textbook.

INSTRUCTIONS:

1. Prepare an income statement. Calculate and record the following component percentages: (a) cost of merchandise sold, (b) gross profit on sales, (c) total expenses, and (d) net income or loss. Round percentage calculations to the nearest 0.1%.
2. Prepare a distribution of net income statement. Net income or loss is to be shared equally.
3. Prepare an owners' equity statement. No additional investments were made.
4. Prepare a balance sheet in report form.

PROBLEM 17-2 Preparing a distribution of net income statement and an owners' equity statement (net income)

Louise Cova and Diane Landon are partners in a merchandising business. The following information was taken from the records on December 31 of the current year.

Partner	Balance of Capital Account January 1	Balance of Drawing Account	Distribution of Net Income
Cova	$138,000.00	$15,260.00	60.0%
Landon	$124,000.00	$16,340.00	40.0%

INSTRUCTIONS:

1. On December 31 the partnership had a net income of $72,400.00. Prepare a distribution of net income statement for the partnership of C.L. Sales.
2. Prepare an owners' equity statement. No additional investments were made.

PROBLEM 17-3 Preparing an owners' equity statement (net loss)

Paul Chapman and Lawrence Jaffa are partners in a merchandising business. The following information was taken from the records on December 31 of the current year.

Partner	Balance of Capital Account	Balance of Drawing Account	Distribution of Net Loss
Chapman	$113,000.00	$12,680.00	$3,400.00
Jaffa	$107,000.00	$13,540.00	$3,400.00

INSTRUCTIONS:

Prepare an owners' equity statement for Riverside Supply. Additional investments made during the year: Paul Chapman, $11,000.00; Lawrence Jaffa, $9,000.00.

ENRICHMENT PROBLEMS

EPT(c,d,e,f,g)

MASTERY PROBLEM 17-M Preparing financial statements

Gallery Furniture prepared the work sheet on the following page for the year ended December 31 of the current year.

INSTRUCTIONS:

1. Prepare an income statement. Calculate and record the following component percentages: (a) cost of merchandise sold, (b) gross profit on sales, (c) total expenses, and (d) net income or loss. Round percentage calculations to the nearest 0.1%.

Gallery Furniture

Work Sheet

For Year Ended December 31, 19--

	ACCOUNT TITLE	TRIAL BALANCE DEBIT	TRIAL BALANCE CREDIT	ADJUSTMENTS DEBIT	ADJUSTMENTS CREDIT	INCOME STATEMENT DEBIT	INCOME STATEMENT CREDIT	BALANCE SHEET DEBIT	BALANCE SHEET CREDIT	
1	Cash	28 792 00						28 792 00		1
2	Petty Cash	500 00						500 00		2
3	Accounts Receivable	12 835 00						12 835 00		3
4	Merchandise Inventory	290 600 00			(a) 14 510 00			276 090 00		4
5	Supplies—Office	5 375 00			(b) 3 360 00			2 015 00		5
6	Supplies—Store	5 840 00			(c) 3 720 00			2 120 00		6
7	Prepaid Insurance	5 145 00			(d) 2 940 00			2 205 00		7
8	Accounts Payable		9 130 00						9 130 00	8
9	Sales Tax Payable		1 072 00						1 072 00	9
10	Jennifer Faust, Capital		142 960 00						142 960 00	10
11	Jennifer Faust, Drawing	18 910 00						18 910 00		11
12	David Mason, Capital		137 450 00						137 450 00	12
13	David Mason, Drawing	18 360 00						18 360 00		13
14	Income Summary			(a) 14 510 00		14 510 00				14
15	Sales		257 300 00				257 300 00			15
16	Purchases	129 280 00				129 280 00				16
17	Advertising Expense	5 585 00				5 585 00				17
18	Credit Card Fee Expense	2 360 00				2 360 00				18
19	Insurance Expense			(d) 2 940 00		2 940 00				19
20	Miscellaneous Expense	2 640 00				2 640 00				20
21	Rent Expense	19 200 00				19 200 00				21
22	Supplies Expense—Office			(b) 3 360 00		3 360 00				22
23	Supplies Expense—Store			(c) 3 720 00		3 720 00				23
24	Utilities Expense	2 490 00				2 490 00				24
25		547 912 00	547 912 00	24 530 00	24 530 00	186 085 00	257 300 00	361 827 00	290 612 00	25
26	Net Income					71 215 00			71 215 00	26
27						257 300 00	257 300 00	361 827 00	361 827 00	27
28										28

2. Prepare a distribution of net income statement. Net income or loss is to be shared equally.
3. Prepare an owners' equity statement. No additional investments were made.
4. Prepare a balance sheet in report form.

CHALLENGE PROBLEM 17-C Preparing financial statements (unequal distribution of net income; additional investment)

Gallery Furniture's work sheet is shown in Mastery Problem 17-M.

INSTRUCTIONS:

1. Prepare a distribution of net income statement. The net income is to be shared as follows: Jennifer Faust, 75.0%; David Mason, 25.0%.
2. Prepare an owners' equity statement. Mr. Mason made an additional investment of $15,000.00 during the year. He had a beginning capital of $122,450.00.

18

Recording Adjusting and Closing Entries for a Partnership

ENABLING PERFORMANCE TASKS

After studying Chapter 18, you will be able to:

a Identify accounting concepts and practices related to adjusting and closing entries for a merchandising business organized as a partnership.

b Record adjusting entries for a merchandising business organized as a partnership.

c Record closing entries for a merchandising business organized as a partnership.

d Prepare a post-closing trial balance for a merchandising business organized as a partnership.

General ledger account balances are changed only by posting journal entries. Two types of journal entries change general ledger account balances at the end of a fiscal period. (1) Adjusting entries bring general ledger account balances up to date. (2) Closing entries prepare temporary accounts for the next fiscal period. *(CONCEPT: Matching Expenses with Revenue)* Information needed for journalizing adjusting entries is taken from the Adjustments columns of a work sheet. Information needed for journalizing closing entries is taken from the Income Statement and Balance Sheet columns of a work sheet and a distribution of net income statement.

RECORDING ADJUSTING ENTRIES

Four adjustments in the partial work sheet's Adjustments columns are shown in Illustration 18-1.

ILLUSTRATION 18-1   Partial work sheet showing adjustments

| | | | | TRIAL BALANCE | | ADJUSTMENTS | |
	ACCOUNT TITLE			DEBIT	CREDIT	DEBIT	CREDIT
4	Merchandise Inventory			225 4 0 0 00			(a) 13 2 0 0 00
5	Supplies—Office			5 4 0 0 00			(b) 3 9 4 0 00
6	Supplies—Store			5 7 8 0 00			(c) 3 2 6 0 00
7	Prepaid Insurance			4 8 4 0 00			(d) 2 6 4 0 00
21	Income Summary					(a) 13 2 0 0 00	
26	Insurance Expense					(d) 2 6 4 0 00	
31	Supplies Expense—Office					(b) 3 9 4 0 00	
32	Supplies Expense—Store					(c) 3 2 6 0 00	
33							

Remember to start a new page for adjusting entries.

Adjusting entries are recorded on the next journal page following the page on which the last daily transaction for the month is recorded. The adjusting entries are entered in the General Debit and Credit columns of a journal. CarLand's four adjusting entries are recorded in a journal as shown in Illustration 18-2 on page 436.

The heading, *Adjusting Entries,* is written in the middle of the journal's Account Title column. This heading explains all of the adjusting entries that follow. Therefore, indicating a source document is unnecessary. The first adjusting entry is recorded on the first two lines below the heading.

Adjusting Entry for Merchandise Inventory

The debit and credit parts of the merchandise inventory adjustment are identified on the work sheet by the letter (a), Illustration 18-1.

ILLUSTRATION 18-2   Adjusting entries recorded in a journal

PAGE *26*

JOURNAL

	DATE		ACCOUNT TITLE	DOC. NO.	POST. REF.	GENERAL DEBIT	GENERAL CREDIT	ACCOUNTS RECEIVABLE DEBIT	ACCOUNTS RECEIVABLE CREDIT	
1			*Adjusting Entries*							1
2	*Dec.*	31	*Income Summary*			13 2 0 0 00				2
3			*Merchandise Inventory*				13 2 0 0 00			3
4		31	*Supplies Expense—Office*			3 9 4 0 00				4
5			*Supplies—Office*				3 9 4 0 00			5
6		31	*Supplies Expense—Store*			3 2 6 0 00				6
7			*Supplies—Store*				3 2 6 0 00			7
8		31	*Insurance Expense*			2 6 4 0 00				8
9			*Prepaid Insurance*				2 6 4 0 00			9

Income Summary

Adj. (a)	13,200.00	

Merchandise Inventory

Bal.	225,400.00	Adj. (a)	13,200.00
(New Bal.	212,200.00)		

The merchandise inventory adjustment includes a debit to Income Summary and a credit to Merchandise Inventory of $13,200.00.

CarLand's adjusting entry for merchandise inventory is shown on lines 2 and 3 of the journal, Illustration 18-2.

The effect of posting the adjusting entry for merchandise inventory is shown in the T accounts.

Adjusting Entry for Office Supplies Inventory

Supplies Expense—Office

Adj. (b)	3,940.00	

Supplies—Office

Bal.	5,400.00	Adj. (b)	3,940.00
(New Bal.	1,460.00)		

The debit and credit parts of the office supplies adjustment are identified on the work sheet by the letter (b), Illustration 18-1. The office supplies inventory adjustment includes a debit to Supplies Expense—Office and a credit to Supplies—Office of $3,940.00.

CarLand's adjusting entry for office supplies inventory is shown on lines 4 and 5 of the journal, Illustration 18-2.

The effect of posting the adjusting entry for office supplies inventory is shown in the T accounts.

Adjusting Entry for Store Supplies Inventory

Supplies Expense—Store

Adj. (c)	3,260.00	

Supplies—Store

Bal.	5,780.00	Adj. (c)	3,260.00
(New Bal.	2,520.00)		

The debit and credit parts of the store supplies adjustment are identified on the work sheet by the letter (c), Illustration 18-1. The store supplies inventory adjustment includes a debit to Supplies Expense—Store and a credit to Supplies—Store of $3,260.00.

CarLand's adjusting entry for store supplies inventory is shown on lines 6 and 7 of the journal, Illustration 18-2.

The effect of posting the adjusting entry for store supplies inventory is shown in the T accounts.

Adjusting Entry for Prepaid Insurance

The debit and credit parts of the prepaid insurance adjustment are identified on the work sheet by the letter (d), Illustration 18-1. The prepaid insurance adjustment includes a debit to Insurance Expense and a credit to Prepaid Insurance of $2,640.00.

CarLand's adjusting entry for prepaid insurance is shown on lines 8 and 9 of the journal, Illustration 18-2.

The effect of posting the adjusting entry for prepaid insurance is shown in the T accounts.

The four adjusting entries for a merchandising business organized as a partnership are summarized in Illustration 18-3.

Insurance Expense		
Adj. (d)	2,640.00	

Prepaid Insurance			
Bal.	4,840.00	Adj. (d)	2,640.00
(New Bal.	2,200.00)		

SUMMARY ILLUSTRATION 18-3

Summary of adjusting entries for a merchandising business organized as a partnership

Adjusting Entry	JOURNAL		
	Account Title	General	
		Debit	Credit
1. Adjust merchandise inventory (increase in inventory)	Merchandise Inventory Income Summary	X	X
(decrease in inventory)	Income Summary Merchandise Inventory	X	X
2. Adjust office supplies inventory	Supplies Expense—Office Supplies—Office	X	X
3. Adjust store supplies inventory	Supplies Expense—Store Supplies—Store	X	X
4. Adjust prepaid insurance	Insurance Expense Prepaid Insurance	X	X

RECORDING CLOSING ENTRIES

At the end of a fiscal period, the temporary accounts are closed to prepare the general ledger for the next fiscal period. *(CONCEPT: Matching Expenses with Revenue)* To close a temporary account, an amount equal to its balance is recorded on the side opposite the balance. CarLand records four kinds of closing entries.

1 An entry to close income statement accounts with credit balances.

2 An entry to close income statement accounts with debit balances.

3 An entry to record net income or loss and close the income summary account.

4 Entries to close the partners' drawing accounts.

The Income Summary Account

A temporary account is used to summarize the closing entries for revenue, cost, and expenses. The account is titled Income Summary because it is used to summarize information about net income. Income Summary is used only at the end of a fiscal period to help prepare other accounts for a new fiscal period. The income summary account is a unique account because it does not have a normal balance side.

Amounts needed for the closing entries are obtained from the Income Statement and Balance Sheet columns of the work sheet and from the distribution of net income statement.

Closing entries are recorded in the General Debit and Credit columns of a journal. The heading, *Closing Entries,* is written in the middle of the journal's Account Title column on the next line following the last adjusting entry. This heading explains all of the closing entries that follow. Therefore, indicating a source document is unnecessary. The first closing entry is recorded on the first two lines below the heading.

Closing Entry for an Income Statement Account with a Credit Balance

CarLand's work sheet has one income statement account with a credit balance, Sales, as shown in Illustration 18-4. This revenue account has a normal credit balance at the end of a fiscal period. This credit balance must be reduced to zero to prepare the account for the next fiscal period. *(CONCEPT: Matching Expenses with Revenue)* The closing entry for Sales is journalized as shown in Illustration 18-4.

To reduce the balance to zero, Sales is debited for the amount of the balance, $352,600.00. Income Summary is credited for $352,600.00 so that debits equal credits in this entry.

Sales			
Closing	352,600.00	Bal.	352,600.00
		(New Bal. zero)	

Income Summary			
Adj. (mdse. inv.)	13,200.00	Closing (revenue)	352,600.00

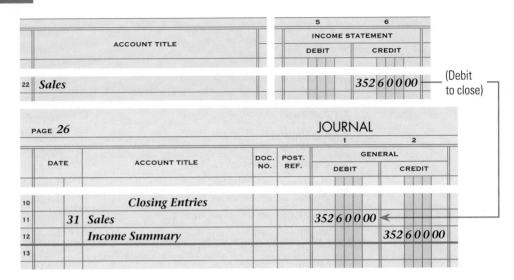

The effect of this closing entry on the general ledger accounts is shown in the T accounts.

The balance of **Sales** is now zero, and the account is ready for the next fiscal period.

Closing Entry for Income Statement Accounts with Debit Balances

The income summary account is used only at the end of the fiscal period to help prepare other accounts for a new fiscal period.

CarLand's work sheet has eleven income statement accounts with debit balances, as shown in Illustration 18-5 on page 440. These eleven accounts are the cost account, **Purchases**, and the ten expense accounts. The cost and expense accounts have normal debit balances at the end of a fiscal period. These debit balances must be reduced to zero to prepare the accounts for the next fiscal period. *(CONCEPT: Matching Expenses with Revenue)* To reduce the balances to zero, the cost and expense accounts are credited for the amount of their balances. The account used for the debit of this closing entry is **Income Summary**. The closing entry for the cost and expense accounts is journalized as shown in Illustration 18-5.

The income summary amount shown on the work sheet, $13,200.00, is the amount of the adjustment for merchandise inventory. **Income Summary** is used to summarize the amounts that contribute to net income. The adjustment for merchandise inventory contributes to net income. However, **Income Summary** is not closed as part of this closing entry. Instead, the account is closed with the third closing entry when net income is recorded.

The debit to **Income Summary** is not entered in the amount column until all cost and expense balances have been journalized and the total amount calculated. The account title and balance of each cost and expense account is written in the Account Title and General Credit columns. After all cost and expense accounts and their

	ACCOUNT TITLE	INCOME STATEMENT	
		5 DEBIT	**6** CREDIT
21	*Income Summary*	13 2 0 0 00	
22	*Sales*		352 6 0 0 00
23	*Purchases*	158 3 0 0 00	
24	*Advertising Expense*	5 5 0 0 00	
25	*Credit Card Fee Expense*	2 8 9 0 00	
26	*Insurance Expense*	2 6 4 0 00	
27	*Miscellaneous Expense*	2 1 8 2 15	
28	*Payroll Taxes Expense*	7 2 9 9 75	
29	*Rent Expense*	18 0 0 0 00	
30	*Salary Expense*	60 1 5 3 00	
31	*Supplies Expense—Office*	3 9 4 0 00	
32	*Supplies Expense—Store*	3 2 6 0 00	
33	*Utilities Expense*	3 1 8 0 00	

(Credit to close)

PAGE *26*   JOURNAL

	DATE	ACCOUNT TITLE	DOC. NO.	POST. REF.	GENERAL **1** DEBIT	GENERAL **2** CREDIT
13	31	*Income Summary*			267 3 4 4 90	
14		*Purchases*				158 3 0 0 00
15		*Advertising Expense*				5 5 0 0 00
16		*Credit Card Fee Expense*				2 8 9 0 00
17		*Insurance Expense*				2 6 4 0 00
18		*Miscellaneous Expense*				2 1 8 2 15
19		*Payroll Taxes Expense*				7 2 9 9 75
20		*Rent Expense*				18 0 0 0 00
21		*Salary Expense*				60 1 5 3 00
22		*Supplies Expense—Office*				3 9 4 0 00
23		*Supplies Expense—Store*				3 2 6 0 00
24		*Utilities Expense*				3 1 8 0 00

balances have been written in the journal, add the credit amounts for this entry. Write the total of the cost and expense accounts, $267,344.90, in the General Debit column on the same line as the account title Income Summary.

The effect of this closing entry on the general ledger accounts is shown in the T accounts on the following page.

The cost account, Purchases, and the expense accounts are now closed and have zero balances. Income Summary has three amounts. (1) A debit of $13,200.00, the amount of the merchandise inventory adjustment. (2) A credit of $352,600.00, the amount of the entry to close the revenue account. (3) A debit of $267,344.90, the total amount of the entry to close the cost and expense accounts. The balance of Income Summary is the net income for the fiscal period, $72,055.10.

FYI

When creating a partnership, the partners should write a business plan to outline the purposes and goals of the business.

Income Summary

Adj. (mdse. inv.)	13,200.00	Closing	
Closing (cost and expenses)	267,344.90	(revenue)	352,600.00
		(New Bal.	*72,055.10)*

Purchases

Bal.	158,300.00	Closing	158,300.00
(New Bal. zero)			

Rent Expense

Bal.	18,000.00	Closing	18,000.00
(New Bal. zero)			

Advertising Expense

Bal.	5,500.00	Closing	5,500.00
(New Bal. zero)			

Salary Expense

Bal.	60,153.00	Closing	60,153.00
(New Bal. zero)			

Credit Card Fee Expense

Bal.	2,890.00	Closing	2,890.00
(New Bal. zero)			

Supplies Expense—Office

Bal.	3,940.00	Closing	3,940.00
(New Bal. zero)			

Insurance Expense

Bal.	2,640.00	Closing	2,640.00
(New Bal. zero)			

Supplies Expense—Store

Bal.	3,260.00	Closing	3,260.00
(New Bal. zero)			

Miscellaneous Expense

Bal.	2,182.15	Closing	2,182.15
(New Bal. zero)			

Utilities Expense

Bal.	3,180.00	Closing	3,180.00
(New Bal. zero)			

Payroll Taxes Expense

Bal.	7,299.75	Closing	7,299.75
(New Bal. zero)			

Closing Entry to Record Net Income or Loss and Close the Income Summary Account

Income Summary

Adj. (mdse. inv.)	13,200.00	Closing	
Closing (cost and expenses)	267,344.90	(revenue)	352,600.00
Closing (net income)	72,055.10	*(New Bal. zero)*	

Amy Kramer, Capital

		Bal.	101,118.00
		Closing (net income)	36,027.55

Dario Mesa, Capital

		Bal.	101,228.00
		Closing (net income)	36,027.55

Net income increases the partners' equity and, therefore, must be credited to the partners' capital accounts. The share of the net income to be recorded for each partner is shown on the distribution of net income statement. The balance of the temporary account Income Summary must be reduced to zero to prepare the account for the next fiscal period. The distribution of net income statement and the closing entry to record net income and close Income Summary are shown in Illustration 18-6 on page 442. The effect of this closing entry on the general ledger accounts is shown in the T accounts.

The credits to the two partners' capital accounts, $36,027.55, record the partners' share of the net income. The debit to the income summary account, $72,055.10, reduces the account balance to zero and prepares the account for the next fiscal period.

If the business has a net loss, the partners' capital accounts are debited for their share of the net loss. Income Summary is credited for the total net loss.

CarLand		
Distribution of Net Income Statement		
For Year Ended December 31, 19--		
Amy Kramer		
50% share of net income	36 0 2 7 55	(Record net income in capital accounts)
Dario Mesa		
50% share of net income	36 0 2 7 55	
Net Income	72 0 5 5 10	(Close Income Summary)

PAGE 26   **JOURNAL**

	DATE	ACCOUNT TITLE	DOC. NO.	POST. REF.	GENERAL DEBIT	GENERAL CREDIT
25	31	Income Summary			72 0 5 5 10	
26		Amy Kramer, Capital				36 0 2 7 55
27		Dario Mesa, Capital				36 0 2 7 55
28						
29						
30						

Closing Entries for the Partners' Drawing Accounts

The partners' drawing accounts are temporary accounts and must begin each fiscal period with zero balances. Because withdrawals are neither a revenue, cost, nor expense, the drawing accounts are not closed through Income Summary. The drawing account balances are closed directly to the partners' capital accounts.

A partial work sheet and the closing entries for the partners' drawing accounts are shown in Illustration 18-7. The closing entry is on lines 28-31 of the journal.

The credits to Amy Kramer, Drawing and Dario Mesa, Drawing reduce the account balances to zero. The accounts are prepared for the next fiscal period. The debits to Amy Kramer, Capital and Dario Mesa, Capital reduce the balances of these accounts by the amount of the partners' withdrawals during the fiscal period.

The effect of these closing entries on the general ledger accounts is shown in the T accounts.

After the closing entry for the partners' drawing accounts, the balances of the partners' capital accounts are the same as reported in the owners' equity section of the balance sheet, Illustration 18-8 on page 444.

Amy Kramer, Capital

Closing (drawing)	18,200.00	Bal.	101,118.00
		Closing (net income)	36,027.55
		(New Bal.	*118,945.55)*

Amy Kramer, Drawing

Bal.	18,200.00	Closing	18,200.00
(New Bal. zero)			

Dario Mesa, Capital

Closing (drawing)	18,600.00	Bal.	101,228.00
		Closing (net income)	36,027.55
		(New Bal.	*118,655.55)*

Dario Mesa, Drawing

Bal.	18,600.00	Closing	18,600.00
(New Bal. zero)			

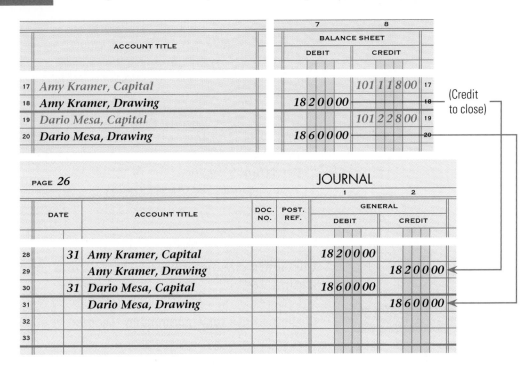

	ACCOUNT TITLE	BALANCE SHEET	
		DEBIT	CREDIT
17	*Amy Kramer, Capital*		101 1 18 00
18	**Amy Kramer, Drawing**	18 20 00 00	
19	*Dario Mesa, Capital*		101 2 28 00
20	**Dario Mesa, Drawing**	18 60 00 00	

(Credit to close)

PAGE 26   JOURNAL

	DATE	ACCOUNT TITLE	DOC. NO.	POST. REF.	GENERAL DEBIT	GENERAL CREDIT
28	31	**Amy Kramer, Capital**			18 20 00 00	
29		**Amy Kramer, Drawing**				18 20 00 00
30	31	**Dario Mesa, Capital**			18 60 00 00	
31		**Dario Mesa, Drawing**				18 60 00 00
32						
33						

■ Judy Sims ■

SOFTWARE SPECTRUM, GARLAND, TEXAS

Judy Sims chairs the Board of Directors and is Chief Executive Officer of Software Spectrum Inc., a company she co-founded in 1983. Software Spectrum is a leading national reseller of microcomputer software and a provider of technical services to large corporations.

Sims majored in accounting at Texas Tech University and worked as a C.P.A. for eleven years for national accounting firms. She advanced to the position of Audit Partner, and provided small and larger corporations with audit services. In 1983, she and two partners pooled $40,000 of personal funds and started Software Spectrum.

"The biggest lesson we learned early was to listen to the customer and quickly make changes in response to their needs," says Sims. "We started as a retail store selling education and entertainment software. But in the first six weeks, the cash register hardly ever rang. We then decided to focus on selling business software to corporations. These corporate customers wanted their software delivered and they wanted to buy it on account. So we changed our policies immediately."

Sims's advice to students is to set goals. She says that you should not just think about goals but actually write them down on paper and review them frequently. "The great thing about our country," says Sims, "is that there are only self-imposed limitations. Don't limit yourself—set high goals."

Sims reports that when the company's focus changed from retail to corporate software sales, they gave up their retail location in a shopping center. That store is now occupied by a business named "Positively Magic." Sims says that that is appropriate because "that initial location was positively magic for us—it was the launching pad for what has grown into a $219 million company."

Personal Visions in Business

ILLUSTRATION 18-8   Owner's equity section of a balance sheet

CarLand		
Balance Sheet		
December 31, 19--		
Owners' Equity		
Amy Kramer, Capital	118 9 4 5 55	
Dario Mesa, Capital	118 6 5 5 55	
Total Owners' Equity		237 6 0 1 10
Total Liabilities and Owners' Equity		252 4 4 5 57

CarLand's closing entries recorded in a journal are shown in Illustration 18-9.

ILLUSTRATION 18-9   Closing entries for a partnership recorded in a journal

PAGE 26 — JOURNAL

	DATE	ACCOUNT TITLE	DOC. NO.	POST. REF.	GENERAL DEBIT	GENERAL CREDIT	ACCOUNTS RECEIVABLE DEBIT	ACCOUNTS RECEIVABLE CREDIT	
10		*Closing Entries*							10
11	31	Sales			352 6 0 0 00				11
12		Income Summary				352 6 0 0 00			12
13	31	Income Summary			267 3 4 4 90				13
14		Purchases				158 3 0 0 00			14
15		Advertising Expense				5 5 0 0 00			15
16		Credit Card Fee Expense				2 8 9 0 00			16
17		Insurance Expense				2 6 4 0 00			17
18		Miscellaneous Expense				2 1 8 2 15			18
19		Payroll Taxes Expense				7 2 9 9 75			19
20		Rent Expense				18 0 0 0 00			20
21		Salary Expense				60 1 5 3 00			21
22		Supplies Expense—Office				3 9 4 0 00			22
23		Supplies Expense—Store				3 2 6 0 00			23
24		Utilities Expense				3 1 8 0 00			24
25	31	Income Summary			72 0 5 5 10				25
26		Amy Kramer, Capital				36 0 2 7 55			26
27		Dario Mesa, Capital				36 0 2 7 55			27
28	31	Amy Kramer, Capital			18 2 0 0 00				28
29		Amy Kramer, Drawing				18 2 0 0 00			29
30	31	Dario Mesa, Capital			18 6 0 0 00				30
31		Dario Mesa, Drawing				18 6 0 0 00			31

The closing entries for a merchandising business organized as a partnership are summarized in Illustration 18-10.

Closing Entry	JOURNAL		
	Account Title	General	
		Debit	Credit
1. Transfers income statement accounts with credit balances to Income Summary	Revenue account Income Summary	X	X
2. Transfers income statement accounts with debit balances to Income Summary	Income Summary Cost and expense accounts	X	X
3. Transfers net income or loss to partners' capital accounts and closes Income Summary	Income Summary Partners' capital accounts (net income)	X	X
	Partners' capital accounts Income Summary (net loss)	X	X
4. Transfers partners' drawing account balances to partners' capital accounts	Partners' capital accounts Partners' drawing accounts	X	X

CHECKING A GENERAL LEDGER'S ACCURACY AFTER POSTING ADJUSTING AND CLOSING ENTRIES

CarLand's 4-column general ledger account form has separate Balance Debit and Balance Credit columns. Each time an entry is posted to a general ledger account, the account balance is calculated. The balance is then recorded in the appropriate balance column. Each general ledger account shows its current balance at all times. When an account is closed, a short line is drawn in both the Balance Debit and Credit columns. The ending balance for one fiscal period is the beginning balance for the next fiscal period.

Completed General Ledger

CarLand's completed general ledger after adjusting and closing entries are posted is shown in Illustration 18-11 on pages 446 through 451.

Balance sheet accounts (asset, liability, and capital accounts) have up-to-date balances to begin the new fiscal period. Balances in the balance sheet accounts agree with the amounts on the balance sheet, Illustration 17-10, Chapter 17. General ledger account balances on

December 31 of one year are the beginning balances for January 1 of the next year.

Income statement accounts (revenue, cost, and expense accounts) have zero balances to begin the new fiscal period. *(CONCEPT: Matching Expenses with Revenue)*

ILLUSTRATION 18-11   General ledger after adjusting and closing entries are posted

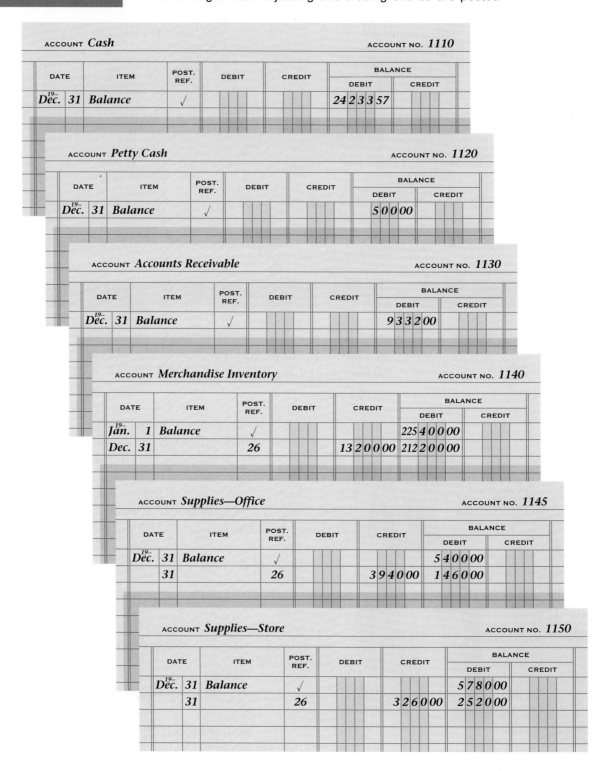

ACCOUNT *Prepaid Insurance*   ACCOUNT NO. *1160*

DATE		ITEM	POST. REF.	DEBIT	CREDIT	BALANCE	
						DEBIT	CREDIT
Dec.¹⁹⁻⁻	31	Balance	✓			4 8 4 0 00	
	31		26		2 6 4 0 00	2 2 0 0 00	

ACCOUNT *Accounts Payable*   ACCOUNT NO. *2110*

DATE		ITEM	POST. REF.	DEBIT	CREDIT	BALANCE	
						DEBIT	CREDIT
Dec.¹⁹⁻⁻	31	Balance	✓				10 4 5 1 90

ACCOUNT *Employee Income Tax Payable*   ACCOUNT NO. *2120*

DATE		ITEM	POST. REF.	DEBIT	CREDIT	BALANCE	
						DEBIT	CREDIT
Dec.¹⁹⁻⁻	31	Balance	✓				4 0 2 00

ACCOUNT *FICA Tax Payable*   ACCOUNT NO. *2130*

DATE		ITEM	POST. REF.	DEBIT	CREDIT	BALANCE	
						DEBIT	CREDIT
Dec.¹⁹⁻⁻	31	Balance	✓				8 3 2 16

ACCOUNT *Sales Tax Payable*   ACCOUNT NO. *2140*

DATE		ITEM	POST. REF.	DEBIT	CREDIT	BALANCE	
						DEBIT	CREDIT
Dec.¹⁹⁻⁻	31	Balance	✓				1 7 6 0 00

ACCOUNT *Unemployment Tax Payable—Federal*   ACCOUNT NO. *2150*

DATE		ITEM	POST. REF.	DEBIT	CREDIT	BALANCE	
						DEBIT	CREDIT
Dec.¹⁹⁻⁻	31	Balance	✓				5 9 15

ACCOUNT *Unemployment Tax Payable—State*   ACCOUNT NO. *2160*

DATE		ITEM	POST. REF.	DEBIT	CREDIT	BALANCE	
						DEBIT	CREDIT
Dec.¹⁹⁻⁻	31	Balance	✓				3 9 9 26

ACCOUNT *Health Insurance Premiums Payable*   ACCOUNT NO. *2170*

DATE	ITEM	POST. REF.	DEBIT	CREDIT	BALANCE DEBIT	BALANCE CREDIT
Dec.19-- 31	Balance	✓				8 4 0 00

ACCOUNT *U.S. Savings Bonds Payable*   ACCOUNT NO. *2180*

DATE	ITEM	POST. REF.	DEBIT	CREDIT	BALANCE DEBIT	BALANCE CREDIT
Dec.19-- 31	Balance	✓				4 0 00

ACCOUNT *United Way Donations Payable*   ACCOUNT NO. *2190*

DATE	ITEM	POST. REF.	DEBIT	CREDIT	BALANCE DEBIT	BALANCE CREDIT
Dec.19-- 31	Balance	✓				6 0 00

ACCOUNT *Amy Kramer, Capital*   ACCOUNT NO. *3110*

DATE	ITEM	POST. REF.	DEBIT	CREDIT	BALANCE DEBIT	BALANCE CREDIT
Dec.19-- 31	Balance	✓				101 1 1 8 00
31		26		36 0 2 7 55		137 1 4 5 55
31		26	18 2 0 0 00			118 9 4 5 55

ACCOUNT *Amy Kramer, Drawing*   ACCOUNT NO. *3120*

DATE	ITEM	POST. REF.	DEBIT	CREDIT	BALANCE DEBIT	BALANCE CREDIT
Dec.19-- 31	Balance	✓			18 2 0 0 00	
31		26		18 2 0 0 00	—	—

ACCOUNT *Dario Mesa, Capital*   ACCOUNT NO. *3130*

DATE	ITEM	POST. REF.	DEBIT	CREDIT	BALANCE DEBIT	BALANCE CREDIT
Dec.19-- 31	Balance	✓				101 2 2 8 00
31		26		36 0 2 7 55		137 2 5 5 55
31		26	18 6 0 0 00			118 6 5 5 55

ACCOUNT *Dario Mesa, Drawing*   ACCOUNT NO. *3140*

DATE	ITEM	POST. REF.	DEBIT	CREDIT	BALANCE DEBIT	BALANCE CREDIT
Dec.19-- 31	Balance	✓			18 6 0 0 00	
31		26		18 6 0 0 00		

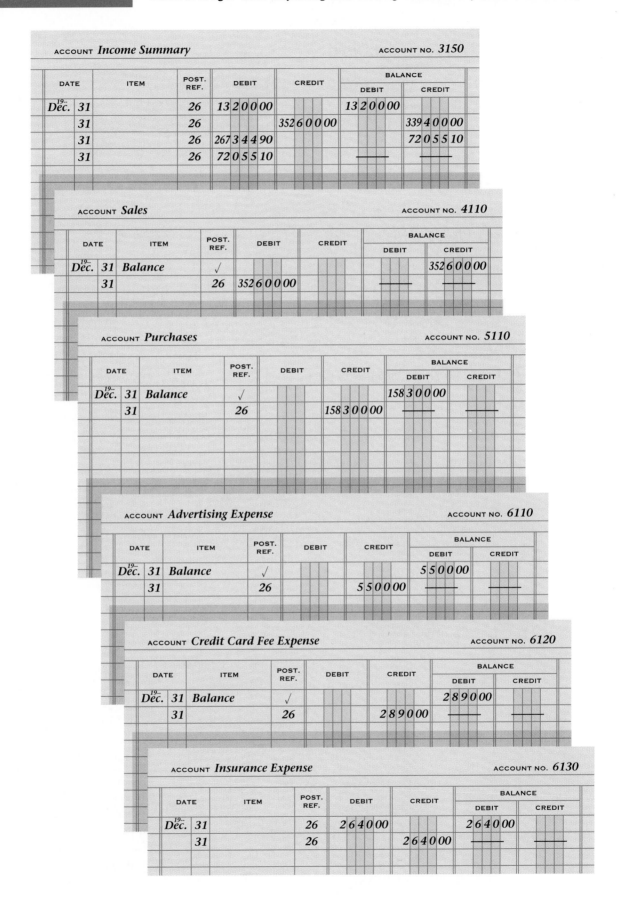

ACCOUNT *Income Summary*   ACCOUNT NO. *3150*

DATE		ITEM	POST. REF.	DEBIT	CREDIT	BALANCE DEBIT	BALANCE CREDIT
Dec.¹⁹⁻⁻	31		26	13 2 0 0 00		13 2 0 0 00	
	31		26		352 6 0 0 00		339 4 0 0 00
	31		26	267 3 4 4 90			72 0 5 5 10
	31		26	72 0 5 5 10		——	——

ACCOUNT *Sales*   ACCOUNT NO. *4110*

DATE		ITEM	POST. REF.	DEBIT	CREDIT	BALANCE DEBIT	BALANCE CREDIT
Dec.¹⁹⁻⁻	31	Balance	✓				352 6 0 0 00
	31		26	352 6 0 0 00		——	——

ACCOUNT *Purchases*   ACCOUNT NO. *5110*

DATE		ITEM	POST. REF.	DEBIT	CREDIT	BALANCE DEBIT	BALANCE CREDIT
Dec.¹⁹⁻⁻	31	Balance	✓			158 3 0 0 00	
	31		26		158 3 0 0 00	——	——

ACCOUNT *Advertising Expense*   ACCOUNT NO. *6110*

DATE		ITEM	POST. REF.	DEBIT	CREDIT	BALANCE DEBIT	BALANCE CREDIT
Dec.¹⁹⁻⁻	31	Balance	✓			5 5 0 0 00	
	31		26		5 5 0 0 00	——	——

ACCOUNT *Credit Card Fee Expense*   ACCOUNT NO. *6120*

DATE		ITEM	POST. REF.	DEBIT	CREDIT	BALANCE DEBIT	BALANCE CREDIT
Dec.¹⁹⁻⁻	31	Balance	✓			2 8 9 0 00	
	31		26		2 8 9 0 00	——	

ACCOUNT *Insurance Expense*   ACCOUNT NO. *6130*

DATE		ITEM	POST. REF.	DEBIT	CREDIT	BALANCE DEBIT	BALANCE CREDIT
Dec.¹⁹⁻⁻	31		26	2 6 4 0 00		2 6 4 0 00	
	31		26		2 6 4 0 00	——	

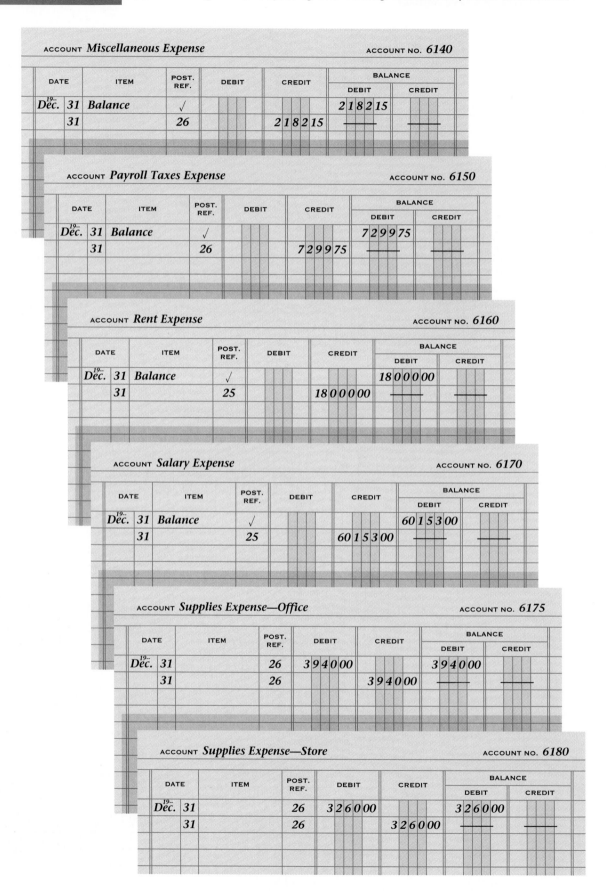

ACCOUNT *Miscellaneous Expense*   ACCOUNT NO. *6140*

DATE	ITEM	POST. REF.	DEBIT	CREDIT	BALANCE DEBIT	BALANCE CREDIT
Dec. 31	Balance	✓			2 1 8 2 15	
31		26		2 1 8 2 15	———	

ACCOUNT *Payroll Taxes Expense*   ACCOUNT NO. *6150*

DATE	ITEM	POST. REF.	DEBIT	CREDIT	BALANCE DEBIT	BALANCE CREDIT
Dec. 31	Balance	✓			7 2 9 9 75	
31		26		7 2 9 9 75	———	

ACCOUNT *Rent Expense*   ACCOUNT NO. *6160*

DATE	ITEM	POST. REF.	DEBIT	CREDIT	BALANCE DEBIT	BALANCE CREDIT
Dec. 31	Balance	✓			18 0 0 0 00	
31		25		18 0 0 0 00	———	

ACCOUNT *Salary Expense*   ACCOUNT NO. *6170*

DATE	ITEM	POST. REF.	DEBIT	CREDIT	BALANCE DEBIT	BALANCE CREDIT
Dec. 31	Balance	✓			60 1 5 3 00	
31		25		60 1 5 3 00	———	

ACCOUNT *Supplies Expense—Office*   ACCOUNT NO. *6175*

DATE	ITEM	POST. REF.	DEBIT	CREDIT	BALANCE DEBIT	BALANCE CREDIT
Dec. 31		26	3 9 4 0 00		3 9 4 0 00	
31		26		3 9 4 0 00	———	

ACCOUNT *Supplies Expense—Store*   ACCOUNT NO. *6180*

DATE	ITEM	POST. REF.	DEBIT	CREDIT	BALANCE DEBIT	BALANCE CREDIT
Dec. 31		26	3 2 6 0 00		3 2 6 0 00	
31		26		3 2 6 0 00	———	

ILLUSTRATION 18-11

General ledger after adjusting and closing entries are posted (concluded)

ACCOUNT *Utilities Expense*							ACCOUNT NO. *6190*	
						BALANCE		
DATE	ITEM	POST. REF.	DEBIT	CREDIT		DEBIT	CREDIT	
Dec.¹⁹⁻⁻ 31	Balance	√				3 1 8 0 00		
31		26		3 1 8 0 00		———	———	

Post-Closing Trial Balance

The post-closing trial balance is prepared to prove the equality of debits and credits in the general ledger. Only accounts with balances are listed.

After adjusting and closing entries have been posted, a post-closing trial balance is prepared. The post-closing trial balance is prepared to prove the equality of debits and credits in the general ledger. Car-Land's post-closing trial balance prepared on December 31 is shown in Illustration 18-12.

All general ledger accounts that have balances are listed on a post-closing trial balance. Accounts are listed in the same order as they appear in the general ledger. Accounts with zero balances are not listed on a post-closing trial balance.

ILLUSTRATION 18-12

Post-closing trial balance

CarLand		
Post-Closing Trial Balance		
December 31, 19--		
ACCOUNT TITLE	**DEBIT**	**CREDIT**
Cash	24 2 3 3 57	
Petty Cash	5 0 0 00	
Accounts Receivable	9 3 3 2 00	
Merchandise Inventory	212 2 0 0 00	
Supplies—Office	1 4 6 0 00	
Supplies—Store	2 5 2 0 00	
Prepaid Insurance	2 2 0 0 00	
Accounts Payable		10 4 5 1 90
Employee Income Tax Payable		4 0 2 00
FICA Tax Payable		8 3 2 16
Sales Tax Payable		1 7 6 0 00
Unemployment Tax Payable—Federal		5 9 15
Unemployment Tax Payable—State		3 9 9 26
Health Insurance Premiums Payable		8 4 0 00
U.S. Savings Bonds Payable		4 0 00
United Way Donations Payable		6 0 00
Amy Kramer, Capital		118 9 4 5 55
Dario Mesa, Capital		118 6 5 5 55
Totals	252 4 4 5 57	252 4 4 5 57

Audit Your Understanding

1. Where is the information obtained for journalizing closing entries?

2. What is the name of the temporary account that is used to summarize the closing entries for revenue, cost, and expenses?

3. How is a temporary account closed?

4. Which accounts are listed on a post-closing trial balance?

Account balances on the post-closing trial balance, Illustration 18-12, agree with the balances on the balance sheet, Illustration 17-10, Chapter 17. Also, because the post-closing trial balance debit and credit balance totals are the same, *$252,445.57,* the equality of debits and credits in the general ledger is proved. The general ledger is ready for the next fiscal period. *(CONCEPT: Accounting Period Cycle)*

SUMMARY OF AN ACCOUNTING CYCLE FOR A MERCHANDISING BUSINESS

Service and merchandising businesses use a similar accounting cycle. The accounting cycles are also similar for a proprietorship and a partnership. Variations occur when subsidiary ledgers are used. Variations also occur in preparing financial statements. CarLand's accounting cycle for a merchandising business is summarized in Illustration 18-13.

QUESTIONS FOR INDIVIDUAL STUDY

EPT(a)

1. What two types of journal entries change general ledger account balances at the end of a fiscal period?

2. Where is the information obtained for journalizing adjusting entries?

3. Where is the information obtained for journalizing closing entries?

4. Where is the explanation for adjusting entries written in a journal?

5. Which accounting concept is being applied when temporary accounts are closed at the end of a fiscal period?

6. What four kinds of closing entries are recorded at the end of a fiscal period?

7. What is the title of the temporary account used to summarize information about net income at the end of a fiscal period?

8. Why is the income summary account considered a unique account?

9. Where is the explanation for closing entries written in a journal?

10. What are the three amounts recorded in the income summary account after closing the revenue, cost, and expense accounts?

11. Why are partners' withdrawals not closed to the income summary account?

12. What is recorded in the Balance Debit and Credit columns of a general ledger account when an account is closed?

13. Which accounting concept is being applied when revenue, cost, and expense accounts begin a new fiscal period with zero balances?

14. What accounts are listed on a post-closing trial balance?

Summary of an accounting cycle for a merchandising business

1 Source documents are checked for accuracy and transactions are analyzed into debit and credit parts.

2 Transactions, from information on source documents, are recorded in a journal.

3 Journal entries are posted to the accounts receivable ledger, the accounts payable ledger, and the general ledger.

4 Schedules of accounts receivable and accounts payable are prepared from the subsidiary ledgers.

5 Work sheet, including a trial balance, is prepared from the general ledger.

6 Financial statements are prepared from the work sheet.

7 Adjusting and closing entries are journalized from the work sheet.

8 Adjusting and closing entries are posted to the general ledger.

9 Post-closing trial balance of the general ledger is prepared.

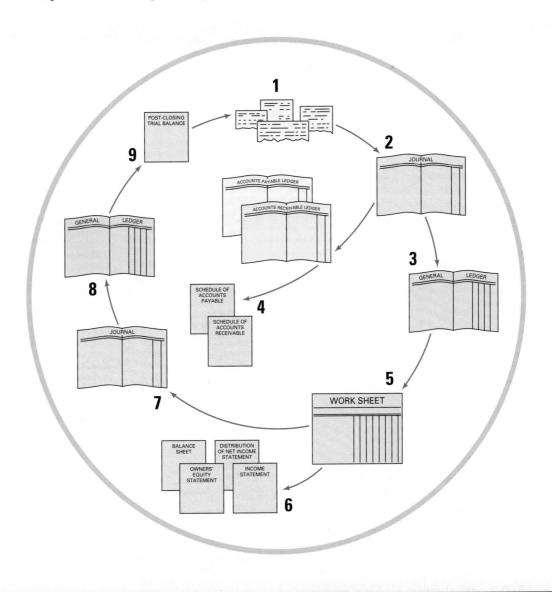

CASE 1 Household Furniture's Trial Balance Debit column of the work sheet shows a debit balance of $2,400.00 for the office supplies account. The ending office supplies inventory is determined to be $1,800.00. The accounting clerk journalized the following adjusting entry: debit Supplies Expense—Office, $1,800.00; credit Supplies—Office, $1,800.00. Susan Gray, partner, discussed the entry with the accounting clerk and suggested that the adjusting entry should have been for $600.00 instead of $1,800.00. The clerk indicated that there is no problem because the amounts will be adjusted

again at the end of the next fiscal period. Do you agree with Miss Gray or the accounting clerk? Explain your answer.

CASE 2 Two businesses have been using different accounting practices. One business first closes the income summary account to record the net income in the capital accounts and then closes the drawing accounts. The other business first closes the drawing accounts and then closes the income summary account to record the net income in the capital accounts. Which practice is correct? Explain.

DRILL 18-D1 Analyzing adjusting entries

TUTORIAL

The following information is related to adjustments needed at the end of a fiscal period for three businesses.

Business	Account Title	Account Balance in General Ledger	Adjustment Information	
			Ending Inventories	Ending Value
1	Merchandise Inventory	$388,000.00	$365,000.00	
	Supplies—Office	4,730.00	2,910.00	
	Supplies—Store	5,230.00	3,470.00	
	Prepaid Insurance	3,360.00		$840.00
2	Merchandise Inventory	$274,000.00	$286,000.00	
	Supplies—Office	3,620.00	1,840.00	
	Supplies—Store	3,950.00	2,110.00	
	Prepaid Insurance	2,850.00		$570.00
3	Merchandise Inventory	$292,000.00	$278,000.00	
	Supplies—Office	4,480.00	2,250.00	
	Supplies—Store	4,130.00	2,320.00	
	Prepaid Insurance	3,200.00		$800.00

INSTRUCTIONS:

1. Prepare eight T accounts for each of the three businesses. (1) Merchandise Inventory. (2) Supplies—Office. (3) Supplies—Store. (4) Prepaid Insurance. (5) Income Summary. (6) Insurance Expense. (7) Supplies Expense—Office. (8) Supplies Expense—Store. For those accounts that have a balance, enter the balance on the proper side of the T account.
2. Enter the adjusting entries in the appropriate T accounts for each business.

DRILL 18-D2 Analyzing closing entries

The following information is from the work sheet of Novak's Sport Center.

	ACCOUNT TITLE	INCOME STATEMENT	
		5 DEBIT	6 CREDIT
21	*Income Summary*	12 0 0 0 00	
22	*Sales*		236 0 0 0 00
23	*Purchases*	94 4 0 0 00	
24	*Advertising Expense*	3 2 5 0 00	
25	*Credit Card Fee Expense*	2 1 3 0 00	
26	*Insurance Expense*	2 5 2 0 00	
27	*Miscellaneous Expense*	1 3 8 0 00	
28	*Rent Expense*	14 4 0 0 00	
29	*Supplies Expense—Office*	2 9 8 0 00	
30	*Supplies Expense—Store*	3 1 2 0 00	

INSTRUCTIONS:

1. Prepare a T account for each account. In each T account, enter the amount that is shown in the Income Statement columns.
2. Enter the debit and credit amounts to close the income statement credit balance account. Enter the debit and credit amounts to close the income statement debit balance accounts.

# APPLICATION PROBLEM
EPT(b,c,d)

PROBLEM 18-1 Journalizing and posting adjusting and closing entries; preparing a post-closing trial balance

AUTOMATED

Use the following partial work sheet of Jewel Box Company for the year ended December 31 of the current year. The general ledger accounts and their balances are in the working papers accompanying this textbook.

	ACCOUNT TITLE	ADJUSTMENTS		INCOME STATEMENT	
		3 DEBIT	4 CREDIT	5 DEBIT	6 CREDIT
4	*Merchandise Inventory*		(a)13 0 0 0 00		
5	*Supplies—Office*		(b) 2 1 4 0 00		
6	*Supplies—Store*		(c) 2 4 5 0 00		
7	*Prepaid Insurance*		(d) 2 6 4 0 00		
21	*Income Summary*	(a)13 0 0 0 00		13 0 0 0 00	
22	*Sales*				316 0 0 0 00
23	*Purchases*			126 4 5 0 00	
24	*Advertising Expense*			4 7 2 0 00	
25	*Credit Card Fee Expense*			3 2 6 0 00	
26	*Insurance Expense*	(d) 2 6 4 0 00		2 6 4 0 00	
27	*Miscellaneous Expense*			1 9 3 0 00	
28	*Payroll Taxes Expense*			6 7 7 3 00	
29	*Rent Expense*			15 6 0 0 00	
30	*Salary Expense*			56 7 8 7 00	
31	*Supplies Expense—Office*	(b) 2 1 4 0 00		2 1 4 0 00	
32	*Supplies Expense—Store*	(c) 2 4 5 0 00		2 4 5 0 00	
33	*Utilities Expense*			2 9 4 0 00	
34		20 2 3 0 00	20 2 3 0 00	238 6 9 0 00	316 0 0 0 00
35	*Net Income*			77 3 1 0 00	
36				316 0 0 0 00	316 0 0 0 00

INSTRUCTIONS:

1. Use page 25 of a journal. Journalize the adjusting entries using information from the partial work sheet.
2. Post the adjusting entries.
3. Continue using page 25 of the journal. Journalize the closing entries using information from the work sheet. The distribution of net income statement shows equal distribution of earnings. The partners' drawing accounts show the following debit balances in the work sheet's Balance Sheet Debit column: Paula Chaney, Drawing, $14,580.00; Scott Chaney, Drawing, $14,720.00.
4. Post the closing entries.
5. Prepare a post-closing trial balance.

ENRICHMENT PROBLEMS

EPT(b,c,d)

MASTERY PROBLEM 18-M Journalizing and posting adjusting and closing entries; preparing a post-closing trial balance

Use the following partial work sheet of Robco Toys for the year ended December 31 of the current year. The general ledger accounts and their balances are in the working papers accompanying this textbook.

AUTOMATED

APPLICATION

	ACCOUNT TITLE	ADJUSTMENTS DEBIT	ADJUSTMENTS CREDIT	INCOME STATEMENT DEBIT	INCOME STATEMENT CREDIT
4	Merchandise Inventory		(a)12 5 0 0 00		
5	Supplies—Office		(b) 2 4 3 0 00		
6	Supplies—Store		(c) 2 2 7 0 00		
7	Prepaid Insurance		(d) 2 2 8 0 00		
21	Income Summary	(a)12 5 0 0 00		12 5 0 0 00	
22	Sales				325 6 3 0 00
23	Purchases			130 4 5 0 00	
24	Advertising Expense			5 1 8 0 00	
25	Credit Card Fee Expense			3 4 2 0 00	
26	Insurance Expense	(d) 2 2 8 0 00		2 2 8 0 00	
27	Miscellaneous Expense			2 0 6 0 00	
28	Payroll Taxes Expense			7 1 2 4 00	
29	Rent Expense			15 6 0 0 00	
30	Salary Expense			59 3 6 0 00	
31	Supplies Expense—Office	(b) 2 4 3 0 00		2 4 3 0 00	
32	Supplies Expense—Store	(c) 2 2 7 0 00		2 2 7 0 00	
33	Utilities Expense			2 8 8 0 00	
34		19 4 8 0 00	19 4 8 0 00	245 5 5 4 00	325 6 3 0 00
35	Net Income			80 0 7 6 00	
36				325 6 3 0 00	325 6 3 0 00
37					

INSTRUCTIONS:

1. Use page 25 of a journal. Journalize the adjusting entries using information from the partial work sheet.
2. Post the adjusting entries.

3. Continue using page 25 of the journal. Journalize the closing entries using information from the work sheet. The distribution of net income statement shows equal distribution of earnings. The partners' drawing accounts show the following debit balances in the work sheet's Balance Sheet Debit column: Marcus Florie, Drawing, $18,230.00; Karen Rader, Drawing, $18,710.00.
4. Post the closing entries.
5. Prepare a post-closing trial balance.

CHALLENGE PROBLEM 18-C Completing end-of-fiscal-period work

AUTOMATED

Plaza Book Center's trial balance is recorded on a 10-column work sheet in the working papers accompanying this textbook. The general ledger accounts and their balances are also given.

INSTRUCTIONS:

1. Use the following adjustment information. Complete the 10-column work sheet.

Adjustment Information, December 31

Merchandise inventory	$204,680.00
Office supplies inventory	2,635.00
Store supplies inventory	2,310.00
Value of prepaid insurance	2,200.00

2. Prepare an income statement from the information on the work sheet. Calculate and record the following component percentages: (a) cost of merchandise sold, (b) gross profit on sales, (c) total expenses, and (d) net income or loss. Round percentage calculations to the nearest 0.1%.
3. Prepare a distribution of net income statement. Net income or loss is to be shared equally.
4. Prepare an owners' equity statement. No additional investments were made.
5. Prepare a balance sheet in report form.
6. Use page 25 of a journal. Journalize the adjusting entries.
7. Post the adjusting entries.
8. Continue using page 25 of the journal. Journalize the closing entries.
9. Post the closing entries.
10. Prepare a post-closing trial balance.

End-of-Fiscal-Period Work for a Partnership

Chapters 16 through 18 describe CarLand's manual accounting procedures for completing end-of-fiscal-period work. Integrating Automated Accounting Topic 6 describes procedures for using automated accounting software to complete CarLand's end-of-fiscal-period work. The Automated Accounting Problems contain instructions for using automated accounting software to solve Application Problem 18-1, Mastery Problem 18-M, and Challenge Problem 18-C, Chapter 18.

COMPLETING END-OF-FISCAL-PERIOD WORK

In automated accounting, end-of-fiscal-period reports are prepared by a computer based on instructions in the computer software. The run date used for all end-of-fiscal-period reports is the ending date of the accounting period. Before printing financial statements, the software is directed to prepare a trial balance. The trial balance is prepared to prove equality of general ledger debits and credits and to plan adjustments to general ledger accounts.

Preparing a Trial Balance

To prepare a trial balance the general ledger data base is retrieved. The Reports menu is selected from the menu bar. The Ledgers command is chosen from the Reports window. Trial Balance is selected from the Report Selection window to display the trial balance. The trial balance is printed as shown in Illustration T6-1.

☞ ☞ FYI ☞ ☞

A trial balance proves the equality of the debits and credits in the general ledger. A trial balance taken after closing entries are performed is a post-closing trial balance. The Trial Balance command must be chosen to display a post-closing trial balance.

ILLUSTRATION T6-1   Trial balance

```
                        CarLand
                     Trial Balance
                       12/31/--
--------------------------------------------------------------
Acct.   Account
Number  Title                           Debit          Credit
--------------------------------------------------------------
1110    Cash                          24233.57
1120    Petty Cash                      500.00
1130    Accounts Receivable            9332.00
1140    Merchandise Inventory        225400.00
1145    Supplies--Office               5400.00
1150    Supplies--Store                5780.00
1160    Prepaid Insurance              4840.00
2110    Accounts Payable                             10451.90
2120    Employee Income Tax Pay.                       402.00
2130    FICA Tax Payable                              832.16
2140    Sales Tax Payable                            1760.00
2150    Unemployment Tax Pay--Fed                      59.15
2160    Unemployment Tax Pay--St.                     399.26
2170    Health Ins. Premiums Pay.                     840.00
2180    U.S. Savings Bonds Pay.                        40.00
2190    United Way Donations Pay.                      60.00
3110    Amy Kramer, Capital                        101118.00
3120    Amy Kramer, Drawing           18200.00
3130    Dario Mesa, Capital                        101228.00
3140    Dario Mesa, Drawing           18600.00
4110    Sales                                      352600.00
5110    Purchases                    158300.00
6110    Advertising Expense            5500.00
6120    Credit Card Fee Expense        2890.00
6140    Miscellaneous Expense          2182.15
6150    Payroll Taxes Expense          7299.75
6160    Rent Expense                  18000.00
6170    Salary Expense                60153.00
6190    Utilities Expense              3180.00
                                    ----------      ----------
        Totals                      569790.47       569790.47
                                    ==========      ==========
```

Recording Adjusting Entries

Adjusting entries are batched and recorded on a general journal input form. CarLand's completed general journal input form for the adjusting entries is shown in Illustration T6-2.

General journal input form with adjustments recorded

RUN DATE 12,31,--
MM DD YY

GENERAL JOURNAL
Input Form

	DATE MM/DD	REFERENCE	ACCOUNT NO.	CUSTOMER/ VENDOR NO.	DEBIT	CREDIT	
1	12 31	Adj.Ent.	3150		13200 00		1
2	/		1140			13200 00	2
3	31	Adj.Ent.	6175		3940 00		3
4	/		1145			3940 00	4
5	31	Adj.Ent.	6180		3260 00		5
6	/		1150			3260 00	6
7	31	Adj.Ent.	6130		2640 00		7
8	/		1160			2640 00	8
25	/						25
				PAGE TOTALS	23040 00	23040 00	
				FINAL TOTALS	23040 00	23040 00	

CarLand has the following adjustment data on December 31.

Adjustment Information, December 31

Merchandise inventory	$212,200.00
Office supplies inventory......................	1,460.00
Store supplies inventory	2,520.00
Value of prepaid insurance...................	2,200.00

The information needed to journalize the adjusting entries is obtained from the trial balance. Income Summary is debited and Merchandise Inventory is credited for $13,200.00, the decrease in merchandise inventory. The journal entry to record this adjustment is on lines 1 and 2 of the general journal input form shown in Illustration T6-2. The abbreviation for adjusting entries, *Adj.Ent.*, is written in the Reference column for each entry.

Supplies Expense—Office is debited and Supplies—Office is credited for $3,940.00, the value of office supplies used. The journal entry to record this adjustment is on lines 3 and 4 of Illustration T6-2.

Supplies Expense—Store is debited and Supplies—Store is credited for $3,260.00, the value of store supplies used. The journal entry to record this adjustment is on lines 5 and 6 of Illustration T6-2.

Insurance Expense is debited and Prepaid Insurance is credited for $2,640.00, the value of insurance used. The journal entry to record this adjustment is on lines 7 and 8 of Illustration T6-2.

After all adjusting entries have been recorded, the Debit and Credit columns are totaled. The totals are entered on the Page Totals and Final Totals lines provided at the bottom of the input

CAREERS IN ACCOUNTING

COMPUTER PROGRAMMER

- *Writes, updates, and maintains computer programs*
- *Enters program codes into computer system and inputs test data into computer*
- *Interprets program operating codes while observing computer monitor screen*
- *Analyzes, reviews, and rewrites programs to increase operating efficiency*
- *Compiles and writes documentation of program development and subsequent revisions*

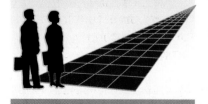

form. The totals are compared to assure that debits equal credits. As the totals are the same, $23,040.00, the adjusting entries on the general journal input form are assumed to be correct.

Processing Adjusting Entries

Dollar and cent signs are not entered on input forms.

The Journals menu is selected from the menu bar. The General Journal command is chosen from the Journals menu to display the data entry window for keying data.

After all lines on the input form have been keyed and posted, the Reports menu is selected from the menu bar. The Journals command is selected to display the Report Selection window. General Journal is selected from the Report Selection window. As CarLand wants to print only the adjusting entries, the abbreviation *Adj.Ent.* is keyed as a Reference restriction. The *Ok* button is pushed to display the general journal report. The report is checked for accuracy by comparing the report totals, $23,040.00, with the totals on the general journal input form. Because the totals are the same, the general journal report is assumed to be correct. The general journal report is printed, as shown in Illustration T6-3, and filed for future reference.

ILLUSTRATION T6-3   General journal report for adjusting entries

```
                              CarLand
                          General Journal
                             12/31/--
-------------------------------------------------------------------------
Date   Refer.   V/C  Acct.  Title                         Debit     Credit
-------------------------------------------------------------------------
12/31  Adj.Ent.       3150  Income Summary             13200.00
12/31  Adj.Ent.       1140  Merchandise Inventory                 13200.00

12/31  Adj.Ent.       6175  Supplies Expense--Office    3940.00
12/31  Adj.Ent.       1145  Supplies--Office                       3940.00

12/31  Adj.Ent.       6180  Supplies Expense--Store     3260.00
12/31  Adj.Ent.       1150  Supplies--Store                        3260.00

12/31  Adj.Ent.       6130  Insurance Expense           2640.00
12/31  Adj.Ent.       1160  Prepaid Insurance                      2640.00
                                                       ---------  ---------
                            Totals                     23040.00   23040.00
                                                       =========  =========
```

PROCESSING FINANCIAL STATEMENTS

To prepare the income statement, the Reports menu is selected from the menu bar. The Financial Statements command is chosen to display the Report Selection window. Income Statement is selected from the Report Selection window. The income statement is printed, as shown in Illustration T6-4 on page 462, and filed for future reference.

To prepare the balance sheet, the same steps are followed as to prepare an income statement. However, Balance Sheet is selected

```
                              CarLand
                          Income Statement
                      For Period Ended 12/31/--
-----------------------------------------------------------------
                        *****Monthly*****    *****Yearly******
                        Amount    Percent    Amount    Percent
-----------------------------------------------------------------
O p e r a t i n g   R e v e n u e
---------------------------------------
Sales                   352600.00  100.00  352600.00   100.00
                        ---------- ------- ---------- ----------
Total Operating Revenue 352600.00  100.00  352600.00   100.00

C o s t   o f   M e r c h a n d i s e   S o l d
--------------------------------------------------
Beginning Inventory     225400.00   63.93  225400.00    63.93
Purchases               158300.00   44.90  158300.00    44.90
                        ---------- ------- ---------- ----------
Merchandise Available for Sale 383700.00 108.82 383700.00 108.82
Less Ending Inventory  -212200.00  -60.18 -212200.00   -60.18
                        ---------- ------- ---------- ----------
Cost of Merchandise Sold 171500.00  48.64  171500.00    48.64
                        ---------- ------- ---------- ----------
Gross Profit            181100.00   51.36  181100.00    51.36

O p e r a t i n g   E x p e n s e s
---------------------------------------
Advertising Expense       5500.00    1.56    5500.00     1.56
Credit Card Fee Expense   2890.00     .82    2890.00      .82
Insurance Expense         2640.00     .75    2640.00      .75
Miscellaneous Expense     2182.15     .62    2182.15      .62
Payroll Taxes Expense     7299.75    2.07    7299.75     2.07
Rent Expense             18000.00    5.10   18000.00     5.10
Salary Expense           60153.00   17.06   60153.00    17.06
Supplies Expense--Office  3940.00    1.12    3940.00     1.12
Supplies Expense--Store   3260.00     .92    3260.00      .92
Utilities Expense         3180.00     .90    3180.00      .90
                        ---------- ------- ---------- ----------
Total Operating Expenses 109044.90  30.93  109044.90    30.93
                        ---------- ------- ---------- ----------
Net Income               72055.10   20.44   72055.10    20.44
                        ========== ======= ========== ==========
```

from the Report Selection window. The balance sheet is printed, as shown in Illustration T6-5, and filed for future reference.

CLOSING TEMPORARY ACCOUNTS

In automated accounting the software contains instructions for closing temporary accounts. After the balance sheet has been prepared, The Options menu is selected from the menu bar. The Period-End Closing command is chosen from the Options menu to close all temporary accounts.

PROCESSING A POST-CLOSING TRIAL BALANCE

After the financial statements have been prepared and period-end closing has been performed, a post-closing trial balance is

```
                              CarLand
                           Balance Sheet
                             12/31/--

          A s s e t s
          ----------
          Cash                            24233.57
          Petty Cash                        500.00
          Accounts Receivable              9332.00
          Merchandise Inventory          212200.00
          Supplies--Office                 1460.00
          Supplies--Store                  2520.00
          Prepaid Insurance                2200.00
                                         ----------
          Total Assets                                 252445.57
                                                       ==========
          L i a b i l i t i e s
          ---------------------
          Accounts Payable                10451.90
          Employee Income Tax Pay.          402.00
          FICA Tax Payable                  832.16
          Sales Tax Payable                1760.00
          Unemployment Tax Pay--Fed          59.15
          Unemployment Tax Pay--St.         399.26
          Health Ins. Premiums Pay.         840.00
          U.S Savings Bonds Pay.             40.00
          United Way Donations Pay.          60.00
                                         ----------
          Total Liabilities                             14844.47

          O w n e r ' s   E q u i t y
          ---------------------------
          Amy Kramer, Capital            101118.00
          Amy Kramer, Drawing            -18200.00
          Dario Mesa, Capital            101228.00
          Dario Mesa, Drawing            -18600.00
          Net Income                      72055.10
                                         ----------
          Total Owner's Equity                         237601.10
                                                       ----------
          Total Liabilities & Equity                   252445.57
                                                       ==========
```

processed. The Reports menu is selected from the menu bar. The Ledgers command is chosen to display the Reports Selection window. Trial Balance is selected from the Report Selection window. The trial balance is printed, as shown in Illustration T6-6 on page 464, and filed for future reference.

OPTIONAL PROBLEM DB-6A

CarLand's general ledger data base is on the accounting textbook template. If you wish to complete Rugcare's end-of-fiscal-period work using automated accounting software, load the *Automated Accounting 6.0* or higher software. Select Data Base 6A (DB-6A) from the template disk. Read the Problem Instructions screen. Follow the procedures described to process CarLand's end-of-fiscal-period work.

```
                              CarLand
                           Trial Balance
                             12/31/--
-------------------------------------------------------------------
Acct.   Account
Number  Title                          Debit          Credit
-------------------------------------------------------------------
1110    Cash                         24233.57
1120    Petty Cash                     500.00
1130    Accounts Receivable           9332.00
1140    Merchandise Inventory       212200.00
1145    Supplies--Office              1460.00
1150    Supplies--Store               2520.00
1160    Prepaid Insurance             2200.00
2110    Accounts Payable                           10451.90
2120    Employee Income Tax Pay.                     402.00
2130    FICA Tax Payable                             832.16
2140    Sales Tax Payable                           1760.00
2150    Unemployment Tax Pay--Fed                     59.15
2160    Unemployment Tax Pay--St.                    399.26
2170    Health Ins. Premiums Pay.                    840.00
2180    U.S. Savings Bonds Pay.                       40.00
2190    United Way Donations Pay.                     60.00
3110    Amy Kramer, Capital                      118945.55
3130    Dario Mesa, Capital                      118655.55
                                     ----------    ----------
        Totals                      252445.57     252445.57
                                     ==========    ==========
```

AUTOMATED ACCOUNTING PROBLEMS

AUTOMATING APPLICATION PROBLEM 18-1 Journalizing and posting adjusting and closing entries; preparing a post-closing trial balance.

INSTRUCTIONS:

1. Use the end-of-fiscal-period work for Problem 18-1, Chapter 18. Use December 31 of the current year as the run date.

2. Load the *Automated Accounting 6.0* or higher software. Select data base F18-1 (First-Year Course Problem 18-1) from the accounting textbook template. Read the Problem Instructions Screen.

3. Select File from the menu bar and choose the Save As menu command. Key the path to the drive and directory that contains your data files. Save the data base with a file name of XXX181 (where XXX are your initials).

4. Display/print a trial balance.

5. Record the adjusting entries on a general ledger input form using the following information. Use the account numbers from the trial balance prepared in Instruction 4.

Adjustment Information, December 31

Merchandise inventory	$283,830.00
Office supplies inventory.	2,570.00
Store supplies inventory	2,130.00
Value of prepaid insurance	1,100.00

6. Key the adjusting entries from the general journal input form.

7. Display/print the general journal report.

8. Display/print the income statement and balance sheet.

9. Perform period-end closing.

10. Display/print the post-closing trial balance.

AUTOMATING MASTERY PROBLEM 18-M Journalizing and posting adjusting and closing entries; preparing a post-closing trial balance

INSTRUCTIONS:

1. Use the end-of-fiscal-period work for Mastery Problem 18-M, Chapter 18. Use December 31 of the current year as the run date.
2. Load the *Automated Accounting 6.0* or higher software. Select data base F18-M (First-Year Course Mastery Problem 18-M) from the accounting textbook template. Read the Problem Instructions screen.
3. Select File from the menu bar and choose the Save As menu command. Key the path to the drive and directory that contains your data files. Save the data base with a file name of XXX18M (where XXX are your initials).
4. Display/print a trial balance.
5. Record the adjusting entries on a general journal input form using the following information. Use the account numbers from the trial balance prepared in Instruction 4.

Adjustment Information, December 31

Merchandise inventory	$276,140.00
Office supplies inventory	2,400.00
Store supplies inventory	2,010.00
Value of prepaid insurance	750.00

6. Key the adjusting entries from the general journal input form.
7. Display/print the general journal report.
8. Display/print the income statement.
9. Display/print the balance sheet.
10. Perform period-end closing.
11. Display/print the post-closing trial balance.

AUTOMATING CHALLENGE PROBLEM 18-C Completing end-of-fiscal-period work

INSTRUCTIONS:

1. Use the end-of-fiscal-period work for Challenge Problem 18-C, Chapter 18. Use December 31 of the current year as the run date.
2. Load the *Automated Accounting 6.0* or higher software. Select data base F18-C from the accounting textbook template. Read the Problem Instructions screen.
3. Select File from the menu bar and choose the Save As menu command. Key the path to the drive and directory that contains your data files. Save the data base with a file name of XXX18C (where XXX are your initials).
4. Display/print a trial balance.
5. Record the adjusting entries on a general journal input form using the following information. Use the account numbers from the trial balance prepared in Instruction 4.

Adjustment Information, December 31

Merchandise inventory	$204,680.00
Office supplies inventory	2,635.00
Store supplies inventory	2,310.00
Value of prepaid insurance	2,200.00

6. Key the adjusting entries from the general journal input form.
7. Display/print the general journal report.
8. Display/print the income statement and balance sheet.
9. Perform period-end closing.
10. Display/print the post-closing trial balance.

An Accounting Cycle for a Partnership: End-of-Fiscal-Period Work

AUTOMATED

The ledgers used in Reinforcement Activity 2, Part A, are needed to complete Reinforcement Activity 2, Part B.

Reinforcement Activity 2, Part B, includes those accounting activities needed to complete the accounting cycle of ClearView Optical.

END-OF-FISCAL-PERIOD WORK

INSTRUCTIONS:

10. Prepare a trial balance on a work sheet. Use December 31 of the current year as the date.

11. Complete the work sheet using the following adjustment information.

Adjustment Information, December 31

Merchandise inventory	$203,200.00
Office supplies inventory	2,370.00
Store supplies inventory	3,240.00
Value of prepaid insurance	260.00

12. Prepare an income statement. Figure and record the following component percentages: (a) cost of merchandise sold, (b) gross profit on sales, (c) total expenses, and (d) net income or loss. Round percentage calculations to the nearest 0.1%.

13. Prepare a distribution of net income statement. Net income or loss is to be shared equally.

14. Prepare an owners' equity statement. No additional investments were made.

15. Prepare a balance sheet in report form.

16. Use page 25 of a journal. Journalize and post the adjusting entries.

17. Continue using page 25 of the journal. Journalize and post the closing entries.

18. Prepare a post-closing trial balance.

Viking Marine is a merchandising business organized as a partnership. This business simulation covers the realistic transactions completed by Viking Marine, which sells personal watercraft and water sports items. Transactions are recorded in a journal similar to the one used by CarLand in Part 3. The following activities are included in the accounting cycle for Viking Marine. This business simulation is available from the publisher in either manual or automated versions.

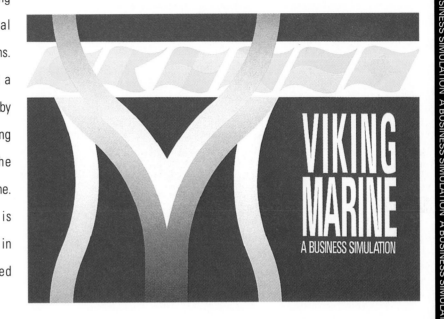

Activities in Viking Marine:

1. Recording transactions in a journal from source documents.

2. Posting items to be posted individually to a general ledger and subsidiary ledger.

3. Recording a payroll in a payroll register. Updating the employee earnings record. Recording payroll journal entries.

4. Posting column totals to a general ledger.

5. Preparing schedules of accounts receivable and accounts payable from subsidiary ledgers.

6. Preparing a trial balance on a work sheet.

7. Planning adjustments and completing a work sheet.

8. Preparing financial statements.

9. Journalizing and posting adjusting entries.

10. Journalizing and posting closing entries.

11. Preparing a post-closing trial balance.

Accounting Concepts

The following accounting concepts and their definitions are provided in this appendix for ready reference.

ACCOUNTING CONCEPTS

Accounting personnel are guided in their work by generally accepted accounting concepts. Ten commonly accepted accounting concepts are described in this appendix. Each concept is fully explained in the text the first time an application of the concept is described. Throughout the textbook, each time a concept application occurs, a concept reference is given, such as *(CONCEPT: Business Entity)*.

1. ACCOUNTING PERIOD CYCLE. [Chapter 8]
   Changes in financial information are reported for a specific period of time in the form of financial statements.

2. ADEQUATE DISCLOSURE. [Chapter 9]
   Financial statements contain all information necessary to understand a business' financial condition.

3. BUSINESS ENTITY. [Chapter 2]
   Financial information is recorded and reported separately from the owner's personal financial information.

4. CONSISTENT REPORTING. [Chapter 8]
The same accounting procedures are followed in the same way in each accounting period.

5. GOING CONCERN. [Chapter 2]
Financial statements are prepared with the expectation that a business will remain in operation indefinitely.

6. HISTORICAL COST. [Chapter 11]
The actual amount paid for merchandise or other items bought is recorded.

7. MATCHING EXPENSES WITH REVENUE. [Chapter 8]
Revenue from business activities and expenses associated with earning that revenue are recorded in the same accounting period.

8. OBJECTIVE EVIDENCE. [Chapter 5]
A source document is prepared for each transaction.

9. REALIZATION OF REVENUE. [Chapter 12]
Revenue is recorded at the time goods or services are sold.

10. UNIT OF MEASUREMENT. [Chapter 2]
Business transactions are stated in numbers that have common values, that is, using a common unit of measurement.

Using a Calculator and Computer Keypad

KINDS OF CALCULATORS

Many different models of calculators, both desktop and hand held, are available. All calculators have their own features and particular placement of operating keys. Therefore, it is necessary to refer to the operator's manual for specific instructions and locations of the operating keys for the calculator being used. A typical keyboard of a desktop calculator is shown in Illustration B-1.

ILLUSTRATION B-1   Typical desktop calculator keyboard

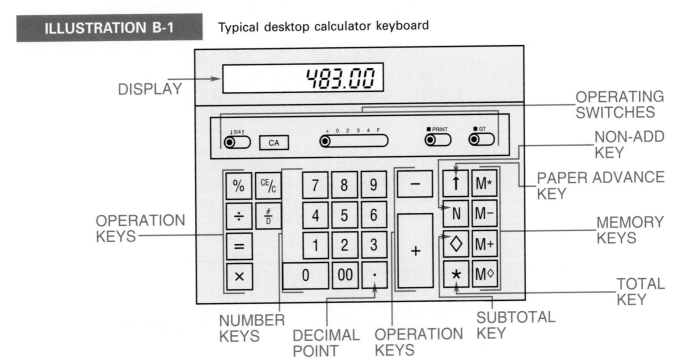

DESKTOP CALCULATOR SETTINGS

Several operating switches on a desktop calculator must be engaged before the calculator will produce the desired results.

The *decimal selector* sets the appropriate decimal places necessary for the numbers that will be entered. For example, if the decimal selector is set at 2, both the numbers entered and the answer will have two decimal places. If the decimal selector is set at F, the calculator automatically sets the decimal places. The F setting allows the answer to be unrounded and carried out to the maximum number of decimal places possible.

The *decimal rounding selector* rounds the answers. The down arrow position will drop any digits beyond the last digit desired. The up arrow position will drop any digits beyond the last digit desired and round the last digit up. In the 5/4 position, the calculator rounds the last desired digit up only when the following digit is 5 or greater. If the following digit is less than 5, the last desired digit remains unchanged.

The *GT* or *grand total switch* in the on position accumulates totals.

KINDS OF COMPUTER KEYBOARDS

The computer has a keypad on the right side of the keyboard called the **numeric keypad.** Even though several styles of keyboards for the IBM® and compatible computers are found, there are two basic layouts for the numeric keypad. The standard layout and enhanced layout are shown in Illustration B-2 on page B-3. On the standard keyboard the directional arrow keys are found on the number keys. To use the numbers, press the key called **Num Lock.** (This key is found above the "7" key.) When the Num Lock is turned on, numbers are entered when the keys on the keypad are pressed. When the Num Lock is off, the arrow, Home, Page Up, Page Down, End, Insert, and Delete keys can be used.

The enhanced keyboards have the arrow keys and the other directional keys mentioned above to the left of the numeric keypad. When using the keypad on an enhanced keyboard, Num Lock can remain on.

The asterisk (*) performs a different function on the computer than the calculator. The asterisk on the calculator is used for the total while the computer uses it for multiplication.

Another difference is the division key. The computer key is the forward slash key (/). The calculator key uses the division key (÷).

TEN-KEY TOUCH SYSTEM

Striking the numbers 0 to 9 on a calculator or numeric keypad without looking at the keyboard is called the **touch system.** Using the touch system develops both speed and accuracy.

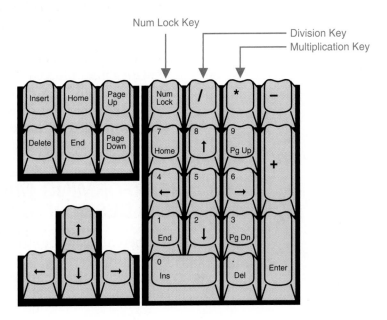

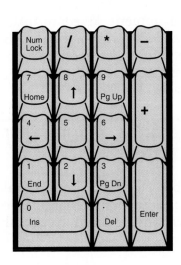

Standard
Keyboard Layout

Enhanced
Keyboard Layout

The 4, 5, and 6 keys are called the **home row.** If the right hand is used for the keyboard, the index finger is placed on the 4 key, the middle finger on the 5 key, and the ring finger on the 6 key. If the left hand is used, the ring finger is placed on the 4 key, the middle finger on the 5 key, and the index finger on the 6 key.

Place the fingers on the home row keys. Curve the fingers and keep the wrist straight. These keys may feel slightly concaved or the 5 key may have a raised dot. The differences in the home row allow the operator to recognize the home row by touch rather than by sight.

Maintain the position of the fingers on the home row. The finger used to strike the 4 key will also strike the 7 key and the 1 key. Stretch the finger up to reach the 7; then stretch the finger down to reach the 1 key. Visualize the position of these keys.

Again, place the fingers on the home row. Stretch the finger that strikes the 5 key up to reach the 8 key, then down to reach the 2 key. Likewise, stretch the finger that strikes the 6 key up to strike the 9 and down to strike the 3 key. This same finger will stretch down again to hit the decimal point.

If the right hand is used, the thumb will be used to strike the 0 and 00 keys and the little finger to strike the addition key. If the left hand is used, the little finger will be used to strike the 0 and 00 keys and the thumb to strike the addition key.

HAND-HELD CALCULATORS

Hand-held calculators are slightly different from desktop calculators, not only in their size and features but also in their operation. Refer to the operator's manual for specific instructions for the calculator being used.

On a hand-held calculator, the numeric keys are usually very close together. In addition, the keys do not respond to touch as easily as on a desktop calculator. Therefore, the touch system is usually not used on a hand-held calculator.

PERFORMING MATHEMATICAL OPERATIONS ON DESKTOP CALCULATORS

Mathematical operations can be performed on a calculator both quickly and efficiently. The basic operations of addition, subtraction, multiplication, and division are used frequently on a calculator.

Addition

Each number to be added is called an **addend.** The answer to an addition problem is called the **sum.**

Addition is performed by entering an addend and striking the addition key (+). All numbers are entered on a calculator in the exact order they are given. To enter the number 4,455.65, strike the 4, 4, 5, 5, decimal, 6, and 5 keys in that order, and then strike the addition key. Commas are not entered. Continue in this manner until all addends have been entered. To obtain the sum, strike the total key on the calculator.

Subtraction

The top number or first number of a subtraction problem is called the **minuend.** The number to be subtracted from the minuend is called the **subtrahend.** The answer to a subtraction problem is called the **difference.**

Subtraction is performed by first entering the minuend and striking the addition key (+). The subtrahend is then entered, followed by the minus key (−), followed by the total key.

Multiplication

The number to be multiplied is called the **multiplicand.** The number of times the multiplicand will be multiplied is called the **multiplier.** The answer to a multiplication problem is called the **product.**

Multiplication is performed by entering the multiplicand and striking the multiplication key (×). The multiplier is then entered, followed by the equals key (=). The calculator will automatically multiply and give the product.

Division

The number to be divided is called the **dividend.** The number the dividend will be divided by is called the **divisor.** The answer to a division problem is called the **quotient.**

Division is performed by entering the dividend and striking the division key (÷). The divisor is then entered, followed by the equals key (=). The calculator will automatically divide and give the quotient.

Correcting Errors

If an error is made while using a calculator, several methods of correction may be used. If an incorrect number has been entered and the addition key or equals key has not yet been struck, strike the clear entry (CE) key one time. This key will clear only the last number that was entered. However, if the clear entry key is depressed more than one time, the entire problem will be cleared on some calculators. If an incorrect number has been entered and the addition key has been struck, strike the minus key one time only. This will automatically subtract the last number added, thus removing it from the total.

PERFORMING MATHEMATICAL OPERATIONS ON COMPUTERS AND HAND-HELD CALCULATORS

On a computer keypad or a hand-held calculator, addition is performed in much the same way as on a desktop calculator. However, after the + key is depressed, the display usually shows the accumulated total. Therefore, the total key is not found. Some computer programs will not calculate the total until Enter is pressed.

Subtraction is performed differently on many computer keypads and hand-held calculators. The minuend is usually entered, followed by the minus (−) key. Then the subtrahend is entered. Pressing either the + key or the = key will display the difference. Some computer programs will not calculate the difference until Enter is pressed.

Multiplication and division are performed the same way on a computer keypad and hand-held calculator as on a desktop calculator. Keep in mind that computers use the * for multiplication and / for division.

SAFETY CONCERNS

Whenever electrical equipment such as a calculator or computer is being operated in a classroom or office, several safety rules apply. These rules protect the operator of the equipment, other persons in the environment, and the equipment itself.

1. Do not unplug equipment by pulling on the electrical cord. Instead, grasp the plug at the outlet and remove it.

2. Do not stretch electrical cords across an aisle where someone might trip over them.

3. Avoid food and beverages near the equipment where a spill might result in an electrical short.

4. Do not attempt to remove the cover of a calculator, computer, or keyboard for any reason while the power is turned on.

5. Do not attempt to repair equipment while it is plugged in.

6. Always turn the power off or unplug equipment when finished using it.

CALCULATION DRILLS

INSTRUCTIONS FOR DESKTOP CALCULATORS

Complete each drill using the touch method. Set the decimal selector at the setting indicated in each drill. Compare the answer on the calculator to the answer in the book. If the two are the same, progress to the next problem. It is not necessary to enter 00 in the cents column if the decimal selector is set at 0-F. However, digits other than zeros in the cents column must be entered preceded by a decimal point.

INSTRUCTIONS FOR COMPUTER KEYPADS

Complete each drill using the touch method. There is no decimal selector on computer keypads. Set the number of decimal places as directed in the instructions for the computer program. In spreadsheets, for example, use the formatting options to set the number of decimal places. When the drill indicates "F" for floating, leave the computer application in its default format. Compare the answer on the computer monitor to the answer in the book. If the two are the same, progress to the next problem. It is not necessary to enter 00 in the cents column. However, digits other than zeros in the cents column must be entered preceded by a decimal point.

DRILL D-1 **Performing addition using the home row keys**
Decimal Selector—2

4.00	44.00	444.00	4,444.00	44,444.00
5.00	55.00	555.00	5,555.00	55,555.00
6.00	66.00	666.00	6,666.00	66,666.00
5.00	45.00	455.00	4,455.00	44,556.00
4.00	46.00	466.00	4,466.00	44,565.00
5.00	54.00	544.00	5,544.00	55,446.00
6.00	56.00	566.00	5,566.00	55,664.00
5.00	65.00	655.00	6,655.00	66,554.00
4.00	64.00	644.00	6,644.00	66,555.00
5.00	66.00	654.00	6,545.00	65,465.00
49.00	561.00	5,649.00	56,540.00	565,470.00

DRILL D-2 Performing addition using the 0, 1, 4, and 7 keys
Decimal Selector—2

4.00	11.00	444.00	4,440.00	44,000.00
7.00	44.00	777.00	7,770.00	77,000.00
4.00	74.00	111.00	1,110.00	11,000.00
1.00	71.00	741.00	4,400.00	41,000.00
4.00	70.00	740.00	1,100.00	71,000.00
7.00	10.00	101.00	4,007.00	10,000.00
4.00	14.00	140.00	7,001.00	10,100.00
1.00	17.00	701.00	1,007.00	40,100.00
4.00	40.00	700.00	1,004.00	70,100.00
7.00	77.00	407.00	7,700.00	74,100.00
43.00	428.00	4,862.00	39,539.00	448,400.00

DRILL D-3 Performing addition using the 2, 5, and 8 keys
Decimal Selector—2

5.00	58.00	588.00	8,888.00	88,855.00
8.00	52.00	522.00	5,555.00	88,822.00
5.00	85.00	888.00	2,222.00	88,852.00
2.00	52.00	222.00	8,525.00	88,222.00
5.00	25.00	258.00	2,585.00	85,258.00
8.00	58.00	852.00	8,258.00	22,255.00
5.00	82.00	225.00	8,585.00	22,288.00
2.00	28.00	885.00	5,258.00	22,258.00
5.00	88.00	882.00	2,852.00	22,888.00
8.00	22.00	228.00	2,288.00	25,852.00
53.00	550.00	5,550.00	55,016.00	555,550.00

DRILL D-4 Performing addition using the 3, 6, 9, and decimal point keys
Decimal Selector—2

6.00	66.66	666.66	6,666.99	66,699.33
9.00	99.99	999.99	9,999.66	99,966.66
6.00	33.33	333.33	3,333.99	33,366.33
3.00	33.66	666.99	3,366.99	36,963.36
6.36	33.99	999.66	6,699.33	69,636.36
3.36	99.66	333.66	9,966.33	33,333.66
9.36	99.33	696.36	9,636.69	66,666.99
9.63	33.36	369.63	3,696.36	99,999.33
6.33	33.69	336.69	6,963.99	96,369.63
9.93	69.63	963.36	6,699.33	36,963.36
68.97	603.30	6,366.33	67,029.66	639,965.01

DRILL D-5 Performing subtraction using all number keys
Decimal Selector—F

456.73	789.01	741.00	852.55	987.98
−123.21	−456.00	−258.10	−369.88	−102.55
333.52	333.01	482.90	482.67	885.43

DRILL D-6   **Performing multiplication using all number keys**
Decimal Selector—F

654.05	975.01	487.10	123.56	803.75
× 12.66	× 27.19	× 30.21	× 50.09	× 1.45
8,280.273	26,510.5219	14,715.291	6,189.1204	1,165.4375

DRILL D-7   **Performing division using all number keys**
Decimal Selector—F

900.56	÷	450.28	=	2.
500.25	÷	100.05	=	5.
135.66	÷	6.65	=	20.4
269.155	÷	105.55	=	2.550023685*
985.66	÷	22.66	=	43.49779346*

Number of decimal places may vary due to machine capacity.

APPENDIX C

Recycling Problems

NOTE: No recycling problems are provided for Chapter 1.

RECYCLING PROBLEM 2-R Determining how transactions change an accounting equation and preparing a balance sheet

Kim Suomi is starting Suomi Service Center, a telephone-answering business. Suomi Service Center uses the accounts shown in the following accounting equation. Use a form similar to the following to complete this problem.

Trans. No.	Assets			= Liabilities	+ Owner's Equity
	Cash +	Supplies +	Prepaid Insurance	= Olson Office Supply	+ Kim Suomi, Capital
Beg. Bal. 1.	0 +700	0	0	0	0 +700 (investment)
New Bal. 2.	700	0	0	0	700

Transactions
1. Received cash from owner as an investment, $700.00.
2. Bought supplies on account from Olson Office Supply, $100.00.
3. Paid cash for insurance, $150.00.
4. Paid cash for supplies, $50.00.
5. Paid cash on account to Olson Office Supply, $50.00.

INSTRUCTIONS:

1. For each transaction, complete the following. Transaction 1 is given as an example.
    a. Analyze the transaction to determine which accounts in the accounting equation are affected.
    b. Write the amount in the appropriate columns, using a plus (+) if the account increases or a minus (−) if the account decreases.
    c. For transactions that change owner's equity, write in parentheses a description of the transaction to the right of the amount.
    d. Calculate the new balance for each account in the accounting equation.
    e. Before going on to the next transaction, determine that the accounting equation is still in balance.
2. Using the final balances in the accounting equation, prepare a balance sheet. Use February 7 of the current year as the date of the balance sheet.

RECYCLING PROBLEM 3-R Determining how transactions change an accounting equation and preparing a balance sheet

Steve Bird operates a service business called Office Plants Company. Office Plants Company uses the accounts shown in the following accounting equation. Use a form similar to the following to complete the problem.

| Trans. No. | Assets | | | = | Liabilities | + | Owner's Equity |
	Cash +	Supplies +	Prepaid Insurance	=	Stanton Company	+	Steve Bird, Capital
Beg. Bal.	1,600	200	400		500		1,700
1.	−90						−90 (expense)
New Bal.	1,510	200	400		500		1,610
2.							

Transactions
1. Paid cash for telephone bill, $90.00.
2. Received cash from sales, $230.00.
3. Paid cash for equipment repair, $25.00.
4. Received cash from owner as an investment, $300.00.
5. Paid cash for rent, $400.00.
6. Received cash from sales, $250.00.
7. Paid cash for advertising, $100.00.
8. Paid cash on account to Stanton Company, $500.00.
9. Paid cash for water bill, $60.00.
10. Paid cash for miscellaneous expense, $10.00.
11. Bought supplies on account from Stanton Company, $300.00.
12. Paid cash for supplies, $200.00.
13. Received cash from sales, $270.00.
14. Paid cash to owner for personal use, $600.00.
15. Paid cash for insurance, $150.00.

INSTRUCTIONS:

1. For each transaction, complete the following. Transaction 1 is given as an example.
    a. Analyze the transaction to determine which accounts in the accounting equation are affected.
    b. Write the amount in the appropriate columns, using a plus (+) if the account increases or a minus (−) if the account decreases.

c. For transactions that change owner's equity, write in parentheses a description of the transaction to the right of the amount.

d. Calculate the new balance for each account in the accounting equation.

e. Before going on to the next transaction, determine that the accounting equation is still in balance.

2. Using the final balances in the accounting equation, prepare a balance sheet. Use the date November 15 of the current year.

RECYCLING PROBLEM 4-R   Analyzing transactions into debit and credit parts

Alicia Valdez owns a business called QuickWash. QuickWash uses the following accounts.

Cash	Sales
Supplies	Advertising Expense
Prepaid Insurance	Miscellaneous Expense
Kishler Office Supplies	Rent Expense
Travis Office Supplies	Repair Expense
Alicia Valdez, Capital	Utilities Expense
Alicia Valdez, Drawing	

Transactions

Mar. 1. Received cash from owner as an investment, $3,000.00.
2. Paid cash for supplies, $60.00.
5. Paid cash for rent, $200.00.
5. Received cash from sales, $350.00.
6. Bought supplies on account from Travis Office Supplies, $500.00.
9. Paid cash for repairs, $10.00.
12. Received cash from sales, $200.00.
13. Paid cash for insurance, $100.00.
17. Bought supplies on account from Kishler Office Supplies, $50.00.
19. Paid cash for miscellaneous expense, $5.00.
19. Received cash from owner as an investment, $800.00.
19. Received cash from sales, $300.00.
20. Paid cash on account to Travis Office Supplies, $50.00.
24. Paid cash for telephone bill (utilities expense), $25.00.
25. Paid cash for advertising, $35.00.
26. Received cash from sales, $320.00.
30. Paid cash to owner for personal use, $500.00.
31. Received cash from sales, $100.00.

INSTRUCTIONS:

1. Prepare a T account for each account.
2. Analyze each transaction into its debit and credit parts. Write the debit and credit amounts in the proper T accounts to show how each transaction changes account balances. Write the date of the transaction in parentheses before each amount.

RECYCLING PROBLEM 5-R   Journalizing transactions

Mary Ching owns a service business called Ching's Accounting. Ching's Accounting uses the following accounts.

Cash	Sales
Supplies	Advertising Expense
Prepaid Insurance	Miscellaneous Expense
West Supplies	Rent Expense
Wilson's Office Supplies	Repair Expense
Mary Ching, Capital	Utilities Expense
Mary Ching, Drawing	

INSTRUCTIONS:

1. Journalize the following transactions completed during October of the current year. Use page 1 of a journal similar to the one described in Chapter 5 for Rugcare. Source documents are abbreviated as follows: check, C; memorandum, M; receipt, R; calculator tape, T.

Oct. 1. Received cash from owner as an investment, $14,000.00. R1.
2. Paid cash for rent, $700.00. C1.
5. Paid cash for supplies, $500.00. C2.
6. Paid cash for insurance, $1,500.00. C3.
7. Bought supplies on account from West Supplies, $2,000.00. M1.
9. Paid cash for miscellaneous expense, $5.00. C4.
12. Paid cash on account to West Supplies, $1,000.00. C5.
12. Received cash from sales, $450.00. T12.
13. Received cash from sales, $400.00. T13.
14. Paid cash for telephone bill, $60.00. C6.
14. Received cash from sales, $480.00. T14.
15. Paid cash for repairs, $80.00. C7.
15. Paid cash to owner for personal use, $400.00. C8.
15. Received cash from sales, $550.00. T15.
16. Received cash from sales, $480.00. T16.
19. Received cash from sales, $380.00. T19.
20. Received cash from sales, $520.00. T20.
21. Bought supplies on account from Wilson's Office Supplies, $600.00. M2.
21. Received cash from sales, $400.00. T21.
22. Paid cash for supplies, $1,200.00. C9.
22. Received cash from sales, $550.00. T22.
23. Received cash from sales, $450.00. T23.

2. Prove and rule page 1 of the journal. Carry the column totals forward to page 2 of the journal.
3. Use page 2 of the journal. Journalize the following transactions completed during October of the current year.

Oct. 26. Paid cash for advertising, $100.00. C10.
26. Bought supplies on account from West Supplies, $60.00. M3.
26. Received cash from sales, $460.00. T26.
27. Received cash from sales, $370.00. T27.
28. Paid cash for electric bill, $40.00. C11.
28. Received cash from sales, $400.00. T28.
29. Paid cash on account to West Supplies, $60.00. C12.
29. Received cash from sales, $330.00. T29.
30. Paid cash for supplies, $50.00. C13.
30. Received cash from sales, $550.00. T30.
31. Paid cash to owner for personal use, $400.00. C14.

4. Prove page 2 of the journal.
5. Prove cash. The beginning cash balance on October 1 is zero. The balance on the next unused check stub is $14,675.00.
6. Rule page 2 of the journal.

RECYCLING PROBLEM 6-R Journalizing and posting to a general ledger

Al Burns owns a service business called Burns Cleaning. Burns Cleaning uses the same journal used by Rugcare in Chapter 6.

INSTRUCTIONS:

1. Open a general ledger account for each of the following accounts.

Assets
110 Cash
120 Supplies
130 Prepaid Insurance

Liabilities
210 Mitchell Office Supplies

Owner's Equity
310 Al Burns, Capital
320 Al Burns, Drawing

Revenue
410 Sales

Expenses
510 Advertising Expense
520 Miscellaneous Expense
530 Rent Expense
540 Utilities Expense

2. Journalize the following transactions completed during November of the current year. Use page 1 of a journal. Source documents are abbreviated as follows: check, C; memorandum, M; receipt, R; calculator tape, T.

Nov. 1. Received cash from owner as an investment, $7,000.00. R1.
   3. Paid cash for insurance, $250.00. C1.
   5. Paid cash for miscellaneous expense, $5.00. C2.
   6. Received cash from sales, $410.00. T6.
   9. Paid cash for rent, $400.00. C3.
   11. Paid cash for supplies, $550.00. C4.
   13. Bought supplies on account from Mitchell Office Supplies, $700.00. M1.
   13. Received cash from sales, $380.00. T13.
   16. Paid cash for electric bill, $50.00. C5.
   18. Paid cash on account to Mitchell Office Supplies, $350.00. C6.
   20. Paid cash for advertising, $35.00. C7.
   20. Received cash from sales, $1,020.00. T20.
   25. Paid cash for supplies, $100.00. C8.
   27. Paid cash for supplies, $120.00. C9.
   27. Received cash from sales, $1,660.00. T27.
   30. Paid cash to owner for personal use, $500.00. C10.
   30. Received cash from sales, $450.00. T30.

3. Prove the journal.
4. Prove cash. The beginning cash balance on November 1 is zero. The balance on the next unused check stub is $8,560.00.
5. Rule the journal.
6. Post from the journal to the general ledger.

RECYCLING PROBLEM 7-R Reconciling a bank statement; journalizing a bank service charge, a dishonored check, and petty cash transactions

Sarah Getz owns a business called Quick Service. Quick Service completed the following transactions during August of the current year.

INSTRUCTIONS:

1. Journalize the following transactions completed during August of the current year. Use page 8 of a journal. Source documents are abbreviated as follows: check, C; memorandum, M.

Aug. 24. Paid cash to establish a petty cash fund, $200.00. C81.
   25. Received notice from the bank of a dishonored check, $50.00, plus $5.00 fee; total, $55.00. M28.
   26. Paid cash for miscellaneous expense, $18.00. C82.
   27. Paid cash for supplies, $60.00. C83.
   28. Paid cash for repairs, $35.00. C84.
   31. Paid cash to owner for personal use, $500.00. C85.
   31. Paid cash to replenish the petty cash fund, $105.00: supplies, $65.00; miscellaneous expense, $40.00. C86.

2. On August 31 of the current year, Quick Service received a bank statement dated August 30. Prepare a bank statement reconciliation. Use August 31 of the current year as the date. The following information is obtained from the August 30 bank statement and from the records of the business.

Bank statement balance	$1,970.00
Bank service charge.	6.00
Outstanding deposit, August 31.	520.00
Outstanding checks, Nos. 85 and 86	
Checkbook balance on Check Stub No. 87	1,891.00

3. Continue using the journal and journalize the following transaction.

Aug. 31. Received bank statement showing August bank service charge, $6.00. M29.

RECYCLING PROBLEM 8-R Completing a work sheet

On May 31 of the current year, ServiceAll has the following general ledger accounts and balances. The business uses a monthly fiscal period.

Account Title	Account Balances	
	Debit	Credit
Cash	$3,900.00	
Petty Cash	100.00	
Supplies	3,400.00	
Prepaid Insurance	850.00	
Gordon Supplies.		$ 170.00
Weil Company		90.00
James McCurdy, Capital.		6,000.00
James McCurdy, Drawing	340.00	
Income Summary	—	—
Sales		3,500.00
Advertising Expense	270.00	
Insurance Expense	—	
Miscellaneous Expense.	120.00	
Rent Expense.	400.00	
Supplies Expense	—	
Utilities Expense	380.00	

INSTRUCTIONS:

1. Prepare the heading and trial balance on a work sheet.
2. Analyze the following adjustment information into debit and credit parts. Record the adjustments on the work sheet.

Adjustment Information, May 31

Supplies on hand	$2,000.00
Value of prepaid insurance	350.00

3. Extend the up-to-date account balances to the Balance Sheet or Income Statement columns.
4. Complete the work sheet.

RECYCLING PROBLEM 9-R Preparing financial statements

See the following page for information obtained from the work sheet of Best Delivery Service for the month ended December 31 of the current year.

INSTRUCTIONS:

1. Prepare an income statement for the month ended December 31 of the current year. Calculate and record the component percentages for total expenses and net income. Round percentage calculations to the nearest 0.1%.
2. Prepare a balance sheet for December 31 of the current year.

APPENDIX C   Recycling Problems

	ACCOUNT TITLE	INCOME STATEMENT DEBIT	INCOME STATEMENT CREDIT	BALANCE SHEET DEBIT	BALANCE SHEET CREDIT	
1	Cash			6 0 7 5 00		1
2	Petty Cash			2 0 0 00		2
3	Supplies			6 3 0 0 00		3
4	Prepaid Insurance			2 1 0 0 00		4
5	Dale Supplies				3 8 0 0 00	5
6	Niles Office Supplies				9 7 0 00	6
7	Evert Pole, Capital				9 7 0 0 00	7
8	Evert Pole, Drawing			1 0 0 0 00		8
9	Income Summary					9
10	Sales		4 5 6 0 00			10
11	Advertising Expense	3 0 0 00				11
12	Insurance Expense	1 5 0 00				12
13	Miscellaneous Expense	1 2 0 00				13
14	Rent Expense	2 5 0 0 00				14
15	Supplies Expense	1 6 5 00				15
16	Utilities Expense	1 2 0 00				16
17		3 3 5 5 00	4 5 6 0 00	15 6 7 5 00	14 4 7 0 00	17
18	Net Income	1 2 0 5 00			1 2 0 5 00	18
19		4 5 6 0 00	4 5 6 0 00	15 6 7 5 00	15 6 7 5 00	19
20						20
21						21
22						22
23						23

RECYCLING PROBLEM 10-R Journalizing adjusting and closing entries

The following information is obtained from the partial work sheet of Lawn Services for the month ended September 30 of the current year.

	ACCOUNT TITLE	ADJUSTMENTS DEBIT	ADJUSTMENTS CREDIT	INCOME STATEMENT DEBIT	INCOME STATEMENT CREDIT	BALANCE SHEET DEBIT	BALANCE SHEET CREDIT	
1	Cash					3 1 5 0 00		1
2	Supplies		(a) 1 7 5 00			6 7 5 00		2
3	Prepaid Insurance		(b) 2 3 0 00			2 5 0 00		3
4	Lodge Supplies						4 5 0 00	4
5	Verner Supplies						1 0 0 00	5
6	Norman Eli, Capital						3 1 3 0 00	6
7	Norman Eli, Drawing					3 1 5 00		7
8	Income Summary							8
9	Sales				1 6 1 5 00			9
10	Insurance Expense	(b) 2 3 0 00		2 3 0 00				10
11	Miscellaneous Expense			7 5 00				11
12	Rent Expense			4 2 5 00				12
13	Supplies Expense	(a) 1 7 5 00		1 7 5 00				13
14		4 0 5 00	4 0 5 00	9 0 5 00	1 6 1 5 00	4 3 9 0 00	3 6 8 0 00	14
15	Net Income			7 1 0 00			7 1 0 00	15
16				1 6 1 5 00	1 6 1 5 00	4 3 9 0 00	4 3 9 0 00	16
17								17
18								18

INSTRUCTIONS:

1. Use page 3 of a journal. Journalize the adjusting entries.

2. Continue to use page 3 of the journal. Journalize the closing entries.

RECYCLING PROBLEM 11-R   Journalizing purchases, cash payments, and other transactions

Eva Akemi and Daniel Marino, partners, own a furniture store.

INSTRUCTIONS:

Journalize the following transactions completed during November of the current year. Use page 11 of a journal similar to the one described in Chapter 11. Source documents are abbreviated as follows: check, C; memorandum, M; purchase invoice, P.

Nov. 2. Paid cash for rent, $1,200.00. C251.
     2. Purchased merchandise on account from Baines Furniture Co., $2,335.00. P88.
     3. Paid cash for office supplies, $66.00. C252.
     5. Paid cash on account to Decor-Concepts, $985.00, covering P85. C253.
     7. Purchased merchandise for cash, $130.00. C254.
     9. Purchased merchandise on account from Metaline Co., $950.00. P89.
     9. Bought store supplies on account from Gateway Supply, $140.00. M40.
   10. Purchased merchandise for cash, $83.00. C255.
   12. Paid cash on account to Furniture Industries, $1,400.00, covering P86. C256.
   12. Bought office supplies on account from Scott Supply, $95.00. M41.
   14. Discovered that a transaction for store supplies bought in October was journalized and posted in error as a debit to Purchases instead of Supplies—Store, $74.00. M42.
   16. Eva Akemi, partner, withdrew cash for personal use, $1,000.00. C257.
   17. Daniel Marino, partner, withdrew cash for personal use, $1,000.00. C258.
   17. Paid cash for advertising, $75.00. C259.
   19. Paid cash on account to Classic Furniture, $1,345.00, covering P87. C260.
   19. Purchased merchandise on account from Metaline Co., $1,250.00. P90.
   20. Daniel Marino, partner, withdrew merchandise for personal use, $152.00. M43.
   22. Purchased merchandise for cash, $60.00. C261.
   24. Paid cash on account to Baines Furniture Co., $2,335.00, covering P88. C262.
   25. Eva Akemi, partner, withdrew merchandise for personal use, $225.00. M44.
   27. Paid cash for store supplies, $78.00. C263.
   30. Paid cash to replenish the petty cash fund, $301.00: office supplies, $78.00; store supplies, $52.00; advertising, $125.00; miscellaneous, $46.00. C264.
   30. Paid cash on account to Metaline Co., $950.00, covering P89. C265.

RECYCLING PROBLEM 12-R   Journalizing sales and cash receipts

Ana Lamas and Alex Keyser, partners, own an office supply store.

INSTRUCTIONS:

1. Journalize the following transactions completed during September of the current year. Use page 9 of a journal similar to the one described in Chapter 12. A 4% sales tax has been added to each sale. Source documents are abbreviated as follows: receipt, R; sales invoice, S; cash register tape, T.

Sept. 1. Sold merchandise on account to Samuel Quist, $75.00, plus sales tax, $3.00; total, $78.00. S53.
     1. Received cash on account from David Plouff, $85.28, covering S49. R85.
     2. Sold merchandise on account to Carmen Estevez, $125.00, plus sales tax, $5.00; total, $130.00. S54.

Sept. 5. Sold merchandise on account to Keith Aldrich, $265.00, plus sales tax, $10.60; total, $275.60. S55.

5. Recorded cash and credit card sales, $1,940.00, plus sales tax, $77.60; total, $2,017.60. T5.

7. Received cash on account from Edward Jarmen, $249.60, covering S50. R86.

9. Sold merchandise on account to Perez Accounting Co., $345.00, plus sales tax, $13.80; total, $358.80. S56.

10. Sold merchandise on account to Nancy Cain, $85.00, plus sales tax, $3.40; total, $88.40. S57.

11. Received cash on account from Bonner Secretarial Service, $249.60, covering S51. R87.

12. Recorded cash and credit card sales, $2,350.00, plus sales tax, $94.00; total, $2,444.00. T12.

14. Received cash on account from David Doran, $187.20, covering S52. R88.

15. Sold merchandise on account to Hazel Ervin, $65.00, plus sales tax, $2.60; total, $67.60. S58.

18. Received cash on account from Samuel Quist, $78.00, covering S53. R89.

19. Recorded cash and credit card sales, $2,450.00, plus sales tax, $98.00; total, $2,548.00. T19.

21. Received cash on account from Carmen Estevez, $130.00, covering S54. R90.

25. Received cash on account from Keith Aldrich, $275.60, covering S55. R91.

26. Recorded cash and credit card sales, $2,140.00, plus sales tax, $85.60; total, $2,225.60. T26.

29. Sold merchandise on account to Susan Gates, $145.00, plus sales tax, $5.80; total, $150.80. S59.

30. Recorded cash and credit card sales, $1,285.00, plus sales tax, $51.40; total, $1,336.40. T30.

2. Total the journal. Prove the equality of debits and credits.

3. Rule the journal.

RECYCLING PROBLEM 13-R Opening accounts and journalizing and posting business transactions

INSTRUCTIONS:

1. Open the following accounts in the general ledger of Catalina Shoes. Record the balances as of September 1 of the current year.

Account No.	Account Title	Account Balance
1110	Cash	$ 13,200.00
1130	Accounts Receivable	441.00
1140	Supplies—Office	1,830.00
1150	Supplies—Store	1,560.00
2110	Accounts Payable	3,820.00
2120	Sales Tax Payable	937.50
3120	Sophia Kizer, Drawing	9,820.00
3140	Brian Rankin, Drawing	9,600.00
4110	Sales	150,000.00
5110	Purchases	88,000.00
6110	Advertising Expense	2,310.00
6140	Miscellaneous Expense	1,260.00
6160	Rent Expense	7,600.00
6190	Utilities Expense	1,620.00

2. Open the following vendor accounts in the accounts payable ledger. Record the balances as of September 1 of the current year.

Vendor No.	Vendor Name	Purchase Invoice No.	Account Balance
210	A & J Shoes........................	P66	$1,480.00
220	Colormate Shoes	—	—
230	Sanz Supply	—	—
240	Suave Shoe Co......................	P65	2,340.00

3. Open the following customer accounts in the accounts receivable ledger. Record the balances as of September 1 of the current year.

Customer No.	Customer Name	Sales Invoice No.	Account Balance
110	Joyce Abler........................	S53	$178.50
120	Helen Gorthy	—	—
130	Joshua Lentz	—	—
140	Earl Ward	S52	262.50

4. Journalize the following transactions completed during September of the current year. Use page 9 of a journal similar to the one described in Chapter 13. A 5% sales tax has been added to each sale. Source documents are abbreviated as follows: check, C; memorandum, M; purchase invoice, P; receipt, R; sales invoice, S; cash register tape, T.

Sept. 1. Paid cash for rent, $950.00. C225.
2. Purchased merchandise on account from Colormate Shoes, $1,650.00. P67.
4. Received cash on account from Earl Ward, $262.50, covering S52. R33.
5. Recorded cash and credit card sales, $3,350.00, plus sales tax, $167.50; total, $3,517.50. T5.
   Posting. Post the items that are to be posted individually.
7. Paid cash for electric bill, $158.10. C226.
9. Bought office supplies on account from Sanz Supply, $135.00. M32.
10. Paid cash on account to Suave Shoe Co., $2,340.00, covering P65. C227.
12. Recorded cash and credit card sales, $4,140.00, plus sales tax, $207.00; total, $4,347.00. T12.
   Posting. Post the items that are to be posted individually.
14. Sold merchandise on account to Helen Gorthy, $260.00, plus sales tax, $13.00; total, $273.00. S54.
15. Sold merchandise on account to Joshua Lentz, $125.00, plus sales tax, $6.25; total, $131.25. S55.
15. Sophia Kizer, partner, withdrew cash for personal use, $1,200.00. C228.
15. Brian Rankin, partner, withdrew cash for personal use, $1,200.00. C229.
18. Purchased merchandise on account from A & J Shoes, $940.00. P68.
19. Recorded cash and credit card sales, $4,080.00, plus sales tax, $204.00; total, $4,284.00. T19.
   Posting. Post the items that are to be posted individually.
21. Discovered that a transaction for office supplies bought for cash was journalized and posted in error as a debit to Supplies—Store instead of Supplies—Office, $118.00. M33.
22. Sophia Kizer, partner, withdrew merchandise for personal use, $125.00. M34.
24. Sold merchandise on account to Earl Ward, $135.00, plus sales tax, $6.75; total, $141.75. S56.
25. Sold merchandise on account to Joyce Abler, $95.00, plus sales tax, $4.75; total, $99.75. S57.
26. Recorded cash and credit card sales, $4,530.00, plus sales tax, $226.50; total, $4,756.50. T26.
   Posting. Post the items that are to be posted individually.
28. Received cash on account from Joyce Abler, $178.50, covering S53. R34.
28. Paid cash on account to A & J Shoes, $1,480.00, covering P66. C230.
30. Paid cash to replenish the petty cash fund, $201.50: office supplies, $42.00; store supplies, $57.50; advertising, $64.00; miscellaneous, $38.00. C231.

Sept. 30. Purchased merchandise on account from Suave Shoe Co., $860.00. P69.

30. Recorded cash and credit card sales, $1,970.00, plus sales tax, $98.50; total, $2,068.50. T30.

Posting. Post the items that are to be posted individually.

5. Total the journal. Prove the equality of debits and credits.
6. Prove cash. The balance on the next unused check stub is $25,084.90.
7. Rule the journal.
8. Post the totals of the special columns of the journal.
9. Prepare a schedule of accounts payable and a schedule of accounts receivable. Prove the accuracy of the subsidiary ledgers by comparing the schedule totals with the balances of the controlling accounts in the general ledger. If the totals are not the same, find and correct the errors.

RECYCLING PROBLEM 14-R Preparing a semimonthly payroll

The following information is for the semimonthly pay period June 1–15 of the current year.

Employee		Marital Status	No. of Allowances	Earnings		Deductions
No.	Name			Regular	Overtime	Health Insurance
3	Cahill, Bryan M.	S	2	$598.40	$40.00	$25.00
4	Dykes, Eleanor S.	M	3	525.60		30.00
7	Holcomb, David K.	S	1	624.00		
1	Kirby, Sharon A.	S	1	552.00	9.30	
5	Mendez, Thomas T.	M	2	545.60		25.00
6	Salassi, Carol W.	M	3	576.00		30.00
8	Tsang, Elaine C.	M	2	651.20	44.40	25.00

INSTRUCTIONS:

1. Prepare a payroll register. The date of payment is June 16. Use the federal income tax withholding tables in Illustration 14-4 to find the income tax withholding for each employee. Calculate FICA tax withholding using an 8% tax rate. None of the employee accumulated earnings has exceeded the FICA tax base.
2. Prepare a check for the total amount of the net pay. Make the check payable to Payroll Account, and sign your name as a partner of Riddley Company. The beginning check stub balance is $7,687.89.
3. Prepare payroll checks for David Holcomb, Check No. 332, and Carol Salassi, Check No. 335. Sign your name as a partner of Riddley Company. Record the two payroll check numbers in the payroll register.

RECYCLING PROBLEM 15-R Journalizing payroll taxes

Johnson Manufacturing completed payroll transactions during the period February 28 to April 30 of the current year. Payroll tax rates are as follows: FICA, 8%; federal unemployment, 0.8%; and state unemployment, 5.4%. No total earnings have exceeded the tax base for calculating unemployment taxes.

INSTRUCTIONS:

1. Journalize the following transactions on page 4 of a journal. Source documents are abbreviated as follows: check, C, and memorandum, M.

Feb. 28. Paid cash for monthly payroll, $3,312.16 (total payroll, $4,298.00, less deductions: employee income tax, $642.00; FICA tax, $343.84). C167.

28. Recorded employer payroll taxes expense. M34.

Mar. 15. Paid cash for liability for employee income tax, $642.00, and for FICA tax, $687.68; total, $1,329.68. C192.
15. 31. Paid cash for monthly payroll, $3,328.84 (total payroll, $4,327.00, less deductions: employee income tax, $652.00; FICA tax, $346.16). C235.
31. Recorded employer payroll taxes expense. M39.
Apr. 15. Paid cash for liability for employee income tax, $652.00, and for FICA tax, $692.32; total, $1,344.32. C251.
30. Paid cash for federal unemployment tax liability for quarter ended March 31, $103.62. C272.
30. Paid cash for state unemployment tax liability for quarter ended March 31, $699.41. C273.

2. Prove and rule the journal.

RECYCLING PROBLEM 16-R Completing a work sheet

On December 31 of the current year, Klimer has the following general ledger accounts and balances.

Account Title	Balance
Cash	$ 19,865.00
Petty Cash	500.00
Accounts Receivable	9,260.00
Merchandise Inventory	226,320.00
Supplies—Office	5,085.00
Supplies—Store	5,420.00
Prepaid Insurance	4,300.00
Accounts Payable	9,720.00
Sales Tax Payable	950.00
Dorothy Klimer, Capital	107,365.00
Dorothy Klimer, Drawing	15,880.00
Howard Klimer, Capital	106,190.00
Howard Klimer, Drawing	15,730.00
Income Summary	—
Sales	189,540.00
Purchases	85,250.00
Advertising Expense	4,735.00
Credit Card Fee Expense	1,930.00
Insurance Expense	—
Miscellaneous Expense	2,360.00
Rent Expense	14,400.00
Supplies Expense—Office	—
Supplies Expense—Store	—
Utilities Expense	2,730.00

INSTRUCTIONS:

Prepare Klimer's work sheet for the fiscal period ended December 31 of the current year.

Adjustment Information, December 31

Merchandise inventory	$218,770.00
Office supplies inventory	2,195.00
Store supplies inventory	2,205.00
Value of prepaid insurance	1,720.00

RECYCLING PROBLEM 17-R Preparing financial statements

Discount Footwear prepared the work sheet on page C-13 for the year ended December 31 of the current year.

Discount Footwear
Work Sheet
For Year Ended December 31, 19--

	TRIAL BALANCE		ADJUSTMENTS		INCOME STATEMENT		BALANCE SHEET	
ACCOUNT TITLE	DEBIT	CREDIT	DEBIT	CREDIT	DEBIT	CREDIT	DEBIT	CREDIT
1 Cash	1939500						1939500	
2 Petty Cash	30000						30000	
3 Accounts Receivable	893000						893000	
4 Merchandise Inventory	25720000			(a) 975000			24745000	
5 Supplies—Office	512000			(b) 298000			214000	
6 Supplies—Store	487500			(c) 314000			173500	
7 Prepaid Insurance	483000			(d) 276000			207000	
8 Accounts Payable		836000						836000
9 Sales Tax Payable		98000						98000
10 Joseph Kane, Capital		11164000						11164000
11 Joseph Kane, Drawing	1584000						1584000	
12 Gail Miles, Capital		11036000						11036000
13 Gail Miles, Drawing	1593000						1593000	
14 Income Summary			(a) 975000		975000			
15 Sales		23545000				23545000		
16 Purchases	10595000				10595000			
17 Advertising Expense	496500				496500			
18 Credit Card Fee Expense	213000				213000			
19 Insurance Expense			(d) 276000		276000			
20 Miscellaneous Expense	228500				228500			
21 Rent Expense	1680000				1680000			
22 Supplies Expense—Office			(b) 298000		298000			
23 Supplies Expense—Store			(c) 314000		314000			
24 Utilities Expense	224000				224000			
25	46679000	46679000	1863000	1863000	15300000	23545000	31379000	23134000
26 Net Income					8245000			8245000
27					23545000	23545000	31379000	31379000
28								

INSTRUCTIONS:

1. Prepare an income statement. Calculate and record the following component percentages: (a) cost of merchandise sold, (b) gross profit on sales, (c) total expenses, and (d) net income or loss. Round percentage calculations to the nearest 0.1%.
2. Prepare a distribution of net income statement. Net income or loss is to be shared equally.
3. Prepare an owners' equity statement. No additional investments were made.
4. Prepare a balance sheet in report form.

RECYCLING PROBLEM 18-R Journalizing adjusting and closing entries

Use the following partial work sheet of Cook & Latzco Paints for the year ended December 31 of the current year.

| | ACCOUNT TITLE | ADJUSTMENTS | | INCOME STATEMENT | |
		DEBIT (3)	CREDIT (4)	DEBIT (5)	CREDIT (6)
4	Merchandise Inventory		(a) 9 8 4 0 00		
5	Supplies—Office		(b) 2 5 1 0 00		
6	Supplies—Store		(c) 2 6 3 0 00		
7	Prepaid Insurance		(d) 2 5 8 0 00		
21	Income Summary	(a) 9 8 4 0 00		9 8 4 0 00	
22	Sales				310 9 2 0 00
23	Purchases			124 3 5 0 00	
24	Advertising Expense			4 7 8 0 00	
25	Credit Card Fee Expense			3 9 8 0 00	
26	Insurance Expense	(d) 2 5 8 0 00		2 5 8 0 00	
27	Miscellaneous Expense			2 1 4 0 00	
28	Payroll Taxes Expense			7 0 7 0 00	
29	Rent Expense			13 2 0 0 00	
30	Salary Expense			58 9 2 0 00	
31	Supplies Expense—Office	(b) 2 5 1 0 00		2 5 1 0 00	
32	Supplies Expense—Store	(c) 2 6 3 0 00		2 6 3 0 00	
33	Utilities Expense			2 7 6 0 00	
34		17 5 6 0 00	17 5 6 0 00	234 7 6 0 00	310 9 2 0 00
35	Net Income			76 1 6 0 00	
36				310 9 2 0 00	310 9 2 0 00
37					
38					
39					
40					
41					

INSTRUCTIONS:

1. Use page 25 of a journal. Journalize the adjusting entries using information from the partial work sheet.
2. Continue using page 25 of the journal. Journalize the closing entries using information from the work sheet. The distribution of net income statement shows equal distribution of earnings. The partners' drawing accounts show the following debit balances in the work sheet's Balance Sheet Debit column: Angela Cook, Drawing, $14,780.00; Alan Latzco, Drawing, $15,120.00.

Answers to
Audit Your Understanding

CHAPTER 1, PAGE 11

1. The language of business.
2. Accountants, bookkeepers, accounting clerks, and other general office workers.
3. The American Institute of Certified Public Accountants (AICPA).

CHAPTER 1, PAGE 13

1. Communication is the transfer of information between two or more individuals.
2. When an individual disregards his or her principles of right and wrong by choosing the wrong action.
3. **(1)** Is the action illegal? **(2)** Does the action violate company or professional standards? **(3)** Who is affected, and how, by the action?

CHAPTER 2, PAGE 21

1. A business owned by one person.
2. Assets = Liabilities + Owner's Equity.
3. Assets.
4. Liabilities and Owner's Equity.

CHAPTER 2, PAGE 26

1. The left side equals the right side.
2. The right side must be increased.
3. An account is increased by the same amount another account on the same side is decreased.

CHAPTER 2, PAGE 29

1. Assets, liabilities, and owner's equity.
2. Assets.
3. Liabilities and owner's equity.
4. Find the errors before completing any more work.

CHAPTER 3, PAGE 41

1. Increased.
2. Decreased.
3. Decreased.

CHAPTER 3, PAGE 43

1. Assets.
2. Liabilities and owner's equity.
3. Total assets.
4. Total liabilities and owner's equity.

CHAPTER 4, PAGE 55

1. $$Assets = Liabilities + Owner's\ Equity$$

2. **(1)** Account balances increase on the normal balance side of an account. **(2)** Account balances decrease on the side opposite the normal balance side of an account.

CHAPTER 4, PAGE 64

1. **(1)** What accounts are affected? **(2)** How is each account classified? **(3)** How is each account balance changed? **(4)** How is each amount entered in the accounts?
2. Debit.
3. Credit.
4. Debit.
5. Credit.
6. Debit.

CHAPTER 5, PAGE 76

1. General Debit, General Credit, Sales Credit, Cash Debit, and Cash Credit.
2. By date.
3. Checks, calculator tapes, receipts, memorandums.
4. Source documents are one way to verify the accuracy of a specific journal entry.

CHAPTER 5, PAGE 83

1. Date, debit, credit, source document.

CHAPTER 5, PAGE 87

1. Cash on hand at the beginning of the month, plus total cash received, less total cash paid.

2. (1) Rule a single line across all amount columns directly below the last entry to indicate that the columns are to be added. **(2)** On the next line, write the date in the Date column. **(3)** Write the word, *Totals*, in the Account Title column. **(4)** Write each column total below the single line. **(5)** Rule double lines below the column totals across all amount columns. The double lines mean that the totals have been verified as correct.

CHAPTER 6, PAGE 103

1. The first digit indicates in which general ledger division the account is located. The second and third digits indicate the location of the account within that division.

2. (1) Write the account title in the heading. **(2)** Write the account number in the heading.

CHAPTER 6, PAGE 112

1. (1) Write the date in the Date column of the account. **(2)** Write the journal page number in the Post. Ref. column of the account. **(3)** Write the amount in the Debit or Credit column. **(4)** Calculate and write the new account balance in the Balance Debit or Balance Credit column. **(5)** Write the account number in the Post. Ref. column of the journal.

CHAPTER 7, PAGE 140

1. Blank endorsement, special endorsement, and restrictive endorsement.

2. (1) Write the amount of the check in the space after the dollar sign at the top of the stub. **(2)** Write the date of the check on the Date line at the top of the stub. **(3)** Write to whom the check is to be paid on the To line at the top of the stub. **(4)** Record the purpose of the check on the For line. **(5)** Write the amount of the check in the amount column at the bottom of the stub on the line with the words "Amt. this Check." **(6)** Calculate the new checking account balance and record the new balance in the amount column on the last line of the stub.

CHAPTER 7, PAGE 147

1. (1) Calculate the adjusted check stub balance. **(2)** Calculate the adjusted bank balance. **(3)** Compare adjusted balances.

2.

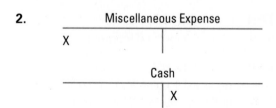

CHAPTER 7, PAGE 153

1.

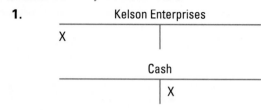

2.

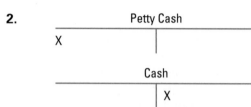

3.

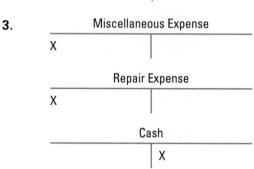

CHAPTER 8, PAGE 183

1. One year.

2. Name of business, name of report, and date of report.

3. (1) What is the balance of the account? **(2)** What should the balance be for this account? **(3)** What must be done to correct the account balance? **(4)** What adjustment is made?

4. Assets, liabilities, and owner's equity accounts.

5. Revenue and expense accounts.

CHAPTER 8, PAGE 187

1. Subtract the smaller total from the larger total to find the difference.

2. The difference between two column totals can be divided evenly by 9.

3. A slide.

CHAPTER 9, PAGE 199

1. Heading, revenue, expenses, and net income or net loss.

2. Total Expenses ÷ Total Sales = Total Expenses Component Percentage.

3. Net Income ÷ Total Sales = Net Income Component Percentage.

CHAPTER 9, PAGE 204

1. Heading, assets, liabilities, and owner's equity.

2. Capital Account Balance + Net Income − Drawing Account Balance = Current Capital.

CHAPTER 10, PAGE 213

1. To update general ledger accounts.
2. Adjustments column of the work sheet.
3. Insurance Expense and Supplies Expense.

CHAPTER 10, PAGE 223

1. Beginning balances.
2. Changes in the owner's capital account for a single fiscal period.
3. **(1)** An entry to close income statement accounts with credit balances. **(2)** An entry to close income statement accounts with debit balances. **(3)** An entry to record net income or net loss and close the income summary account. **(4)** An entry to close the drawing account.

CHAPTER 10, PAGE 227

1. To assure a reader that a balance has not been omitted.
2. Only those with balances (permanent accounts).
3. Because they are closed and have zero balances.

CHAPTER 11, PAGE 253

1. To save time and space in journalizing transactions.
2.

Purchases	
dr.	cr.
+	−

Accounts Payable	
dr.	cr.
−	+

3. To show that no account title needs to be written.
4. To show that amounts on that line are not to be posted individually.
5. A business purchases merchandise to sell but buys supplies for use in the business. Supplies are not intended for sale.

CHAPTER 11, PAGE 259

1. Cash is decreased by a credit.
2. Cash and merchandise.
3. A journal entry made to correct an error in the ledger.

CHAPTER 12, PAGE 273

1. Price of Goods × Sales Tax Rate = Sales Tax
2.

Sales Tax Payable	
dr.	cr.
−	+

Accounts Receivable	
dr.	cr.
+	−

3. Cash is increased; Accounts Receivable and the customer's account are decreased.

CHAPTER 12, PAGE 277

1. The columns are totaled and the equality of debits and credits is verified.
2. **(1)** Write the page number at the top of the journal. **(2)** Write the date in the Date column. **(3)** Write the words, Brought Forward, in the Account Title column. A check mark is also placed in the Post. Ref. column to show that nothing on this line needs to be posted. **(4)** Record the column totals brought forward from page 21 of the journal.
3. Cash on hand at the beginning of the month, *plus* total cash received during the month, *less* total cash paid during the month, *equals* cash balance on hand at end of the month. Cash is proved if the balance on the next unused check stub is the same as the cash proof.

CHAPTER 13, PAGE 290

1. An account in a general ledger that summarizes all accounts in a subsidiary ledger.
2. The balance of a controlling account equals the total of all account balances in its related subsidiary ledger.
3. Debit, Credit, Debit Balance, and Credit Balance.
4. Accounts for vendors from whom items are purchased or bought on account.
5. Accounts for charge customers.

CHAPTER 13, PAGE 298

1. Credit Balance. Because accounts payable are liabilities and liabilities have normal credit balances.
2. By writing the vendor name and vendor number on the heading of the ledger account.
3. **(1)** Write the date in the Date column of the account. **(2)** Write the journal page number in the Post. Ref. column of the account. **(3)** Write the credit amount in the Credit amount column of the account. **(4)** Add the amount in the Credit amount column to the previous balance in the Credit Balance column. Write the new account balance in the Credit Balance column. **(5)** Write the vendor number in the Post. Ref. column of the journal. The vendor number shows that the posting for this entry is completed.
4. Debit Balance. Because accounts receivable are assets and assets have normal debit balances.

CHAPTER 13, PAGE 302

1. By preparing a schedule of accounts receivable and schedule of accounts payable.
2. All vendor accounts that have balances.
3. When the total of the schedule of accounts receivable equals the balance of the accounts receivable general ledger account.

CHAPTER 14, PAGE 330

1. The total amount earned by all employees for a pay period.
2. Overtime hours X overtime rate (time and one half).
3. 3½.
4. $400.00.

CHAPTER 14, PAGE 334

1. Marital status and withholding allowance.
2. Both the employer and employee.
3. Employer.
4. Employer.

CHAPTER 14, PAGE 341

1. The total earnings and payroll withholdings of all employees.
2. By using tax tables provided by the federal government.
3. By subtracting total deductions from total earnings.

CHAPTER 14, PAGE 344

1. To enable the company to complete required tax forms at the end of the year.
2. Recording information on several forms with one writing.

CHAPTER 15, PAGE 359

1. Salary Expense.
2. Employee Income Tax Payable.
3. FICA Tax Payable.

CHAPTER 15, PAGE 363

1. Employers must pay 8% of each employee's total earnings up to the tax base.
2. Employers must pay 0.8% of total earnings of each employee up to a base of $7,000.00.

CHAPTER 15, PAGE 367

1. Federal income tax and FICA taxes.
2. By January 31.
3. Federal income tax and FICA employee and employer taxes.

CHAPTER 16, PAGE 398

1. A columnar form on which the financial information needed to prepare financial statements is summarized.
2. To prove the equality of debits and credits in the general ledger.
3. Merchandise Inventory.
4. Merchandise Inventory and Income Summary.

CHAPTER 16, PAGE 399

1. Income Statement Debit or Credit column.
2. When the Income Statement Debit column total (costs and expenses) is larger than the Credit column total (revenue).
3. Balance Sheet Debit.

CHAPTER 16, PAGE 404

1. Trial Balance Debit and Credit columns; Adjustments Debit and Credit columns; Adjusted Trial Balance Debit and Credit columns; Income Statement Debit and Credit columns; and Balance Sheet Debit and Credit columns.
2. Trial balance amounts after adjustments are extended to the Adjusted Trial Balance columns and the Adjusted Trial Balance columns are proved before extending amounts to the Income Statement and Balance Sheet columns.

CHAPTER 17, PAGE 420

1. The cost of merchandise sold section.
2. Beginning merchandise inventory, *plus* purchases, *equals* total cost of merchandise available for sale, *less* ending merchandise inventory, *equals* cost of merchandise sold.
3. By comparing it with the amount calculated on the work sheet.
4. Net loss.

CHAPTER 17, PAGE 428

1. Each partner's share of net income or net loss.
2. Beginning capital, additional investments, and withdrawal of assets.
3. Schedules of accounts receivable and schedule of accounts payable.

CHAPTER 18, PAGE 437

1. Insurance Expense and Income Summary.
2. Because the explanation "Adjusting Entries" is recorded in the Account Title column to explain all of the adjusting entries that follow.
3. Adjusting entry for merchandise inventory.

CHAPTER 18, PAGE 452

1. Income Statement and Balance Sheet columns of the work sheet and a distribution of net income statement.
2. Income Summary.
3. An amount equal to its balance is recorded on the side opposite the balance.
4. General ledger accounts with balances.

Glossary

Account: a record summarizing all the information pertaining to a single item in the accounting equation. (p. 22)

Accountant: a person who plans, summarizes, analyzes, and interprets accounting information. (p. 6)

Account balance: the amount in an account. (p. 22)

Accounting: planning, recording, analyzing, and interpreting financial information. (p. 5)

Accounting clerk: a person who records, sorts, and files accounting information. (p. 7)

Accounting cycle: the series of accounting activities included in recording financial information for a fiscal period. (p. 227)

Accounting equation: an equation showing the relationship among assets, liabilities, and owner's equity. (p. 21)

Accounting period: see *fiscal period.*

Accounting records: organized summaries of a business' financial activities. (p. 5)

Accounting system: a planned process for providing financial information that will be useful to management. (p. 5)

Account number: the number assigned to an account. (p. 100)

Accounts payable ledger: a subsidiary ledger containing only accounts for vendors from whom items are purchased or bought on account. (p. 285)

Accounts receivable ledger: a subsidiary ledger containing only accounts for charge customers. (p. 285)

Account title: the name given to an account. (p. 22)

Addend: each number to be added. (p. B-4)

Adjusting entries: journal entries recorded to update general ledger accounts at the end of a fiscal period. (p. 211)

Adjustments: changes recorded on a work sheet to update general ledger accounts at the end of a fiscal period. (p. 175)

Asset: anything of value that is owned. (p. 20)

Automated accounting: an accounting system in which data are recorded and reported mostly by using automated machines. (p. 123)

Automated accounting system: a collection of computer programs designed to computerize accounting procedures. (p. 124)

Automatic check deposit: depositing payroll checks directly to an employee's checking or savings account in a specific bank. (p. 340)

Balance ruled account: see *account.*

Balance sheet: a financial statement that reports assets, liabilities, and owner's equity on a specific date. (p. 26)

Bank statement: a report of deposits, withdrawals, and bank balance sent to a depositor by a bank. (p. 140)

Batch: a group of journal entries. (p. 309)

Blank endorsement: an endorsement consisting of only the endorser's signature. (p. 137)

Bookkeeper: a person who does general accounting work plus some summarizing and analyzing of accounting information. (p. 7)

Business ethics: the use of personal ethics in making business decisions. (p. 12)

Capital: the account used to summarize the owner's equity in the business. (p. 202)

Cash sale: a sale in which cash is received for the total amount of the sale at the time of the transaction. (p. 268)

Cell: the space on an electronic spreadsheet where a column intersects with a row. (p. 145)

Cell address: the column letter and row number of a cell. (p. 145)

Charge sale: see *sale on account*.

Chart of accounts: a list of accounts used by a business. (p. 55)

Check: a business form ordering a bank to pay cash from a bank account. (p. 74)

Checking account: a bank account from which payments can be ordered by a depositor. (p. 135)

Closing entries: journal entries used to prepare temporary accounts for a new fiscal period. (p. 215)

Component percentage: the percentage relationship between one financial statement item and the total that includes that item. (p. 197)

Computer program: a set of instructions followed by a computer to process data. (p. 124)

Contra account: an account that reduces a related account on a financial statement. (p. 63)

Controlling account: an account in a general ledger that summarizes all accounts in a subsidiary ledger. (p. 285)

Correcting entry: a journal entry made to correct an error in the ledger. (p. 258)

Cost of goods sold: see *cost of merchandise sold*.

Cost of merchandise: the price a business pays for goods it purchases to sell. (p. 247)

Cost of merchandise sold: the total original price of all merchandise sold during a fiscal period. (pp. 411–412)

Credit: an amount recorded on the right side of a T account. (p. 54)

Credit card sale: a sale in which a credit card is used for the total amount of the sale at the time of the transaction. (p. 268)

Customer: a person or business to whom merchandise or services are sold. (p. 267)

Data base: a prearranged file in which data can be entered and retrieved. (p. 124)

Debit: an amount recorded on the left side of a T account. (p. 54)

Difference: the answer to a subtraction problem. (p. B-4)

Dishonored check: a check that a bank refuses to pay. (p. 146)

Distribution of net income statement: a partnership financial statement showing distribution of net income or net loss to partners. (p. 419)

Dividend: the number to be divided. (p. B-5)

Divisor: the number the dividend will be divided by. (p. B-5)

Double-entry accounting: the recording of debit and credit parts of a transaction. (p. 74)

Electronic funds transfer: a computerized cash payment system that uses electronic impulses to transfer funds. (p. 148)

Electronic spreadsheet: a group of rows and columns displayed on a computer monitor. (p. 145)

Employee earnings record: a business form used to record details affecting payments made to an employee. (p. 341)

Endorsement: a signature or stamp on the back of a check transferring ownership. (p. 137)

Endorsement in full: see *special endorsement*.

Entry: information for each transaction recorded in a journal. (p. 74)

Equities: financial rights to the assets of a business. (p. 21)

Ethics: the principles of right and wrong that guide an individual in making decisions. (p. 12)

Exhibit: see *supporting schedule*.

Expense: a decrease in owner's equity resulting from the operation of a business. (p. 38)

Face amount: see *principal of a note*.

Federal Insurance Contributions Act: see *FICA tax*.

Federal unemployment tax: a federal tax used for state and federal administrative expenses of the unemployment program. (pp. 333–334)

FICA tax: a federal tax paid by employees and employers for old-age, survivors, disability, and hospitalization insurance. (p. 333)

File maintenance: the procedure for arranging accounts in a general ledger, assigning account numbers, and keeping records current. (pp. 101–104)

Fiscal period: the length of time for which a business summarizes and reports financial information. (p. 171)

General amount column: a journal amount column that is not headed with an account title. (p. 73)

General ledger: a ledger that contains all accounts needed to prepare financial statements. (p. 100)

General office clerk: a person who does general kinds of office tasks, including some accounting tasks. (p. 8)

Gross earnings: see *total earnings*.

Gross pay: see *total earnings*.

Gross profit on sales: the revenue remaining after cost of merchandise sold has been deducted. (p. 414)

Income statement: a financial statement showing the revenue and expenses for a fiscal period. (p. 178)

Internal Revenue Service (IRS): the branch of the U.S. Treasury Department concerned with enforcement and collection of income taxes. (p. 171)

Inventory: the amount of goods on hand. (p. 393)

Invoice: a form describing the goods sold, the quantity, and the price. (p. 249)

Journal: a form for recording transactions in chronological order. (p. 73)

Journal entry: see *entry*.

Journalizing: recording transactions in a journal. (p. 73)

Ledger: a group of accounts. (p. 100)

Liability: an amount owed by a business. (p. 21)

Management accountant: see *private accountant*.

Manual accounting: an accounting system in which data are recorded and reported mostly by hand. (p. 123)

Markup: the amount added to the cost of merchandise to establish the selling price. (p. 247)

Medicare: the federal health insurance program for people who have reached retirement age. (p. 332)

Memorandum: a form on which a brief message is written describing a transaction. (p. 76)

Menu: a list of options from which an activity may be selected. (p. 126)

Merchandise: goods that a merchandising business purchases to sell. (p. 246)

Merchandise inventory: the amount of goods on hand for sale to customers. (p. 393)

Merchandising business: a business that purchases and sells goods. (p. 246)

Minuend: the top number or first number of a subtraction problem. (p. B-4)

Multiplicand: the number to be multiplied. (p. B-4)

Multiplier: the number of times the multiplicand will be multiplied. (p. B-4)

Net income: the difference between total revenue and total expenses when total revenue is greater. (p. 180)

Net loss: the difference between total revenue and total expenses when total expenses is greater. (p. 182)

Net pay: the total earnings paid to an employee after payroll taxes and other deductions. (p. 337)

Nominal account: see *temporary accounts*.

Opening an account: Writing an account title and number on the heading of an account. (p. 102)

Owner's equity: the amount remaining after the value of all liabilities is subtracted from the value of all assets. (p. 21)

Owners' equity statement: a financial statement that summarizes the changes in owners' equity during a fiscal period. (p. 421)

Partner: each member of a partnership. (p. 246)

Partnership: a business in which two or more persons combine their assets and skills. (p. 246)

Pay period: the period covered by a salary payment. (p. 327)

Payroll: the total amount earned by all employees for a pay period. (p. 327)

Payroll register: a business form used to record payroll information. (p. 334)

Payroll taxes: taxes based on the payroll of a business. (p. 330)

Pegboard: a special device used to write the same information at one time on several forms. (p. 343)

Permanent accounts: accounts used to accumulate information from one fiscal period to the next. (p. 214)

Petty cash: an amount of cash kept on hand and used for making small payments. (p. 149)

Petty cash slip: a form showing proof of a petty cash payment. (p. 151)

Post-closing trial balance: a trial balance prepared after the closing entries are posted. (pp. 226, 237)

Postdated check: a check with a future date on it. (p. 139)

Posting: transferring information from a journal entry to a ledger account. (p. 103)

Principal of a note: the original amount of a note. (p. 103)

Private accountant: an accountant who is employed by a single business. (p. 7)

Product: the answer to a multiplication problem. (p. B-4)

Profit: see *net income*.

Proprietorship: a business owned by one person. (p. 20)

Proving cash: determining that the amount of cash agrees with the accounting records. (p. 86)

Public accounting firm: a business selling accounting services to the general public. (p. 6)

Purchase invoice: an invoice used as a source document for recording a purchase on account transaction. (p. 249)

Purchase on account: a transaction in which the merchandise purchased is to be paid for later. (p. 249)

Quotient: the answer to a division problem. (p. B-5)

Real accounts: see *permanent accounts*.

Receipt: a business form giving written acknowledgement for cash received. (p. 75)

Restrictive endorsement: an endorsement restricting further transfer of a check's ownership. (p. 138)

Revenue: an increase in owner's equity resulting from the operation of a business. (p. 37)

Run date: the date to be printed on reports prepared by a computer. (p. 125)

Salary: the money paid for employee services. (p. 327)

Sale on account: a sale for which cash will be received at a later date. (p. 269)

Sales invoice: an invoice used as a source document for recording a sale on account. (p. 269)

Sales slip: see *sales invoice*.

Sales tax: a tax on a sale of merchandise or services. (p. 267)

Schedule of accounts payable: a listing of vendor accounts, account balances, and total amount due all vendors. (p. 301)

Schedule of accounts receivable: a listing of customer accounts, account balances, and total amount due from all customers. (p. 301)

Service business: a business that performs an activity for a fee. (p. 20)

Social security taxes: see *FICA tax*.

Software: programs used to direct the operations of a computer. (p. 124)

Sole proprietorship: see *proprietorship*.

Source document: a business paper from which information is obtained for a journal entry. (p. 74)

Special amount column: a journal amount column headed with an account title. (p. 73)

Special endorsement: an endorsement indicating a new owner of a check. (p. 137)

State unemployment tax: a state tax used to pay benefits to unemployed workers. (p. 334)

Subsidiary ledger: a ledger that is summarized in a single general ledger account. (p. 285)

Subtrahend: the number to be subtracted from the minuend. (p. B-4)

Sum: the answer to an addition problem. (p. B-4)

Supplementary report: see *supporting schedule*.

Supporting schedule: a report prepared to give details about an item on a principal financial statement. (p. 428)

T account: an accounting device used to analyze transactions. (p. 53)

Tax base: the maximum amount of earnings on which a tax is calculated. (p. 336)

Template: a model of a computer application stored on a computer disk for repeated use. (p. 124)

Temporary accounts: accounts used to accumulate information until it is transferred to the owner's capital account. (p. 215)

Terms of sale: an agreement between a buyer and a seller about payment for merchandise. (p. 250)

Total earnings: the total pay due for a pay period before deductions. (p. 329)

Transaction: a business activity that changes assets, liabilities, or owner's equity. (p. 21)

Trial balance: a proof of the equality of debits and credits in a general ledger. (p. 172)

Vendor: a business from which merchandise is purchased or supplies or other assets are bought. (p. 248)

Vertical analysis: see *component percentage*.

Withdrawal: asset taken out of a business for the owner's personal use. (p. 40)

Withholding allowance: a deduction from total earnings for each person legally supported by a taxpayer. (p. 332)

Work sheet: a columnar accounting form used to summarize the general ledger information needed to prepare financial statements. (p. 172)

Index

Bold page numbers indicate illustrations.